The CELTIC Football Companion

DAVID DOCHERTY

FOREWORD
JOHN C. McGINN

PUBLISHED BY JOHN DONALD PUBLISHERS LTD
WITH THE APPROVAL OF
CELTIC FOOTBALL CLUB

For Sandra, Elaine and Ailsa

John Donald Publishers Ltd.,
138 St. Stephen Street,
Edinburgh EH3 5AA.

ISBN 0 85976 173 8

The Publishers would like to thank D. C. Thomson & Co. Ltd., Dundee for kindly supplying many of the illustrations used in this book.

Phototypeset by Newtext Composition Ltd., Glasgow.
Printed in Great Britain by Bell & Bain Ltd., Glasgow.

Foreword

I am delighted to be given the opportunity to write this foreword because I am quite satisfied that readers of this book will find a fund of statistical information that will put an end to many arguments concerning the club.

As you read through the book season by season over the last forty years or so, you seem to focus on the period you can remember best. For readers like myself, old enough to have seen the start of this period as a youngster, it brings back memories of games, good and bad, which for one reason or another have stuck in the mind.

It also illustrates very dramatically the change in Celtic fortunes from a rather barren disappointing period in the years immediately after the war, to the highly successful period from the mid sixties onwards which produced that unforgettable run of nine League Championships in succession, not to mention the clean sweep season of 1966-67 which included the coveted European Cup.

What I think the reader will find is that having read the book through it will then become a reference type book for the facts and figures that seem to be so essential nowadays. However, when you refer to the book to elicit some fact or other, you again become engrossed in the events surrounding that particular period. It's an endless fascination recalling in print games and players from the past, the appearances in each season and the goalscorers.

The author has clearly worked very hard to make this book possible and has taken great care with all his statistics. If, however, any odd error has gone through undetected, I hope that readers will understand that a mistake can elude the most painstaking care, especially in a book of this type.

John C. McGinn,
Chairman

Acknowledgements

I would like to thank the following organisations and people who have helped in the production of this book: the *Glasgow Herald* and the *Daily Record* and *Sunday Mail* for permission to quote extracts from contemporary newspaper reports; D. C. Thomson Organisation and particularly Ian Bruce of the *Sunday Post* in Glasgow for kind permission to reproduce the many illustrations of theirs in the book; and Harry Davidson of the *Daily Record,* Bob Carroll, Sean Fallon, Duncan Hart and my family for their support and encouragement.

David Docherty

The Celtic squad in 1930-31. Back row: Cook, Cavanagh, Smith, Wilson. Middle row: McGonigle, Geatons, O'Hare, Thomson, Whitelaw, Hughes. Front row: R. Thomson, A. Thomson, McGrory, McStay, Scarff, Napier. Standing: Quinn (trainer).

Contents

Celtic, Scottish Cup Winners for the 15th time in Season 1936-37. Back row: C. Geatons, R. Hogg, J. Kennaway, R. Morrison, W. Buchan, G. Paterson. Front row: William Maley (Secretary and Manager), J. Delaney, J. McGrory, W. Lyon, J. Crum, F. Murphy, J. McMenemy (trainer).

Introduction

Celtic Football Club was founded in November 1887. Now nearly one hundred years later they have long been established as one of the world's most famous club sides.

The club had its origin in charity. Brother Walfrid, a member of the teaching institute of Marist Brothers, promoted on 6th November 1887 the formation of a football team with the title of Celtic Football and Athletic Club. Their main object to raise funds for meals for needy children of the East End of Glasgow. The motion was agreed unanimously and the very first colours were white shirts with green collars and a Celtic cross in red and green on the right breast.

The first ground was situated to the East of Janefield Cemetery and was secured on 13th November for an annual rent of £50. The official opening took place on 8th May 1888 which was also the opening date of the Glasgow Exhibition and a crowd of 3,000 watched a match between Hibs and Cowlairs which ended 0-0. Their first home match was on May 28th when they beat Rangers 5-2 before a crowd of 2,000. In their very first year of existence the club gave over £400 in charity. In 1892 the club moved to its present site off London Road, which was then a brickfield half-filled with water to a depth of more than 40 feet and needed 100,000 cartloads of material to raise the level. Today it can fairly lay claim to be one of the most famous Stadia in the World.

Celtic reached the final of the Scottish Cup in their very first year of existence. They were beaten 2-1 by Third Lanark in a replay which was ordered after a protest concerning ground conditions after the first match which Third Lanark won 3-0. Celtic were one of the ten founder members of the Scottish League in 1890-91 and their first official League match resulted in a 5-0 victory over Hearts at Tynecastle on 23rd August 1890. They finished 3rd in their first season despite having 4 points deducted for playing an ineligible goalkeeper named Bell.

It is only right in any book about Celtic to recall the players who overcame all of the early difficulties to launch what has become an institution in Scotland. The following players took part in their very first Scottish Cup Final in February 1889 – John Kelly; Gallacher, McKeown; W. Maley, James Kelly, McLaren; McCallum, Dunbar, Groves, Coleman, T. Maley.

Over the years Celtic have contributed many players to the Scottish international team; Jimmy McMenemy, Jimmy Quinn, Jimmy McGrory, John Thomson, Bobby Evans, Billy McNeill, Pat Crerand, Jimmy Johnstone, Kenny Dalglish, Danny McGrain and Paul McStay to mention but a few. Even back in 1889 two Celtic players – James Kelly and McLaren were in the Scotland team which beat England 3-2 at Kensington Oval; the winning goal being scored by McLaren with the last kick of the match. Celtic players have also represented Ireland (both North and South) and Iceland.

The first major trophy the club won was the Glasgow Cup in 1891 when they beat Third Lanark 4-0 in the Final. The first Scottish Cup success came in 1892 when they beat Queens Park 5-1 at the first Ibrox in front of a crowd of 20,000. The team was Cullen; Doyle, Reynolds; Gallacher, Kelly, Maley; Campbell, Dowds, McCallum, McMahon and Brady. The goalscorers were Campbell (2), McMahon (2) and an own goal.

Celtic's first League Championship success came in season 1893 and they took the title 3 more times before the end of the century. In 1893 they played a friendly against Clyde under artificial light on Christmas night but the experiment was not a success.

Celtic had turned themselves into a limited company on 4th March 1897. In that same year former player Willie Maley was appointed Secretary at a salary of £150 per year. He later became Secretary-Manager and was to stay with club in that capacity until February 1939, a total association of 52 years. Below is Willie Maley's full record of success:

16 League Championships: 1898, 1905, 1906, 1907, 1908, 1909, 1910, 1914, 1915, 1916, 1917, 1919, 1922, 1926, 1936, 1938.

14 Scottish Cups: 1899, 1900, 1904, 1907, 1908, 1911, 1912, 1914, 1923, 1925, 1927, 1931, 1933, 1937.

In addition the Glasgow Cup was won 14 times and the Glasgow Charity Cup on 18 occasions. They also won the Empire Exhibition Trophy in 1938. They won 3 League and Cup "doubles" under Maley. The Maley family hold another unique record. In 1904 while Willie was leading Celtic to success in the Scottish Cup his brother Tom took Manchester City to victory in the F.A. Cup.

The club's success continued unabated throughout the Twenties and Thirties. They won the Scottish Cup for the 11th time in 1925 in what came to be known as "Gallacher's Final". Opponents Dundee were leading 1-0 until 7 minutes from the end when Gallacher scored a sensational equaliser and McGrory popped up to head in McFarlane's free-kick in the dying seconds. Jimmy McGrory was a phenomenon. He joined the club in season 1922-23, spent a season on loan to Clydebank then returned to Celtic Park. He scored an amazing 410 goals in 408 matches to become the only British player to average more than a goal a game over a complete career; a record which is unlikely to be beaten. He scored 8 goals in a League match against Dunfermline Athletic on 14th January 1928. He was unfortunate to be a contemporary of the enigmatic Hughie Gallacher and this cost him many international honours. McGrory missed the victorious Scottish Cup Final of 1927 through injury but he was in the sides which beat Motherwell in both 1931 and 1933.

Another legendary figure of the same time was goalkeeper John Thomson who on the afternoon of Saturday September 5th 1931, at the age of 22, received fatal head injuries in a Rangers v Celtic Scottish League match at Ibrox Park. Sam English, the Rangers centre-forward, suddenly darted through with the ball. As he was in the very act of shooting Thomson flung himself fearlessly at his feet and against all the odds got to the ball in time to deflect it and save his charge – at the cost of his life.

Thomson was buried the following Thursday at Cardenden. His funeral was one of the most extraordinary ever recorded in Britain. Coal mines throughout the district closed down for the day. The railways laid on excursion specials to take 5,000 people to the graveside from Glasgow alone. One train had a special van attached to carry wreathes which had been sent from all parts of England and Scotland. Thomson's International cap which he had received only a fortnight before was placed on the coffin. Thomson's replacement in goal was Joe Kennaway, a Canadian, who was discovered during the club's first ever tour of North America in the summer of 1931.

Celtic won the League Championship in 1936 and 1938 and in that same year they became the Winners of the Empire Exhibition Cup which was staged at Ibrox and involved four Scottish and four English clubs. They beat Sunderland, the 1936 English league Champions and 1937 F.A. Cup Winners, 3-0 after their first game was drawn then knocked out Hearts 1-0 in the Semi-Final before beating Everton 1-0 after extra-time in the Final. The team was: Kennaway; Hogg, Morrison; Geatons, Lyons, Paterson; Delaney, McDonald, Crum, Divers and Murphy. Johnny Crum was the scorer against Everton. It was an important win for Celtic in their jubilee year. The club's record attendance was set on 1st January 1938 when 92,000 watched their match with Rangers.

During the season Jimmy McGrory retired and became Manager of Kilmarnock taking the Rugby Park club to the Scottish Cup Final in his first season after beating Celtic 2-1 in the 3rd Round of the competition. Celtic played Clyde on Saturday 2nd September 1939 on the eve of the outbreak of the Second World War and immediately afterwards the competition was abandoned. Ex-player Jimmy McStay succeeded Willie Maley as Manager, then in July 1945 with the resumption of football, Jimmy McGrory was invited back to Parkhead to become only the third Manager in the history of the club.

The Celtic Football Companion starts after the Second World War, with season 1946-47 and continues season by season to 1985-86. Each competitive match in the major competitions is fully covered giving both teams, the score, the scorers and times of goals and attendance. Occasionally, after consulting various sources it has not been possible to track down information. When this happens the letters NA have been inserted = not available. Some of the more important and interesting matches carry a short match summary which has been collated using contemporary newspaper reports. It is hoped memories will stir and forgotten heroes will be remembered as you turn the pages and that friendly disagreement in pub or club, can be easily resolved by reference to the pages of the book.

A historic occasion. Celtic have just become the first British side to win the European Cup on the 25th May, 1967, and Billy McNeill is mobbed by the happy fans.

Season 1946-47

Celtic finished a disappointing seventh in this first post-war campaign. In a season in which they used no fewer than 30 players they suffered particularly heavy reversals both home and away to Aberdeen – losing 11 goals in the two matches. They collected only 5 points out of the 24 available against the 6 teams who finished above them. Even their best win of the season, a 4-1 home victory over Hibs in November, received criticism in the press for their robust, uncompromising play throughout. They failed to qualify from their League Cup Section – Hibs finishing top – and they suffered the indignity of losing to a 'B' Divison side, Dundee, in their first Scottish Cup tie. They also lost out to a Jimmy Caskie goal in a closely contested Glasgow Cup Final with Rangers. More encouragingly they won both Friendly matches, away, against English opposition: 2-1 against Aston Villa and 3-1 against Leeds United.

Evans had a promising season and Miller, though hard pressed throughout, continually picked up man of the match nominations and earned International recognition as a result. The arrival of Jerry McAloon from Brentford, in October, in a straight exchange for George Paterson, added much-needed firepower to the attack and he finished as top scorer with 12 League goals in his 19 matches.

League:	Seventh
League Cup:	Failed to qualify from Section
Scottish Cup:	First Round

LEAGUE DIVISION A

August 10
CELTIC (1) 1 MORTON (0) 2
Rae (30) Neil (46), Garth (69)

CELTIC: Miller; Hogg, Milne; W. Gallacher, Corbett, McAuley; Sirrell, Kiernan, Rae, Bogan, Shields

MORTON: McFeat; Westwater, Fyfe; Campbell, Kelly, Aird; McKillop, Divers, Neil, Garth, McGarry

Attendance: 35,000

August 14th
CLYDE (2) 2 CELTIC (0) 2
Dixon 2 Cantwell 2

CLYDE: Sweeney; Duffy, Galbraith; Campbell, McCormack, Long; Hepburn, Donaldson, Mathie, Wallace, Dixon

CELTIC: Miller, Hogg, Milne; W. Gallacher, Corbett, McAuley; Sirrell, Kiernan, Cantwell, Bogan, Shields

Attendance: 15,000

August 17th
ABERDEEN (3) 6 CELTIC (2) 2
Harris (10), Hamilton (13) Kiernan 2 (15, 19)
Williams (14), Kiddie (55),
Baird 2 (70, 78)

ABERDEEN: Johnstone; Cowie, McKenna; Dunlop, Waddell, McCall; A. Kiddie, Hamilton, Harris, Baird, Williams

CELTIC: Miller; Hogg, Milne; W. Gallacher, Corbett, McAuley; Sirrell, Kiernan, Cantwell, Bogan, Shields

Attendance: 35,000

August 21st
CELTIC (2) 2 HEARTS (2) 3
Kiernan (18), Wardhaugh (13), Kelly 2
Evans (21) (32, 49)

CELTIC: Miller; Hogg, Milne; W. Gallacher, Corbett, McAuley; Sirrell, Kiernan, Cantwell, Bogan, Evans

HEARTS: Brown; McSpadyen, McLure; Cox, Baxter, Miller; Sloane, Walker, Kelly, McCrae, Wardhaugh

Attendance: 30,000

August 28th
HAMILTON ACADEMICALS (2) 2 — CELTIC (1) 2
Devlin (2, 35) — Cantwell (17), Kiernan (90 pen)

HAMILTON: Campbell; McGurk, Devine; Lindsay, Rothera, Johnstone; Fearn, McFarlane, Devlin, Daly, McLaughlin

CELTIC: Miller; Hogg, Milne; Sirrell, Corbett, McAuley; Hazlett, Kiernan, Cantwell, Bogan, Evans

Attendance: n.a.

August 31st
ST MIRREN (0) 0 — CELTIC (1) 1
Cantwell (9)

ST MIRREN: Newlands; Telfer, Lindsay; Hunter, Drinkwater, Scott; Crowe, Telford, Aikman, Deakin, McLaren

CELTIC; Miller; Lamb, Milne; W. Gallacher, Corbett, McAuley; Cantwell, Kiernan, Rae, Bogan, Evans

Attendance: 12,000

September 4th
CELTIC (1) 1 — THIRD LANARK (0) 4
Cantwell (33) — Venters (49), Henderson 2 (61, 86), Mitchell (76)

CELTIC: Miller; McDonald, Milne; W. Gallacher, Corbett, McAuley; Rae, Kiernan, Cantwell, Bogan, Evans

THIRD LANARK: Petrie; Carabine, Kelly; Bolt, Barclay, Mooney; McCulloch, Ayton, Henderson, Venters, Mitchell

Attendance: n.a.

September 7th
CELTIC (1) 2 — RANGERS (2) 3
Kiernan (29), Bogan (58) — Duncanson 2 (10, 30), Parlane (58)

CELTIC: Miller; McDonald, Milne; McMillan, Corbett, McAuley; Bogan; Kiernan, Cantwell, W. Gallacher, Hazlett

RANGERS: Brown; Gray, Shaw; Cox, Young, Symon; Stead, Gillick, Parlane, Duncanson, Caskie

Attendance: n.a.

Playing with something like the fighting spirit of their teams of the past, Celtic came near to achieving their first home win of the Season. They had three penalty claims turned down and seemed particularly unlucky not to be awarded one late in the game when Young's arm stopped Bogan's cross-shot. In Kiernan, the home side had the cleverest individual player on the field – in the first-half especially he had Symon running round in circles and labouring in his rear. Rangers were overwhelmingly superior in the art of making the telling pass.

September 14th
QUEEN OF THE SOUTH (1) 3 — CELTIC (1) 1
Fitzsimmons (28), Armstrong 2 (77, 85) — Kiernan (34)

QUEEN OF THE SOUTH: Henderson; Savage, Dryburgh; Fitzsimmons, Denmark, Holt; Oakes, Dempsey, Armstrong, Law, Johnstone

CELTIC: Miller; McDonald, Milne; Lynch, Corbett, Baillie; Bogan, Kiernan, Cantwell, W. Gallacher, Hazlett

Attendance: 15,000

October 4th: George Paterson was transferred to Brentford in exchange for Jerry McAloon.

October 8th: Chic Geatons was appointed coach at Parkhead.

October 19th: Willie Miller was in the Scotland team beaten 3-1 by Wales in Cardiff.

November 2nd
FALKIRK (0) 1 — CELTIC (2) 4
Fitzsimmons (57) — Rae 2 (20, 55), McAloon (28), Evans (65)

FALKIRK: Dawson; McPhee, Stewart; Telfer, R. Henderson, Sinclair; J. Henderson, Allison, Wardlaw, Fitzsimmons, Fiddes

CELTIC: Miller; Hogg, McDonald; Lynch, McMillan, Milne; Evans, Kiernan, Rae, McAloon, Hazlett

Attendance: 15,000

League positions

	P	W	D	L	F	A	Pts
1 Hibernian	11	8	0	3	30	10	16
2 Rangers	11	8	0	3	34	14	16
3 Aberdeen	11	6	3	2	21	13	15
4 Clyde	10	6	2	2	23	13	14
5 Partick Thistle	11	6	2	3	27	19	14
13 CELTIC	10	2	2	6	18	26	6

November 9th
CELTIC (2) 4 — HIBERNIAN (0) 1
Evans (20), Kiernan (41), McAloon 2 (52, 83) — Weir (82)

CELTIC: Miller; Hogg, McDonald; Lynch, Corbett, Milne; Evans, Kiernan, Rae, McAloon, Hazlett

HIBERNIAN: Kerr; Howie, Shaw; Fraser, Aird, Kean; Smith, Buchanan, Weir, Turnbull, Aitkenhead

Attendance: 45,000

November 16th
PARTICK THISTLE (2) 4 — CELTIC (1) 1
Glover (19), Chisholm (23), O'Donnell (68), Sharp (86) — McAloon (31)

PARTICK THISTLE: Nimmo; McGowan, Curran; Hewitt, Husband, Brown; Glover, O'Donnell, Mathie, Sharp, Chisholm

CELTIC: Miller; Hogg, McDonald; Lynch, Corbett, Milne; Evans, Kiernan, Rae, McAloon, Hazlett

Attendance: 40,000

November 23rd
MOTHERWELL (1) 1 CELTIC (0) 2
Brown (4) McAloon (59), Rae (86)

MOTHERWELL: Johnstone; Kilmarnock, Shaw; McLeod, Paton, Redpath; Humphreys, Watson, Brown, Bremner, Barclay

CELTIC: Miller; Hogg, McDonald; Lynch, McMillan, Milne; J. Jordan, Kiernan, Rae, McAloon, Hazlett

Attendance: 15,000

November 30th
CELTIC (3) 4 KILMARNOCK (0) 2
Rae (20), Kiernan 2 (35, 49) Collins 2 (46, 47)
McAloon (44)

CELTIC: Miller; Hogg, McDonald; Lynch, McMillan, Milne; J. Jordan, Kiernan, Rae, McAloon, Hazlett

KILMARNOCK: Downie; Dornan, Landsborough; Devlin, Thyne, Davie; Stevenson, Turnbull, Collins, McAvoy, Kirkpatrick

Attendance: 15,000

December 7th
MORTON (1) 2 CELTIC (1) 1
McInnes (39), Jordan (31)
McKillop (46)

MORTON: McFeat; Maley, Fyfe; Mitchell, Aird, Whyte; McKillop, Divers, Henderson, McGarritty, McInnes

CELTIC: Miller; Hogg, McDonald; Lynch, McMillan, Milne; J. Jordan, Kiernan, Rae, McAloon, Hazlett

Attendance: n.a.

December 14th
CELTIC (1) 3 CLYDE (3) 3
Airlie 2 (16, 60) Galletly (18), Dixon
McCormack o.g. (86) (22), Johnstone (41)

CELTIC: Miller; Hogg, Mallan; Lynch, McMillan, Milne; Evans, Kiernan, Airlie, McAloon, Hazlett

CLYDE: Sweeney; Duffy, Galbraith; Campbell, McCormack, Long; Galletly, Gourlay, Johnstone, Dixon, Cameron

Attendance: 18,000

December 21st
HEARTS (1) 2 CELTIC (1) 1
Walker (37), Airlie (55)
McCrae (89)

HEARTS: Brown; McSpadyen, McKenzie; Cox, Baxter, Miller; McFarlane, Wardhaugh, Currie, McCrae, Walker

CELTIC: Miller; Hogg, Mallan; Lynch, McMillan, Milne; Evans, Kiernan, Airlie, McAloon, Hazlett

Attendance: n.a.

December 25th
CELTIC (1) 1 QUEENS PARK (0) 0
Rae (24)

CELTIC: Miller; Hogg, Mallan; Lynch, McMillan, Milne; Evans, Kiernan, Rae, Airlie, Hazlett

QUEENS PARK: R. Simpson; J. Mitchell, W. Johnstone; D. Letham, J. Whigham, I. Harnett; L. Hodge, A. Aitken, C. Liddell, J. McAuley, H.G. Millar

Attendance: n.a.

December 28th
CELTIC (0) 2 HAMILTON ACADEMICALS (1) 1
McAloon 2 (79, 80) Ogilvie (45)

CELTIC: Miller; Hogg, Mallan; Lynch, McMillan, Milne; Evans, McAloon, Airlie, W. Gallacher, Hazlett

HAMILTON: Campbell; McGurk, Johnstone; Stewart, Daly, McFarlane; Ogilvie, Bremner, Smith, Gillan, Fitzsimmons

Attendance: 15,000

League positions

	P	W	D	L	F	A	Pts
1 Rangers	19	14	2	3	55	21	30
2 Aberdeen	19	11	5	3	37	21	27
3 Hibernian	19	11	4	4	46	22	26
4 Morton	19	9	5	5	39	29	23
5 Hearts	19	9	5	5	31	28	23
9 CELTIC	19	7	3	9	37	42	17

January 1st
RANGERS (0) 1 CELTIC (1) 1
Gillick (60) Hazlett (10)

RANGERS: Brown; Young, Shaw; McColl, Woodburn, Rae; Waddell, Gillick, Thornton, Duncanson, McNee

CELTIC: Miller; Hogg, Mallan; Lynch, McMillan, Milne; Evans, McAloon, Airlie, W. Gallacher, Hazlett

Attendance: 85,000

A record crowd for a club game in Britain this season witnessed a game of punishing pace and he-man exchanges. The visitors opened the scoring – a terrific 30-yard free-kick by Lynch was on its way to the net when Brown turned the ball out but young Hazlett was following up and scored. From the start of the second half Rangers took the initiative and after 15 minutes Waddell tricked Mallan and crossed to the far post where Duncanson headed the ball back for Gillick to prod into the net. Late in the game a Gallacher cross came back off the face of the bar and was scrambled clear by Shaw.

January 2nd
CELTIC (0) 1 ABERDEEN (1) 5
Hazlett (85) Hamilton 4 (39, 46, 47, 58), Harris

CELTIC: Miller; Hogg, Mallan; Lynch, McMillan, Milne; Evans, McAloon, Airlie, W. Gallacher, Hazlett

ABERDEEN: Watson; Cooper, Cowie; McLaughlin, Dunlop, Taylor; Kiddie, Hamilton, Harris, Williams, McCall

Attendance: n.a.

January 4th
CELTIC (2) 2 — QUEEN OF THE SOUTH (0) 0
McAloon (13), Rae (28 pen)

CELTIC: Miller; Hogg, Mallan; W. Gallacher, McMillan, Milne; Docherty, McAloon, Rae, Evans, O'Sullivan

QUEEN OF THE SOUTH: Wilson; Dryburgh, Savage; Haxton, Barbour, Collier; Cummings, Armstrong, Houliston, Dempsey, Johnstone

Attendance: 10,000

January 11th
QUEENS PARK (1) 1 — CELTIC (2) 3
Whigham (16 pen) — Rae 2 (3, 24), McAloon (74)

QUEENS PARK: R. Simpson; J. Mitchell, W. Johntone; D. Letham, J. Whigham, I. Harnett; J. Farquhar, A. Aitken, C. Liddell, A. McAuley, W. McPhail

CELTIC: Miller; Hogg, Mallan; W. Gallacher, Corbett, Milne; Docherty, McAloon, Rae, Evans, O'Sullivan

Attendance: 12,000
Gallacher was ordered off in the first half

January 18th
THIRD LANARK 0 — CELTIC 0

THIRD LANARK: Fraser; Balunas, Kelly; Bolt, Palmer, Mooney; Bogan, McDonald, McCulloch, Ayton, Mitchell

CELTIC: Miller; Hogg, Mallan; W. Gallacher, Corbett, Milne; Docherty, McAloon, Rae, Evans, O'Sullivan.

Attendance: 30,000
League positions

	P	W	D	L	F	A	Pts
1 Rangers	27	19	4	4	66	23	42
2 Hibernian	25	14	6	5	59	31	34
3 Hearts	26	13	6	7	43	39	32
4 Aberdeen	24	13	5	6	44	32	31
5 Partick Thistle	24	14	2	8	62	43	30
10 CELTIC	24	9	5	10	44	49	23

February 22nd
CELTIC (2) 2 — ST MIRREN (0) 1
Kiernan (2), Hazlett (17) — Deakin (55)

CELTIC: Miller; Hogg, Mallan; Lynch, Corbett, McAuley; Hazlett, Kiernan, Rae, Evans, O'Sullivan

ST MIRREN: Newlands; Telfer, Drinkwater; Stenhouse, Roy, Cunningham; Milne, Aikman, Telford, Deakin, Crowe

Attendance: 9,900

March 22nd
CELTIC (1) 2 — PARTICK THISTLE (0) 0
Evans (42), Curran o.g. (76)

CELTIC: Miller; Hogg, Mallan; R. Quinn, Corbett, Milne; F. Quinn, McAloon, Kiernan, Evans, Hazlett

PARTICK THISTLE: Steadward; McGowan, Curran; Hewitt, Husband, Brown; Glover, O'Donnell, Mathie, Sharp, Chisholm

Attendance: 15,000

March 29th
KILMARNOCK (0) 1 — CELTIC (2) 2
McLeish n.a. — Kiernan (4), McAloon n.a.

KILMARNOCK: Downie; Landsborough, Hood; Turnbull, Thyne, Devlin; McLeish, Reid, Collins, McAvoy, Drury

CELTIC: Miller; Hogg, Mallan; R. Quinn, Corbett, Milne; F. Quinn, McAloon, Kiernan, Evans, Hazlett

Attendance: 12,000

April 12th: Miller was in the Scotland team which drew 1-1 with England at Wembley.

April 12th
HIBERNIAN (1) 2 — CELTIC (0) 0
L. Johnston (32), Reilly (85)

HIBERNIAN: Kerr; Govan, Shaw; Howie, Aird, Kean; Reilly, Finnigan, Johnston, Turnbull, Ormond

CELTIC: Ugolini; Hogg, Mallan; McPhail, Corbett, Milne; F. Quinn, McAloon, Kiernan, Evans, Cannon

Attendance: 25,000

April 26th: Celtic announced that Hugh Docherty was returning to Ireland.

April 26th
CELTIC 0 — FALKIRK 0

CELTIC: Miller; Hogg, Mallan; McPhail, Corbett, Milne; F. Quinn, McAloon, Bogan, Evans, Cannon

FALKIRK: J. Dawson; Fiddes, Whyte; Doig, Thomson, Telfer; Campbell, Aitken, Wardlaw, Henderson, K. Dawson

Attendance: 15,000

May 3rd
CELTIC (2) 3 — MOTHERWELL (1) 2
Sirrell (35), McAloon (42), Rae (59 pen) — Watson (40), Humphries (74)

CELTIC: Miller; Hogg, Milne; McPhail, Corbett, McAuley; F. Quinn, McAloon, Rae, Sirrell, Cannon

MOTHERWELL: Johnstone; Kilmarnock, Shaw; McLeod, Paton, Redpath; McRoberts, Watson, Humphries, Bremner, Barclay

Attendance: 7,000
Watson and Sirrell were ordered off

April 26th: Willie Miller was in the Scottish League team which beat the Irish League 7-4 in Belfast.

May 18th: Miller was in the Scotland team beaten 2-1 by Belgium in Brussels.

May 24th: Miller was in the Scotland team which won 6-0 away against Luxembourg.

Scottish League Division A

	P	W	D	L	F	A	Pts
1 Rangers	30	21	4	5	76	26	46
2 Hibernian	30	19	6	5	69	33	44
3 Aberdeen	30	16	7	7	58	41	39
4 Hearts	30	16	6	8	52	43	38
5 Partick Thistle	30	16	3	11	74	59	35
6 Morton	30	12	10	8	58	45	34
7 CELTIC	30	13	6	11	53	55	32
8 Motherwell	30	12	5	13	58	54	29
9 Third Lanark	30	11	6	13	56	64	28
10 Clyde	30	9	9	12	55	65	27
11 Falkirk	30	8	10	12	62	61	26
12 Queen of the South	30	9	8	13	44	69	26
13 Queens Park	30	8	6	16	47	60	22
14 St Mirren	30	9	4	17	47	65	22
15 Kilmarnock	30	6	9	15	44	66	21
16 Hamilton	30	2	7	21	38	85	11

LEAGUE CUP

September 21st

HIBERNIAN (1) 4 — CELTIC (1) 2

Aitkenhead (10), Weir (50), Cuthbertson (52), Buchanan (63) — Bogan (27), W. Gallacher (75)

HIBERNIAN: Kerr; Howie, Shaw; Kean, Aird, Cairns; Reilly, Buchanan, Weir, Cuthbertson, Aitkenhead

CELTIC: Miller; Hogg, Milne; Lynch, Corbett, McAuley; Bogan, Kiernan, Rae, W. Gallacher, Hazlett

Attendance: 20,000

September 28th

CELTIC 0 — THIRD LANARK 0

CELTIC: Miller; Hogg, Milne; Lynch, McMillan, McAuley; Bogan, Kiernan, Rae, Sirrell, Paton

THIRD LANARK: Petrie; Balunas, Kelly; Bolt, Barclay, Mooney; McCulloch, Ayton, Henderson, Morrison, Mitchell

Attendance: 15,000

October 5th

HAMILTON ACADEMICALS (1) 2 — CELTIC (1) 2

Bremner (21), Devlin (81) — Kiernan 2 (31, 88)

HAMILTON: Jenkins; McGurk, Johnstone; Daly, Rothera, Lindsay; McGuigan, Bremner, Devlin, Gillan, Devine

CELTIC: Miller; Hogg, Milne; Lynch, McMillan, McAuley; Bogan, Kiernan, Cantwell, McAloon, Paton

Attendance: 18,000

October 12th

CELTIC (1) 1 — HIBERNIAN (1) 1

McAloon (1) — Weir (30)

CELTIC: Miller; Hogg, McDonald; Lynch, McMillan, McAuley; Bogan, Kiernan, Rae, McAloon, Paton

HIBERNIAN: Kerr; Howie, Shaw; Finnigan, Aird, Kean; Smith, Buchanan, Weir, Cuthbertson, Aitkenhead

Attendance: n.a.

October 19th

THIRD LANARK (2) 2 — CELTIC (2) 3

Ayton (3), Mason (23) — Kiernan 2 (33, 60 pen), Bogan (40)

THIRD LANARK: Petrie; Balunus, Kelly; Bolt, Palmer, Mooney; McCulloch, Mason, Carabine, Ayton, Middleton

CELTIC: Ugolini; Hogg, McDonald; Lynch, McMillan, McAuley; Bogan, Kiernan, Rae, McAloon, Paton

Attendance: 35,000

October 26th

CELTIC (1) 3 — HAMILTON ACADEMICALS (1) 1

Rae (7), Kiernan 2 (72, 74) — Devlin (5)

CELTIC: Miller; Hogg, McDonald; Lynch, McMillan, Milne; Bogan, Kiernan, Rae, McAloon, Hazlett

HAMILTON: Jenkins; McGurk, Johnstone; Lindsay, Rothera, Irvine; McGuigan, Bremner, Devlin, Gillan, Devine

Attendance: 15,000

SECTION TABLE

	P	W	D	L	F	A	Pts
Hibernian	6	4	1	1	16	9	9
Celtic	6	2	3	1	11	10	7
Hamilton	6	2	1	3	14	16	5
Third Lanark	6	1	1	4	8	14	3

Qualifiers: HIBERNIAN

SCOTTISH CUP

First Round, January 25th

DUNDEE (1) 2 — CELTIC (0) 1

Ewen (13), Turnbull (58) — McAloon (86)

DUNDEE: Bennett; Follon, Ancell; McKenzie, Gray, Smith; Gunn, Pattillo, Turnbull, Ewen, Juliusson

CELTIC: Miller; Hogg, Mallan; Lynch, Corbett, Milne; Docherty, Kiernan, Rae, McAloon, Evans

Attendance: 36,000

APPEARANCES	League	League Cup	Scottish Cup
Miller	29	4	1
Hogg	26	6	1
Milne	29	3	1
W. Gallacher	14	–	–
Corbett	19	1	1
McAuley	10	6	–
Sirrell	6	1	–
Kiernan	22	6	1
Rae	15	5	1
Bogan	10	6	–
Shields	3	–	–
Cantwell	8	1	–
Evans	21	–	1
Hazlett	18	1	–
Lamb	1	–	–
McDonald	9	3	–
McMillan	12	5	–
Lynch	14	6	1
Baillie	1	–	–
McAloon	19	4	1
Jordan	3	–	–

APPEARANCES	League	League Cup	Scottish Cup
Mallan	14	–	1
Airlie	6	–	–
Docherty	3	–	1
O'Sullivan	4	–	–
R. Quinn	2	–	–
F. Quinn	5	–	–
Ugolini	1	2	–
McPhail	3	–	–
Cannon	3	–	–
J. Gallacher	–	1	–
Paton	–	5	–
McAra	–	–	–

GOALSCORERS

League: McAloon 12, Kiernan 11, Rae 10, Cantwell 5, Evans 4, Airlie 3, Hazlett 3, Own Goals 2, Sirrell 1, Jordan 1, Bogan 1.

League Cup: Kiernan 5, Bogan 2, Rae 1, J. Gallacher 1, Cantwell 1, McAloon 1.

Scottish Cup: McAloon 1.

Geatons is seen donning John Thomson the Celtic goalkeepers jersey after the accident on 5th September, 1931, which resulted in the goalkeeper's tragic death at the age of 22 in a league match at Ibrox against Rangers.

Season 1947- 48

This was probably Celtic's worst-ever League season. They never picked up after a bad start and won only 10 of their 30 matches – 5 at home and 5 away. Undoubtedly their most important win was at Dundee on 17th April when a hat-trick from big-money signing Jock Weir gave them a 3-2 win and took away all possible relegation fears. They lost both Old Firm clashes. They scored only 41 League goals and Tommy McDonald, who was given a free transfer at the end of the season, finished as top scorer with 7 goals. Jock Weir was signed from Blackburn Rovers in February, and at the end of the season Charlie Tully was signed from Belfast Celtic. Tommy Kiernan was transferred to Stoke City for £8,000 just after the start of the season. Willie Miller again represented Scotland and he also played for the Scottish League, as did McAuley and Bogan.

Celtic failed to qualify from their very tough League Cup Section which included Rangers, Dundee and Third Lanark but they did manage a 2-0 home victory over eventual Section winners Rangers.

They also managed to reach the Semi-Final of the Scottish Cup, beating Cowdenbeath, Motherwell and Montrose en route, but they lost to Morton in extra time at Ibrox.

League:	Twelfth
League Cup:	Failed to qualify from Section
Scottish Cup:	Semi-Finalists

LEAGUE DIVISION A

August 13th
AIRDRIE (1) 3 — CELTIC (1) 2
Picken (10), Flavell (59), Cooke (65) — McAuley (40), Kiernan (67 pen)

AIRDRIE: Moodie; Peters, Cunningham; Stevenson, Kelly, Whyte; McCulloch, Picken, Flavell, Brown, Cooke

CELTIC: Miller; Hogg, Mallan; McPhail, Corbett, McAuley; Hazlett, Evans, Kiernan, Sirrell, Paton

Attendance: 20,000

August 27th
CELTIC (3) 4 — QUEENS PARK (0) 0
Paton (10), Rae (24)
McPhail (25), Evans (84)

CELTIC: Miller; Boden, Mallan; McPhail, Corbett, McAuley; Bogan, R. Quinn, Rae, Evans, Paton
QUEENS PARK: R. Simpson; D. Dow, A. Carmichael; D. Letham, A. Miller, J. Hardie; J. Alexander, H.G. Miller, J. Farquhar, R. Gunn, J.M. Brown

Attendance: n.a.

September 20th
RANGERS (1) 2 — CELTIC (0) 0
Williamson (16),
Findlay (77)

RANGERS: Brown; Young, Shaw: McColl, Woodburn, Cox; Waddell, Findlay, Williamson, Thornton, Duncanson

CELTIC: Miller; Ferguson, Milne; R. Quinn, Corbett, McAuley; Bogan, McAloon, J. Gallacher, Evans, Kapler

Attendance: 50,000

Waddell had something of a field day against Milne and it was only splendid goalkeeping by Miller and a magnificent display by Corbett, who was as often at right or left-back as he was at centre-half, that prevented a rout.

September 25th: Tommy Kiernan was transferred to Stoke City for £8,000.

September 27th
CELTIC (0) 0 — MOTHERWELL (1) 1
Humphries (15)

CELTIC: Miller; Ferguson, Milne; R. Quinn, Corbett, McAuley; Bogan, Sirrell, J. Gallacher, Evans, Paton

MOTHERWELL: Johnston; Kilmarnock, Shaw; McLeod, Paton, Redpath; Waters, Watson, Humphries, Bremner, Barclay

Attendance: 25,000

October 1st: Pat McDonald joined Dunfermline Athletic.

October 4th
ABERDEEN (1) 2 — CELTIC (0) 0
Kiddie (19), Baird (76)

ABERDEEN: Johnstone; Cowie, McKenna; McLaughlin, Waddell, Taylor; Kiddie, Baird, Williams, Harris, Millar

CELTIC: Ugolini; Ferguson, Mallan; R. Quinn, Corbett, McAuley; Hazlett, Bogan, Rae, Evans, Paton

Attendance: 25,000

October 4th: Willie Miller was in goal for Scotland against Ireland in Belfast. Ireland won 2-0.

October 11th
CELTIC (1) 3 — MORTON (2) 2
Bogan (13), Paton (67) McLaughlin (79) — McKillop (18), Cupples (28)

CELTIC: Miller; Hogg, Milne; Boden, Corbett, McAuley; Hazlett, Bogan, McLaughlin, Evans, Paton

MORTON: McFeat; Maley, Fyfe; Campbell, Whigham, Daly; Cupples, Orr, McKillop, Henderson, Liddell

Attendance: 14,000

October 18th
CLYDE (1) 2 — CELTIC (0) 0
Johnston (14), Fitzsimmons (59)

CLYDE: Sweeney; Gibson, Deans; Gourlay, McCormack, Long; Riley, Campbell, Johnston, McPhail, Fitzsimmons

CELTIC: Miller; Mallan, Milne; McPhail, Corbett, McAuley; Paton, Bogan, McLaughlin, Evans, Kapler

Attendance: 20,000

October 24th: Celtic signed Tommy McDonald from Third Lanark

October 25th
CELTIC (2) 4 — QUEEN OF THE SOUTH (1) 3
Sirrell (33), McDonald (43), Paton 2 (49, 89) — Houliston 2 (16, 50), Brown (62)

CELTIC: Miller; Mallan, Milne; McPhail, Corbett, McAuley; Bogan, T. McDonald, Evans, Sirrell, Paton

QUEEN OF THE SOUTH: Henderson; Savage, James; Scott, Aird, Sharp; Nutley, Brown, Houliston, Jenkins, Johnstone

Attendance: 12,000

League positions

	P	W	D	L	F	A	Pts
1 Partick Thistle	8	7	0	1	24	8	14
2 Motherwell	8	7	0	1	23	11	14
3 Hibernian	8	5	1	2	20	9	11
4 Dundee	8	5	0	3	17	11	10
5 Rangers	5	4	0	1	11	5	8
10 CELTIC	8	3	0	5	13	15	6

November 8th
CELTIC (0) 0 — FALKIRK (1) 3
Aikman 2 (10, 89), Corbett o.g. (69)

CELTIC: Miller; Mallan, Milne; McPhail, Corbett, McAuley; Bogan, Gallacher, Evans, Sirrell, Paton

FALKIRK: J. Dawson; Whyte, McPhee; Bolt, Fiddes, Whitelaw; Allison, Fleck, Aikman, J. Henderson, K. Dawson

Attendance: 15,000

November 12th: Willie Miller was in the Scotland team beaten 2-1 by Wales at Hampden Park.

November 12th: Celtic signed Frank Walsh from Kilmarnock.

November 15th
PARTICK THISTLE (2) 3 — CELTIC (1) 5
O'Donnell (13), Wright 2 (7 pen, 55) — McDonald 2 (20, 74), Corbett (56 pen), Walsh (60), Bogan (68)

PARTICK THISTLE: Henderson; McGowan, Curran; Brown, Forsyth, Husband; Wright, O'Donnell, Candlin, Sharp, Smith

CELTIC: Ugolini; Mallan, Milne; McPhail, Corbett, McAuley; Bogan, McDonald, Walsh, Evans, Paton

Attendance: 32,000

November 22nd
ST MIRREN (1) 1 — CELTIC (0) 2
Smith (10) — McAuley (60), Walsh (83)

ST MIRREN: Rennie; Smith, Lindsay; W. Reid, Telfer, Martin; Burrell, Crowe, Jack, Deakin, Lesz

CELTIC: Ugolini; Mallan, Milne; McPhail, Corbett, McAuley; Bogan, McDonald, Walsh, Evans, Paton

Attendance: 23,000

December 6th
CELTIC (1) 1 — DUNDEE (1) 1
McDonald (13) — Juliusson (41)

CELTIC: Miller; Mallan, Milne; McPhail, Corbett, McAuley; Bogan, McDonald, Walsh, Evans, Paton

DUNDEE: Lynch; Follon, Ancell; Cowie, Boyd, Gallacher; Gunn, Ewan, Juliusson, Pattilo, Hill

Attendance: 25,000

December 13th
HIBERNIAN (0) 1 — CELTIC (0) 1
McAuley o.g. (48) — Paton (75)

HIBERNIAN: Brown; Govan, Shaw; Finnigan, Aird, Buchanan; Smith, Combe, Linwood, Cuthbertson, Ormond

CELTIC: Miller; Mallan, Milne; McPhail, Corbett, McAuley; Bogan, McDonald, Walsh, Evans, Paton

Attendance: 38,000

December 20th
CELTIC 0 — AIRDRIE 0

CELTIC: Miller; Mallan, Milne; McPhail, Corbett, McAuley; Bogan, McDonald, Walsh, Evans, Paton

AIRDRIE: Moodie; Peters, Higgins; Stevenson, Kelly, Black; McCulloch, Murray, H. Watson, Duncan, G. Watson

Attendance: n.a.

December 25th
CELTIC (2) 4 — HEARTS (1) 2
McDonald 2 (12, 88), Bogan (13), Walsh (87) — Martin 2 (13, 59)

CELTIC: Miller; Mallan, Milne; McPhail, Corbett, McAuley; Bogan, McDonald, Walsh, Evans, Paton

HEARTS: Brown; Mathieson, McKenzie; Dougan, Parker, Laing; Sloan, Martin, Flavell, Dixon, Williams

Attendance:

December 27th
QUEENS PARK (1) 3 — CELTIC (2) 2
Farquhar 2 (30 pen, 51), Cunningham (82) — Paton (15), McDonald (40)

QUEENS PARK: R. Simpson; D. Dow, A. Carmichael; D. McBain, D. Letham, S. Cowan; G. Cunningham, J. Farquhar, A. Aitken, J. Hardy, J.M. Brown

CELTIC: Miller; Mallan, Milne; McPhail, Corbett, McAuley; Bogan, McDonald, Walsh, Evans, Paton

Attendance: 18,000

League positions

	P	W	D	L	F	A	Pts
1 Rangers	15	13	1	1	36	11	27
2 Hibernian	17	11	3	3	50	15	25
3 Partick Thistle	17	10	2	5	40	25	22
4 Motherwell	16	9	1	6	30	23	19
5 Dundee	17	8	2	7	37	31	18
8 CELTIC	16	6	3	7	28	29	15

January 2nd
CELTIC (0) 0 — RANGERS (3) 4
McColl (9), Thornton (26), Rutherford (38), Duncanson (80)

CELTIC: Miller; Mallan, Milne; McPhail, Corbett, McAuley; Bogan, McDonald, Walsh, Evans, Paton

RANGERS: Brown; Cox, Shaw; McColl, Young, Rae; Rutherford, Gillick, Thornton, Duncanson, Caskie

Attendance: 60,000

Rangers meandered back to the top of A Division. A cracking first-time shot by Thornton taken on the half turn in 26 minutes, after Rutherford's corner-kick, ended the match as a contest.

January 3rd
HEARTS (0) 1 — CELTIC (0) 0
Flavell (50)

HEARTS: Brown; Mathieson, McKenzie; Cox, Parker, Laing; McFarlane, Hamilton, Flavell, Dixon, Williams

CELTIC: Miller; Mallan, Milne; McMillan, Corbett, McAuley; Mitchell, Gallacher, Rae, Evans, Paton

Attendance: 37,000

January 10th
CELTIC (0) 1 — ABERDEEN (0) 0
Corbett (55 pen)

CELTIC: Miller; Ferguson, Milne; McPhail, Corbett, McAuley; Paton, McDonald, Gormley, Gallacher, Kapler

ABERDEEN: Johnstone; Cooper, McKenna; Cowie, Dunlop, Taylor; A. Kiddie, McLaughlin, Kelly, Harris, Miller

Attendance: 18,000

Jan 14: Miller and McAuley were in the Scottish League team which beat the Irish League 3-0 at Parkhead.

January 17th
MORTON (2) 4 — CELTIC (0) 0
Divers (20), Orr 2 (44, 54), Cupples (52)

MORTON: Cowan; Mitchell, Whigham; Campbell, Miller, Whyte; Hepburn, Divers, Cupples, Orr, Liddell

CELTIC: Miller; Hogg, Ferguson; McMillan, Corbett, McAuley; Paton, Gallacher, Walsh, McPhail, Kapler

Attendance: 12,000

January 24th
CELTIC (1) 1 — PARTICK THISTLE (2) 2
McPhail (26) — Glover (10), Walker (38)

CELTIC: Miller; Hogg, Milne; McMillan, Corbett, McAuley; Paton, McPhail, Rae, Evans, Kapler

PARTICK THISTLE: Henderson; McGowan, Husband; Davidson, Forsyth, Hewitt; Glover, Brown, Mathie, Sharp, Walker

Attendance: 15,000

January 31st
CELTIC 0 — CLYDE 0

CELTIC: Miller; Mallan, Milne; McMillan, Corbett, McAuley; Bogan, McPhail, Evans, McDonald, Paton

CLYDE: Gullan; Gibson, Deans; McCormack, Milligan, Campbell; Galletly, Riley, Johnston, Garth, Fitzsimmons

Attendance: 20,000. McAuley was ordered off

February 14th
QUEEN OF THE SOUTH (2) 2 — CELTIC (0) 0
Houliston 2 (65, 80)

QUEEN OF THE SOUTH: Henderson; Fulton, James; Hamilton, Aird, Law; Stephens, Brown, Houliston, Jenkins, Johnstone

CELTIC: Miller; Mallan, Milne; McMillan, Corbett, McAuley; Bogan, McPhail, Evans, W. Gallacher, Paton

Attendance: 13,500

February 17th: Celtic signed Jock Weir from Blackburn Rovers for £7,000.

February 28th
FALKIRK (0) 0 — CELTIC (0) 1
Corbett (89 pen)

FALKIRK: J. Dawson; Whyte, McPhee; Doig, Fiddes, Whitelaw; Allison, Fleck, Aikman, J. Henderson, K. Dawson

CELTIC: Miller; Mallan, Milne; W. Gallacher, Corbett, McAuley; Bogan, McPhail, Weir, McDonald, Paton

Attendance: 20,000

League positions

	P	W	D	L	F	A	Pts
1 Hibernian	24	17	4	3	69	20	38
2 Rangers	22	18	1	3	54	19	37
3 Partick Thistle	25	13	3	9	48	35	29
4 Dundee	24	12	3	9	52	37	27
5 Motherwell	22	12	1	9	40	31	25
10 CELTIC	24	8	4	12	31	42	20

March 1st: Celtic announced that all of the regular first team – with the exception of Willie Miller – and most of the Parkhead staff were to become full-timers.

March 13th
CELTIC 0 — ST MIRREN 0

CELTIC: Miller; Mallan, Milne; W. Gallacher, Corbett, Baillie; Bogan, McPhail, Weir, Evans, Paton

ST MIRREN: Kirk; Smith, Lindsay; Drinkwater, Telfer, Martin; Burrell, Crowe, Milne, Deakin, Lesz

Attendance: 45,000

March 17th: Willie Miller and Tommy Bogan were in the Scottish League team which drew 1-1 with the English League at Newcastle.

March 20th
MOTHERWELL (0) 0 — CELTIC (3) 3
McPhail 2 (17, 33), Weir (43)

MOTHERWELL: Johnstone; Kilmarnock, Shaw; McLeod, A. Paton, Redpath; Watters, W. Paton, Humphries, Bremner, Barclay

CELTIC: Miller; Mallan, Milne; W. Gallacher, Corbett, Baillie; Bogan, McPhail, Weir, Evans, Paton

Attendance: 20,000

March 29th
THIRD LANARK (1) 5 — CELTIC (0) 1
Stirling (36), Staroscik 2 (58, n.a.), Mitchell (n.a.) — Evans (69)

THIRD LANARK: Petrie; Balunas, Kelly; Mooney, Barclay, Harrower; Staroscik, Mason, Stirling, Ayton, Mitchell

CELTIC: Miller; Mallan, Milne; W. Gallacher, Corbett, Baillie; Paton, McDonald, Walsh, Evans, Kapier

Attendance: 25,000

April 3rd
CELTIC (2) 2 — HIBERNIAN (1) 4
Lavery (23), Evans (35) — Linwood 2 (15, 82), Turnbull 2 (54, 65 pen)

CELTIC: Miller; Fraser, McAuley; W. Gallacher, Mallan, Baillie; Bogan, McPhail, Lavery, Evans, Paton

HIBERNIAN: Farm; Govan, Shaw; Kean, Howie, Buchanan; Smith, Combe, Linwood, Cuthbertson, Turnbull

Attendance: 25,000

April 10th
CELTIC (0) 1 — THIRD LANARK (1) 3
Bogan (89) — W. Gallacher o.g. (10), Mason (10), Orr (83)

CELTIC: Miller; Mallan, McAuley; W. Gallacher, Corbett, Baillie; Bogan, McPhail, Weir, Evans, Kapler

THIRD LANARK: Petrie; Balunas, Kelly; Mooney, Barclay, Harrower; Staroscik, Mason, Stirling, Orr, Mitchell

Attendance: 19,000

April 17th
DUNDEE (1) 2 — CELTIC (2) 3
Ewen (44), Mackay (60) — Weir 3 (14, 67, 88)

DUNDEE: Brown; Follon, Irvine; Gallacher, Gray, Boyd; Gunn, Pattillo, Stewart, Ewen, Mackay

CELTIC: Miller; Hogg, Mallan; Evans, Corbett, McAuley; Weir, McPhail, Lavery, Gallacher, Paton

Attendance: 31,000

Scottish League Division A

	P	W	D	L	F	A	Pts
1 Hibernian	30	22	4	4	86	27	48
2 Rangers	30	21	4	5	64	28	46
3 Partick Thistle	30	16	4	10	61	42	36
4 Dundee	30	15	3	12	67	51	33
5 St Mirren	30	13	5	12	54	58	31
6 Clyde	30	12	7	11	52	57	31
7 Falkirk	30	10	10	10	55	48	30
8 Motherwell	30	13	3	14	45	47	29
9 Hearts	30	10	8	12	37	42	28
10 Aberdeen	30	10	7	13	45	45	27
11 Third Lanark	30	10	6	14	56	73	26
12 CELTIC	30	10	5	15	41	56	25
13 Queen of the South	30	10	5	15	49	74	25
14 Morton	30	9	6	15	47	43	24
15 Airdrie	30	7	7	16	39	78	21
16 Queens Park	30	9	2	19	45	75	20

April 24th: Willie Miller was in the Scottish League Team which beat the League of Ireland 2-0 in Dublin.

May 3rd: Celtic freed Tommy McDonald, Joe Rae, George Hazlett, R. Quinn, Joe McLaughlin, F. Walsh and B. Cannon. Rae joined Rosario F.C. of Argentina and Hazlett joined Belfast Celtic.

June 20th: Charlie Tully was signed from Belfast Celtic for a fee between £8,000 and £9,000.

LEAGUE CUP

August 9th
RANGERS (0) 2 — CELTIC (0) 0
Williamson 2 (61, 71)

RANGERS: Brown; Cox, Shaw; McColl, Woodburn, Rae; Waddell, Gillick, Williamson, Thornton, Duncanson

CELTIC: Miller; Hogg, Mallan; McPhail, Corbett, McAuley; F. Quinn, McAloon, Kiernan, Sirrell, Paton

Attendance: 75,000

Never before had so big a crowd watched a game on the opening day of the season in Britain. Both Rangers' goals, within 10 minutes of each other in the second half, were made by Duncanson and finished off by Williamson. Apart from a 20-yard drive from Sirrell that bounced from the post with Brown helpless, Celtic's forwards never looked like scoring.

August 16th
CELTIC (1) 1 — DUNDEE (1) 1
Paton (44) — Turnbull (12)

CELTIC: Miller; Hogg, Mallan; McPhail, Corbett, McAuley; Kiernan, Sirrell, J. Gallacher, Evans, Paton

DUNDEE: Lynch; Follon, Ancell; Cowie, Gray, Boyd; Gunn, Ewen, Turnbull, Pattillo, Hill

Attendance: 35,000

August 23rd
CELTIC (2) 3 — THIRD LANARK (0) 1
J. Gallacher 2 (1, 22), R. Quinn (85) — McCulloch (61)

CELTIC: Miller; Boden, Mallan; McPhail, Corbett, McAuley; Bogan, R. Quinn, J. Gallacher, Evans, Paton

THIRD LANARK: Fraser; Middleton, Kelly; Baillie, Palmer, Mooney; McCulloch, Mason, Reid, Ayton, Mitchell

Attendance: 25,000

August 30th
CELTIC (0) 2 — RANGERS (0) 0
J. Gallacher (52), Paton (58)

CELTIC: Miller; Hogg, Mallan; McPhail, Corbett, McAuley; Bogan, R. Quinn, J. Gallacher, Evans, Paton

RANGERS: Brown; Cox, Shaw; Watkins, Woodburn, Rae; Waddell, Gillick, Williamson, Thornton, Duncanson

Attendance: 50,000

Rangers' cloak of invincibility was torn in shreds by Celtic. The keystone of Celtic's victory was the excellent play of their half-back line. The zest and cleverness of McPhail and McAuley made Gillick and Thornton their direct opponents look jaded.

September 6th
DUNDEE (3) 4 — CELTIC (1) 1
Pattillo (5), Ewen 2 (26, 37 pen), Juliusson (47) — Bogan (30)

DUNDEE: Lynch; Follon, Ancell; Cowie, Boyd, R. Smith; Gray, Ewen, Turnbull, Pattillo, Juliusson

CELTIC: Miller; Hogg, P. McDonald; McPhail, Corbett, McAuley; Bogan, R. Quinn, Rae, Evans, Paton

Attendance: 35,000

September 13th (Hampden Park)
THIRD LANARK (2) 3 — CELTIC (2) 2
McCulloch (3), McDonald 2 (17, 46) — J. Gallacher (8), Palmer o.g. (15)

THIRD LANARK: Fraser; Balunas, Kelly; McMillan, Palmer, Mooney; Staroscik, Mason, McCulloch, McDonald, Mitchell

CELTIC: Miller; Boden, Milne; McPhail, Corbett, McAuley; P. McDonald, Sirrell, J. Gallacher, Evans, Kapler

Attendance: 25,000

SECTION TABLE

	P	W	D	L	F	A	Pts
Rangers	6	4	1	1	12	4	9
Dundee	6	2	2	2	12	13	6
CELTIC	6	2	1	3	9	11	5
Third Lanark	6	2	0	4	12	17	4

SCOTTISH CUP

Second Round February 7th
CELTIC (1) 3 COWDENBEATH (0) 0
McPhail 2 (3, 63),
W. Gallacher (57)

CELTIC: Miller; Mallan, Milne; McMillan, Corbett, McAuley; Bogan, McPhail, Evans, W. Gallacher, Paton

COWDENBEATH: Shaw; Hamilton, Elliot; Shankland, Brawley, Boyd; Hope, Cowan, Jones, McCreadie, Kesley

Attendance: 19,931

Third Round February 21st
CELTIC (0) 1 MOTHERWELL (0) 0
Paton (78)

CELTIC: Miller; Mallan, Milne; McMillan, Corbett, McAuley; Bogan, McPhail, Weir, McDonald, Paton

MOTHERWELL: Johnston; Kilmarnock, Shaw; McLeod, Paton, Redpath; Waters, Robertson, Humphries, Bremner, Barclay

Attendance: 55,231

Fourth Round March 6th
CELTIC (2) 4 MONTROSE (0) 0
McPhail 2 (28, 49),
Weir (34),
Paton (71)

CELTIC: Miller; Mallan, Milne; W. Gallacher, Corbett, McAuley; Bogan, McPhail, Weir, Evans, Paton

MONTROSE: Cook; Calder, Costello; Wotherspoon, Jolly, Cabrelli; Munro, Jeffrey, Scobie, Mitchell, Lawrie

Attendance: 39,077

Semi-Final March 27th at Ibrox
MORTON (0) 1 CELTIC (0) 0
Murphy (112)
After Extra Time

MORTON: Cowan; Mitchell, Whigham; Campbell, Miller, Whyte; Hepburn, Murphy, Cupples, McGarrity, Liddell

CELTIC: Miller; Mallan, Milne; W. Gallacher, Corbett, Baillie; Bogan, McPhail, Weir, Evans, Paton

Attendance: 80,000

Before the interval Mitchell cut off the goal-line a ball which, shot from the touchline by McPhail, had beaten Cowan. The defences sealed all approaches in the second half, Miller, Morton's centre-half, being particularly dominating. In extra time Morton lasted the strenuous pace the better. Only Milne, Corbett and McPhail were consistently good for Celtic. Murphy scored the only goal of the game for Morton in extra time.

Appearances	League	League Cup	Scottish Cup
Miller	27	6	4
Hogg	5	4	–
Mallan	24	4	4
McPhail	24	6	4
Corbett	29	6	4
McAuley	27	6	3
Hazlett	3	–	–
Evans	27	5	3
Kiernan	1	2	–
Sirrell	4	3	–
Paton	28	5	4
Boden	2	2	–
Bogan	23	3	4
R. Quinn	4	3	–
Rae	4	1	–
Ferguson	5	–	–
Milne	23	1	4
McAloon	1	1	–
J. Gallacher	7	4	–
Kapler	6	1	–
Ugolini	3	–	–
McLaughlin	2	–	–
T. McDonald	13	–	1
Walsh	10	–	–
McMillan	5	–	2
Mitchell	1	–	–
Gormley	1	–	–
W. Gallacher	7	–	3
Weir	5	–	3
Baillie	5	–	1
Fraser	1	–	–
Lavery	2	–	–
F. Quinn	–	1	–
P. McDonald	–	2	–

GOALSCORERS:

League: McDonald 7, Paton 6, Weir 4, Bogan 4, McPhail 4, Evans 3, Walsh 3, Corbett 3 (3 pens), McAuley 2, Lavery 1, Sirrell 1, McLaughlin 1, Rae 1, Kiernan 1 (pen)

League Cup: J. Gallacher 4, Paton 2, R. Quinn 1, Bogan 1, Own Goal 1

Scottish Cup: McPhail 4, Paton 2, W. Gallacher 1, Weir 1

Season 1948-49

Celtic picked up 6 more points than in the previous season and finished 6 places higher up the table. They won 12 of their matches but the fans had to wait until December 18th for their first home win in the competition. They lost both matches against Rangers but they did manage the double over four teams – Clyde, Hearts, Motherwell and Partick Thistle. Rangers won the title by a point from Dundee. Celtic scored 48 goals – Jackie Gallacher was top scorer with 12 – and the defence had tightened up considerably. Only Tully played in all 30 matches.

Leslie Johnston was signed from Clyde for £12,000 and Celtic made a highly publicised but unsuccessful attempt to sign England International Wilf Mannion from Middlesbrough. Bobby Hogg, Tommy Bogan, Duncan McMillan and Willie Corbett all left the club during the season.

Celtic again failed to qualify from their League Cup Section. They won their first 3 matches against Hibs, Clyde and Rangers but lost all three of the returns.

They were knocked out of the Scottish Cup in the first round by B Division Dundee United.

League:	Sixth
League Cup:	Failed to qualify from Section
Scottish Cup:	First Round

LEAGUE DIVISION A

August 9th: John Bonnar was signed from Arbroath.

August 14th
CELTIC 0 MORTON 0

CELTIC: Miller; Milne, Mallan; Evans, Boden, McAuley; Weir, McPhail, Lavery, Tully, Paton

MORTON: Cowan; Mitchell, Whigham; Campbell, Miller, Whyte; Hepburn, Murphy, Farquhar, Orr, Mochan

Attendance: 60,000

August 18th
ABERDEEN (0) 1 CELTIC (0) 0
Williams (55)

ABERDEEN: Johnstone; McLaughlin, McKenna; Stenhouse, Roy, Waddell; Harris, Hamilton, Williams, Baird, Pearson

CELTIC: Miller; Milne, Mallan; Evans, Boden, McAuley; Weir, McPhail, Lavery, Tully, Paton

Attendance: 35,000

August 21st
CELTIC (0) 0 RANGERS (1) 1
Findlay (6)

CELTIC: Miller; Milne, Mallan; Evans, Boden, McAuley; Docherty, McPhail, Weir, Tully, Paton

RANGERS: Brown; Young, Shaw; McColl, Woodburn, Cox; Rutherford, Gillick, Thornton, Findlay, Duncanson

Mallan missed a penalty.

Attendance: 50,000. Tommy Docherty's debut.

August 28th
HEARTS (1) 1 CELTIC (2) 2
Flavell (25) McPhail 2 (27 pen, 37)

HEARTS: Brown; Laing, McKenzie; Cox, Parker, Dougan; Sloan, Conn, Flavell, Urquhart, Williams

CELTIC: Miller; Milne, Mallan; Evans, Boden, McAuley; Weir, McPhail, J. Gallacher, Tully, Paton

Attendance: 40,000

September 1st
CELTIC (2) 2 — J. Gallacher 2 (24, 43)
QUEEN OF THE SOUTH (1) 2 — Jenkins (30), Johnstone (80)

CELTIC: Miller; Milne, Mallan; Evans, McMillan, McAuley; Weir, McPhail, J. Gallacher, Tully, Paton

QUEEN OF THE SOUTH: Henderson; Sharp, James; McBain, Aird, Hamilton; McCulloch, Turnbull, Houliston, Jenkins, Johnstone

Attendance: 40,000

September 4th
ALBION ROVERS (1) 3 — Wallace 2 (29, 84), Love (81)
CELTIC (2) 3 — Weir 2 (25, 68), Tully (28)

ALBION ROVERS: McGregor; Paterson, English; Martin, Stein, Kerr; Craig, Dixon, Wallace, Love, J. Smith

CELTIC: Miller; Milne, Mallan; Evans, McMillan, McAuley; Weir, Bogan, J. Gallacher, Tully, Paton

Attendance: 25,000

September 12th: Celtic made a bid of £12,000 for Wilf Mannion of Middlesbrough.

September 24th: There was press speculation that Leeds United were ready to make a £20,000 bid for both Evans and Tully.

September 30th: Tommy Bogan was transferred to Preston North End.

October 14th: A Celtic bid of two players and a sum of money for Wilf Mannion was rejected by Middlesbrough.

October 23rd
CELTIC (0) 0
DUNDEE (1) 1 — Gerrie (35)

CELTIC: Miller; Milne, Mallan; Docherty, Boden, Baillie; Weir, McPhail, J. Gallacher, Tully, Paton

DUNDEE: Brown, Follon, Ancell; Gallacher, Gray, Boyd; Gunn, Pattillo, Gerrie, Smith, Andrews

Attendance: 28,000

October 23rd: Bobby Evans was in the Scotland team which beat Wales 3-1 in Cardiff.

October 26th: Celtic signed Leslie Johnston of Clyde for £12,000.

October 30th
HIBERNIAN (0) 1 — Cuthbertson (57)
CELTIC (1) 2 — Johnston 2 (15, 75)

HIBERNIAN: Kerr; Govan, Howie; Buchanan, Aird, Kean; Smith, Turnbull, Linwood, Cuthbertson, Reilly

CELTIC: Miller; Milne, McGuire; Evans, Boden, Baillie; Weir, Tully, J. Gallacher, Johnstone, Paton

Attendance: 35,000

League positions

	P	W	D	L	F	A	Pts
1 Hibernian	8	5	2	1	27	16	12
2 St Mirren	7	5	1	1	13	8	11
3 East Fife	7	5	0	2	17	10	10
4 Falkirk	8	4	1	3	23	14	9
5 Rangers	7	3	3	1	10	9	9
9 CELTIC	8	2	3	3	9	10	7

November 6th
CLYDE (0) 0
CELTIC (3) 4 — J. Gallacher 2 (10, 22), Paton 2 (25, 50)

CLYDE; Gullan; Gibson, Deans; Dunn, McCormack, Campbell; Davies, Wright, Ackerman, Garth, Galletly

CELTIC: Bonnar; McGuire, Milne; Docherty, Boden, Baillie; Sirrell, Tully, J. Gallacher, Johnston, Paton

Attendance: 35,000

November 6th: Miller and Evans were in the Scottish League team which beat the Irish League 1-0 in Belfast.

November 13th
CELTIC (0) 0
EAST FIFE (1) 1 — Duncan (10)

CELTIC: Bonnar; McGuire, Milne; Evans, Boden, Baillie; Sirrell, Tully, J. Gallacher, Johnston, Paton

EAST FIFE: Clark; Proudfoot, Stewart; Philp, Finlay, Aitken; Adams, Fleming, Morris, Brown, Duncan

Attendance: 55,000

November 17th: Bobby Evans was in the Scotland team which beat Ireland 3-2 at Hampden Park.

November 19th: Bobby Hogg was given a free transfer after 18 seasons with the club. He later joined Alloa Athletic.

November 20th:
THIRD LANARK (3) 3 — Scott 2 (14, 39), Baillie o.g. (43)
CELTIC (2) 2 — Paton (4), J. Gallacher (15)

THIRD LANARK: Fraser; Balunas, Kelly; Orr, Barclay, Harrower; Downs, Mason, Scott, Bogan, Staroscik

CELTIC: Miller; McGuire, Milne; Evans, Boden, Baillie; Weir, Tully, J. Gallacher, Johnston, Paton

Attendance: 30,000

November 27th
CELTIC (2) 4 — J. Gallacher 3 (3, 25, 79), Weir (68)
FALKIRK (4) 4 — Allison (17), Logan (29), K. Dawson (35), Inglis (40)

CELTIC: Miller; McGuire, Milne; Evans, T. Docherty, McAuley; Weir, Tully, J. Gallacher, Johnston, Paton

FALKIRK: J. Dawson; Whyte, McPhee; Fiddes, Henderson, Telfer; Allison, Ackerman, Inglis, Logan, K. Dawson

Attendance: 30,000

December 4th
PARTICK THISTLE (1) 1 CELTIC (0) 2
Sharp (27) Weir (70), Johnston (86)

PARTICK THISTLE: Henderson; McGowan, Pirrie; Brown, Davidson, Candlin; McKenzie, Wilson, O'Donnell, Sharp, Walker

CELTIC: Miller; McGuire, Milne; Evans, Boden, McAuley; Weir, Johnston, J. Gallacher, Tully, Paton

Attendance: 36,000

December 11th
ST MIRREN (1) 1 CELTIC (1) 1
Reid (12) Tully (24)

ST MIRREN: Kirk; Lapsley, Martin; Drinkwater, Telfer, Willie Reid; Burrell, Stewart, Telford, Davie, Lesz

CELTIC: Miller; Milne, Mallan; Evans, Boden, McAuley; Weir, Johnston, J. Gallacher, Tully, Paton

Attendance: 35,000

December 18th
CELTIC (1) 3 MOTHERWELL (0) 2
Johnston (32), McAuley (52 pen) Paton (75) Mathie 2 (68, 90)

CELTIC: Miller; Milne, Mallan; Evans, Boden, McAuley; Weir, Johnston, J. Gallacher, Tully, Paton

MOTHERWELL: Johnstone; Kilmarnock, Shaw; Russell, Paton, Redpath; Goodall, Watson, Mathie, Bremner, Barclay

Attendance: 40,000

Leading positions

	P	W	D	L	F	A	Pts
1 Hibernian	15	8	4	3	40	30	20
2 Rangers	13	8	3	2	25	16	19
3 Dundee	12	7	3	2	25	14	17
4 St Mirren	14	7	3	4	23	18	17
5 Falkirk	14	6	4	4	40	30	16
7. CELTIC	15	5	5	5	25	22	15

December 25th
CELTIC (3) 3 ABERDEEN (0) 0
McPhail (15), Paton 2 (18, 21)

CELTIC: Miller; Milne, Mallan; Evans, Boden, McAuley; Weir, Johnston, McPhail, Tully, Paton

ABERDEEN: Curran; Massie, McKenna; Stenhouse, Waddell, McLaughlin; Rice, Hamilton, Kelly, Harris, Williams

Attendance: 35,000

January 1st
RANGERS (3) 4 CELTIC (0) 0
Thornton (3), Duncanson 3 (26, 43, 88)

RANGERS: Brown; Young, Shaw; McColl, Woodburn, Cox; Waddell, Paton, Thornton, Duncanson, Rutherford

CELTIC: Miller; Milne, Mallan; Evans, Boden, McAuley; Weir, Johnston, J. Gallacher, Tully, Paton

Attendance: 85,000

Rangers played football of the highest quality in difficult conditions. The left-wing of Duncanson and Rutherford was a tremendous success. The outside-left gave Milne, the Celtic right-back, a roasting. McColl took full revenge on Tully for the latter's joy day at his expense earlier in the season.

January 3rd
CELTIC (1) 2 HEARTS (0) 0
Tully (44), J. Gallacher (52)

CELTIC; Miller; Boden, Mallan; Evans, McPhail, McAuley; Weir, Johnston, J. Gallacher, Tully, Paton

HEARTS: Brown; Mathieson, McKenzie; Parker, Dougan, Laing; McFarlane, Conn, Bauld, Wardhaugh, Flavell

Attendance: 50,000

January 8th
MORTON 0 CELTIC 0

MORTON: Clark; Henderson, Fyfe; G. Mitchell, Miller, Whyte; Stevenson, Divers, Liddell, Orr, Alexander

CELTIC: Miller; Boden, Mallan; Evans, McPhail; McAuley; Weir, W. Gallacher, Johnston, Tully, Paton

Attendance: 18,000

January 15th
CELTIC (2) 3 ALBION ROVERS (0) 0
Docherty (8), J. Gallacher (18), Weir (83)

CELTIC: Miller; Boden, Mallan; Docherty, McPhail, McAuley; Weir, W. Gallacher, J. Gallacher, Tully, Paton

ALBION ROVERS: McGregor; Muir, English; Imrie, Stein, McLeod; McKinnon, Hunter, Love, Wallace, Smith

Attendance: 15,000

January 29th
QUEEN OF THE SOUTH (1) 1 CELTIC (0) 0
Jenkins (7)

QUEEN OF THE SOUTH: Henderson; McCall, James; McBain, Aird, Hamilton; McCulloch, G. Brown, C. Brown, Jenkins, Johnstone

CELTIC: Miller; Boden, Mallan; Evans, McPhail, McAuley; Sirrell, Johnston, J. Gallacher, Tully, Paton

Attendance: 16,500

February 5th: Dan Lavery joined Glentoran on loan.

February 12th
CELTIC (0) 1 — HIBERNIAN (2) 2
McPhail (62 pen) — Smith (70,) Plumb (36)

CELTIC: Miller; McGuire, Milne; McPhail, Boden, McAuley; Weir, Evans, Johnston, W. Gallacher, Tully

HIBERNIAN: Kerr; Govan, Cairns; Gallacher, Kean, Buchanan; Smith, Combe, Plumb, Turnbull, Ormond

Attendance: 37,000

February 21st: it was reported that Celtic were ready to exchange Bobby Evans for Irish International goalkeeper, Fred Hinton of Fulham.

February 26th
EAST FIFE (1) 3 — CELTIC (0) 2
Duncan (15), Black (66), Fleming (77) — Johnston (58), Docherty (80)

EAST FIFE: Niven; Laird, Stewart; Philp, Finlay, Hudson; Black, Fleming, Morris, Brown, Duncan

CELTIC: Bonnar; Mallan, Milne; McPhail, Boden, Baillie; Weir, Docherty, Johnston, Tully, Paton

Attendance: 18,000

March 8th: Duncan McMillan was transferred to Grimsby Town.

March 12th
FALKIRK (0) 1 — CELTIC (1) 1
Inglis (62) — Docherty (16)

FALKIRK: J. Dawson; Whyte, McPhee; Fiddes, Henderson, Whitelaw; Alison, Inglis, Aikman, Logan, K. Dawson

CELTIC: Bonnar; Mallan, Milne; McPhail, Boden, McAuley; Weir, Docherty, Johnston, Tully, Paton

Attendance: 15,000

League positions

	P	W	D	L	F	A	Pts
1 Hibernian	23	17	4	2	64	24	38
2 Rangers	22	17	3	2	45	20	37
3 Hearts	24	16	2	6	64	29	34
4 Dundee	23	11	7	5	41	26	29
5 CELTIC	24	11	6	7	40	42	28

March 19th
CELTIC (0) 3 — PARTICK THISTLE (0) 0
Weir 2 (64, 83), J. Gallacher (88)

CELTIC: Bonnar; Mallan, Milne; McPhail, Boden, McAuley; Weir, Evans, Johnston, Tully, J. Gallacher

PARTICK THISTLE: Henderson; McGowan, Gibb; Hewitt, Davidson, Wilson; McKenzie, Howitt, O'Donnell, Sharp, Walker

Attendance: 25,000

March 23rd: Jimmy Mallan was in the Scottish League team beaten 3-0 by the English League at Ibrox.

March 26th
CELTIC (1) 2 — ST MIRREN (0) 1
Weir (23), Lapsley o.g. (48) — Milne (49)

CELTIC: Bonnar; Mallan, Milne; McPhail, Boden, McAuley; Weir, Evans, J. Gallacher, Johnston, Tully

ST MIRREN: Kirk; Lapsley, Martin; Drinkwater, Telfer, Reid; Burrell, Guthrie, Milne, Deakin, Lesz

Attendance:

April 2nd
MOTHERWELL (0) 0 — CELTIC (0) 1
J. Gallacher (62)

MOTHERWELL: Johnstone; Kilmarnock, Shaw; McLeod, Paton, Russell; Goodall, Bremner, Watson, McCall, Aitkenhead

CELTIC: Bonnar; McGuire, Milne; Evans, Boden, McAuley; Weir, McPhail, J. Gallacher, Johnston, Tully

Attendance: 20,000

April 9th: Bobby Evans was in the Scotland team which beat England 3-1 at Wembley.

April 11th
DUNDEE (1) 3 — CELTIC (2) 2
Stott (43), Gerrie 2 (76 n.a.) — Johnston 2 (15, 17)

DUNDEE: Lynch; Gray, Boyd; Gallacher, Cowie, Rattray; Gunn, Ewen, Stott, Gerrie, Hill

CELTIC: Bonnar; Mallan, Milne; McPhail, Boden, McAuley; Weir, T. Docherty, Johnston, W. Gallacher, Tully

Attendance: 29,000

April 16th
CELTIC (1) 1 — THIRD LANARK (2) 2
Tully (17) — Scott (9), Staroscik (21)

CELTIC: Bonnar; Mallan, McGuire; Evans, Boden, McAuley; J. Weir, D. Weir, Johnston, Docherty, Tully

THIRD LANARK: Fraser; Balunas, Harrower; Orr, Christie, Mooney; Bogan, Mason, Scott, Henderson, Staroscik

Attendance: 30,000

April 18th
CELTIC (1) 2 — CLYDE (0) 1
Weir (26), Johnston (83) — Linwood (82)

CELTIC: Miller; McGuire, Baillie; Evans, Boden, McAuley; Johnston, J. Docherty, J. Weir, Tully, Paton

CLYDE: Gullan; Gibson, Deans; Campbell, McCormack, Long; Davies, Wright, Linwood, Garth, Galletly

Attendance: 25,000

April 27th: Bobby Evans was in the Scotland team which beat France 2-0 at Hampden Park.

May 7th: Willie Corbett joined Preston North End.

May 10th: Sirrell, Kapier and W. Gallacher were given free transfers.

Scottish League Division A

	P	W	D	L	F	A	Pts
1 Rangers	30	20	6	4	63	32	46
2 Dundee	30	20	5	5	71	48	45
3 Hibernian	30	17	5	8	75	52	39
4 East Fife	30	16	3	11	64	46	35
5 Falkirk	30	12	8	10	70	54	32
6 CELTIC	30	12	7	11	48	40	31
7 Third Lanark	30	13	5	12	56	52	31
8 Hearts	30	12	6	12	64	54	30
9 St Mirren	30	13	4	13	51	47	30
10 Queen of the South	30	11	8	11	47	53	30
11 Partick Thistle	30	9	9	12	50	63	27
12 Motherwell	30	10	5	15	44	49	25
13 Aberdeen	30	7	11	12	39	48	25
14 Clyde	30	9	6	15	50	67	24
15 Morton	30	7	8	15	39	51	22
16 Albion Rovers	30	3	2	25	30	105	8

LEAGUE CUP

September 11th
CELTIC (1) 1 — HIBERNIAN (0) 0
Weir (3)

CELTIC: Miller; Milne, Mallan; Evans, Boden, McAuley; Weir, W. Gallacher, J. Gallacher, Tully, Paton

HIBERNIAN: Kerr; Howie, Shaw; Finnigan, Aird, Buchanan; Smith, Combe, Linwood, Turnbull, Reilly

Attendance: 55,000

September 18th
CLYDE (0) 0 — CELTIC (2) 2
J. Gallacher (2), W. Gallacher (20)

CLYDE: Gullan; Gibson, Deans; Dunn, McCormack, Campbell; Davies, Wright, Johnston, Garth, Galletly

CELTIC: Miller; Milne, Mallan; Evans, Boden, McAuley; Weir, W. Gallacher, J. Gallacher, Tully, Paton

Attendance: 25,000

September 25th
CELTIC (2) 3 — RANGERS (1) 1
J. Gallacher (39), W. Gallacher (44), Weir (70) — Findlay (10)

CELTIC: Miller; Milne, Mallan; Evans, Boden, McAuley; Weir, W. Gallacher, J. Gallacher, Tully, Paton

RANGERS: Brown; Lindsay, Shaw; McColl, Young, Cox; Waddell, Findlay, Thornton, Duncanson, Gillick

Attendance: 65,000

In 10 minutes Miller made his one mistake of the match by dropping the ball at Findlay's feet for a cheap score. In 39 minutes Tully trailed half of the Rangers' defenders after him, gesticulated to Paton where the pass would go and served him perfectly. When Young had to go for the winger J. Gallacher had an easy task to shoot the ball home. One minute from half-time after Thornton had hit the post, came another splendid goal for Celtic. Evans swerved through and guided the ball to Tully, and when the latter's headed pass continued the operation W. Gallacher was in the centre-forward position to score. The deciding goal 20 minutes from the end led to heated protests from Rangers. There may have been some justification in their claim that Brown was impeded by J. Gallacher before Weir shot home.

October 2nd
HIBERNIAN (1) 4 — CELTIC (2) 2
Linwood (10), Smith 2 (73 pen, 89), Reilly (66) — J. Gallacher 2 (35, 56),

HIBERNIAN: Kerr; Howie, Shaw; Buchanan, Aird, Kean; Smith, Combe, Linwood, Cuthbertson, Reilly

CELTIC: Miller; Milne, Mallan; Evans, Boden, McAuley; Weir, W. Gallacher, J. Gallacher, Tully, Paton

Attendance: 53,000 (a record)

October 9th
CELTIC (2) 3 — CLYDE (4) 6
J. Gallacher 3 (11, 35, 69) — Wright 3 (2, 24, 50), Ackerman (33), Campbell (38), Garth (66 pen)

CELTIC: Miller; Milne, Mallan; Evans, McGrory, McAuley; Weir, W. Gallacher, J. Gallacher, Sirrell, Paton

CLYDE: Grant; Gibson, Deans; Dunn, McCormack, Campbell; Davies, Wright, Ackerman, Garth, Galletly

Attendance: 22,000

October 16th
RANGERS (1) 2 — CELTIC (0) 1
Williamson (39), Waddell (72) — McPhail (49 pen)

RANGERS: Brown; Young, Shaw; Cox, Woodburn, Rae; Waddell, Thornton, Williamson, Marshall, Duncanson

CELTIC: Miller; Milne, Mallan; Evans, Boden, McAuley; Weir, McPhail, J. Gallacher, Tully, Paton

Attendance: 105,000 — biggest of the season in Britain

Rangers' opening goal in 39 minutes was extremely fortuitous. Williamson's back was to the Celtic goal when 20 yards out he lunged in to block Boden's clearance and fortunately the ball struck his boot, rose in the air, and sailed over Miller's head. Celtic's goal, 4 minutes after half-time, was the cause of much complaint as Rangers appealed to the referee that Woodburn's tackle on Gallacher was fair. McPhail scored from the spot. Celtic questioned the validity of

Waddell's score 18 minutes from the end but his anticipation of Thornton's pass was timed to perfection.

SECTION TABLE

	P	W	D	L	F	A	Pts
Rangers	6	3	2	1	8	6	8
Hibernian	6	3	1	2	12	5	7
CELTIC	6	3	0	3	12	13	6
Clyde	6	1	1	4	9	17	3

Qualifier: RANGERS

SCOTTISH CUP

First Round January 22nd
DUNDEE UNITED (2) 4 CELTIC (1) 3
McKay 2 (20, 75 pen), Dickson (25) Cruikshank (80)
Tully (29), J. Gallacher 2 (56, 76)

DUNDEE UNITED: Edmiston; Berrie, Jardine; Ogilvie, Ross, Grant; Quinn, Dickson, McKay, Mitchell, Cruikshank

CELTIC: Miller; Boden, Mallan; Evans, McPhail, McAuley; Weir, Johnston, J. Gallacher, Tully, Paton

Attendance: 25,000

Appearances	League	League Cup	Scottish Cup
Miller	21	6	1
Milne	24	6	1
Mallan	21	6	1
Evans	24	6	1
Boden	27	5	1
McAuley	24	6	1
J. Weir	27	6	1
McPhail	18	1	–
Lavery	2	–	–
Tully	30	5	1
Paton	24	6	1
T. Docherty	9	–	–
J. Gallacher	19	6	1
McMillan	2	–	–
Bogan	1	–	–
Baillie	7	–	–
McGuire	10	–	–
Johnston	22	–	1
Bonnar	9	–	–
Sirrell	3	1	–
W. Gallacher	4	5	–
D. Weir	1	–	–
J. Docherty	1	–	–
McGrory	–	1	–

GOALSCORERS:
League: J. Gallacher 12, J.Weir 9, Johnston 8, Paton 6, McPhail 4 (2 pens), Tully 4, T. Docherty, 3, McAuley 1 (pen), Own Goals 1

League Cup: J. Gallacher 7, J. Weir 2, W. Gallacher 2, McPhail 1 (pen)

Scottish Cup: J. Gallacher 2, Tully 1

The Celtic team in 1947-48. Back row: Hogg (Capt.), Mallan, Miller, Gallacher, Corbett, Milne. Front row: Docherty, McAloon, Rae, Evans and O'Sullivan.

Season 1949-50

Celtic's League form showed a slight improvement from the previous season. 14 of the 30 matches were won and they finished 5th in the table behind Champions Rangers, Hibs, Hearts and East Fife. They went through the whole campaign without a home defeat but they won only 3 away matches. They scored 51 League goals but managed only 14 away from home – their lowest-ever total. Mike Haughney and John McPhail finished as joint top scorers with 12 apiece. Bobby Evans and Alec Boden each played in 27 matches. Leslie Johnston and Tommy Docherty were transferred south of the border and Sean Fallon was signed from Glenavon at the end of March for £5,000.

For the third season in succession Celtic drew Rangers in their League Cup Section and although they managed to beat them at home, as in the previous two seasons, they again failed to qualify.

They lost to Aberdeen in the Third Round of the Scottish Cup in front of their own fans after beating Brechin City and Third Lanark (after a replay).

League:	Fifth
League Cup:	Failed to qualify from Section
Scottish Cup:	Third Round

LEAGUE DIVISION A

August 28th: Bill Rennett was signed from Lochee Harp.

September 9th: Johnny Paton was transferred to Brentford for £5,000.

September 10th
QUEEN OF THE SOUTH (0) 0 — CELTIC (2) 2
Taylor (13), Haughney (30)

QUEEN OF THE SOUTH: Henderson; McCardle, James; McBain, Waldie, Gibson; Houliston, Jack Brown, James Brown, Neilson, Johnstone

CELTIC: Miller; McGuire, Baillie; Evans, Boden, McAuley; Collins, McPhail, Haughney, Taylor, Tully

Attendance: 20,250

September 17th
CELTIC (2) 3 — HEARTS (2) 2
Haughney (7), Taylor (31), Collins (69) — Wardhaugh 2 (25, 39)

CELTIC: Miller; McGuire, Baillie; Evans, Boden, McAuley; Weir, Collins, Haughney, Taylor, Tully

HEARTS: Brown; Parker, Mathieson; Cox, Henderson, Dougan; Sloan, Currie, Bauld, Wardhaugh, Flavell

Attendance: n.a.

September 24th
RANGERS (2) 4 — CELTIC (0) 0
Rutherford (6), Findlay (43), Waddell (85 pen), Williamson (88)

RANGERS: Brown; Young, Shaw: McColl, Woodburn, Rae; Waddell, Findlay, Williamson, Cox, Rutherford

CELTIC: Miller; McGuire, Milne; Evans, Boden, Baillie; Collins, McPhail, Haughney, Taylor, Rennett

Attendance: 64,000

The absence in Rangers' team of Thornton and Duncanson and of McAuley and Tully from Celtic undoubtedly reduced the skill element. Rangers dominated proceedings throughout with goals from Rutherford, Findlay, Waddell from the penalty spot and Williamson.

The Celtic team which beat Rangers 3-2 in the 1949-50 Glasgow Charity Cup Final. Back row: Haughney, Milne, Bonnar, Evans, McGrory, Baillie. Front row: Collins, Fernie, McPhail, Peacock and Tully.

October 1st
CELTIC (2) 2 — RAITH ROVERS (2) 2
Taylor (4), Haughney (36) — Penman 2 (34, 44)

CELTIC: Miller; Boden, Mallan; Cairney, McGrory, Baillie; Collins, Johnston, Haughney, Taylor, Rennett

RAITH ROVERS: Westland; McLure, McNaught; Young, Colville, Till; Smith, Maule, Goldie, McLaughlin, Penman

Attendance: 15,000

October 1st: Bobby Evans was in the Scotland team which beat Ireland 8-2 in Belfast.

October 8th
MOTHERWELL (0) 1 — CELTIC (2) 2
Waters (53) — Collins (12), McPhail (15)

MOTHERWELL: Hamilton; Kilmarnock, Higgins; W. Paton, A. Paton, Redpath; Watters, Watson, Mathie, Robertson, Aitkenhead

CELTIC: Miller; Boden, Milne; Evans, McGrory, McAuley; Collins, McPhail, Haughney, Taylor, Tully

Attendance: 30,000

October 15th
CELTIC (1) 4 — ABERDEEN (1) 2
Collins (36), McPhail (77), Haughney 2 (80,89) — Kelly (6), Rice (85)

CELTIC: Miller; Boden, Milne; Evans, McGrory, McAuley; Collins, McPhail, Haughney, Taylor, Tully

ABERDEEN: Curran; Emery, McKenna; Anderson, Waddell, Harris; Rice, Hamilton, Kelly, Yorston, Hather

Attendance: 30,000

October 19th: Bobby Evans was in the Scottish League team which beat the League of Ireland 1-0 in Dublin.

October 22nd
DUNDEE (3) 3 — CELTIC (0) 0
Rattray (1), Gerrie (11), Gunn (17)

DUNDEE: Lynch; Follon, Cowan; Gallacher, Cowie, Boyd; Gunn, Rattray, Fraser, Gerrie, Andrews

CELTIC: Miller; Mallan, Milne; Evans, Boden, McAuley; Collins, McPhail, Haughney, Taylor, Tully

Attendance: 35,000

October 28th: Leslie Johnston was transferred to Stoke City for £9,000

October 29th
CELTIC (0) 2 — HIBERNIAN (2) 2
McPhail (62), Evans (89) — Reilly (17), Smith (33)

CELTIC; Miller; Mallan, Milne; Evans, McGrory, McAuley; Collins, McPhail, Haughney, Tully, Rennett

HIBERNIAN: Younger; Govan, Cairns; Combe, Paterson, Buchanan; Smith, Johnstone, Reilly, Turnbull, Ormond

Attendance: 55,000

League positions

	P	W	D	L	F	A	Pts
1 St Mirren	8	4	3	1	21	13	11
2 Rangers	5	5	0	0	12	1	10
3 Dundee	7	4	2	1	18	10	10
4 CELTIC	8	4	2	2	15	16	10
5 Hibernian	6	4	1	1	16	7	9

November 4th: Tommy Docherty joined Preston North End for £5,000.

November 5th
CELTIC (1) 4 — CLYDE (1) 1
Rennett 3 (39, 57, 87), Haughney (78) — Ackerman (57)

CELTIC: Miller; Boden, Mallan; Evans, McGrory, McAuley; Collins, McPhail, Haughney, Tully, Rennett

CLYDE: Hewkins; Gibson, Mennie; Campbell, Milligan, Haddock; Galletly, Ackerman, Linwood, McPhail, Shepherd

Attendance: 25,000. McPhail missed a penalty

November 9th: Evans and McPhail were in the Scotland team which beat Wales 2-0 at Hampden Park. McPhail scored the opening goal.

November 9th: Charlie Tully was in the Ireland team beaten 9-2 by England at Maine Road, Manchester.

November 12th
STIRLING ALBION (1) 2 — CELTIC (1) 1
Jones 2 (24, 80) — McPhail (32)

STIRLING ALBION: Gerhard; Muir, McKeown; Bain, Whiteford, Wilson; Dick, Keith, Jones, Martin, Szpula

CELTIC: Miller; Boden, Milne; Evans, McGrory, McAuley; Collins, McPhail, Haughney, Tully, Rennett

Attendance: 25,000 (Ground record)

November 19th
CELTIC (1) 2 — THIRD LANARK (1) 1
McPhail (33), Haughney (71) — Cuthbertson (28)

CELTIC: Miller; Boden, Milne; Evans, McGrory, Baillie; Collins, McPhail, Haughney, Tully, Rennett

THIRD LANARK: Fraser; Balunas, Kelly; Mooney, Barclay, Harrower; Friel, Cuthbertson, Scott, Henderson, McLeod

Attendance: 28,000

November 26th
FALKIRK (0) 1 — CELTIC (0) 1
McGrory o.g. (73) — Haughney (65)

FALKIRK: Nicol; Whyte, McPhee; J. Gallacher, Henderson, Whitelaw; Fiddes, W. Gallacher, Silcock, Dawson, Alison

CELTIC: Miller; Boden, Milne; Evans, McGrory, Baillie; Collins, Haughney, Weir, Tully, Rennett

Attendance: 20,000

December 3rd
CELTIC (0) 1 PARTICK THISTLE (0) 0
Rennett (63)

CELTIC: Miller; Boden, Milne; Evans, McGrory, Baillie; Haughney, McPhail, Weir, Tully, Rennett

PARTICK THISTLE: Ledgerwood; McGowan, Gibb; Davidson, Kinnell, Hewitt; Thomson, Brown, Stott, Howitt, Walker

Attendance: 25,000. McPhail missed a penalty.

December 10th
CELTIC 0 ST MIRREN 0

CELTIC: Miller; Boden, Milne; Evans, McGrory, Baillie; Weir, McPhail, Haughney, Tully, Rennett

ST MIRREN: Kirk; Lapsley, Martin; Drinkwater, Telfer, Reid; Milne, Burrell, Henderson, Davie, Lesz

Attendance: 28,000

December 17th
EAST FIFE (1) 5 CELTIC (1) 1
Duncan (22), Black (48), Fleming (52), Morris 2 (60, 86) Gallacher (40)

EAST FIFE: Niven; Laird, Stewart; Philp, Finlay, Aitken; Black, Fleming, Morris, Brown, Duncan

CELTIC: Miller; Boden, Milne; Evans, McGrory, Baillie; Collins, McPhail, Gallacher, Tully, Haughney

Attendance: 14,000

December 24th
CELTIC (2) 3 QUEEN OF THE SOUTH (0) 0
Collins (2), Haughney 2 (35,48)

CELTIC: Miller; Boden, Milne; Evans, McGrory, Baillie; Collins, McPhail, Haughney, Tully, Rennett

QUEEN OF THE SOUTH: Henderson; Sharp, James; McBain, Waldie, Hamilton; Wooton, McKinnon, C. Brown, J. Brown, Johnstone

Attendance: 15,000

League positions

	P	W	D	L	F	A	Pts
1 Hibernian	14	12	1	1	40	14	25
2 Rangers	13	11	0	2	27	13	22
3 Hearts	15	10	1	4	43	18	21
4 Dundee	15	8	4	3	30	17	20
5 CELTIC	16	8	4	4	28	26	20

December 20th: 18-year old goalkeeper George Hunter was signed from Neilston Juniors.

December 31st
HEARTS (1) 4 CELTIC (0) 2
Bauld 2 (25, 63), Parker (60), Milne o.g. (84) Collins 2 (49, 66)

HEARTS: Brown; Parker, McKenzie; Cox, Dougan, Laing; Sloan, Conn, Bauld, Wardhaugh, Flavell

CELTIC: Miller; Boden, Milne; Evans, McGrory, Baillie; Weir, Collins, Haughney, Tully, Rennett

Attendance: 44,000

January 2nd
CELTIC (1) 1 RANGERS (0) 1
Weir (36) McCulloch (82)

CELTIC: Bonnar; Boden, Mallan; Evans, McGrory, Baillie; Collins, Haughney, Weir, Taylor, Tully

RANGERS: Brown; Young, Shaw; McColl, Woodburn, Cox; McCulloch, Findlay, Thornton, Johnson, Marshall

Attendance: 65,000

Celtic's goal in 36 minutes was the result of a defensive mistake by Woodburn who should have intercepted Taylor's through pass to Weir. 8 minutes from time Mallan astonishingly lost his balance, completely missed the ball and McCulloch, far and away Rangers' best forward, accepted the Ne'erday gift and equalised.

January 3rd
RAITH ROVERS (1) 1 CELTIC (1) 1
McLaughlin (19) Haughney (10)

RAITH ROVERS: McGregor; McSpadyen, McNaught; Till, Colville, Leigh; Kelly, Maule, Collins, McLaughlin, Stirling

CELTIC: Bonnar; McGuire, Mallan; Evans, McGrory, Baillie; Taylor, Haughney, Weir, Peacock, Tully

Attendance: 10,000

January 7th
CELTIC (3) 3 MOTHERWELL (0) 1
Kilmarnock o.g. (15), Taylor (37), McAuley (44) McLeod (51)

CELTIC: Bonnar; Boden, Mallan; Evans, McGrory, Baillie; Collins, Taylor, Weir, McAuley, Tully

MOTHERWELL: Hamilton; Kilmarnock, Higgins; McLeod, Paton, Redpath; McCall, Watson, Kelly, Bremner, Aitkenhead

Attendance: 25,000

January 14th
ABERDEEN (2) 4 CELTIC (0) 0
Baird (7), Pearson (12), Hather (55), Emery (89 pen)

ABERDEEN: Watson; Emery, McKenna; Anderson, McKenzie, Harris; Hather, Yorston, Hamilton, Baird, Pearson

CELTIC: Bonnar; Boden, Mallan; Evans, McGrory, Baillie; Collins, Taylor, Weir, McAuley, Tully

Attendance: 25,000

January 21st
CELTIC (1) 2 — DUNDEE (0) 0
Tully (17), Evans (90)

CELTIC: Bonnar; Boden, McAuley; Evans, McGrory, Baillie; Collins, McPhail, Weir, Taylor, Tully

DUNDEE: Lynch; Follon, Cowan; Cowie, Pattillo, Boyd; Gunn, Toner, Gerrie, Ewen, Andrews

Attendance: 25,000

February 4th
HIBERNIAN (2) 4 — CELTIC (1) 1
Turnbull 4 (22 pen, 44 pen, 51, 71 pen) — Collins (32 pen)

HIBERNIAN: Younger; Govan, Clark; Combe, Cairns, Buchanan; Smith, Johnstone, Reilly, Turnbull, Ormond

CELTIC: Bonnar; Boden, McAuley; Evans, McGrory, Baillie; Collins, McPhail, Weir, Taylor, Tully

Attendance: 38,000

February 18th
CELTIC (2) 2 — STIRLING ALBION (0) 1
Weir 2 (10 secs, 9) — Inglis (85)

CELTIC: Bonnar; Boden, McAuley; Toner, McGrory, Baillie; Collins, McPhail, Weir, Haughney, Tully

STIRLING ALBION: Little; McKeown, Clark; Bain, Rodgers, Guy; Laird, Martin, Inglis, Dick, Miller

Attendance: 25,000. Miller missed a penalty

League positions

	P	W	D	L	F	A	Pts
1 Hibernian	27	18	5	4	84	29	41
2 Rangers	25	15	6	4	55	25	36
3 East Fife	26	15	3	8	60	42	33
4 Hearts	26	13	6	7	61	43	32
5 Raith Rovers	26	10	6	10	39	45	26
13 CELTIC	24	7	6	11	38	44	20

March 4th
CELTIC (1) 4 — FALKIRK (2) 3
Weir (4), McPhail 3 (64, 70 pen, 71) — Wright (23), Fiddes 2 (38, 83 pen)

CELTIC: Bonnar; Boden, McAuley; Evans, Toner, Baillie; Weir, Haughney, McPhail, Tully, Rennett

FALKIRK: Nicol; Fiddes, Whitelaw; J. Gallacher, Henderson, McCabe; Souness, Wright, Plumb, Anderson, Dawson

Attendance: 20,000

March 11th
THIRD LANARK (1) 1 — CELTIC (0) 0
Staroscik (9)

THIRD LANARK: Goram; Balunas, Harrower; Orr, Christie, Mooney; Staroscik, Mason, Cuthbertson, Henderson, Dalziel

CELTIC: Bonnar; Boden, McAuley; Evans, McGrory, Baillie; Collins, Taylor, McPhail, J. Docherty, Rennett

Attendance: 20,000

March 18th
ST MIRREN (0) 0 — CELTIC (0) 1
Haughney (71)

ST MIRREN: Kirk; Lapsley, Martin; Drinkwater, Telfer, Reid; Burrell, Lawson, Jones, Neilson, Brown

CELTIC: Bonnar; Boden, McAuley; Evans, McGrory, Baillie; Collins, Fernie, McPhail, Peacock, Haughney

Attendance: 20,000

March 22nd: Bobby Evans was in the Scottish League team beaten 3-1 by the English League at Middlesbrough.

March 25th
CELTIC (2) 4 — EAST FIFE (1) 1
McPhail 4 (24, 44, 82 pen, 84) — Brown (5)

CELTIC: Bonnar; Boden, McAuley; Evans, McGrory, Baillie; Collins, Fernie, McPhail, Peacock, Tully

EAST FIFE: Niven; Laird, Stewart; Philp, Finlay, Aitken; Black, Fleming, Morris, Brown, Duncan

Attendance: 25,000

March 27th: Sean Fallon was signed from Glenavon for £5,000.

April 10th
PARTICK THISTLE (1) 1 — CELTIC (0) 0
Stott (19)

PARTICK THISTLE: Henderson; McGowan, McCreadie; Davidson, Kinnell, Hewitt; McKenzie, McCallum, Stott, Sharp, Walker

CELTIC: Bonnar; Boden, Milne; Evans, McGrory, Baillie; Collins, Fernie, McPhail, Peacock, Haughney

Attendance: 34,000

April 15th
CLYDE (1) 2 — CELTIC (1) 2
Fallon o.g. (34), Linwood (85) — Fernie (29), Tully (88)

CLYDE: Hewkins; Lindsay, S. Dunn; J. Dunn, Milligan, Haddock; Galletly, Ackerman, Linwood, Davies, Barclay

CELTIC: Bonnar; Fallon, Milne; Mallan, McGrory, Baillie; Collins, Fernie, McPhail, Tully, Rennett

Attendance: 20,000

April 26th: Bobby Evans was in the Scotland team which beat Switzerland 3-1 at Hampden Park.

May 25th: Bobby Evans was in the Scotland team which drew 2-2 with Portugal in Lisbon.

Scottish League Division A

	P	W	D	L	F	A	Pts
1 Rangers	30	22	6	2	58	26	50
2 Hibernian	30	22	5	3	86	34	49
3 Hearts	30	20	3	7	86	40	43
4 East Fife	30	15	7	8	58	43	37
5 CELTIC	30	14	7	9	51	50	35
6 Dundee	30	12	7	11	49	46	31
7 Partick Thistle	30	13	3	14	55	45	29
8 Aberdeen	30	11	4	15	48	56	26
9 Raith Rovers	30	9	8	13	45	54	26
10 Motherwell	30	10	5	15	53	58	25
11 St Mirren	30	8	9	13	42	49	25
12 Third Lanark	30	11	3	16	44	62	25
13 Clyde	30	10	4	16	56	73	24
14 Falkirk	30	7	10	13	48	72	24
15 Queen of the South	30	5	6	19	31	63	16
16 Stirling Albion	30	6	3	21	38	77	15

LEAGUE CUP

August 13th
CELTIC (2) 3 — RANGERS (1) 2
McPhail 2 (22, 30), Haughney (70) — Waddell (12 pen), Thornton (65)

CELTIC: Miller; McGuire, Baillie; Evans, Boden, McAuley; Collins, McPhail, Johnston, Tully, Haughney

RANGERS: Brown; Young, Shaw; McColl, Woodburn, Cox; Waddell, Findlay, Thornton, Duncanson, Rutherford

Attendance: 70,000

This was McAuley's match. He sold more dummies to Findlay than are usually bought in an entire season and he prompted and spurred Tully, a collaborator in Rangers' defeat. Both Collins and Haughney made their first appearance in senior football. Collins showed fine intelligence in parting with the ball at exactly the right moment and Haughney was concerned in the scoring of all Celtic's goals.

August 17th
ABERDEEN (2) 4 — CELTIC (3) 5
Emery (1), Yorston (6), Kelly (49), Harris (76) — Haughney 3 (2, 10, 16), Collins (64), McPhail (86)

ABERDEEN: Curran; Emery, McKenna; Anderson, McKenzie, Waddell; Rice, Yorston, Kelly, Harris, Pearson

CELTIC: Miller; McGuire, Baillie; Evans, Boden, McAuley; Collins, McPhail, Johnston, Tully, Haughney

Attendance: n.a.

August 20th
ST MIRREN (1) 1 — CELTIC (0) 0
Deakin (20)

ST MIRREN: Miller; Lapsley, Martin; Crowe, Telfer, Reid; Burrell, Stewart, Milne, Deakin, Lesz

CELTIC: Miller; McGuire, Baillie; Evans, Boden, Milne; Collins, McPhail, Johnston, Tully, Haughney

Attendance: 42,000

August 27th
RANGERS (1) 2 — CELTIC (0) 0
Findlay (40), Waddell (82)

RANGERS: Brown; Young, Shaw; Cox, Woodburn, Rae; Waddell, Findlay, Thornton, Duncanson, Rutherford

CELTIC: Miller; Mallan, Baillie; Evans, Boden, McAuley; Collins, McPhail, Johnston, Tully, Haughney

Attendance: 95,000

In 40 minutes Findlay scored for Rangers. 10 minutes after half-time Rangers were awarded a penalty-kick after Waddell had been tackled by Boden but Young hit the crossbar from the spot. Rangers scored the decisive second goal late on by Willie Waddell. The Celtic fans were unhappy throughout at many of the referees decisions.

August 31st
CELTIC (1) 1 — ABERDEEN (2) 3
Haughney (6) — Pearson (10), Kelly (15), Yorston (78)

CELTIC: Miller; Mallan, Baillie; Evans, Boden, McAuley; Collins, McPhail, Haughney, Peacock, Tully

ABERDEEN: Curran; Emery, McKenna; Anderson, Roy, Harris; Kiddie, Yorston, Kelly, Smith, Pearson

Attendance: 15,000

September 3rd
CELTIC (3) 4 — ST MIRREN (0) 1
Haughney (25), Tully (30), McAuley (44), McPhail (61) — Davie (58)

CELTIC: Miller; McGuire, Baillie; Evans, McGrory, McAuley; Collins, McPhail, Haughney, Taylor, Tully

ST MIRREN: Miller; Lapsley, Martin; Crowe, Telfer, Reid; Burrell, Stewart, Milne, Davie, Lesz

Attendance: 30,000

SECTION TABLE

	P	W	D	L	F	A	Pts
Rangers	6	3	2	1	15	8	8
CELTIC	6	3	0	3	13	13	6
Aberdeen	6	2	1	3	12	14	5
St Mirren	6	2	1	3	7	12	5

Qualifier: RANGERS

SCOTTISH CUP

First Round January 28th
BRECHIN CITY (0) 0 CELTIC (1) 3
Weir 2 (30, 62), McPhail (73)

BRECHIN: Shaw; Paterson, Atkinson; Bennett, Smith, Mitchell; Fraser, Robbie, Paris, Hind, Henderson

CELTIC: Bonnar; Boden, McAuley; Evans, McGrory, Baillie; Collins, McPhail, Weir, Taylor, Tully

Attendance: 6,500

Second Round February 15th
THIRD LANARK (1) 1 CELTIC (0) 1
Orr (29) Weir (58)

THIRD LANARK: Goram; Balunas, Crawford; Mooney, Christie, Harrower; Henderson, Mason, Cuthbertson, Orr, Scott

CELTIC: Bonnar; Boden, McAuley; Evans, McGrory, Baillie; Collins, McPhail, Weir, Taylor, Tully

Attendance: 35,000

Second Round Replay February 20th
CELTIC (1) 4 THIRD LANARK (0) 1
McPhail 3 (4, 86, 90), Tully (63) Mitchell (55)

CELTIC: Bonnar; Boden, McAuley; Evans, McGrory, Baillie; Collins, McPhail, Weir, Haughney, Tully

THIRD LANARK: Goram; Balunas, Crawford; Mooney, Christie, Harrower; Henderson, Mason, Mitchell, Cuthbertson, Staroscik

Attendance: 33,000

Third Round February 25th
CELTIC (0) 0 ABERDEEN (1) 1
Anderson (35)

CELTIC: Bonnar; Boden, McAuley; Evans, McGrory, Baillie; Collins, McPhail, Weir, Tully, Rennett

ABERDEEN: Watson; Emery, McKenna; Anderson, McKenzie, Harris; Stenhouse, Yorston, Hamilton, Baird, Pearson

Attendance: 65,112

Appearances	League	League Cup	Scottish Cup
Miller	17	6	–
McGuire	4	4	–
Baillie	24	6	4
Evans	27	6	4
Boden	27	5	4
McAuley	17	5	4
Collins	26	6	4
McPhail	22	6	4
Haughney	23	6	1
Taylor	14	1	2
Tully	25	6	4
J. Weir	13	–	4
Milne	15	1	–
Rennett	14	–	1
Mallan	9	2	–
Cairney	1	–	–
McGrory	25	1	4
Johnston	1	4	–
Gallacher	1	–	–
Bonnar	13	–	4
Peacock	4	1	–
Toner	2	–	–
J. Docherty	1	–	–
Fernie	4	–	–
Fallon	1	–	–

GOALSCORERS

League: Haughney 12, McPhail 12 (2 pens), Collins 7(1 pen), Taylor 4, Rennett 4, J. Weir 4, Evans 2, Tully 2, Gallacher 1, McAuley 1, Fernie 1, Own Goal 1

League Cup: Haughney 6, McPhail 4, Tully 1, McAuley 1, Collins 1

Scottish Cup: McPhail 4, J. Weir 3, Tully 1

Willie Maley, associated with the Club for 52 years as player, secretary and manager.

Season 1950-51

Although their away form had improved, Celtic's home form was very patchy, with only 6 wins, and they finished 7th in the League table behind Hibs, Rangers, Dundee, Hearts, Aberdeen and Partick Thistle. Their best sequence of results was 10 matches without defeat between October 21st and December 30th. They were in fourth place in the table on December 30th. But the New Year started disastrously with 5 straight defeats. They scored 48 goals and Bobby Collins finished as top scorer with 15. Only Bertie Peacock played in every match. Miller, McAuley and Jackie Gallacher all left Celtic Park – Miller to Clyde before the season had begun. Goalkeeper George Hunter, formerly of Neilston Juniors, proved to be the find of the season and he went on to win a Scottish Cup Winner's medal after only 16 senior appearances.

The Club won the Scottish Cup for the first time since 1937. They beat East Fife (after a replay), Duns, Hearts and Aberdeen. Raith Rovers were overcome in the Semi-Final in a 5-goal thriller, and although they did not produce their best form in the Final itself against Motherwell in front of a crowd of 131,943, a 12th-minute goal from captain John McPhail ensured that the Cup returned to Parkhead for the 16th time. The Cup victory was more than ample revenge for the League Cup Quarter-Final defeat at the hands of Motherwell whom they faced after going through their six Section matches undefeated.

They undertook a 9-match tour of North America and Canada at the end of the season remaining undefeated until their final match against English First Division side Fulham in Montreal: 2-3.

League:	Seventh
League Cup:	Quarter-Finalists
Scottish Cup:	Winners
St Mungo's Cup:	Winners

LEAGUE DIVISION A

August 1st: Willie Miller joined Clyde.

August 8th: Chic Geatons resigned as Coach.

September 9th
CELTIC (1) 3 — MORTON (2) 4
McPhail 3 (30, 61 pen, 84 pen) — Mochan 3 (32, 53, 86), Orr (35 pen)

CELTIC: Bonnar; Haughney, Milne; Evans, McGrory, Baillie; Collins, Fernie, McPhail, Peacock, Tully

MORTON: Cowan; Mitchell, Whigham; Hunter, Batton, Whyte; Alexander, Orr, Mochan, McGarritty, McVinish

Attendance: 45,000

September 23rd
CELTIC (0) 3 — RANGERS (0) 2
D. Weir (60), McPhail (80 pen), Peacock (85) — Rae (61), Thornton (74)

CELTIC: Bonnar; Fallon, Milne; Evans, Mallan, Baillie; Collins, D. Weir, McPhail, Peacock, Tully

RANGERS: Brown; Young, Lindsay; McColl, Woodburn, Cox; Rutherford, Findlay, Thornton, Johnson, Rae

Attendance: 53,789

16 minutes were left for play when the extraordinary heading ability of Thornton gave Rangers the lead from a Rutherford corner and a Findlay glance. In the 80th minute a Tully cross was intercepted by Woodburn. The referee, with a clear view, immediately signalled for

a penalty to the consternation of Rangers and the surprise of most of the spectators. The jubilant Celts struck again five minutes from time and again a Tully cross led to the goal.

September 30th
RAITH ROVERS (1) 1 — CELTIC (2) 2
Young (4) — J. Weir (12), Peacock (37)

RAITH ROVERS: Johnstone; McLure, McNaught; McLaughlin, Woodcock, Colville; Mitchell, Keith, Young, Murray, Brander

CELTIC: Bonnar; Fallon, Milne; Evans, Mallan, Millsop; J. Weir, D. Weir, McPhail, Peacock, Tully

Attendance: 13,500

September 27th: Evans and McPhail were in the Scottish League team which beat the Irish League 4-0 in Belfast.

October 7th
CELTIC (2) 2 — RAITH ROVERS (1) 3
Peacock 2 (11, 36) — Penman (22), McLaughlin 2 (75, 80)

CELTIC: Bonnar; Fallon, Milne; Evans, Mallan, Millsop; Collins, D. Weir, McPhail, Peacock, Tully

RAITH ROVERS: Johnstone; McLure, McNaught; McLaughlin, Colville, Leigh; Branden, Maule, Young, Murray, Penman

Attendance: 20,000

October 14th
ABERDEEN (0) 2 — CELTIC (0) 1
Hamilton 2 (76, 84) — McPhail (89)

ABERDEEN: Martin; Emery, Shaw; Anderson, Young, Glen; Boyd, Yorston, Hamilton, Baird, Hather

CELTIC: Bonnar; Fallon, Milne; Evans, Mallan, Baillie; Collins, D. Weir, McPhail, Peacock, Tully

Attendance: 30,000

October 21st
CELTIC 0 — DUNDEE 0

CELTIC: Bonnar; Fallon, Milne; Evans, Mallan, Baillie; Millsop, Fernie, J. Weir, Peacock, Tully

DUNDEE: Lynch; Follon, Cowan; Cowie, Boyd, Craig; Gunn, Toner, Williams, Gerrie, Andrews

Attendance: 30,000

October 21st: McPhail and Collins were in the Scotland team which beat Wales 3-1 in Cardiff.

October 28th
MORTON (0) 0 — CELTIC (1) 2
Collins (22), McPhail (63)

MORTON: Cowan; Mitchell, Whigham; G. Mitchell, Thom, Whyte; Alexander, Cupples, Mochan, McGarritty, McVinish

CELTIC: Bonnar; Fallon, Milne; Evans, Mallan, Baillie; J. Weir, Collins, McPhail, Peacock, Tully

Attendance: 20,000

League positions

	P	W	D	L	F	A	Pts
1 Dundee	8	5	2	1	12	6	12
2 Hearts	8	5	1	2	17	10	11
3 Morton	8	5	1	2	19	13	11
4 Aberdeen	7	5	0	2	18	14	10
5 Raith Rovers	8	4	1	3	17	15	9
9 CELTIC	7	3	1	3	13	12	7

November 1st: Collins and McPhail were in the Scotland team which beat Ireland 6-1 at Hampden Park. McPhail scored 2 of the goals.

November 4th
CLYDE (1) 1 — CELTIC (1) 3
Buchanan (13) — J. Weir (11), McPhail (49), Collins (75)

CLYDE: Allan; Lindsay, Mennie; J. Dunn, Somerville, Long; Davies, Bolton, Buchanan, McPhail, Ring

CELTIC: Bonnar; Fallon, Milne; Evans, Mallan, Baillie; J. Weir, Collins, McPhail, Peacock, Tully

Attendance: 30,000

November 11th
CELTIC (2) 3 — FALKIRK (0) 0
McPhail (15), Collins (22 pen), Peacock (80)

CELTIC: Bonnar; Fallon, Milne; Evans, Mallan, Baillie; J. Weir, Collins, McPhail, Peacock, Tully

FALKIRK: Barrie; Fiddes, Wilson; Gallacher, Henderson, Whitelaw; Morrison, Johnson, Plumb, Wright, Brown

Attendance: 12,000

November 18th
AIRDRIE (0) 2, — CELTIC (2) 4
Picken (47), McMillan (78) — Collins 2 (33 pen, 55), McPhail (41), Tully (81)

AIRDRIE: Fraser; Kelly, Elliot; Cairns, Dingwall, T. Brown; Picken, Welsh, Orr, Cunningham, McMillan

CELTIC: Bonnar; Fallon, Milne; Evans, Mallan, Baillie; J. Weir, Collins, McPhail, Peacock, Tully

Attendance: 20,000

November 25th
CELTIC (1) 1 — THIRD LANARK (0) 1
McPhail (20) — Cuthbertson (57)

CELTIC: Bonnar; Fallon, Milne; Evans, Mallan, Baillie; J. Weir, Collins, McPhail, Peacock, Tully

THIRD LANARK: Simpson; Balunas, Harrower; Adams, Samuel, Orr; McCall, Mason, Cuthbertson, Dick, Staroscik

Attendance: 15,000

The Celtic team in 1954. Back row: Mike Haughney, Frank Meechan, John Bonnar, Bobby Collins, Bobby Evans, Bert Peacock. Front row: Willie Fernie, Sean Fallon, Jock Stein, Charlie Tully and Neil Mochan.

Referee Mowat blows for time-up and Tully hugs McPhail, the scorer of the only goal. Celtic had just won the 1951 Scottish Cup Final, defeating Motherwell by 1 goal to 0.

November 29th: Evans and McPhail were in the Scottish League team which beat the English League 1-0 at Ibrox. McPhail scored the only goal.

December 2nd
PARTICK THISLTE (0) 0 CELTIC (0) 1
J. Weir (80)

PARTICK THISTLE: Ledgerwood; McGowan, Gibb; Davidson, Forsyth, Hewitt; McKenzie, McCallum, O'Donnell, Sharp, Walker

CELTIC: Bonnar; Fallon, Milne; Evans, Mallan, Baillie; J. Weir, Collins, McPhail, Peacock, Tully

Attendance: 38,000

December 9th
ST MIRREN 0 CELTIC 0

ST MIRREN: Kirk; Lapsley, Drinkwater; Neilson, Telfer, Johnston; Blyth, Anderson, Rennie, Duncanson, Lesz

CELTIC: Bonnar; Fallon, Milne; Evans, Mallan, Baillie; J. Weir, Collins, McPhail, Peacock, Tully

Attendance: 30,000

December 13th: Evans, Collins and McPhail were in the Scotland team which was beaten 1-0 by Austria at Hampden Park.

December 15th: Pat McAuley was transferred to Luton Town.

December 16th
CELTIC (3) 6 EAST FIFE (1) 2
McPhail 3 (6 secs, 11, 80), Collins 3 (32, 59, 84)
Morris (24), Duncan (74)

CELTIC: Bonnar; Fallon, Milne; Evans, Mallan, Baillie; J. Weir, Collins, McPhail, Peacock, Tully

EAST FIFE: Easson; Weir, Proudfoot; Philip, Finlay, McLennan; Black, Fleming, Morris, Bonthrone, Duncan

Attendance: 18,000

December 30th
CELTIC (1) 2 HEARTS (1) 2
McAlindon 2 (18, 54)
Wardhaugh (37), Bauld (55)

CELTIC: Bonnar; Fallon, Milne; Evans, Mallan, Baillie; J. Weir, Collins, McAlindon, Peacock, Tully

HEARTS: Brown; Parker, McKenzie; Cox, Dougan, Laing; Sloan, Conn, Bauld, Wardhaugh, Cumming

Attendance: 40,000

League positions

	P	W	D	L	F	A	Pts
1 Dundee	17	10	4	3	27	12	24
2 Aberdeen	16	10	2	4	37	23	22
3 Hibernian	13	10	1	2	36	10	21
4 CELTIC	15	8	4	3	33	20	20
5 Hearts	17	8	4	5	34	28	20

January 1st
RANGERS (1) 1 CELTIC (0) 0
Waddell (23)

RANGERS: Brown; Young, Shaw; McColl, Woodburn, Cox; Waddell, Findlay, Simpson, Thornton, Paton

CELTIC: Bonnar; Fallon, Milne; Evans, Mallan, Baillie; J. Weir, Collins, McPhail, Peacock, Tully

Attendance: 55,000

Not a game to remember. The conditions were appalling, the centre of the field dotted with puddles and the wings hard and greasy. In addition there was far too much fouling and far too much latitude allowed by the referee. Although Celtic played more combined football on the deplorable pitch, they had no such powerful raider as Waddell and no such steady back as Young.

January 6th
MOTHERWELL (1) 2 CELTIC (0) 1
Watson (36), Forrest (74)
J. Weir (70)

MOTHERWELL: Johnstone; Kilmarnock, Shaw; McLeod, Paton, Redpath; Watters, Forrest, Kelly, Watson, Aitkenhead

CELTIC: Bonnar; Fallon, Rollo; Evans, Mallan, Baillie; J. Weir, Boden, McAlindon, Peacock, Tully

Attendance: 25,500

January 13th
CELTIC (2) 3 ABERDEEN (1) 4
Collins (12 pen), Tully 2 (16, 80)
Yorston (24), Emery 2 (62, 79 pen) Delaney (68)

CELTIC: Bonnar; Fallon, Rollo; Evans, Mallan, Baillie; J. Weir, Collins, McAlindon, Peacock, Tully

ABERDEEN: Watson; Emery, Shaw; Anderson, Young, Harris; Delaney, Yorston, Hamilton, Baird, Pearson

Attendance: 60,000

January 17th: Bobby Collins was in the Scottish League team which beat the League of Ireland 7-0 at Parkhead. He scored one of the goals.

January 20th
DUNDEE (0) 3 CELTIC (1) 1
Boyd 2 (64, 72 pen), Ziesing (66)
Frew o.g. (19)

DUNDEE: Lynch; Frew, Cowan; Irvine, Cowie, Boyd; Hill, Ewen, Ziesing, Steel, Christie

CELTIC: Bonnar; Fallon, Rollo; Evans, McGrory, Baillie; J. Weir, Collins, Haughney, Peacock, McDowall

Attendance: 28,000

February 3rd
CELTIC (0) 0 HIBERNIAN (0) 1
Turnbull (49)

CELTIC: Hunter; Fallon, Rollo; Evans, Boden, Baillie; Collins, Fernie, J. Weir, Peacock, Tully

HIBERNIAN: Younger; Govan, Ogilvie; Buchanan, Paterson, Gallacher; Smith, Johnstone, Reilly, Turnbull, Ormond

Attendance: 60,000

February 17th
FALKIRK (0) 0 — CELTIC (2) 2
Haughney (3), Collins (43)

FALKIRK: Scott; Fiddes, McPhee; Gallacher, Henderson, Whitelaw; Morrison, Wright, Plumb, Johnson, Brown

CELTIC: Hunter; Fallon, Rollo; Evans, Boden, Baillie; J. Weir, Collins, Haughney, Peacock, Fernie

Attendance: 12,000

March 3rd
THIRD LANARK (2) 2 — CELTIC (0) 0
Dick (38), Boden o.g. (42)

THIRD LANARK: Petrie; Balunas, Harrower; Orr, Samuel, Aitken; Henderson, Mason, Cuthbertson, Dick, Bradley

CELTIC: Hunter; Fallon, Rollo; Evans, Boden, Baillie; J. Weir, Collins, Haughney, Peacock, Tully

Attendance: 35,000

League positions

	P	W	D	L	F	A	Pts
1 Hibernian	22	16	2	4	58	21	34
2 Dundee	24	14	5	5	39	20	33
3 Aberdeen	25	14	4	7	55	41	32
4 Hearts	23	12	4	7	53	32	28
5 Rangers	22	11	4	7	44	28	26
7 CELTIC	22	9	4	11	40	33	22

March 17th
CELTIC (0) 2 — ST MIRREN (0) 1
Collins (61 pen), J. Weir (66) — Duncanson (72)

CELTIC: Hunter; Fallon, Rollo; Evans, Boden, Baillie; J. Weir, Collins, McPhail, Peacock, Tully

ST MIRREN: Kirk; Lapsley, Drinkwater; Neilson, Telfer, Johnston; Rice, Duncanson, Crowe, Reid, Lesz

Attendance: 30,000

March 24th
EAST FIFE (1) 3 — CELTIC (0) 0
Duncan (10 pen) Fleming 2 (47, 67)

EAST FIFE: Curran; Finlay, Stewart; Christie, Aird, McLennan; Stewart, Fleming, Gardiner, Black, Duncan

CELTIC: Hunter; Fallon, Rollo; Evans, Boden, Baillie; J. Weir, Collins, Fernie, Peacock, Tully

Attendance: 13,000

April 7th
HEARTS (1) 1 — CELTIC (0) 1
Conn (4) — Collins (48)

HEARTS: Brown; Parker, Adie; Whitehead, Dougan, Laing; Sloan, Conn, Bauld, Wardhaugh, Cumming

CELTIC: Hunter; Fallon, Rollo; Evans, Boden, Baillie; Collins, Fernie, McAlindon, Peacock, Tully

Attendance: 17,000

April 11th
CELTIC (0) 0 — AIRDRIE (0) 1
Welsh (60)

CELTIC: Hunter; Fallon, Rollo; Millsop, Boden, Baillie; Collins, Fernie, Haughney, Peacock, Tully

AIRDRIE: Fraser; T. Brown, Elliot; Cairns, Kelly, Shankland; W. Brown, Docherty, McGurn, Welsh, McCulloch

Attendance: n.a.

April 14th: Bobby Evans was in the Scotland team which beat England 3-2 at Wembley.

April 16th
CELTIC (0) 0 — PARTICK THISTLE (1) 3
Stott 2 (8, 75), Kinnell (86)

CELTIC: Hunter; Fallon, Rollo; Millsop, McGrory, Baillie; J. Weir, Collins, McAlindon, Peacock, Tully

PARTICK THISTLE: Ledgerwood; McGowan, Gibb; Thomson, Forsyth, Hewitt; McKenzie, Kinnell, Stott, Sharp, Walker

Attendance: n.a.

April 25th
CELTIC (0) 3 — MOTHERWELL (0) 1
Collins 2 (59 pen, 65 pen), J. Weir (74) — Aitken (80)

CELTIC: Hunter; Fallon, Rollo; Evans, Boden, Baillie; J. Weir, Collins, McPhail, Peacock, Tully

MOTHERWELL: Johnstone; Kilmarnock, Shaw; McLeod, Paton, Redpath; Forrest, Aitken, Kelly, Watson, J. Johnston

Attendance: n.a.

April 28th
CELTIC (0) 1 — CLYDE (0) 0
Collins (78)

CELTIC: Hunter; Mallan, Rollo; Evans, Boden, Baillie; J. Weir, Collins, McPhail, Peacock, Tully

CLYDE: Miller; Lindsay, Haddock; Campbell, Sommerville, Long; Buchanan, Bolton, Clifford, Robertson, Ring

Attendance: 24,000

April 30th
HIBERNIAN (1) 3 — CELTIC (0) 1
Buchanan (24), Reilly 2 (70, n.a.) — J. Weir (90)

HIBERNIAN: Younger; Howie, Cairns; Gallacher, Paterson, Buchanan; Smith, Johnstone, Reilly, Turnbull, Combe

CELTIC: Hunter; Haughney, Rollo; Evans, Mallan, Baillie; J. Weir, Collins, Walsh, Peacock, Millsop

Attendance: 22,000

Scottish League Division A

	P	W	D	L	F	A	Pts
1 Hibernian	30	22	4	4	78	26	48
2 Rangers	30	17	4	9	64	37	38
3 Dundee	30	15	8	7	47	30	38
4 Hearts	30	16	5	9	72	45	37
5 Aberdeen	30	15	5	10	61	50	35
6 Partick Thistle	30	13	7	10	57	48	33
7 CELTIC	30	12	5	13	48	46	29
8 Raith Rovers	30	13	2	15	52	52	28
9 Motherwell	30	11	6	13	58	65	28
10 East Fife	30	10	8	12	48	66	28
11 St Mirren	30	9	7	14	35	51	25
12 Morton	30	10	4	16	47	59	24
13 Third Lanark	30	11	2	17	40	51	24
14 Airdrie	30	10	4	16	52	67	24
15 Clyde	30	8	7	15	37	57	23
16 Falkirk	30	7	4	19	35	81	18

May 7th: Jackie Gallacher was given a free transfer. He later joined Alloa Athletic.

LEAGUE CUP

August 12th
CELTIC (2) 2 — EAST FIFE (0) 0
Peacock (20), McPhail (30)

CELTIC: Bonnar; Haughney, Milne; Evans, McGrory, Baillie; Collins, Fernie, McPhail, Peacock, Tully

EAST FIFE: Niven; Laird, Stewart; Philp, Finlay, Hudson; Black, Fleming, Morris, Bonthrone, Duncan

Attendance: 60,000

August 16th
THIRD LANARK (0) 1 — CELTIC (1) 2
Staroscik (55) — Collins (5), Fernie (52)

THIRD LANARK: Simpson; Balunas, Harrower; Orr, Christie, Mooney; Henderson, Mason, Muir, Cuthbertson, Staroscik

CELTIC: Bonnar; Haughney, Milne; Evans, McGrory, Baillie; Collins, Fernie, McPhail, Peacock, Tully

Attendance: 40,000

August 19th
CELTIC (1) 2 — RAITH ROVERS (1) 1
McPhail 2 (33, 88) — Leigh (41)

CELTIC: Bonnar; Haughney, Milne; Evans, McGrory, Baillie; Collins, Fernie, McPhail, Peacock, Tully

RAITH ROVERS: Johnstone; McLure, McNaught; Till, Colville, Young; Leigh, Keith, McLaughlin, Maule, Penman

Attendance: 35,000

August 26th
EAST FIFE (0) 1 — CELTIC (1) 1
Duncan (60 — McPhail (24)

EAST FIFE: Niven; Proudfoot, Stewart; Philp, Weir, Addison; Black, Fleming, Gardiner, Bonthrone, Duncan

CELTIC: Bonnar; Haughney, Milne; Evans, McGrory, Baillie; Collins, Fernie, McPhail, Peacock, Tully

Attendance: 15,000

August 30th
CELTIC (1) 3 — THIRD LANARK (1) 1
McPhail 2 (8 pen, 78 pen), Collins (69) — Cuthbertson (32)

CELTIC: Bonnar; Haughney, Milne; Evans, McGrory, Baillie; Collins, Fernie, McPhail, Peacock, Tully

THIRD LANARK: Simpson; Balunas, Harrower; Orr, Samuel, Mooney; Henderson, Mason, Muir, Cuthbertson Staroscik

Attendance: 30,000

September 2nd
RAITH ROVERS (0) 2 — CELTIC (2) 2
Henderson (57), Penman (65) — Collins (22), Peacock (30)

RAITH ROVERS: Johnstone; McLure, McNaught; Till, Colville, Leigh; Henderson, Mitchell, Young, Maule, Penman

CELTIC: Bonnar; Haughney, Milne; Evans, McGrory, Baillie; Collins, Fernie, McPhail, Peacock, Tully

Attendance: 16,000

SECTION TABLE

	P	W	D	L	F	A	Pts
CELTIC	6	4	2	0	12	6	10
Third Lanark	6	2	1	3	13	13	5
East Fife	6	1	3	2	13	15	5
Raith Rovers	6	1	2	3	10	14	4

Qualifier: CELTIC

Quarter-Final First Leg September 16th
CELTIC (1) 1 — MOTHERWELL (2) 4
McPhail (2) — Watson (8), Haughney o.g. (38), Forrest (50), Hunter (60)

CELTIC: Bonnar; Haughney, Milne; Evans, McGrory, Baillie; Collins, Fernie, McPhail, Peacock, J. Weir

MOTHERWELL: Hamilton; Kilmarnock, Shaw; McLeod, Paton, Redpath; Hunter, Forrest, Kelly, Watson, Aitkenhead

Attendance: 50,000

McPhail (24)

MOTHERWELL: Hamilton; Kilmarnock, Shaw; McLeod, Paton, Redpath; Hunter, Forrest, Kelly, Watson, Aitkenhead

CELTIC: Bonnar; Fallon, Milne; Boden, Mallan, Baillie; Collins, Evans, McPhail, Peacock, Tully

Attendance: 29,000. Motherwell won 4-2 on aggregate.

SCOTTISH CUP

First Round January 27th
EAST FIFE (2) 2 — CELTIC (1) 2
Black (24), Duncan (40) — J. Weir (38), Collins (80)

EAST FIFE: Easson; Proudfoot, Stewart; Philp, Finlay, Christie; Black, Fleming, Morris, Bonthrone, Duncan

CELTIC: Bonnar; Fallon, Rollo; Evans, McGrory, Baillie; Collins, Millsop, J. Weir, Peacock, Tully

Attendance: 14,000

First Round Replay January 31st
CELTIC (4) 4 — EAST FIFE (0) 2
McPhail 2 (12, 25), Peacock (15), Collins (34 — Bonthrone (55), Morris (60)

CELTIC: Hunter; Fallon, Rollo; Evans, McGrory, Baillie; J. Weir, Collins, McPhail, Peacock, Tully

EAST FIFE: Easson; Finlay, Proudfoot; Philp, Weir, Christie; Black, Fleming, Morris, Gardner, Bonthrone

Attendance: 36,000

Second Round February 10th
CELTIC (2) 4 — DUNS (0) 0
J. Weir 2 (21, 43), Peacock (72), D. Weir (82)

CELTIC: Hunter; Fallon, Rollo; Evans, Boden, Baillie; J. Weir, Collins, D. Weir, Peacock, Haughney

DUNS: Gowans; Farmer, John Smith; Sharp, J.Smith, McFeat; Mitchell, Robertson, Spiers, Cannon, Walters

Attendance: 22,907

Third Round February 24th
HEARTS (1) 1 — CELTIC (2) 2
Conn (21) — J. Weir (13), McPhail (36)

HEARTS: Brown; Parker, McKenzie; Cox, Dougan, Laing; Sloan, Conn, Bauld, Wardhaugh, Cumming

CELTIC: Hunter; Fallon, Rollo; Evans, Boden, Baillie; J. Weir, Collins, McPhail, Peacock, Tully

Attendance: 47,000

Fourth Round March 10th
CELTIC (2) 3 — ABERDEEN (0) 0
McPhail 2 (15, 81), Tully (42)

CELTIC: Hunter; Fallon, Rollo; Evans, Boden, Baillie; J. Weir, Collins, McPhail, Peacock, Tully

ABERDEEN: Martin; McKenna, Shaw; Anderson, Young, Harris; Delaney, Yorston, Bogan, Baird, Pearson

Attendance: 75,000

Semi-Final March 31st at Hampden Park
CELTIC (2) 3 — RAITH ROVERS (1) 2
J. Weir (7), McPhail (40), Tully (81) — Boden o.g. (35), Penman (80)

CELTIC: Hunter; Fallon, Rollo; Evans, Boden, Baillie; J. Weir, Collins, McPhail, Peacock, Tully

RAITH ROVERS: Johnstone; McLure, McNaught; McLaughlin, Colville, Leigh; Maule, Young, Penman, Murray, Brander

Attendance: 84,237

Raith Rovers made a splendid attempt to save the day at Hampden Park when in the last 8 minutes they did everything but score, but the play of Celtic will be remembered. Tully played some delightful football throughout and practically the only orthodox item he contributed to the game was his straightforward swing at the ball when he scored the winning goal 9 minutes from time.

Final April 21st at Hampden Park
CELTIC (1) 1 — MOTHERWELL (0) 0
McPhail (12)

CELTIC: Hunter; Fallon, Rollo; Evans, Boden, Baillie; J. Weir, Collins, McPhail, Peacock, Tully

MOTHERWELL: Johnstone; Kilmarnock, Shaw; McLeod, Paton, Redpath; Humphries, Forrest, Kelly, Watson, Aitkenhead

Attendance: 131,943

There have been many better Cup Finals but few better goals have been scored than McPhail's which gave Celtic the trophy for the 16th time and for the 3rd time at Motherwell's expense.

Appearances	League	League Cup	Scottish Cup
Bonnar	19	8	1
Haughney	6	7	1
Milne	16	8	–
Evans	28	8	7
McGrory	3	7	2
Baillie	28	8	7
Collins	27	8	7
Fernie	7	7	–
McPhail	17	8	5
Peacock	30	8	7
Tully	27	7	6
Fallon	27	1	7
Mallan	19	1	–
D. Weir	4	–	1
Millsop	6	–	1
J. Weir	24	1	7
McAlindon	5	–	–
Rollo	14	–	7
Boden	10	1	5
McDowall	1	–	–
Hunter	11	–	6
Walsh	1	–	–

GOALSCORERS:
League: Collins 15 (6 pens), McPhail 13 (3 pens), J. Weir 7, Peacock 5, Tully 3, McAlindon 2, D. Weir 1, Haughney 1, Own Goal 1
League Cup: McPhail 8 (2 pens), Collins 3, Peacock 2, Fernie 1
Scottish Cup: McPhail 7, J. Weir 5, Tully 2, Collins 2, Peacock 2, D Weir 1.

Season 1951-52

Celtic had another poor League season – particularly away from home where they won only 3 times – and they could manage only 9th place in the table – 17 points behind Champions Hibernian. January proved to be a particularly disastrous month. They managed the double over only two teams – Aberdeen and Partick Thistle. Bobby Collins again finished as top scorer with 12 of their 52 goals. He, Fallon and Baillie played in all 30 matches. A comparatively unknown centre-half, Jock Stein, was signed from Welsh League club Llanelly at the beginning of December. Evans, Baillie, Rollo, Collins, Fallon, Peacock and Tully all received representative honours during the season.

Celtic marched to the Semi-Final of the League Cup after topping a Section which included Morton, Third Lanark and Airdrie and then beating Forfar on a 5-2 aggregate in the Quarter-Final, but they were well beaten by Rangers in the Semi-Final match at Hampden.

They fell at the first hurdle in their defence of the Scottish Cup – losing to Third Lanark after extra time in a replay at Cathkin Park.

League:	Ninth
League Cup:	Semi-Finalists
Scottish Cup:	First Round

LEAGUE DIVISION A

August 5th: Giles Heron, a trialist from Jamaica, was signed up as a full-timer.

August 27th: Goalkeeper Andrew Bell was signed from Arthurlie.

September 8th
MOTHERWELL (2) 2 — CELTIC (0) 2
Kelly 2 (7, 35) — Peacock (70), Tully (86)

MOTHERWELL: Johnstone; Kilmarnock, Shaw; McLeod, Paton, Redpath; Humphries, Forrest, Kelly, Watson, Aitkenhead
CELTIC: Bonnar; Fallon, Rollo; Evans, Boden, Baillie; Collins, Walsh, McPhail, Peacock, Tully
Attendance: 28,000

September 22nd
RANGERS (0) 1 — CELTIC (1) 1
Findlay (63) — Collins (21)

RANGERS: Brown; Young, Little; McColl, Woodburn, Cox; Waddell, Findlay, Gardiner, Thornton, Hubbard
CELTIC: Devanney; Fallon, Rollo; Evans, Boden, Baillie; Collins, Walsh, McPhail, Peacock, Tully
Attendance: 86,000

Rangers made it clear in the press and in their match programme that such things as banners, party tune singing and foul language would not be tolerated. Collins' goal was the most memorable feature of a most satisfying match. It was the more remarkable in that it was scored when Celtic had only 10 players on the field, McPhail having gone off with a nasty head cut in the 18th minute.

September 26th: Rollo, Baillie and Collins were in the Scottish League team which beat the Irish League 3-0 at Ibrox Park.

September 29th
CELTIC (0) 1 — HEARTS (1) 3
Peacock (53) — Bauld (34), Wardhaugh (55), Conn (69)

CELTIC: Bonnar; Fallon, Rollo; Evans, Boden, Baillie; Collins, D. Weir, Walsh, Peacock, Tully

HEARTS: Brown; Parker, McKenzie; Adie, Milne, Laing; Durkin, Conn, Bauld, Wardhaugh, Urquhart
Attendance: 50,000

October 6th: Bobby Evans was in the Scotland team which beat Ireland 3-0 in Belfast. Peacock and Tully were in the Ireland team.

October 10th
MORTON (0) 0 — CELTIC (1) 1
Millsop (25)
MORTON: Cowan; Mitchell, Batton; Little, Thom, Hunter; Garth, Orr, Linwood, McGarritty, Alexander
CELTIC: Bonnar; Fallon, Rollo; Evans, Boden, Baillie; Millsop, Collins, J. Weir, Peacock, Tully
Attendance: n.a.

October 17th: Sean Fallon was in the Eire team which beat Germany 3-2 in Dublin.

October 20th
DUNDEE (1) 2 — CELTIC (1) 1
Christie (35), Pattillo (48) — Merchant o.g. (5)
DUNDEE: Brown; Follon, Cowan; Gallacher, Merchant, Cowie; Toner, Pattillo, Flavell, Steel, Christie
CELTIC: Bell; Fallon, Rollo; Evans, Mallan, Baillie; Collins, Boden, McPhail, Peacock, Millsop
Attendance: 32,000

October 27th
CELTIC (1) 1 — HIBERNIAN (0) 1
McPhail (15) — Ormond (78)
CELTIC: Bell; Fallon, Rollo; Evans, Mallan, Baillie; Collins, Walsh, McPhail, Peacock, Tully
HIBERNIAN: Younger; Govan, Howie; Buchanan, Paterson, Combe; Smith, Johnstone, Reilly, Turnbull, Ormond
Attendance: 40,000
League positions

	P	W	D	L	F	A	Pts
1 East Fife	9	6	2	1	22	14	14
2 Hibernian	8	5	3	0	23	9	13
3 St Mirren	8	4	1	3	15	14	9
4 Third Lanark	8	3	2	3	16	13	8
5 Hearts	8	3	2	3	13	12	8
14 CELTIC	6	1	3	2	7	9	5

October 31st: Evans and Baillie were in the Scottish League team which was beaten 2-1 by the English League in Sheffield.

November 3rd
CELTIC (2) 2 — THIRD LANARK (1) 2
Walsh (16), Harrower o.g. (22) — Smellie (29), Dick (60)
CELTIC: Bell; Fallon, Rollo; Evans, Mallan, Baillie; Collins, Walsh, McAlindon, McPhail, Tully
THIRD LANARK: Petrie; Balunas, Harrower; Mooney, Aitken, McCall; Smellie, Dick, Cuthbertson, Henderson, McLeod
Attendance: n.a. Tully was ordered off.

November 10th
STIRLING ALBION (0) 2 CELTIC (0) 1
Smith (51), Anderson (52) — McAlindon (47)
STIRLING ALBION: Jenkins; J. Henderson, Hadden; Mitchell, Paton, Wilson; McFarlane, Bain, G. Henderson, Smith, Anderson
CELTIC: Bell; Fallon, Rollo; Evans, Boden, Baillie; Collins, Walsh, McAlindon, McPhail, Tully
Attendance: n.a.

November 17th
CELTIC (2) 3 — AIRDRIE (0) 1
Walsh (9), Peacock (10), McPhail (58) — McMillan (67)
CELTIC: Bell; Fallon, Rollo; Evans, Boden, Baillie; Collins, Walsh, McPhail, Peacock, Tully
AIRDRIE: Fraser; T. Brown, Elliot; Cairns, Rodger, Shankland; W. Brown, McMillan, Quinn, Welsh, McCulloch
Attendance: 20,000

November 21st: Charlie Tully was suspended for 1 month for his ordering off v. Third Lanark.

November 24th
QUEEN OF THE SOUTH (3) 4 — CELTIC (0) 0
Inglis (5), Patterson (21), Rothera (38), Neilson (60)
QUEEN OF THE SOUTH: Henderson; Sharp, Binning; McBain, Aird, Greenock; Inglis, Rothera, Patterson, Neilson, Oakes
CELTIC: Bell; Fallon, Rollo; Evans, Boden, Baillie; Collins, Walsh, McPhail, Peacock, McAlindon
Attendance: 14,500

December 1st
CELTIC (2) 2 — PARTICK THISTLE (0) 1
Collins (6), Walsh (14) — Stott (53)
CELTIC: Bell; Fallon, Rollo; Evans, Boden, Baillie; Collins, Walsh, Heron, Peacock, Lafferty
PARTICK THISTLE: Ledgerwood; McGowan, Gibb; Thomson, Davidson, Mathers; McKenzie, Anderson, Stott, Sharp, Walker
Attendance: 30,000

December 4th: Jock Stein was signed from Welsh Non-League club Llanelly.

December 8th
CELTIC (2) 2 — ST MIRREN (0) 1
Lafferty 2 (22, 42) — Gemmell (70)

CELTIC: Bell; Fallon, Rollo; Evans, Stein, Baillie; Collins, Walsh, Lafferty, Peacock, McPhail

ST MIRREN: Lynch; Lapsley, Drinkwater; Neilson, Telfer, Reid; Rice, Anderson, Stewart, Gemmell, Blyth

Attendance: 20,000

December 15th

EAST FIFE (2) 3	CELTIC (0) 1
J. Stewart (23), Gardiner 2 (33, 86)	Walsh (57)

EAST FIFE: Curran; Finlay, S. Stewart; Whyte, Aird, McLennan; J. Stewart, Fleming, Gardiner, Bonthrone, Duncan

CELTIC: Bell; Fallon, Rollo; Evans, Stein, Baillie; Collins, Walsh, Lafferty, Peacock, Fernie

Attendance: 15,000

December 22nd

CELTIC (1) 2	MOTHERWELL (0) 1
Lafferty (17), Peacock (59)	Kelly (57)

CELTIC: Bell; Fallon, Jack; Evans, Stein, Baillie; Collins, Walsh, Lafferty, Peacock, Tully

MOTHERWELL: Johnstone; Kilmarnock, Shaw; McLeod, Paton, Redpath; Hunter, Aitken, Kelly, Watson, Aitkenhead

Attendance: 28,000

December 29th

ABERDEEN (1) 3	CELTIC (3) 4
Baird (4), Emery (82 pen), Yorston (89)	Collins 2 (1 pen, 24 pen), McKenna o.g. (26), Walsh (65)

ABERDEEN: Watson; Emery, McKenna; Lowrie, Thomson, Harris; Boyd, Yorston, Hamilton, Baird, Pearson

CELTIC: Bell; Fallon, Jack; Evans, Stein, Baillie; Collins, Walsh, J. Weir, Peacock, Tully

Attendance: 25,000

League positions

	P	W	D	L	F	A	Pts
1 Hibernian	17	11	4	2	50	18	26
2 East Fife	18	11	3	4	46	33	25
3 Hearts	17	10	3	4	46	25	23
4 Rangers	14	8	4	2	29	13	20
5 Aberdeen	16	6	5	5	37	32	17
9 CELTIC	15	5	5	5	24	28	15

January 1st

CELTIC (1) 1	RANGERS (2) 4
Tully (20)	Liddell (15), Paton 2 (21, 62), Waddell (71)

CELTIC: Bell; Fallon, Jack; Evans, Stein, Baillie; Collins, Walsh, J. Weir, Peacock, Tully

RANGERS: Brown; Young, Shaw; McColl, Woodburn, Prentice; Waddell, Paton, Thornton, Cox, Liddell

Attendance: 45,000

Rangers gained a richly deserved victory in view of the fact that they played with 10 men for almost the last half-hour of the match after Shaw had been stretchered off. Celtic's inexperienced youngster Jack had little answer to Waddell's speed and ball control.

January 2nd

HEARTS (0) 2	CELTIC (0) 1
Parker (48 pen), Whittle (65)	Collins (80 pen)

HEARTS: Brown; Parker, Adie; Glidden, Milne, Laing; Rutherford, Whittle, Bauld, Wardhaugh, Urquhart

CELTIC: Bonnar; Fallon, Rollo; Evans, Stein, Baillie; Collins, Walsh, Lafferty, Peacock, Tully

Attendance: n.a.

January 12th

RAITH ROVERS (1) 1	CELTIC (0) 0
Kelly (32)	

RAITH ROVERS: Johnstone; McLure, McNaught; Young, Colville, Leigh; Wood, Maule, Copland, Kelly, Penman

CELTIC: Bell; Fallon, Rollo; Evans, Stein, Baillie; Collins, Peacock, Lafferty, Morrison, Tully

Attendance: 16,000

January 19th

CELTIC (1) 1	DUNDEE (1) 1
Walsh (6)	Steel (16)

CELTIC: Bonnar; Fallon, Rollo; Evans, Stein, Baillie; Collins, Walsh, McPhail, Tully, Peacock

DUNDEE: Brown; Pattillo, Frew; Gallacher, Cowie, Boyd; Burrell, Henderson, Flavell, Steel, Hill

Attendance: 35,000

February 2nd

HIBERNIAN (1) 3	CELTIC (1) 1
Turnbull (12), Reilly (56), Johnstone (85)	Walsh (38)

HIBERNIAN: Younger; Govan, Howie; Buchanan, Paterson, Gallacher; Smith, Johnstone, Reilly, Turnbull, Combe

CELTIC: Bonnar; Fallon, Rollo; Evans, Stein, Baillie; Collins, Walsh, McPhail, Tully, Peacock

Attendance: 40,000

February 16th

CELTIC (1) 3	STIRLING ALBION (0) 1
Collins 2 (28 pen, 66), McPhail (65)	Anderson (68)

CELTIC: Bonnar; Fallon, Baillie; Evans, Stein, Millsop; Collins, Walsh, McPhail, Peacock, Tully

STIRLING ALBION: Jenkins; J. Henderson, Hadden; Smith, Paton, Rutherford; Bertolini, McFarlane, G. Henderson, Silcock, Anderson

Attendance: 20,000

February 23rd
CELTIC (0) 0 — RAITH ROVERS (1) 1
Kelly (21)

CELTIC: Bonnar; Fallon, Baillie; Evans, Stein, Millsop; Collins, Walsh, McPhail, Peacock, Haughney

RAITH ROVERS: Johnstone; McLure, McNaught; Young, Colville, Leigh; Maule, McEwan, Penman, Kelly, McIntyre

Attendance: 20,000

February 27th
AIRDRIE (1) 2 — CELTIC (0) 1
Welsh (9), Lennox (69) — Collins (53)

AIRDRIE: Fraser; T. Brown, J. Murray; Cairns, Rodger, Shankland; W. Brown, McMillan, Lennox, Welsh, Seawright

CELTIC: Bonnar; Fallon, Baillie; Evans, Stein, Millsop; J. Weir, Collins, McAlindon, McPhail, Peacock

Attendance: n.a.

March 1st
CELTIC (4) 6 — QUEEN OF THE SOUTH (1) 1
J. Weir 2 (15, 66), McPhail (22), Collins (28), Tully (31), Peacock (58) — Brown (29)

CELTIC: Bonnar; Fallon, Baillie; Evans, Stein, Millsop; J. Weir, Collins, McPhail, Peacock, Tully

QUEEN OF THE SOUTH: Henderson; Smyth, Binning; Rothera, Waldie, Greenock; Oakes, Brown, Patterson, Neilson, Johnstone

Attendance: n.a.

League positions

	P	W	D	L	F	A	Pts
1 Hibernian	27	18	5	4	84	29	41
2 Rangers	25	15	6	4	55	25	36
3 East Fife	26	15	3	8	60	42	33
4 Hearts	26	13	6	7	61	43	32
5 Raith Rovers	26	10	6	10	39	45	26
13 CELTIC	24	7	6	11	38	44	20

March 5th
CELTIC (1) 2 — MORTON (1) 2
McPhail (28), Peacock (90) — Orr 2 (42, 52)

CELTIC: Bonnar; Fallon, Baillie; Fernie, Stein, Millsop; J. Weir, Collins, McPhail, Peacock, Tully

MORTON: Cowan; Mitchell, Whigham; Little, Thom, Hunter; Garth, Orr, Linwood, McGarritty, McVinish

Attendance: 12,000

March 8th
PARTICK THISTLE (1) 2 — CELTIC (4) 4
Stott (2), McCreadie (87) — McPhail 2 (6, 41), Millsop (30), Collins (37)

PARTICK THISTLE: Ledgerwood; McGowan, Collins; Crawford, Kinnell, Mathers; Miller, Gillick, Stott, Sharp, McCreadie

CELTIC: Bonnar; Fallon, Baillie; Fernie, Stein, Millsop; J. Weir, Collins, McPhail, Peacock, Tully

Attendance: 30,000

March 15th
ST MIRREN (2) 3 — CELTIC (1) 1
Stewart (4), Rice (35), Wilson (82) — McPhail (6)

ST MIRREN: Lynch; Ashe, Cunningham; Crowe, Telfer, Reid; Rice, Wilson, Stewart, Williamson, Duncanson

CELTIC: Bonnar; Fallon, Baillie; Evans, Stein, Millsop; J. Weir, Collins, McPhail, Peacock, Tully

Attendance: 37,000

March 17th: Bobby Collins was in the Scottish League team which beat the League of Ireland 2-0 in Dublin.

March 22nd
CELTIC (2) 2 — EAST FIFE (0) 1
Tully (29), McPhail (43) — Gardiner (69)

CELTIC: Bonnar; Fallon, Baillie; Fernie, Stein, Millsop; J. Weir, Collins, McPhail, Boden, Tully

EAST FIFE: Curran; Weir, S. Stewart; Christie, Finlay, Whyte; J. Stewart, Fleming, Gardiner, McLennan, Duncan

Attendance: 30,000

March 29th
CELTIC (2) 2 — ABERDEEN (0) 0
J. Weir (3), McPhail (4)

CELTIC: Bonnar; Fallon, Baillie; Fernie, Boden, Millsop; J. Weir, Collins, McPhail, Walsh, Tully

ABERDEEN: Martin; Young, Shaw; Samuels, Thomson, Harris; Boyd, Yorston, Rodger, Baird, Hather

Attendance: 18,000

April 12th
THIRD LANARK (2) 3 — CELTIC (1) 3
Dick (2 (10, 34), Fallon o.g. (67) — Collins 2 (18, 82 pen), McPhail (87)

THIRD LANARK: Robertson; Balunas, Cairns; Mooney, Forsyth, Harrower; Goodall, Mason, Dick, Henderson, McLeod

CELTIC: Bonnar; Fallon, Baillie; Fernie, Boden, Millsop; J. Weir, Collins, McPhail, Walsh, Tully

Attendance: 35,000

Scottish League Division A

	P	W	D	L	F	A	Pts
1 Hibernian	30	20	5	5	92	36	45
2 Rangers	30	16	9	5	61	31	41
3 East Fife	30	17	3	10	71	49	37
4 Hearts	30	14	7	9	69	53	35
5 Raith Rovers	30	14	5	11	43	42	33
6 Partick Thistle	30	12	7	11	48	51	31
7 Motherwell	30	12	7	11	51	57	31
8 Dundee	30	11	6	13	53	52	28
9 CELTIC	30	10	8	12	52	55	28
10 Queen of the South	30	10	8	12	50	60	28
11 Aberdeen	30	10	7	13	65	58	27
12 Third Lanark	30	9	8	13	51	62	26
13 Airdrie	30	11	4	15	54	69	26
14 St Mirren	30	10	5	15	43	48	25
15 Morton	30	9	6	15	49	56	24
16 Stirling Albion	30	5	5	20	36	99	15

LEAGUE CUP

August 11th
CELTIC (0) 1 — THIRD LANARK (1) 1
Fallon (55) — Henderson (14)

CELTIC: Bonnar; Haughney, Rollo; Evans, Mallan, Baillie; Collins, Walsh, Fallon, Peacock, Tully

THIRD LANARK: Petrie; Balunas, Harrower; Mooney, Samuel, Aitken; Henderson, Currie, Goodall, Dick, McCall

Attendance: 45,000

August 15th
AIRDRIE (1) 1 — CELTIC (1) 1
Shields (40) — Peacock (8)

AIRDRIE: Fraser; T. Brown, Elliot; Cairns, Dingwall, Shankland; W. Brown, Baird, McGurn, Shields, McCulloch

CELTIC: Bonnar; Haughney, Rollo; Evans, Mallan, Baillie; Collins, Walsh, Fallon, Peacock, Tully

Attendance: n.a.

August 18th
CELTIC (2) 2 — MORTON (0) 0
Evans (29), Heron (35)

CELTIC: Bonnar; Fallon, Rollo; Evans, Mallan, Baillie; Collins, Walsh, Heron, Peacock, Tully

MORTON: Cowan; Mitchell, Whigham; Little, Thom, Hunter; Cupples, Gourlay, Gibson, McGarritty, McVinish

Attendance: 40,000

August 25th
THIRD LANARK (0) 0 — CELTIC (1) 1
Walsh (40)

THIRD LANARK: Petrie; Balunas, Harrower; Mooney, Samuel, Aitken; Henderson, Gibson, Currie, Dick, McCall

CELTIC: Bonnar; Fallon, Rollo; Evans, Mallan, Baillie; Collins, Walsh, Heron, Peacock, Tully

Attendance: 35,000

August 29th
CELTIC (2) 2 — AIRDRIE (0) 0
Walsh (10), Heron (38)

CELTIC: Bonnar; Fallon, Rollo; Evans, Mallan, Baillie; Collins, Walsh, Heron, Peacock, Tully

AIRDRIE: Fraser; T. Brown, Elliot; Cairns, Dingwall, Shankland; McMillan, Baird, McGurn, Shields, McCulloch

Attendance: 25,000. Brown was carried off after 20 minutes

September 1st
MORTON (1) 2 — CELTIC (0) 0
Orr 2 (10, 48)

MORTON: Cowan; Mitchell, Whigham; Little, Thom, Hunter; Garth, Orr, Linwood, McGarritty, McVinish

CELTIC: Bonnar; Fallon, Rollo; Evans, Mallan, Baillie; Collins, Walsh, Heron, Peacock, Tully

Attendance: n.a.

SECTION TABLE

	P	W	D	L	F	A	Pts
CELTIC	6	3	2	1	7	4	8
Morton	6	4	0	2	12	8	8
Third Lanark	6	2	1	3	11	9	5
Airdrie	6	1	1	4	5	14	3

Qualifier: CELTIC

Quarter-Final First Leg September 15th
CELTIC (2) 4 — FORFAR ATHLETIC (0) 1
Peacock (31), Collins (44), Baillie (51), Walsh (71) — Cunningham (87)

CELTIC: Devanney; Fallon, Rollo; Evans, Mallan, Baillie; Collins, Walsh, McPhail, Peacock, Tully

FORFAR: Ingram; McNellis, McLuskey; McLean, McKenzie, Falconer; Adams, Fearns, Lawrence, Cunningham, Meechan

Attendance: 28,000

Quarter-Final Second Leg September 19th
FORFAR ATHLETIC (1) 1 — CELTIC (1) 1
McLean (35) — Peacock (42)

FORFAR: Ingram; McNellis, McLuskey; McLean, McKenzie, Hamilton; Adams, Fearn, Lawrence, Cunningham, Meechan

CELTIC: Devanney; Fallon, Rollo; Evans, Mallan, Baillie; Millsop, Walsh, McPhail, Peacock, Tully

Attendance: 6,900. Celtic won 5-2 on aggregate.

Semi-Final October 13th at Hampden Park
CELTIC (0) 0 — RANGERS (2) 3
Thornton (15), Johnson (44), Findlay (53)

CELTIC: Bonnar; Fallon, Rollo; Evans, Boden, Baillie; J. Weir, Collins, McPhail, Peacock, Tully

RANGERS: Brown; Young, Little; McColl, Woodburn, Cox; Waddell, Findlay, Thornton, Johnson, Rutherford

Attendance: 83,235

Rangers' standard of play in the first half must have been a revelation to the thousands who had been lamenting their recent displays. Brown was beaten twice in the match and did not lose a goal – Tully hit the bar in the first half and Boden did likewise, from outside-left, in the second.

SCOTTISH CUP

First Round January 30th
CELTIC 0 THIRD LANARK 0

CELTIC: Bonnar; Fallon, Rollo; Evans, Stein, Baillie; Collins, Walsh, McPhail, Tully, Peacock

THIRD LANARK: Robertson; Balunas, Cairns; Mooney, Forsyth, Harrower; Henderson, Docherty, Cuthbertson, Dick, McLeod

Attendance: 24,000

First Round Replay February 4th
THIRD LANARK (1) 2 CELTIC (0) 1
Dick (23), Docherty (108) Rollo (29)
After Extra Time

THIRD LANARK: Robertson; Balunas, Cairns; Mooney, Forsyth, Harrower; Henderson, Docherty, Cuthbertson, Dick, McLeod

CELTIC: Bonnar; Fallon, Rollo; Evans, Stein, Baillie; Collins, Walsh, McPhail, Peacock, Tully

Attendance: 27,344

Appearances	League	League Cup	Scottish Cup
Bonnar	16	7	2
Fallon	30	9	2
Rollo	17	9	2
Evans	25	9	2
Boden	12	1	–
Baillie	30	9	2
Collins	30	8	2
Walsh	21	8	2
McPhail	21	3	2
Peacock	25	9	2
Tully	23	9	2
Devanney	1	2	–
D. Weir	1	–	–
Millsop	12	1	–
J. Weir	11	1	–
Bell	13	–	–
Mallan	3	8	–
McAlindon	4	–	–
Heron	1	4	–
Lafferty	6	–	–
Stein	17	–	2
Fernie	6	–	–
Jack	3	–	–
Morrison	1	–	–
Haughney	1	2	–

GOALSCORERS
League: Collins 12 (4 pens), McPhail 11, Walsh 7, Peacock 6, Tully 4, Lafferty 3, J. Weir 3, Own Goals 3, Millsop 2, McAlindon 1
League Cup: Peacock 3, Walsh 3, Heron 2, Fallon 1, Evans 1, Collins 1, Baillie 1
Scottish Cup: Rollo 1

Jubilation at the 1951 Scottish Cup success. John McPhail is chaired by his team-mates, Hunter, Weir, Rollo, Collins, Baillie, Boden, Fallon, Tully and Peacock.

Season 1952-53

What was otherwise a very mediocre domestic season was enlivened right at the end with Celtic winning the prestigious Coronation Cup. They had started their League campaign well and stood 3rd in the table at the end of December, but after losing the Ne'erday fixture at Ibrox they won only 2 of their next 11 matches and eventually finished 8th in the table – 14 points behind Rangers who won the championship on goal average from Hibs. Astonishingly only 5 points separated 4th-placed Hearts and relegated Motherwell in 15th place. Celtic's most impressive victory during the season was their 5-0 home win over Dundee in December. The fact that Dundee won the return fixture by 4-0 underlines the erratic form of the Parkhead team. Only Bobby Evans played in all 30 matches. Bertie Peacock was top scorer with 8 goals followed by Fernie, Tully and Walsh – all on 7. Neil Mochan was signed from Middlesbrough at the end of the season. Sadly young Jackie Millsop died in Glasgow Royal Infirmary following an operation for appendicitis.

Celtic finished second to Hibs in the League Cup Section Table with 4 wins from their 6 matches including a double over St Mirren whom they beat in all 4 meetings during the season.

The Scottish Cup trail ended at Ibrox at the Quarter-Final stage. In the previous Round against Falkirk at Brockville Charlie Tully performed the unique feat of scoring with 2 successive corner-kicks. After his first kick had entered the net the referee awarded a retake for an infringement and Tully duly repeated his performance to put Celtic back into the game which they eventually won 3-2. Celtic won the Coronation Cup defeating Hibernian 2-0 in the Final at Hampden Park before a huge crowd of 117,060.

League:	Eighth
League Cup:	Failed to qualify from Section
Scottish Cup:	Quarter-Finalists
Coronation Cup:	Winners

LEAGUE DIVISION A

September 3rd: Joe Baillie was in the Scottish League team which beat the Irish League 5-1 in Belfast.

September 6th

CELTIC (3) 5	FALKIRK (0) 3
McPhail 3 (10, 18, 89),	Plumb 2 (47, 61),
Fernie (13), Tully (80)	Morrison (55)

CELTIC: Bonnar; Boden, Fallon; Evans, Stein, Baillie; Walsh, Fernie, McPhail, Tully, Millsop

FALKIRK: Scott; McKenzie, Rae; Gallacher, Wilson, Hunter; Brown, Morrison, Plumb, McCabe, Delaney

Attendance: 20,000

September 13th

RAITH ROVERS (0) 1	CELTIC (0) 1
McEwan (54)	Tully (60)

RAITH ROVERS: Stewart; McLure, McNaught; Young, Colville, Leigh; Wood, McEwan, Penman, Cockburn, McIntyre

CELTIC: Bonnar; Boden, Fallon; Evans, Stein, Baillie; Walsh, Fernie, McPhail, Tully, Peacock

Attendance: 10,000

September 17th: Jackie Millsop died in Glasgow Royal Infirmary following an operation for appendicitis. He was 21.

September 20th

CELTIC (2) 2	RANGERS (0) 1
Walsh (4), Rollo (10)	Liddell (72)

CELTIC: Bonnar; Boden, Meechan; Evans, Stein, Baillie; Rollo, Walsh, Fallon, Tully, Peacock

RANGERS: Niven; Young, Little; McColl, Woodburn, Cox; McCulloch, Grierson, Thornton, Prentice, Liddell

Attendance: 48,000

If only for the fact that they scored one of the finest goals ever seen in Scottish football Celtic deserved their victory. In 4 minutes after Fallon had fallen over the ball some 30 yards from Rangers' goal Walsh's speed enabled him to beat McColl to the ball, his intelligent control baffled Woodburn and his accuracy and power of shot from 18 yards gave Niven no chance.

September 24th: Alec Boden was in the Scottish League team which was beaten 3-0 by the Welsh League in Cardiff.

September 27th
ABERDEEN (2) 2 — CELTIC (1) 2
Boyd (3), Hamilton (21) — Peacock (39), Fallon (66)

ABERDEEN: Martin; Mitchell, Smith; Harris, Young, Wallace; Boyd, Yorston, Hamilton, Hay, Hather

CELTIC: Bonnar; Boden, Meechan; Evans, Stein, Baillie; Rollo, Walsh, Fallon, Tully, Peacock

Attendance: 27,000

October 4th
CELTIC (2) 3 — MOTHERWELL (0) 0
Peacock (2), Fallon (13), Walsh (69 pen)

CELTIC: Bonnar; Boden, Meechan; Evans, Stein, Baillie; Hepburn, Walsh, Fallon, Fernie, Peacock

MOTHERWELL: Johnstone; Kilmarnock, Shaw; Cox, Paton, Redpath; Sloan, Humphries, Kelly, Forrest, Aitkenhead

Attendance: 30,000

October 4th: Charlie Tully scored both of Ireland's goals in a 2-2 draw with England in Belfast.

October 8th: Bobby Evans was in the Scottish League team which beat the League of Ireland 5-1 in Glasgow.

October 11th
CLYDE (0) 1 — CELTIC (1) 2
Campbell (85) — Peacock 2 (15, 88)

CLYDE: Wilson; Lindsay, Haddock; Campbell, Keogh, Long; Buchanan, Baird, McPhail, Robertson, Ring

CELTIC: Bonnar; Boden, Meechan; Evans, Stein, Baillie; Hepburn, Walsh, Fallon, Tully, Peacock

Attendance: 31,000

October 16th: Jock Weir was transferred to Falkirk.

October 18th
CELTIC (1) 1 — QUEEN OF THE SOUTH (0) 1
Peacock (45) — Patterson (57)

CELTIC: Bonnar; Boden, Meechan; Evans, Stein, Baillie; Hepburn, Walsh, Fallon, Tully, Peacock

QUEEN OF THE SOUTH: Henderson; Sharpe, Binning; McBain, Smith, Greenock; Oakes, Neilston, Patterson, Brown, Johnstone

Attendance: 25,000

October 25th
HEARTS (0) 1 — CELTIC (0) 0
Urquhart (85)

HEARTS: Watters; Parker, McKenzie; Glidden, Milne, Laing; Whittle, Conn, Bauld, Wardhaugh, Urquhart

CELTIC: Hunter; Haughney, Meechan; Evans, Stein, Baillie; Fernie, Walsh, Fallon, Tully, Peacock

Attendance: 40,000

November 1st
ST MIRREN (0) 1 — CELTIC (1) 2
Telfer (79 pen) — Fernie (13), Duncan (63)

ST MIRREN: Park; Lapsley, Ashe; Neilson, Telfer, Reid; Blyth, McGill, Stewart, Gemmell, Anderson

CELTIC: Hunter; Boden, Fallon; Evans, Stein, Baillie; Duncan, Fernie, McPhail, Tully, Peacock

Attendance: 36,000

League positions

	P	W	D	L	F	A	Pts
1 East Fife	9	7	1	1	26	15	15
2 CELTIC	9	5	3	2	18	11	13
3 St Mirren	9	5	2	2	19	11	12
4 Hibernian	7	5	0	2	20	14	10
5 Aberdeen	9	4	2	3	28	21	10

November 5th: Charlie Tully was in the Ireland team which drew 1-1 with Scotland at Hampden Park.

November 8th
CELTIC (1) 5 — THIRD LANARK (2) 4
Peacock (14), Lafferty (50), Walsh (72), Forsyth o.g. (75), Tully (89) — Cuthbertson 2 (16, 59), Dick 2 (32, 57)

CELTIC: Hunter; Boden, Fallon; Evans, Stein, Baillie; Walsh, Fernie, Lafferty, Tully, Peacock

THIRD LANARK: Robertson; Balunas, Harrower; Docherty, Forsyth, Mooney; Brown, Dick, Dobbie, Cuthbertson, McLeod

Attendance: 30,000

November 11th: Peacock and Tully were in the Ireland team which was beaten 3-1 by France in Paris, Tully scored Ireland's goal.

November 15th
PARTICK THISTLE (1) 3 — CELTIC (0) 0
Stott 2 (24, 57), Howitt (74)

PARTICK THISTLE: Ledgerwood; McGowan, McNab; Crawford, Davidson, Kerr; McKenzie, Howitt, Stott, Sharp, Walker

CELTIC: Hunter; Boden, Meechan; Evans, Stein, Baillie; Walsh, Fernie, McPhail, Tully, Peacock

Attendance: 38,500

November 16th: Sean Fallon scored Eire's goal in a 1-1 draw with France in Dublin.

November 22nd
AIRDRIE 0 CELTIC 0

AIRDRIE: Fraser; Pryde, Cross; Cairns, McGuire, McCulloch; Campbell, McMillan, Baird, Welsh, Seawright

CELTIC: Hunter; Boden, Fallon; Evans, Stein, Baillie; Hepburn, Fernie, McPhail, Walsh, Peacock

Attendance: 18,000

December 6th
HIBERNIAN (0) 1 CELTIC (1) 1
Reilly (59) McIlroy (30)

HIBERNIAN: Younger; Govan, Howie; Buchanan, Paterson, Combe; Smith, Johnstone, Reilly, Turnbull, Ormond

CELTIC: Hunter; Boden, Fallon; Evans, Stein, Rollo; McPhail, Fernie, McIlroy, Walsh, Peacock

Attendance: 32,000

December 13th
CELTIC (1) 5 DUNDEE (0) 0
Tully (10),
Fernie 3 (57, 50, 77),
McIlroy (88)

CELTIC: Hunter; Boden, Fallon; Evans, Stein, Peacock; Collins, Fernie, McIlroy, Walsh, Tully

DUNDEE: R. Henderson; Frew, Cowan; Gallacher, Boyd, Cowie; Stables, A. Henderson, Flavell, Steel, Christie

Attendance: 25,000

December 20th
FALKIRK (1) 2 CELTIC (1) 3
Dunlop (26), Collins (15), McIlroy
Delaney (73) (59), Peacock (61)

FALKIRK: McFeat; McDonald, Rae; Gallacher, McKenzie, Hunter; Delaney, Dunlop, Weir, Campbell, Brown

CELTIC: Hunter; Boden, Fallon; Evans, Stein, Jack; Collins, Fernie, McIlroy, Tully, Peacock

Attendance: 14,000

December 27th
CELTIC (0) 0 RAITH ROVERS (1) 1
Copland (24)

CELTIC: Hunter; Mallan, Meechan; Evans, Stein, Peacock; Collins, Fernie, McIlroy, Tully, Duncan

RAITH ROVERS: Johnstone; McLure, McNaught; Young, Colville, Williamson; Maule, Kelly, Copland, McEwan, Penman

Attendance: 25,000

League positions

	P	W	D	L	F	A	Pts
1 East Fife	16	10	3	3	41	29	23
2 Hibernian	15	10	1	4	46	28	21
3 CELTIC	16	8	5	3	32	22	21
4 St Mirren	17	8	5	4	26	20	21
5 Rangers	13	8	2	3	37	22	18

January 1st
RANGERS (0) 1 CELTIC (0) 0
Simpson (53)

RANGERS: Niven; Young, Little; McColl, Woodburn, Cox; Waddell, Grierson, Simpson, Prentice, Hubbard

CELTIC: Hunter; Haughney, Meechan; Evans, Stein, Rollo; Collins, Fernie, McIlroy, Peacock, Tully

Attendance: 73,000

There was little sustained attacking play on either side. Evans, Stein and Rollo mopped up almost every inside-forward move and only the sprightly little Hubbard's darts and the crosses of Waddell were dangerous to Celtic.

January 10th
MOTHERWELL (0) 4 CELTIC (1) 2
Robinson (55), Fernie (20),
Humphries (75) Peacock (57)
Aitkenhead 2 (61, 89 pen)

MOTHERWELL: Johnstone; Kilmarnock, Shaw; Forrest, Paton, Cox; Sloan, Humphries, Kelly, Robinson, Aitkenhead

CELTIC: Hunter; Haughney, Meechan; Evans, Stein, Rollo; Collins, Fernie, McIlroy, Tully, Peacock

Attendance: 20,300

January 17th
CELTIC (1) 2 CLYDE (0) 4
McGrory (22), Baird (59),
Tully (82) Ring 3 (65, 70, 89)

CELTIC: Hunter; Haughney, Meechan; Evans, Stein, Jack; Hepburn, Fernie, McGrory, Collins, Tully

CLYDE: Wilson; Murphy, Haddock; Anderson, Campbell, Long; Buchanan; Baird, McPhail, Robertson, Ring

Attendance: 30,000

January 31st
QUEEN OF THE SOUTH (1) 2 CELTIC (0) 1
Patterson 2 (38, 69) Tully (84)

QUEEN OF THE SOUTH: Henderson; Sharpe, Binning; McBain, Smith, Greenock; Oakes, Black, Patterson, Cruikshanks, Johnstone

CELTIC: Bonnar; Meechan, Fallon; Evans, Stein, Jack; Collins, Fernie, McGrory, Peacock, Tully
Attendance:

February 14th
CELTIC (1) 1 — HEARTS (1) 1
McPhail (12 pen) — Wardhaugh (15)

CELTIC: Bonnar; Boden, Meechan; Evans, Stein, Fernie; Walsh, McPhail, McGrory, Tully, Peacock

HEARTS: Watters; Parker, McKenzie; Laing, Dougan, Armstrong; Souness, Conn, Bauld, Wardhaugh, Urquhart

Attendance: 30,000

February 28th
THIRD LANARK (1) 1 — CELTIC (1) 3
Dobbie (17) — Walsh (40), McGrory 2 (65, 85)

THIRD LANARK: Robertson; Balunas, Phillips; Mooney, Samuel, Henderson; Wilson, Docherty, Dobbie, Dick, Barclay

CELTIC: Hunter; Haughney, Meechan; Evans, Stein, McPhail; Collins, Walsh, McGrory, Fernie, Tully

Attendance: 30,000

League positions

	P	W	D	L	F	A	Pts
1 Hibernian	22	15	2	5	73	41	32
2 East Fife	23	12	6	5	51	39	30
3 Rangers	20	12	5	3	52	26	29
4 St Mirren	24	10	6	8	40	38	26
5 Clyde	25	11	4	10	68	61	26
6 CELTIC	22	9	6	7	41	35	24

March 7th
CELTIC (2) 3 — PARTICK THISTLE (0) 1
Tully (12), Walsh 2 (28, 47) — Walker (79)

CELTIC: Hunter; Haughney, Meechan; Evans, McIlroy, McPhail; Collins, Fernie, McGrory, Walsh, Tully

PARTICK THISTLE: Bell, McGowan, Gibb; Crawford, Davidson, McNab; McKenzie, Howitt, Stott, Sharp, Walker

Attendance: 35,000

March 12th: John McAlindon was transferred to Worcester City.

March 18th
CELTIC (0) 0 — AIRDRIE (1) 1
McCulloch (22)

CELTIC: Hunter; Haughney, Meechan; Evans, Stein, McPhail; Collins, Fernie, McGrory, Walsh, Tully

AIRDRIE: Fraser; Pryde, T. Brown; Cairns, Rodger, Shankland; Storrier, McMillan, Lennox, Docherty, McCulloch

Attendance: n.a.

March 21st
EAST FIFE (3) 4 — CELTIC (0) 1
Gardiner (32), J. Stewart (35), Emery (44 pen), Fleming (52) — Finlay o.g. (69)

EAST FIFE: Curran; Emery, S. Stewart; Christie, Finlay, McLennan; J. Stewart, Fleming, Bonthrone, Gardiner, Duncan

CELTIC: Hunter; Haughney, Meechan; Evans, Stein, McPhail; Walsh, Fernie, McGrory, Duffy, Tully

Attendance: 13,000

March 25th: Evans, Collins and Fernie were in the Scottish League team which beat the English League 1-0 at Ibrox.

March 28th
CELTIC (0) 1 — HIBERNIAN (2) 3
Collins (75 pen) — Johnstone 2 (23, 85), Reilly (43)

CELTIC: Hunter; Haughney, Fallon; Evans, Stein, McPhail; Collins, Walsh, McGrory, Fernie, Tully

HIBERNIAN: Younger; Govan, Clark; Gallacher, Paterson, Ward; Smith, Johnstone, Reilly, Turnbull, Combe

Attendance: n.a.

April 4th
DUNDEE (3) 4 — CELTIC (0) 0
Flavell (18), Toner (27), Henderson 2 (44, 88)

DUNDEE: Brown; Fallon, Cowan; Gallacher, Cowie, Ziesing; Toner, Henderson, Flavell, Steel, Hill

CELTIC: Bonnar; Haughney, Fallon; Evans, McIlroy, Stein; Walsh, Duffy, McPhail, Fernie, Tully

Attendance: 28,000

April 11th
CELTIC (2) 3 — ST MIRREN (1) 2
Fernie (13), Fallon (26), Collins (83) — Gemmell 2 (3, 85)

CELTIC: Bonnar; Haughney, Meechan; Evans, Stein, Conroy; Collins, Fernie, Fallon, McPhail, Peacock

ST MIRREN: Park; Lapsley, Johnston; Neilson, Telfer, Moore; Blyth, Cross, Wilson, Gemmell, Anderson

Attendance: 10,000

April 15th
CELTIC (0) 1 — ABERDEEN (2) 3
McPhail (48) — Hamilton 2 (40, 42), Yorston (85)

CELTIC: Bonnar; Haughney, Meechan; Evans, Stein, McGrory; Collins, Walsh, Fallon, McPhail, Peacock

ABERDEEN: Martin; Mitchell, Smith; Harris, Young, Allister; Rodger, Young, Buckley, Hamilton, Hather

Attendance: 10,000

April 15th Charlie Tully was in the Ireland team which was beaten 3-2 by Wales in Belfast.

April 18th
CELTIC (1) 1 — EAST FIFE (0) 1
Walsh (32) — Gardiner (48)

CELTIC: Bonnar; Haughney, Fallon; Evans, Jack, McGrory; Hepburn, Collins, Walsh, Peacock, Tully

EAST FIFE: Curran; Emery, S. Stewart; Christie, Finlay, McLellan; J. Stewart, Fleming, Bonthrone, Gardiner, Matthew

Attendance: 20,000

Scottish League Division A

	P	W	D	L	F	A	Pts
1 Rangers	30	18	7	5	80	39	43
2 Hibernian	30	19	5	6	93	51	43
3 East Fife	30	16	7	7	72	48	39
4 Hearts	30	12	6	12	59	50	30
5 Clyde	30	13	4	13	78	78	30
6 St Mirren	30	11	8	11	52	58	30
7 Dundee	30	9	11	10	44	37	29
8 CELTIC	30	11	7	12	51	54	29
9 Partick Thistle	30	10	9	11	55	63	29
10 Queen of the South	30	10	8	12	43	61	28
11 Aberdeen	30	11	5	14	64	68	27
12 Raith Rovers	30	9	8	13	47	53	26
13 Falkirk	30	11	4	15	53	63	26
14 Airdrie	30	10	6	14	53	75	26
15 Motherwell	30	10	5	15	57	80	25
16 Third Lanark	30	8	4	18	52	75	20

May 6th: Bobby Evans was in the Scotland team which was beaten 2-1 by Sweden at Hampden Park.

May 8th: Neil Mochan was signed from Middlesbrough for £8,000.

May 9th: Celtic offered Morton £4,000 for goalkeeper Jimmy Cowan.

June 17th: The great Patsy Gallagher died.

LEAGUE CUP

August 9th
ST MIRREN (0) 0 — CELTIC (1)1
McDonald (6)

ST MIRREN: Pirrie; Lapsley, Cunningham; Neilson, Telfer, Martin; Rice, Wilson, Stewart, Williamson, Duncanson

CELTIC: Bonnar; Boden, Fallon; Evans, Stein, Baillie; Weir, McPhail, McDonald, Tully, Peacock

Attendance: 25,000

August 13th
CELTIC (1) 2 — PARTICK THISTLE (0) 5
Tully (77½), McDonald (79) — Walker 2 (n.a.), Stott 3 (77, 78, 90)

CELTIC: Bonnar; Boden, Fallon; Evans, Stein, Baillie; Weir, McPhail, McDonald, Tully, Peacock

PARTICK THISTLE: Ledgerwood; McGowan, Gibb; Davidson, Crawford, Mathers; McCallum, Harvey, Stott, Sharp, Walker

Attendance: 40,000

August 16th
CELTIC (0) 1 — HIBERNIAN (0) 0
McPhail (80)

CELTIC: Bonnar; Boden, Fallon; Evans, Stein, Baillie; Millsop, Fernie, McPhail, Tully, Haughney

HIBERNIAN: Younger; Govan, Howie; Buchanan, Paterson, Gallagher; Smith, Combe, Reilly, Turnbull, Ormond

Attendance: 49,000

August 23rd
CELTIC (2) 3 — ST MIRREN (0) 1
McPhail (7), Peacock (28), Fernie (60) — Lapsley (75)

CELTIC: Bonnar; Boden, Fallon; Evans, Stein, Baillie; Millsop, Fernie, McPhail, Tully, Peacock

ST MIRREN: Lornie; Lapsley, Cunningham; Neilson, Telfer, Reid; Blyth, Wilson, Stewart, McGill, Duncanson

Attendance: 25,000

August 27th
PARTICK THISTLE (0) 0 — CELTIC (0) 1
Peacock (67)

PARTICK THISTLE: Ledgerwood; McGowan, McCreadie; Thomson, Davidson, Mathers; McKenzie, Howitt, Stott, Sharp, Walker

CELTIC: Bonnar; Boden, Fallon; Evans, Stein, Baillie; Walsh, Fernie, White, Tully, Peacock

Attendance: 30,000

August 30th
HIBERNIAN (2) 3 — CELTIC (0) 0
Turnbull (19), Reilly 2 (28, 78)

HIBERNIAN: Younger; Govan, Clark; Buchanan, Howie, Combe; Smith, Johnstone, Reilly, Turnbull, Ormond

CELTIC; Bonnar; Meechan, Fallon; Evans, Boden, Baillie; Millsop, Fernie, Walsh, Tully, Peacock

Attendance: 51,000

SECTION TABLE

	P	W	D	L	F	A	Pts
Hibernian	6	5	0	1	17	8	10
CELTIC	6	4	0	2	8	9	8
St Mirren	6	2	1	3	13	13	5
Partick Thistle	6	1	1	4	10	18	3

Qualifier: HIBERNIAN

SCOTTISH CUP

First Round January 24th
EYEMOUTH (0) 0 CELTIC (3) 4
McGrory 4 (3, 12, 40, 88)

EYEMOUTH: Paterson; Sinclair, Muirhead; Grant, Nairn, Schumacher; Burns, Houston, Scott, Ridley, Armstrong

CELTIC: Bonnar; Meechan, Rollo; Evans, Stein, Jack; Collins, Fernie, McGrory, Peacock, Tully

Attendance: 4,131

Second Round February 7th
STIRLING ALBION (0) 1 CELTIC (1) 1
Chalmers (82) McGrory (15)

STIRLING ALBION: Jenkins; Gibson, Forsyth; Fleming, Christie, Smith; McFarlane, Chalmers, Henderson, McQueen, Anderson

CELTIC: Bonnar; Boden, Fallon; Evans, Stein, Jack; Collins, Fernie, McGrory, McPhail, Tully

Attendance: 24,763

Second Round Replay February 11th
CELTIC (0) 3 STIRLING ALBION (0) 0
McGrory 2 (50, n.a.),
Peacock (65)

CELTIC: Bonnar; Boden, Meechan; Evans, Stein, Fernie; Collins, McPhail, McGrory, Tully, Peacock

STIRLING ALBION: Jenkins; Gibson, Forsyth; Fleming, Christie, Smith; McFarlane, Chalmers, Henderson, McQueen, Anderson

Attendance: 24,500

Third Round February 21st
FALKIRK (2) 2 CELTIC (0) 3
Weir (5), Campbell (18) Tully (53), Fernie (59),
McGrory (66)

FALKIRK: McFeat; McDonald, Rae; Gallacher, McKenzie, Hunter; Delaney, Dunlop, Weir, Campbell, J. Brown

CELTIC: Bonnar; Haughney, Meechan; Evans, Stein, McPhail; Collins, Walsh, McGrory, Fernie, Tully

Attendance: 23,100

Fourth Round March 14th
RANGERS (1) 2 CELTIC (0) 0
Prentice (10),
Grierson (88)

RANGERS: Niven; Young, Little; McColl, Woodburn, Cox; Paton, Grierson, Simpson, Prentice, Hubbard

CELTIC: Hunter; Haughney, Meechan; Evans, Stein, McPhail; Collins, Fernie, McGrory, Walsh, Tully

Attendance: 95,000

An early goal by Prentice allowed Rangers to control this match. Young, who was a superbly constructive player and Little, consistently successful against Collins, formed with their centre-half a barrier which Celtic found difficult to penetrate. Rangers, however, survived a remarkable minute just before the interval in which Collins shot against a post, Tully shot against Niven from only 6 yards and another Collins shot that had the goalkeeper beaten was headed out from under the crossbar by Little. Grierson made sure for the home side with a late goal in the 88th minute.

CORONATION CUP

First Round May 11th at Hampden Park
CELTIC (1) 1 ARSENAL (0) 0
Collins (23)

CELTIC: Bonnar; Haughney, Rollo; Evans, Stein, McPhail; Collins, Walsh, Mochan, Peacock, Tully

ARSENAL: Swindin; Wade, Chenhall; Forbes, Dodgin, Mercer; Roper, Goring, Holton, Lishman, Marden

Attendance: 59,500

Celtic not only beat English Division 1 Champions Arsenal but taught them how to play football. Had Arsenal lost by 5 or 6 goals they could have had no valid complaint. Celtic's shooting was a revelation. On at least a dozen occasions the ball whistled inches high or wide of the Arsenal goal and on as many more Swindin saved superbly.

Semi-Final May 16th at Hampden Park
CELTIC (1) 2 MANCHESTER
Peacock (24), UNITED (0) 1
Mochan (53) Rowley (77)

CELTIC: Bonnar; Haughney, Rollo; Evans, Stein, McPhail; Collins, Walsh, Mochan, Peacock, Tully

MANCHESTER UNITED: Crompton; McNulty, Aston; Carey, Chilton, Gibson; Violett, Downie, Rowley, Pearson, Byrne

Attendance: 73,000

Though they did not play with the brilliance that astounded Arsenal, Celtic beat Manchester United with a display that was perhaps the more creditable in view of the very difficult conditions. Wing-halves Evans and McPhail inspired their side to victory and Peacock was the forward who caused the United defence most concern.

Final May 20th at Hampden Park
CELTIC (1) 2 HIBERNIAN (0) 0
Mochan (28), Walsh (87)

CELTIC: Bonnar; Haughney, Rollo; Evans, Stein, McPhail; Collins, Walsh, Mochan, Peacock, Fernie

HIBERNIAN: Younger; Govan, Paterson; Buchanan, Howie, Combe; Smith, Johnstone, Reilly, Turnbull, Ormond

Attendance: 117,060

Celtic, who only a few weeks ago were the despair of their huge following, confounded everyone by winning the Coronation Cup. Just before the competition began Celtic signed Mochan from Middlesbrough and it was he who set his side on the road to victory with a magnificent goal in the 28th minute of the first half. Bonnar undoubtedly saved Celtic from defeat in a second half that was – even more than the first in which Celtic were the superior side – almost one-way traffic, so persistent were the Hibs attackers. His saves from Johnstone, Turnbull and Buchanan were uncanny.

APPEARANCES	League	League Cup	Scottish Cup	Coronation Cup
Bonnar	13	6	4	3
Boden	15	6	2	–
Fallon	20	6	1	–
Evans	30	6	5	3
Stein	28	5	5	3
Baillie	12	6	–	–
Walsh	22	2	2	3
Fernie	24	4	5	1
McPhail	15	4	4	3
Tully	25	6	5	2
Millsop	1	3	–	–
Peacock	22	5	2	3
Meechan	19	1	4	–
Rollo	5	–	1	3
Hepburn	6	–	–	–
Hunter	17	–	1	–

APPEARANCES	League	League Cup	Scottish Cup	Coronation Cup
Haughney	13	1	2	3
Duncan	2	–	–	–
Lafferty	1	–	–	–
McIlroy	8	–	–	–
Collins	14	–	5	3
Jack	4	–	2	–
Mallan	1	–	–	–
McGrory	10	–	5	–
Duffy	2	–	–	–
Conroy	1	–	–	–
Weir	–	2	–	–
McDonald	–	2	–	–
Mochan	–	–	–	3

GOALSCORERS:

League: Peacock 8, Fernie 7, Tully 7, Walsh 7 (1 pen), McPhail 5 (1 pen), Fallon 3, McIlroy 3, Collins 3 (1 pen), McGrory 3, Own Goals 2, Rollo 1, Duncan 1, Lafferty 1

League Cup: McDonald 2, McPhail 2, Peacock 2, Tully 1, Fernie 1

Scottish Cup: McGrory 8, Peacock 1, Tully 1, Fernie 1

Coronation Cup: Mochan 2, Collins 1, Peacock 1, Walsh 1

The team bus leaves Hampden Park after Celtic had defeated Aberdeen 2-1 in the 1954 Scottish Cup Final. Jock Stein shows the Cup to the waiting fans.

Season 1953-54

This was Celtic's most successful season for 40 years and ended with both the League Championship and the Scottish Cup being won (Celtic's 4th double).

The basis of their Championship win was their superb home form where they collected 29 of the possible 30 points. By sharp contrast away from home they won only one match in the first 7 months, but after beating Airdrie 6-0 on March 17th they won at Firhill, Love Street, Brockville and Easter Road, scoring 12 goals for the loss of only 2. They topped the table for the first time on April 9th and ended the season 5 points ahead of runners-up Hearts and 9 ahead of Rangers. Bertie Peacock played in all 30 matches with Bobby Evans missing only one. Their goals total shot up to 72 with Neil Mochan scoring 20 and Collins and Fernie each getting 10. The signing of Mochan from Middlesbrough at the tail-end of the previous season had been a masterstroke.

The Scottish Cup was also won in fine style. Celtic beat Falkirk, Stirling Albion and Hamilton in the early Rounds – all away from home. They let Motherwell off the hook in their first Semi-Final clash but made no mistake in the replay, winning 3-1. They faced Aberdeen in the Final on April 24th. An all-ticket crowd of nearly 130,000 saw a hard, fast game featuring magnificent half-back play. Fernie set up the winning goal for Fallon which gave Celtic the trophy for the 17th time.

There had been no indication of the glory to come when Celtic finished bottom of their League Cup Section at the end of August.

League:	Champions
League Cup:	Failed to qualify from Section
Scottish Cup:	Winners

LEAGUE DIVISION A

August 10th: Tony Hepburn joined Dumbarton.

August 31st: Jimmy Mallan joined St Mirren after being released by the club. Vincent Ryan joined the club from Home Farm, Dublin.

September 5th
HAMILTON ACADEMICALS (1) 2 — CELTIC (0) 0
Young (40), Scott (62)

HAMILTON: Ritchie; Bathgate, Johnstone; Wilson, G. Scott, Martin; Young, Todd, J. Scott, Brown, Cunning

CELTIC: Bell; Haughney, Meechan; Evans, Stein, Baillie; Collins, Walsh, McPhail, Peacock, Fernie

Attendance: 20,000

September 12th
CELTIC (0) 1 — CLYDE (0) 0
Collins (87)

CELTIC: Bell; Haughney, Fallon; Evans, Stein, McPhail; Collins, Fernie, Walsh, Peacock, Duncan

CLYDE: Wilson; Murphy, Haddock; Anderson, Campbell, Long; Buchanan, Baird, McPhail, Robertson, Ring

Attendance: 23,000

September 19th
RANGERS (1) 1 — CELTIC (1) 1
Paton (21) — Duncan (23)

RANGERS: Niven; Caldow, Little; McColl, Woodburn, Cox; Waddell, Grierson, Paton, Prentice, Hubbard

CELTIC: Bell; Haughney, Fallon; Evans, Stein, Peacock; Collins, Walsh, McPhail, Tully, Duncan

Attendance: 59,000

September 26th
CELTIC (2) 3 ABERDEEN (0) 0
Collins 3 (8 pen, 44 pen, 67 pen)

CELTIC: Bell; Haughney, Fallon; Evans, Stein, Peacock; Collins, Walsh, Duncan, Tully, Mochan

ABERDEEN: Martin; Mitchell, Caldwell; Allister, Young, Glen; Leggat, Smith, Buckley, Hay, Hather

Attendance: 26,000

October 3rd: Evans and McPhail were in the Scotland team which beat Ireland 3-1 in Belfast. Tully represented Ireland.

October 10th
CELTIC (1) 3 RAITH ROVERS (0) 0
Fernie 2 (6, 67), Collins (69)

CELTIC: Hunter; Haughney, Fallon; Evans, Stein, Peacock; Collins, Fernie, McPhail, Walsh, Duncan

RAITH ROVERS: Johnstone; Kirk, McNaught; Leigh, Colville, Williamson; McEwan, Young, Copland, Kelly, Scott

Attendance: 20,000

October 17th
QUEEN OF THE SOUTH (0) 2 CELTIC (0) 1
Rothera (60), Patterson (70) Collins (51 pen)

QUEEN OF THE SOUTH: Henderson; Sharpe, Binning; Brown, Smith, Greenock; Black, McGill, Patterson, Rothera, Oakes

CELTIC: Hunter; Haughney, Rollo; Evans, McIlroy, Peacock; Higgins, Collins, McPhail, Walsh, Duncan

Attendance: 16,000

October 24th
CELTIC (2) 2 HEARTS (0) 0
McPhail (21), Walsh (29)

CELTIC: Hunter; Haughney, Fallon; Evans, Stein, Peacock; Collins, Fernie, McPhail, Walsh, Mochan

HEARTS: Watters; Parker, Adie; Armstrong, Dougan, Laing; Rutherford, Conn, Wardhaugh, Cumming, Urquhart

Attendance: 30,000

October 31st
DUNDEE (0) 1 CELTIC (1) 1
Cowie (64) McPhail (22)

DUNDEE: Brown; Frew, Cowan; Gallacher, Malloy, Cowie; Burrell, Henderson, Turnbull, Steel, Christie

CELTIC: Bonnar; Haughney, Meechan; Evans, Stein, Peacock; Collins, Fernie, McPhail, Walsh, Tully

Attendance: 27,000

League positions

	P	W	D	L	F	A	Pts
1 Queen of the South	9	7	1	1	26	12	15
2 Dundee	9	4	3	2	13	11	11
3 CELTIC	8	4	2	2	12	6	10
4 Hearts	9	4	2	3	18	13	10
5 Raith Rovers	9	4	2	3	19	16	10

November 4th: Bobby Evans was in the Scotland team which drew 3-3 with Wales at Hampden Park.

November 7th
CELTIC (1) 2 HIBERNIAN (0) 2
Collins (20), Stein (83) Reilly 2 (69, 70)

CELTIC: Bonnar; Haughney, Meechan; Evans, Stein, Peacock; Collins, Fernie, McPhail, Walsh, Tully

HIBERNIAN: Younger; McFarlane, Paterson; Buchanan, Howie, Combe; Smith, Johnstone, Reilly, Turnbull, Duchart

Attendance: 40,000. Charie Tully was carried off in the 35th minute.

November 14th
EAST FIFE (2) 4 CELTIC (1) 1
Bonthrone (6), Fleming 3 (20, 58, 74) Fernie (42)

EAST FIFE: Curran; Emery, S. Stewart; Christie, Finlay, McLennan; J. Stewart, Fleming, Bonthrone, Gardiner, Matthew

CELTIC: Bonnar; Haughney, Meechan; Evans, Stein, Peacock; Collins, Fernie, McPhail, Walsh, Duncan

Attendance: 15,000

November 21st
CELTIC (2) 4 AIRDRIE (1) 1
McPhail (4), Mochan 3 (15, 79, 89) Welsh (44)

CELTIC: Bonnar; Haughney, Meechan; Evans, Stein, Peacock; Collins, Fernie, McPhail, Walsh, Mochan

AIRDRIE: Fraser; Pryde, Cross; Cairns, Rodger, Quinn; Quigley, McMillan, Baird, Welsh, McCulloch

Attendance: 20,000

November 28th
CELTIC (2) 2 PARTICK THISTLE (1) 1
Fernie 2 (4, 34) Sharp (3)

CELTIC: Bonnar; Haughney, Meechan; Evans, Stein, Peacock; Collins, Fernie, McPhail, Walsh, Mochan

PARTICK THISTLE: Smith; McGowan, Kerr; Crawford, Davidson, Mathers; McKenzie, Howitt, Sharp, Wright, Walker

Attendance: 27,000

December 5th
STIRLING ALBION (1) 2 — CELTIC (0) 1
Bain (44), Kelly (67) — Peacock (48)

STIRLING ALBION: Jenkins; Ferguson, Whitehead; Bain, Milligan, Smith; Chalmers, Williamson, Kelly, Rattray, Allan

CELTIC: Bonnar; Haughney, Meechan; Evans, Stein, Peacock; Collins, Fernie, Hemple, Walsh, Mochan

Attendance: 18,000

December 12th
CELTIC (0) 4 — ST MIRREN (0) 0
Walsh 2 (46, 63), Mochan (53), Hemple (71)

CELTIC: Bonnar; Haughney, Meechan; Evans, Stein, Peacock; Collins, Fernie, Hemple, Walsh, Mochan

ST MIRREN: Park; Lapsley, McDonald; Wilson, Telfer, Johnston; Blyth, Gemmell, Stewart, McGill, McGuigan

Attendance: 25,000

December 15th: John McDonald was transferred to St Mirren.

December 26th
CLYDE (0) 1 — CELTIC (3) 7
Carr (80) — Mochan 2 (31, 79), Hemple (43), Higgins 2 (44, 62), Collins 2 (81, 86)

CLYDE: Wilson; Murphy, Haddock; Campbell, Anderson, Baird; Hill, Robertson, Buchanan, Carr, Ring

CELTIC: Bonnar; Haughney, Meechan; Evans, Stein, Peacock; Higgins, Fernie, Hemple, Collins, Mochan

Attendance: 21,500

League positions

	P	W	D	L	F	A	Pts
1 Queen of the South	17	11	2	4	46	25	24
2 Dundee	16	8	5	3	22	17	21
3 Hearts	17	8	4	5	39	26	20
4 CELTIC	15	8	3	4	33	17	19
5 Aberdeen	16	8	3	5	40	22	19

January 1st
CELTIC (0) 1 — RANGERS (0) 0
Mochan (60)

CELTIC: Bonnar; Haughney, Meechan; Stein, Evans, Peacock; Higgins, Fernie, McPhail, Collins, Mochan

RANGERS: Brown; Young, Little; McColl, Woodburn, Cox; Waddell, Grierson, Gardiner, Prentice, Hubbard

Attendance: n.a.

A magnificent display by Rangers' defence almost baulked Celtic of a thoroughly deserved victory. Never had Woodburn in particular served his club more capably. It was cruel luck for him that his only mistake enabled Mochan to score 15 minutes after half-time, and even that error was partly caused by Young's failure to clear. Celtic were immeasurably superior at inside-forward – Collins and Fernie were a splendid combination. Evans and Peacock had unflagging energy. Meechan was the master of Waddell, and Haughney was just as much the master of Hubbard.

January 2nd
ABERDEEN (1) 2 — CELTIC (0) 0
Buckley 2 (8, 46)

ABERDEEN: Morrison; Mitchell, Caldwell; O'Neil, Young, Glen; Leggat, Hamilton, Buckley, Hay, Hather

CELTIC: Bonnar; Haughney, Meechan; Evans, Stein, Peacock; Collins, Fernie, Hemple, Walsh, Mochan

Attendance: 30,000

January 9th
CELTIC (0) 1 — FALKIRK (0) 0
Higgins (57)

CELTIC: Bonnar; Haughney, Meechan; Evans, Stein, Peacock; Higgins, Fernie, McPhail, Collins, Mochan

FALKIRK: McFeat; McDonald, Rae; Gallacher, McKenzie, Black; Sinclair, Morrison, Plumb, McCrae, Kelly

Attendance: 28,000

January 16th
RAITH ROVERS (1) 2 — CELTIC (0) 0
Copland 2 (13, 84)

RAITH ROVERS: Drummond; McLure, McNaught; McNeil, Colville, Leigh; McEwan, Young, Copland, Kelly, Duncan

CELTIC: Bonnar; Haughney, Meechan; Evans, Stein, Peacock; Higgins, Fernie, McPhail, Collins, Mochan

Attendance: 13,000

January 23rd
CELTIC (2) 3 — QUEEN OF THE SOUTH (0) 1
McPhail (16), Mochan 2 (30, 54) — McGill (56)

CELTIC: Bonnar; Haughney, Meechan; Evans, Stein, Peacock; Higgins, Fernie, McPhail, Collins, Mochan

QUEEN OF THE SOUTH: Henderson; Sharpe, Binning; McBain, Hollywood, Greenock; Black, McGill, Brown, Rothera, Oakes

Attendance: 28,000

February 6th
HEARTS (0) 3 — CELTIC (0) 2
Bauld 2 (46, 59), Wardhaugh (87) — Haughney 2 (69 pen, 82 pen)

HEARTS: Watters; Parker, Adie; Laing, Glidden, Cumming; Souness, Conn, Bauld, Wardhaugh, Urquhart

CELTIC: Hunter; Haughney, Meechan; Evans, Stein, Peacock; Collins, Fernie, Walsh, Tully, Mochan

Attendance: 47,519

February 20th
CELTIC (4) 5 — DUNDEE (1) 1
Mochan 2 (7, 37), Walsh (17), Fernie (44), Higgins (82) — Merchant (25)

CELTIC: Bell; Haughney, Meechan; Evans, Stein, Peacock; Higgins, Fernie, Walsh, Tully, Mochan

DUNDEE: Brown; Fallon, Frew; Ziesing, Malloy, Cowie; Carmichael, Gallacher, Merchant, Steel, Flavell

Attendance: 32,000

League positions

	P	W	D	L	F	A	Pts
1 Hearts	25	14	6	5	63	38	34
2 CELTIC	22	12	3	7	45	26	27
3 Aberdeen	23	12	3	8	57	39	27
4 Queen of the South	23	12	3	8	58	42	27
5 Clyde	24	11	4	9	49	57	26

March 6th
CELTIC (2) 4 — EAST FIFE (1) 1
Higgins 2 (3, 54), Fernie (14), Walsh (87) — Christie (35)

CELTIC: Bell; Haughney, Meechan; Evans, Stein, Peacock; Higgins, Fernie, Walsh, Tully, Mochan

EAST FIFE: Curran; Emery, S. Stewart; Christie, Finlay, McLennan; J. Stewart, Fleming, Gardiner, Bonthrone, Matthew

Attendance: 25,000

March 17th: Mike Haughney was in the Scottish League team which beat the League of Ireland 3-1 in Dublin.

March 17th
AIRDRIE (0) 0 — CELTIC (3) 6
Mochan 3 (7, 25, n.a.), Fallon (45), Higgins (50), Fernie (n.a. pen)

AIRDRIE: Walker; T. Brown, Shanks; McLure, Rodger, Gordon; Cairns, Quinn, Baird, Cross, McCulloch

CELTIC: Bonnar; Boden, Meechan; Evans, McIlroy, Peacock; Higgins, Fernie, Fallon, Collins, Mochan

Attendance: 13,000

March 20th
PARTICK THISTLE (1) 1 — CELTIC (0) 3
Sharp (31) — Fallon 2 (64, 87), Fernie (72)

PARTICK THISTLE: Ledgerwood; McGowan, Kerr; Harvey, Davidson, Mathers; McKenzie, Howitt, Sharp, Wright, McInnes

CELTIC: Bonnar; Haughney, Meechan; Evans, Stein, Peacock; Higgins, Fernie, Fallon, Walsh, Mochan

Attendance: 30,000

March 29th
CELTIC (2) 4 — STIRLING ALBION (0) 0
Mochan 2 (25, 68), Fallon (31), Fernie (65)

CELTIC: Bonnar; Boden, Meechan; Evans, Stein, Peacock; Higgins, Fernie, Fallon, Collins, Mochan

STIRLING ALBION: Jenkins; Ferguson, Whitehead; McKechnie, Milligan, Swanson; Jackson, Chalmers, Kelly, Rattray, Brander

Attendance: n.a.

April 7th
ST MIRREN (1) 1 — CELTIC (2) 3
McGill (45) — Tully (13), Collins (17), Haughney (62 pen)

ST MIRREN: Park; Lapsley, Mallan; J. Neilson, Telfer, Johnston; McMaster, McGill, Stewart, Gemmell, McGuigan

CELTIC: Bonnar; Haughney, Meechan; Evans, Stein, Peacock; Collins, Fernie, Fallon, Tully, Mochan

Attendance: 18,000

April 14th
FALKIRK (0) 0 — CELTIC (1) 3
Fallon (10), Mochan 2 (58, 86)

FALKIRK: McFeat; Sievwright, Rae; Black, Ralston, J. Hunter; Sinclair, Morrison, Plumb, McCrae, Kelly

CELTIC: Bonnar; Haughney, Meechan; Evans, Stein, Peacock; Higgins, Fernie, Fallon, Tully, Mochan

Attendance: 22,000

April 17th
HIBERNIAN (0) 0 — CELTIC (1) 3
Mochan 2 (1, 48), Higgins (86)

HIBERNIAN: Younger; MacFarlane, Paterson; Gallagher, Ward, Combe; Johnstone, Preston, Thomson, Turnbull, Ormond

CELTIC: Bonnar; Haughney, Meechan; Evans, Stein, Peacock; Higgins, Fernie, Fallon, Tully, Mochan

Attendance: 45,000

April 25th: Ian White was signed from St Anthony's.

April 26th
CELTIC (1) 1 — HAMILTON ACADEMICALS (0) 0
Haughney (9)

CELTIC: Bonnar; Ryan, Meechan; Haughney, McIlroy, Peacock; Higgins, Collins, Fallon, Tully, Mochan

HAMILTON: Houston; Ferguson, Johnston; Stirling, Scott, Martin; Rae, Walker, Todd, Brown, Crawford

Attendance: 20,000

The successful Celtic line-up of season 1953/54. League Champions and Scottish Cup Winners.

Scottish League Division A

	P	W	D	L	F	A	Pts
1 CELTIC	30	20	3	7	72	29	43
2 Hearts	30	16	6	8	70	45	38
3 Partick Thistle	30	17	1	12	76	54	35
4 Rangers	30	13	8	9	56	35	34
5 Hibernian	30	15	4	11	72	51	34
6 East Fife	30	13	8	9	55	45	34
7 Dundee	30	14	6	10	46	47	34
8 Clyde	30	15	4	11	64	67	34
9 Aberdeen	30	15	3	12	66	51	33
10 Queen of the South	30	14	4	12	72	58	32
11 St Mirren	30	12	4	14	44	54	28
12 Raith Rovers	30	10	6	14	56	60	26
13 Falkirk	30	9	7	14	47	61	25
14 Stirling Albion	30	10	4	16	39	62	24
15 Airdrie	30	5	5	20	41	92	15
16 Hamilton	30	4	3	23	29	94	11

May 1st: Rollo, Hunter, Hepburn, Murphy and Duffy were all given free transfers.

April 28th: Evans, Stein and Fernie were in the Scottish League team which was beaten 4-0 by the English League at Stamford Bridge.

May 5th: Bobby Evans was in the Scotland team which beat Norway 1-0 at Hampden Park.

May 14th: St Mirren signed John McGrory who had been on loan to Albion Rovers.

May 19th: Neil Mochan was in the Scotland team which drew 1-1 with Norway in Oslo.

May 25th: Evans and Fernie were in the Scotland team which beat Finland 2-1 in Helsinki.

May 20th: Evans, Fernie and Mochan were included in Scotland's pool of 12 players for the World Cup Finals in Switzerland.

June 16th: Fernie and Mochan were in the Scotland team which was beaten 1-0 by Austria in the World Cup Finals in Zurich.

June 19th: Fernie and Mochan were in the Scotland team which was beaten 7-0 by Uruguay in the World Cup Finals in Basle.

LEAGUE CUP

August 8th
CELTIC (0) 0 ABERDEEN (0) 1
Brown (63)

CELTIC: Bonnar; Haughney, Rollo; Evans, Stein, McPhail; Tully, Walsh, Mochan, Peacock, Fernie

ABERDEEN: Martin; Mitchell, Smith; Harris, Young Allister; Brown, Yorston, Buckley, Hamilton, Hather

Attendance: 55,000

August 12th
EAST FIFE (0) 1 CELTIC (0) 1
Fleming (81) Peacock (69)

EAST FIFE: Curran; Emery, S. Stewart; Christie, Finlay, McLennan; J. Stewart, Fleming, Bonthrone, Gardiner, Matthew

CELTIC: Bonnar; Haughney, Rollo; Evans, Stein, McPhail; Collins, Walsh, Mochan, Peacock, Fernie

Attendance: 16,000

August 15th
AIRDRIE (1) 2 CELTIC (0) 1
McCulloch 2 (11 pen, 83) Walsh (84)

AIRDRIE: Fraser; Pryde, Cross; Henderson, Rodger, Cairns; Quigley, Quinn, Baird, Docherty, McCulloch

CELTIC: Bonnar; Haughney, Rollo; Evans, Stein, McPhail; Collins, Walsh, Mochan, Peacock, Fernie

Attendance: 22,000

August 22nd
ABERDEEN (2) 5 CELTIC (1) 2
Yorston 2 (12, 43), Walsh (27), Mochan (89)
Buckley 2 (64, 86),
Hather (73)

ABERDEEN: Morrison; Mitchell, Caldwell; Harris, Smith, Allister; Dunbar, Yorston, Buckley, Hamilton, Hather

CELTIC: Hunter; Haughney, Rollo; Evans, Stein, McPhail; Walsh, Fernie, White, Peacock, Mochan

Attendance: 30,000

August 26th
CELTIC (0) 0 EAST FIFE (1) 1
Luke (28)

CELTIC: Bonnar; Haughney, Meechan; Evans, Stein, McPhail; Collins, Fernie, Mochan, Peacock, McMillan

EAST FIFE: Curran; Emery, S. Stewart; Christie, Finlay, McLennan; J. Stewart, Fleming, Gardiner, Luke, Matthew

Attendance: n.a.

August 29th
CELTIC (2) 2 AIRDRIE (0) 0
Walsh (13), McPhail (27)

CELTIC: Bonnar; Haughney, Meechan; Evans, McIlroy, Baillie; Collins, Walsh, McPhail, Peacock, McMillan

AIRDRIE: Fraser; Henderson, Cross; Cairns, Rodger, Docherty; Quigley, McMillan, Baird, Quinn, McCulloch

Attendance: 18,000

SECTION TABLE

	P	W	D	L	F	A	Pts
East Fife	6	4	1	1	14	9	9
Aberdeen	6	3	0	3	14	12	6
Airdrie	6	3	0	3	11	14	6
CELTIC	6	1	1	4	6	10	3

Qualifier: EAST FIFE

SCOTTISH CUP

Second Round February 17th
FALKIRK (1) 1 — CELTIC (1) 2
Aikman (30) — Fernie (10), Higgins (46)

FALKIRK: McFeat; McDonald, Rae; Black, McKenzie, Hunter; J. Sinclair, Morrison, Aikman, McCrae, Kelly

CELTIC: Bell; Haughney, Meechan; Evans, Stein, Peacock; Higgins, Fernie, Walsh, Tully, Mochan

Attendance: 22,000

Third Round February 27th
STIRLING ALBION (2) 3 — CELTIC (3) 4
Rattray 2 (7, 25), Kelly (80) — Haughney (29 pen), Higgins (33), Mochan 2 (36, 50)

STIRLING ALBION: Jenkins; Ferguson, Whitehead; Smith, Milligan, Swanson; Chalmers, Williamson, Kelly, Rattray, Brander

CELTIC: Bell; Haughney, Meechan; Evans, Stein, Peacock; Higgins, Fernie, Walsh, Tully, Mochan

Attendance: 25,750

Fourth Round March 13th
HAMILTON ACADEMICALS (0) 1 — CELTIC (1) 2
Todd (78) — Haughney (9 pen), Fernie (75)

HAMILTON: Houston; Shearer, J. Young; Barrett, Scott, Martin; Todd, Walker, Stott, Brown, Crawford

CELTIC: Bell; Haughney, Meechan; Evans, Stein, Peacock; Higgins, Fernie, Walsh, Tully, Mochan

Attendance: 22,000

Semi-Final March 27th at Hampden Park
CELTIC (1) 2 — MOTHERWELL (1) 2
Mochan (24), Fallon (55) — Humphries (22), Aitken (88)

CELTIC: Bonnar; Haughney, Meechan; Evans, Stein, Peacock; Higgins, Fernie, Fallon, Tully, Mochan

MOTHERWELL: Johnstone; Kilmarnock, Shaw; Cox, Paton, Redpath; Sloan, Forrest, Humphries, Aitken, Aitkenhead

Attendance: 100,000

When Fallon scored a 2nd and leading goal for Celtic 10 minutes after half-time few would have given Motherwell a chance of saving the day, but save it they did, and they might even have won it in a breathtaking rally in the final quarter of an hour.

Semi-Final Replay April 5th at Hampden Park
CELTIC (1) 3 — MOTHERWELL (1) 1
Kilmarnock o.g. (22), Fernie (52), Mochan (70) — Hunter (34)

CELTIC: Bonnar; Haughney, Meechan; Evans, Stein, Peacock; Higgins, Fernie, Fallon, Duncan, Mochan

MOTHERWELL: Johnstone; Kilmarnock, Higgins; Cox, Paton, Redpath; Sloan, Forrest, Hunter, Humphries, Aitkenhead

Attendance: 92,662

Motherwell on this occasion did not match their rivals for stamina and were a well beaten side in the end. Motherwell played particularly well in the first half in which they had to face a strong wind and though Celtic had by far the greater share of the attacking in that period the Division B leaders must have been thoroughly satisfied to retire on level terms. 20 minutes from time Motherwell were down and almost out. Johnstone could not get his hands to a cross from Higgins and Mochan lobbed into the net. 3 minutes from time Haughney missed a penalty kick by crashing the ball high over the bar after Paton had floored Duncan. Jock Stein was the outstanding player afield.

Final April 24th at Hampden Park
ABERDEEN (0) 1 — CELTIC (0) 2
Buckley (52) — Young o.g. (51), Fallon (63)

ABERDEEN: Martin; Mitchell, Caldwell; Allister, Young, Glen; Leggat, Hamilton, Buckley, Clunie, Hather

CELTIC: Bonnar; Haughney, Meechan; Evans, Stein, Peacock; Higgins, Fernie, Fallon, Tully, Mochan

Attendance: 129,926. *Referee:* C.E. Faultless

Deprived of the services of O'Neil, Aberdeen were not inspired by their inside-forwards, for which the perpetually active wing-halves Evans and Peacock must receive great credit. The threat of Buckley had been anticipated, and Stein employed all his resources of positional sense to counterbalance his disadvantage in pace; Evans in particular was frequently present to assist his centre-half. 18 minutes after the restart Fernie went off on a dribble. In towards goal and along the goal-line he went with an Aberdeen player making unsuccessful attempts to tackle him from behind. Just when he seemed to have lost control, he recovered magnificently and there was a chipped pass laid on for Fallon, plumb in the centre of the goal, to score what proved to be the Cup winning goal. The gestures of the Aberdeen players at the end of a gruelling and always interesting match were admirable – a spontaneous display of gracefulness in defeat.

Appearances	League	League Cup	Scottish Cup
Bell	6	–	3
Haughney	28	6	6
Meechan	24	2	6
Evans	29	6	6
Stein	27	5	6
Baillie	1	1	–
Collins	25	4	–
McPhail	15	6	–
Peacock	30	6	6
Fernie	26	5	6
Fallon	12	–	3
Walsh	19	5	3
Duncan	6	–	1
Tully	11	1	5
Mochan	22	5	6
Hunter	4	1	–
Rollo	1	4	–
McIlroy	3	1	–
Higgins	14	–	6
Bonnar	20	5	3
Hemple	4	–	–
Boden	2	–	–
Ryan	1	–	–
White	–	1	–
McMillan	–	2	–

GOALSCORERS

League: Mochan 20, Collins 10 (4 pens), Fernie 10 (1 pen), Higgins 8, Walsh 5, Fallon 5, Haughney 4 (3 pens), McPhail 4, Hemple 2, Tully 1, Duncan 1, Stein 1, Peacock 1

League Cup: Walsh 3, Peacock 1, Mochan 1, McPhail 1

Scottish Cup: Mochan 4, Fernie 3, Fallon 2, Higgins 2, Haughney 2 (2 pens), Own Goals 2

The Celtic team in 1958. Back row: Mackay, Smith, Beattie, McNeil, Colrain, Mochan. Front row: Fernie, Tully, Peacock, Wilson and Auld.

Season 1954-55

Celtic just failed to repeat their feats of the previous season. They finished with 3 more points than in their previous Championship-winning season but they had to settle for the runners-up spot 3 points behind Aberdeen. They lost only 3 matches during the campaign – at home against Hibs and away against Partick Thistle and Rangers – but the fact that they drew 8 matches to Aberdeen's 1 proved crucial. They did the double over 6 teams including the new champions and had a number of fine wins, no more so than their 5-0 thrashing of Hibs at Easter Road in December and their 3-0 win at Tynecastle in the last match of the season. They used 21 players during the campaign and both Haughney and Evans were ever-presents. Jimmy Walsh was top scorer with 19 of their 76 goals.

For the 7th time in 9 seasons they failed to qualify for the latter stages of the League Cup, finishing behind Hearts and Dundee in their section.

They reached their 26th Scottish Cup Final by beating Alloa, Kilmarnock (after a replay), Hamilton and Airdrie. Comeback man John McPhail scoring both goals in the Semi-Final replay. In one of the poorer Finals they should have built up a comfortable lead of 3 or 4 goals over Clyde. Instead they led for almost 50 minutes by 1 goal scored by Jimmy Walsh before Clyde's Archie Robertson, aided and abetted by the unfortunate John Bonnar scored a sensational late equaliser to earn his side a replay. Celtic sprang a surprise by dropping Collins for the replay and Clyde went on to win the Cup by a goal scrambled in by international winger Tommy Ring. With only 4 minutes to go only a brilliant save by goalkeeper Ken Hewkins prevented John McPhail from heading an equaliser which on the balance of play would have been undeserved.

League:	Runners-up
League Cup:	Failed to qualify from Section
Scottish Cup:	Finalists

LEAGUE DIVISION A

August 6th: Sam Hemple was transferred to Albion Rovers.

September 11th
CLYDE (0) 2 — CELTIC (1) 2
Ring (54), Hill (86) — Fernie (41), Walsh (67)

CLYDE: Wilson; Murphy, Ferrier; Gallacher, Anderson, Laing; Granville, Robertson, Hill, Carmichael, Ring

CELTIC: Bonnar; Haughney, Meechan; Evans, Stein, Peacock; Higgins, Boden, Fallon, Fernie, Walsh

Attendance: 30,000

September 15th: Mike Haughney was in the Scottish League team which beat the Irish League 5-1 in Belfast.

September 18th
CELTIC (0) 2 — RANGERS (0) 0
Walsh (59), Higgins (89)

CELTIC: Bonnar; Haughney, Fallon; Evans, Stein, Peacock; Higgins, Boden, Walsh, Fernie, Mochan

RANGERS: Niven; Young, Little; McColl, Stanners, Rae; McCulloch, Grierson, Simpson, Prentice, Hubbard

Attendance: 45,000

Bonnar twice saved the day for Celtic – when he baulked McCulloch in the middle of the penalty area, and when, 3 minutes from time, he saved magnificently at the corner of the post a shot from Simpson which he probably did not see until the last possible moment. In the final minute Higgins scored a 2nd Celtic goal, and for all Rangers' late rally the result was not unfair.

September 25th
RAITH ROVERS (0) 1 — CELTIC (0) 3
Kelly (75) — Haughney 2 (55 pen, 70 pen), Mochan (67)

RAITH ROVERS: Drummond; Kirk, McNaught; Young, Colville, Leigh; McIntyre, Kelly, Copland, Buchan, Duncan

CELTIC: Bell; Haughney, Fallon; Evans, Stein, Peacock; Higgins, Boden, Walsh, Fernie, Mochan

Attendance: 16,000

October 2nd
CELTIC (3) 6 — KILMARNOCK (1) 3
Walsh (6), Higgins 2 (23, 40), Mochan (56), Fernie 2 (59, 71) — Curlett (1), Mays (65), Henaughan (66)

CELTIC: Bonnar; Haughney, Fallon; Evans, Stein, Conroy; Higgins, Boden, Walsh, Fernie, Mochan

KILMARNOCK: Brown; Collins, Rollo; Russell, Thyne, Middlemass; Mays, Murray, Imrie, Curlett, Henaughan

Attendance: 30,000

October 2nd: Bertie Peacock was in the Ireland team which was beaten 2-0 by England in Belfast.

October 9th
ABERDEEN (0) 0 — CELTIC (0) 2
Mochan (57), Haughney (71 pen)

ABERDEEN: Martin; Mitchell, Smith; Wallace, Young, Glen; Leggat, Yorston, Buckley, O'Neill, Hather

CELTIC: Bonnar; Haughney, Fallon; Evans, Stein, Peacock; Higgins, Tully, Walsh, Fernie, Mochan

Attendance: 38,000

October 16th: Willie Fernie was in the Scotland team which beat Wales 1-0 in Cardiff.

October 16th
CELTIC (0) 1 — QUEEN OF THE SOUTH (1) 1,
Higgins (89½) — Black (32)

CELTIC: McMahon; Haughney, Fallon; Evans, Stein, Peacock; Higgins, Tully, Walsh, Smith, Mochan

QUEEN OF THE SOUTH: Henderson; Sharpe, Binning; McBain, Smith, Greenock; Black, McGill, Patterson, Brown, Oakes

Attendance: 22,000

October 30th
CELTIC (2) 3 — FALKIRK (0) 1
Walsh (10), Higgins (16), Haughney (61 pen) — McCrae (73)

CELTIC: Bonnar; Haughney, Fallon; Evans, Stein, Peacock; Higgins, Tully, Walsh, Fernie, Mochan

FALKIRK: Slater; Parker, Rae; Black, Ralston, Campbell; Plumb, Ormond, Davidson, Morrison, McCrae

Attendance: 30,000

League positions

	P	W	D	L	F	A	Pts
1 Aberdeen	8	6	0	2	21	6	12
2 CELTIC	7	5	2	0	19	8	12
3 Clyde	8	5	2	1	25	14	12
4 Rangers	7	4	1	2	23	10	9
5 St Mirren	7	4	1	2	16	15	9

November 1st: Joe Baillie was transferred to Wolves for £4,000

November 3rd: Evans and Fernie were in the Scotland team which drew 2-2 with Ireland at Hampden Park. Bertie Peacock was in the Ireland team.

November 6th
ST MIRREN (1) 1 — CELTIC (1) 1
Callan (49) — Walsh (23)

ST MIRREN: Lornie; Lapsley, Cunningham; Neilson, Telfer, Johnston; McMaster, Holmes, McDonald, Gemmell, Callan

CELTIC: Bonnar; Haughney, Fallon; Evans, Stein, Peacock; Higgins, Tully, Walsh, Fernie, Collins

Attendance: 35,000

November 13th
CELTIC (5) 7 — STIRLING ALBION (0) 0
Fernie (2), Walsh 3 (6, 51, 72), Higgins 2 (30, 43), Tully (35)

CELTIC: Bonnar; Haughney, Fallon; Evans, Stein, Peacock; Higgins, Fernie, Walsh, Tully, Collins

STIRLING ALBION: Nicol; Gibson, Whitehead; Bain, McQueen, Docherty; Chalmers, Smith, Williamson, McGill, Brander

Attendance: 15,000

November 18th: Mike Haughney was in the Scottish League team which beat the League of Ireland 5-0 at Shawfield.

November 20th
PARTICK THISTLE (2) 4 — CELTIC (2) 2
Howitt (3), Smith (5), Sharp 2 (49, 69) — Walsh (23), Collins (44)

PARTICK THISTLE: Ledgerwood; McGowan, Gibb; Thomson, Davidson, D. Wright; McKenzie, Howitt, Smith, Sharp, McParland

CELTIC: Bonnar; Haughney, Fallon; Evans, Stein, Peacock; Higgins, Tully, Walsh, Fernie, Collins

Attendance: 33,000

November 27th
MOTHERWELL (0) 2 — CELTIC (0) 2
Hunter (72), Humphries (86) — Higgins (49), Walsh (65)

MOTHERWELL: McIntyre; Kilmarnock, Shaw; Cox, Paton, Redpath; Hunter, Aitken, Humphries, Forrest, Aitkenhead

CELTIC: Bonnar; Haughney, Fallon; Evans, Boden, Peacock; Higgins, Smith, Walsh, Fernie, Collins

Attendance: 20,000

December 4th
CELTIC (1) 2 — EAST FIFE (0) 2
Walsh (27), Mochan (51) — Fleming 2 (67, 80)

CELTIC: Bonnar; Haughney, Fallon; Evans, Stein, Peacock; Higgins, Tully, Walsh, Fernie, Mochan

EAST FIFE: Curran; Emery, S. Stewart; Christie, Finlay, McLennan; J. Stewart, Fleming, Gardiner, Leishman, Bonthrone

Attendance: 23,500

December 11th
HIBERNIAN (0) 0 — CELTIC (1) 5
Walsh 2 (2, 58), Fernie 2 (49, 56), Higgins (74)

HIBERNIAN: Younger; Ward, Paterson; Grant, Plenderleith, Combe; Smith, Johnstone, Reilly, Preston, Ormond

CELTIC: Bell; Haughney, Meechan, Evans, Stein, Peacock; Higgins, Tully, Walsh, Fernie, Collins

Attendance: 33,000

December 18th
CELTIC (1) 4 — DUNDEE (0) 1
Haughney (30 pen), Fernie (52), Rowan (73), Malloy o.g. (74) — Merchant (85)

CELTIC: Bell; Haughney, Meechan; Evans, Stein, Peacock; Rowan, Tully, Walsh, Fernie, Collins

DUNDEE: Brown; Gray, Irvine; Gallacher, Malloy, Cowie; Carmichael, Henderson, Merchant, Roy, Christie

Attendance: 14,000

December 25th
CELTIC (1) 2 — CLYDE (1) 2
Boden (41), Collins (51) — Buchanan (20), Robertson (85 pen)

CELTIC: Bell; Haughney, Meechan; Evans, Stein, Peacock; Boden, Tully, Walsh, Fernie, Collins

CLYDE: Wilson; Murphy, Haddock; Gallacher, Anderson, Laing; Buchanan, Divers, Hill, Robertson, Ring

Attendance: 31,000

League positions

	P	W	D	L	F	A	Pts
1 Aberdeen	16	13	0	3	39	13	26
2 Rangers	15	10	2	3	44	18	22
3 CELTIC	15	8	6	1	44	20	22
4 St Mirren	15	10	2	3	38	25	22
5 Hibernian	16	10	1	5	37	29	21

January 1st
RANGERS (1) 4 — CELTIC (1) 1
Simpson (9), Hubbard 3 (72, 80, 89 pen) — Fernie (32)

RANGERS: Niven; Little, Cox; Pryde, Young, Rae; McCulloch, Prentice, Simpson, Grierson, Hubbard

CELTIC: Bell; Haughney, Meechan; Evans, Stein, Peacock; Boden, Tully, Walsh, Fernie, Collins

Attendance: 65,000

In the 9th minute Stein sliced a clearance straight to the feet of Grierson, who promptly and accurately gave Simpson a scoring chance which he gratefully accepted. On practically the only occasion when Walsh beat Young, the centre-half brought him down and Fernie lobbed the free-kick over the defensive wall and away from the searching fingers of Niven. In 72 minutes Hubbard jinked past Haughney, Stein and Bell before walking the ball into the net. 7 minutes later Simpson, closely challenged by Stein, chipped his pass so precisely that Hubbard, intelligently placed in the centre, had merely to direct the ball into the gaping goal. A minute from time Hubbard completed his hat-trick when he converted a penalty after Grierson had been brought down in the box.

January 3rd
CELTIC (2) 4 — RAITH ROVERS (0) 1
Evans (20), Collins (34), Walsh (50), Tully (70) — Young (52)

CELTIC: Bell; Haughney, Meechan; Evans, Stein, Peacock; Collins, Tully, Walsh, Fernie, Mochan

RAITH ROVERS: Johnstone; Kirk, McLure; Bain, Colville, Leigh; Rice, Thomson, Copland, Young, Duncan

Attendance: n.a.

January 8th
KILMARNOCK (0) 1 — CELTIC (0) 2
Murray (65) — Mackay o.g. (53), Tully (71)

KILMARNOCK: Brown; Collins, Rollo; Curlett, Dougan, Mackay; Murray, Harvey, Flavell, Jack, Henaughan

CELTIC: Bell; Haughney, Meechan; Evans, Stein, Peacock; Boden, Tully, Walsh, Fernie, Mochan

Attendance: 24,518

January 22nd
QUEEN OF THE SOUTH (0) 0 — CELTIC (0) 2
Fernie 2 (76, 79)

QUEEN OF THE SOUTH: Henderson; Sharpe, Binning; Rothera, Smith, Greenock; Black, McGill, Patterson, Brown, Oakes

CELTIC: Bonnar; Haughney, Meechan; Evans, Stein, Peacock; Collins, Walsh, Fallon, Fernie, Mochan

Attendance: 12,500

January 29th
CELTIC (0) 2 — HEARTS (0) 0
Walsh 2 (48, 90)

CELTIC: Bonnar; Haughney, Meechan; Evans, Stein, Peacock; Higgins, Walsh, Fallon, Fernie, Collins

HEARTS: Duff; Parker, McKenzie; Mackay, Glidden, Cumming; Souness, Conn, Bauld, Wardhaugh, Urquhart

Attendance: 49,300

February 12th
FALKIRK (0) 1 — CELTIC (1) 1
Morrison (87) — Fernie (21)

FALKIRK: Slater; Parker, Rae; Black, McKenzie, Campbell; Ormond, Morrison, Davidson, McCrae, Taylor

CELTIC: Bonnar; Haughney, Meechan; Evans, Stein, Peacock; Collins, Walsh, Fallon, Fernie, Mochan

Attendance: 20,223

February 26th
CELTIC (3) 5 — ST MIRREN (2) 2
Walsh (9), Fernie (20), Collins (27), Smith (65), Haughney (73 pen) — Wilson (14), McGuigan (30)

CELTIC: Bonnar; Haughney, Meechan; Evans, Stein, Peacock; Walsh, Smith, Fallon, Fernie, Collins

ST MIRREN: Lornie; Lapsley, Johnston; Neilson, Telfer, Holmes; McGuigan, Wilson, Anderson, Gemmell, Callan

Attendance: 36,000

League positions

	P	W	D	L	F	A	Pts
1 Aberdeen	23	19	1	3	58	18	39
2 CELTIC	22	13	7	2	61	29	33
3 Clyde	23	10	8	5	53	39	28
4 St Mirren	22	11	6	5	47	37	28
5 Rangers	21	12	3	6	52	25	27

March 9th
STIRLING ALBION (2) 2 — CELTIC (0) 3
Smith (28), McGill (40) — Haughney (47 pen), Boden (80), Stein (88)

STIRLING ALBION: Mitchell; Gibson, McNicol; McKechnie, Williamson, Docherty; Laird, Smith, Andrews, McGill, Paterson

CELTIC: Bonnar; Haughney, Meechan; Evans, Stein, Peacock; Walsh, Tully, Fallon, Boden, Collins

Attendance: 6,000

March 12th
CELTIC 0 — PARTICK THISTLE 0

CELTIC: Bonnar; Haughney, Meechan; Evans, Stein, Peacock; Walsh, Tully, Fallon, Fernie, Collins

PARTICK THISTLE: Ledgerwood; Kerr, Donlevy; Harvey, Davidson, Wright; McKenzie, Howitt, Smith, McParland, Crowe

Attendance: 38,000

March 16th: Evans and Collins were in the Scottish League team which beat the English league 3-2 at Hampden Park. Collins scored one of the goals.

March 19th
CELTIC (0) 1 — MOTHERWELL (0) 0
Mochan (52)

CELTIC: Bonnar; Haughney, Meechan; Evans, Stein, Peacock; Collins, Walsh, Fallon, Mochan, Tully

MOTHERWELL: McIntyre; Kilmarnock, Shaw; Mason, Paton, Redpath; Hunter, Aitken, McSeveney, Humphries, Williams

Attendance: 35,000

March 30th
EAST FIFE (1) 3 — CELTIC (1) 4
Plumb 3 (38, 71, 86) — Walsh 2 (29, 64), Mochan 2 (69, 84)

EAST FIFE: Curran; Emery, S. Stewart; Bonthrone, Finlay, McLennan; Wilson, J. Stewart, Plumb, Leishman, Hill

CELTIC: Bonnar; Haughney, Meechan; Evans, Stein, Peacock; Collins, Walsh, Mochan, McPhail, Tully

Attendance: n.a.

April 2nd
CELTIC (1) 1 — HIBERNIAN (1) 2
Tully (40) — Smith (23), Fraser (69)

CELTIC: Bonnar; Haughney, Meechan; Evans, Stein, Peacock; Collins, Reid, McPhail, Mochan, Tully

HIBERNIAN: Younger; Paterson, McFarlane; Thomson, Plenderleith, Preston; Smith, Combe, Fraser, Turnbull, Ormond

Attendance: 31,000

April 9th
DUNDEE (0) 0 — CELTIC (1) 1
Reid (27)

DUNDEE: Brown; Gray, Irvine; Gallacher, Malloy, Cowie; Walker, Roy, Chalmers, Henderson, Christie

CELTIC: Bonnar; Haughney, Meechan; Conroy, Evans, Peacock; Walsh, Reid, McPhail, Mochan, Tully

Attendance: 23,000

April 16th
CELTIC (1) 2 — ABERDEEN (0) 1
McPhail 2 (22, 60) — Leggat (80)

CELTIC: Bonnar; Haughney, Meechan; Evans, Stein, Peacock; Collins, Reid, McPhail, Mochan, Tully

ABERDEEN: Martin; Paterson, Caldwell; O'Neil, Young, Glen; Leggat, Yorston, Buckley, Wishart, Hather

Attendance: 40,000

April 30th
HEARTS (0) 0 — CELTIC (1) 3
Mochan 2 (6, 81), Collins (50)

HEARTS: Watters; Parker, McKenzie; Armstrong, Glidden, Cumming; Souness, Urquhart, Murray, Wardhaugh, Crawford

CELTIC: Bonnar; Haughney, Fallon; Evans, Stein, Peacock; Collins, Fernie, Walsh, Tully, Mochan

Attendance: 18,000

Scottish League Division A

	P	W	D	L	F	A	Pts
1 Aberdeen	30	24	1	5	73	46	49
2 CELTIC	30	19	8	3	76	37	46
3 Rangers	30	19	3	8	67	33	41
4 Hearts	30	16	7	7	74	45	39
5 Hibernian	30	15	4	11	64	54	34
6 St Mirren	30	12	8	10	55	54	32
7 Clyde	30	11	9	10	59	50	31
8 Dundee	30	13	4	13	48	48	30
9 Partick Thistle	30	11	7	12	49	61	29
10 Kilmarnock	30	10	6	14	46	58	26
11 East Fife	30	9	6	15	51	62	24
12 Falkirk	30	8	8	14	42	54	24
13 Queen of the South	30	9	6	15	38	56	24
14 Raith Rovers	30	10	3	17	49	57	23
15 Motherwell	30	9	4	17	42	62	22
16 Stirling Albion	30	2	2	26	29	105	6

May 4th: Bobby Evans was in the Scotland team which beat Portugal 3-0 at Hampden Park.

May 19th: Celtic freed Jim Duncan.

May 15th: Evans and Collins were in the Scotland team which drew 2-2 with Yugoslavia in Belgrade.

May 19th: Evans and Collins were in the Scotland team which beat Austria 4-1 in Vienna.

May 28th: Sean Fallon was in the Eire team which was beaten 2-1 by Germany in Hamburg.

May 29th: Evans and Collins were in the Scotland team which was beaten 3-1 by Hungary in Budapest.

LEAGUE CUP

August 14th
CELTIC (3) 3 — FALKIRK (0) 0
Higgins (10), Fallon 2 (35, 44)

CELTIC: Bonnar; Haughney, Meechan; Evans, Stein, Peacock; Higgins, Fernie, Fallon, Tully, Mochan

FALKIRK: Slater; Sievwright, Rae; Black, McKenzie, Hunter; Sinclair, Morrison, Ormond, McCrae, Kelly

Attendance: 46,000

August 18th
DUNDEE (2) 3 — CELTIC (0) 1
Henderson (14), Merchant (33), Roy (60) — Mochan (53)

DUNDEE: Brown; Gray, Irvine; Gallacher, Malloy, Craig; Christie, Henderson, Merchant, Roy, Hill

CELTIC: Bonnar; Haughney, Meechan; Evans, Stein, Peacock; Higgins, Fernie, Fallon, Tully, Mochan

Attendance: 28,000

August 21st
CELTIC (0) 1 — HEARTS (2) 2
Higgins (67) — Wardhaugh (27), Peacock o.g. (37)

CELTIC: Bonnar; Haughney, Meechan; Evans, Stein, Peacock; Higgins, Fernie, Fallon, Tully, Mochan

HEARTS: Duff; Parker, Adie; Mackay, Glidden, Cumming; Blackwood, Conn, Bauld, Wardhaugh, Urquhart

Attendance: 55,000

August 28th
FALKIRK (1) 2 — CELTIC (2) 2
Plumb (7), Sinclair (80) — Fernie (19), Haughney (40 pen)

FALKIRK: Slater; Sievwright, Rae; Black, Ralston, Campbell; Sinclair, Morrison, Plumb, Ormond, Kelly

CELTIC: Bonnar; Haughney, Meechan; Evans, Stein, Peacock; Higgins, Fernie, Fallon, Tully, Mochan

Attendance: 15,000

September 1st
CELTIC (0) 0 — DUNDEE (1) 1
Malloy (23 pen)

CELTIC: Bonnar; Haughney, Jack; Evans, Stein, Peacock; Collins, Walsh, Fallon, Tully, Mochan

DUNDEE: Brown; Gray, Irvine; Gallacher, Malloy, Craig; Christie, Easson, Henderson, Roy, Hill

Attendance: 30,000

September 4th
HEARTS (0) 3 — CELTIC (1) 2
Wardhaugh (47), Laing (51 pen), Bauld (73) — Tully (6), Collins (52)

HEARTS: Duff; Parker, Adie; Laing, Glidden, Cumming; Blackwood, Conn, Bauld, Wardhaugh, Urquhart

CELTIC: Bonnar; Haughney, Baillie; Evans, Stein, Peacock; Collins, Fernie, Fallon, Tully, Duncan

Attendance: 32,000

SECTION TABLE

	P	W	D	L	F	A	Pts
Hearts	6	5	0	1	19	11	10
Dundee	6	4	0	2	12	10	8
CELTIC	6	1	1	4	9	11	3
Falkirk	6	1	1	4	10	18	3

SCOTTISH CUP

Fifth Round February 5th
ALLOA ATHLETIC (1) 2 CELTIC (1) 4
Lynch (25), Kiernan (59) Haughney (45 pen), Walsh 2 (55, 87), Peacock (75)

ALLOA: McInnes; Farrell, Kerr; A. Miller, Wilson, Lynch; McKinstray, Keirnan, Wishart, G. Miller, Davidson

CELTIC: Bonnar; Haughney, Meechan; Evans, Stein, Peacock; Collins, Walsh, Fallon, Fernie, Mochan

Attendance: 15,000 (excluding Stand)

Sixth Round February 19th
KILMARNOCK (0) 1 CELTIC (1) 1
Henaughan (49) Smith (31)

KILMARNOCK: Brown; Collins, Rollo; Curlett, Dougan, Mackay; Murray, Harvey, Flavell, Jack, Henaughan

CELTIC: Bonnar; Haughney, Meechan; Evans, Stein, Peacock; Smith, Walsh, Fallon, Fernie, Collins

Attendance: 30,000

Sixth Round Replay February 23rd
CELTIC (0) 1 KILMARNOCK (0) 0
Walsh (49)

CELTIC: Bonnar; Haughney, Meechan; Evans, Stein, Peacock; Smith, Walsh, Fallon, Fernie, Collins

KILMARNOCK: Brown; Baillie, Rollo; Curlett, Dougan, McKay; Murray, Harvey, Flavell, Jack, Henaughan

Attendance: 40,000

Seventh Round March 5th
CELTIC (1) 2 HAMILTON ACADEMICALS (1) 1
Collins (36), Fernie (60) F. Quinn (44)

CELTIC: Bonnar; Haughney, Meechan; Evans, Stein, Peacock; Tully, Smith, Fallon, Fernie, Collins

HAMILTON: Houston; Shearer, R. Quinn; Barrett, Boyd, Martin; F. Quinn, Walker, Cron, Reid, Armit

Attendance: 49,000

Semi-Final March 26th at Hampden Park
AIRDRIE (1) 2 CELTIC (1) 2
Reid (15 secs), Welsh (68) Fernie (17), Walsh (55)

AIRDRIE: Walker; Shanks, Gordon; Quinn, Baillie, Cairns; Reid, Welsh, Baird, McMillan, McCulloch

CELTIC: Bonnar; Haughney, Meechan; Evans, Stein, Peacock; Collins, Fernie, Walsh, Mochan, Tully

Attendance: 80,040

Had McMillan's header in the closing minute at Hampden been a foot lower, Celtic would have been out of the Scottish Cup. Apart from thrills in the goalmouth there were many pleasing spells of polished football. Before thousands of spectators were in the ground Celtic were a goal down. Long before half-time, however, they had taken command. Baillie was undergoing an ordeal as Fernie and Mochan joined Walsh in the centre. At half-time the score was 1-1 and 9-0 for Celtic in corner-kicks. Straight after the interval Reid hit Bonnar's left-hand post but the keeper managed to gather the rebound. 22 minutes from the end, and after Baird had emulated some of the Celtic finishing by shooting wildly when clean through, Evans missed McCulloch's apology of a cross and Welsh scooped the ball past Bonnar.

Semi-Final Replay April 4th at Hampden Park
CELTIC (0) 2 AIRDRIE (0) 0
McPhail 2 (48, 52)

CELTIC: Bonnar; Haughney, Meechan; Evans, Stein, Peacock; Collins, Fernie, McPhail, Walsh, Tully

AIRDRIE: Walker; Shanks, Gordon; Quinn, Baillie, Cairns; Reid, Welsh, Baird, McMillan, McCulloch

Attendance: 71,000

McPhail in only his 3rd first-team game of the season – his first was only a week before at Methil – scored in the 3rd and 7th minutes of the second half to knock Airdrie out of the Cup. McPhail's astute sense of position and his intelligent distribution of the ball were the factors which softened the Division B team for the final punch. Celtic in the end won very easily.

Final April 23rd at Hampden Park
CELTIC (1) 1 CLYDE (0) 1
Walsh (38) Robertson (87)

CELTIC: Bonnar; Haughney, Meechan; Evans, Stein, Peacock; Collins, Fernie, McPhail, Walsh, Tully

CLYDE: Hewkins; Murphy, Haddock; Granville, Anderson, Laing; Divers, Robertson, Hill, Brown, Ring

Attendance: 106,234. *Referee:* C. E. Faultless (Giffnock)

This was the first Scottish Cup Final to be televised live.

Celtic should have had the Cup won before half an hour had gone. In the period Clyde had their goal exposed on several occasions, particularly by the clever passing of McPhail and Tully, but only Walsh seemed prepared to shoot. Celtic went ahead when Fernie made a delightful pass through the centre and Walsh, intelligently anticipating the low, true pass scored immaculately. They lost a chance to consolidate when both McPhail and Walsh failed to make contact with Tully's pass when only 3 yards from goal. Robertson it was who, from a corner-kick 3 minutes from time, drew the match. He was unwittingly assisted by Bonnar, who misjudged his leap for the ball, which dropped under the bar and was turned into the net by the goalkeeper.

Final Replay April 28th at Hampden Park
CLYDE (0) 1 CELTIC (0) 0
Ring (52)

CELTIC: Bonnar; Haughney, Meechan; Evans, Stein, Peacock; Walsh, Fernie, Fallon, McPhail, Tully

CLYDE: Hewkins; Murphy, Haddock; Granville, Anderson, Laing; Divers, Robertson, Hill, Brown, Ring

Attendance: 68,831 *Referee:* C. E. Faultless (Giffnock)

Clyde won the Cup for the 2nd time in their history. The quality of play, on Clyde's part, was tremendously improved from the previous Saturday. They deservedly won the Cup though they withstood a terrific barrage in the final 5 minutes during which a magnificent save by Hewkins prevented McPhail equalising with a header from a Tully lob. Walsh and Tully were Celtic's best forwards but received scant service.

APPEARANCES	League	League Cup	Scottish Cup
Bonnar	22	6	8
Haughney	30	6	8
Meechan	18	4	8
Evans	30	6	8
Stein	28	6	8
Peacock	29	6	8
Higgins	14	4	–
Boden	9	–	–
Fallon	20	6	5
Fernie	23	5	8
Walsh	28	1	7
Mochan	17	5	2
Bell	7	–	–
Conroy	2	–	–
Tully	21	6	5
McMahon	1	–	–
Smith	3	–	3
Collins	20	2	7
McPhail	4	–	3
Rowan	1	–	–
Reid	3	–	–
Jack	–	1	–
Baillie	–	1	–
Duncan	–	1	–

GOALSCORERS

League: Walsh 19, Fernie 12, Higgins 9, Mochan 9, Haughney 7 (7 pens), Collins 5, Tully 4, Boden 2, Own Goals 2, McPhail 2, Rowan 1, Evans 1, Smith 1, Stein 1, Reid 1

League Cup: Higgins 2, Fallon 2, Mochan 1, Fernie 1, Haughney 1 (pen), Tully 1, Collins 1

Scottish Cup: Walsh 5, Fernie 2, McPhail 2, Haughney 1 (pen), Peacock 1, Smith 1, Collins 1

The Celtic team of 1959. Back row: McNeill, Mochan, Haffey, McKay, Evans, Peacock. Front row: Carroll, McVittie, Byrne, Colrain and Mackle.

Season 1955-56

Celtic finished a creditable 5th in the 'A' League, which had been extended to 18 clubs, behind Rangers, Aberdeen, Hearts and Hibs. Mainly as a result of 6 consecutive away wins they stood on top of the table at the half-way stage but their form dipped sharply in the New Year and they collected only 16 points from their last 17 matches to fall out of the Championship race. Team selections were very erratic and by the end of the season they had used 30 different players. Bertie Peacock made 33 appearances followed by Willie Fernie on 32 and Beattie, Mochan and Evans on 31. Neil Mochan was top scorer with 15 goals. John McPhail was amongst the end-of-season free transfers.

Ater a fine 4-1 win over Rangers at Ibrox Celtic looked set to qualify for the Quarter-Finals of the League Cup but Rangers reversed the result only 4 days later, largely as a result of an injury to Stein, and eventually topped the Section by a point. (Celtic did gain some revenge in the Glasgow Cup Final, beating the Ibrox team 5-3 in a replay on Boxing Day.)

They reached the Scottish Cup Final for the 3rd successive season, beating Morton, Ayr United, Airdrie and Clyde en route but they suffered their 9th Final defeat – at the hands, or rather feet, of Hearts. The Celtic team selection which contained the previously untried right-wing partnership of Craig and Haughney was the main talking point among the fans, pre-match, but the experiment proved to be a flop, the team as a whole did not compete on the day, and the Cup went to Tynecastle for the 1st time in 50 years.

League:	Fifth
League Cup:	Failed to qualify from Section
Scottish Cup:	Runners-up

September 7th: Evans and Collins were in the Scottish League team which beat the Irish League 3-0 at Ibrox.

LEAGUE DIVISION A

September 10th
FALKIRK (2) 3 — CELTIC (1) 1
O'Hara (24), McCormack (30), Wright (62) — Mochan (16)

FALKIRK: Hamilton; Parker, Rae; Fletcher, Colville, McIntosh; Sinclair, McCormack, Wright, McCrae, O'Hara

CELTIC: Beattie; Haughney, Fallon; Evans, Jack, Peacock; Craig, Boden, McPhail, Smith, Mochan

Attendance: 10,000

September 17th
CELTIC (0) 3 — STIRLING ALBION (0) 0
Tully 2 (47, 78), McPhail (50)

CELTIC: Beattie; Haughney, Fallon; Fernie, Evans, Peacock; Smith, Collins, McPhail, Tully, Mochan

STIRLING ALBION: Mitchell; Gibson, McNicol; Smith, Milligan, Rankine; Paterson, McGill, Kerr, Philliben, Liddell

Attendance: 14,000

September 21st: Evans and Collins were in the Scottish League team which beat the League of Ireland 4-2 in Dublin. Collins scored 2 of the goals.

September 24th
RANGERS 0 — CELTIC 0

RANGERS: Niven; Caldow, Little; McColl, Young, Rae; Scott, Baird, Simpson, Prentice, Hubbard

CELTIC: Beattie; Boden, Fallon; Fernie, Evans, Peacock; Docherty, Collins, Haughney, Smith, Mochan

Attendance: 47,000

The wind, the rain, the slippery turf and the skidding ball all contributed to make the players' task difficult. There was no doubt, however, who contributed most of the football in the match. Fernie, the individualist, proved that even in difficult conditions the ball can be mastered. Niven had the save of the match from almost the only worthwhile shot when he tipped over a left-foot shot from Docherty in the first half. Scott missed a great chance from a Simpson cross, when unmarked, in the first half.

October 1st
CELTIC (1) 2 — RAITH ROVERS (0) 0
McVittie (7), Sharkey (86)

CELTIC: Beattie; Boden, Fallon; Reid, Evans, Peacock; Collins, McVittie, Sharkey, Fernie, Tully

RAITH ROVERS: Drummond; Weir, McLure; Bain, McNaught, Leigh; McMillan, McEwan, Copland, Thomson, Scott

Attendance: 15,000

October 8th
HEARTS (2) 2 — CELTIC (0) 1
Urquhart (28), Conn (43) — Fernie (75)

HEARTS: Duff; Parker, Kirk; Mackay, Glidden, Cumming; Hamilton, Conn, Bauld, Wardhaugh, Urquhart

CELTIC: Beattie; Boden, Fallon; Whyte, Jack, Mochan; Higgins, Fernie, Sharkey, Rowan, Tully

Attendance: 30,000

October 8th: Evans and Collins were in the Scotland team which was beaten 2-1 by Ireland in Belfast. Bertie Peacock was in the Ireland team.

October 11th: Evans and Collins were in the Scottish League team which beat the Danish Football Combination 4-0 in Copenhagen.

October 15th
CELTIC (1) 2 — MOTHERWELL (1) 2
Fernie (22), McVittie (66) — Gardiner (43), Aitken (89)

CELTIC: Beattie; Boden, Mochan; Whyte, Evans, Peacock; Collins, McVittie, Sharkey, Fernie, Tully

MOTHERWELL: Weir; Kilmarnock, Shaw; Aitken, Paton, McFadyen; Sloan, Toner, Gardiner, Reid, Williams

Attendance: 22,000

October 22nd
CLYDE (1) 1 — CELTIC (1) 3
Walsh (20) — Higgins (50), Fernie (67 pen), McPhail (43)

CLYDE: Wilson; Murphy, Ferrier; Gallacher, Anderson, Laing; McHard, McPhail, Lennox, Carmichael, Ring

CELTIC: Beattie; Boden, Mochan; Fernie, Evans, Peacock; Higgins, Collins, Walsh, Smith, Tully

Attendance: 25,000

October 26th: Evans and Collins were in the Scottish League team which was beaten 4-2 by the English League at Hillsborough, Sheffield. Collins scored one of the goals.

October 29th
CELTIC (1) 4 — DUNFERMLINE (2) 2
Walsh 3 (51, 64, 83), Tully (41) — Peebles (16), Dickson (38)

CELTIC: Beattie; Boden, Mochan; Fernie, Evans, Peacock; Higgins, Collins, Walsh, Smith, Tully

DUNFERMLINE: Mackin; Laird, Williamson; Samuel, Duthie, Baikie; Peebles, O'Brien, Dickson, Reilly, Mailer

Attendance: 28,000

League positions

	P	W	D	L	F	A	Pts
1 Queen of the South	8	6	0	2	20	10	12
2 CELTIC	8	4	2	2	16	10	10
3 Raith Rovers	8	4	2	2	17	14	10
4 Aberdeen	5	4	1	0	15	5	9
5 Falkirk	8	4	1	3	15	17	9

November 2nd: Peacock and Tully were in the Ireland team which was beaten 3-0 by England at Wembley.

November 5th
CELTIC 0 — EAST FIFE 0

CELTIC: Beattie; Boden, Mochan; Fernie, Evans, Peacock; Collins, McVittie, Walsh, Smith, Tully

EAST FIFE: Curran; Adie, S. Stewart; Christie, Finlay, McLennan; Wright, Kirkwood, Plumb, Bonthrone, Matthew

Attendance: 27,000

November 9th: Evans and Collins were in the Scotland team which beat Wales 2-0 at Hampden Park.

November 12th
DUNDEE (0) 1 — CELTIC (1) 2
Malloy (88 pen) — Mochan 2 (15, 67)

DUNDEE: Brown; Reid, Irvine; Black, Malloy, Cowie; Chalmers, Stables, Ritchie, Smith, Christie

CELTIC: Beattie; Boden, Meechan; Whyte, Evans, Peacock; Collins, Fernie, Walsh, Smith, Mochan

Attendance: 24,000

November 19th
CELTIC (1) 3 — ST MIRREN (0) 0
Fernie (42), Sharkey (67), Mochan (82)

CELTIC: Beattie; Meechan, Fallon; Whyte, Evans, Peacock; Collins, Fernie, Sharkey, Walsh, Mochan

ST MIRREN: Lornie; Lapsley, Mallan; Connor, Telfer, Holmes; Rodger, Laird, Brown, Gemmell, McLeod

Attendance: 29,000

November 26th
AIRDRIE (0) 1 — CELTIC (0) 2
McCulloch (89) — Welsh o.g. (59), Sharkey (73)

AIRDRIE: Walker; Miller, Neville; Quinn, Quigley, Price; Reid, McMillan, Baird, Welsh, McCulloch

CELTIC: Beattie; Boden, Meechan; Whyte, Evans, Peacock; Collins, Fernie, Sharkey, Walsh, Mochan

Attendance: 17,500. Beattie saved a McMillan penalty kick

December 3rd
STIRLING ALBION (0) 0 — CELTIC (2) 3
Mochan (16), Fernie (33), Walsh (70)

STIRLING ALBION: Robertson; Gibson, Milligan; McKechnie, McNicol, Swanson; Philliben, Smith, Henderson, Rankine, Pattison

CELTIC: Beattie; Boden, Meechan; Whyte, Evans, Peacock; Collins, Fernie, Sharkey, Walsh, Mochan

Attendance: 11,000

December 10th
CELTIC (0) 0 — KILMARNOCK (2) 2
Curlett 2 (4, 38)

CELTIC: Beattie; Haughney, Meechan; Conroy, Evans, Peacock; Higgins, Fernie, Sharkey, Collins, Mochan

KILMARNOCK: Brown; Watson, Rollo; Taggart, Toner, Mackay; Mays, Harvey, Curlett, Beattie, Fletcher

Attendance: 15,000

December 17th
CELTIC (2) 5 — PARTICK THISTLE (0) 1
Mochan 3 (3, 27, 83), Sharkey (78), Haughney (80 pen) — McParland (60)

CELTIC: Beattie; Haughney, Goldie; Evans, Stein, Peacock; Higgins, Fernie, Sharkey, Collins, Mochan

PARTICK THISTLE: Smith; Kerr, Gibb; Thomson, Davidson, Mathers; McKenzie, McInnes, Smith, Wright, McParland

Attendance: 20,500

December 24th
HIBERNIAN (1) 2 — CELTIC (1) 3
Combe (43), Turnbull (76) — Mochan 2 (20, 59), Sharkey (61)

HIBERNIAN: Younger; MacFarlane, Paterson; Thomson, Plenderleith, Preston; Smith, Combe, Reilly, Turnbull, Ormond

CELTIC: Beattie; Haughney, Goldie; Evans, Stein, Peacock; Walsh, Fernie, Sharkey, Collins, Mochan

Attendance: 29,000

League positions

	P	W	D	L	F	A	Pts
1 CELTIC	16	10	3	3	34	17	23
2 Hearts	15	10	1	4	38	21	21
3 Rangers	14	7	6	1	34	15	20
4 Hibernian	15	9	2	4	38	27	20
5 Falkirk	16	8	4	4	36	28	20

December 31st
QUEEN OF THE SOUTH (1) 1 — CELTIC (0) 3
Patterson (43) — Mochan (50), Sharkey (55), Collins (60)

QUEEN OF THE SOUTH: Henderson; Sharpe, Binning; Sweeney, Smith, Whitehead; Black, McGill, Patterson, Rothera, McGuire

CELTIC: Beattie; Haughney, Fallon; Whyte, Evans, Peacock; Walsh, Fernie, Sharkey, Collins, Mochan

Attendance: 12,500

January 2nd
CELTIC (0) 0 — RANGERS (1) 1
Kichenbrand (27)

CELTIC: Beattie; Haughney, Fallon; Evans, Stein, Peacock; McVittie, Fernie, Sharkey, Collins, Mochan

RANGERS: Brown; Caldow, Little; McColl, Elliot, Rae; Scott, Simpson, Kichenbrand, Baird, Hubbard

Attendance: 47,000

Celtic and Rangers continued to provide the unpredictable. Rangers were handicapped for 60 minutes of the game by an injury to Rae who had to go to the wing. Beattie was involved in the foolish loss of a goal in the 27th minute. Kichenbrand was faster than Stein in chasing a high punt by Simpson. Beattie rushed out some 18 yards from his line and Kichenbrand accurately lobbed the ball past him into the unguarded net. Rangers were lucky when 3 minutes from time Caldow pulled Mochan down in the box and escaped punishment.

January 7th
ABERDEEN (1) 1 — CELTIC (0) 0
Leggat (41)

ABERDEEN: Martin; MacFarlane, Caldwell; Allister, Young, Glen; Leggat, Yorston, Allan, Wishart, Hather

CELTIC: Beattie; Haughney, Fallon; Evans, Stein, Peacock; Smith, Fernie, Sharkey, Collins, Mochan

Attendance: 36,000

January 21st
RAITH ROVERS (1) 1 — CELTIC (1) 1
Copland (41) — Sharkey (25)

RAITH ROVERS: Stewart; Polland, McLure; Young, McNaught, Leigh; McEwan, Kelly, Copland, Thomson, McMillan

CELTIC: Beattie; Haughney, Fallon; Boden, Evans, Peacock; Walsh, Fernie, Sharkey, Collins, Mochan

Attendance: 16,000

January 28th
CELTIC (0) 1 HEARTS (1) 1
Walsh (48) Young (1)

CELTIC: Beattie; Haughney, Goldie; Evans, Stein, Peacock; Collins, Fernie, Sharkey, Walsh, Mochan

HEARTS: Duff; Kirk, McKenzie; Mackay, Glidden, Cumming; Crawford, Conn, Young, Wardhaugh, Urquhart

Attendance: 40,000

February 11th
MOTHERWELL (0) 2 CELTIC (0) 2
Gardiner (74 pen), Forrest (82) Tully (64), Smith (67)

MOTHERWELL: Weir; Kilmarnock, McSeveney; Forrest, Paton, Aitken; Kerr, Reid, Gardiner, McFadyen, Aitkenhead

CELTIC: Beattie; Haughney, Fallon; Goldie, Evans, Peacock; Collins, Fernie, McAlindon, Tully, Smith

Attendance: 19,000

February 25th
CELTIC (1) 4 CLYDE (1) 1
Haughney (44), Mochan (56), Collins (57), Walsh (62) Ring (8)

CELTIC: Beattie; Haughney, Fallon; Boden, Evans, Peacock; Collins, Smith, Walsh, Tully, Mochan

CLYDE: Watson; W. Currie, Haddock; Gallacher, Walters, Laing; D. Currie, Divers, McPhail, Innes, Ring

Attendance: 30,000

League positions

	P	W	D	L	F	A	Pts
1 Rangers	21	14	6	1	51	16	34
2 Hearts	23	14	5	4	69	28	33
3 Aberdeen	23	13	7	3	65	33	33
4 Hibernian	23	14	3	6	63	36	31
5 CELTIC	23	12	6	5	45	25	30

March 7th
DUNFERMLINE (1) 1 CELTIC (0) 1
Dickson (28) Collins (81)

DUNFERMLINE: Mackin; Laird, Williamson; Samuel, Colville, Mailer; McKinlay, O'Brien, Dickson, Reilly, Anderson

CELTIC: Beattie; Haughney, Fallon; Boden, Evans, Peacock; Collins, Fernie, Walsh, Tully, Mochan

Attendance: 10,000

March 10th
EAST FIFE (2) 3 CELTIC (0) 0
Plumb 2 (5, 70), J. Stewart (35)

EAST FIFE: Currie; Adie, S. Stewart; Christie, Finlay, McLennan; J. Stewart, Leishman, Plumb, Bonthrone, Matthew

CELTIC: Beattie; Haughney, Fallon; Boden, Evans, Peacock; Craig, Fernie, Mochan, Tully, Collins

Attendance: 11,000

March 12th: Evans and Collins were in the Scotland team which beat the South Africans 2-1 at Ibrox Park. Collins scored what proved to be the winning goal.

March 17th
CELTIC (1) 1 DUNDEE (0) 0
Collins (38)

CELTIC: Beattie; Haughney, Fallon; Evans, Stein, Peacock; Collins, Fernie, Sharkey, Smith, Tully

DUNDEE: Brown; Gray, Irvine; Gallacher, Black, Cowie; Stables, Henderson, Merchant, O'Hara, Chalmers

Attendance: 24,000

March 28th
ST MIRREN (0) 0 CELTIC (0) 2
Peacock (52), Mochan (74)

ST MIRREN: Lornie; Lapsley, Mallan; Neilson, Telfer, Johnston; McGill, Bryceland, Melrose, Gemmell, Callan

CELTIC: Beattie; Haughney, Goldie; Boden, Evans, Peacock; Craig, Collins, Mochan, Fernie, Tully

Attendance: 10,000

March 31st
CELTIC (1) 3 AIRDRIE (0) 1
Mochan 2 (40, 85), McAlindon (87) Baird (61)

CELTIC: Beattie; Haughney, Meechan; Goldie, Evans, Peacock; McAlindon, Collins, Mochan, Fernie, Tully

AIRDRIE: Goldie; Miller, McNeil; Price, Quigley, Davidson; Shaw, Rankin, Baird, McMillan, McCulloch

Attendance: 20,000

April 10th
CELTIC (0) 1 ABERDEEN (0) 1
McAlindon (46) Yorston (68)

CELTIC: Beattie; Haughney, Fallon; Goldie, Evans, Peacock; McAlindon, Craig, Mochan, Fernie, Tully

ABERDEEN: Martin; Mitchell, Caldwell; Wilson, Young, Glen; Leggat, Yorston, Allan, Wishart, Boyd

Attendance: 14,000

April 13th
KILMARNOCK 0 CELTIC 0

KILMARNOCK: Brown; Collins, Watson; Stewart, Toner, Mackay; Mays, Fletcher, Curlett, Lawlor, Flavell

CELTIC: Beattie; Haughney, Fallon; Smith, Jack, Peacock; McAlindon, Sharkey, Mochan, Fernie, Tully

Attendance: n.a.

April 14th: Bobby Evans was in the Scotland team which drew 1-1 with England at Hampden Park.

April 23rd
PARTICK THISTLE (0) 2 CELTIC (0) 0
Crawford (55),
Haughney o.g. (84)

PARTICK THISTLE: W. Smith; Kerr, Gibb; Harvey, Davidson, Mathers; McKenzie, Wright, G. Smith, Crawford, Ewing

CELTIC: Beattie; Haughney, Kennedy; Goldie, Evans, Peacock; Craig, Smith, Mochan, Fernie, Tully

Attendance: n.a.

April 25th
CELTIC (0) 0 HIBERNIAN (1) 3
Reilly 3 (38, 54, 66)

CELTIC: Bonnar; Haughney, Fallon; Goldie, Evans, Peacock; Craig, Fernie, Sharkey, Walsh, Mochan

HIBERNIAN: Younger; McFarlane, Paterson; Buchanan, Grant, Combe; Fraser, Turnbull, Reilly, Harrower, Ormond

Attendance: 9,500

April 28th
CELTIC (1) 1 QUEEN OF THE SOUTH (2) 3
Walsh (1)
Black (8)
Rothera 2 (33, 85)

CELTIC: Bonnar; Haughney, Fallon; Goldie, Evans, Peacock; Higgins, Fernie, Sharkey, Walsh, Mochan

QUEEN OF THE SOUTH: Henderson; Sharpe, Binning; Whitehead, Smith, Gibson; Black, McGill, Patterson, Rothera, Oakes

Attendance: 9,000

April 30th
CELTIC (1) 1 FALKIRK (0) 0
Fernie (44)

CELTIC: Bonnar; Haughney, Fallon; Boden, Jack, Peacock; Higgins, Fernie, Sharkey, Walsh, Mochan

FALKIRK: Slater; Fletcher, McIntosh; Thomson, Cartmell, Campbell; Sinclair, Ormond, Davidson, McCrae, Anderson

Attendance: 4,000

Scottish League Division A

	P	W	D	L	F	A	Pts
1 Rangers	34	22	8	4	85	27	52
2 Aberdeen	34	18	10	6	87	50	46
3 Hearts	34	19	7	8	99	47	45
4 Hibernian	34	19	7	8	86	50	45
5 CELTIC	34	16	9	9	55	39	41
6 Queen of the South	34	16	5	13	69	73	37
7 Airdrie	34	14	8	12	85	96	36
8 Kilmarnock	34	12	10	12	52	45	34
9 Partick Thistle	34	13	7	14	62	60	33
10 Motherwell	34	11	11	12	53	59	33
11 Raith Rovers	34	12	9	13	58	75	33
12 East Fife	34	13	5	16	61	69	31
13 Dundee	34	12	6	16	56	65	30
14 Falkirk	34	11	6	17	58	75	28
15 St Mirren	34	10	7	17	57	70	27
16 Dunfermline	34	10	6	18	42	82	26
17 Clyde	34	8	6	20	50	74	22
18 Stirling Albion	34	4	5	25	23	82	13

April 30th: Celtic freed John McPhail, White, Fletcher and Rowan.

May 2nd: Bobby Evans was in the Scotland team which drew 1-1 with Austria at Hampden Park.

May 6th: Billy McPhail was signed from Clyde for £2,500.

June 12th: Jim Docherty joined Alloa Athletic.

LEAGUE CUP

August 13th
CELTIC (2) 4 QUEEN OF THE SOUTH (1) 2
Mochan (30 secs),
Walsh (32),
Collins (46),
Fernie (47)
Patterson 2 (16, 88)

CELTIC: Bonnar; Haughney, Fallon; Evans, Stein, McPhail; Collins, Fernie, Walsh, Tully, Mochan

QUEEN OF THE SOUTH: Henderson; Sharpe, Whitehead; King, Smith, Gibson; Black, McGill, Patterson, Rothera, Oakes

Attendance: 40,000

August 17th
QUEEN OF THE SOUTH (0) 0 CELTIC (0) 2
Walsh (60),
Sharpe o.g. (62)

QUEEN OF THE SOUTH: Henderson; Sharpe, Whitehead; King, Smith, Gibson; Black, McGill, Patterson, Rothera, Oakes

CELTIC: Bonnar; Haughney, Fallon; Conroy, Evans, Peacock; Collins, Fernie, McAlindon, Walsh, Mochan

Attendance: 12,000

August 20th
CELTIC (3) 5 — FALKIRK (0) 1
Collins 2 (6, 22), Tully (34), Mochan (82), Fernie (85) — Morrison (87)

CELTIC: Bonnar; Haughney, Fallon; Evans, Stein, Peacock; Collins, Fernie, Walsh, Tully, Mochan

FALKIRK: Slater; Parker, Rae; Fletcher, Colville, Campbell; Sinclair, Morrison, Ormond, McCrae, O'Hara

Attendance: 40,000

August 27th
RANGERS (1) 1 — CELTIC (3) 4
Fallon o.g. (35) — McPhail (16), Smith 2 (28, 41), Mochan (52)

RANGERS: Niven; Caldow, Little; McColl, Young, Baird; Scott, Simpson, Murray, McMillan, Hubbard

CELTIC: Bonnar; Haughney, Fallon; Evans, Stein, Peacock; Collins, Fernie, Mochan, Smith, McPhail

Attendance: 75,000

This was a brilliant display by Celtic at Ibrox. McPhail scored the first goal in 16 minutes, whipping round Caldow and smashing a right-foot shot over Niven's head. 12 minutes later Smith increased their lead when he scored from a Mochan pass. 10 minutes from half-time Fallon and Scott collided as they went for a Baird free-kick and Scott received the congratulations for a goal which may well have been unwittingly scored by the back. In another 6 minutes McPhail's astute pass was glided round the struggling Baird by Smith and from 22 yards he shot so powerfully that Niven, though he had anticipated the direction, could not prevent a goal. 7 minutes after the interval Mochan took Celtic's total to 4 when he scored with a bullet-like right-foot shot.

August 31st
CELTIC (0) 0 — RANGERS (1) 4
Baird 2 (4, 49), Simpson (77), Murray (80)

CELTIC: Bonnar; Haughney, Fallon; Evans, Stein, Peacock; Collins, McVittie, Mochan, Smith, McPhail

RANGERS: Niven; Caldow, Little; McColl, Young, Rae; Scott, Simpson, Murray, Baird, Hubbard

Attendance: 61,000

An injury to Stein, 10 minutes from half-time, handicapped the home side. He had to go to outside-left, Evans taking over at centre-half. That apart, this was revenge with a vengeance for Rangers. Rangers increased their lead in the 49th minute when Celtic half-cleared and Baird rushed in and shot with his left foot from 8 yards past a helpless Bonnar. The limping Stein nearly scored with a glancing header from a Mochan corner. Rangers were well on top in the closing 15 minutes and scored twice more. Near the end Scott struck the post and crossbar in quick succession. Rangers had taken the lead in the 4th minute when Baird, taking a return pass from Simpson, shot a splendid goal from 20 yards.

September 3rd
FALKIRK (1) 1 — CELTIC (0) 1
Morrison (20) — Mochan (68)

FALKIRK: Hamilton; Parker, Rae; Fletcher, Colville, McIntosh; Sinclair, Morrison, Wright, McCrae, O'Hara

CELTIC: Beattie; Haughney, Meechan; Smith, Evans, Peacock; Collins, Fernie, Docherty, Tully, Mochan

Attendance: 17,000. Rae was ordered off.

SECTION TABLE

	P	W	D	L	F	A	Pts
Rangers	6	5	0	1	22	8	10
CELTIC	6	4	1	1	16	9	9
Falkirk	6	2	1	3	12	15	5
Queen of the South	6	0	0	6	3	21	0

Qualifier: RANGERS

SCOTTISH CUP

Fifth Round February 4th
MORTON (0) 0 — CELTIC (2) 2
Tully (28), Collins (35)

MORTON: Harvey; McCabe, Baird; Simpson, Lewis, Hinshelwood; Kerr, Fleming, McGhee, Orr, Gibson

CELTIC: Beattie; Haughney, Goldie; Evans, Boden, Peacock; Collins, Fernie, Sharkey, Tully, Mochan

Attendance: 17,000

Sixth Round February 18th
AYR UNITED (0) 0 — CELTIC (1) 3
Collins 2 (40, 89), Mochan (90)

AYR UNITED: Round; Leckie, Thomson; Strickland, Gallacher, Haugh; Japp, McMillan, Price, Stevenson, Beattie

CELTIC: Beattie; Haughney, Fallon; Boden, Evans, Peacock; Collins, Smith, McAlindon, Tully, Mochan

Attendance: 24,000

Quarter-Final March 3rd
CELTIC (1) 2 — AIRDRIE (0) 1
Collins (10), Tully (77) — Baird (74)

CELTIC: Beattie; Haughney, Fallon; Boden, Evans, Peacock; Collins, Fernie, Walsh, Tully, Mochan

AIRDRIE: Walker; Miller, McNeil; Quinn, Quigley, Price; Duncan, Rankine, Baird, McMillan, McCulloch

Attendance: 59,000

Semi-Final March 24th at Hampden Park
CELTIC (2) 2 — CLYDE (1) 1
Sharkey (2), Haughney (19 pen) — McPhail (20)

CLYDE: Watson; Murphy, Haddock; Gallacher, Keogh, Laing; Hill, Robertson, McPhail, Ring, Kemp

CELTIC: Beattie; Haughney, Fallon; Boden, Evans, Peacock; Collins, Walsh, Sharkey, Fernie, Tully

Attendance: 65,200

In view of the fact that Clyde were baulked of a goal, by virtue of a goal-line clearance on 2 occasions and because twice more luck rather than able defence prevented them from scoring, the Cup holders were unfortunate to lose. Early in the first half Keogh and Hill gave the impression that they were not going to tolerate the intricate ball-play of Fernie, and before half-time one or the other had brought him down 7 times. One of Keogh's offences resulted in a penalty kick from which Haughney scored in the 19th minute. Keogh had a dreadful first half, for it was his ill-advised and ill-directed pass that cost his side the opening goal in the 2nd minute. Clyde's goal, scored by McPhail less than a minute after Celtic's 2nd, also resulted from a defensive error. Evans ducked a long upfield punt without apparently signalling his intention to Beattie, and McPhail beat the goalkeeper as they collided in the penalty area.

Final April 21st at Hampden Park

HEARTS (1) 3 — CELTIC (0) 1
Crawford 2 (19, 49), Conn (81) — Haughney (53)

HEARTS: Duff; Kirk, McKenzie; Mackay, Glidden, Cumming; Young, Conn, Bauld, Wardhaugh, Crawford

CELTIC: Beattie; Meechan, Fallon; Smith, Evans, Peacock; Craig, Haughney, Mochan, Fernie, Tully

Attendance: 132,842. *Referee:* R. H. Davidson (Airdrie)

Celtic were, through no fault of their own, handicapped by the absence of Stein and Collins, but the fielding on the right flank of their team, of players who had either little or no experience of the positions this season proved crucial. Fernie chose the very day Celtic needed him most to play well short of his best. At the end of the day Hearts had deservedly beaten a side who had never forced their goalkeeper to save.

APPEARANCES	League	League Cup	Scottish Cup
Beattie	31	1	5
Haughney	24	6	5
Fallon	20	5	3
Evans	31	6	5
Jack	4	–	–
Peacock	33	5	5
Craig	1	–	1
Boden	17	–	4
McPhail	2	3	–
Smith	13	3	2
Mochan	31	6	4
Fernie	32	5	5
Collins	26	6	4
Tully	17	3	5
Docherty	1	1	–
Reid	1	–	–
McVittie	4	1	–
Sharkey	19	–	2
Whyte	7	–	–
Higgins	7	–	–
Rowan	1	–	–
Walsh	16	3	2
Meechan	6	1	1
Conroy	1	1	–
Goldie	10	–	1
Stein	6	4	–
McAlindon	4	1	1
Craig	5	–	–
Kennedy	1	–	–
Bonnar	3	5	–

GOALSCORERS

League: Mochan 15, Sharkey 7, Walsh 7, Fernie 6 (1 pen), Tully 4, Collins 4, McPhail 2, McVittie 2, McAlindon 2, Haughney 2 (1 pen), Higgins 1, Smith 1, Peacock 1, Own Goal 1

League Cup: Mochan 4, Collins 3, Walsh 2, Fernie 2, Smith 2, Tully 1, McPhail 1, Own Goal 1

Scottish Cup: Collins 4, Tully 2, Haughney 2 (1 pen), Mochan 1, Sharkey 1

Season 1956-57

For the second successive season Celtic finished 5th in the table – behind Rangers, Hearts, Kilmarnock and Raith Rovers. Their home form was impressive with only 2 defeats, but as in the previous season their away form nose-dived in the New Year and they collected only 3 points from a possible 20. Mike Haughney was the only ever-present and Neil Mochan finished as top scorer with 11. Evans, Collins, Fernie and Peacock all received International honours during a season which saw Jock Stein announce his retirement from the playing side through injury.

Celtic won the League Cup for the first time, beating Partick Thistle after a replay. They topped a very tough Section which included Rangers, Aberdeen and East Fife – without losing a match. Dunfermline were beaten 6-3 on aggregate in the Quarter-Final and ex-Shawfield star Billy McPhail scored the 2 goals which defeated his former club in the Semi-Final. Celtic should have won their first meeting with an injury struck Partick Thistle with some ease. Instead it took two brilliant saves from Beattie to avert an embarrassing defeat. However, they made no mistake in the replay, winning decisively with 2 goals from McPhail and another from Collins without any reply from Thistle.

They reached the Semi-Final of the Scottish Cup but lost to Kilmarnock after a replay. Their best performance in the competition was their win at Ibrox in a Sixth-Round Replay after Rangers had fought back from being 2 goals down to snatch a sensational 4-4 draw at Parkhead.

Celtic undertook their 3rd tour of North America and Canada and played 7 matches, winning 5 and losing twice to Tottenham Hotspur in Vancouver and Toronto (3-6, 1-3). They gained some revenge by beating them 2-0 in Montreal in their last match. Mike Haughney decided to emigrate to the U.S. prior to the tour.

League:	Fifth
League Cup:	Winners
Scottish Cup:	Semi-Finalists

SCOTTISH FIRST DIVISION

July 13th: Trainer Alex Dowdalls left Parkhead for Leicester City.

September 5th: Evans and Collins were in the Scottish League team which beat the Irish League 7-1 in Belfast.

September 8th
CELTIC (1) 2 QUEENS PARK (0) 0
Mochan (3), Collins (89)

CELTIC: Beattie; Haughney, Fallon; Evans, Jack, Peacock; Mochan, Collins, McPhail, Fernie, Tully

QUEENS PARK: F. Crampsey; I. Harnett, W. Hastie; R. Cromar, J. Valentine, A. Glen; G. Herd, W. Omand, C. Church, J. Devine, N. Hopper

Attendance: 28,000

September 22nd
CELTIC (0) 0 RANGERS (1) 2
Murray (31), Scott (71)

CELTIC: Beattie; Haughney, Fallon; Evans, Jack, Peacock; Higgins, Collins, McPhail, Fernie, Mochan

RANGERS: Niven; Shearer, Little; McColl, Young, Logie; Scott, Grierson, Murray, Baird, Hubbard

Attendance: 53,000

The speed of Scott and the skill of Hubbard troubled the Celtic defence throughout. Nineteen free-kicks were awarded against Rangers in the match for infringements other than offside, a high proportion of them against Baird. Before Murray headed the first goal in 32 minutes Celtic were deprived of scores only by superb saves by Niven. Young was a majestic figure in defence for Rangers.

The Celtic team group, Season 1956-57, who won the League Cup. Back row: Craig, Meechan, Jack, Bonnar, Evans, Haughney, Fallon. Middle row: W. Johnstone (trainer), Goldie, Boden, Walsh, McCreadie, Auld, McKay, McAlinden, J. McGrory (manager) and J. Gribben (asst. trainer). Front row: Ryan, Fernie, Collins, Peacock, McPhail, Tully and Mochan.

September 26th: Evans and Collins were in the Scottish League team which beat the League of Ireland 3-1 at Shawfield. Collins scored one of the goals.

September 29th
MOTHERWELL (1) 1 CELTIC (0) 0
Quinn (15)
MOTHERWELL: Weir; McSeveney, Holton; Aitken, Paton, Forrest; Hunter, Quinn, Gardiner, McCann, Rea
CELTIC: Beattie; Haughney, Fallon; Evans, Jack, Peacock; Mochan, Collins, McPhail, Fernie, Tully
Attendance: 18,000

October 13th
FALKIRK (0) 0 CELTIC (0) 1
Collins (60)
FALKIRK: Brown; Parker, Rae; Thomson, Cosker, McIntosh; Sinclair, Wright, McCole, Prentice, O'Hara
CELTIC: Beattie; Haughney, Fallon; Evans, Jack, Peacock; Craig, Walsh, McPhail, Collins, Fernie
Attendance: 20,000

October 20th
CELTIC (1) 1 RAITH ROVERS (1) 1
McPhail (25) Williamson (40)
CELTIC: Beattie; Haughney, Fallon; Evans, Jack, Peacock; Craig, Smith, McPhail, Tully, Walsh
RAITH ROVERS: Drummond; Polland, Bain; Young, McNaught, Leigh; McEwan, Kelly, Copland, Williamson, Urquhart
Attendance: 16,000

League positions

	P	W	D	L	F	A	Pts
1 Hearts	8	6	1	1	20	15	13
2 Motherwell	7	5	2	0	21	8	12
3 Raith Rovers	8	3	4	1	22	16	10
4 Rangers	6	4	1	1	14	7	9
5 East Fife	8	3	3	2	21	17	9
12 CELTIC	5	2	1	2	4	4	5

October 20th: Collins and Fernie were in the Scotland team which drew 2-2 with Wales in Cardiff. Fernie scored Scotland's first goal.

November 3rd
DUNDEE (1) 2 CELTIC (0) 1
Black (11), O'Hara (58) Mochan (59)
DUNDEE: Brown; Reid, Cox; Henderson, McKenzie, Cowie; Chalmers, Black, Watt, O'Hara, Christie
CELTIC: Beattie; Haughney, Fallon; Smith, Jack, Peacock; Tully, Collins, McPhail, Fernie, Mochan
Attendance: 22,000. Bobby Collins was carried off after 22 minutes with a broken ankle.

November 7th: Willie Fernie was in the Scotland team which beat Ireland 1-0 at Hampden Park.

November 10th
CELTIC (2) 4 EAST FIFE (0) 0
Mochan (21), Haughney 44 (pen), Ryan (50), Higgins (54)
CELTIC: Beattie; Haughney, Kennedy; Smith, Jack, Peacock; Higgins, Ryan, Mochan, Fernie, Tully
EAST FIFE: McCluskey; Wilkie, S. Stewart; Fox, Christie, Cox; J. Stewart, Leishman, Plumb, Bonthrone, Matthew
Attendance: 17,000

November 17th
AYR UNITED (0) 1 CELTIC (1) 3
Price (77) McPhail (24), Tully (68), Haughney (73 pen)
AYR UNITED: Round; Bell, Thomson; Boden, Gallagher, Haugh; Japp, Paton, Price, Murray, Beattie
CELTIC: Beattie; Haughney, Fallon; Smith, Jack, Peacock; Tully, Ryan, McPhail, Fernie, Mochan
Attendance: 17,000

November 21st: Willie Fernie was in the Scotland team which beat Yugoslavia 2-0 at Hampden Park.

November 24th
CELTIC (0) 1 PARTICK THISTLE (1) 1
Mochan (62) McIntosh (27)
CELTIC: Beattie; Haughney, Fallon; Evans, Jack, Peacock; Tully, Ryan, McPhail, Fernie, Mochan
PARTICK THISTLE: Smith; Kerr, Baird; Wright, McNab, Mathers; McKenzie, Smith, Hogan, McIntosh, Ewing
Attendance: 20,000

December 1st
CELTIC (0) 1 HEARTS (0) 1
McPhail (63) Wardhaugh (75)
CELTIC: Beattie: Haughney, Fallon; Evans, Jack, Peacock; Higgins, Ryan, McPhail, Fernie, Mochan
HEARTS: Marshall; Kirk, McKenzie; Mackay, Milne, Cumming; Hamilton, Young, Bauld, Wardhaugh, Crawford
Attendance: 32,000

December 8th
ST MIRREN (0) 0 CELTIC (0) 2
Mochan (74), Higgins (84)
ST MIRREN: Forsyth; Lapsley, McTurk; Dallas, Telfer, Johnston; Devine, Wilson, Humphries, Holmes, McGill
CELTIC: Beattie; Haughney, Meechan; Evans, Jack, Peacock; Higgins, Ryan, Mochan, Sharkey, Fernie
Attendance: 21,500

December 15th
CELTIC (1) 3 — DUNFERMLINE (0) 1
Higgins (6), Mochan (60), Fernie (89) — McWilliams (46)

CELTIC: Beattie; Haughney, Meechan; Evans, Jack, Peacock; Higgins, Ryan, Mochan, Fernie, Tully

DUNFERMLINE: Mackin; Laird, Duthie; Mailer, Colville, Melrose; Peebles, O'Brien, McWilliams, Reilly, Anderson

Attendance: 11,000

December 22nd
AIRDRIE (3) 3 — CELTIC (4) 7
McMillan (4), Rankin (14), McNeil (30) — Higgins 4 (11, 17, 29, 42), Ryan (71), Fernie 2 (75, 77)

AIRDRIE: Goldie; Kilmarnock, Shanks; Price, Quigley, Slingsby; Rankin, McMillan, Baird, McNeil, McCulloch

CELTIC: Beattie; Haughney, Meechan; Evans, Jack, Peacock; Higgins, Ryan, Mochan, Fernie, Tully

Attendance: 16,000

December 29th
HIBERNIAN (1) 3 — CELTIC (1) 3
Fraser (25), Thomson (63), Reilly (81) — Ryan (44), Smith (71), Mochan (72)

HIBERNIAN: Wren; Grant, Paterson; Nicol, Plenderleith, Hughes; Fraser, Turnbull, Reilly, Thomson, Ormond

CELTIC: Beattie; Haughney, Meechan; Evans, Jack, Peacock; Smith, Ryan, Mochan, Fernie, Tully

Attendance: 31,000

League positions

	P	W	D	L	F	A	Pts
1 Hearts	17	13	2	2	46	31	26
2 Motherwell	16	10	3	3	43	26	23
3 Rangers	15	10	1	4	44	26	21
4 Raith Rovers	17	8	5	4	43	28	21
5 Dundee	14	8	3	3	28	18	19
7 CELTIC	14	7	4	3	29	16	18

January 1st
RANGERS (1) 2 — CELTIC (0) 0
Murray (12), Simpson (70)

RANGERS: Niven; Shearer, Caldow; McColl, Young, Logie; Scott, Simpson, Murray, Baird, Hubbard

CELTIC: Beattie; Haughney, Meechan; Evans, Jack, Peacock; Smith, Ryan, Mochan, Fernie, Tully

Attendance: 60,000

Celtic were lucky that Rangers did not take much heavier toll of them. Celtic's outstanding player was Jack. Time and again he prevented goals with strong, well-timed tackles. Rangers' backs and half-backs gave most of the Celtic players a lesson in going determinedly for the ball. Both Rangers' goals were scored from positions close in on goal, Murray's from Baird's pass and Simpson's from Murray's deflection from Shearer's free-kick. Fernie squandered Celtic's best chance 3 minutes from time when he intercepted a poor back pass and missed an unguarded goal.

January 2nd
CELTIC (1) 1 — KILMARNOCK (0) 1
Mochan (42) — Mays (60)

CELTIC: Beattie; Haughney, Kennedy; Evans, Jack, Peacock; Smith, Ryan, Mochan, Fernie, Tully

KILMARNOCK: Brown; Collins, Watson; Stewart, Toner, Mackay; Muir, Harvey, Mays, Black, Burns

Attendance: n.a.

January 5th
QUEENS PARK (0) 2 — CELTIC (0) 0
Church 2 (62, 65)

QUEENS PARK: F. Crampsey; I. Harnett, W. Hastie; R. Cromar, J. Valentine, A. Glen; N. Hopper, M. Darroch, A. McEwan, J. Devine, C. Church

CELTIC: Beattie: Haughney, Meechan; Evans, Jack, Peacock; Smith, Ryan, Mochan, Fernie, Tully

Attendance: 21,174

January 12th
CELTIC (1) 2 — MOTHERWELL (1) 1
Haughney (18), Sharkey (55) — Gardiner (15)

CELTIC: Beattie; Haughney, Kennedy; Evans, Jack, Peacock; Higgins, Ryan, Sharkey, Fernie, Mochan

MOTHERWELL: Weir; McSeveney, Holton; Aitken, Paton, Forrest; J. Hunter, Quinn, Gardiner, McCann, Reid

Attendance: 32,000

January 19th
QUEEN OF THE SOUTH (1) 4 — CELTIC (1) 3
Jack o.g. (44), Whitehead (52), Patterson (56), McGill (61) — Binning o.g. (35), Higgins (75), Mochan (87)

QUEEN OF THE SOUTH: Selkirk; Sharpe, Binning; Whitehead, Smith, Greenock; Black, McGill, Patterson, McMillan, McGuire

CELTIC: Beattie; Haughney, Kennedy; Evans, Jack, Peacock; Higgins, Tully, Sharkey, Fernie, Mochan

Attendance: 11,000

January 26th
CELTIC (1) 4 — FALKIRK (0) 0
Mochan (12), McPhail (66), Higgins (78), Irvine o.g. (85)

CELTIC: Beattie; Haughney, Fallon; Evans, Jack, Peacock; Higgins, Fernie, McPhail, Mochan, Collins

FALKIRK: Slater; Parker, Rae; Neil, Irvine, Prentice; Moran, Grierson, Merchant, Wright, O'Hara
Attendance: 18,000

January 29th: Jock Stein announced his retirement through injury. He was offered a coaching position by the Club.

February 9th
RAITH ROVERS (1) 3 — CELTIC (1) 1
Urquhart (16), Williamson (35), Copland (85) — Fernie (9)

RAITH ROVERS: Drummond; Polland, Bain; Young, McNaught, Leigh; McEwan, Kelly, Copland, Williamson, Urquhart

CELTIC: Beattie; Haughney, Fallon; Evans, Jack, Peacock; Higgins, Fernie, McPhail, Mochan, Collins
Attendance: 20,000

February 23rd
CELTIC (2) 2 — ABERDEEN (1) 1
McPhail (20), Mochan (37) — Allister (38)

CELTIC: Beattie; Haughney, Fallon; Evans, Jack, Peacock; Tully, Fernie, McPhail, Mochan, Collins

ABERDEEN: Martin; Mitchell, Caldwell; Allister, Young, Glen; Leggat, Brownlie, Davidson, Wishart, Mulhall
Attendance: 12,000

League positions

	P	W	D	L	F	A	Pts
1 Hearts	26	18	5	3	66	40	41
2 Rangers	23	16	2	5	61	34	34
3 Motherwell	24	15	4	5	60	37	34
4 Raith Rovers	25	13	7	5	70	40	33
5 Kilmarnock	25	11	9	5	44	28	31
8 CELTIC	22	10	5	7	42	30	25

March 6th
CELTIC (1) 1 — DUNDEE (0) 1
Haughney (32 pen) — O'Hara (78)

CELTIC: Beattie; Haughney, Fallon; Evans, Jack, Peacock; Higgins, Fernie, McPhail, Mochan, Collins

DUNDEE: Brown; Reid, Cox; Henderson, Ferguson, Black; Chalmers, Cousin, Birse, O'Hara, Christie
Attendance: 7000

March 9th
EAST FIFE (0) 2 — CELTIC (0) 0
Gillon (48), Matthew (70)

EAST FIFE: McCluskey; Wilkie, S. Stewart; Skinner, Christie, Cox; J. Stewart, Leishman, Gillon, Bonthrone, Matthew

CELTIC: Beattie; Haughney, Fallon; Evans, Jack, Peacock; McAlindon, Fernie, Byrne, Mochan, Collins
Attendance: 9000

March 14th: Collins and Fernie were in the Scottish League team which beat the English League 3-2 at Ibrox Park. Both Fernie and Collins scored.

March 16th
CELTIC (1) 4 — AYR UNITED (0) 0
Haughney (44 pen), Byrne 2 (46, 66), Collins (74)

CELTIC: Beattie; Haughney, Fallon; Evans, Jack, Peacock; Higgins, Collins, Byrne, Mochan, Tully

AYR UNITED: Travers; Paterson, Thomson; Graynor, Boden, Haugh; Price, Paton, Whittle, McMillan, Beattie
Attendance: 10,000

March 30th
HEARTS (2) 3 — CELTIC (0) 1
Bauld (2), Young (13), Crawford (76) — Collins (63)

HEARTS: Marshall; Kirk, McKenzie; Parker, Milne, Mackay; Hamilton, Conn, Bauld, Young, Crawford

CELTIC: Beattie; Haughney, Meechan; Evans, Jack, Peacock; Higgins, Fernie, Byrne, Collins, Mochan
Attendance: 25,000

April 6th: Collins and Fernie were in the Scotland team which was beaten 2-1 by England at Wembley.

April 10th:
PARTICK THISTLE (2) 3 — CELTIC (1) 1
Smith (2), Ewing (4), Hogan (80) — Byrne (43)

PARTICK THISTLE: Ledgerwood; Collins, Baird; Harvey, Davidson, Kerr; McKenzie, Smith, Hogan, McIntosh, Ewing

CELTIC: Beattie; Haughney, Fallon; Evans, Jack, Mochan; Collins, Fernie, Higgins, Byrne, Tully
Attendance: 18,000

April 10th: Bertie Peacock was in the Ireland team which drew 0-0 with Wales in Belfast.

April 13th
DUNFERMLINE (0) 0 — CELTIC (1) 1
McAlindon (11)

DUNFERMLINE: Mackin; Laird, Duthie; Samuel, Colville, Mailer; McKinlay, Miller, Dickson, Reilly, Anderson

CELTIC: Beattie; Haughney, Fallon; Evans, Jack, Peacock; Fernie, Collins, McAlindon, Smith, Tully
Attendance: 12,000

April 17th
CELTIC (1) 2 — ST MIRREN (3) 3
Haughney (39 pen), Fernie (50) — Bryceland (17), Devine (36), Holmes (40)

CELTIC: Beattie; Haughney, Fallon; Evans, Jack, Peacock; Higgins, Fernie, Mochan, Collins, Tully

ST MIRREN: Forsyth; Lapsley, Wilson; Buchanan, Telfer, Johnston; Flavell, Bryceland, McKay, Holmes, Devine

Attendance: n.a. Haughney missed a penalty

April 20th
CELTIC (0) 3 — AIRDRIE (0) 0
Haughney (61 pen), McAlindon (77), Collins (78)

CELTIC: Bonnar; Haughney, Fallon; Evans, Jack, Peacock; Collins, Fernie, McAlindon, Smith, Mochan

AIRDRIE: Walker; Kilmarnock, Shanks; Price, Quigley, Quinn; Rankin, Welsh, Baird, Duncan, McLean

Attendance: 6,000

April 22nd
ABERDEEN (0) 0 — CELTIC (0) 1
Higgins (85)

ABERDEEN: Martin; Caldwell, Hogg; Allister, Young, Brownlie; Leggat, Ward, Davidson, Wishart, Hather

CELTIC: McCreadie; Haughney, Fallon; Evans, Jack, Mochan; Higgins, Fernie, Ryan, Collins, Tully

Attendance: 15,000

April 25th: Bertie Peacock was in the Ireland team which was beaten 1-0 by Italy in Rome.

April 26th
KILMARNOCK 0 — CELTIC 0

KILMARNOCK: Brown; Collins, J. Stewart; R. Stewart, Toner, Taggart; Mays, Harvey, Curlett, Black, Muir

CELTIC: Bonnar; Haughney, Fallon; Evans, Jack, Mochan; Higgins, Fernie, Ryan, Collins, Tully

Attendance: n.a.

April 27th
CELTIC (0) 2 — HIBERNIAN (0) 1
Fernie (71), Haughney (87 pen) — Fraser (69)

CELTIC: Bonnar; Haughney, Fallon; Evans, Jack, Peacock; Higgins, Fernie, Ryan, Collins, Mochan

HIBERNIAN: Leslie; Muir, Boyle; Nicol, Plenderleith, Preston; Smith, Turnbull, Fraser, Harrower, Aitken

Attendance: 12,000

May 3rd: Sammy Wilson was signed from Falkirk.

April 29th
CELTIC 0 — QUEEN OF THE SOUTH 0

CELTIC: Bonnar; Haughney, Goldie; Evans, Meechan, Peacock; Higgins, Fernie, Byrne, Collins, Mochan

QUEEN OF THE SOUTH: Morrow; Sharpe, Binning; Whitehead, Smith, Greenock; Black, McGill, Patterson, King, McGuire

Attendance: 3,000.

Scottish First Division

	P	W	D	L	F	A	Pts
1 Rangers	34	26	3	5	96	48	55
2 Hearts	34	24	5	5	81	48	53
3 Kilmarnock	34	16	10	8	57	39	42
4 Raith Rovers	34	16	7	11	84	58	39
5 CELTIC	34	15	8	11	58	43	38
6 Aberdeen	34	18	2	14	79	59	38
7 Motherwell	34	16	5	13	72	66	37
8 Partick Thistle	34	13	8	13	53	51	34
9 Hibernian	34	12	9	13	69	56	33
10 Dundee	34	13	6	15	55	61	32
11 Airdrie	34	13	4	17	77	89	30
12 St Mirren	34	12	6	16	58	72	30
13 Queens Park	34	11	7	16	55	59	29
14 Falkirk	34	10	8	16	51	70	28
15 East Fife	34	10	6	18	59	82	26
16 Queen of the South	34	10	5	19	54	96	25
17 Dunfermline	34	9	6	19	54	74	24
18 Ayr United	34	7	5	22	48	89	19

May 1st: Celtic freed McCreadie, Reid and McAlindon.

May 1st: Bertie Peacock was in the Ireland team which beat Portugal 3-0 in Belfast.

May 3rd: Sammy Wilson was signed from Falkirk.

May 8th: Bobby Collins was in the Scotland team which beat Spain 4-2 in a World Cup Qualifier at Hampden Park.

May 19th: Collins was in the Scotland team which beat Switzerland 2-1 in a World Cup Qualifier in Basle.

May 22nd: Evans and Collins were in the Scotland team which beat World Champions West Germany 3-1 in Stuttgart.

May 26th: Evans and Collins were in the Scotland team which was beaten 4-1 by Spain in Madrid.

LEAGUE CUP

August 11th
ABERDEEN (0) 1 — CELTIC (1) 2
Yorston (85) — Fernie (34), Higgins (63)

ABERDEEN: Morrison; Mitchell, Caldwell; Wilson, Young, Glen; Leggat, Yorston, Buckley, Wishart, Hather

CELTIC: Beattie; Haughney, Fallon; Evans, Jack, Peacock; Higgins, Collins, McPhail, Fernie, Tully

Attendance: 35,000

August 15th
CELTIC (1) 2 — RANGERS (1) 1
Collins (38), Tully (68) — Murray (44)

CELTIC: Beattie; Haughney, Fallon; Evans, Jack, Peacock; Higgins, Collins, McPhail, Fernie, Tully

RANGERS: Niven; Shearer, Little; McColl, Young, Rae; Scott, Simpson, Murray, Baird, Hubbard

Attendance: 45,000

Niven might have been beaten on 3 occasions had Evans, Peacock and Fernie been accurate in finishing. Then in the 38th minute McPhail guided a Haughney pass into Collins' path and Niven was decisively beaten. Shortly after a fine angular shot by Scott hit the crossbar.

Murray equalised just on half-time after a goalmouth scramble. In the 65th minute Young upset Higgins, and Haughney shot the penalty-kick over the crossbar. 3 minutes later Tully hooked a lobbed shot past Niven for the 2nd Celtic goal.

August 18th
CELTIC (1) 2 — EAST FIFE (1) 1
Fernie (15), McPhail (57) — Bonthrone (2)

CELTIC: Beattie; Haughney, Kennedy; Evans, Jack, Peacock; Higgins, Collins, McPhail, Fernie, Tully

EAST FIFE: Watters; Adie, S. Stewart; Cox, Christie, McLennan; J. Stewart, Leishman, Wright, Bonthrone, Matthew

Attendance: 28,000

August 25th
CELTIC (1) 3 — ABERDEEN (1) 2
Collins (15), Tully (77), Fernie (85) — Leggat (7), Davidson (57)

CELTIC: Beattie; Haughney, Fallon; Evans, Jack, Peacock; Smith, Collins, McPhail, Fernie, Tully

ABERDEEN: Morrison; Mitchell, Hogg; Allister, Glen, Brownlie; Leggat, Yorston, Davidson, Hay, Hather

Attendance: 36,000

August 29th
RANGERS 0 — CELTIC 0

RANGERS: Niven; Caldow, Little; McColl, Young, Shearer; Scott, Paton, Murray, Simpson, Hubbard

CELTIC: Beattie; Haughney, Fallon; Evans, Jack, Peacock; Tully, Collins, McPhail, Fernie, Mochan

Attendance: 84,000

Celtic made a promising start and Mochan twice had Niven in difficulty within 5 minutes with accurate crosses. Celtic were much more dangerous, and the energetic and clever play of their forwards gave the home defence many moments of anxiety. Towards the interval a tremendous shot by McColl from 35 yards was only a foot wide. At the start of the second-half Fallon denied Rangers a goal when he headed an overhead kick from Scott off the line. In the 52nd minute a Mochan shot struck the post. Near the end Peacock started a splendid Celtic move with a pass to Tully. The outside-right transferred the ball to McPhail, who in turn sent it to Fernie 2 yards from goal, but the inside-left lofted high over when scoring looked easier.

September 1st
EAST FIFE (0) 0 — CELTIC (0) 1
McPhail (62)

EAST FIFE: McCluskey; Adie, S. Stewart; Cox, Christie, McLennan; J. Stewart, Wilson, Plumb, Leishman, Keddie

CELTIC: Beattie; Haughney, Fallon; Evans, Jack, Peacock; Smith, Collins, McPhail, Fernie, Mochan

Attendance: 16,535

SECTION TABLE

	P	W	D	L	F	A	Pts
CELTIC	6	5	1	0	10	5	11
Rangers	6	4	1	1	18	6	9
Aberdeen	6	1	0	5	11	18	2
East Fife	6	1	0	5	5	15	2

Qualifier: CELTIC

Quarter-Final First Leg September 12th
CELTIC (2) 6 — DUNFERMLINE (0) 0
Collins (24), Colville o.g. (32), Mochan 2 (55, 67), McPhail 2 (57, 89)

CELTIC: Beattie; Haughney, Fallon; Evans, Jack, Peacock; Mochan, Collins, McPhail, Fernie, Tully

DUNFERMLINE: Mackin; Woods, Duthie; Samuel, Colville, Baikie; McWilliam, Millar, Dickson, Reilly, Anderson

Attendance: 23,000

Quarter-Final Second Leg September 15th
DUNFERMLINE (1) 3 — CELTIC (0) 0
Anderson 2 (35, 75), Reilly (85)

DUNFERMLINE: Mackin; Burns, Duthie; Samuel, Colville, Melrose; Peebles, Millar, McWilliams, Reilly, Anderson

CELTIC: Beattie; Haughney, Fallon; Evans, Jack, Peacock; Mochan, Collins, Walsh, Fernie, Smith

Attendance: 16,000. Celtic won 6-3 on aggregate

Semi-Final October 6th at Hampden Park
CELTIC (1) 2 — CLYDE (0) 0
McPhail 2 (25, 46)

CELTIC: Beattie; Haughney, Fallon; Evans, Jack, Peacock; Smith, Collins, McPhail, Fernie, Mochan

CLYDE: Watson; Murphy, Haddock; Clinton, Finlay, Keogh; Rowan, Robertson, McHard, Innes, Ring

Attendance: 36,697

Billy McPhail played a prominent part in Celtic's victory. He scored both goals and came within inches of scoring 2 more. Beattie was called on to make one fine save – a leap to his left and a deflection of a header from Innes that looked certain to score. Later Watson made an equally fine save from McPhail.

Final October 27th at Hampden Park
CELTIC 0 PARTICK THISTLE 0
After Extra Time

CELTIC: Beattie; Haughney, Fallon; Evans, Jack, Peacock; Walsh, Collins, McPhail, Tully, Fernie

PARTICK THISTLE: Ledgerwood; Kerr, Gibb; Collins, Davidson, Mathers; McKenzie, Smith, Hogan Wright, Ewing

Attendance: 58,794. *Referee:* J. A. Mowat (Rutherglen)

Against a sorely handicapped side Beattie had to effect 2 of the best saves of the day to avert a defeat that would have been humiliating for Celtic. For the extra time Thistle relieved the injured Smith of his ordeal and played on with 10 men. They probably felt that Celtic might play for a week and not score. Fernie had a goal disallowed for offside. Beattie saved from McKenzie. Walsh shot into the side net and Beattie had to make a desperate last-second backward jump to prevent Hogan's corner-kick curling into the far corner of the net.

Final Replay October 31st at Hampden Park
CELTIC (0) 3 PARTICK THISTLE (0) 0
McPhail 2 (49, 52),
Collins (61)

CELTIC: Beattie; Haughney, Fallon; Evans, Jack, Peacock; Tully, Collins, McPhail, Fernie, Mochan

PARTICK THISTLE: Ledgerwood; Kerr, Gibb; Collins, Crawford, Mathers; McKenzie, Wright, Hogan, McParland, Ewing

Attendance: 31,156. *Referee:* J. A. Mowat (Rutherglen)

Celtic won the League Cup for the first time when they decisively defeated Partick Thistle at Hampden. In a dull first half, only when Tully was brought into the scheme of things was there an obvious menace to Thistle. Within 4 minutes of the start of the second half Celtic scored the goal that altered the whole complexion of the game. McPhail hooked the ball over Ledgerwood's head as the goalkeeper tried desperately to retrieve a pass-back blunder. Within 12 minutes Celtic were 3 up. Kerr hit a clearance too square and Tully clipped the ball to Mochan. He survived Gibb's belated tackle near the corner flag and squared the pass to McPhail standing in the clear to score. Then a pass from Evans let Collins through for a fast low shot out of Ledgerwood's reach. Celtic, with Mochan for Walsh their single personnel change, were generally the faster, stronger side.

SCOTTISH CUP

Fifth Round February 2nd
FORRES MECHANICS (0) 0 CELTIC (2) 5
Higgins (16),
Mochan (26),
McPhail 3 (46, 62, 73)

FORRES: Wisniewski; Hazle, Shaw; Clark, Roy, MacIntosh; Johnston, Preston, MacRae, Hay, Wallace

CELTIC: Beattie; Haughney, Fallon; Evans, Jack, Peacock; Higgins, Fernie, McPhail, Mochan, Collins

Attendance: 7,000

Sixth Round February 16th
CELTIC (2) 4 RANGERS (2) 4
McPhail (10), Higgins (15), Collins (75), Fernie (81)
Morrison (7), Simpson (14), Hubbard (83 pen), Murray (85)

CELTIC: Beattie; Haughney, Fallon; Evans, Jack, Peacock; Higgins, Fernie, McPhail, Mochan, Collins

RANGERS: Niven; Shearer, Caldow; McColl, Davis, Baird; Scott, Simpson, Murray, Morrison, Hubbard

Attendance: 50,000

This was an exhilarating match with 4 goals inside 9 minutes of the first half and 4 more in 11 minutes of the 2nd. Early in the second half Fallon made the save of the day by heading over the crossbar a Scott corner-kick propelled beyond Beattie's reach by Simpson. With 7 minutes remaining for play Baird pumped the ball upfield. Hubbard, in attempting to jump, was clumsily barged by Jack. The little winger converted the penalty-kick himself. 2 minutes later Rangers were on equal terms when Murray side-footed home Hubbard's corner-kick.

Sixth Round Replay February 20th
RANGERS (0) 0 CELTIC (2) 2
Higgins (15),
Mochan (35)

RANGERS: Niven; Shearer, Caldow; McColl, Davis, Baird; Scott, Simpson, Murray, Morrison, Hubbard

CELTIC: Beattie; Haughney, Fallon; Evans, Jack, Peacock; Higgins, Fernie, McPhail, Mochan, Collins

Attendance: 88,000

On a heavily sanded, frosty pitch Celtic played almost all of the football in the match. Almost from the start Rangers' players indulged in coarse tackling. Fernie suffered the worse treatment. The shocking climax came five minutes from time when Higgins was flattened by a bull-like rush by Shearer just as he was about to shoot well inside the penalty area.

Quarter-Final March 2nd
CELTIC (2) 2 ST MIRREN (0) 1
Peacock (12), Higgins (40)
Holmes (52)

CELTIC: Beattie; Haughney, Fallon; Evans, Jack, Peacock; Higgins, Fernie, McPhail, Mochan, Collins

ST MIRREN: Forsyth; Lapsley, J. Wilson; S. Wilson, Dallas, Johnstone; Devine, Gemmell, Telfer, Holmes, McCulloch

Attendance: 49,000

Semi-Final March 23rd at Hampden Park
CELTIC (0) 1 KILMARNOCK (1) 1
Higgins (84)
Mays (35)

CELTIC: Beattie; Haughney, Fallon; Evans, Jack, Peacock; Higgins, Fernie, Byrne, Mochan, Collins

KILMARNOCK: Brown; Collins, J. Stewart; R. Stewart, Dougan, Mackay; Mays, Harvey, Curlett, Black, Burns

Attendance: 109,145

The best football of the Semi-Final was played by Celtic in the opening 20 minutes. They had many shots at Brown's goal – Mochan most of them. Collins was unlucky when he beat Brown from Mochan's pass but his shot struck the crossbar. Dougan, deputising for Toner, was most impressive in the Kilmarnock defence. For long periods in the second half Celtic hemmed their opponents into their own half of the field. 6 minutes from the end Killie's Collins conceded a corner. Mochan's kick sailed over the leaping Brown and Higgins headed an equalising goal that was greeted with near bedlam on the terracing. Less than a minute later, with the Celtic defence spreadeagled, Mays was left with the chance of the match but ballooned the ball over.

Semi-Final Replay March 27th at Hampden Park

KILMARNOCK (2) 3	CELTIC (1) 1
Mays 2 (23, 44),	Collins (34)
Black (51)	

KILMARNOCK: Brown; Collins, J. Stewart; R. Stewart, Toner, Mackay; Mays, Harvey, Curlett, Black, Burns

CELTIC: Beattie; Haughney, Fallon; Evans, Jack, Peacock; Higgins, Fernie, Byrne, Mochan, Collins

Attendance: 76,963

Kilmarnock won a match astonishing for the number of blunders perpetrated by Celtic. Kilmarnock, committed to defence for most of the game, did not have more than 7 or 8 shots in the 90 minutes. They scored 3 goals and might have scored as many more again.

Celtic had little luck in the second half. In the 51st minute Beattie advanced to baulk Black, foolishly used his foot instead of his hands, lost the ball and left the inside-left with a vacant goal. Not long after the 3rd goal it seemed apparent that even such enthusiastic players as Peacock and Evans had accepted defeat.

Appearances	League	League Cup	Scottish Cup
Beattie	29	11	6
Haughney	34	11	6
Fallon	22	10	6
Evans	31	11	6
Jack	33	11	6
Peacock	31	11	6
Mochan	31	6	6
Collins	20	11	6
McPhail	13	10	4
Fernie	32	11	6
Tully	21	8	–
Higgins	19	3	6
Craig	2	–	–
Walsh	2	2	–
Smith	10	4	–
Kennedy	4	1	–
Ryan	15	–	–
Meechan	8	–	–
Sharkey	3	–	–
McAlindon	3	–	–
Byrne	5	–	2
Bonnar	4	–	–
McCreadie	1	–	–
Goldie	1	–	–

GOALSCORERS:

League: Mochan 11, Higgins 10, Haughney 8 (7 pens), Fernie 6, Collins 5, McPhail 5, Ryan 3, Byrne 3, McAlindon 2, Own Goals 2, Tully 1, Smith 1, Sharkey 1.

League Cup: McPhail 8, Collins 4, Fernie 3, Tully 2, Mochan 2, Higgins 1, Own Goal 1

Scottish Cup: Higgins 5, McPhail 4, Collins 2, Mochan 2, Peacock 1, Fernie 1.

Season 1957-58

Celtic finished 3rd in the League table behind run-away winners Hearts and Rangers. They had an amazing run of 10 consecutive away wins but their home form, although improving towards the end of the season, started disastrously with only 1 win in their first 10 matches between October 12th and January 18th. They completed the double over 6 teams and twice scored 6 goals against Clyde. They scored an amazing 84 goals – their highest post-war total. Sammy Wilson was top scorer with 23 goals, followed by Bobby Collins with 19. Wilson, Evans and Beattie missed only 1 match of the 34.

Celtic retained the League Cup, thrashing Rangers 7-1 in the Final in front of a crowd of 82,293. They topped their Section which included Hibs, Airdrie and East Fife. Third Lanark were soundly beaten in both legs of the Quarter-Final and Clyde, badly affected by an outbreak of influenza on the eve of the match, were beaten 4-2 in the Semi-Final at Ibrox. The Final turned into a personal nightmare for Rangers new centre-half John Valentine who found Billy McPhail in unstoppable form. Celtic led 2-0 at half-time but they really went to town in the final 21 minutes of the match – scoring 4 times to inflict their heaviest ever defeat on their great rivals. The unfortunate Valentine was made the scapegoat and never played for Rangers again. Celtic scored a total of 38 goals in their 10 matches in the competition, Billy McPhail leading the field with 14.

League: Third
League Cup: Winners
Scottish Cup: Third Round

SCOTTISH FIRST DIVISION

August 28th: Newcastle bid £8,000 for Willie Fernie.

September 7th
FALKIRK (0) 0 — CELTIC (1) 1
Fernie (44)

FALKIRK: Slater; Parker, Rae; Wright, Irvine, Prentice; Murray, McMillan, Merchant, Moran, O'Hara

CELTIC: Beattie; Donnelly, Fallon; Fernie, Evans, Peacock; Tully, Collins, Conway, Wilson, Auld

Attendance: 14,000

September 17th: Evans and Collins were in the Scottish League team which beat the League of Ireland 5-1 in Dublin. Collins scored a hat-trick.

September 21st
RANGERS (1) 2 — CELTIC (1) 3
Simpson 2 (39, 68) — Collins (19), McPhail (54), Wilson (64)

RANGERS: Ritchie; Shearer, Caldow; McColl, Valentine, Austin; Scott, Simpson, Murray, Baird, Hubbard

CELTIC: Beattie; Donnelly, Fallon; Fernie, Evans, Peacock; Sharkey, Collins, McPhail, Smith, Tully

Attendance: 60,000

October 5th: Evans and Collins were in the Scotland team which drew 1-1 with Ireland in Belfast. Peacock was in the Ireland team.

October 9th: Evans and Collins were in the Scottish League team which beat the Irish League 7-0 at Ibrox Park. Collins scored one of the goals from the penalty spot.

October 12th
CELTIC (1) 1 — RAITH ROVERS (0) 1
Mochan (9) — Copland (70)

CELTIC: Beattie; Donnelly, Fallon; Fernie, Evans, Peacock; Tully, Collins, Mochan, Wilson, Smith

RAITH ROVERS: Drummond; Polland, Williamson; Young, McNaught, Leigh; McEwan, Kerray, Copland, Kelly, Urquhart

Attendance: 20,000

October 26th
THIRD LANARK (0) 0 CELTIC (0) 2
Collins 2 (60, 85)

THIRD LANARK: Robertson; Cosker, Brown; Smith, Lewis, Kelly; W. Craig, R. Craig, Allan, Slingsby, Callan

CELTIC: Beattie; Goldie, Fallon; Fernie, Evans, Peacock; Tully, Collins, McPhail, Wilson, Mochan

Attendance: 24,000

League positions

	P	W	D	L	F	A	Pts
1 Hearts	7	6	1	0	32	5	13
2 Raith Rovers	8	4	1	3	14	9	11
3 Hibernian	8	5	1	2	15	10	11
4 Clyde	6	5	0	1	18	7	10
5 Kilmarnock	6	5	0	1	17	11	10
7 CELTIC	4	3	1	0	7	3	7

November 2nd
CELTIC (2) 4 KILMARNOCK (0) 0
Mochan 2 (28, 73), Wilson (43), McPhail (86)

CELTIC: Beattie; Goldie, Fallon; Fernie, Evans, Peacock; Tully, Collins, McPhail, Wilson, Mochan

KILMARNOCK: Brown; J. Stewart, Mackay; R. Stewart, Toner, Kennedy; Muir, Beattie, Mays, Black, Burns

Attendance: 35,000

November 6th: Bertie Peacock was in the Ireland team which beat England 3-2 at Wembley.

November 6th: Fernie, Evans and Collins were in the Scotland team which beat Switzerland 3-2 at Hampden Park.

November 7th: Billy McPhail was selected for the Scotland team to play Wales on November 13th.

November 8th: Jim Sharkey was transferred to Airdrie.

November 9th
EAST FIFE (0) 0 CELTIC (0) 3
Mochan (58), McPhail 2 (85, 89)

EAST FIFE: Allan; Wilkie, S. Stewart; Christie, Bowie, Neilson; Ingram, Leishman, Buchart, Bonthrone, Birse

CELTIC: Beattie; Donnelly, Fallon; Fernie, Evans, Peacock; Tully, Collins, McPhail, Wilson, Mochan

Attendance: 9,000

November 10th: Billy McPhail had to call off international duty with an ankle injury. He never got another chance.

November 13th: Scotland drew 1-1 with Wales at Hampden Park. Evans, Fernie and Collins were in the team. Collins scored Scotland's goal.

November 16th
CELTIC (1) 2 ST MIRREN (1) 2
Divers (21), Wilson (47) McGill (40), McKay (50)

CELTIC: Beattie; Donnelly, Fallon; Fernie, Evans, Peacock; Tully, Divers, McPhail, Wilson, Mochan

ST MIRREN: Forsyth; Higgins, Wilson; Neilson, Buchanan, Johnston; Devine, Gemmell, McKay, McGill, McCulloch

Attendance: 30,000

November 23rd
HIBERNIAN (0) 0 CELTIC (0) 1
Wilson (64)

HIBERNIAN: Leslie; Grant, Muir; Turnbull, Paterson, Baxter; Reilly, Harrower, Baker, Preston, Ormond

CELTIC: Beattie; Donnelly, Fallon; Fernie, Evans, Peacock; Tully, Collins, McPhail, Wilson, Mochan

Attendance: 40,000

November 30th
AIRDRIE (0) 2 CELTIC (2) 5
Price (61), Caven (63) Collins 2 (22 pen, 80), Peacock (36), Wilson 2 (60, 82)

AIRDRIE: Goldie; Reid, Shanks; Price, McPhail, Quinn; Rankin, Caven, Sharkey, McMillan, Ormond

CELTIC: Beattie; Donnelly, Fallon; Fernie, Evans, Peacock; Tully, Collins, McPhail, Wilson, Mochan

Attendance: 22,000

December 7th
CELTIC 0 DUNDEE 0

CELTIC: Beattie; Donnelly, Fallon; Fernie, Evans, Peacock; Jackson, Collins, McPhail, Wilson, Mochan

DUNDEE: Brown; Reid, Cox; Black, McKenzie, Cowie; Christie, Cousin, Henderson, Sneddon, Robertson

Attendance: 20,000

December 14th
CLYDE (2) 3 CELTIC (3) 6
Robertson 2 (34, 40), Keogh (64) McPhail 2 (3, 16), Clinton o.g. (23), Smith 2 (57, 89), Wilson (72)

CLYDE: McCulloch; Murphy, Haddock; Walters, Finlay, Clinton; Herd, Currie, Keogh, Robertson, Ring

CELTIC: Beattie; Donnelly, Fallon; Fernie, Evans, Peacock; Smith, Collins, McPhail, Wilson, Mochan

Attendance: 26,500

December 16th: Smith and Mochan played for a Glasgow Select against Kilmarnock in a match for the victims of the Muirkirk Disaster.

Willie Fernie scores the seventh and last goal against Rangers from the penalty spot in the 1957/58 League Cup Final.

December 21st
CELTIC (0) 2 — PARTICK THISTLE (2) 3
Mochan 2 (54, 59) — Mathers (11), Harvey (38), Kerr (84)

CELTIC: Beattie; Donnelly, Fallon; Fernie, Evans, Peacock; Smith, Collins, McPhail, Wilson, Mochan

PARTICK THISTLE: Thomson; Collins, Baird; Mathers, Davidson, Donlevy; Smith, Harvey, Kerr, Wright, McParland

Attendance: 18,000. Fernie was carried off after 45 minutes.

December 25th
CELTIC (0) 1 — QUEEN OF THE SOUTH (2) 2
Conway (68) — Patterson 2 (2, 34)

CELTIC: Beattie; Donnelly, Fallon; Jack, Evans, Peacock; Smith, Collins, Conway, Wilson, Mochan

QUEEN OF THE SOUTH: W. Smith; Sharpe, Binning; Whitehead, A. Smith, Greenock; Black, Crosbie, Patterson, Tasker, Oakes

Attendance: 15,000

December 28th
CELTIC (0) 0 — HEARTS (0) 2
Wardhaugh (65), Young (88)

CELTIC: Beattie; Fallon, Kennedy; Smith, Evans, Peacock; Conway, Collins, Ryan, Wilson, Mochan

HEARTS: Marshall; Kirk, Thomson; Mackay, Milne, Bowman; Blackwood, Murray, Young, Wardhaugh, Crawford

Attendance: 43,000. Collins missed a penalty

Young of Hearts was the star of the show, displaying consummate skill on a treacherous greasy surface. His duel of wits with Evans was fascinating throughout. It was his superbly judged flick which gave Wardhaugh his goal, and Young himself headed the decisive score 2 minutes from time. Smith, combining zeal and skill, had his best display for Celtic to date.

League positions

	P	W	D	L	F	A	Pts
1 Hearts	17	14	2	1	71	14	30
2 Hibernian	17	11	1	5	39	24	23
3 Clyde	17	10	0	5	46	26	20
4 Raith Rovers	17	8	4	5	32	22	20
5 CELTIC	14	8	3	3	31	17	19

January 1st
CELTIC (0) 0 — RANGERS (1) 1
Scott (19)

CELTIC: Beattie; Fallon, Kennedy; Smith, Evans, Peacock; McVittie, Colrain, Ryan, Wilson, Mochan

RANGERS: Ritchie; Shearer, Caldow; McColl, Telfer, Baird; Scott, Millar, Murray, Brand, Wilson

Attendance: 50,000

A remarkable save by Ritchie midway through the 2nd half was the principal factor in Rangers' success. McVittie's shot was placed carefully and cleverly far to the right of the goalkeeper but with nimbleness and courage he dived headlong and collared the ball when all of the Celtic legions were crying 'goal'. Rangers seemed the better able to master the difficult conditions. The Murray-led line was always the more dangerous. Scott, who scored the goal in the 19th minute, Millar and Wilson were forwards of distinction.

January 2nd
QUEENS PARK (0) 0 — CELTIC (2) 3
Wilson 2 (23, 35), McVittie (82)

QUEENS PARK: W. Pinkerton; I. Harnett, W. Hastie; R. Cromar, R. McKinven, J. Robb; C. Church, J. Coates, B. Kingsmore, G. McKenzie, E. Perry

CELTIC: Beattie; Fallon, Kennedy; Smith, Evans, Peacock; McVittie, Colrain, Ryan, Wilson, Mochan

Attendance: 10,000

January 4th
CELTIC (0) 2 — FALKIRK (1) 2
Byrne (56), Colrain (79) — McCole 2 (17, 78)

CELTIC: Beattie; Fallon, Kennedy; Smith, Evans, Peacock; Ryan, Colrain, Byrne, Wilson, Mochan

FALKIRK: Slater; Parker, McIntosh; McCormack, Irvine, McMillan; Murray, Grierson, McCole, Moran, O'Hara

Attendance: 18,000

January 11th
MOTHERWELL (1) 1 — CELTIC (1) 3
Quinn (40 pen) — Mochan (25), Collins (65), Holton o.g. (80)

MOTHERWELL: H. Weir; McSeveney, Holton; Aitken, Martis, McCann; Kerr, Quinn, Gardiner, McPhee, A. Weir

CELTIC: Beattie; Donnelly, Fallon; Smith, Evans, Peacock; Collins, Ryan, Byrne, Wilson, Mochan

Attendance: 16,000

January 18th
CELTIC (1) 1 — ABERDEEN (0) 1
Collins (28) — Ewen (84)

CELTIC: Beattie; Donnelly, Fallon; Smith, Evans, Peacock; Collins, Ryan, Byrne, Wilson, Auld

ABERDEEN: Morrison; Caldwell, J. Hogg; Brownlie, Clunie, Allister; Ewen, W. Hogg, Davidson, Wishart, Hather

Attendance: 20,000

January 25th
RAITH ROVERS (0) 1 — CELTIC (2) 2
Young (49) — Collins (2), Byrne (12)

The Celtic team which won the 1957/58 League Cup Final. Back row: Donnelly, Evans, Fallon, Beattie, McPhail, Fernie. Front row: McGrory (manager), Tully, Collins, Peacock, Wilson, Mochan

RAITH ROVERS: Thorburn; McGregor, Polland; Young, McNaught, Leigh; McEwan, Kelly, Copland, Williamson, Urquhart

CELTIC: Beattie; Donnelly, Fallon; Fernie, Evans, Peacock; Collins, Smith, Byrne, Wilson, Mochan

Attendance: 10,000

February 22nd
KILMARNOCK (0) 1 — CELTIC (1) 1
McBride (65) — Wilson (21)

KILMARNOCK: Brown; Collins, J. Stewart; Falls, Toner, Kennedy; Muir, Harvey, Wentzel, McBride, Black

CELTIC: Beattie; Donnelly, Fallon; Fernie, Evans, Peacock; Collins, Smith, McPhail, Wilson, Byrne

Attendance: 21,000

League positions

	P	W	D	L	F	A	Pts
1 Hearts	24	21	2	1	100	17	44
2 Rangers	19	13	3	3	54	29	29
3 Clyde	21	14	1	6	52	36	29
4 CELTIC	21	11	6	4	43	24	28
5 Hibernian	24	12	3	9	51	42	27

March 5th
CELTIC (0) 4 — EAST FIFE (0) 0
Byrne 3 (60, 71, 85), Collins (69)

CELTIC: Beattie; Donnelly, Fallon; Fernie, Evans, Peacock; Collins, Smith, Byrne, Wilson, Mochan

EAST FIFE: McCluskey; Adie, Cox; Neilson, Christie, Mochan; Bonthrone, Ingram, Gillon, Leishman, Matthew

Attendance: 4,000

March 8th
ST MIRREN (1) 1 — CELTIC (0) 1
Bryceland (29) — Collins (76 pen)

ST MIRREN: Lornie; Lapsley, McTurk; Neilson, Buchanan, Johnston; Bryceland, Ryan, Wilson, Gemmell, Miller

CELTIC: Beattie; Donnelly, Fallon; Fernie, Evans, Peacock; Collins, Smith, Byrne, Wilson, Tully

Attendance: 12,000

March 14th
HEARTS (2) 5 — CELTIC (1) 3
Crawford 2 (4, 46), Blackwood (7), Murray 2 (52, 77) — Byrne (31), Collins (56 pen), Smith (75)

HEARTS: Marshall; Kirk, Thomson; Mackay, Milne, Bowman; Blackwood, Murray, Young, Wardhaugh, Crawford

CELTIC: Beattie; Donnelly, Fallon; Fernie, Evans, Peacock; Collins, Smith, McPhail, Wilson, Byrne

Attendance: 30,000

Hearts ended Celtic's unbeaten away record in a display of brilliant football all the more commendable after injury to Mackay in 13 minutes. Celtic fought back from 1-4 to 3-4, the first team to score 3 goals against Hearts in the League this season, but after 77 minutes Murray widened the margin again.

March 19th
CELTIC (2) 4 — HIBERNIAN (0) 0
Wilson 3 (25, 43, 60), McPhail (67)

CELTIC: Beattie; Meechan, Fallon; Fernie, Evans, Peacock; McVittie, Collins, McPhail, Wilson, Byrne

HIBERNIAN: Leslie; Grant, MacFarlane; Turnbull, Paterson, Baxter; Frye, Thomson, Fraser, Preston, Ormond

Attendance: n.a.

March 22nd
CELTIC (2) 4 — AIRDRIE (1) 2
Byrne (28), Collins 3 (31, 53 pen, 55) — McGill (35), Ormond (62)

CELTIC: Beattie; Donnelly, Fallon; Fernie, Evans, Peacock; McVittie, Collins, McPhail, Wilson, Byrne

AIRDRIE: Wallace; Miller, Shanks; Price, Baillie, Quinn; Rankin, McGill, Caven, McMillan, Ormond

Attendance: 15,000

March 26th: Evans and Collins were in the Scottish League team beaten 4-1 by the English League at Newcastle.

March 29th
DUNDEE (2) 5 — CELTIC (2) 3
Sneddon (15), Bonthrone (18), Cousin (42), Curlett 2 (60, 79) — Collins (13 pen), McVittie (40), Wilson (85)

DUNDEE: Brown; Hamilton, Cox; Henderson, McKenzie, Cowie; Curlett, Bonthrone, Cousin, Sneddon, Christie

CELTIC: Beattie; Meechan, Mochan; Fernie, Evans, Peacock; Collins, McVittie, McPhail, Wilson, Byrne

Attendance: 5,000

April 5th
ABERDEEN (0) 0 — CELTIC (0) 1
Byrne (77)

ABERDEEN: Morrison; Walker, Hogg; Burns, Clunie, Glen; Leggat, Brownlie, Davidson, Wishart, Hather

CELTIC: Beattie; Meechan, Mochan; Smith, Evans, Peacock; Collins, McVittie, Byrne, Wilson, Fernie

Attendance: 12,000

April 7th
CELTIC (1) 5 — QUEENS PARK (1) 1
Wilson 2 (44, 47), McVittie (59), Byrne (66), Smith (70) — McEwan (10)

CELTIC: Beattie; Meechan, Mochan; Smith, Evans, Conroy; McVittie, Collins, Byrne, Wilson, Fernie

QUEENS PARK: F. Crampsey; I. Harnett, J. Kerr; R. Cromar, R. Drainer, D. Holt; C. Church, J. Robb, A. McEwan, R. McKinven, J. Lindsay

Attendance: 4,000. Holt was carried off

April 9th
CELTIC (3) 6 — CLYDE (2) 2
Fernie (17), McVittie (40), Wilson (44), McPhail (70), Collins 2 (80, 84) — Ring (6), Currie (39)

CELTIC: Beattie; Meechan, Mochan; Smith, Evans, Conroy; McVittie, Collins, McPhail, Wilson, Fernie

CLYDE: McCulloch; Murphy, Haddock; Walters, Finlay, Clinton; Herd, Currie, Coyle, Robertson, Ring

Attendance: n.a.

April 9th: Bertie Peacock was in the Ireland team which drew 0-0 with Wales in Belfast.

April 12th
PARTICK THISTLE (0) 0 — CELTIC (0) 1
Collins (72)

PARTICK THISTLE: Rennucci; Kerr, Baird; Mathers, Davidson, Donlevy; Anderson, Bell, Keenan, McParland, Ewing

CELTIC: Beattie; Meechan, Mochan; Smith, Evans, Peacock; McVittie, Collins, McPhail, Wilson, Fernie

Attendance: 26,000

April 16th
QUEEN OF THE SOUTH (3) 4 — CELTIC (1) 3
Patterson (8 pen), Ewing (16), Black (17), Rankin (56) — McPhail (4), Wilson 2 (61, 70)

QUEEN OF THE SOUTH: Smith; Sharpe, Binning; Whitehead, Elliot, Greenock; Black, Rankin, Patterson, Ewing, Tasker

CELTIC: Beattie; Meechan, Mochan; Smith, Jack, Conroy; McVittie, Collins, McPhail, Wilson, Fernie

Attendance: 7,000

April 19th: Bobby Evans was in the Scotland team beaten 4-0 by England at Hampden Park.

April 21st
CELTIC (2) 2 — MOTHERWELL (0) 2
Wilson 2 (1, 42) — W. Hunter 2 (48, 71)

CELTIC: Beattie; Meechan, Mochan; Smith, Evans, Peacock; Collins, Colrain, McPhail, Wilson, Fernie

MOTHERWELL: H. Weir, McSeveney, Holton; Aitken, Martis, McCann; J. Hunter, Quinn, St John, W. Hunter, A. Weir

Attendance: n.a.

April 30th
CELTIC (2) 4 — THIRD LANARK (1) 1
Peacock (15), Wilson 2 (19, 47), Collins (65 pen) — Allan (34)

CELTIC: Haffey; Meechan, Mochan; Smith, Evans, Peacock; Collins, Fernie, McPhail, Wilson, McVittie

THIRD LANARK: Ramage; Smith, Brown; Higgins, Lewis, Slingsby; W. Craig, R. Craig, Allan, Gray McInnes

Attendance: n.a.

Scottish First Division

	P	W	D	L	F	A	Pts
1 Hearts	34	29	4	1	132	29	62
2 Rangers	34	22	5	7	89	49	49
3 CELTIC	34	19	8	7	84	47	46
4 Clyde	34	18	6	10	84	61	42
5 Kilmarnock	34	14	9	11	60	55	37
6 Partick Thistle	34	17	3	14	69	71	37
7 Raith Rovers	34	14	7	13	66	56	35
8 Motherwell	34	12	8	14	68	67	32
9 Hibernian	34	13	5	16	59	60	31
10 Falkirk	34	11	9	14	64	82	31
11 Dundee	34	13	5	16	49	65	31
12 Aberdeen	34	14	2	18	68	76	30
13 St Mirren	34	11	8	15	59	66	30
14 Third Lanark	34	13	4	17	69	88	30
15 Queen of the South	34	12	7	17	61	72	29
16 Airdrie	34	13	2	19	71	92	28
17 East Fife	34	10	3	21	45	88	23
18 Queens Park	34	4	1	29	41	114	9

April 30th: Celtic freed Bonnar, Goldie, White and Haughney.

May 7th: Evans and Collins were in the Scotland team which drew 1-1 with Hungary at Hampden Park.

June 1st: Evans and Collins were in the Scotland team which beat Poland 2-1 in Warsaw. Collins scored both Scotland goals.

June 8th: Evans and Collins were in the Scotland team which drew 1-1 with Yugoslavia in a World Cup match in Vasteraas, Sweden.

June 11th: Evans, Collins and Fernie were in the Scotland team beaten 3-2 by Paraguay in a World Cup match in Norrkoping, Sweden. Collins scored one of the goals.

June 15th: Evans and Collins were in the Scotland team beaten 2-1 by France in the World Cup match in Orebro, Sweden.

Bertie Peacock played 4 times for Ireland in the World Cup Finals in Sweden.

LEAGUE CUP

August 10th
CELTIC (0) 3 AIRDRIE (0) 2
McPhail (54), Mochan (76), Peacock (82) Caven (56), Rankin (62)

CELTIC: Beattie; Meechan, Fallon; Fernie, Evans, Peacock; Tully, Collins, McPhail, Smith, Mochan

AIRDRIE: Walker; Quigley, Shanks; Price, Baillie, Quinn; Rankin, Welsh, Caven, Duncan, McLean

Attendance: 38,000

August 14th
EAST FIFE (1) 1 CELTIC (1) 4
Bonthrone (40 pen) McPhail 3 (36, 79, 84), Collins (42)

EAST FIFE: McQueen; Wilkie, Stewart; Christie, Bowie, Cox; Ingram, Leishman, Duchart, Bonthrone, Matthew

CELTIC: Beattie; Meechan, Fallon; Wilson, Evans, Peacock; Tully, Collins, McPhail, Sharkey, Mochan

Attendance: n.a.

August 17th
HIBERNIAN (2) 3 CELTIC (1) 1
Ormond (5), Meechan o.g. (12), Fraser (88) Collins (18)

HIBERNIAN: Leslie; Muir, Boyle; Nicol, Plenderleith, Preston; Smith, Marshall, Fraser, Harrower, Ormond

CELTIC: Beattie; Meechan, Fallon; Fernie, Evans, Peacock; Tully, Collins, McPhail, Sharkey, Mochan

Attendance: 35,000

August 24th
AIRDRIE (1) 1 CELTIC (1) 2
Caven (20) Smith (45), Fernie (72)

AIRDRIE: Walker; Kilmarnock, Shanks; Price, Quigley, Quinn; Rankin, Welsh, Caven, Duncan, McLean

CELTIC: Beattie; Donnelly, Fallon; Fernie, Evans, Peacock; Tully, Collins, McPhail, Smith, Auld

Attendance: 16,000

August 28th
CELTIC (3) 6 EAST FIFE (1) 1
McPhail 2 (3, 25), Wilson 2 (52, 72), Auld (32), Collins (61) Matthew (29)

CELTIC: Beattie; Donnelly, Fallon; Fernie, Evans, Peacock; Tully, Collins, McPhail, Wilson, Auld

EAST FIFE: McCluskey; S. Stewart, Cox; Neilson, Christie, Bonthrone; Ingram, Leishman, Birse, Duchart, Matthew

Attendance: 18,000

August 31st
CELTIC (0) 2 HIBERNIAN (0) 0
Wilson (47), McPhail (58)

CELTIC: Beattie; Donnelly, Fallon; Fernie, Evans, Peacock; Tully, Collins, McPhail, Wilson, Auld

HIBERNIAN: Leslie; MacFarlane, Boyle; Nicol, Grant, Preston; Smith, Turnbull, Fraser, Harrower, Ormond

Attendance: 50,000

SECTION TABLE

	P	W	D	L	F	A	Pts
CELTIC	6	5	0	1	18	8	10
Hibernian	6	3	1	2	15	10	7
Airdrie	6	3	0	3	20	13	6
East Fife	6	0	1	5	6	28	1

Qualifier: CELTIC

Quarter-Final First Leg September 11th
CELTIC (4) 6 THIRD LANARK (0) 1
McPhail 2 (21, 38), Collins 2 (12, 67), Wilson (28), Auld (82) Craig (68)

CELTIC: Beattie; Donnelly, Fallon; Fernie, Evans, Peacock; Tully, Collins, McPhail, Wilson, Auld

THIRD LANARK: Robertson; Smith, Brown; Kelly, Lewis, Slingsby; W. Craig, R. Craig, Allan, Cunningham, McInnes

Attendance: 20,000

Quarter-Final Second Leg September 14th
THIRD LANARK (0) 0 CELTIC (1) 3
Collins (30), McPhail (56), Wilson (73)

THIRD LANARK: Robertson; Smith, Brown; Kelly, Lewis, Slingsby; W. Craig, R. Craig, Catterson, Callaghan, McInnes

CELTIC: Beattie; Donnelly, Fallon; Fernie, Evans, Peacock; Tully, Collins, McPhail, Wilson, Auld

Attendance: 20,000. Celtic won 9-1 on aggregate

Semi Final September 28th at Ibrox Park
CELTIC (2) 4 CLYDE (1) 2
Wilson (12), McPhail (41), Collins (55), Fernie (58) Robertson (44), Innes (50)

CELTIC: Beattie; Donnelly, Fallon; Fernie, Evans, Peacock; Smith, Collins, McPhail, Wilson, Auld

CLYDE: McCulloch; Murphy, Weir; Walters, Finlay, Haddock; Herd, Robertson, Keogh, Innes, Ring

Attendance: 42,000

Clyde were doubly unfortunate. A few hours before their most important match of the season they learned that three of their players – Watson, Clinton and Currie – had contracted influenza and they were forced to make several changes in their team. On the field itself they had the misfortune to meet Collins in his most irrepressible mood. He was one of the schemers in 3 of Celtic's 4 goals and he scored one himself with a shot which had not been rivalled for spectacle at Ibrox in years. Clyde, although beaten, were by no means disgraced by the result.

Final October 19th at Hampden Park
CELTIC (2) 7 RANGERS (0) 1
Wilson (23), McPhail 3 (53, 69, 81), Mochan 2 (44, 74), Fernie (90 pen) — Simpson (59)

CELTIC: Beattie; Donnelly, Fallon; Fernie, Evans, Peacock; Tully, Collins, McPhail, Wilson, Mochan

RANGERS: Niven; Shearer, Caldow; McColl, Valentine, Davis; Scott, Simpson, Murray, Baird, Hubbard

Attendance: 82,293. *Referee:* J.A. Mowat (Rutherglen)

Celtic proved conclusively the value of concentration on discipline and on the arts and crafts of the game to the exclusion of so-called power play. Not since the brilliant Coronation Cup days at Hampden had Celtic played football of such quality. Valentine, not so long before a commanding figure on this same ground, was a forlorn, bewitched centre-half, repeatedly beaten in the air and on the ground in a variety of ways. In the first 20 minutes Celtic might have scored at least 4 goals. First Collins and then Tully hit the wood around Niven. They opened the scoring in 23 minutes when McPhail headed down to Wilson and the inside-right, without waiting for the ball to touch the ground, bulged the net from 12 yards. Next the crossbar stopped another 30-yard free-kick by Collins. Mochan scored a 2nd in the 2nd last minute of the first half. McPhail, after engaging in a heading movement with Wilson, lofted the ball over Shearer to the galloping outside-left. Mochan cut in and from the near touchline hurtled his shot into the far corner of the net. Rangers started the second half with Murray, a knee bandaged, at outside-left. In the 53rd minute McPhail made it 3-0 when he headed in a Collins cross. 5 minutes later Simpson, with an exhilarating dive and header, scored from McColl's cross. In the final 21 minutes McPhail (now toying with Valentine), Mochan, McPhail again and Fernie from a penalty-kick completed the humiliation.

SCOTTISH CUP

First Round February 1st
AIRDRIE (0) 3 CELTIC (3) 4
McGill 2 (50, 65), McMillan (81 pen) — Collins (8), Fernie (12), Byrne 2 (36, 48)

AIRDRIE: Goldie; Kilmarnock, Shanks; Price, Baillie, Quinn; McMillan, McGill, Caven, Rankin, Ormond

CELTIC: Beattie; Donnelly, Fallon; Fernie, Evans, Peacock; Collins, Smith, Byrne, Wilson, Mochan

Attendance: 26,000

Second Round February 15th
CELTIC (3) 7 STIRLING ALBION (1) 2
Smith 2 (10, 33), Mochan (39), Wilson 2 (61), 81), Byrne (85, 88) — Ryce (5), Grant (58)

CELTIC: Beattie; Donnelly, Fallon; Fernie, Evans, Peacock; Collins, Smith, Byrne, Wilson, Mochan

STIRLING ALBION: Smith; Gibson, Beacham; McKechnie, Menzies, Pierson; Grant, Ryce, Benvie, Spence, Rodger

Attendance: 30,200

Third Round March 1st
CELTIC (0) 0 CLYDE (2) 2
Ring (10), Currie (25)

CELTIC: Beattie; Donnelly, Fallon; Smith, Evans, Peacock; Collins, Fernie, Byrne, Wilson, Mochan

CLYDE: McCulloch; Murphy, Haddock; Walters, Finlay, Clinton; Herd, Currie, Coyle, Robertson, Ring

Attendance: 65,000

Appearances	League	League Cup	Scottish Cup
Beattie	33	10	3
Donnelly	19	7	3
Fallon	26	10	3
Fernie	27	9	3
Evans	33	10	3
Peacock	31	10	3
Tully	10	9	–
Collins	30	10	3
Conway	3	–	–
Wilson	33	7	3
Auld	2	6	–
Sharkey	1	2	–
McPhail	20	10	–
Smith	23	3	3
Mochan	26	4	3
Goldie	2	–	–
Divers	1	–	–
Jackson	1	–	–
Jack	2	–	–
Kennedy	4	–	–
Ryan	6	–	–
McVittie	11	–	–
Colrain	4	–	–
Byrne	13	–	3
Meechan	9	3	–
Conroy	3	–	–
Haffey	1	–	–

GOALSCORERS:

League: Wilson 23, Collins 19 (6 pens), Byrne 9, McPhail 9, Mochan 7, Smith 4, McVittie 4, Fernie 2, Peacock 2, Own Goals 2, Divers 1, Conway 1, Colrain 1

League Cup: McPhail 14, Wilson 7, Collins 7, Mochan 3, Fernie 3 (1 pen), Auld 2, Smith 1, Peacock 1

Scottish Cup: Byrne 4, Smith 2, Wilson 2, Collins 1, Fernie 1, Mochan 1

Season 1958-59

Celtic dropped to 6th place in the League Table. They lost only 2 home matches but their away form was very poor and they recorded only 3 wins in their 17 matches. They only managed to complete the double over two teams – Kilmarnock and Stirling Albion. The team selections were again very erratic. 21 different players were used in only the first 8 matches. McNeill, Crerand and Chalmers all made their League debuts during the season. Another debutant, Duncan McKay, ended his first season by playing for Scotland against England at Wembley and going on his country's European Tour together wtih colleagues Evans, Smith and Auld. Bobby Collins and Willie Fernie were both transferred to English clubs early in the season. Neil Mochan made 33 League appearances and John Colrain finished as top scorer with 14 of the club's 70 goals. John Higgins was forced, through injury, to give up the game and Charlie Tully announced his retirement at the end of the season – he later took over as player-manager of Cork Hibs.

Celtic topped a League Cup Section which included Clyde, St Mirren and Airdrie. They ran up 10 goals in their two Quarter-Final matches with Cowdenbeath but were shocked by Partick Thistle in the Semi-Final at Ibrox despite the Firhill team losing their goalkeeper, Ledgerwood, 4 minutes after half-time.

They reached the Semi-Final of the Scottish Cup after beating Albion Rovers, Clyde – thanks to a goal by Peacock in extra time in a replay at Shawfield – Rangers and Stirling Albion. However, they were thoroughly beaten by a rampant St Mirren who went on to lift the trophy, beating Aberdeen 3-1 in the Final.

League:	Sixth
League Cup:	Semi-Finalists
Scottish Cup:	Semi-Finalists

SCOTTISH FIRST DIVISION

August 18th: John Bonnar joined Dumbarton on a free transfer.

August 20th
CLYDE (0) 2 — CELTIC (0) 1
Coyle (85), Currie (86) — Auld (60)

CLYDE: McCulloch; Murphy, Haddock; Walters, Finlay, White; Herd, Currie, Coyle, Robertson, Ring

CELTIC: Beattie; McKay, Mochan; Fernie, Evans, Peacock; Tully, Collins, Byrne, Wilson, Auld

Attendance: n.a. Evans was off the field, injured, for 65 minutes.

August 28th: Billy McPhail gave up the game through injury.

September 3rd: Bobby Collins was in the Scottish League team which beat the Irish League 5-0 in Belfast. He scored one of the goals.

September 6th
CELTIC (1) 2 — RANGERS (1) 2
Collins (28), Smith (63) — Hubbard (41 pen), Brand (76)

CELTIC: Beattie; McKay, Mochan; Fernie, McNeill, Peacock; Smith, Tully, Conway, Collins, Auld

RANGERS: Niven; Shearer, Caldow; McColl, Telfer, Davis; Scott, Brand, Murray, Wilson, Hubbard

Attendance: 50,000

Celtic fans were unhappy at the penalty-kick awarded to Rangers in the 41st minute. McNeill appeared to slide in a foot from just the rear of Wilson and prod the ball away just as the inside-left drew back his foot to shoot, and Brand seemed to throw himself towards Beattie as the goalkeeper bent to pick up the ball. Hubbard converted the penalty. 27 minutes from time Scott fouled Mochan, the free-kick reached Conway, and he transferred it to Smith who warded off Telfer's attempted tackle to run in and beat the advancing Niven. Brand made the score 2-2 thirteen minutes later.

Collins had opened the scoring for Celtic in the 28th minute.

September 12th: Bobby Collins joined Everton for £25,000.

September 13th
KILMARNOCK (1) 1 — McBride (28)
CELTIC (2) 4 — Smith (10), Colrain 2 (20, 83), Auld (89 pen)

KILMARNOCK: J. Brown; Collins, Watson; Kennedy, Toner, Mackay; H. Brown, Henaughan, McBride, Black, Muir

CELTIC: Beattie; McKay, Mochan; Fernie, McNeill, Peacock; Smith, Tully, Colrain, Wilson, Auld

Attendance: 20,000

September 20th
CELTIC (1) 3 — Fernie 2 (13, 68), Smith (64)
RAITH ROVERS (1) 1 — McEwan (23)

CELTIC: Beattie; McKay, Mochan; Smith, Jack, Peacock; Tully, Fernie, Colrain, Wilson, Auld

RAITH ROVERS: Thorburn; McGregor, Polland; Leigh, McNaught, Baxter; McEwan, Kerray, Dobbie, Wallace, Urquhart

Attendance: 30,000

September 27th
ABERDEEN (2) 3 — Glen (8), Little (11), Mulhall (55)
CELTIC (0) 1 — Peacock (82)

ABERDEEN: Morrison; Clydesdale, Hogg; Burns, Clunie, Glen; Ewen, Little, Davidson, Wishart, Mulhall

CELTIC: Beattie; McKay, Mochan; Smith, McNeill, Peacock; Tully, Fernie, Colrain, Wilson, Auld

Attendance: 20,000

October 4th
CELTIC (1) 3 — Divers (17), Conway (57), Auld (86)
QUEEN OF THE SOUTH (1) 1 — McGill (20)

CELTIC: Beattie; Donnelly, Mochan; Crerand, McNeill, Smith; Colrain, Fernie, Conway, Divers, Auld

QUEEN OF THE SOUTH: Gebbie; Sharpe, Smith; Knox, Elliot, Greenock; McGill, Black, Patterson, Garrett, King

Attendance: 20,000

October 4th: Bertie Peacock was in the Ireland team which drew 3-3 with England in Belfast.

October 9th: Fernie and Auld were in the Scottish League team which drew 1-1 with the English League at Ibrox Park.

October 11th
CELTIC (3) 3 — Divers 2 (1, 39), Fernie (25)
FALKIRK (2) 4 — White (9), Wright (33), McCulloch (77), Moran (90)

CELTIC: Beattie; Donnelly, Mochan; Crerand, McNeill, Smith; Colrain, Fernie, Conway, Divers, Auld

FALKIRK: Slater; Richmond, Hunter; Wright, Prentice, Price; McCulloch, White, Grierson, Moran, Lachlan

Attendance: 23,000

October 16th: Charlie Tully was in the Ireland team beaten 6-2 by Spain in Madrid.

October 18th
AIRDRIE (0) 1 — McNeill o.g. (66)
CELTIC (2) 4 — Fernie (6), Byrne (41), Smith (65), Divers (84)

AIRDRIE: Wallace; Neil, Miller; Quinn, Baillie, Johnstone; Sharkey, McGill, Black, Rankin, Ormond

CELTIC: Beattie; McKay, Mochan; Fernie, McNeill, Smith; Higgins, Jackson, Byrne, Divers, Auld

Attendance: 16,000

October 25th
CELTIC (2) 3 — Wilson (26 pen), Mochan (32), Auld (53 pen)
THIRD LANARK (1) 1 — Allan (2)

CELTIC: Beattie; McKay, Mochan; Fernie, McNeill, Smith; Higgins, Jackson, Byrne, Wilson, Auld

THIRD LANARK: Ramage; Smith, Brown; Kelly, Cosker, Slingsby; W. Craig, R. Craig, Allan, Dick, Christie

Attendance: 20,000

League positions

	P	W	D	L	F	A	Pts
1 Hearts	8	6	2	0	30	13	14
2 Motherwell	9	5	3	1	27	12	13
3 Aberdeen	9	6	0	3	24	9	12
4 Airdrie	9	6	0	3	21	19	12
5 CELTIC	9	5	1	3	24	16	11

November 1st
DUNDEE (1) 1 — McNeill o.g. (28)
CELTIC (0) 1 — Higgins (63)

DUNDEE: Brown; Reid, Cox; Henderson, Gabriel, Cowie; McGeachie, Cousin, Curlett, Sneddon, Robertson

CELTIC: Beattie; McKay, Mochan; Fernie, McNeill, Peacock; Higgins, Jackson, Conway, Wilson, Auld

Attendance: 22,500

November 5th: Bertie Peacock was in the Ireland team which drew 2-2 with Scotland at Hampden Park.

November 8th
DUNFERMLINE (0) 1 — CELTIC (0) 0
Rattray (60)

DUNFERMLINE: Connachan; Duthie, Sweeney; Higgins, Colville, Rattray; Peebles, Dickson, Watson, Napier, Melrose

CELTIC: Beattie; McKay, Mochan; Fernie, McNeill, Peacock; Higgins, Jackson, Conway, McVittie, Auld

Attendance: 16,500

November 15th
CELTIC (1) 3 — ST MIRREN (3) 3
Auld 2 (28, 78 pen), McGugan o.g. (46) — Lapsley (15), Campbell (18), Laird (39)

CELTIC: Beattie; McKay, Mochan; Fernie, McNeill, Peacock; Higgins, Jackson, Conway, McVittie, Auld

ST MIRREN: Forsyth; Lapsley, Wilson; Boonan, McGugan, Gregal; Flynn, Bryceland, Ryan, Laird, Campbell

Attendance: 17,000

November 22nd
PARTICK THISTLE (0) 2 — CELTIC (0) 0
Smith (55), Kerr (70)

PARTICK THISTLE: Freebairn; Hogan, Baird; Mathers, Davidson, Donlevy; McKenzie, Smith, Kerr, Wilson, McParland

CELTIC: Beattie; McKay, Mochan; Fernie, McNeill, Peacock; McVittie, Jackson, Conway, Colrain, Auld

Attendance: 24,794

November 29th
HIBERNIAN (2) 3 — CELTIC (2) 2
Baker 3 (12, 40, 74) — Colrain (5), Higgins (6)

HIBERNIAN: Leslie; Young, McLelland; Nicol, Plenderleith, Preston; Smith, Fox, Baker, Gibson, Ormond

CELTIC: Beattie; McKay, Mochan; Crerand, McNeill, Peacock; Higgins, McVittie, Conway, Colrain, Auld

Attendance: 22,000

December 1st: Willie Fernie was transferred to Middlesbrough for £17,500.

December 6th
CELTIC (2) 2 — MOTHERWELL (0) 0
Auld (20), Divers (29)

Match abandoned after 83 minutes due to fog. It was replayed on January 2nd.

CELTIC: Beattie; McKay, Mochan; Smith, Evans, Peacock; McVittie, Jackson, Colrain, Divers, Auld

MOTHERWELL: H. Weir; McSeveney, Holton; Aitken, Martis, McCann; A. Weir, W. Reid, St John, Quinn, Hunter

Attendance: 26,000

December 13th
CELTIC (4) 7 — STIRLING ALBION (0) 3
Colrain 3 (13, 52, 70), Divers 2 (25, 44), Jackson (33), McVittie (55) — Gilmour 2 (63, 65), Spence (83)

CELTIC: Beattie; McKay, Mochan; Smith, Evans, Peacock; McVittie, Jackson, Colrain, Divers, Auld

STIRLING ALBION: Smith; Gibson, Pettigrew; McKechnie, Menzies, Pierson; Ryce, Benvie, Gilmour, Spence, McPhee

Attendance: 13,000

December 10th: Duncan McKay was in the Scotland Under-23 team beaten 1-0 by Wales.

December 20th
HEARTS (1) 1 — CELTIC (0) 1
Blackwood (21) — Higgins (59)

HEARTS: Brown; Kirk, Thomson; Bowman, Milne, Cumming; Paton, Murray, Bauld, Blackwood, Hamilton

CELTIC: Beattie; McKay, Mochan; Smith, Evans, Peacock; Higgins, Jackson, Colrain, Divers, McVittie

Attendance: 25,000

December 27th (1) 3 — CLYDE (1) 1
McVittie (8), Colrain 2 (54, 72) — Coyle (7)

CELTIC: Beattie; McKay, Mochan; Smith, Evans, Peacock; McVittie, Jackson, Colrain, Divers, Auld

CLYDE: McCulloch; Murphy, Haddock; Walters, Finlay, Clinton; Herd, Currie, Coyle, Robertson, Ring

Attendance: 20,000

League positions

	P	W	D	L	F	A	Pts
1 Rangers	18	11	5	2	59	29	27
2 Airdrie	18	12	2	4	40	28	26
3 Hearts	18	10	5	3	58	31	25
4 Motherwell	17	9	6	2	50	25	24
5 Dundee	18	9	5	4	36	28	23
6 CELTIC	17	7	4	6	41	31	18

January 1st
RANGERS (1) 2 — CELTIC (1) 1
Matthew (19), Caldow (63 pen) — Peacock (15)

RANGERS: Niven; Shearer, Caldow; McColl, Telfer, Stevenson; Scott, McMillan, Murray, Brand, Matthew

CELTIC: Beattie; McKay, Mochan; Smith, Evans, Peacock; McVittie, Jackson, Colrain, Divers, Auld

Attendance: 55,000

Peacock began the scoring in 15 minutes with a low shot which was deflected by Telfer past Niven. 4 minutes later Rangers equalised through Matthew after Beattie had saved from the outside-left. Caldow shot the home team ahead from the penalty-spot after Mochan armed away a shot from Scott with no apparent danger to

Beattie. 10 minutes from time it was touch and go whether the referee would abandon the match as a dreadful gale was sweeping over a pitch which had long since become a quagmire. Celtic made tremendous efforts to neutralise Rangers' 2-1 lead. 5 minutes from time they were awarded a penalty. Auld had to search for the penalty spot in the morass but his shot struck the crossbar and was cleared.

January 2nd
CELTIC (2) 3 — MOTHERWELL (0) 3
Divers 2 (10, 42), Colrain (68) — Quinn 2 (56 pen, 90) St John (80)

CELTIC: Beattie; McKay, Kennedy; Smith, Evans, Peacock; Higgins, Jackson, Colrain, Divers, Auld

MOTHERWELL: Weir; McSeveney, McCallum; Stenhouse, Martis, McCann; S. Reid, Forrest, St John, Quinn, A. Weir

Attendance: 36,000

January 21st
CELTIC (0) 2 — KILMARNOCK (0) 0
Peacock (47), Dougan o.g. (89)

CELTIC: Haffey; McKay, Mochan; Smith, Evans, Peacock; Higgins, Jackson, Colrain, Divers, Auld

KILMARNOCK: Brown; Toner, Watson; Beattie, Dougan, Stewart; Mays, Wentzel, McBride, Black, Grant

Attendance: 9,000

January 24th
QUEEN OF THE SOUTH (1) 2 — CELTIC (1) 2
Garrett (34), King (47) — Auld (16), Colrain (65)

QUEEN OF THE SOUTH: W. Smith; Sharpe, Greenock; Patterson, A. Smith, O'Hara; Oakes, Knox, Garrett, Ewing, King

CELTIC: Haffey; McKay, Mochan; McNeill, Evans, Smith; Slater, Jackson, Colrain, Divers, Auld

Attendance: 7,500

February 7th
FALKIRK (2) 3 — CELTIC (1) 2
McCulloch (21), Moran (32), Murray (54) — Colrain (12), Divers (70)

FALKIRK: Slater; Thomson, Hunter; McCormack, Richmond, Prentice; Murray, Wright, White, Moran, McCulloch

CELTIC: Haffey; McKay, Mochan; Smith, Evans, Peacock; Slater, Wilson, Colrain, Divers, Auld

Attendance: 11,500

February 21st
THIRD LANARK (1) 1 — CELTIC (0) 1
R. Craig (12) — McVittie (80)

THIRD LANARK: Ramage; Caldwell, Brown; Kelly, McCallum, Robb; R. Craig, Goodfellow, Dick, Gray, Christie

CELTIC: Haffey; McKay, Mochan; Smith, Evans, Peacock; Wilson, Jackson, Colrain, Divers, McVittie

Attendance: 18,000

League positions

	P	W	D	L	F	A	Pts
1 Rangers	26	17	6	3	75	37	40
2 Motherwell	26	13	8	5	67	43	34
3 Hearts	25	14	5	6	71	43	33
4 Airdrie	26	14	2	10	53	50	30
5 Partick Thistle	26	13	4	9	47	38	30
10 CELTIC	23	8	7	8	52	42	23

March 4th
CELTIC (0) 1 — DUNDEE (1) 1
Mochan (48 pen) — Bonthrone (17)

CELTIC: Haffey; McKay, Mochan; Smith, Evans, Crerand; Higgins, Jackson, Lochead, Wilson, Divers

DUNDEE: Brown; Hamilton, Cox; Henderson, Gabriel, Curlett; McGeachie, Bonthrone, Cousin, Sneddon, Robertson

Attendance: 9,000

March 7th
CELTIC (1) 3 — DUNFERMLINE (0) 1
Mochan (18 pen), Jackson 2 (79, 88) — Duthie (81 pen)

CELTIC: Haffey; McKay, Mochan; Smith, Evans, McNeill; Colrain, Jackson, Lochead, Wilson, Divers

DUNFERMLINE: Connachan; Duthie, Sweeney; Williamson, Colville, Rattray; Peebles, Logan, Dickson, Smith, Melrose

Attendance: 14,000

March 10th
CELTIC (1) 1 — AIRDRIE (1) 2
Colrain (34) — McGill (25), Black (61)

CELTIC: Haffey; McKay, Mochan; Smith, Evans, Peacock; McVittie, Chalmers, Colrain, Wilson, Auld

AIRDRIE: Wallace; Miller, Johnstone; Quinn, Neil, Stewart; Sharkey, McGill, Black, Storrie, Ormond

Attendance: 4,000

March 11th: A Rangers/Celtic select beat Inverness Caledonian 4-2 in a floodlit friendly in Inverness. Jim Conway scored one of the goals.

March 18th
ST MIRREN (1) 1 — CELTIC (0) 0
Miller (30)

ST MIRREN: Walker; Lapsley, Wilson; Neilson, McGugan, Leishman; Rodger, Laird, Baker, Gemmell, Miller

CELTIC: Haffey; McKay, Mochan; Smith, Evans, Peacock; McVittie, Jackson, Byrne, Wilson, Divers

Attendance: n.a.

March 21st
CELTIC (1) 2 PARTICK THISTLE (0) 0
Slater (27), Colrain (49)

CELTIC: Haffey; McKay, Mochan; Smith, Evans, Peacock; Slater, Colrain, Lochead, Wilson, Divers

PARTICK THISTLE: Ledgerwood; Hogan, Baird; McParland, Kennedy, Brown; McKenzie, Thomson, Kerr, Wilson, Fleming

Attendance: 15,000

March 25th
CELTIC (1) 4 ABERDEEN (0) 0
Lochead (28), Mochan (59 pen), Colrain (61), McVittie (64)

CELTIC: Haffey; McKay, Mochan; McNeill, Evans, Peacock; McVittie, Colrain, Lochead, Divers, Auld

ABERDEEN: Ogston; Walker, Hogg; Caldwell, Gibson, Glen; Ewen, Little, Baird, Wishart, Paterson

Attendance: 6,000

March 28th
CELTIC (0) 3 HIBERNIAN (0) 0
Wilson 2 (55, 57), Lochead (66)

CELTIC: Beattie; McKay, Mochan; Smith, Evans, Peacock; McVittie, Colrain, Lochead, Wilson, Divers

HIBERNIAN: Wren; Grant, McLelland; Turnbull, Paterson, Nicol; Fraser, Aitken, Fox, Gibson, Ormond

Attendance: 18,000

April 6th
RAITH ROVERS (1) 3 CELTIC (0) 1
Conn (17), McFarlane (70), Urquhart (73) Mochan (71 pen)

RAITH ROVERS: Drummond; Polland, MacFarlane; Young, McNaught, Baxter; McEwan, Conn, Kerray, Urquhart, Gardiner

CELTIC: Haffey; McKay, Mochan; Smith, Evans, Peacock; McVittie, Colrain, Lochead, Divers, Auld

Attendance: 8,000

April 11th
STIRLING ALBION (0) 0 CELTIC (1) 1
McVittie (43)

STIRLING ALBION: Stewart; Hailstones, Pettigrew; Bell, Sinclair, Pierson; Benvie, Simpson, Gilmour, Spence, Callan

CELTIC: Haffey; Donnelly, Mochan; Smith, McNeill, Peacock; Slater, McVittie, Lochead, Colrain, Auld

Attendance: 7,500

April 11th: McKay and Evans were in the Scotland team beaten 1-0 by England at Wembley.

April 8th
MOTHERWELL (2) 2 CELTIC (0) 0
S. Reid., A. Weir

MOTHERWELL: H. Weir; McSeveney, Forrest; Aitken, Martis, McCann; Hunter, S. Reid, St John, Quinn, A. Weir

CELTIC: Haffey; Kurila, Mochan; Smith, McNeill, Peacock; McVittie, Colrain, Conway, Divers, Auld

Attendance: n.a.

April 18th
CELTIC (0) 2 HEARTS (1) 1
Auld (53), Smith (67) Rankin (25)

CELTIC: Haffey; Donnelly, Mochan; McKay, Evans, Peacock; Smith, McVittie, Byrne, Colrain, Auld

HEARTS: Marshall; McIntosh, Lough; Thomson, Milne, Cumming; Blackwood, Murray, Young, Rankin, Hamilton

Attendance: 19,500

Scottish First Division

	P	W	D	L	F	A	Pts
1 Rangers	34	21	8	5	92	51	50
2 Hearts	34	21	6	7	92	51	48
3 Motherwell	34	18	8	8	83	50	44
4 Dundee	34	16	9	9	61	51	41
5 Airdrie	34	15	7	12	64	62	37
6 CELTIC	34	14	8	12	70	53	36
7 St Mirren	34	14	7	13	71	74	35
8 Kilmarnock	34	13	8	13	58	51	34
9 Partick Thistle	34	14	6	14	59	66	34
10 Hibernian	34	13	6	15	68	70	32
11 Third Lanark	34	11	10	13	74	83	32
12 Stirling Albion	34	11	8	15	54	64	30
13 Aberdeen	34	12	5	17	63	66	29
14 Raith Rovers	34	10	9	15	60	70	29
15 Clyde	34	12	4	18	62	66	28
16 Dunfermline	34	10	8	16	68	87	28
17 Falkirk	34	10	7	17	58	79	27
18 Queen of the South	34	6	6	22	38	101	18

April 22nd: Bertie Peacock scored one of Ireland's goals in a 4-1 win over Wales in Belfast.

April 27th: McKay, Evans, Smith and Auld were in the Scotland European Tour party.

April 30th: Celtic freed Higgins, Meechan, Jack and Colquhoun. Higgins had to give up the game through injury. Charlie Tully announced his retirement.

May 6th: Bobby Evans and Duncan McKay were in the Scotland team which beat Germany 3-2 at Hampden Park.

May 27th: McKay, Evans, Smith and Auld were in the Scotland team which beat Holland 2-1 in Amsterdam. Bertie Auld was ordered off.

June 3rd: McKay, Smith, Evans and Auld were in the Scotland team beaten 1-0 by Portugal in Lisbon.

LEAGUE CUP

August 9th
CLYDE (1) 1 — CELTIC (2) 4
Ring (26) — Tully (29), Collins (39), Wilson (49), Auld (61)

CLYDE: McCulloch; Murphy, Haddock; White, Finlay, Clinton; Herd, Currie, Coyle, Robertson, Ring

CELTIC: Beattie; McKay, Mochan; Fernie, Evans, Peacock; Tully, Collins, Conway, Wilson, Auld

Attendance: 26,500

August 13th
CELTIC (3) 3 — AIRDRIE (2) 3
Auld (17), Conway (29), Collins (30) — Rankin (26), Storrie (40), McGill (71)

CELTIC: Beattie; McKay, Kennedy; Fernie, Evans, Peacock; Tully, Collins, Conway, Wilson, Auld

AIRDRIE: Wallace; Miller, Shanks; Quinn, Baillie, Johnstone; Rankin, McGill, Sharkey, Storrie, G. Ormond

Attendance: n.a.

August 16th
CELTIC (1) 3 — ST MIRREN (0) 0
Collins (39), Conway (59), Tully (64)

CELTIC: Beattie; McKay, Mochan; Fernie, Evans, Peacock; Tully, Collins, Conway, Wilson, Auld

ST MIRREN: Forsyth; Lapsley, McTurk; Neilson, McGugan, Gregal; Bryceland, Ryan, Wilson, Gemmell, Miller

Attendance: n.a.

August 23rd
CELTIC (2) 2 — CLYDE (0) 0
Wilson (4), Auld (35)

CELTIC: Haffey; McKay, Mochan; Fernie, McNeill, Peacock; Tully, Collins, Conway, Wilson, Auld

CLYDE: McCulloch; Murphy, Haddock; Walters, Finlay, White; Herd, Currie, Coyle, Robertson, Ring

Attendance: 39,000. Billy McNeill made his debut

August 27th
AIRDRIE (0) 1 — CELTIC (2) 2
McGill (72) — Peacock (26), Conway (38)

AIRDRIE: Wallace; Miller, Shanks; Rankin, Baillie, Johnstone; Blair, McGill, Black, Welsh, G. Ormond

CELTIC: Haffey; McKay, Mochan; Fernie, McNeill, Peacock; Tully, Collins, Conway, Wilson, Auld

Attendance: 15,000

August 30th
ST MIRREN (3) 6 — CELTIC (2) 3
Bryceland 3 (34, 70, 78), Gemmell (40), Lapsley (43), Neilson (64) — Collins 2 (7 pen, 87 pen), Auld (25)

ST MIRREN: Forsyth; Lapsley, McTurk; Neilson, McGugan, Thomson; Ryan, Bryceland, Wilson, Gemmell, Miller

CELTIC: Haffey; McKay, Mochan; Fernie, McNeill, Peacock; Tully, Collins, Conway, Wilson, Auld

Attendance: 20,000

SECTION TABLE

	P	W	D	L	F	A	Pts
CELTIC	6	4	1	1	17	11	9
Clyde	6	4	0	2	15	11	8
St Mirren	6	3	0	3	15	19	6
Airdrie	6	0	1	5	12	18	1

Qualifier: CELTIC

Quarter-Final First Leg September 10th
CELTIC (1) 2 — COWDENBEATH (0) 0
Collins (31), Auld (67)

CELTIC: Beattie; McKay, Mochan; Fernie, McNeill, Peacock; Smith, Tully, Jackson, Collins, Auld

COWDENBEATH: Dorman; Lindsay, R. Campbell; Clark, Ross, Murphy; Millar, McWilliams, Craig, Gilfillan, G. Campbell

Attendance: n.a.

Quarter-Final Second Leg September 17th
COWDENBEATH (0) 1 — CELTIC (6) 8
Craig (82) — Wilson 4 (3, 37, 43, 65), Colrain 2 (14, 64), McGill o.g. (39), Auld (42)

COWDENBEATH: Dorman; Lindsay, Clark; Harrower, Ross, Murphy; Millar, McGill, Gilfillan, Craig, McWilliams

CELTIC: Beattie; McKay, Mochan; Smith, McNeill, Peacock; Tully, Fernie, Colrain, Wilson, Auld

Attendance: 10,000. Celtic won 10-1 on aggregate.

Semi-Final October 1st at Ibrox Park
CELTIC (0) 1 — PARTICK THISTLE (0) 2
Conway (88) — McParland (72), McKenzie (81)

CELTIC: Beattie; Donnelly, Mochan; Smith, McNeill, Peacock; Tully, Fernie, Conway, Divers, Auld

PARTICK THISTLE: Ledgerwood; Hogan, Baird; Mathers, Crawford, Donlevy; McKenzie, Wright, Kerr, Smith, McParland

Attendance: 45,000. Ledgerwood was carried off in the 49th minute. Wright took over in goal. Ledgerwood eventually resumed at outside-right.

Thistle's victory at Ibrox was as heroic as it was unexpected. When Ledgerwood was hurt and left the field 4 minutes after the interval few would have thought much of Thistle's chances, but with the re-appearance of the goalkeeper 11 minutes later at outside-right and the switching of McKenzie from the right to left, Thistle quickly adapted to their handicap and went on to shock the Cup holders with their positive play.

SCOTTISH CUP

First Round January 31st
CELTIC (1) 4 — ALBION ROVERS (0) 0
Jackson (35), Wilson 2 (58, 84), Kerr o.g. (80)

CELTIC: Haffey; McKay, Mochan; Smith, Evans, Peacock; Tully, Jackson, Colrain, Wilson, Auld

ALBION ROVERS: Torrance; Kerr, Gallacher; McPhail, Herbert, Kiernan; Duncan, Glancy, Fagan, Carmichael, Bingham

Attendance: 27,000

Second Round February 18th
CELTIC (0) 1 — CLYDE (0) 1
McVittie (53) — Ring (75)

CELTIC: Haffey; McKay, Mochan; Smith, Evans, Peacock; McVittie, Paton, Colrain, Divers, Conway

CLYDE: McCulloch; Murphy, Haddock; Walters, Finlay, Clinton; Herd, White, Coyle, Robertson, Ring

Attendance: 32,000

Second Round Replay February 23rd
CLYDE (2) 3 — CELTIC (2) 4
Robertson (22), White (28), Ring (53) — Wilson 2 (26, 56), McVittie (30), Peacock (93)

After Extra Time

CLYDE: McCulloch; Murphy, Haddock; Walters, Finlay, Clinton; Herd, White, Coyle, Robertson, Ring

CELTIC: Haffey; McKay, Mochan; Smith, Evans, Peacock; McVittie, Colrain, Lochead, Wilson, Auld

Attendance: 26,087

Third Round February 28th
CELTIC (1) 2 — RANGERS (0) 1
Divers (44), McVittie (47) — Murray (90)

CELTIC: Haffey; McKay, Mochan; Smith, Evans, Peacock; McVittie, Jackson, Lochead, Wilson, Divers

RANGERS: Niven; Shearer, Caldow; Davis, Telfer, Stevenson; Scott, McMillan, Murray, Wilson, Matthew

Attendance: 42,500

Rangers were hot favourites for the match but Divers headed Celtic into the lead a minute before the interval. McVittie added a 2nd shortly after the restart. Divers might have scored 3 but for ill-luck. 11 minutes from time Haffey pulled off a save in a million when he diverted a fast-flying header from Murray one-handed. Murray's headed goal after a minute of overtime proved meaningless.

Fourth Round March 14th
STIRLING ALBION (0) 1 — CELTIC (2) 3
Kilgannon (81) — Divers (17), Wilson (35), Lochead (47)

STIRLING ALBION: Stewart; Hailstones, Pettigrew; McKechnie, Sinclair, Pierson; Benvie, Kilgannon, Gilmour, Spence, McPhee

CELTIC: Haffey; McKay,, Mochan; Smith, Evans, Peacock; McVittie, Jackson, Lochead, Wilson, Divers

Attendance: 28,000

Semi-Final April 4th at Hampden Park
ST MIRREN (3) 4 — CELTIC (0) 0
Miller 2 (16, 33), Baker (38), Bryceland (89)

CELTIC: Haffey; McKay, Mochan; Smith, Evans, Peacock; McVittie, Jackson, Lochead, Wilson, Divers

ST MIRREN: Walker; Lapsley, Wilson; Neilson, McGuigan, Leishman; Rodger, Bryceland, Baker, Gemmell, Miller

Attendance: 73,885

The individual ability of the speedy Baker was itself a sore strain on Celtic. Gemmell, a delightful manipulator and passer of the ball, so built the attacks that Evans, who seldom had been so harrassed repeatedly had to face two St Mirren players going through the middle. Lochead, when St Mirren led by only 1 goal, fluffed his shot from only 4 yards straight at the goalkeeper, and repeatedly a Celtic forward passed the ball when he should have shot. When Bryceland scored the 4th goal in the final minutes the Celtic end of the terracing was almost bare. In the end Celtic were thoroughly beaten – indeed, almost humiliated – so deplorable was their forwards' display.

Appearances	League	League Cup	Scottish Cup
Beattie	20	6	–
McKay	30	8	6
Mochan	33	8	6
Evans	20	3	6
Fernie	12	9	–
Peacock	27	9	6
Tully	5	9	1
Collins	2	7	–
Byrne	5	–	–
Wilson	14	7	5
Auld	27	9	2
McNeill	17	6	–
Smith	27	3	6
Conway	9	7	1
Colrain	25	1	3
Jack	1	–	–
Donnelly	4	1	–
Crerand	4	–	–
Divers	20	1	4
Higgins	10	–	–
Jackson	17	1	4
McVittie	17	–	5
Kennedy	1	1	–
Haffey	14	3	6
Slater	4	–	–
Lochead	7	–	4
Chalmers	1	–	–
Kurila	1	–	–
Paton	–	–	1

GOALSCORERS:
League: Colrain 14, Divers 9, Auld 8 (3 pens), Smith 5, Mochan 5 (4 pens), McVittie 5, Fernie 4, Peacock 3, Wilson 3 (1 pen), Higgins 3, Jackson 3, Lochead 2, Own Goals 2, Slater 1, Collins 1, Conway 1, Byrne 1

League Cup: Wilson 6, Collins 6 (2 pens), Auld 6, Conway 4, Colrain 2, Tully 2, Peacock 1, Own Goal 1

Scottish Cup: Wilson 5, McVittie 3, Divers 2, Jackson 1, Peacock 1, Lochead 1, Own Goal 1

Celtic team group, August 1959. Back row: McNeill, Donnelly, Carroll, Fallon, Haffey, Kennedy, McKay. Middle row: Colrain, Curran, Lochhead, Crerand, Evans, Conway, Mochan, McVittie. Front row: Smith, Divers, Jackson, Peacock, Mackle, Byrne and O'Hara.

Season 1959-60

Celtic lost 13 matches during the season and slipped to 9th place in the table – 21 points behind Championship-winning Hearts. They had impressive home wins over Kilmarnock, Motherwell and Third Lanark but they suffered from a very leaky defence and conceded a total of 59 goals in their 34 matches. They used 28 different players during the season with Fallon, Gallagher and Carroll all making their first appearances. Bertie Peacock made most appearances (33) and Steve Chalmers finished as top scorer with 14 goals followed by Mochan on 13 and Divers on 12. Eric Smith and long-serving Bobby Evans were both transferred to English clubs at the end of the season.

Celtic got off to a terrible start in their League Cup Section, losing their first 3 matches and eventually finishing 3rd in their group behind Raith Rovers and Airdrie.

They reached the Semi-Final of the Scottish Cup but lost to Rangers after a replay. Their Second Round tie with St Mirren went to 3 matches. Neil Mochan scored all 5 goals in the 2nd replay to take them through to the Third Round against Elgin City, from the Highland League, who came within 6 minutes of causing a major upset.

Celtic played 3 friendlies against English clubs, beating Everton and losing to Wolves at Celtic Park and to Sunderland at Roker Park. They wore numbers for the first time in a friendly match against Sparta Rotterdam in May. Later that month they undertook a 3-match tour of Ireland, winning all 3 matches and scoring 15 goals.

League:	Ninth
League Cup:	Failed to qualify from Section
Scottish Cup:	Semi-Finalists

SCOTTISH FIRST DIVISION

August 10th: Dick Beattie was transferred to Portsmouth.

August 19th
CELTIC (1) 2 — KILMARNOCK (0) 0
Conway (10), Divers (61)

CELTIC: Haffey; McNeill, Mochan; McKay, Evans, Peacock; Carroll, O'Hara, Conway, Divers, Mackle

KILMARNOCK: Brown; Watson, Cook; R. Stewart, Toner, Kennedy; Copland, McInally, McBride, Black, McPike

Attendance: n.a.

September 5th
RANGERS (1) 3 — CELTIC (1) 1
Wilson (9), Scott (65), Millar (76) — Jackson (72)

RANGERS: Niven; Shearer, Little; Davis, Telfer, Stevenson; Scott, Wilson, Millar, Baird, Matthew

CELTIC: Haffey; McNeill, Kennedy; McKay, Evans, Peacock; McVittie, Jackson, Conway, Divers, Auld

Attendance: 65,000

Davie Wilson scored in the 9th minute, Millar having beaten Evans in the jump for a long corner-kick by Matthew which passed right across Haffey's front. In 65 minutes Millar sent another cross over to the far post and Haffey, by this time not fully fit after a clash with Baird, unwisely used only his left hand to try to stop Scott's header. Jackson scored Celtic's goal in 72 minutes with a fine left-foot shot but 4 minutes later Millar turned and twisted his way all of 40 yards, Evans chasing hard after him, before he shot Rangers' 3rd goal. The Celtic trainer was summoned to attend to Jackson (twice), Haffey, Auld and Kennedy. Not once did Rangers' trainer have to appear on the field.

September 2nd: Bobby Evans was in the Scottish League team which beat the League of Ireland 4-1 in Dublin.

September 12th
CELTIC (0) 3 — HEARTS (3) 4
Auld (51), Divers (67), Conway (69) — Hamilton (10), Murray (18), Young (21), Blackwood (87)

CELTIC: Haffey; McNeill, Donnelly; McKay, Evans, Peacock; Auld, Jackson, Conway, Divers, Mackle

HEARTS: Marshall; Kirk, Thomson; Bowman, Milne, Cumming; Smith, Murray, Young, Blackwood, Hamilton

Attendance: 40,000

Celtic sensationally fought back to equalise and came within an ace of taking the lead before Blackwood's late winner.

September 19th
RAITH ROVERS (0) 0 — CELTIC (1) 3
Jackson (20), Chalmers 2 (51, 83)

RAITH ROVERS: Drummond; Polland, MacFarlane; Leigh, McNaught, Baxter; Kerray, Conn, White, Mochan, Urquhart

CELTIC: Haffey; McNeill, Mochan; Smith, Evans, Peacock; Chalmers, Jackson, Conway, Divers, Auld

Attendance: 13,000

September 26th
CELTIC (1) 1 — CLYDE (0) 1
Mackle (44) — Meek (58)

CELTIC: Fallon; Curran, Mochan; Smith, Evans, Peacock; Chalmers, Jackson, Conway, Divers, Mackle

CLYDE: Thomson; Walters, Haddock; White, Sim, McPhail; Wilson, Herd, Meek, Currie, Shearer

Attendance: 27,000

October 3rd
ARBROATH (0) 0 — CELTIC (2) 5
Chalmers 2 (6, 63), Jackson 2 (35, 83), Conway (53)

ARBROATH: Williamson; McLevy, Young; Wright, Fraser, Davidson; Shireffs, Brown, Easson, Hay, Quinn

CELTIC: Fallon; Curran, Mochan; Smith, McNeill, Clark; Chalmers, Jackson, Conway, Divers, Auld

Attendance: 9,000

October 3rd: Bobby Evans was in the Scotland team which beat Ireland 4-0 in Belfast. Bertie Peacock represented Ireland.

October 10th
CELTIC (1) 1 — ABERDEEN (0) 1
Conway (23) — Baird (80)

CELTIC: Fallon; Curran, Mochan; Smith, Evans, Clark; Chalmers, Jackson, Conway, Peacock, Auld

ABERDEEN: Ogston; Cadenhead, Hogg; Burns, Clunie, Glen; Ewen, Little, Baird, Wishart, Mulhall

Attendance: 25,000

October 14th: Bobby Evans was in the Scottish League team which beat the Irish League 7-1 at Ibrox Park.

October 17th
THIRD LANARK (1) 4 — CELTIC (1) 2
Gray 2 (39, 49), McInnes (70), I. Hilley (84) — Divers (45), Jackson (89)

THIRD LANARK: Robertson; Lewis, Brown; Reilly, McCallum, Cunningham; McInnes, Craig, D. Hilley, Gray, I. Hilley

CELTIC: Fallon; McKay, Mochan; Smith, Evans, Peacock; Slater, Jackson, Conway, Divers, Auld

Attendance: 22,000

October 18th: Charlie Tully joined Cork Hibs as manager.

October 24th
CELTIC (3) 5 — MOTHERWELL (0) 1
Divers 2 (5, 77), Jackson (15), Auld (34), Colrain (62) — St John (71)

CELTIC: Fallon; McKay, Mochan; Smith, Evans, Peacock; Chalmers, Jackson, Colrain, Divers, Auld

MOTHERWELL: H. Weir; Forrest, McCallum; Aitken, Martis, McCann; Hunter, S. Reid, St John, Quinn, A. Weir

Attendance: 25,000

October 31st
HIBERNIAN (0) 3 — CELTIC (2) 3
Baker 2 (47, 59), Johnstone (85) — Peacock (25), Jackson (29), Colrain (55)

HIBERNIAN: Wilson; Grant, McLelland; Young, Plenderleith, Baxter; McLeod, Johnstone, Baker, Preston, Ormond

CELTIC: Fallon; McKay, Mochan; Smith, Evans, Peacock; Chalmers, Jackson, Colrain, Divers, Auld

Attendance: 28,000

League positions

	P	W	D	L	F	A	Pts
1 Hearts	10	8	2	0	36	17	18
2 Rangers	10	7	0	3	23	13	14
3 Clyde	10	4	4	2	19	14	12
4 Third Lanark	10	6	0	4	28	22	12
5 St Mirren	10	5	1	4	31	19	11
6 CELTIC	10	4	3	3	26	17	11

November 4th: Evans and Auld were in the Scotland team which drew 1-1 with Wales at Hampden Park.

November 7th
CELTIC (0) 2 — AYR UNITED (1) 3
Auld (60), Divers (67) — McMillan 2 (30, 49), McGhee (84)

CELTIC: Fallon; McKay, Donnelly; Smith, Evans, Peacock; Chalmers, Jackson, Colrain, Divers, Auld

AYR UNITED: Hamilton; Burn, G. McIntyre; W. McIntyre, Paterson, Elliot; Fulton, McMillan, Price, Paton, McGhee

Attendance: 23,000

November 14th
CELTIC (3) 4 — DUNFERMLINE (2) 2
Divers 3 (12, 14, 30), Jackson (75) — Melrose (33), Wardhaugh (45)

CELTIC: Fallon; McKay, Mochan; Smith, Evans, Peacock; Chalmers, Jackson, Colrain, Divers, Auld

DUNFERMLINE: Connachan; Ferguson, Miller; Stevenson, Colville, Rattray; Peebles, Thomson, Dickson, Wardhaugh, Melrose

Attendance: 16,000

November 18th: Bertie Peacock was in the Ireland team beaten 2-1 by England at Wembley.

November 21st
STIRLING ALBION (2) 2 — CELTIC (2) 2
McPhee (13), Peacock o.g. (38) — Colrain (8), Bell o.g. (33)

STIRLING ALBION: Morrison; McKeachie, Pettigrew; Bell, Little, Johnstone; Colquhoun, Benvie, Gilmour, Napier, McPhee

CELTIC: Fallon; Donnelly, Mochan; McKay, Evans, Peacock; Chalmers, Jackson, Colrain, Divers, Auld

Attendance: 18,000

November 25th: Matt McVittie was transferred to St Johnstone.

November 25th: Duncan McKay was in the Scotland Under-23 team which drew 1-1 with Wales Under-23s in Wrexham.

November 28th
PARTICK THISTLE (2) 3 — CELTIC (1) 1
Fleming (10), Smith 2 (40, 85) — Divers (42)

PARTICK THISTLE: Fleck; Muir, Baird; Wright, Harvey, Donlevy; Fleming, Simpson, Smith, McParland, Devine

CELTIC: Fallon; Donnelly, Mochan; McKay, Evans, Peacock; Chalmers, Jackson, Colrain, O'Hara, Auld

Attendance: 30,000

December 5th
CELTIC (1) 2 — DUNDEE (0) 3
Chalmers (38), Mochan (66 pen) — Bonthrone (48), Robertson (64), Henderson (74)

CELTIC: Fallon; Donnelly, Mochan; Crerand, Evans, Peacock; Chalmers, Smith, Lochead, Divers, Auld

DUNDEE: Liney; Hamilton, Cox; Gabriel, Smith, Cowie; Penman, Bonthrone, Cousin, Henderson, Robertson

Attendance: 10,000

December 12th
CELTIC 0 — AIRDRIE 0

CELTIC: Haffey; McKay, Kennedy; McNeill, Evans, Peacock; Auld, Smith, Colrain, Mochan, Byrne

AIRDRIE: Leslie; Miller, Shanks; Quinn, J. Stewart, Quigley; Duncan, McGill, Baillie, Storrie, A. Stewart

Attendance: 13,000

December 17th: Celtic made a bid for Jackie Mudie of Blackpool.

December 19th
ST MIRREN (0) 0 — CELTIC (0) 3
O'Hara (49), Colrain (87), Mochan (88)

ST MIRREN: Forsyth; Wilson, Riddell; Gregal, McGugan, Thomson; Rodger, Bryceland, Baker, Gemmell, Miller

CELTIC: Haffey; McKay, Kennedy; McNeill, Evans, Peacock; Auld, O'Hara, Colrain, Mochan, Byrne

Attendance: 19,000

December 26th
KILMARNOCK (1) 2 — CELTIC (1) 1
Kerr (30), Black (85) — Mochan (44)

KILMARNOCK: Brown; Richmond, Watson; Beattie, Toner, Kennedy; Wentzel, McInally, Kerr, Black, Muir

CELTIC: Haffey; McKay, Kennedy; McNeill, Evans, Peacock; Auld, Smith, Colrain, Mochan, Byrne

Attendance: 15,000

League positions

	P	W	D	L	F	A	Pts
1 Hearts	18	13	3	2	52	30	29
2 Rangers	18	13	0	5	51	18	26
3 Kilmarnock	18	11	1	6	32	31	23
4 Hibernian	18	10	2	6	68	44	22
5 Dundee	18	9	3	6	37	29	21
11 CELTIC	18	6	5	17	31	32	17

January 1st
CELTIC (0) 0 — RANGERS (0) 1
Millar (89½)

CELTIC: Haffey; McKay, Kennedy; McNeill, Evans, Peacock; Auld, Smith, Carroll, Mochan, Byrne

RANGERS: Niven; Shearer, Little; Davis, Paterson, Stevenson; Brand, Baird, Millar, Wilson, Hume

Attendance: 50,000

Less than half a minute from time at Celtic Park Millar gave Rangers their 5th successive win. Evans had dived low to head out from his penalty area and Baird immediately prodded the ball forward to Millar who shot high and hard with his left foot as Haffey, somewhat hesitatingly, left his goal to narrow the angle. Celtic prevailed upon the referee to consult the linesman on the stand side, appealing that Millar had been offside, but the score stood. Just before Millar's goal Davis cleared on the goal-line a header from Carroll that had beaten his goalkeeper. In the 15th minute of the second half Haffey diverted for a corner-kick a penalty kick shot hard to his right by Little.

January 2nd
HEARTS (1) 3 — CELTIC (1) 1
Smith (6), Bauld (60), Thomson (72 pen) — Peacock (37)

HEARTS: Marshall; Kirk, Thomson; Cumming, Milne, Bowman; Smith, Young, Bauld, Blackwood, Hamilton

CELTIC: Haffey; McKay, Kennedy; McNeill, Evans, Peacock; Carroll, Smith, Byrne, Mochan, Auld

Attendance: 28,000

January 9th
CELTIC (0) 1 — RAITH ROVERS (0) 0
Mochan (64)

CELTIC: Haffey; McKay, Kennedy; McNeill, Evans, Peacock; Carroll, Smith, Byrne, Mochan, Auld

RAITH ROVERS: Thorburn; Polland, Mochan; Young, McNaught, Baxter; Wallace, Conn, Kerray, Spence, Urquhart

Attendance: 15,000

January 16th
CLYDE (3) 3 — CELTIC (2) 3
McLaughlin 2 (9, 40), Robertson (33) — Mochan (4 pen), Byrne 2 (36, 74)

CLYDE: McCulloch; McGregor, Haddock; White, Finlay, McPhail; A. Wilson, Herd, McLaughlin, Robertson, Shearer

CELTIC: Haffey; McKay, Kennedy; Crerand, Kurila, Peacock; Carroll, O'Hara, Byrne, Mochan, Divers

Attendance: 25,000

January 23rd
CELTIC (2) 4 — ARBROATH (0) 0
Divers 2 (27, 89), Byrne (40), Carroll (61)

CELTIC: Haffey; McKay, Kennedy; Crerand, Evans, Peacock; Carroll, O'Hara, Byrne, Mochan, Divers

ARBROATH: Williamson; McLevy, Young; McLean, Fraser, Wright; Shireffs, Brown, Easson, Grierson, Quinn

Attendance: 16,000

February 6th
ABERDEEN (1) 3 — CELTIC (1) 2
Kinnell (35), Davidson (52), Brownlie (88) — Mochan (30 pen, 71 pen)

ABERDEEN: Ogston; Cadenhead, Hogg; Burns, Clunie, Kinnell; Brownlie, Little, Davidson, Wishart, Mulhall

CELTIC: Haffey; McKay, Kennedy; Crerand, Evans, Peacock; Carroll, O'Hara, Byrne, Mochan, Divers.

Attendance: 14,000

League positions

	P	W	D	L	F	A	Pts
1 Hearts	26	18	6	2	79	39	42
2 Rangers	24	16	3	5	63	22	35
3 Kilmarnock	24	17	1	6	49	33	35
4 Dundee	25	12	6	7	47	36	30
5 Clyde	25	11	8	6	58	49	30
11 CELTIC	24	8	6	10	52	42	22

March 7th
CELTIC (1) 1 — HIBERNIAN (0) 0
Conway (8)

CELTIC: Haffey; McKay, Kennedy; McNeill, Evans, Peacock; Auld, Smith, Conway, Chalmers, Byrne

HIBERNIAN: Muirhead; Grant, McLelland; Young, Plenderleith, Hughes; McLeod, Johnstone, Baker, Fox, Ormond

Attendance: 19,000

March 13th: Jock Stein was appointed manager of Dunfermline Athletic.

March 16th
AYR UNITED (1) 1 — CELTIC (0) 1
W. McIntyre (40) — Crerand (70)

AYR UNITED: Hamilton; Burn, Thomson; W. McIntyre, Paterson, Telfer; A. McIntyre, McMillan, Price, Paton, McGhee

CELTIC: Haffey; McKay, Kennedy; Crerand, Evans, Peacock; Smith, Colrain, Conway, Divers, Byrne

Attendance: n.a.

March 19th
DUNFERMLINE (1) 3 — CELTIC (1) 2
Dickson (15 secs), Melrose 2 (50, 52) — Conway (19), Byrne (62)

DUNFERMLINE: Connachan; Fraser, Sweeney; Wardhaugh, Stevenson, Mailer; Peebles, A. Smith, Dickson, Kerray, Melrose

CELTIC: Haffey; McKay, Kennedy; McNeill, Evans, Peacock; Conway, Smith, Mochan, Divers, Byrne

Attendance: 10,000. This was Jock Stein's first match as Dunfermline's manager.

March 21st
MOTHERWELL (0) 1 — CELTIC (1) 2
McPhee (48) — Mochan 2 (24, 60)

MOTHERWELL: H. Weir; Strachan, Reid; Aitken, Martis, Forrest; Hunter, Quinn, Young, McPhee, A. Weir

CELTIC: Haffey; McKay, Kennedy; Crerand, McNeill, Peacock; Smith, Colrain, Mochan, Divers, Byrne

Attendance: n.a.

March 26th
CELTIC (0) 1 — STIRLING ALBION (0) 1
Mochan (82) — Glancey (78)

CELTIC: Haffey; McKay, Kennedy; McNeill, Evans, Peacock; Smith, Colrain, Mochan, Divers, Conway

STIRLING ALBION: Morrison; McKechnie, Pettigrew; Pierson, Bell, Johnstone; Hill, Bonthrone, Gilmour, Glancey, Colquhoun

Attendance: 12,000

March 23rd: Bobby Evans was in the Scottish League team which was beaten 1-0 by the English League at Highbury.

March 28th
CELTIC (2) 4 — THIRD LANARK (0) 0
Colrain (10), Chalmers 2 (25, 54), Mochan (87 pen)

CELTIC: Haffey; McKay, Kennedy; Crerand, McNeill, Peacock; Smith, Colrain, Mochan, Chalmers, Byrne

THIRD LANARK: Robertson; Lewis, Caldwell; Reilly, Robb, Cunningham; Goodfellow, Hilley, Harley, Gray, Fraser

Attendance: 8,000

March 29th: Johnny Kelly was signed from Crewe Alexandria.

April 9th: Haffey, McKay and Evans were in the Scotland team which drew 1-1 with England at Hampden. Haffey saved a penalty from Charlton.

April 12th
CELTIC (0) 2 — PARTICK THISTLE (2) 4
Chalmers 2 (70, 85) — McParland (20), Smith 3 (40, 54, 65)

CELTIC: Fallon; McKay, Kennedy; McNeill, Evans, Peacock; Chalmers, Colrain, Mochan, Divers, Gallagher

PARTICK THISTLE: Freebairn; Hogan, Baird; Brown, Harvey, Donlevy; McKenzie, McParland, Smith, Hastings, Fleming

Attendance: 5,000

April 16th
DUNDEE (2) 2 — CELTIC (0) 0
Gilzean (23), Robertson (41)

DUNDEE: Liney; Hamilton, Cox; Ure, Smith, Cowie; Penman, McGeachie, Gilzean, Cousin, Robertson

CELTIC: Haffey; McKay, Kennedy; McNeill, Evans, Peacock; Carroll, Chalmers, Mochan, Colrain, Gallagher

Attendance: 15,000

April 18th
AIRDRIE (2) 2 — CELTIC (1) 5
Rankin (34), Stewart (49) — Welsh o.g. (17), Chalmers 3 (71, 74, 81) Mochan (65)

AIRDRIE: Beaton; Neil, Shanks; McNeill, Baillie, Welsh; Duncan, Rankin, Sharkey, Ormond, Stewart

CELTIC: Fallon; McKay, Kennedy; Crerand, Evans, Peacock; Carroll, Chalmers, Mochan, Divers, Gallagher

Attendance: 4,000

April 30th
CELTIC (3) 3 — ST MIRREN (0) 3
Mochan (3), Chalmers 2 (33, 41) — Gemmell (78), Baker (80), Miller (82)

CELTIC: Fallon; McKay, Kennedy; McNeill, Evans, Peacock; Carroll, Chalmers, Mochan, Gallagher, Divers

ST MIRREN: Walker; Wilson, McTurk; Doonan, McGugan, Gregal; Rodger, Bryceland, Baker, Gemmell, Miller

Attendance: 10,000

Scottish First Division

	P	W	D	L	F	A	Pts
1 Hearts	34	23	8	3	102	51	54
2 Kilmarnock	34	24	2	8	67	45	50
3 Rangers	34	17	8	9	72	38	42
4 Dundee	34	16	10	8	70	49	42
5 Motherwell	34	16	8	10	71	61	40
6 Clyde	34	15	9	10	77	69	39
7 Hibernian	34	14	7	13	106	85	35
8 Ayr	34	14	6	14	65	73	34
9 CELTIC	34	12	9	13	73	59	33
10 Partick Thistle	34	14	4	16	54	78	32
11 Raith Rovers	34	14	3	17	64	62	31
12 Third Lanark	34	13	4	17	75	83	30
13 Dunfermline	34	10	9	15	72	80	29
14 St Mirren	34	11	6	17	78	86	28
15 Aberdeen	34	11	6	17	54	72	28
16 Airdrie	34	11	6	17	56	80	28
17 Stirling Albion	34	7	8	19	55	72	22
18 Arbroath	34	4	7	23	38	106	15

May 4th: McKay and Evans were in the Scotland team beaten 3-2 by Poland at Hampden Park.

May 29th: McKay and Evans were in the Scotland team beaten 4-1 by Austria in Vienna.

June 5th: McKay and Evans were in the Scotland team which drew 3-3 with Hungary in Budapest.

June 8th: McKay and Evans were in the Scotland team beaten 4-2 by Turkey in Ankara.

May 11th: Eric Smith was transferred to Leeds United for £11,000.

May 20th: Bobby Evans was transferred to Chelsea.

LEAGUE CUP

August 8th
RAITH ROVERS (2) 2 — CELTIC (0) 1
MacFarlane (33 pen), Conn (45) — Mackle (60)

RAITH ROVERS: Drummond; Polland, MacFarlane; Young, McNaught, Leigh; Kerray, Conn, White, McKinven, Urquhart

CELTIC: Haffey; McNeill, Mochan; McKay, Evans, Peacock; Smith, McVittie, Byrne, Colrain, Mackle
Attendance: 17,000

August 12th
CELTIC (0) 1 PARTICK THISTLE (0) 2
Mochan (51 pen) Wilson (65), Fleming (77)

CELTIC: Haffey; McNeill, Mochan; McKay, Evans, Smith; Carroll, Colrain, Byrne, Divers, Mackle
PARTICK THISTLE: Freebairn; Hogan, Baird; Harvey, Davidson, Donlevy; McKenzie, McParland, Smith, Wilson, Fleming
Attendance: 25,000

August 15th
AIRDRIE (2) 4 CELTIC (2) 2
Storrie 3 (17, 20, 77), McGill (50) Carroll (4), Baillie o.g. (14)

AIRDRIE: Thomson; Neil, Shanks; Quinn, Baillie, J. Stewart; Rankin, Storrie, Sharkey, McGill, A. Stewart
CELTIC: Haffey; McNeill, Mochan; McKay, Evans, Smith; Carroll, McVittie, Colrain, Divers, Byrne
Attendance: 15,000

August 22nd
CELTIC (1) 1 RAITH ROVERS (0) 0
MacFarlane o.g. (36)

CELTIC: Haffey; McNeill, Kennedy; McKay, Evans, Peacock; McVittie, O'Hara, Conway, Gallagher, Auld
RAITH ROVERS: Drummond; Polland, MacFarlane; Young, McNaught, Leigh; Kerray, Conn, White, McKinven, Urquhart
Attendance: 24,000

August 26th
PARTICK THISTLE (0) 0 CELTIC (1) 2
Jackson (9, 89)

PARTICK THISTLE: Freebairn; Hogan, Baird; Wright, Harvey, Donlevy; McKenzie, McParland, Keenan, Smith, Fleming
CELTIC: Haffey; McNeill, Kennedy; McKay, Evans, Peacock; McVittie, Jackson, Conway, O'Hara, Auld
Attendance: 20,000

August 29th
CELTIC (1) 2 AIRDRIE (1) 2
Divers (32), Auld (60 pen) Sharkey (16), McGill (75)

CELTIC: Haffey; McNeill, Kennedy; Mckay, Evans, Peacock; McVittie, Jackson, Lochead, Divers, Auld
AIRDRIE: Wallace; Neil, Miller; Quinn, Baillie, Welsh; Blair, McGill, Sharkey, Rankin, Ormond
Attendance: 24,500

SECTION TABLE

	P	W	D	L	F	A	Pts
Raith Rovers	6	5	0	1	13	5	10
Airdrie	6	2	2	2	12	10	6
CELTIC	6	2	1	3	9	10	5
Partick Thistle	6	1	1	4	3	12	3

Qualifier: RAITH ROVERS

SCOTTISH CUP

Second Round February 13th
ST MIRREN (0) 1 CELTIC (0) 1
Rodger (63) Byrne (64)

ST MIRREN: Walker; McTurk, Wilson; McGugan, Tierney, Riddell; Rodger, Bryceland, Baker, Gemmell, Miller
CELTIC: Haffey; McKay, Kennedy; McNeill, Evans, Peacock; Smith, Colrain, Mochan, Divers, Byrne
Attendance: 37,000

Second Round Replay February 24th
CELTIC (1) 4 ST MIRREN (3) 4
Mochan 2 (25, 85), Divers 2 (49, 105) Miller (36), Rodger (44), Baker (45), Bryceland (98)
After Extra Time

CELTIC: Haffey; McKay, Kennedy; McNeill, Evans, Peacock; Smith, Colrain, Mochan, Divers, Byrne
ST MIRREN; Walker; McTurk, Wilson; McGugan, Tierney, Riddell; Rodger, Bryceland, Baker, Gemmell, Miller
Attendance: 38,000

Second Round Second Replay February 29th
CELTIC (3) 5 ST MIRREN (0) 2
Mochan 5 (7, 12 pen, 40, 54, 81) Gemmell (61), Rodger (79)

CELTIC: Haffey; McKay, Kennedy; McNeill, Evans, Peacock; Smith, Colrain, Mochan, Divers, Byrne
ST MIRREN: Walker; Wilson, Riddell; Neilson, Tierney, McGugan; Rodger, Bryceland, Baker, Gemmell, Miller
Attendance: 51,000

Third Round March 5th
ELGIN CITY (0) 1 CELTIC (0) 2
Grant (65) Divers (84), Smith (88)

ELGIN CITY: Jenkins; Coghill, Harper; Cormie, McCall, Brander; Castell, Roy, Davidson, Clyne, Grant
CELTIC: Haffey; McKay, Kennedy; McNeill, Evans, Peacock; Smith, Colrain, Mochan, Divers, Byrne
Attendance: 12,000

Fourth Round March 12th
CELTIC (1) 2 PARTICK THISTLE (0) 0
Smith (19), Colrain (66)

CELTIC: Haffey; McKay, Kennedy; McNeill, Evans, Peacock; Smith, Colrain, Mochan, Divers, Auld

PARTICK THISTLE: Curran; Brown, Baird, Wright, Hogan, Donlevy; McKenzie, McParland, Smith, Fleming, Devine

Attendance: 41,000

Semi-Final April 2nd at Hampden Park

RANGERS (0) 1 — CELTIC (1) 1

Millar (68) — Chalmers (25)

RANGERS: Niven; Caldow, Little; Davis, Paterson, Stevenson; Scott, McMillan, Millar, Baird, Wilson

CELTIC: Haffey; McKay, Kennedy; McNeill, Evans, Peacock; Chalmers, Colrain, Mochan, Divers, Byrne

Attendance: 79,786

Much of the goalmouth excitement was the result of miskicks and misses. Chalmers headed Celtic's goal in 25 minutes from Colrain's corner-kick when Rangers, not for the first time, left a player unmarked for a cross. Rangers' goal came from a header. 22 minutes from time, during a period of clear Rangers' superiority, Wilson crossed hard from the left corner of the field and Millar scored a magnificent goal from no fewer than 15 yards. Haffey made saves from McMillan, Scott and Millar which saved the day for his side.

Semi-Final Replay April 6th at Hampden Park

RANGERS (1) 4 — CELTIC (1) 1

Wilson 2 (27, 71), Millar 2 (49, 79) — Mochan (33)

RANGERS: Ritchie; Caldow, Little; Davis, Paterson, Stevenson; Scott, McMillan, Millar, Baird, Wilson

CELTIC: Haffey; McKay, Kennedy; McNeill, Evans, Peacock; Chalmers, Colrain, Mochan, Jackson, Divers

Attendance: 70,977

Few could have foreseen the events of the second half, during which the Celtic defence played like novices. In 71 minutes Wilson headed almost out of Haffey's hands an orthodox cross by Scott while Kennedy and Scott acted as spectators. In 79 minutes Baird, now at right-half for Davis who had been taken off on a stretcher, dropped a cross into Celtic's goal area for Millar to head in another goal. Millar once again proved to be Evans's bogey man.

Appearances	League	League Cup	Scottish Cup
Haffey	20	6	7
McNeill	19	6	7
Mochan	29	3	7
McKay	29	6	7
Evans	30	6	7
Peacock	33	4	7
Carroll	10	2	–
O'Hara	6	2	–
Conway	12	2	–
Divers	23	3	7
Mackle	3	2	–
Kennedy	20	3	7
McVittie	1	5	–
Jackson	13	2	1
Auld	20	3	1
Donnelly	5	–	–
Smith	21	3	5
Chalmers	17	–	2
Fallon	14	–	–
Curran	3	–	–
Clark	2	–	–
Slater	1	–	–
Colrain	17	3	7
Crerand	8	–	–
Lochead	1	1	–
Byrne	14	3	5
Kurila	1	–	–
Gallagher	4	1	–

GOALSCORERS:

League: Chalmers 14, Mochan 13 (4 pens), Divers 12, Jackson 8, Conway 6, Colrain 5, Byrne 4, Auld 3, Peacock 2, Own Goals 2, Mackle 1, O'Hara 1, Crerand 1, Carroll 1

League Cup: Jackson 2, Own Goals 2, Mackle 1, Mochan 1 (pen), Carroll 1, Divers 1, Auld 1 (pen)

Scottish Cup: Mochan 8 (1 pen), Divers 3, Smith 2, Byrne 1, Colrain 1, Chalmers 1

Season 1960-61

After a poor start which saw Celtic go without a win in their first 5 matches, the return of Willie Fernie to Parkhead sparked off an immediate revival and they went on to lose only 6 of their remaining 29 matches, eventually finishing 4th in the table behind Rangers, Kilmarnock and Third Lanark. The period from mid-January to the end of April was particularly successful with only 1 defeat in 13 matches. 17-year old John Hughes burst onto the scene and Pat Crerand, who established himself in the side during the season, made such good progress that he was capped by Scotland 3 times, beginning with the World Cup match with Eire on May 3rd. Billy McNeill also progressed to the full Scotland side although he would wish to forget his debut against England at Wembley. Frank Haffey had even better reasons for forgetting that particular match. Neil Mochan was transferred to Dundee United in November and Bertie Peacock – after 12 seasons with the club – Auld and Conway were all transferred at the end of the season. McKay, Kennedy and Chalmers all played in 32 matches, Chalmers finishing as top scorer with 20 goals.

Celtic took 7 points from their first 4 League Cup matches including wins at Cathkin Park and Ibrox but a slip-up, at home, against Partick Thistle meant that they had to win their last home match against Rangers to go through to the Quarter-Finals. They took an early lead through Chalmers, but goals from Davis and Brand put them out of the competition for another season.

They reached their first Scottish Cup Final for 5 years but lost out to Dunfermline, managed by former Celt Jock Stein. Their toughest tie along the way was the Fourth Round meeting with Hibs.

They took part in the Friendship Cup but lost to French club Sedan in the First Round.

League:	Fourth
League Cup:	Failed to qualify from Section
Scottish Cup:	Runners-up

SCOTTISH FIRST DIVISION

August 24th
KILMARNOCK (0) 2 — CELTIC (1) 2
McInally 2 (49, 68) — Carroll (31), Mochan (80)

KILMARNOCK: Brown; Richmond, Watson; Beattie, Toner, Kennedy; Muir, McInally, Kerr, Black, McIlroy

CELTIC: Fallon; McKay, Kennedy; Crerand, McNeill, Peacock; Carroll, Chalmers, Hughes, Divers, Mochan

Attendance: 20,000

September 10th
CELTIC (0) 1 — RANGERS (1) 5
Chalmers (89) — Scott (2), Millar (65), Brand (78), Wilson (84), Davis (86)

CELTIC: Fallon; McKay, Kennedy; Crerand, Kurila, Peacock; Conway, Chalmers, Carroll, Divers, Hughes

RANGERS: Ritchie; Shearer, Caldow; Davis, Paterson, Baxter; Scott, McMillan, Millar, Brand, Wilson

Attendance: 40,000

For more than an hour it was anybody's game but after Rangers scored their 2nd goal in 65 minutes they romped into an unassailable position.

September 17th
THIRD LANARK (1) 2 — CELTIC (0) 0
Goodfellow (36), Harley (83)

THIRD LANARK: Robertson; McGillvray, Caldwell; Reilly, McCormack, Cunningham; Goodfellow, Hilley, Harley, Gray, McInnes

CELTIC: Fallon; McKay, Kennedy; Crerand, McNeill, Peacock; Carroll, Chalmers, Hughes, Divers, Auld
Attendance: 15,000

September 24th
CELTIC 0 ABERDEEN 0
CELTIC: Fallon; McKay, Kennedy; Crerand, McNeill, Peacock; Conway, Gallagher, Carroll, Divers, Auld
ABERDEEN: Ogston; Bennett, Hogg; Brownlie, Kinnell, Fraser; Ewen, Davidson, Little, Cooke, Mulhall
Attendance: 19,000

October 1st
AIRDRIE (2) 2 CELTIC (0) 0
Caven (14), Storrie (44)
AIRDRIE: Leslie; Shanks, Keenan; Stewart, Johnstone, McNeill; Sharkey, Storrie, Caven, Rankin, Duncan
CELTIC: Goldie; McKay, Kennedy; Crerand, McNeill, Peacock; Carroll, Divers, Mochan, Chalmers, Byrne
Attendance: 12,000

October 5th: Pat Crerand was in the Scottish League team which beat the League of Ireland 5-1 at Parkhead.

October 6th: Willie Fernie returned to Celtic from Middlesbrough.

October 8th
CELTIC (3) 4 ST MIRREN (0) 2
Auld 2 (5, 72), Divers (16), Chalmers (44) Rodger 2 (55, 68)
CELTIC: Haffey; McKay, Kennedy; Crerand, McNeill, Clark; Chalmers, Fernie, Carroll, Divers, Auld
ST MIRREN: Williamson; Doonan, Wilson; Thomson, Clunie, Riddell; Rodger, Kerrigan, Baker, Gemmell, Miller
Attendance: 32,000

October 8th: Bertie Peacock was in the Ireland team beaten 5-2 by England in Belfast.

October 15th
HIBERNIAN (0) 0 CELTIC (2) 6
Carroll 2 (14, 18), Fernie (49), Auld (51), Chalmers 2 (52, 62)
HIBERNIAN: Muirhead; Fraser, McLelland; Falconer, Baird, Hughes; Buchanan, McLeod, Baker, Stevenson, Ormond
CELTIC: Haffey; McKay, Kennedy; Crerand, McNeill, Peacock; Chalmers, Fernie, Carroll, Divers, Auld
Attendance: 28,000

October 22nd
CLYDE (0) 0 CELTIC (3) 3
Auld (7), Carroll (43), Peacock (44 pen)
CLYDE: McCulloch; Cameron, Haddock; Sim, Finlay, Clinton; Wilson, Robertson, Gallagher, Thomson, Boyd
CELTIC: Haffey; Donnelly, Kennedy; Crerand, McNeill, Peacock; Chalmers, Fernie, Carroll, Divers. Auld
Attendance: 23,500

League positions

	P	W	D	L	F	A	Pts
1 Rangers	7	6	0	1	26	10	12
2 Dundee	8	5	1	2	15	11	11
3 Aberdeen	8	3	4	1	18	14	10
4 Third Lanark	8	5	0	3	25	20	10
5 Kilmarnock	8	3	4	1	12	10	10
10 CELTIC	8	3	2	2	16	13	8

October 22nd: Duncan McKay was in the Scotland team beaten 2-0 by Wales in Cardiff.

October 26th: Bertie Peacock was in the Ireland team beaten 4-3 by West Germany in Belfast.

October 29th
CELTIC (1) 2 AYR UNITED (0) 0
Carroll (22), Divers (47)
CELTIC: Haffey; McKay, Kennedy; Crerand, McNeill, Peacock; Chalmers, Fernie, Carroll, Divers, Auld
AYR UNITED: Hamilton; Burn, Thomson; W. McIntyre, McLean, Walker; A. McIntyre, McMillan, Fulton, Christie, McGhee
Attendance: 16,000

November 5th
RAITH ROVERS (0) 2 CELTIC (1) 2
Spence 2 (62, 68) Fernie (16), Chalmers (77)
RAITH ROVERS: Thorburn; Wilson, Mochan; Polland, McNaught, Duffy; Wallace, Spence, Easson, Kelly, Matthew
CELTIC: Haffey; McKay, Kennedy; Jackson, McNeill, Peacock; Chalmers, Fernie, Carroll, Divers, Auld
Attendance: 10,000

November 9th: McKay was in the Scotland team which beat Ireland 5-2 at Hampden Park. Peacock was in the Ireland team.

November 12th
CELTIC (0) 0 PARTICK THISTLE (0) 1
Hogan (73)
CELTIC: Haffey; McKay, Kennedy; Kurila, McNeill, Peacock; Chalmers, Fernie, Carroll, Divers, Auld
PARTICK THISTLE: Freebairn; Muir, Brown; Cunningham, Harvey, Donlevy; Ewing, Smith, Hogan, Duffy, McParland
Attendance: 23,000

November 17th: Neil Mochan signed for Dundee United for £1,500.

November 18th: Hearts called off a swop deal involving John Colrain and Ian Crawford. Colrain then joined Clyde for £5,000.

November 19th
DUNFERMLINE (1) 2 — CELTIC (2) 2
Dickson 2 (40, 66) — Carroll (3), Chalmers (41)

DUNFERMLINE: Connachan; Fraser, Cunningham; Mailer, Stevenson, Miller; McDonald, Smith, Dickson, Melrose, Peebles

CELTIC: Haffey; McKay, Kennedy; Crerand, McNeill, Peacock; Chalmers, Fernie, Carroll, Divers, Auld

Attendance: 11,000

November 26th
ST JOHNSTONE (0) 2 — CELTIC (1) 1
McKinven (72), Gardiner (80) — Chalmers (2)

ST JOHNSTONE: Taylor; McFadyen, Lachlan; Walker, Little, McKinven; Newlands, Docherty, Gardiner, Innes, McVittie

CELTIC: Haffey; McKay, Kennedy; Crerand, McNeill, Peacock; Chalmers, Fernie, Carroll, Divers, Auld

Attendance: 15,000

December 10th
CELTIC (0) 1 — DUNDEE UNITED (1) 1
Hughes (48) — Irvine (3)

CELTIC: Haffey; McKay, Kennedy; Crerand, McNeill, Peacock; Conway, Chalmers, Hughes, Divers, Auld

DUNDEE UNITED: Ugolini; Graham, Roe; Neilson, Yeats, Briggs; Irvine, Gillespie, Mochan, Howieson, Ormond

Attendance: 15,000

December 17th
HEARTS (1) 2 — CELTIC (1) 1
Crawford 2 (18, 64) — Crerand (35)

HEARTS: Marshall; Kirk, Holt; Ferguson, Cumming, Higgins; Hamilton, Finlay, Blackwood, Crawford, McFadzean

CELTIC: Haffey; McKay, Kennedy; Crerand, McNeill, Peacock; Chalmers, Fernie, Hughes, Divers, Auld

Attendance: 24,000

December 24th
CELTIC (1) 1 — MOTHERWELL (0) 0
Divers (9)

CELTIC: Haffey; McKay, Kennedy; Crerand, McNeill, Peacock; Carroll, Chalmers, Kelly, Divers, Byrne

MOTHERWELL: H. Weir; Delaney, I. Weir; McCann, Martis, McPhee; Lindsay, Quinn, St John, Hunter, A. Weir

Attendance: 20,500

League positions

	P	W	D	L	F	A	Pts
1 Rangers	16	13	0	3	52	18	26
2 Kilmarnock	17	9	6	2	36	26	24
3 Aberdeen	17	7	7	3	37	34	21
4 Third Lanark	17	10	0	7	50	44	20
5 Partick Thistle	17	9	2	6	29	30	20
12 CELTIC	16	5	5	6	26	23	15

December 26th
CELTIC (2) 2 — DUNDEE (0) 1
Conway (10), Byrne (42) — Robertson (62)

CELTIC: Haffey; McKay, Kennedy; Crerand, McNeill, Peacock; Carroll, Chalmers, Conway, Kelly, Byrne

DUNDEE: Horsburgh; Reid, Cox; Seith, Ure, Cowie; Crichton, Cousin, Waddell, Gilzean, Robertson

Attendance: 11,000

December 31st
CELTIC (0) 3 — KILMARNOCK (1) 2
Chalmers 2 (59, 60), Gallagher (85) — Brown (2), Kennedy (50)

CELTIC: Haffey; McKay, Kennedy; Crerand, McNeill, Peacock; Chalmers, Divers, Conway, Gallagher, Byrne

KILMARNOCK: McLaughlin; Richmond, Watson; Davidson, Toner, Beattie; Brown, McInally, Kerr, Kennedy, Muir

Attendance: 30,000

January 2nd
RANGERS (0) 2 — CELTIC (1) 1
Brand (62), Wilson (80) — Divers (28)

RANGERS: Niven; Shearer, Caldow; Davis, Paterson, Baxter; Scott, McMillan, Millar, Brand, Wilson

CELTIC: Haffey; McKay, Kennedy; Crerand, McNeill, Peacock; Chalmers, Divers, Conway, Fernie, Byrne

Attendance: 79,000

Celtic led 1-0 at half-time, Divers having scored in 28 minutes after Baxter had chosen to indulge in frills of ball control almost on his own penalty spot. An error of judgement by Haffey lost Celtic the match – Scott sent over an orthodox high cross which the goalkeeper missed completely and Wilson headed into the net. Byrne had been the best winger of the 4 until injured in the 30th minute of the 1st half.

January 7th
CELTIC (2) 2 — THIRD LANARK (2) 3
Divers (13), Chalmers (28) — Harley 2 (15, 35), Goodfellow (70)

CELTIC: Haffey; McKay, Kennedy; Crerand, McNeill, Peacock; Gallagher, Divers, Conway, Chalmers, Fernie

THIRD LANARK: Robertson; McGillivray, Lewis; Reilly, McCormack, Cunningham; Goodfellow, Hilley, Harley, Gray, McInnes

Attendance: 22,000

January 14th
ABERDEEN (0) 1 — CELTIC (2) 3
Brownlie (66) — Gallagher (37), Chalmers (42), Divers (83)

ABERDEEN: Ogston; Bennett, Sim; Burns, Coutts, Kinnell; Ewen, Brownlie, Little, Cooke, Mulhall

CELTIC: Haffey; McKay, Kennedy; Crerand, McNeill, Peacock; Gallagher, Divers, Hughes, Chalmers, Auld

Attendance: 22,000

January 18th: Billy McNeill was in the Scotland Under-23 team which beat the Second Division Select 10-2 at Brockville. He scored with a penalty.

January 21st
CELTIC (2) 4 — AIRDRIE (0) 0
Divers (14), Chalmers 2 (32, 83), Crerand (77)

CELTIC: Haffey; McKay, Kennedy; Crerand, McNeill, Clark; Gallagher, Divers, Hughes, Chalmers, Auld

AIRDRIE: Leslie; Shanks, Ross; Quinn, Stewart, McNeill; Sharkey, Storrie, Caven, Rankin, Duncan

Attendance: 21,000

February 4th
ST MIRREN (0) 2 — CELTIC (1) 1
Kerrigan (49), Bryceland (89) — Peacock (38 pen)

ST MIRREN: Brown; R. Campbell, Wilson; Stewart, Clunie, Riddell; R. Campbell, Bryceland, Kerrigan, McTavish, Miller

CELTIC: Haffey; McKay, Kennedy; Crerand, McNeill, Peacock; Gallagher, Divers, Hughes, Fernie, Auld

Attendance: 27,000

February 18th
CELTIC (2) 2 — HIBERNIAN (0) 0
Chalmers 2 (11, 16)

CELTIC: Haffey; McKay Kennedy; Crerand, McNamee, Peacock; Gallagher, Fernie, Hughes, Chalmers, Byrne

HIBERNIAN: Simpson; Fraser, McLelland; Grant, Easton, Baird; McLeod, Preston, Baker, Baxter, Ormond

Attendance: 33,000

League positions

	P	W	D	L	F	A	Pts
1 Rangers	25	18	3	4	68	29	39
2 Kilmarnock	25	13	7	5	56	39	33
3 Motherwell	24	12	5	7	51	37	29
4 Aberdeen	24	11	7	6	55	50	29
5 Third Lanark	24	12	2	8	67	61	26
7 CELTIC	24	10	5	9	44	34	25

February 27th
CELTIC (2) 6 — CLYDE (1) 1
Byrne (40), Peacock (44), Gallagher (51), Chalmers (66), Hughes 2 (71, 73) — Robertson (8)

CELTIC: Haffey; McKay, Kennedy; Crerand, McNeill, Peacock; Gallagher, Fernie, Hughes, Chalmers, Byrne

CLYDE: McCulloch; Cameron, Haddock; Colrain, Finlay, Clinton; McLean, Herd, McLaughlin, Robertson, Steel

Attendance: n.a.

March 4th
AYR UNITED (1) 1 — CELTIC (0) 3
Fulton (41) — McNeill (55), Peacock (74 pen), Fernie (82)

AYR UNITED: Gallagher; Burn, G. McIntyre; W. McIntyre, McLean, Curlett; A. McIntyre, McMillan, McGuinness, McGhee, Fulton

CELTIC: Haffey; McKay, Kennedy; Crerand, McNeill, Peacock; Gallagher, Fernie, Hughes, Chalmers, Byrne

Attendance: 15,500

March 18th
PARTICK THISTLE (1) 1 — CELTIC (2)2
McBride (41) — Byrne (17), Chalmers (43)

PARTICK THISTLE: Freebairn; Hogan, Brown; Wright, McKinnon, Donlevy; Ewing, Smith, McBride, Duffy, McParland

CELTIC: Haffey; McKay, Kennedy; Crerand, McNeill, Clark; Gallagher, Fernie, Hughes, Chalmers, Byrne

Attendance: 27,000

March 20th
CELTIC (1) 1 — RAITH ROVERS (0) 1
Chalmers (22) — Fox (74)

CELTIC: Haffey; McKay, Kennedy; Crerand, McNeill, Clark; Gallagher, Fernie, Hughes, Chalmers, Byrne

RAITH ROVERS: Thorburn; McDonald, McNaught; Stein, Polland, Leigh; Buchanan, Fox, Wallace, Benvie, Urquhart

Attendance: n.a.

March 22nd: Crerand and McNeill were in the Scottish League team which beat the English League 3-2 at Ibrox.

March 25th
CELTIC (0) 2 — DUNFERMLINE (1) 1
Fernie (52), Byrne (57) — Melrose (19)

CELTIC: Haffey; McKay, Kennedy; Crerand, McNeill, Clark; Gallagher, Fernie, Hughes, Chalmers, Byrne

DUNFERMLINE: Connachan; Fraser, Cunningham; Mailer, Williamson, Miller; Peebles, Smith, Dickson, McLindon, Melrose

Attendance: 20,000

April 5th
CELTIC (0) 1 — ST JOHNSTONE (1) 1
Fernie (60) — Gardiner (34)

CELTIC: Haffey; McKay, Kennedy; Crerand, McNeill, Clark; Gallagher, Chalmers, Hughes, Fernie, Byrne

ST JOHNSTONE: Taylor; McFadyen, Lachlan; Little, Ferguson, McKinven; Newlands, Gardiner, Walker, Innes, Carr

Attendance: 8,000

April 8th
DUNDEE (0) 0 — CELTIC (1) 1
Chalmers (30)

DUNDEE: Liney; Hamilton, Cox; Seith, Ure, Cowie; Penman, Cousin, Gilzean, Wishart, Robertson

CELTIC: Haffey; McKay, Kennedy; Crerand, McNeill, Clark; Gallagher, Fernie, Hughes, Chalmers, Byrne

Attendance: 17,500

April 10th
DUNDEE UNITED (1) 1 — CELTIC (0) 1
Ormond (28) — Hughes (82)

DUNDEE UNITED: Brown; Graham, Briggs; Neilson, Smith, Fraser; Bonar, Gillespie, Mochan, Howieson, Ormond

CELTIC: Haffey; McKay, Kennedy; Crerand, McNeill, Clark; Gallagher, Chalmers, Hughes, Fernie, Byrne

Attendance: 15,000

April 15th: Haffey and McNeill were in the Scotland team beaten 9-3 by England at Wembley.

April 25th: Bertie Peacock was in the Ireland team beaten 3-2 by Italy in Bologna.

April 25th: Jim Kennedy was rushed to hospital with appendicitis and missed the Scottish Cup Final Replay with Dunfermline. 19-year old Willie O'Neil took his place for his first senior appearance for the club.

April 29th
MOTHERWELL (2) 2 — CELTIC (1) 2
Roberts 2 (5, 45) — Chalmers (17), Fernie (85)

MOTHERWELL: Wylie; Delaney, Strachan; Aitken, Martis, McPhee; Lindsay, St John, Roberts, Quinn, Hunter

CELTIC: Haffey; McKay, O'Neill; Crerand, McNeill, Clark; Chalmers, Carroll, Hughes, Fernie, Byrne

Attendance: 14,000

April 30th: Jim Conway was transferred to Norwich City for £12,000.

May 1st: Bertie Auld joined Birmingham City for £15,000.

May 2nd
CELTIC (1) 1 — HEARTS (2) 3
Divers (24) — Wallace (16), Davidson 2 (23, 85)

CELTIC: Haffey; Curran, O'Neill; Kelly, Kurila, Clark; Carroll, Divers, Hughes, Chalmers, Byrne

HEARTS: Marshall; Kirk, Ferguson; Higgins, Polland, Cumming; Henderson, Davidson, Wallace, Docherty, Hamilton

Attendance: 7,000

Scottish First Division

	P	W	D	L	F	A	Pts
1 Rangers	34	23	5	6	88	46	51
2 Kilmarnock	34	21	8	5	77	45	50
3 Third Lanark	34	20	2	12	100	80	42
4 CELTIC	34	15	9	10	64	46	39
5 Motherwell	34	15	8	11	70	57	38
6 Aberdeen	34	14	8	12	72	72	36
7 Hibernian	34	15	4	15	66	69	34
8 Hearts	34	13	8	13	51	51	34
9 Dundee United	34	13	7	14	60	58	33
10 Dundee	34	13	6	15	61	53	32
11 Partick Thistle	34	13	6	15	59	69	32
12 Dunfermline	34	12	7	15	65	81	31
13 Airdrie	34	10	10	14	61	71	30
14 St Mirren	34	11	7	16	53	58	29
15 St Johnstone	34	10	9	15	47	63	29
16 Raith Rovers	34	10	7	17	46	67	27
17 Clyde	34	6	11	17	55	77	23
18 Ayr United	34	5	12	17	51	81	22

May 2nd: Lochead, Mackle and Connor were given free transfers.

May 3rd: Crerand and McNeill were in the Scotland team which beat Eire 4-1 at Hampden Park.

May 3rd: Bertie Peacock was in the Ireland team beaten 2-1 by Greece in Athens.

May 7th: Crerand and McNeill were in the Scotland team which beat Eire 3-0 in Dublin.

May 10th: Peacock was in the Ireland team beaten 2-1 by West Germany in Berlin.

May 14th: Crerand and McNeill were in the Scotland team beaten 4-0 by Czechoslovakia in Bratislava. Crerand was ordered off in the 38th minute together with Kvasnak of Czechoslovakia.

May 18th: Bertie Peacock joined Coleraine.

LEAGUE CUP

August 13th
CELTIC (0) 2 THIRD LANARK (0) 0
Hughes (50), Mochan (74)

CELTIC: Haffey; McKay, Kennedy; Crerand, McNeill, Peacock; Carroll, Chalmers, Hughes, Mochan, Divers

THIRD LANARK: Robertson; McGillivray, Caldow; Reilly, Robb, Cunningham; Hilley, Brims, Harley, Gray, Goodfellow

Attendance: 25,000

August 17th
PARTICK THISTLE (0) 1 CELTIC (0) 1
Smith (56) Carroll (81)

PARTICK THISTLE: Freebairn; Hogan, Baird; Wright, Harvey, Donlevy; McKenzie, McParland, Smith, Hastings, Fleming

CELTIC: Haffey; McKay, Kennedy; Crerand, McNeill, Peacock; Carroll, Chalmers, Hughes, Divers, Mochan

Attendance: 20,000

August 20th
RANGERS (1) 2 CELTIC (3) 3
Millar (36), Brand (61) Carroll (15), Divers (25), Hughes (44)

RANGERS: Ritchie; Shearer, Caldow; Davis, Baillie, Baxter; Scott, Baird, Millar, Brand, Wilson

CELTIC: Haffey; McKay, Kennedy; Crerand, McNeill, Peacock; Carroll, Chalmers, Hughes, Divers, Mochan

Attendance: 60,000

Hughes, only seventeen, caused havoc in Rangers' defence. The even bigger, heavier Baillie was time and again confused as his much more nimble opponent beat him for speed and control of the ball. In the 2nd half Haffey, who had broken a toe earlier, was in constant peril, but he was beaten only once – by Brand.

August 27th
THIRD LANARK (0) 1 CELTIC (3) 3
Goodfellow (59) Divers (6), Hughes 2 (20, 23)

THIRD LANARK: Robertson; McGillivray, Caldwell; Reilly, Robb, Cunningham; Goodfellow, Hilley, Harley, Gray, McInnes

CELTIC: Fallon; McKay, Kennedy; Crerand, McNeill, Peacock; Conway, Chalmers, Hughes, Divers, Mochan

Attendance: 31,000

August 31st
CELTIC (0) 1 PARTICK THISTLE (2) 2
Hughes (73) Smith 2 (10, 34)

CELTIC: Fallon; McKay, Kennedy; Crerand, Kurila, Peacock; Carroll, Chalmers, Hughes, Divers, Mochan

PARTICK THISTLE: Freebairn; Hogan, Baird; Wright, Harvey, Donlevy; Fleming, McParland, Smith, Hastings, Ferns

Attendance: 26,000

September 3rd
CELTIC (1) 1 RANGERS (0) 2
Chalmers (2) Davis (48), Brand (70)

CELTIC: Fallon; McKay, Kennedy; Crerand, Kurila, Peacock; Carroll, Chalmers, Hughes, Divers, Mochan

RANGERS: Ritchie; Shearer, Caldow; Davis, Paterson, Baxter; Scott, McMillan, Millar, Brand, Wilson

Attendance: n.a.

Rangers were indeed fortunate to be only 1 goal down at the interval – a goal by Chalmers after only 2 minutes which they claimed, with some justification, was offside. Paterson, taking the minimum of risks and blocking the middle successfully if unattractively, kept Rangers in the game. Shortly after half-time Davis headed the equaliser – Brand dummied the ball and deceived Fallon. 20 minutes from time Millar beat Kurila in the air and enabled Brand to shoot from 16 yards, so fast that Fallon was beaten where he stood.

SECTION TABLE

	P	W	D	L	F	A	Pts
Rangers	6	4	0	2	15	10	8
CELTIC	6	3	1	2	11	8	7
Third Lanark	6	3	0	3	12	10	6
Partick Thistle	6	1	1	4	6	16	3

Qualifier: RANGERS

SCOTTISH CUP

First Round January 28th
FALKIRK (0) 1 CELTIC (2) 3
McMillan (69 pen) Thomson o.g. (10), Peacock 2 (20 pen, 75 pen)

FALKIRK: Whigham; Thomson, McIntosh; McCarry, Lowry, Pierson; Lambie, McMillan, Moran, Reid, Duchart

CELTIC: Haffey; McKay, Kennedy; Crerand, McNeill, Peacock; Gallagher, Divers, Hughes, Fernie, Auld

Attendance: 20,300

Second Round February 11th
CELTIC (4) 6 MONTROSE (0) 0
McCorquodale o.g. (1), Hughes 2 (10, 27), Chalmers 2 (11, 75), Byrne (56)

CELTIC: Haffey; McKay, Kennedy; Crerand, McNeill, Peacock; Gallagher, Divers, Hughes, Chalmers, Byrne

MONTROSE: Grieve; Russell, Ogilvie; Cross, Nicoll, McCorquodale; Riddle, Dunn, J. Kemp, Sandeman, R. Kemp

Attendance: 26,000

Third Round February 25th

RAITH ROVERS (1) 1 — CELTIC (3) 4

Wallace (13) — Chalmers (7), Leigh o.g. (14), Fernie (26), Hughes (90)

RAITH ROVERS: Thorburn; McDonald, McNaught; Leigh, Polland, Duffy; Peebles, Easson, Wallace, Malcolm, Matthew

CELTIC: Haffey; McKay, Kennedy; Crerand, McNeill, Peacock; Gallagher, Fernie, Hughes, Chalmers, Byrne

Attendance: 19,359

Fourth Round March 11th

CELTIC (0) 1 — HIBERNIAN (0) 1

Chalmers (85) — Kinloch (47)

CELTIC: Haffey; McKay, Kennedy; Crerand, McNeill, Peacock; Gallagher, Fernie, Hughes, Chalmers, Byrne

HIBERNIAN: Simpson; Fraser, McLelland; Baxter, Easton, Baird; McLeod, Kinloch, Baker, Preston, Stevenson

Attendance: 56,000

Fourth Round Replay March 15th

HIBERNIAN (0) 0 — CELTIC (0) 1

Clark (104)

After Extra Time

HIBERNIAN: Simpson; Fraser, McLelland; Baxter, Easton, Baird; McLeod, Kinloch, Baker, Preston, Stevenson

CELTIC: Haffey; McKay, Kennedy; Crerand, McNeill, Clark; Gallagher, Fernie, Hughes, Chalmers, Byrne

Attendance: 39,243

Semi-Final April 1st at Hampden Park

CELTIC (4) 4 — AIRDRIE (0) 0

Hughes 2 (19, 24), Chalmers (37), Fernie (42)

CELTIC: Haffey; McKay, Kennedy; Crerand, McNeill, Clark; Gallagher, Fernie, Hughes, Chalmers, Byrne

AIRDRIE: Leslie; Shanks, Keenan; Stewart, Johnstone, McNeill; Rankin, Storrie, Sharkey, Caven, Duncan

Attendance: 72,612

For only about 20 minutes was this Semi-Final a contest. During that period Haffey made two exceptionally fine saves from Storrie. In the 37th minute Chalmers raced through the middle of Airdrie's defence as Gallagher thrust the ball into his path and Leslie was defeated by his cleverly lofted shot which Chalmers directed over him. Airdrie might have lost 3 more goals before Fernie, 3 minutes from half-time, meandered in from the right and baffled both Leslie and Shanks with an almost cheeky flick with the outside of his foot.

Final April 22nd at Hampden Park

CELTIC 0 — DUNFERMLINE 0

CELTIC: Haffey; McKay, Kennedy; Crerand, McNeill, Clark; Gallagher, Fernie, Hughes, Chalmers, Byrne

DUNFERMLINE: Connachan; Fraser, Cunningham; Mailer, Williamson, Miller; Peebles, Smith, Dickson, McLindon, Melrose

Attendance: 113,328 *Referee:* H. Phillips

This match, although goalless, was thoroughly entertaining. Connachan entitled himself to the freedom of Dunfermline for his impeccable display. One save from a Hughes header was world-class. But an even more valuable save was that of Haffey as the final minutes ticked away when he saved a venomous low shot from Peebles, Dunfermline, even when their centre-half Williamson was absent through injury for the last 13 minutes, maintained their studied pattern of play. Hughes more than once was unlucky in his individual sorties. Byrne was the recipient, time and again, of magnificent passes from Crerand but rarely turned the defence.

Final Replay April 26th at Hampden Park

CELTIC (0) 0 — DUNFERMLINE (0) 2

Thomson (67), Dickson (88)

CELTIC: Haffey; McKay, O'Neill; Crerand, McNeill, Clark; Gallagher, Fernie, Hughes, Chalmers, Byrne

DUNFERMLINE: Connachan; Fraser, Cunningham; Mailer, Miller, Sweeney; Peebles, Smith, Thomson, Dickson, Melrose

Attendance: 87,866 *Referee:* H. Phillips

Dunfermline won the Scottish Cup – a remarkable achievement, for never before this season had the Fife club reached the Semi-Final let alone the Final. A headed goal by Thomson put Dunfermline ahead in 67 minutes after terrific Celtic pressure. Magnificent goal-keeping by Connachan denied Celtic time and time again before Haffey made a shocking blunder 2 minutes from the end and presented Dickson with a decisive 2nd goal. Although the reconstructed Dunfermline defence played with enormous zeal, Celtic lost the Final through their own forward deficiencies. Celtic's front line were much too individualistic, and only when Crerand decided to make his great late efforts did the Dunfermline defence look like wilting.

APPEARANCES	League	League Cup	Scottish Cup
Fallon	4	3	–
McKay	32	6	8
Kennedy	32	6	7
Crerand	31	6	8
McNeill	31	4	8
Peacock	24	6	4
Carroll	17	5	–
Chalmers	32	6	7
Hughes	19	6	8
Divers	23	6	2
Mochan	2	6	–
Kurila	3	2	–
Conway	7	1	–
Auld	15	–	1
Gallagher	15	–	8
Goldie	1	–	–
Byrne	16	–	7
Haffey	29	3	8
Clark	10	–	4
Fernie	22	–	7
Donnelly	1	–	–
Jackson	1	–	–
Kelly	3	–	–
McNamee	1	–	–
O'Neill	2	–	1
Curran	1	–	–

GOALSCORERS:

League: Chalmers 20, Divers 8, Carroll 6, Fernie 6, Auld 4, Peacock 4 (3 pens), Hughes 4, Byrne 4, Gallagher 3, Crerand 2, McNeill 1, Conway 1, Mochan 1

League Cup: Hughes 5, Carroll 2, Divers 2, Mochan 1, Chalmers 1

Scottish Cup: Hughes 5, Chalmers 5, Own Goals 3, Fernie 2, Peacock 2 (2 pens), Byrne 1, Clark 1

The Celtic team in 1960-61. Back row: McKay, Kennedy, Haffey, Crerand, McNeill, Clark. Front row: Gallagher, Fernie, Hughes, Chalmers and Byrne.

Season 1961-62

Celtic finished 3rd in the table – 5 points behind Rangers and 8 points behind Dundee who won their first-ever Championship. The Parkhead team won 19 of their matches and completed the double over Dundee United, Dunfermline, Partick Thistle, St Johnstone and St Mirren. They lost only 1 home game – their final one against Raith Rovers. Late goals from Brogan and McNeill gave them a home victory over Dundee in March and both Old Firm meetings were drawn. Frank Brogan scored their 5,000th League goal in the match at Firhill on April 4th. Johnny Divers was their only ever-present and he finished as top scorer with 19 goals followed by Hughes on 18. Bobby Lennox made his first-team debut during the season.

Celtic were beaten home and away by St Johnstone which prevented their qualification to the later stages of the League Cup. This was their 11th such failure in 16 seasons.

They reached the Semi-Final of the Scottish Cup but surprisingly lost to St Mirren whom they had beaten 5-0 at Love Street only 5 days previously. The Paisley side, showing 6 team changes, were 3 goals up after only 33 minutes. Hearts were beaten 4-3 at Tynecastle in the Fourth Round and Third Lanark were beaten 4-0 in a Quarter-Final replay at Hampden Park after a 4-4 draw at Parkhead.

League:	Third
League Cup:	Failed to qualify from Section
Scottish Cup:	Semi-Finalists

SCOTTISH FIRST DIVISION

August 5th: Pat Crerand was suspended for a month for being ordered off in a five-a-side tournament at Brockville Park, Falkirk.

August 7th: Frank Connor who had been given a free transfer was recalled because of an injury to Frank Haffey.

August 23rd
KILMARNOCK (2) 3 — CELTIC (1) 2
McInally (4), Muir (31), Black (56) — Divers (29), Chalmers (60)

KILMARNOCK: McLaughlin; Richmond, Watson; Davidson, Toner, Beattie; McIlroy, Mason, Black, McInally, Muir

CELTIC: Connor; Donnelly, Kennedy; Jackson, McNeill, Clark; Carroll, Fernie, Hughes, Divers, Chalmers

Attendance: 20,000

September 9th
CELTIC (0) 1 — THIRD LANARK (0) 0
Divers (72)

CELTIC: Connor; McKay, Kennedy; Crerand, McNeill, Price; Chalmers, Jackson, Hughes, Divers, Fernie

THIRD LANARK: Robertson; McGillivray, Lewis; Reilly, McCormick, Cunningham; Goodfellow, Hilley, Harley, Gray, McInnes

Attendance: 29,000

September 16th
RANGERS (1) 2 — CELTIC (1) 2
Christie (5), Baxter (88) — Divers (23), Fernie (48)

RANGERS: Ritchie; Shearer, Caldow; Davis, Paterson, Baxter; Scott, McMillan, Christie, Brand, Wilson

CELTIC: Haffey; McKay, Kennedy; Crerand, McNeill, Price; Chalmers, Jackson, Hughes, Divers, Fernie

Attendance: 70,000. 2 people were killed and 60 hurt when the crowd broke a barrier at the end of the match

Rangers were the superior team in the first-half. Christie chasing every ball was a constant menace to Celtic defenders as he sought to add to the goal he headed from a cross by Wilson after 5 minutes' play. Divers, taking the home defence by surprise after 28 minutes, scored from a pass by Chalmers. 3 minutes after the interval Celtic took the lead when Fernie was in position to jab the ball past Ritchie from close range after Shearer blocked a shot from Chalmers. 2 minutes from the end Rangers equalised through Baxter with a shot from 25 yards.

September 23rd
CELTIC (2) 3 DUNDEE UNITED (1) 1
Hughes (13), Chalmers (45), Jackson (70) Gillespie (40)

CELTIC: Haffey; McKay, Kennedy; Crerand, McNeill, Price; Chalmers, Jackson, Hughes, Divers, Carroll

DUNDEE UNITED: Ugolini; Graham, Briggs; Neilson, Smith, Fraser; Bonnar, McMichael, Carlyle, Gillespie, Mochan

Attendance: 24,000

September 26th: McKay, Crerand and McNeill were in the Scotland team which beat Czechoslovakia 3-2 at Hampden Park in a World Cup Qualifier.

September 30th
FALKIRK (1) 3 CELTIC (1) 1
Duchart (9), Oliver (50), Murray (52) Hughes (14)

FALKIRK: Whigham; Rae, Hunter; Pierson, Thomson, McIntosh; Oliver, Reid, Duchart, Murray, Ormond

CELTIC: Haffey; McKay, Kennedy; Crerand, McNeill, Price; Chalmers, Jackson, Hughes, Divers, Carroll

Attendance: 13,000

October 7th: McKay, Crerand and McNeill were in the Scotland team which beat Ireland 6-1 in Belfast.

October 14th
CELTIC (3) 5 STIRLING ALBION (0) 0
Carroll (13), Hughes 3 (22, 30, 52), Divers (77)

CELTIC: Haffey; McKay, Kennedy; Crerand, McNeill, Price; Chalmers, Jackson, Hughes, Divers, Carroll

STIRLING ALBION: Wren; McGuinness, Pettigrew; Myles, J. Sinclair, McGregor; W. Sinclair, Addison, Gilmour, Dyson, Lawlor

Attendance: 22,000

October 18th
ST JOHNSTONE (0) 0 CELTIC (1) 3
Divers (2), Jackson (72), Carroll (74)

ST JOHNSTONE: Taylor; McFadyen, Lachlan; Little, Ferguson, Rattray; Walker, Rankin, Gardiner, Bell, McVittie

CELTIC: Haffey; McKay, Kennedy; Crerand, McNeill, Price; Chalmers, Jackson, Hughes, Divers, Carroll

Attendance: 7,000

October 21st
HEARTS (2) 2 CELTIC (0) 1
Wallace (14), Elliott (43) Hughes (58)

HEARTS: Marshall; Kirk, Holt; Cumming, Polland, Higgins; Ferguson, Elliot, Wallace, Gordon, Hamilton

CELTIC: Haffey; McKay, Kennedy; Crerand, McNeill, Price; Chalmers, Jackson, Hughes, Divers, Carroll

Attendance: 22,000

October 28th
CELTIC (1) 2 DUNFERMLINE (1) 1
Carroll 2 (24, 77) McDonald (29)

CELTIC: Haffey; McKay, Kennedy; Crerand, McNamee, Price; Chalmers, Jackson, Hughes, Divers, Carroll

DUNFERMLINE: Connachan; Fraser, Cunningham; Mailer, Williamson, Miller; McDonald, Peebles, Dickson, Smith, Melrose

Attendance: 26,000

League positions

	P	W	D	L	F	A	Pts
1 Dundee	9	8	0	1	27	14	16
2 Kilmarnock	9	6	1	2	22	16	13
3 Rangers	7	4	3	0	22	7	11
4 CELTIC	9	5	1	3	20	12	11
5 Third Lanark	9	5	1	3	22	14	11

November 4th
DUNDEE (1) 2 CELTIC (1) 1
Wishart (8), Gilzean (58) Carroll (21)

DUNDEE: Liney; Hamilton, Cox; Seith, Ure, Wishart; Smith, Penman, Cousin, Gilzean, Robertson

CELTIC: Haffey; McKay, Kennedy; Crerand, McNamee, Clark; Chalmers, Jackson, Hughes, Divers, Carroll

Attendance: 24,500

November 8th: Pat Crerand was in the Scotland team which beat Wales 2-0 at Hampden Park.

November 15th
CELTIC (3) 7 ST MIRREN (0) 1
Chalmers 2 (18, 40), Carroll 2 (20, 55), Jackson 2 (53, 61), Hughes (69) Beck (80)

CELTIC: Haffey; McKay, Kennedy; Crerand, McNamee, Price; Chalmers, Jackson, Hughes, Divers, Carroll

ST MIRREN: Williamson; Campbell, Wilson; Henderson, Clunie, McTavish; Rodger, Beck, Kerrigan, Gemmell, Miller

Attendance: 22,000

November 18th
CELTIC (1) 3 — AIRDRIE (0) 0
Jackson 2 (26, 68), Hughes (85)

CELTIC: Haffey; McKay, Kennedy; Crerand, McNamee, Price; Chalmers, Jackson, Hughes, Divers, Carroll

AIRDRIE: Dempster; Shanks, Ross; Hinshelwood, Johnstone, McNeill; Murray, Storrie, Caven, Reid, Newlands

Attendance: 26,000

November 25th
ABERDEEN 0 — CELTIC 0

ABERDEEN: Ogston; Bennett, Cadenhead; Burns, Kinnell, Fraser; Callaghan, Brownlie, Little, Baird, Mulhall

CELTIC: Haffey; McKay, Kennedy; Crerand, McNeill, Price; Chalmers, Jackson, Hughes, Divers, Carroll

Attendance: 15,000

November 29th: Pat Crerand was in the Scotland team which was beaten 4-2 by Czechoslovakia in a World Cup play-off in Brussels.

December 2nd
CELTIC (2) 5 — PARTICK THISTLE (0) 1
Hughes (14), Jackson (23), Chalmers 2 (52, 86), Divers (77) — McParland (62)

CELTIC: Haffey; McKay, Kennedy; Crerand, McNeill, Price; Chalmers, Jackson, Hughes, Divers, Carroll

PARTICK THISTLE: Gray; Hogan, Brown; Harvey, McKinnon, Cunningham; Williamson, McBride, McParland, Duffy, Ewing

Attendance: 20,000

December 16th
CELTIC (1) 4 — HIBERNIAN (2) 3
Divers 3 (23, 58, 79), Hughes (54) — Falconer 2 (21, 77), Stevenson (40)

CELTIC: Haffey; McKay, Kennedy; Crerand, McNeill, Price; Chalmers, Jackson, Hughes, Divers, Carroll

HIBERNIAN: Simpson; Fraser, McLelland; Preston, Easton, Grant; Stevenson, Gibson, Baker, Falconer, McLeod

Attendance: 28,000

December 23rd
RAITH ROVERS (0) 0 — CELTIC (2) 4
Chalmers (28), Carroll (41), Divers 2 (57, 59)

RAITH ROVERS: Thorburn; Wilson, Mochan; Clinton, Forsyth, Leigh; Adamson, Fox, White, Benvie, Malcolm

CELTIC: Haffey; McKay, Kennedy; Crerand, McNeill, Price; Chalmers, Jackson, Hughes, Divers, Carroll

Attendance: 14,000

League positions

	P	W	D	L	F	A	Pts
1 Dundee	16	13	2	1	50	25	28
2 CELTIC	16	10	2	4	44	19	22
3 Rangers	15	9	3	3	38	19	21
4 Partick Thistle	17	10	1	6	37	32	21
5 Dunfermline	17	8	4	5	37	22	20

January 6th
CELTIC (1) 2 — KILMARNOCK (1) 2
Carroll (31), Chalmers (47) — Kerr (34), McIlroy (80)

CELTIC: Haffey; McKay, Kennedy; Crerand, McNeill, Price; Chalmers, Jackson, Hughes, Divers, Carroll

KILMARNOCK: Forsyth; Richmond, Watson; Davidson, Toner, Beattie; McInally, Yard, Kerr, Sneddon, McIlroy

Attendance: 35,000

January 10th
THIRD LANARK (0) 1 — CELTIC (0) 1
Gray (90) — Chalmers (89)

THIRD LANARK: Robertson; McCallum, Lewis; Reilly, McCormick, Cunningham; Goodfellow, Hilley, Harley, Gray, Fletcher

CELTIC: Haffey; McKay, Kennedy; Crerand, McNeill, Price; Chalmers, Jackson, Hughes, Divers, Carroll

Attendance: n.a.

January 13th
DUNDEE UNITED (1) 4 — CELTIC (4) 5
Irvine 3 (23, 67, 73), Carlyle (81) — Jackson 2 (13, 21), Hughes 2 (14, 60), Crerand (46)

DUNDEE UNITED: Brown; Gordon, Briggs; Neilson, Smith, Fraser; Carlyle, Brodie, Mochan, Irvine, Gillespie

CELTIC: Haffey; McKay, Kennedy; Crerand, McNeill, Price; Chalmers, Jackson, Hughes, Divers, Carroll

Attendance: 20,000

January 20th
CELTIC (3) 3 — FALKIRK (0) 0
Divers (21), Jackson (29), Crerand (43 pen)

CELTIC: Haffey; McKay, Kennedy; Crerand, McNeill, Price; Chalmers, Jackson, Hughes, Divers, Carroll

FALKIRK: Whigham; Lambie, McIntosh; Thomson, Milne, Pierson; Reid, Harrower, Duchart, Innes, Oliver

Attendance: 27,000

January 22nd
CELTIC (1) 1 — MOTHERWELL (0) 1
Jackson (37) — Young (89)

CELTIC: Haffey; McKay, Kennedy; Crerand, McNeill, Price; Chalmers, Jackson, Hughes, Divers, Carroll

MOTHERWELL: Weir; Delaney, McCallum; Aitken, Martis, McCann; Young, Quinn, Roberts, Hunter, McPhee

Attendance: 23,000

February 3rd
CELTIC (1) 3 — ST JOHNSTONE (0) 1
Divers 2 (5, 76), Hughes (71) — Thomson (75)

CELTIC: Haffey; McKay, Kennedy; Crerand, McNeill, Price; Carroll, Jackson, Hughes, Divers, Byrne

ST JOHNSTONE: Taylor; McFadyen, Lachlan; Little, Ferguson, McKinven; Thomson, Rankin, Kemp, Donlevy, Henderson

Attendance: 19,000

February 5th: Kennedy and Carroll were in the Scottish League team which played a Scotland XI in an international trial at Hampden Park. Carroll scored one of the goals in a 2-2 draw.

February 10th
STIRLING ALBION (0) 1 CELTIC (0) 0
Lawlor (49)

STIRLING ALBION: J. Brown; D. Brown, McGuinness; Rowan, Weir, Johnstone; Kilgannon, Spence, Park, Maxwell, Lawlor

CELTIC: Haffey; McKay, Kennedy; Clark, McNamee, Price; Carroll, Jackson, Hughes, Divers, Byrne

Attendance: 11,000

February 21st
CELTIC (1) 2 — HEARTS (1) 2
Divers (4), Hughes (65) — Paton 2 (44, 51)

CELTIC: Haffey; McKay, Kennedy; Crerand, McNeill, Price; Brogan, Chalmers, Hughes, Divers, Carroll

HEARTS: Marshall; Polland, Holt; Ferguson, Cumming, Higgins; Rodger, Blackwood, Paton, Gordon, Hamilton

Attendance: 23,000

February 24th
DUNFERMLINE (0) 0 — CELTIC (0) 3
Divers (60), Hughes 2 (77, 86)

DUNFERMLINE: Connachan; Fraser, Cunningham; Thomson, Williamson, Miller; McDonald, Smith, Dickson, Melrose, Peebles

CELTIC: Haffey; McKay, Kennedy; Crerand, McNeill, Clark; Jackson, Chalmers, Hughes, Divers, Brogan

Attendance: 15,000

League positions

	P	W	D	L	F	A	Pts
1 Dundee	24	18	3	3	62	36	39
2 Rangers	24	17	4	3	65	24	38
3 CELTIC	25	14	6	5	64	31	34
4 Hearts	26	14	5	7	47	37	33
5 Dunfermline	25	14	4	7	59	35	32

February 23rd: McNeill and Hughes were in the Scotland Under-23 team beaten 4-2 by the England Under-23s at Pittodrie. Hughes scored one of Scotland's goals.

March 3rd
CELTIC (0) 2 — DUNDEE (0) 1
Brogan (80), McNeill (85) — Wishart (56)

CELTIC: Haffey; McKay, Kennedy; Crerand, McNeill, Price; Brogan, Lennox, Hughes, Divers, Carroll

DUNDEE: Liney; Hamilton, Cox; Seith, Ure, Brown; Smith, Cousin, Wishart, Gilzean, Robertson

Attendance: 39,000

Late in the game Celtic, 0-1 down and practically devoid of ideas in forward play, scored twice to record a sensational victory. Lennox found the pace of his first Scottish League game overwhelming, and none of his forward colleagues was capable of coaxing him into confidence.

March 17th
AIRDRIE (0) 1 — CELTIC (0) 0
Murray (51)

AIRDRIE: Dempster; Jonquin, Shanks; Reid, Hannah, Stewart; Murray, Storrie, Tees, Hume, Duncan

CELTIC: Haffey; McKay, Kennedy; Crerand, McNeill, Clark; Carroll, Chalmers, Hughes, Divers, Byrne

Attendance: 24,000

March 24th
CELTIC (1) 2 — ABERDEEN (0) 0
Brogan 2 (42, 59)

CELTIC: Haffey; McKay, O'Neill; Crerand, McNeill, Clark; Brogan, Chalmers, Hughes, Divers, Byrne

ABERDEEN: Ogston; Shewan, Hogg; Brownlie, Kinnell, Fraser; Cummings, Little, Callaghan, Cooke, Thom

Attendance: 21,000

March 26th
ST MIRREN (0) 0 — CELTIC (4) 5
Divers 2 (7, 68), Carroll (13), Chalmers 2 (17, 22)

ST MIRREN: Williamson; Nelson, Wilson; Fernie, Clunie, McTavish; Henderson, Gemmell, McDonald, R. Campbell, Miller

CELTIC: Haffey; McKay, O'Neill; Crerand, McNeill, Clark; Brogan, Chalmers, Carroll, Divers, Byrne

Attendance: n.a.

April 4th
PARTICK THISTLE (0) 1 CELTIC (1) 2
Hainey (56) Brogan (31), Hughes (84)

PARTICK THISTLE: Niven; Muir, Brown; Harvey, McKinnon, Cunningham; Smith, McBride, Hainey, Duffy, McParland

CELTIC: Haffey; Donnelly, Kennedy; Crerand, McNeill, Clark; Brogan, Chalmers, Hughes, Divers, Byrne

Attendance: 7,200. Frank Brogan's goal was Celtic's 5,000th League goal

April 7th
HIBERNIAN (0) 1 CELTIC (0) 1
Falconer (81) Divers (78)

HIBERNIAN: Simpson; Fraser, McLelland; Preston, Easton, McLeod; Scott, Baker, Marjoribanks, Falconer, Stevenson

CELTIC: Haffey; McKay, Kennedy; Crerand, McNeill, Clark; Brogan, Chalmers, Hughes, Divers, Byrne

Attendance: 50,000

April 9th
CELTIC (1) 1 RANGERS (0) 1
Hughes (43) Wilson (78)

CELTIC: Haffey; Donnelly, Kennedy; McKay, McNeill, Clark; Chalmers, Carroll, Hughes, Divers, Brogan

RANGERS: Ritchie; Shearer, Caldow; Davis, McKinnon, Baxter; Henderson, Greig, Millar, Brand, Wilson

Attendance: 50,000

Rangers were outplayed for most of the game but were able to salvage the point which kept them ahead of the table. On a surface made treacherous by heavy rain Celtic adopted the proper tactics of moving the ball swiftly from man to man and employing their wingers to full advantage. The only Rangers' forward who caused any discomfort to them was the diminutive Henderson. McKinnon had an unhappy match against Hughes.

April 14th: Crerand and McNeill were in the Scotland team which beat England 2-0 at Hampden Park.

April 21st
CELTIC (0) 0 RAITH ROVERS (0) 1
Adamson (17)

CELTIC: Haffey; McKay, Kennedy; Crerand, McNeill, Clark; Brogan, Chalmers, Carroll, Divers, Byrne

RAITH ROVERS: Thorburn; Stevenson, Mochan; Stein, Forsyth, Leigh; Adamson, Kerr, Gilfillan, McFadzean, Urquhart

Attendance: 11,000

April 23rd
MOTHERWELL (0) 0 CELTIC (2) 4
Carroll 2 (6, 38), Delaney o.g. (84), Chalmers (87)

MOTHERWELL: Wylie; Delaney, Thomson; Aitken, Martis, McPhee; Lindsay, Quinn, Strachan, Hunter, Roberts

CELTIC: Haffey; McKay, Kennedy; Crerand, McNeill, Clark; Chalmers, Gallagher, Carroll, Divers, Brogan

Attendance: n.a.

Scottish First Division

	P	W	D	L	F	A	Pts
1 Dundee	34	25	4	5	80	46	54
2 Rangers	34	22	7	5	84	31	51
3 CELTIC	34	19	8	7	81	37	46
4 Dunfermline	34	19	5	10	77	46	43
5 Kilmarnock	34	16	10	8	74	58	42
6 Hearts	34	16	6	12	54	49	38
7 Partick Thistle	34	16	3	15	60	55	35
8 Hibernian	34	14	5	15	58	72	33
9 Motherwell	34	13	6	15	65	62	32
10 Dundee United	34	13	6	15	70	71	32
11 Third Lanark	34	13	5	16	59	60	31
12 Aberdeen	34	10	9	15	60	73	29
13 Raith Rovers	34	10	7	17	51	73	27
14 Falkirk	34	11	4	19	45	68	26
15 Airdrie	34	9	7	18	57	78	25
16 St Mirren	34	10	5	19	52	80	25
17 St Johnstone	34	9	7	18	35	61	25
18 Stirling Albion	34	6	6	22	34	76	18

May 2nd: Crerand and McNeill were in the Scotland team beaten 3-2 by Uruguay at Hampden Park.

May 2nd: John Kurila was given a free transfer.

LEAGUE CUP

August 12th
PARTICK THISTLE (0) 2 CELTIC (1) 3
McBride 2 (50, 66) Jackson 2 (2, 80), Hughes (57)

PARTICK THISTLE: Gray; Muir, Brown; Harvey, McKinnon, Donlevy; Smith, Wright, McBride, Duffy, McParland

CELTIC: Connor; McKay, Kennedy; Kurila, McNeill, Clark; Carroll, Jackson, Hughes, Divers, Chalmers

Attendance: 33,549

August 16th
CELTIC (0) 0 ST JOHNSTONE (0) 1
Grant (75)

CELTIC: Connor; McKay, Kennedy; Kurila, McNeill, Clark; Carroll, Jackson, Hughes, Divers, Chalmers

ST JOHNSTONE: Taylor; McFadyen, Lachlan; Little, Ferguson, McKinven; McVittie, Gardiner, Grant, Bell, Henderson

Attendance: 23,000

August 19th
HIBERNIAN (1) 2 — CELTIC (1) 2
Kinloch 2 (9, 77) — Hughes (8), Chalmers (52)

HIBERNIAN: Simpson; Fraser, Grant; Baxter, Easton, Baird; Stevenson, Gibson, Kinloch, Preston, McLeod

CELTIC: Connor; Donnelly, Kennedy; Price, McNeill, Clark; Carroll, Fernie, Hughes, Divers, Chalmers

Attendance: 28,000

August 26th
CELTIC (1) 3 — PARTICK THISTLE (0) 2
Hughes 2 (34, 69), Carroll (76) — McBride (65), Smith (86 pen)

CELTIC: Connor; McKay, Kennedy; Jackson, McNeill, Clark; Carroll, Fernie, Hughes, Divers, Chalmers

PARTICK THISTLE: Freebairn; Muir, Brown; Cunningham, McKinnon, Donlevy; Smith, McBride, Hainey, Duffy, McParland

Attendance: 27,000

August 30th
ST JOHNSTONE (2) 2 — CELTIC (0) 0
Gardiner (16), Wright (35)

ST JOHNSTONE: Taylor; McFadyen, Lachlan; Little, Ferguson, McKinven; Menzies, Wright, Gardiner, Bell, Henderson

CELTIC: Connor; McKay, Kennedy; Jackson, McNeill, Clark; Carroll, Fernie, Hughes, Divers, Chalmers

Attendance: n.a.

September 2nd
CELTIC (1) 2 — HIBERNIAN (0) 1
Divers 2 (5, 71) — Gibson (76)

CELTIC: Connor; McKay, Kennedy; Crerand, McNeill, Price; Chalmers, Jackson, Hughes, Divers, Fernie

HIBERNIAN: Simpson; Hughes, McLelland; Baxter, Grant, Baird; Scott, Stevenson, Fraser, Gibson, McLeod

Attendance: 31,000

SECTION TABLE

	P	W	D	L	F	A	Pts
St Johnstone	6	3	2	1	9	8	8
CELTIC	6	3	1	2	10	10	7
Hibernian	6	2	2	2	11	9	6
Partick Thistle	6	1	1	4	10	13	3

Qualifier: ST JOHNSTONE

SCOTTISH CUP

First Round December 13th
CELTIC (2) 5 — COWDENBEATH (0) 1
Jackson (23), Hughes (36), Chalmers 2 (57, 70), Divers (80) — Black (61)

CELTIC: Haffey; McKay, Kennedy; Crerand, McNeill, Price; Chalmers, Jackson, Hughes, Divers, Carroll

COWDENBEATH: Drummond; Anderson, Jack; Dawson, McGregor, Stirling; Kerr, Alison, Black, Fraser, McIntosh

Attendance: 19,000

Second Round January 27th
MORTON (1) 1 — CELTIC (1) 3
Turner (36) — Carroll (15), Divers (56), Jackson (83)

MORTON: Flood; Boyd, Caldwell; Kelly, Kiernan, Cowie; Robertson, Turner, Ferguson, McGraw, O'Hara

CELTIC: Haffey; McKay, Kennedy; Crerand, McNeill, Price; Chalmers, Jackson, Hughes, Divers, Carroll

Attendance: 21,000

Fourth Round February 17th
HEARTS (1) 3 — CELTIC (1) 4
Blackwood (21), Hamilton (71), Paton (82) — Divers 2 (12, 79), Chalmers (75), Crerand (86 pen)

HEARTS: Marshall; Kirk, Holt; Ferguson, Cumming, Higgins; Rodger, Wallace, Paton, Blackwood, Hamilton

CELTIC: Haffey; McKay, Kennedy; Crerand, McNeill, Price; Chalmers, Jackson, Hughes, Divers, Carroll

Attendance: 35,045

Quarter-Final March 10th
CELTIC (1) 4 — THIRD LANARK (3) 4
Chalmers 2 (10, 48), Brogan (60), Hughes (66) — Gray 3 (18, 38, 81), Harley (16)

CELTIC: Haffey; McKay, Kennedy; Crerand, McNeill, Clark; Brogan, Chalmers, Hughes, Divers, Carroll

THIRD LANARK: Robertson; McGillivray, Cunningham; Reilly, McCormick, Robb; Goodfellow, Hilley, Harley, Gray, McInnes

Attendance: 42,500

Quarter-Final Replay March 14th at Hampden Park for ground safety reasons
THIRD LANARK (0) 0 — CELTIC (0) 4
Chalmers (56), Hughes 2 (70, 74), Byrne (83)

THIRD LANARK: Robertson; McGillivray, Lewis; Reilly, McCormick, Cunningham; Goodfellow, Hilley, Harley, Gray, McInnes

CELTIC: Haffey; McKay, Kennedy; Crerand, McNeill, Clark; Brogan, Chalmers, Hughes, Divers, Byrne

Attendance: 51,518

Semi-Final March 31st at Ibrox Park

CELTIC (0) 1 — ST MIRREN (3) 3

Byrne (83) — Fernie (7), Kerrigan (32), Beck (33)

CELTIC: Haffey; McKay, Kennedy; Crerand, McNeill, Clark; Brogan, Chalmers, Hughes, Divers, Byrne

ST MIRREN: Williamson; Campbell, Wilson; Stewart, Clunie, McLean; Henderson, Bryceland, Kerrigan, Fernie, Beck

Attendance: 56,000

St Mirren's success at Ibrox was thoroughly deserved. They were the superior team in every way and played with assurance from start to finish. This was one of Celtic's poorest displays of the season. They were shaky in defence and most disappointing in attack of which they had a near monopoly in the second half. In a well-balanced St Mirren side 3 players were outstanding – former Celt, Fernie, Clunie and Williamson. After the interval Celtic made determined efforts to break through but their only reward was a goal scored by Byrne 7 minutes from the end.

APPEARANCES	League	League Cup	Scottish Cup
Connor	2	6	–
Donnelly	3	1	–
Kennedy	32	6	6
Jackson	24	5	3
McNeill	29	6	6
Clark	12	5	3
Carroll	28	5	4
Fernie	3	4	–
Hughes	31	6	6
Divers	34	6	6
Chalmers	31	6	6
McKay	32	5	6
Crerand	31	1	6
Price	23	2	3
Haffey	32	–	6
McNamee	5	–	–
Byrne	8	–	2
Brogan	10	–	3
Lennox	1	–	–
O'Neill	2	–	–
Gallagher	1	–	–

GOALSCORERS:

League: Divers 19, Hughes 18, Chalmers 12, Carroll 12, Jackson 11, Brogan 4, Crerand 2 (1 pen), McNeill 1, Fernie 1, Own Goal 1

League Cup: Hughes 4, Jackson 2, Divers 2, Chalmers 1, Carroll 1

Scottish Cup: Chalmers 6, Hughes 5, Divers 4, Jackson 2, Carroll 1, Brogan 1, Byrne 1, Crerand (1 pen)

Celtic team group, March 1962. Back row: Kennedy, McKay, Haffey, Crerand, McNeill, Clark. Front row: Rooney (trainer), Carroll, Chalmers, Hughes, Divers and Byrne.

Season 1962-63

Celtic finished 4th in the League Championship behind Rangers, Kilmarnock and Partick Thistle. They won only one of their first 7 home games up to December 9th and paradoxically lost only one of 9 away games in the same period. However, their home form picked up and after beating Dunfermline at Parkhead on Boxing Day they remained undefeated for the rest of the season, dropping only 1 point from 20. This was the year of the very severe winter and the season had to be extended until the end of May. At one period Celtic were unable to play a League match for 2 months. Their highest League win was 7-0 away against St Mirren. They also scored 6 goals at Airdrie and 5 at Aberdeen, Partick Thistle and Queen of the South. Both Jimmy Johnstone and John Cushley made their League debut against Kilmarnock at Rugby Park on March 27th but it was no dream start – Killie scored 6 without reply. Bobby Murdoch, Tommy Gemmell and Ian Young also made their League debuts during the season. Frank Haffey played most League matches with 33 and Bobby Craig finished as top scorer with 13 goals followed by Hughes, Divers and Chalmers – all on 11.

The lure of English football proved to be too strong for Pat Crerand and he left for Manchester United at the beginning of February for a fee of £56,000.

Celtic finished in the runners-up spot in their League Cup Qualifying group – behind Hearts and ahead of both Dundee clubs.

The club reached their 29th Scottish Cup Final. Celtic, who included Johnstone in their line-up after only two league appearances, were not able to take advantage of the fact that Rangers were effectively reduced to 10 men by an injury to McLean just after half-time. The match ended 1-1 and they were well beaten in the replay. It was remarkable that this was the first time the clubs had met in a Scottish Cup Final for 35 years.

At the beginning of September they entertained Spanish giants Real Madrid at Celtic Park in a Friendly watched by a crowd of 72,000, losing 3-1.

They had their first experience of top-level European competition during the season but were unfortunate to draw Fairs Cities Cup holders Valencia in the First Round. Although things might have been very different had John Clark not missed a 17th-minute penalty at Parkhead.

League:	Fourth
League Cup:	Failed to qualify from Section
Scottish Cup:	Runners-up
Fairs Cities Cup:	First Round

SCOTTISH FIRST DIVISION

August 22nd
FALKIRK (0) 1 — CELTIC (2) 3
Hamilton (85) — Jackson (11), Byrne (19), Hughes (59)

FALKIRK: Whigham; Rae, Hunter; Pierson, Lowry, McCarry; Lambie, Reid, Hamilton, Fulton, Adams

CELTIC: Haffey; McKay, Kennedy; Crerand, McNeill, McNamee; Chalmers, Divers, Hughes, Jackson, Byrne

Attendance: 5,000

September 8th
CELTIC (0) 0 — RANGERS (0) 1
Henderson (84)

CELTIC: Haffey; McKay, Kennedy; Crerand, McNeill, Price; Lennox, Gallagher, Hughes, Murdoch, Byrne

RANGERS: Ritchie; Shearer, Caldow; Davis, McKinnon, Baxter; Henderson, Greig, Millar, Brand, Wilson

Attendance: 72,000

With 6 minutes remaining for play Henderson, operating on the left flank, had the better of a tackle with McKay, shook himself free of the back's despairing clutch at his jersey and shot from about 10 yards. It was not a powerful shot and Haffey had it covered but in the goalmouth flurry the ball was deflected the other way. Kennedy, with a despairing lunge, could do no more than batter it into the net.

September 15th
CLYDE (0) 1 — Currie (50)
CELTIC (3) 3 — Divers 2 (10, 13), Chalmers (17)

CLYDE: McCulloch; Gray, Finnigan; White, Finlay, McHugh; Grant, Currie, Colrain, Thomson, Steel

CELTIC: Haffey; McKay, Kennedy; Crerand, McNeill, Price; Chalmers, Gallagher, Carroll, Divers, Byrne

Attendance: 23,000

September 22nd
CELTIC (0) 1 — Hughes (49)
ABERDEEN (2) 2 — Cooke (10), Cummings (18)

CELTIC: Haffey; McKay, Kennedy; Crerand, McNeill, Price; Chalmers, Divers, Hughes, Murdoch, Carroll

ABERDEEN: Ogston; Bennett, Hogg; Kinnell, Coutts, Smith; Cummings, Allan, Winchester, Cooke, Thom

Attendance: 29,000

September 29th
RAITH ROVERS (0) 0
CELTIC (1) 2 — Murdoch (30), McNeill (77 pen)

RAITH ROVERS: Thorburn; Wilson, McGuire; Stein, Burrows, Leigh; Adamson, Smith, Menzies, McFadzean, McNamee

CELTIC: Haffey; McKay, Kennedy; Crerand, McNeill, O'Neill; Chalmers, Murdoch, Hughes, Gallagher, Byrne

Attendance: 9,000

October 6th
CELTIC (0) 1 — Carroll (46)
KILMARNOCK (0) 1 — Kerr (55)

CELTIC: Haffey; McKay, Kennedy; Crerand, McNeill, O'Neill; Chalmers, Jackson, Carroll, Murdoch, Byrne

KILMARNOCK: McLaughlin; Richmond, Watson; O'Connor, McGrory, Beattie; Brown, Black, Kerr, Sneddon, McIlroy

Attendance: 36,000

October 13th
MOTHERWELL (0) 0
CELTIC (0) 2 — Gallagher (59), Carroll (69)

MOTHERWELL: Wylie; McSeveney, R. McCallum; Aitken, Martis, Roberts; Lindsay, Quinn, Stewart, McCann, Hunter

CELTIC: Haffey; McKay, Kennedy; Crerand, McNeill, O'Neill; Chalmers, Lennox, Carroll, Gallagher, Brogan

Attendance: 18,000

October 20th
CELTIC (1) 1 — Chalmers (35)
DUNDEE UNITED (0) 0

CELTIC: Haffey; McKay, O'Neill; Clark, McNamee, Price; Chalmers, Divers, Carroll, Gallagher, Brogan

DUNDEE UNITED: Davie; Millar, Briggs; Neilson, Smith, Fraser; Carlyle, Gillespie, Howieson, Mitchell, Irvine

Attendance: 21,000

October 20th: Pat Crerand was in the Scotland team which beat Wales 3-2 in Cardiff.

October 24th: Bobby Craig was signed from Blackburn Rovers for £15,000 in time to play against Valencia in the Fairs Cities Cup tie.

October 27th
AIRDRIE (1) 1 — Duncan (45)
CELTIC (1) 6 — Divers 2 (41, 74), Craig 2 (63, 66), Chalmers (65), Gallagher (88)

AIRDRIE: Samson; Shanks, Keenan; Stewart, Hannah, Reid; Newlands, Rowan, Tees, Duncan, Coats

CELTIC: Haffey; McKay, O'Neill; Crerand, McNamee, Price; Chalmers, Craig, Divers, Gallagher, Byrne

Attendance: 16,000

League positions

	P	W	D	L	F	A	Pts
1 Rangers	9	8	1	0	28	8	17
2 Hearts	8	6	2	0	26	10	14
3 CELTIC	9	6	1	2	19	7	13
4 Dunfermline	9	6	1	2	21	9	13
5 Partick Thistle	9	6	1	2	21	11	13

November 3rd
ST MIRREN (0) 0
CELTIC (3) 7 — Chalmers 3 (22, 45, 65), Divers (29), McKay (56 pen), Price (80), Gallagher (89)

ST MIRREN: Williamson; Murray, McTavish; R. Campbell, Clunie, McLean; Provan, Kerrigan, White, B. Campbell, Robertson

CELTIC: Haffey; McKay, O'Neill; Crerand, McNamee, Price; Chalmers, Craig, Divers, Gallagher, Byrne

Attendance: 25,000

November 4th: Steve Chalmers was called into the Scotland team against Ireland to replace the injured Davie Wilson of Rangers.

November 5th: Chalmers had to call off through injury.

November 7th: Scotland beat Ireland 5-1 at Hampden Park. Pat Crerand was in the team.

November 10th
CELTIC (0) 0 — QUEEN OF SOUTH (1) 1
Murphy (42 pen)

CELTIC: Haffey; O'Neill, Kennedy; Crerand, McNeill, Price; Carroll, Craig, Divers, Gallagher, Jeffrey

QUEEN OF THE SOUTH: Farm; Morrison, Kerr; Irving, Rugg, Anderson; Hannigan, Martin, Frye, Murphy, Murray

Attendance: 29,000

November 14th: Kennedy and Crerand were in the Scottish League team which was beaten 4-3 by the Italian League in Rome. Divers came on as a substitute and scored one of the Scottish League's goals.

November 17th
DUNDEE 0 — CELTIC 0

DUNDEE: Slater; Hamilton, Cox; Seith, Ure, Wishart; Smith, Penman, Gilzean, Cousin, Houston

CELTIC: Haffey; Young, Kennedy; Crerand, McNeill, O'Neill; Murdoch, Craig, Divers, Gallagher, Byrne

Attendance: 14,000

November 24th
CELTIC (0) 0 — PARTICK THISTLE (2) 2
Hogan (2), Cowan (26)

CELTIC: Haffey; Young, Kennedy; Crerand, McNeill, O'Neill; Chalmers, Murdoch, Divers, Gallagher, Jeffrey

PARTICK THISTLE: Niven; Hogan, Brown; McParland, Harvey, Cunningham; Cowan, Whitelaw, Hainey, Duffy, Smith

Attendance: 40,000

November 28th: Kennedy, Crerand, Chalmers and Divers were in the Scottish League team which beat the League of Ireland 11-0 at Parkhead. Divers scored a hat-trick and Crerand scored from the penalty-spot.

December 1st
HIBERNIAN (0) 1 — CELTIC (0) 1
Stevenson (76) — Murdoch (75)

HIBERNIAN: Simpson; Fraser, McLelland; Grant, Hughes, McLeod; Scott, Falconer, Preston, Byrne, M. Stevenson

CELTIC: Haffey; McKay, Kennedy; Crerand, McNeill, Price; Chalmers, Craig, Divers, Murdoch, Jeffrey

Attendance: 20,000

December 8th
CELTIC (2) 2 — HEARTS (1) 2
Hughes (5), Price (42) — Davidson (41), J. Hamilton (81)

CELTIC: Haffey; McKay, Kennedy; Crerand, McNeill, Price; Chalmers, Divers, Hughes, Murdoch, Brogan

HEARTS: Marshall; Polland, Holt; Ferguson, Cumming, Higgins; Rodger, W. Hamilton, Davidson, Wallace, J. Hamilton

Attendance: 30,000

December 15th
THIRD LANARK (0) 2 — CELTIC (0) 0
Gray (55), Cunningham (74)

THIRD LANARK: Robertson; McGillivray, Cunningham; Reilly, McCormick, Baird; Goodfellow, Spence, Grant, Gray, McInnes

CELTIC: Haffey; McKay, Kennedy; McNeill, McNamee, Price; Chalmers, Craig, Divers, Gallagher, Brogan

Attendance: 15,000

December 26th
CELTIC (1) 2 — DUNFERMLINE (1) 1
McLean o.g. (9), Hughes (61) — Sinclair (4)

CELTIC: Haffey; McKay, Kennedy; Crerand, McNeill, Price; Chalmers, Gallagher, Hughes, Divers, Brogan

DUNFERMLINE: Herriot; Callaghan, Cunningham; Thomson, McLean, Miller; Edwards, Peebles, Smith, Sinclair, Melrose

Attendance: n.a.

December 29th
CELTIC (1) 2 — FALKIRK (0) 1
Hughes 2 (43, 53) — Lambie (74)

CELTIC: Haffey; McKay, Kennedy; Crerand, McNeill, Price; Chalmers, Murdoch, Hughes, Gallagher, Brogan

FALKIRK: Whigham; Rae, Hunter; Pierson, Thomson, Fulton; Lambie, Redpath, Bain, Maxwell, Adam

Attendance: 18,000

League positions

	P	W	D	L	F	A	Pts
1 Rangers	17	13	3	1	50	16	29
2 Partick Thistle	17	13	2	2	37	16	28
3 Aberdeen	17	10	4	3	43	18	24
4 Hearts	16	9	6	2	42	19	24
5 CELTIC	18	9	4	5	33	17	22

January 1st
RANGERS (1) 4 — CELTIC (0) 0
Davis (12), Millar (68), Greig (70), Wilson (80)

RANGERS: Ritchie; Shearer, Caldow; Davis, McKinnon, Baxter; Scott, Greig, Millar, Brand, Wilson

CELTIC: Haffey; McKay, Kennedy; Crerand, McNeill, Price; Chalmers, Murdoch, Hughes, Gallagher, Brogan

Attendance: 55,000

In 12 minutes from the 68th to the 80th Millar, Greig and Wilson severely punished a Celtic defence that had been vulnerable throughout. Rangers – Davis, Baxter, Millar and Wilson in particular – played much splendid football on a ground which was iron-hard and slippery. Brogan was far and away the best Celtic player, but the outside-left received nothing of the service on which Wilson prospered.

January 5th
ABERDEEN (0) 1 — CELTIC (4) 5
Winchester (66) — Hughes 3 (14, 33, 82), Craig 2 (18, 19)

ABERDEEN: Ogston; Bennett, Hogg; Kinnell, Coutts, Smith; Cummings, Allan, Winchester, Cooke, Thom

CELTIC: Haffey; Young, Gemmell; McNamee, McNeill, Price; Gallagher, Craig, Hughes, Divers, Chalmers

Attendance: 16,000

February 1st: Bobby Carroll joined St Mirren for £7,000.

February 3rd: Pat Crerand was transferred to Manchester United for £56,000.

February 28th: Pat Crerand was included in the Rest of the World pool of 28 for the match against England at Wembley.

March 2nd
CELTIC (1) 3 — AIRDRIE (1) 1
Divers 2 (13, 61), Thomson o.g. (62) — Rowan (45)

CELTIC: Haffey; Young, Kennedy; McNamee, McNeill, Price; Murdoch, Craig, Hughes, Divers, Brogan

AIRDRIE: Samson; Jonquin, Keenan; Hosie, Thomson, Reid; Newlands, Rowan, Tees, Murray, Duncan

Attendance: 23,000

League positions

	P	W	D	L	F	A	Pts
1 Rangers	18	14	3	1	54	16	31
2 Partick Thistle	19	14	3	2	40	18	31
3 Kilmarnock	21	11	5	5	58	28	27
4 Aberdeen	20	11	4	5	45	24	26
5 CELTIC	21	11	4	6	41	23	26

March 9th
CELTIC (1) 1 — ST MIRREN (1) 1
Murdoch (25) — Beck (28)

CELTIC: Haffey; McKay, Kennedy; McNamee, McNeill, Price; Murdoch, Craig, Hughes, Divers, Brogan

ST MIRREN: Beattie; Murray, Riddell; R. Campbell, Clunie, Gray; Carroll, Kerrigan, White, Beck, Robertson

Attendance: 25,000

March 16th
QUEEN OF SOUTH (2) 2 — CELTIC (2) 5
Murphy (35 pen), Murray (44) — Craig 3 (1, 13, 46), Brogan (63), McNamee (86)

QUEEN OF THE SOUTH: Farm; Morrison, Kerr; Patterson, Rugg, Murphy; Martin, Murray, Frye, Anderson, McLean

CELTIC: Haffey; McKay, Gemmell; McNamee, McNeill, Price; Murdoch, Craig, Byrne, Divers, Brogan

Attendance: 8,000

March 19th
CELTIC (0) 4 — RAITH ROVERS (0) 1
Brogan 2 (60, 65), McNamee (69), Chalmers (88) — McFadzean (47)

CELTIC: Haffey; McKay, Kennedy; McNamee, McNeill, Price; Gallagher, Craig, Chalmers, Divers, Brogan

RAITH ROVERS: Muirhead; Wilson, Haig; Stein, Bolton, Burrows; Lourie, Menzies, Gilfillan, McFadzean, McNamee

Attendance: 8,000

March 23rd
CELTIC (3) 4 — DUNDEE (0) 1
Hughes (20), Brogan (33), Seith o.g. (38), Craig (80) — Gilzean (61)

CELTIC: Haffey; McKay, Kennedy; McNamee, McNeill, Price; Murdoch, Craig, Hughes, Divers, Brogan

DUNDEE: Slater; Hamilton, Cox; Seith, Ure, Wishart; Smith, Penman, Cousin, Gilzean, Robertson

Attendance: 42,000

March 27th
KILMARNOCK (2) 6 CELTIC (0) 0
Mason (8), Sneddon (31), Black 2 (46, 57), Kerr 2 (51 pen, 80)

KILMARNOCK: Forsyth; Richmond, Watson; Murray, McGrory, Beattie; Brown, Mason, Kerr, Sneddon, Black

CELTIC: Madden; Young, Kennedy; McKay, Cushley, Price; Johnstone, Craig, Chalmers, Gallagher, Brogan

Attendance: n.a.

April 2nd
PARTICK THISTLE (0) 1 CELTIC (4) 5
Fleming (76) Craig 2 (1, 47), Murdoch (24), McKay (42 pen), Divers (44)

PARTICK THISTLE: Niven; Muir, Brown; Harvey, McKinnon, Cunningham; Cowan, Fleming, Smith, Duffy, McParland

CELTIC: Haffey; McKay, O'Neill; McNamee, McNeill, Price; Chalmers, Craig, Divers, Murdoch, Brogan

Attendance: n.a.

April 5th: Mike Jackson was transferred to St Johnstone.

April 6th
CELTIC (1) 2 HIBERNIAN (0) 0
Price (27), McKay (57 pen)

CELTIC: Haffey; McKay, O'Neill; McNamee, McCarron, Price; Chalmers, Craig, Divers, Lennox, Jeffrey

HIBERNIAN: Simpson; Cameron, Davin; Grant, Toner, Leishman; O'Rourke, M. Stevenson, Baker, Preston, E. Stevenson

Attendance: 14,000

April 20th
CELTIC (2) 2 THIRD LANARK (1) 1
Craig 2 (25, 35) Cunningham (27)

CELTIC: Haffey; McKay, O'Neill; McNamee, McNeill, Price; Chalmers, Craig, Divers, Murdoch, Brogan

THIRD LANARK: Robertson; McGillivray, Davis; Reilly, Lewis, Baird; Goodfellow, Spence, Cunningham, McMorran, McInnes

Attendance: 14,000

April 27th
DUNFERMLINE (0) 1 CELTIC (1) 1
Kerray (48) Divers (21)

DUNFERMLINE: Connachan; W. Callaghan, Lunn; Thomson, McLean, Miller; Edwards, Peebles, Kerray, Paton, T. Callaghan

CELTIC: Haffey; McKay, O'Neill; McNamee, McNeill, Price; Chalmers, Murdoch, Hughes, Divers, Brogan

Attendance: 12,000

April 29th
HEARTS (2) 4 CELTIC (0) 3
Rodger 2 (23, 38), Higgins (70), Hamilton (78) Chalmers (54), Divers (56), Johnstone (60)

HEARTS: Marshall; Shevlane, Holt; Ferguson, Barry, Higgins; Rodger, Wallace, Paton, Davidson, J. Hamilton

CELTIC: Haffey; McKay, Kennedy; McNamee, Cushley, Price; Johnstone, Lennox, Divers, Chalmers, Brogan

Attendance: n.a.

May 6th
CELTIC (1) 2 CLYDE (0) 0
McKay (32 pen), Hughes (80)

CELTIC: Haffey; McKay, Kennedy; McNamee, McNeill, Clark; Johnstone, Murdoch, Hughes, Divers, Chalmers

CLYDE: McCulloch; White, Blain; Murray, Fraser, Currie; Ferguson, McHugh, McFarlane, Reid, Blair

Attendance: n.a.

May 9th: Alec Byrne was given a free transfer.

May 11th
DUNDEE UNITED (1) 3 CELTIC (0) 0
Gillespie (34), Brodie (57), Carlyle (74)

DUNDEE UNITED: Davie; Millar, Gordon; Fraser, Smith, Briggs; Carlyle, Gillespie, Brodie, Irvine, Mitchell

CELTIC: Haffey; McKay, Kennedy; McNamee, McNeill, Price; Johnstone, Murdoch, Hughes, Divers, Chalmers

Attendance: 12,000

May 13th
CELTIC (3) 6 MOTHERWELL (0) 0
Chalmers 3 (7, 29, 55), Craig (44), Thomson o.g. (63), Divers (87)

CELTIC: Haffey; McKay, Kennedy; McNamee, McNeill, Price; Brogan, Craig, Divers, Chalmers, Hughes

MOTHERWELL: Wylie; Delaney, M. Thomson; Aitken, W. McCallum, Murray; Lindsay, McBride, Russell, McCann, I. Thomson

Attendance: n.a.

Scottish First Division

	P	W	D	L	F	A	Pts
1 Rangers	34	25	7	2	94	28	57
2 Kilmarnock	34	20	8	6	92	40	48
3 Partick Thistle	34	20	6	8	66	44	46
4 CELTIC	34	19	6	9	76	44	44
5 Hearts	34	17	9	8	85	59	43
6 Aberdeen	34	17	7	10	70	47	41
7 Dundee United	34	15	11	8	67	52	41
8 Dunfermline	34	13	8	13	50	47	34
9 Dundee	34	12	9	13	60	49	33
10 Motherwell	34	10	11	13	60	63	31
11 Airdrie	34	14	2	18	52	76	30
12 St Mirren	34	10	8	16	52	72	28
13 Falkirk	34	12	3	19	54	69	27
14 Third Lanark	34	9	8	17	56	68	26
15 Queen of the South	34	10	6	18	36	75	26
16 Hibernian	34	8	9	17	47	67	25
17 Clyde	34	9	5	20	49	83	23
18 Raith Rovers	34	2	5	27	35	118	9

May 31st: Paddy Turner was signed from Morton for £10,000.

June 4th: Benny Rooney was given a free transfer.

June 9th: Billy McNeill was in the Scotland team which was beaten 1-0 by the Republic of Ireland in Dublin.

June 13th: Billy McNeill was in the Scotland team which beat Spain 6-2 in Madrid.

LEAGUE CUP

August 11th
CELTIC (1) 3 — HEARTS (1) 1
Murdoch (7), Gallagher (48), Hughes (55) — Paton (22)

CELTIC: Haffey; McKay, Kennedy; Crerand, McNeill, Price; Lennox, Gallagher, Hughes, Murdoch, Byrne

HEARTS: Marshall; Ferguson, Holt; Polland, Barry, Cumming; Rodger, J. Hamilton, Davidson, Wallace, Paton

Attendance: 41,000. Divers forgot his boots and was dropped

August 15th
DUNDEE (0) 1 — CELTIC (0) 0
Smith (60)

DUNDEE: Slater; Hamilton, Cox; Seith, Ure, Wishart; Smith, Penman, Cousin, Gilzean, Robertson

CELTIC: Haffey; McKay, Kennedy; Crerand, McNeill, Price; Lennox, Gallagher, Hughes, Murdoch, Byrne

Attendance: n.a.

August 18th
CELTIC (1) 4 — DUNDEE UNITED (0) 0
Hughes 2 (4, 68), Crerand (63 pen), Gallagher (71)

CELTIC: Haffey; McKay, Kennedy; Crerand, McNeill, Price; Chalmers, Gallagher, Hughes, Murdoch, Byrne

DUNDEE UNITED: McKay; Millar, Gordon; Neilson, Smith, Fraser; Mochan, Brodie, Irvine, Gillespie, Pattie

Attendance: 35,000

August 25th
HEARTS (2) 3 — CELTIC (0) 2
Paton (13), Wallace 2 (19, 50 pen) — Murdoch (60), Hughes (88)

HEARTS: Marshall; Polland, Holt; Ferguson, Barry, Cumming; Rodger, Paton, Davidson, Wallace, Hamilton

CELTIC: Haffey; Mackay, Kennedy; Crerand, McNeill, Price; Lennox, Gallagher, Hughes, Murdoch, Byrne

Attendance: 33,000

August 29th
CELTIC (1) 3 — DUNDEE (0) 0
Gallagher (1), Hughes 2 (83, 87)

CELTIC: Haffey; McKay, Kennedy; Crerand, McNeill, Price; Lennox, Gallagher, Hughes, Murdoch, Byrne

DUNDEE: Slater; Hamilton, Cox; Seith, Ure, Wishart; Smith, Penman, Cameron, Cousin, Robertson

Attendance: 28,000

September 1st
DUNDEE UNITED 0 — CELTIC 0

DUNDEE UNITED: Mackay; Millar, Gordon; Neilson, D. Smith, Fraser; Riddell, Carlyle, Mochan, Brodie, R. Smith

CELTIC: Haffey; McKay, Kennedy; Crerand, McNeill, Price; Lennox, Gallagher, Hughes, Murdoch, Byrne

Attendance: 24,000

SECTION TABLE

	P	W	D	L	F	A	Pts
Hearts	6	4	0	2	11	8	8
CELTIC	6	3	1	2	12	5	7
Dundee United	6	2	1	3	7	11	5
Dundee	6	2	0	4	5	11	4

Qualifier: HEARTS

SCOTTISH CUP

First Round January 28th
FALKIRK (0) 0 — CELTIC (1) 2
Hughes (15), Gallagher (89)

FALKIRK: Whigham; Rae, Hunter; Pierson, Thomson, Fulton; Lambie, Redpath, Bain, Maxwell, Henderson

CELTIC: Haffey; Young, Gemmell; McNamee, McNeill, Price; Gallagher, Craig, Hughes, Divers, Chalmers

Attendance: 13,500

Second Round March 6th
CELTIC (1) 3 — HEARTS (1) 1
Murdoch (36), McNamee (55), Hughes (73) — Wallace (10)

CELTIC: Haffey; McKay, Kennedy; McNamee, McNeill, Price; Murdoch, Craig, Hughes, Divers, Brogan

HEARTS: Marshall; Polland, Holt; Ferguson, Barry, Higgins; Paton, Wallace, Davidson, Gordon, Cumming

Attendance: 38,000

Third Round March 13th
CELTIC (2) 6 — GALA FAIRYDEAN (0) 0
Hughes 2, Murdoch 3, Divers 1

CELTIC: Haffey; McKay, Kennedy; McNamee, McNeill, Price; Gallagher, Murdoch, Hughes, Divers, Brogan

GALA: Drummond; Ballantyne, Peden; Lyall, Oliver, Brims; Hunter, McCrae, Buchanan, French, Reid

Attendance: n.a.

Fourth Round March 30th
ST MIRREN (0) 0 — CELTIC (1) 1
Brogan (8)

ST MIRREN: Beattie; Murray, Riddell; R. Campbell, Clunie, McTavish; Carroll, Quinn, White, Beck, Robertson

CELTIC: Haffey; McKay, Kennedy; McNamee, McNeill, Price; Chalmers, Murdoch, Hughes, Divers, Brogan

Attendance: 34,988

Semi-Final April 13th at Ibrox Park
CELTIC (1) 5 — RAITH ROVERS (1) 2
Divers (10), McKay 2 (51 pen, 57 pen), Chalmers (70), Brogan (84) — McDonald (16), Gilfillan (64)

RAITH ROVERS: Thorburn; Stevenson, Clinton; Wilson, Bolton, Burrows; Lourie, McDonald, Gilfillan, Smith, Adamson

CELTIC: Haffey; McKay, O'Neill; McNamee, McNeill, Price; Chalmers, Murdoch, Divers, Gallagher, Brogan

Attendance: 35,681

Only when McKay scored with 2 penalties in the space of 6 minutes in the second half did Celtic fully imprint their personality on a game devoid of excitement and finesse. Celtic should surely have put the game beyond doubt by the interval but for wanton disregard of their opportunities.

Final May 4th at Hampden Park
RANGERS (1) 1 — CELTIC (1) 1
Brand (43) — Murdoch (45)

RANGERS: Ritchie; Shearer, Provan; Greig, McKinnon, Baxter; Henderson, McLean, Millar, Brand, Wilson

CELTIC: Haffey; McKay, Kennedy; McNamee, McNeill, Price; Johnstone, Murdoch, Hughes, Divers, Brogan

Attendance: 129,527. *Referee:* T. Wharton (Clarkston)

Haffey was the man of the match although in the rain and wind of Hampden this was hardly a goalkeeper's day. His diverting of a second half shot of Brand was the best of the many he made. McLean was injured for most of the second half but it was when he was banished to outside-left and Wilson moved to centre-forward that Rangers looked most dangerous. Baxter was not permitted to exert his usual influence. McNamee along with McNeill, a commanding centre-half, and the cool Price formed the superior half-back line.

Final Replay May 15th at Hampden Park
RANGERS (2) 3 — CELTIC (0) 0
Brand 2 (7, 71), Wilson (44)

RANGERS: Ritchie; Shearer, Provan; Greig, McKinnon, Baxter; Henderson, McMillan, Millar, Brand, Wilson

CELTIC: Haffey; McKay, Kennedy; McNamee, McNeill, Price; Craig, Murdoch, Divers, Chalmers, Hughes

Attendance: 120,263. *Referee:* T. Wharton (Clarkston).

Rangers not only defeated but completely outclassed Celtic. McMillan's recall to the top class led to a feast of fine football in the first half. Henderson had never played so succcessfully against Kennedy. The outside-right's cross after Millar had passed down the touch-line was swept past Haffey in the 7th minute by Brand. In the last minute of the first half Millar passed to Brand, who, as McKay retreated, closed in and shot. Haffey could not hold the fast, low shot and Wilson took the easy scoring chance in his stride. Once Brand, with his left foot from 25 yards, had surprised Haffey with a shot which dropped as it came to the goalkeeper, Rangers toyed with their opponents. 25 minutes from the end thousands of disappointed Celtic supporters streamed from the ground.

FAIRS CITIES CUP

First Round September 26th
VALENCIA 4 CELTIC 2
Coll 2, Guillot, Urtiaja Mestre o.g., Carroll

VALENCIA: Zamora; Piquer, Guincola; Mestre, Sistre, Chicao; Fasha, Ribewes, Urtiaja, Guillot, Coll

CELTIC: Fallon; McKay, Kennedy; Crerand, McNeill, O'Neill; Chalmers, Jackson, Carroll, Gallagher, Byrne

Attendance: 40,000

Celtic emerged from the First Leg with a 2-goal deficit. They gained their 1st goal when a Carroll shot went into the net off Mestre and Carroll also scored a 2nd. Chalmers had the ball in Valencia's net after 70 minutes but was ruled offside, and 2 Celtic penalty claims were turned down.

First Round Second Leg October 24th
CELTIC (0) 2 VALENCIA (0) 2
Verdu o.g. (48), Crerand (85) Guillot (63), Waldo (80)

CELTIC: Haffey; McKay, O'Neill; Crerand, McNamee, Clark; Chalmers, Craig, Divers, Gallagher, Byrne

VALENCIA: Zamora; Verdu, Mestre; Chicao, Piquer, Recaman; Ribelles, Roberto, Walso, Guillot, Ficha

Attendance: 45,000

The score correctly reflected the run of play. Only Chalmers and Byrne were the masters of their immediate opponents. New boy Craig, Divers and Gallagher made little or no impact on the game. Celtic spurned an opportunity to go ahead in the 17th minute when Clark missed a penalty. Each side scored twice and the second half. Valencia progressed to the next round on a 6-4 aggregate.

Appearances	League	League Cup	Scottish Cup	Fairs Cup
Haffey	33	6	7	1
McKay	29	6	6	2
Kennedy	25	6	5	1
Crerand	17	6	–	2
McNeill	28	6	7	1
McNamee	19	–	7	1
Chalmers	27	1	4	2
Divers	27	–	7	1
Hughes	16	6	6	–
Jackson	2	–	–	1
Byrne	9	6	–	2
Price	27	6	7	–
Lennox	4	5	–	–
Gallagher	17	6	3	2
Murdoch	19	6	6	–
Carroll	6	–	–	1
O'Neill	13	–	1	2
Brogan	18	–	5	–
Clark	2	–	–	1
Craig	17	–	3	1
Jeffrey	4	–	–	–
Young	5	–	1	–
Gemmell	2	–	1	–
Madden	1	–	–	–
Cushley	2	–	–	–
Johnstone	4	–	1	–
McCarron	1	–	–	–

GOALSCORERS:

League: Craig 13, Hughes 11, Divers 11, Chalmers 11, Murdoch 4, McKay 4 (4 pens), Brogan 4, Own Goals 4, Gallagher 3, Price 3, Carroll 2, McNamee 2, Byrne 1, McNeill 1 (pen), Jackson 1, Johnstone 1

League Cup: Hughes 6, Gallagher 3, Murdoch 2, Crerand 1 (pen)

Scottish Cup: Murdoch 5, Hughes 4, Divers 2, Brogan 2, McKay 2 (2 pens), Gallagher 1, McNamee 1, Chalmers 1

Fairs Cup: Own Goals 2, Crerand 1, Carroll 1

Celtic team group of 1958. Back row: Mackay, Jackson, Beattie, McNeill, Conway, Mochan. Front row: Fernie, Higgins, Peacock, Wilson and Auld.

Season 1963-64

Celtic finished 3rd in the table behind Rangers and Kilmarnock. For the 3rd successive season they won 19 of their 34 matches. 22 different players were used in only their first 6 matches but despite their constant team changes they lost only 1 home match and 5 away – 4 by the odd goal. They scored a remarkable 89 goals during the campaign and had a 9-0 win over Airdrie, a 7-0 win over Falkirk and 5 goal wins over 2nd placed Kilmarnock, Hibs, Partick Thistle and East Stirling. Steve Chalmers was their only ever-present and he finished as top scorer with 28 goals. An end-of-season clear-out saw McNamee, Frank Brogan, Price and Turner all leave the club.

Only 2 of the 6 League Cup group matches were won. Rangers beat Celtic by 3 clear goals both home and away, and Celtic eventually finished 5 points adrift of the Ibrox club who went on to win the trophy.

Celtic reached the Fourth Round of the Scottish Cup after beating Eyemouth, Morton and Airdrie but lost to Rangers at Ibrox in front of a crowd of 84,724.

In only their 2nd season of European competition Celtic had an incredible run to the Semi-Final of the Cup Winners Cup. Swiss Cup holders Basle were beaten 10-1 on aggregate in the First Round. A 3-0 home win effectively eliminated Dinamo Zagreb in the Second Round and a goal from John Hughes gave them a superb win in Bratislava which took them through to the Semi-Final on a 2-0 aggregate. They built up a 3-0 First-Leg lead against Hungary's M.T.K. and they looked set for the Final but their European inexperience was fully evidenced in the return leg which turned into a nightmare.

League:	Third
League Cup:	Failed to qualify from Section
Scottish Cup:	Fourth Round
Cup Winners Cup:	Semi-Finalists

SCOTTISH FIRST DIVISION

August 6th: Celtic swopped Bobby Craig for Bobby Young of St Johnstone.

August 21st
CELTIC (1) 4 QUEEN OF SOUTH (0) 0
Turner (27), Jeffrey (56),
Chalmers 2 (75, 83)

CELTIC: Haffey; McKay, Gemmell; Clark, McNeill, Price; Brogan, Turner, Divers, Chalmers, Jeffrey

QUEEN OF THE SOUTH: Farm; Morrison, Kerr; Irving, Rugg, McNaught; McDonald, Hannigan, Thomson, Gardner, Murphy

Attendance: n.a.

September 4th: McNeill and Divers were in the Scottish League side which beat the Irish League 4-1 in Belfast. Divers scored 2 goals.

September 7th
RANGERS (0) 2 CELTIC (1) 1
McLean (52), Brand (65) Chalmers (11)

RANGERS: Ritchie; Shearer, Provan; Greig, McKinnon, Baxter; Henderson, McLean, Forrest, Brand, Wilson

CELTIC: Haffey; McKay, Gemmell; Clark, McNeill, O'Neill; Lennox, Turner, Divers, Chalmers, Brogan

Attendance: 55,000

Of the 3 matches since the start of the season this was the liveliest and most entertaining, Rangers proving once again how difficult they were to beat. Haffey effected a brilliant point-blank save from Baxter but had no chance when McLean levelled the scores after an 11th minute goal by Chalmers for Celtic. The tall inside-right gallloped into an open space in pursuit of a ball released perfectly by Forrest and guided it out of Haffey's reach. In the 65th minute Brand raced into ideal position for a pass from Forrest and again Haffey was powerless to prevent a score.

September 14th
CELTIC (4) 4 — THIRD LANARK (3) 4
Divers (7), Lennox (9), Turner (12), Brogan (14 pen) — Anderson 2 (18, 33), Buckley (40), Graham (50)

CELTIC: Haffey; McKay, Gemmell; Clark, McNeill, O'Neill; Lennox, Turner, Divers, Chalmers, Brogan

THIRD LANARK: Mitchell; McGillivray, Davis; Dickson, Lewis, McLeod; Graham, Anderson, Cunningham, McMorran, Buckley

Attendance: 19,000

September 21st
FALKIRK (0) 1 — CELTIC (0) 0
Fulton (74)

FALKIRK: Whigham; Lambie, Hunter; Pierson, Rae, Fulton; O'Donnell, Redpath, Davidson, Maxwell, Gillespie

CELTIC: Haffey; McKay, Gemmell; J. Brogan, McNeill, Clark; Lennox, Chalmers, Hughes, Divers, F. Brogan

Attendance: 11,000

September 28th
ST MIRREN (1) 2 — CELTIC (1) 1
Kerrigan (20), White (59) — Chalmers (28)

ST MIRREN: Dempster; Murray, Wilson; Campbell, Clunie, McTavish; Kerrigan, Carroll, White, Beck, J. Robertson

CELTIC: Haffey; McKay, Gemmell; McNamee, McNeill, J. Brogan; Lennox, Turner, Divers, Chalmers, F. Brogan

Attendance: 16,000

October 5th
CELTIC (1) 2 — DUNFERMLINE (0) 2
Murdoch (7), Brogan (51) — Kerray (58), Peebles (62)

CELTIC: Fallon; Young, Gemmell; McKay, Cushley, Kennedy; Johnstone, Murdoch, Chalmers, Turner, Brogan

DUNFERMLINE: Herriot; Callaghan, Lunn; Thomson, McLean, Miller; Edwards, Peebles, Dickson, Kerray, Melrose

Attendance: 17,000

October 12th
CELTIC (1) 3 — ABERDEEN (0) 0
McKay (18 pen), Chalmers 2 (63, 65)

CELTIC: Haffey; Young, Gemmell; McKay, Cushley, Kennedy; Johnstone, Murdoch, Chalmers, Divers, Hughes

ABERDEEN: Ogston; Bennett, Hogg; Kinnell, Coutts, Smith; Cummings, Morrison, Little, Wilson, Thom

Attendance: 15,000

October 19th
DUNDEE UNITED (0) 0 — CELTIC (1) 3
Fraser o.g. (37), Hughes (57), Murdoch (73)

DUNDEE UNITED: Davie; Smith, Briggs; Neilson, Moore, Fraser; Simpson, Millar, Gillespie, Irvine, Mitchell

CELTIC: Haffey; Young, Gemmell; Clark, McNeill, Kennedy; Johnstone, Murdoch, Chalmers, Divers, Hughes

Attendance: 16,000

League positions

	P	W	D	L	F	A	Pts
1 Rangers	8	7	1	0	26	3	15
2 Kilmarnock	9	7	1	1	20	9	15
3 Dundee	9	6	2	1	23	10	14
4 Dunfermline	9	5	3	1	19	9	13
5 Hearts	9	5	2	2	20	13	12
7 CELTIC	8	3	2	3	10	11	8

October 26th
CELTIC (6) 9 — AIRDRIE (0) 0
Gallagher (17), Hughes 3 (22, 40, 64), Murdoch (34), Divers 3 (41, 55, 59), Chalmers (45)

CELTIC: Haffey; Young, Gemmell; Clark, McNeill, Kennedy; Gallagher, Murdoch, Chalmers, Divers, Hughes

AIRDRIE: McKenzie; Black, Keenan; Rowan, Hannah, Johnstone; McColl, Murray, Boyd, Reid, Jeffrey

Attendance: 13,000. Haffey missed a penalty

November 2nd
EAST STIRLING (0) 1 — CELTIC (3) 5
Kemp (49) — Divers (14), Chalmers 3 (37, 41, 85), Hughes (79)

EAST STIRLING: Swan; McNab, McQueen; Collumbine, Craig, McPhee; Hamill, Sandeman, Coburn, Kemp, McIntosh

CELTIC: Haffey; Young, Gemmell; Clark, McNeill, Kennedy; Gallagher, Murdoch, Chalmers, Divers, Hughes

Attendance: 7,000. McNeill was ordered off

November 9th
CELTIC (2) 5 — PARTICK THISTLE (3) 3
Chalmers 3 (18, 67, 88), Johnstone (21), Hughes (73) — Cowan 2 (30, 35), Hainey (33)

CELTIC: Haffey; Young, Gemmell; Clark, Cushley, Kennedy; Johnstone, Murdoch, Chalmers, Divers, Hughes

PARTICK THISTLE: Niven; Hogan, Tinney; Close, Harvey, Cunningham; Cowan, Yard, Hainey, Duffy, McParland

Attendance: 28,000

November 16th

HIBERNIAN (0) 1 — CELTIC (1) 1

Hamilton (55) — Murdoch (41)

HIBERNIAN: Simpson; Fraser, Parke; Grant, Easton, Baxter; Scott, Quinn, Martin, Hamilton, Stevenson

CELTIC: Fallon; Young, Gemmell; Clark, McNeill, Kennedy; Johnstone, Murdoch, Chalmers, Divers, Hughes

Attendance: 25,000

November 20th: Kennedy and McNeill were in the Scotland team which beat Wales 2-1 at Hampden Park.

November 23rd

CELTIC (2) 5 — KILMARNOCK (0) 0

Divers (8),
Hughes 3 (43, 60, 85),
Johnstone (86)

CELTIC: Fallon; Young, Gemmell; Clark, McNeill, Kennedy; Johnstone, Murdoch, Chalmers, Divers, Hughes

KILMARNOCK: Forsyth; King, Watson; O'Connor, McGrory, Beattie; Brown, McInally, McFadzean, Sneddon, McIlroy

Attendance: 28,000

November 30th

DUNDEE (1) 1 — CELTIC (1) 1

Penman (25 pen) — Murdoch (35)

DUNDEE: Slater; Hamilton, Cox; Seith, Ryden, Stuart; Penman, Waddell, Cousin, Gilzean, Robertson

CELTIC: Fallon; Young, Gemmell; Clark, McNeill, Kennedy; Gallagher, Murdoch, Chalmers, Divers, Hughes

Attendance: 25,000

December 7th

CELTIC (2) 3 — ST JOHNSTONE (1) 1

Murdoch 3 (27, 38, 67) — Flanagan (3)

CELTIC: Fallon; Young, Gemmell; Clark, McNeill, Kennedy; Johnstone, Murdoch, Chalmers, Divers, Lennox

ST JOHNSTONE: Fallon; McFadyen, Richmond; Townsend, McKinven, McCarry; Flanagan, Harrower, McIntyre, Craig, Kemp

Attendance: 24,000. Harrower was sent off

December 14th

HEARTS (1) 1 — CELTIC (1) 1

White (22) — Divers (41)

HEARTS: Cruikshank; Shevlane, Holt; Polland, Barry, Cumming; Hamilton, Wallace, White, Gordon, Traynor

CELTIC: Fallon; Young, Gemmell; Clark, Cushley, Kennedy; Johnstone, Murdoch, Chalmers, Divers, Lennox

Attendance: 23,000. Polland was carried off in the 45th minute

December 21st

CELTIC (1) 2 — MOTHERWELL (0) 1

Divers (38), Clark (67) — McBride (82)

CELTIC: Fallon; Young, Gemmell; Clark, McNeill, Kennedy; Johnstone, Murdoch, Chalmers, Divers, Lennox

MOTHERWELL: Wylie; Thomson, McCallum; Aitken, Delaney, Murray; Carlyle, McCann, McBride, Weir, Lindsay

Attendance: 25,000

December 28th

QUEEN OF THE SOUTH (0) 0 — CELTIC (1) 2

Johnstone (31),
Chalmers (88)

QUEEN OF THE SOUTH: Ball; Kerr, McNaught; Irving, Rugg, Murphy; Hannigan, Currie, Coates, McChesney, Law

CELTIC: Fallon; Young, Gemmell; Clark, McNeill, Kennedy; Johnstone, Murdoch, Chalmers, Divers, Hughes

Attendance: 7,000

League positions

	P	W	D	L	F	A	Pts
1 Kilmarnock	18	13	3	2	41	20	29
2 Rangers	18	12	4	2	47	17	28
3 CELTIC	18	10	5	3	52	20	25
4 Dunfermline	17	9	6	2	37	16	24
5 Dundee	18	10	4	4	44	23	24

January 1st

CELTIC (0) 0 — RANGERS (0) 1

Millar (65)

CELTIC: Fallon; Young, Gemmell; Clark, McNeill, Kennedy; Johnstone, Murdoch, Chalmers, Divers, Hughes

RANGERS: Ritchie; Provan, Caldow; Davis, McKinnon, Baxter; Henderson, Greig, Millar, McLean, Brand

Attendance: 65,000

Celtic had several chances to score but a mixture of bad luck, hesitancy at the vital moment and fine saves by Ritchie thwarted all their efforts. The players who most often sparked life into the match were the 2 outside-rights.

January 2nd
THIRD LANARK (1) 1 CELTIC (0) 1
Murray (13) Divers (65)

THIRD LANARK: Paul; McGillivray, Davis; Brownlie, McCormick, Geddes; Graham, Cunningham, Murray, Paterson, Buckley

CELTIC: Fallon; Young; Gemmell; J. Brogan, Cushley, Kennedy; Johnstone, Divers, Chalmers, Gallagher, Hughes

Attendance: n.a.

January 4th
CELTIC (6) 7 FALKIRK (0) 0
Johnstone (8),
Chalmers 3 (11, 26, 72),
Hughes (28),
Divers 2 (32, 36)

CELTIC: Fallon; Young, Gemmell; Clark, McNeill, Kennedy; Johnstone, Murdoch, Chalmers, Divers, Hughes

FALKIRK: Whigham; Donnachie, Stewart; Pierson, Lowry, Fulton; Foley, Redpath, Wilson, Maxwell, Gourlay

Attendance: 16,000

January 18th
CELTIC (1) 3 ST MIRREN (0) 0
Chalmers (10),
Johnstone (73),
Divers (89)

CELTIC: Fallon; Young, Gemmell; Clark, McNeill, Kennedy; Johnstone, Murdoch, Chalmers, Divers, Hughes

ST MIRREN: Beattie; Murray, Wilson; Clark, Gray, Ross; T. Robertson, Carroll, Queen, Beck, J. Robertson

Attendance: 20,000. Clark of St Mirren was ordered off

Feburary 1st
DUNFERMLINE (1) 1 CELTIC (0) 0
McNeill o.g. (11)

DUNFERMLINE: Herriot; W. Callaghan, Lunn; Smith, McLean, Miller; Edwards, Peebles, Dickson, Kerray, T. Callaghan

CELTIC: Fallon; Young, Gemmell; Clark, McNeill, Kennedy; Johnstone, Murdoch, Chalmers, Gallagher, Hughes

Attendance: 16,000

February 8th
ABERDEEN (0) 0 CELTIC (1) 3
Smith o.g. (16),
Brogan (61), Divers (72)

ABERDEEN: Ogston; Shewan, Hogg; Burns, Coutts, Smith; Kerrigan, Cooke, Little, Winchester, Hume

CELTIC: Fallon; Young, Gemmell; Clark, McNeill, Kennedy; Johnstone, Murdoch, Chalmers, Divers, Brogan

Attendance: 18,000

February 10th: Neil Mochan came back to Parkhead, as assistant to coach Sean Fallon.

February 19th
CELTIC (1) 1 DUNDEE UNITED (0) 0
Chalmers (31)

CELTIC: Fallon; Young, Gemmell; Henderson, McNeill, Kennedy; Johnstone, Turner, Chalmers, Divers, Brogan

DUNDEE UNITED: Davie; Millar, Gordon; Neilson, D. Smith, Fraser; Gillespie, McKinlay, Howieson, Irvine, R. Smith

Attendance: 10,000

February 22nd
AIRDRIE (0) 0 CELTIC (1) 2
Brogan 2 (20, 48)

AIRDRIE: Samson; Jonquin, Keenan; Stewart, Hannah, Reid; McColl, Rowan, Marshall, Murray, Newlands

CELTIC: Fallon; Young, Gemmell; Henderson, McNeill, Kennedy; Gallagher, Turner, Chalmers, Divers, Brogan

Attendance: 8,000

February 29th
CELTIC (3) 5 EAST STIRLING (1) 2
Chalmers 3 (1, 21, 59), Coburn (44), Kemp (87)
Murdoch 2 (37, 72 pen)

CELTIC: Fallon; Young, Gemmell; Clark, McNamee, Kennedy; Johnstone, Murdoch, Chalmers, Divers, Hughes

EAST STIRLING: Arrol; Miller, McQueen; Collumbine, Craig, Frickleton; Munro, Sandeman, Coburn, Kemp, McIntosh

Attendance: 15,000

League positions

	P	W	D	L	F	A	Pts
1 Rangers	27	20	4	3	71	26	44
2 Kilmarnock	27	19	5	3	65	31	43
3 CELTIC	27	16	6	5	74	25	38
4 Hearts	27	15	8	4	61	30	38
5 Dundee	27	16	5	6	79	37	37

March 11th
PARTICK THISTLE (0) 2 CELTIC (1) 2
Duffy (50, Cowan (55) Divers (28),
Murdoch (78)

PARTICK THISTLE: Niven; Campbell, Tinney; McParland, Harvey, Closs; Cowan, Hainey, Davidson, Duffy, Fleming

CELTIC: Fallon; Young, Gemmell; McKay, McNeill, Kennedy; Johnstone, Murdoch, Chalmers, Divers, Hughes

Attendance: n.a.

March 14th
CELTIC (1) 5 HIBERNIAN (0) 0
Murdoch 2 (3 pen, 89),
Chalmers 2 (56, 88),
Divers (85)

CELTIC: Fallon; Young, Gemmell; McKay, McNeill, Kennedy; Johnstone, Murdoch, Chalmers, Divers, Hughes

HIBERNIAN: Simpson; Fraser, Baxter; Stanton, J. Grant, Preston; Hamilton, Quinn, Scott, Martin, John Grant

Attendance: 11,000

March 21st
KILMARNOCK (1) 4 CELTIC (0) 0
Murray 2 (16, 64),
McInally 2 (66, 72)

KILMARNOCK: Forsyth; King, Watson; McFadzean, McGrory, Beattie; Black, McInally, Murray, Sneddon, McIlroy

CELTIC: Fallon; Young, Gemmell; Clark, McNeill, Kennedy; Johnstone, Murdoch, Chalmers, Divers, Hughes

Attendance: 12,000

March 28th
MOTHERWELL (0) 0 CELTIC (3) 4
Murdoch (2),
Johnstone (14),
Chalmers 2 (18, 70)

MOTHERWELL: Wylie; Delaney, McCallum; Murray, Martis, McCann; Lindsay, Thomson, McBride, Robertson, Weir

CELTIC: Fallon; Young, O'Neill; Clark, McNeill, Kennedy; Johnstone, Murdoch, Chalmers, Gallagher, Hughes

Attendance: 8,000

April 1st
CELTIC (0) 2 DUNDEE (1) 1
Gallagher (75), Gilzean (18)
Chalmers (89)

CELTIC: Fallon; Young, O'Neill; Clark, McNeill, Kennedy; Johnstone, Murdoch, Chalmers, Gallagher, Hughes

DUNDEE: Slater; Hamilton, Cox; Seith, Ryden, Stuart; Penman, Cousin, Cameron, Gilzean, Robertson

Attendance: n.a.

April 4th
ST JOHNSTONE (0) 1 CELTIC (1) 1
Kemp (49) Murdoch (13)

ST JOHNSTONE: Fallon; McFadyen, Richmond; McCarry, McKinven, Renton; McIntyre, Harrower, Donnelly, Ferguson, Kemp

CELTIC: Fallon; Young, O'Neill; Clark, McNeill, Kennedy; Johnstone, Murdoch, Chalmers, Gallagher, Divers

Attendance: 9,500. Renton missed a last-minute penalty

April 11th: Kennedy and McNeill were in the Scotland team which beat England 1-0 at Hampden Park.

April 17th: John McNamee was transferred to Hibernian for £17,000.

April 18th
CELTIC (1) 1 HEARTS (0) 1
Chalmers (7) Hamilton (65)

CELTIC: Fallon; Young, Gemmell; Clark, McNeill, Kennedy; Johnstone, Murdoch, Chalmers, Gallagher, Hughes

HEARTS: Cruikshank; Shevlane, Holt; Polland, Anderson, Higgins; Hamilton, Wallace, White, Sandeman, Traynor

Attendance: 21,000

Scottish First Division

	P	W	D	L	F	A	Pts
1 Rangers	34	25	5	4	85	31	55
2 Kilmarnock	34	22	5	7	77	40	49
3 CELTIC	34	19	9	6	89	34	47
4 Hearts	34	19	9	6	74	40	47
5 Dunfermline	34	18	9	7	64	33	45
6 Dundee	34	20	5	9	94	50	45
7 Partick Thistle	34	15	5	14	55	54	35
8 Dundee United	34	13	8	13	65	49	34
9 Aberdeen	34	12	8	14	53	53	32
10 Hibernian	34	12	6	16	59	66	30
11 Motherwell	34	9	11	14	51	62	29
12 St Mirren	34	12	5	17	44	74	29
13 St Johnstone	34	11	6	17	54	70	28
14 Falkirk	34	11	6	17	54	84	28
15 Airdrie	34	11	4	19	52	97	26
16 Third Lanark	34	9	7	18	47	74	25
17 Queen of the South	34	5	6	23	40	92	16
18 East Stirling	34	5	2	27	37	91	12

April 30th: Billy Price was given a free transfer.

May 12th: Kennedy and McNeill were in the Scotland team which drew 2-2 with West Germany in Hanover.

June 8th: Frank Brogan was transferred to Ipswich Town for £12,000.

June 16th: Paddy Turner was transferred to Glentoran for £1,000.

LEAGUE CUP

August 10th
CELTIC (0) 0 — RANGERS (1) 3
Forrest 2 (29, 62), McLean (56)

CELTIC: Haffey; McKay, Gemmell; McNamee, McNeill, Price; Johnstone, Turner, Hughes, Chalmers, Murdoch

RANGERS: Ritchie; Shearer, Provan; Greig, McKinnon, Baxter; Henderson, McLean, Forrest, Brand, Wilson

Attendance: 60,000

Celtic had opportunities to win in the first 25 minutes but the match ended with Rangers completely on top and even toying with their opponents.

August 14th
KILMARNOCK (0) 0 — CELTIC (0) 0

KILMARNOCK: Forsyth; King, Watson; Murray, McGrory, O'Connor; Brown, McInally, Yard, Hamilton, Black

CELTIC: Haffey; McKay, Gemmell; Clark, McNeill, Price; Johnstone, Turner, Hughes, Chalmers, Murdoch

Attendance: 23,000

August 17th
CELTIC (1) 1 — QUEEN OF THE SOUTH (1) 1
Brogan (8) — McDonald (28)

CELTIC: Haffey; McKay, Gemmell; McNamee, McNeill, Clark; Chalmers, Murdoch, Hughes, Turner, Brogan

QUEEN OF THE SOUTH: Farm; Morrison, Kerr; Irving, Rugg, McNaught; McDonald, Hannigan, Thomson, Gardner, Steel

Attendance: 18,000. There was an anti-Kelly demonstration after the match.

August 24th
RANGERS (1) 3 — CELTIC (0) 0
Wilson (38), Brand (54 pen), Forrest (61)

RANGERS: Ritchie; Shearer, Provan; Greig, McKinnon, Baxter; Henderson, McLean, Forrest, Brand, Wilson

CELTIC: Haffey; McKay, Gemmell; Clark, McNeill, Price; Gallagher, Turner, Divers, Chalmers, Jeffrey

Attendance: 65,000

Celtic's lack of punch in attack was again apparent. In the 1st half Rangers made poor use of a strong wind. Against the run of play Rangers scored 7 minutes before the interval when Wilson got his head to a corner-kick by Henderson. They took command of the game in 54 minutes when Brand scored with a penalty-kick after Forrest had his feet pulled from him by McNeill, who had an uncertain afternoon. He was again outwitted in 61 minutes by Forrest, who with a quick wheel 10 yards out shot past Haffey. This 3rd reverse took much of the heart out of Celtic, and before the close it was obvious that there was only 1 team.

August 28th
CELTIC (1) 2 — KILMARNOCK (0) 0
Divers (14), Gallagher (75)

CELTIC: Haffey; McKay, Gemmell; Clark, McNeill, Price; Gallagher, Turner, Divers, Chalmers, Jeffrey

KILMARNOCK: Forsyth; King, Richmond; Murray, McGrory, Beattie; Brown, Sneddon, Yard, McFadzean, Black

Attendance: 12,000. McKay missed a penalty

August 31st
QUEEN OF THE SOUTH (1) 2 — CELTIC (2) 3
McDonald (14), Gardner (83) — Chalmers 2 (15, 62), Gallagher (36 pen)

QUEEN OF THE SOUTH: Wright; Morrison, Kerr; Irving, Rugg, Murphy; Hannigan, McDonald, Thomson, Gardner, Muir

CELTIC: Haffey; McKay, Gemmell; Clark, McNeill, Price; Gallagher, Turner, Divers, Chalmers, Jeffrey

Attendance: 6,500

SECTION TABLE

	P	W	D	L	F	A	Pts
Rangers	6	5	1	0	22	7	11
Kilmarnock	6	2	2	2	9	9	6
CELTIC	6	2	2	2	6	9	6
Queen of the South	6	0	1	5	8	20	1

SCOTTISH CUP

First Round January 11th
CELTIC (0) 3 — EYEMOUTH (0) 0
Chalmers 2 (49, 79), Gallagher (68)

CELTIC: Fallon; Young, Gemmell; Clark, McNeill, Kennedy; Johnstone, Turner, Chalmers, Gallagher, Hughes

EYEMOUTH: Drummond; Paterson, Blackwood; D. Martin, J. Martin, Ross; Graham, Birrell, Steedman, McNeill, Hunter

Attendance: 17,000

Second Round January 25th
MORTON (1) 1 — CELTIC (1) 3
McGraw (22) — Hughes (35), Gallagher (52), Johnstone (55)

MORTON: Miller; Boyd, Mallan; Reilly, Kiernan, Strachan; Stevenson, Campbell, Caven, McGraw, Wilson

CELTIC: Fallon; Young, Gemmell; Clark, McNeill, Kennedy; Johnstone, Murdoch, Chalmers, Gallagher, Hughes

Attendance: 21,000

Third Round February 15th
CELTIC (1) 4 — AIRDRIE (0) 1
Chalmers (9), Murdoch (47 pen), Johnstone (80), Hughes (88) — Rowan (54)

CELTIC: Fallon; Young, Gemmell; Clark, McNeill, Kennedy; Johnstone, Murdoch, Chalmers, Divers, Hughes

AIRDRIE: Samson; Jonquin, Keenan; Stewart, Hannah, Reid; Ferguson, Hastings, Rowan, Murray, Newlands

Attendance: 32,000

Fourth Round March 7th
RANGERS (1) 2 — CELTIC (0) 0
Forrest (44), Henderson (46)

RANGERS: Ritchie; Shearer, Provan; Greig, McKinnon, Baxter; Henderson, McMillan, Forrest, Brand, Wilson

CELTIC: Fallon; Young, Gemmell; Murdoch, McNeill, Kennedy; Brogan, Johnstone, Chalmers, Divers, Hughes

Attendance: 84,724

Before the match Rangers lined up and applauded Celtic onto the field in appreciation of their victory in Bratislava. Rangers' progress did suffer from an unexpectedly lifeless display by Baxter and the fact that Wilson and Forrest were marked out of the game by Young and McNeill. McNeill could not be blamed for the 1st goal which Forrest headed home when Fallon allowed Wilson's corner-kick to bounce out of his hands. Henderson's goal, a minute after the interval, was brilliantly taken. Receiving the ball from Forrest 40 yards out, he ran through a retreating Celtic defence and from the penalty-spot drove the ball past Fallon with his left foot.

EUROPEAN CUP WINNERS' CUP

First Round First Leg September 17th
BASLE (Switzerland) (0) 1 — CELTIC (2) 5
Blumer (78) — Divers (21), Hughes 3 (43, 65, 77), Lennox (52)

BASLE: Stettler; Furi, Michaud; Stocker, Weber, Porlezza; Simonet, Odermatt, Pfirtar, Blumer, Baumann

CELTIC: Haffey; McKay, Gemmell; McNamee, McNeill, Clark; Lennox, Chalmers, Hughes, Divers, Brogan

Attendance: 15,000

Celtic made virtually certain of a place in the next round with a competent display which was far above the standard of the Swiss side. In the 2nd half the superior pace and stamina of Celtic were more than the Basle side could cope with.

First Round Second Leg October 10th
CELTIC (2) 5 — BASLE (0) 0
Johnstone (3), Divers 2 (42, 88), Murdoch (62), Chalmers (78)

CELTIC: Haffey; Young, Gemmell; McKay, McNeill, Kennedy; Johnstone, Murdoch, Chalmers, Divers, Hughes

BASLE: Stettler, Furi, Michaud; Stocker, Buri, Porlezza; Luth, Odermatt, Pfirtar, Noeffel, Mazzola

Attendance: 8,000

Celtic knocked the heart out of the return game by scoring a goal in the 3rd minute. They went on to score 4 more goals against a weak Basle side and the final aggregate of 10-1 confirmed their total superiority.

Second Round First Leg December 4th
CELTIC (2) 3 — DINAMO ZAGREB (Yugoslavia) (0) 0
Chalmers 2 (10, 13), Hughes (62)

CELTIC: Fallon; Young, Gemmell; Clark, McNeill, Kennedy; Johnstone, Murdoch, Chalmers, Divers, Hughes

DINAMO ZAGREB: Crnkovic; Belin, Braun; Markovic, Benco, Kasunovic; Kobescak, Zambata, Raus, Lamza, Ribic

Attendance: 42,000

Celtic were immeasurably superior to their opponents. They were quicker to the ball, used it more imaginatively, tackled tenaciously and in general moved more purposefully than the Yugoslavs.

Second Round Second Leg December 11th
DINAMO ZAGREB (0) 2 — CELTIC (1) 1
Lamza (62), Zambata (85) — Murdoch (41)

DINAMO ZAGREB: Skoric; Belin, Braun; Ramljak, Kasunovic, Benco; Kobescak, Zambata, Raus, Lamza, Ribic

CELTIC: Fallon; Young, Gemmell; Clark, McNeill, Kennedy; Johnstone, Murdoch, Chalmers, Divers, Hughes

Attendance: 10,000

Before Celtic had taken an overall lead of 4-0 in 41 minutes Dinamo had done most of the attacking and Celtic at times had 10 men back in defence. It was against the run of play when Celtic scored. Chalmers pushed through a pass to Murdoch who scored from 20 yards with a fine shot. In the end it needed sturdy defensive work to keep their opponents' score down to 2 goals. Celtic won 4-2 on aggregate.

Third Round First Leg February 26th
CELTIC (0) 1 SLOVAN BRATISLAVA
Murdoch (71 pen) (Czechoslovakia) (0) 0

CELTIC: Fallon; Young, Gemmell; Clark, McNeill, Kennedy; Johnstone, Murdoch, Chalmers, Divers, Hughes

SLOVAN: Schroif; Urban, Filo; Horvath, Popluhar, Peter Molnar; Cvetler, Obert, Hrdlicka, Paul Molnar, Jokl

Attendance: 53,000

One goal, and that from a penalty kick, was all Celtic had to show for almost 90 minutes of attacking football. Celtic's aim to score goals was thwarted mainly by poor finishing. They had some bad luck but their attacks lacked method. Chalmers lacked support, the promise of Hughes' play in the 1st half faded in the second and Johnstone did not come onto a game until the last 20 minutes.

Third Round Second Leg March 4th
SLOVAN BRATISLAVA CELTIC (0) 1
(0) 0 Hughes (85)

SLOVAN: Schroif; Urban, Filo; Horvath, Popluhar, Peter Molnar; Moravcik, Obert, Hrdlicka, Paul Molnar, Cvetler

CELTIC: Fallon; Young, Gemmell; Clark, McNeill, Kennedy; Johnstone, Murdoch, Chalmers, Divers, Hughes

Attendance: 30,000

Hughes' goal, scored with only 5 minutes remaining, came after he had beaten Moravcik and then run half the length of the pitch. After evading a tackle by Popluhar he then flicked the ball past Schroif as the goalkeeper came out to intercept. The match was a triumph for the Celtic team against the Czech side, who had just returned home from a highly successful tour of South America. Celtic won 2-0 on aggregate.

Semi-Final First Leg April 15th
CELTIC (1) 3 M.T.K. BUDAPEST
Johnstone (41), (Hungary) (0) 0
Chalmers 2 (65, 76)

CELTIC: Fallon; Young, Gemmell; Clark, McNeill, Kennedy; Johnstone, Murdoch, Chalmers, Gallagher, Hughes

M.T.K.: Kovalik; Keszel, Jenei; Nagy, Danszi, Vasas; Torok, Takacs, Bodor, Kuti, Dinyes

Attendance: 51,000

Determination, relentless aggression and pace. These qualities and teamwork enabled Celtic to overwhelm M.T.K. The game boiled over in the second-half into a rousing Cup-tie. Johnstone and Chalmers in particular deserved the applause, not just because they scored the goals but because they, more than any other forwards, were constant thorns in the side of M.T.K.'s defence.

Semi-Final Second Leg April 29th
M.T.K. BUDAPEST CELTIC (0) 0
(1) 4
Kuti 2 (11, 71),
Vasas (47 pen),
Sandor (61)

M.T.K.: Kovalik; Keszei, Jenei; Nagy, Danszi, Vasas; Sandor, Takacs, Bodor, Kuti, Halapi

CELTIC: Fallon; Young, Gemmell; Clark, McNeill, Kennedy; Johnstone, Murdoch, Chalmers, Gallagher, Hughes

Attendance: 10,000

The Hungarians, realising they had nothing to lose, went into the attack straight from the start and it came as no real surprise when they scored in 11 minutes. Just before half-time Johnstone and Hughes each had the ball in the net but the referee disallowed both for offside. In the 2nd minute of the 2nd half Gemmell punched a net-bound shot over the bar and from the resultant penalty kick Vasas scored. After Sandor's goal M.T.K. went all out for the vital 4th and in 71 minutes they got it, Kuti easily beating Fallon from close range. M.T.K. won 4-3 on aggregate.

Appearances	League	League Cup	Scottish Cup	Cup Winners Cup
Haffey	10	6	–	2
McKay	9	6	–	2
Gemmell	31	6	4	8
Clark	26	5	3	7
McNeill	28	6	4	8
Price	1	5	–	–
F. Brogan	9	1	1	1
Turner	7	6	1	–
Divers	29	3	2	6
Chalmers	34	6	4	8
Jeffrey	1	3	–	–
O'Neill	5	–	–	–
Lennox	7	–	–	1
J. Brogan	3	–	–	–
Hughes	22	3	4	8
McNamee	2	2	–	1
Fallon	24	–	4	6
Young	29	–	4	7
Cushley	5	–	–	–
Kennedy	29	–	4	7
Johnstone	25	2	4	7
Murdoch	26	3	3	7
Gallagher	10	3	2	2
Henderson	2	–	–	–

GOALSCORERS

League: Chalmers 28, Divers 15, Murdoch 15 (2 pens), Hughes 10, Johnstone 6, F. Brogan 5 (1 pen), Turner 2, Gallagher 2, Own Goals 2, Jeffrey 1, Lennox 1, McKay 1 (pen), Clark 1

League Cup: Chalmers 2, Gallagher 2 (1 pen), Divers 1, F. Brogan 1

Scottish Cup: Chalmers 3, Gallagher 2, Hughes 2, Johnstone 2, Murdoch 1 (pen)

Cup Winners Cup: Chalmers 5, Hughes 5, Murdoch 3, Divers 3, Johnstone 2, Lennox 1

Celtic defeat Dunfermline Athletic 3-2 in the 1965 Scottish Cup Final at Hampden Park before 108,000 spectators.

Season 1964-65

At the end of January the club announced that former team captain Jock Stein, the manager of Hibernian, would be taking over as Manager (their 4th), with Jimmy McGrory, Manager since July 1945, becoming the club's P.R.O. The appointment of Stein had an immediate effect and the club went on to win the Scottish Cup for the first time since Stein himself lifted the trophy 11 years previously. In McGrory's time in charge the club had played 601 League matches, winning 282, drawing 134 and losing 185. They won the League Championship in 1954, the Scottish Cup in 1951 and 1954, the Scottish League Cup in 1956 and 1957, the St Mungo's Cup in 1951 and the Coronation Cup in 1953.

13 League defeats saw the club slip to 8th place in the Championship which was won in dramatic fashion by Kilmarnock. Stein's 1st match in charge was won 6-0 at Airdrie with Bertie Auld scoring 5 goals, but only 2 of the remaining 8 matches were won as the new Manager tried to sort out the immediate problems on the playing side in time for the next season. At the beginning of the season the club made an unsuccessful attempt to bring the legendary Alfredo di Stefano to Parkhead. Former Internationals Frank Haffey and Duncan McKay left the club and former star Bertie Auld became Manager McGrory's last signing when he returned from Birmingham City. Jock Stein's 1st move in the transfer market was to sign Motherwell's Joe McBride – so impressive in the Scottish Cup Semi-Final clashes – at the end of the season. Billy McNeill became Scotland's first-ever Player of the Year and John Hughes finished as the club's top scorer with 22 goals.

Celtic reached their 3rd Scottish League Cup Final, but an injury to McNeill in the final group match against Kilmarnock put him out of action for nearly 3 months including the Final against Rangers where his undoubted talent and experience were sorely missed.

A brilliant headed goal by Billy McNeill won the Scottish Cup Final against Dunfermline – Celtic's first major trophy win in 7 years and revenge for their Final defeat at the hands of the Fife club, then managed by Jock Stein, 4 years previously.

They beat Leixoes of Portugal in the First Round of the Fairs Cities Cup but found Barcelona too experienced and well organised and never looked capable of pulling back the 2-goal first-leg deficit.

League:	Eighth
League Cup:	Finalists
Scottish Cup:	Winners
Fairs Cities Cup:	Second Round

SCOTTISH FIRST DIVISION

August 19th
MOTHERWELL (0) 1
Lindsay (72)

CELTIC (0) 3
Murdoch (45), Chalmers (67), Lennox (74)

MOTHERWELL: Wylie; Thomson, McCallum; McCann, Delaney, Murray; Carlyle, Weir, McBride, Hunter, Lindsay

CELTIC: Fallon; Young, Gemmell; Clark, McNeill, Kennedy; Johnstone, Murdoch, Chalmers, Divers, Lennox

Attendance: 13,000

September 5th
CELTIC (1) 3 — RANGERS (0) 1
Chalmers 2 (35, 50), Hughes (56) — Wilson (82)

CELTIC: Fallon; Young, Gemmell; Brogan, Cushley, Kennedy; Johnstone, Divers, Chalmers, Gallagher, Hughes

RANGERS: Ritchie; Hynd, Provan; Greig, McKinnon, Baxter; Henderson, McLean, Forrest, Brand, Wilson

Attendance: 58,000. Gallagher missed a penalty

Celtic recorded an emphatic victory over Rangers after 90 minutes of excitement on a pitch soaked by incessant heavy rain. Rangers' defence was too often outwitted by the massive Hughes and the diminutive Johnstone.

September 12th
CLYDE (1) 1 — CELTIC (0) 1
McFarlane (13) — Chalmers (83)

CLYDE: McCulloch; Glasgow, Mulheron; McHugh, Fraser, White; Bryce, Gilroy, McFarlane, Hood, Hastings

CELTIC: Fallon; Young, Gemmell; Clark, Cushley, Kennedy; Johnstone, Murdoch, Chalmers, Gallagher, Lennox

Attendance: 22,000

September 19th
CELTIC (0) 1 — DUNDEE UNITED (0) 1
Chalmers (62) — Graham (48)

CELTIC: Fallon; Young, Gemmell; Clark, Kennedy, Brogan; Johnstone, Murdoch, Chalmers, Gallagher, Hughes

DUNDEE UNITED: Davie; Millar, Briggs; Neilson, Smith, Fraser; Graham, Rooney, Howieson, Gillespie, Thom

Attendance: 26,500

September 26th
HEARTS (3) 4 — CELTIC (0) 2
Hamilton (4), Wallace (6), Gordon 2 (15, 87) — Murdoch (69), Lennox (89)

HEARTS: Cruikshank; Ferguson, Shevlane; Polland, Anderson, Higgins; Ford, Hamilton, Wallace, Gordon, Traynor

CELTIC: Fallon; McKay, Gemmell; Clark, Young, Kennedy; Curley, Murdoch, Chalmers, Johnstone, Lennox

Attendance: 22,000

September 27th: Republic of Ireland international winger Joe Haverty of Millwall joined Celtic for one month's trial.

October 3rd: Kennedy and Chalmers were in the Scotland team which was beaten 3-2 by Wales in Cardiff. Chalmers scored one of Scotland's goals.

October 9th: Frank Haffey decided against a transfer to Third Lanark and joined Swindon Town instead.

October 10th
ABERDEEN (1) 1 — CELTIC (1) 3
Kerrigan (12 pen) — Hughes (33), Murdoch (67), Chalmers (78)

ABERDEEN: Ogston; Shewan, Hogg; Cooke, Coutts, Smith; Hume, Kerrigan, Kerr, Little, McIntosh

CELTIC: Fallon; Young, Gemmell; Clark, Cushley, Kennedy; Johnstone, Murdoch, Chalmers, Divers, Hughes

Attendance: 12,000

October 10th: Partick Thistle made a move to sign both Johnny Divers and John Hughes.

October 12th
CELTIC (1) 1 — MORTON (0) 0
Divers (5)

CELTIC: Fallon; Young, Gemmell; Clark, Cushley, Kennedy; Johnstone, Murdoch, Chalmers, Divers, Hughes

MORTON: Sorensen; Boyd, Johansen; Reilly, Kiernan, Strachan; Campbell, Stevenson, Harper, Bertelsen, Wilson

Attendance: 35,000

October 17th
CELTIC (3) 4 — ST MIRREN (1) 1
Divers 2 (10, 12), Hughes (16), Murdoch (71) — Gemmell (28)

CELTIC: Fallon; Young, Gemmell; Clark, Cushley, Kennedy; Hughes, Murdoch, Chalmers, Divers, Haverty

ST MIRREN: Liney; Murray, Wilson; Ross, Clunie, Gray; Robertson, Beck, McIntyre, Gemmell, Quinn

Attendance: 23,000

League positions

	P	W	D	L	F	A	Pts
1 Kilmarnock	8	7	1	0	14	3	15
2 Hearts	9	6	3	0	29	11	15
3 Hibernian	9	7	0	2	22	14	14
4 Dunfermline	9	5	2	2	22	10	12
5 Morton	9	5	2	2	13	7	12
6 CELTIC	8	5	2	1	18	11	12

October 21st: Kennedy and Chalmers were in the Scotland team which beat Finland 3-1 in a World Cup Qualifier at Hampden Park. Chalmers scored Scotland's 2nd goal.

October 28th
KILMARNOCK (3) 5 — CELTIC (0) 2
McInally 2 (8, 37), Hamilton (26), McFadzean 2 (53, 54) — Gemmell (62), Gallagher (78)

KILMARNOCK: Forsyth; King, Watson; Murray, McGrory, Beattie; McIlroy, McInally, Hamilton, McFadzean, Sneddon

CELTIC: Fallon; Young, Gemmell; Brogan, Cushley, Kennedy; Johnstone, Murdoch, Chalmers, Gallagher, Lennox

Attendance: 16,000

October 31st
CELTIC (0) 2 — AIRDRIE (0) 1
Chalmers 2 (77, 82) — Reid (87)

CELTIC: Fallon; Young, Gemmell; Clark, Cushley, Kennedy; Johnstone, Murdoch, Chalmers, Gallagher, Lennox

AIRDRIE: Samson; Jonquin, Keenan; Brown, Hannah, Marshall; Ferguson, Murray, Moonie, Reid, McKay

Attendance: 12,000

November 1st: Celtic were set to pay £26,000 for Harry Hood of Clyde, but Hood turned Celtic down.

November 6th: Duncan McKay was transferred to Third Lanark.

November 7th
ST JOHNSTONE (3) 3 — CELTIC (0) 0
McCarry (1), Kerray (10), McGrogan (30)

ST JOHNSTONE: McVittie; McFadyen, W. Coburn; McCarry, McKinven, Renton; Flanagan, Duffy, J. Coburn, Kerray, McGrogan

CELTIC: Fallon; Young, Gemmell; Murdoch, Cushley, Kennedy; Hughes, Johnstone, Chalmers, Divers, Lennox

Attendance: 11,000

November 11th: Jim Kennedy played for the Scotland XI which beat Tottenham Hotspur 6-2 at White Hart Lane in a Testimonial for the dependants of the late John White.

November 13th: Hugh Maxwell was signed from Falkirk for £15,000.

November 14th
CELTIC (0) 0 — DUNDEE (1) 2
Penman (22), Murray (88)

CELTIC: Fallon; Young, Gemmell; Clark, Cushley, Kennedy; Johnstone, Murdoch, Chalmers, Maxwell, Hughes

DUNDEE: Donaldson; Hamilton, Beattie; Cousin, Easton, Stuart; Murray, Penman, Harley, Gilzean, Robertson

Attendance: 14,500

November 21st
CELTIC (1) 3 — FALKIRK (0) 0
Maxwell (10 secs), Hughes 2 (52, 78)

CELTIC: Simpson; Young, Gemmell; Murdoch, McNeill, Kennedy; Johnstone, Gallagher, Chalmers, Maxwell, Hughes

FALKIRK: Whigham; Lambie, Hunter; Pierson, Markie, Fulton; Houston, Allan, Gourlay, Moran, Scott

Attendance: 16,000

November 25th: Jim Kennedy was in the Scotland team which beat Northern Ireland 3-2 at Hampden Park.

November 28th
THIRD LANARK (0) 0 — CELTIC (1) 3
Murdoch (6), Hughes (75), Baillie o.g. (77)

THIRD LANARK: Williams; McKay, Little; Connell, Baillie, Geddes; Todd, Murray, Cullen, Black, Kirk

CELTIC: Simpson; Young, Gemmell; Murdoch, McNeill, Kennedy; Johnstone, Gallagher, Hughes, Maxwell, Lennox

Attendance: 11,000

December 12th
PARTICK THISTLE (1) 2 — CELTIC (2) 4
Ewing (16), Young o.g. (85) — Gallagher (21), Hughes 2 (37, 77), Maxwell (81)

PARTICK THISTLE: Niven; Hogan, Tinney; Davis, Harvey, Staite; McParland, Cunningham, McLindon, Hainey, Ewing

CELTIC: Simpson; Young, Gemmell; Clark, McNeill, O'Neill; Johnstone, Murdoch, Hughes, Maxwell, Gallagher

Attendance: n.a.

December 19th
CELTIC (1) 1 — DUNFERMLINE (1) 2
Gallagher (40) — Sinclair (3), Ferguson (82)

CELTIC: Simpson; Young, Gemmell; Clark, McNeill, Kennedy; Johnstone, Murdoch, Hughes, Maxwell, Gallagher

DUNFERMLINE: Herriot; W. Callaghan, Lunn; Smith, McLean, T. Callaghan; Edwards, Paton, McLaughlin, Ferguson, Sinclair

Attendance: 15,000

League positions

	P	W	D	L	F	A	Pts
1 Hearts	18	13	4	1	56	23	30
2 Kilmarnock	18	13	4	1	35	15	30
3 Hibernian	17	12	2	3	39	22	26
4 Dunfermline	16	10	2	4	35	18	22
5 CELTIC	17	10	2	5	35	25	22

December 26th
CELTIC (1) 2 — MOTHERWELL (0) 0
Hughes 2 (26, 50)

CELTIC: Simpson; Young, O'Neill; Clark, McNeill, Kennedy; Johnstone, Murdoch, Hughes, Divers, Lennox

MOTHERWELL: Wylie; Thomson, R. McCallum; Murray, Delaney, W. McCallum; Coakley, McCann, McBride, Ramsay, Hunter

Attendance: 9,500. Hughes played in training shoes

January 1st
RANGERS (1) 1 CELTIC (0) 0
Forrest (32)

RANGERS: Ritchie; Provan, Caldow; Greig, McKinnon, Wood; Wilson, Millar, Forrest, Beck, Johnston

CELTIC: Simpson; Young, Gemmell; Clark, McNeill, Kennedy; Johnstone, Murdoch, Hughes, Divers, Gallagher

Attendance: 64,400

Jimmy Johnstone was ordered off for the 2nd time in his career. Murdoch shot over the bar a penalty-kick awarded 6 minutes from time when McKinnon brought down Hughes well inside the area. Rangers were sluggish and their forwards lacked ideas. Johnston was the most purposeful of the 5 but the absence of Baxter could be felt.

January 2nd
CELTIC (1) 1 CLYDE (1) 1
Hughes (4) Gilroy (44)

CELTIC: Simpson; Young, Gemmell; Clark, McNeill, Kennedy; Lennox, Maxwell, Hughes, Divers, Gallagher

CLYDE: McCulloch; Glasgow, Mulheron; McHugh, Fraser, White; Bryce, Gilroy, Knox, McLean, Hastings

Attendance: 13,500

January 9th
DUNDEE UNITED (2) 3 CELTIC (1) 1
Dossing 2 (15, 18), Mitchell (90) Hughes (20)

DUNDEE UNITED: Mackay; Millar, Briggs; Munro, Smith, Gillespie; Dick, Berg, Dossing, Mitchell, Persson

CELTIC: Simpson; Young, Gemmell; Clark, McNeill, Brogan; Johnstone, Murdoch, Hughes, Divers, Gallagher

Attendance: 18,000

January 14th: Bertie Auld rejoined Celtic from Birmingham City for £12,000.

January 16th
CELTIC (1) 1 HEARTS (2) 2
Gemmell (28) Hamilton 2 (4, 37)

Fallon: Young, Gemmell; Brogan, McNeill, Kennedy; Johnstone, Murdoch, Hughes, Gallagher, Auld

HEARTS: Cruikshank; Shevlane, Holt; Ferguson, Anderson, Higgins; Hamilton, Jensen, Wallace, Gordon, Traynor

Attendance: 21,000

January 21st: Celtic made enquiries about signing Johnny Crossan from Standard Liège.

January 23rd
MORTON (0) 3 CELTIC (2) 3
Bertelsen 2 (77, 83), Strachan (82) Lennox (29), Hughes (43), Gemmell (65)

MORTON: E. Sorensen; Boyd, Johansen; Smith, Kiernan, Strachan; Bertelsen. J. Sorensen, Caven, McGraw, Stevenson

CELTIC: Fallon; Young, Gemmell; Brogan, McNeill, Clark; Johnstone, Murdoch, Hughes, Lennox, Auld

Attendance: 17,000

January 30th
CELTIC (3) 8 ABERDEEN (0) 0
Hughes 5 (28, 36, 62, 80, 86), Auld (41 pen), Murdoch (70), Lennox (76)

CELTIC: Fallon; Young, Gemmell; Clark, McNeill, Brogan; Chalmers, Murdoch, Hughes, Lennox, Auld

ABERDEEN: Ogston; Bennett, Shewan; Paterson, McCormick, Smith; Fraser, Winchester, Ravn, Kerrigan, Mortensen

Attendance: 14,000

January 31st: It was announced that Jock Stein of Hibernian would become Celtic's new manager with Chief Coach Sean Fallon becoming his Assistant. Jimmy McGrory was to become the club's Public Relations Officer.

February 13th
ST MIRREN (1) 1 CELTIC (2) 5
Carroll (5) Chalmers (10), Lennox (36), Brogan (52), Hughes (64), Murdoch (71)

ST MIRREN: Liney; Murray, Riddell; Gray, Clunie, Wilson; Robertson, Carroll, Hughes, Queen, Gemmell

CELTIC: Fallon; Young, Gemmell; Clark, McNeill, Brogan; Chalmers, Murdoch, Hughes, Lennox, Auld

Attendance: 12,000

February 27th
CELTIC (1) 2 KILMARNOCK (0) 0
Chalmers (16), Hughes (50)

CELTIC: Fallon; Young, Gemmell; Clark, McNeill, Brogan; Chalmers, Murdoch, Hughes, Lennox, Auld

KILMARNOCK: Forsyth; King, Watson; Murray, McGrory, Beattie; McIlroy, McInally, Hamilton, McFadzean, Sneddon

Attendance: 23,000

League positions

	P	W	D	L	F	A	Pts
1 Hearts	26	16	5	5	67	39	37
2 Dunfermline	24	16	3	5	57	25	35
3 Hibernian	25	16	3	6	58	34	35
4 Kilmarnock	26	15	5	6	45	28	35
5 Rangers	23	12	7	4	58	23	31
7 CELTIC	25	13	4	8	56	38	30

March 10th
AIRDRIE (0) 0 — CELTIC (2) 6
Hughes (25), Auld 5 (41, 55, 62, 82 pen, 86 pen)

AIRDRIE: Samson; Jonquin, Caldwell; Rowan, Hannah, Reid; Ferguson, McMillan, Moonie, Murray, Newlands

CELTIC: Fallon; Young, Gemmell; Clark, McNeill, Brogan; Chalmers, Murdoch, Hughes, Lennox, Auld

Attendance: This was Jock Stein's first game as Manager

March 13th
CELTIC (0) 0 — ST JOHNSTONE (0) 1
Duffy (49)

CELTIC: Fallon; Young, Gemmell; Clark, McNeill, Brogan; Chalmers, Murdoch, Hughes, Lennox, Auld

ST JOHNSTONE: McVittie; McFadyen, Coburn; Richmond, McKinven, Renton; Kerray, Whitelaw, McCarry, Duffy, McGrogan

Attendance: 18,000. Auld missed a penalty

March 20th
DUNDEE (1) 3 — CELTIC (1) 3
Cameron 2 (32, 72), Murdoch o.g. (68) — Lennox 2 (3, 54), Johnstone (62)

DUNDEE: Donaldson; Hamilton, Cox; Cousin, Easton, Stuart; Murray, Penman, Cameron, Cooke, Robertson

CELTIC: Fallon; Young, Kennedy; Murdoch, McNeill, Clark; Johnstone, Chalmers, Hughes, Lennox, Auld

Attendance: 18,000

March 22nd
CELTIC (2) 2 — HIBERNIAN (4) 4
Lennox 2 (35, 42) — Martin 3 (13, 19, 40), Young o.g. (22)

CELTIC: Fallon; Young, Kennedy; Brogan, McNeill, Clark; Chalmers, Murdoch, Hughes, Maxwell, Lennox

HIBERNIAN: Wilson; Fraser, Davis; Stanton, McNamee, Baxter; Martin, Quinn, Cormack, Hamilton, Stevenson

Attendance: 19,000

April 3rd
CELTIC (0) 1 — THIRD LANARK (0) 0
D. McKay o.g. (81)

CELTIC: Fallon; Young, Gemmell; Murdoch, McNeill, Clark; Chalmers, Gallagher, Hughes, Lennox, Auld

THIRD LANARK: Williams, D. McKay, May; Connell, Little, A. McKay; McGuire, Jackson, Murray, Fyfe, Kirk

Attendance: 12,000

April 7th
HIBERNIAN (0) 0 — CELTIC (3) 4
Auld 2 (22, 54), Chalmers (28), Murdoch (33)

HIBERNIAN: Wilson; Simpson, Davis; Stanton, McNamee, Baxter; Cormack, Hamilton, Scott, Quinn, Martin

CELTIC: Fallon; Young, Gemmell; Murdoch, McNeill, Clark; Chalmers, Gallagher, Hughes, Lennox, Auld

Attendance: 16,500

April 10th: Billy McNeill was in the Scotland team which drew 2-2 with England at Wembley.

April 14th
FALKIRK (4) 6 — CELTIC (1) 2
Moran 2 (3, 81), Halliday (7), Wilson (20), Graham (26), Fulton (62) — Auld 2 (22, 86 pen)

FALKIRK: Whigham; Lambie, Hunter; Houston, Baillie, Fulton; Graham, Gourlay, Wilson, Moran, Halliday

CELTIC: Fallon; Young, Gemmell; Murdoch, Cushley, O'Neill; Johnstone, Gallagher, Hughes, Lennox, Auld

Attendance: n.a.

April 17th
CELTIC (0) 1 — PARTICK THISTLE (0) 2
Chalmers (81) — Gibb (51), Hogan (70)

CELTIC: Fallon; Young, Kennedy; Murdoch, McNeill, Clark; Johnstone, Lennox, Chalmers, Auld, Hughes

PARTICK THISTLE: Gray; Campbell, Muir; Gibb, Harvey, Cunningham; Cowan, Hainey, Hogan, Ewing, McParland

Attendance: 11,500

April 27th: Billy McNeill was named as Scotland's Player of the Year, the first time such an award had been made.

April 28th
DUNFERMLINE (2) 5 CELTIC (1) 1
Clark o.g. (39), Hughes (45)
McLaughlin 2 (42, 55),
Melrose (46),
Ferguson (62)

DUNFERMLINE: Herriot; Thomson, W. Callaghan; Smith, Fraser, T. Callaghan; Edwards, Ferguson, McLaughlin, Sinclair, Melrose

CELTIC: Fallon; Gemmell, O'Neill; Clark, McNeill, Brogan; Johnstone, Murdoch, Hughes, Maxwell, Lennox

Attendance: 10,000. Maxwell missed a 2nd minute penalty.

Scottish First Division

	P	W	D	L	F	A	Pts
1 Kilmarnock	34	22	6	6	62	33	50
2 Hearts	34	22	6	6	90	49	50
3 Dunfermline	34	22	5	7	83	36	49
4 Hibernian	34	21	4	9	75	47	46
5 Rangers	34	18	8	8	78	35	44
6 Dundee	34	15	10	9	86	63	40
7 Clyde	34	17	6	11	64	58	40
8 CELTIC	34	16	5	13	76	57	37
9 Dundee United	34	15	6	13	59	51	36
10 Morton	34	13	7	14	54	54	33
11 Partick Thistle	34	11	10	13	57	58	32
12 Aberdeen	34	12	8	14	59	75	32
13 St Johnstone	34	9	11	14	57	62	29
14 Motherwell	34	10	8	16	45	54	28
15 St Mirren	34	9	6	19	38	70	24
16 Falkirk	34	7	7	20	43	85	21
17 Airdrie	34	5	4	25	48	110	14
18 Third Lanark	34	3	1	30	22	99	7

May 12th: Ian McColl quit as Scotland team Manager. Jock Stein was named as temporary boss for the World Cup Qualifiers against Poland and Finland.

May 23rd: McNeill and Hughes were in the Scotland team which drew 1-1 with Poland in Warsaw.

May 27th: Scotland beat Finland 2-1 in Helsinki. McNeill and Hughes were in the team.

June 5th: Celtic signed Joe McBride from Motherwell for £22,500.

June 11th: Hugh Maxwell was transferred to St Johnstone for £10,000.

June 22nd: It was reported that Ronnie Simpson was to join Ayr United.

LEAGUE CUP

August 8th
CELTIC 0 PARTICK THISTLE 0

CELTIC: Fallon; Young, Gemmell; Clark, McNeill, Kennedy; Johnstone, Murdoch, Chalmers, Gallagher, Lennox

PARTICK THISTLE: Niven; Hogan, Tinney; McParland, Harvey, Staite; Cowan, Ewing, Hainey, Duffy, Fleming

Attendance: 29,000

August 12th
HEARTS (0) 0 CELTIC (1) 3
Murdoch 2 (32, 70 pen),
Chalmers (59)

HEARTS: Cruikshank; Shevlane, Holt; Polland, Barry, Higgins; Hamilton, Cumming, Murphy, Sandeman, Traynor

CELTIC: Fallon; Young, Gemmell; Clark, McNeill, Brogan; Johnstone, Murdoch, Chalmers, Gallagher, Lennox

Attendance: 20,000

August 15th
CELTIC (1) 4 KILMARNOCK (0) 1
Gallagher 2 (42, 63), Watson (62)
Chalmers (77),
Johnstone (79)

CELTIC: Fallon; Young, Gemmell; Clark, McNeill, Brogan; Johnstone, Murdoch, Chalmers, Gallagher, Lennox

KILMARNOCK: Forsyth; King, Watson; O'Connor, McGrory, Beattie; Murray, Brown, McInally, Sneddon, McIlroy

Attendance: 23,000

August 22nd
PARTICK THISTLE (1) 1 CELTIC (1) 5
Duffy (39) Gallagher (24),
Chalmers 3 (47, 52, 86),
Johnstone (48)

PARTICK THISTLE: Gray; Hogan, Tinney; Davis, Harvey, Staite; Ewing, Cunningham, Hainey, Duffy, McParland

CELTIC: Fallon; Young, Gemmell; Clark, McNeill, Kennedy; Johnstone, Murdoch, Chalmers, Gallagher, Lennox

Attendance: 28,000

August 26th
CELTIC (3) 6 HEARTS (0) 1
Murdoch 3 (2, 47 pen, Wallace (52)
76 pen),
Gallagher 2 (41, 78),
Kennedy (24)

CELTIC: Fallon; Young, Gemmell; Clark, McNeill, Kennedy; Johnstone, Murdoch, Chalmers, Gallagher, Lennox

HEARTS: Cruikshank; Ferguson, Holt; Polland, Barry, Higgins; Hamilton, Wallace, White, Gordon, Traynor

Attendance: 28,000

August 29th
KILMARNOCK (0) 2 CELTIC (0) 0
Hamilton (51 pen),
McIlroy (90)

KILMARNOCK: Forsyth; King, Watson; O'Connor, McGrory, Beattie; Murray, McInally, Hamilton, Sneddon, McIlroy

CELTIC: Fallon; Young, Gemmell; Clark, McNeill, Kennedy; Johnstone, Murdoch, Chalmers, Gallagher, Hughes

Attendance: 18,000. McNeill and Murdoch were both carried off

SECTION TABLE

	P	W	D	L	F	A	Pts
CELTIC	6	4	1	1	18	5	9
Kilmarnock	6	3	2	1	9	5	8
Partick Thistle	6	1	2	3	6	14	4
Hearts	6	1	1	4	7	16	3

Qualifier: CELTIC

Quarter-Final First Leg September 9th
EAST FIFE (1) 2 CELTIC (0) 0
Christie (24), Waddell (64)

EAST FIFE: Kruzycki; Stirrat, Smith; Walker, Young, Donnelly; Broome, Dewar, Christie, Stewart, Waddell

CELTIC: Fallon; Young, Gemmell; Brogan, Cushley, Kennedy; Johnstone, Divers, Chalmers, Gallagher, Hughes

Attendance: n.a.

Quarter-Final Second Leg September 16th
CELTIC (3) 6 EAST FIFE (0) 0
Chalmers 5 (9, 41, 46, 58, 81), Kennedy (15)

CELTIC: Fallon; Young, Gemmell; Clark, Cushley, Kennedy; Johnstone, Murdoch, Chalmers, Gallagher, Hughes

EAST FIFE: Kruzycki; Stirrat, Smith; Walker, Young, Donnelly; Broome, Dewar, Christie, Stewart, Waddell

Attendance: 32,000. Celtic won 6-2 on aggregate.

Semi-Final at Ibrox Park September 29th
CELTIC (0) 2 MORTON (0) 0
Lennox (54),
Gallagher (88)

CELTIC: Fallon; Young, Gemmell; Clark, Cushley, Kennedy; Johnstone, Murdoch, Chalmers, Gallagher, Lennox

MORTON: Sorensen; Boyd, Johansen; Reilly, Kiernan, Strachan; Wilson, Smith, Stevenson, Bertelsen, McBeth

Attendance: 60,000

Celtic went through to the Final of the League Cup for the 1st time since their overwhelming win against Rangers in 1957-58 but they had to fight hard for the honour. Indeed, only when Gallagher scored their 2nd goal 2 minutes from the end could they afford to relax against a team who were their equals in every respect bar scoring.

Final at Hampden Park October 24th
RANGERS (0) 2 CELTIC (0) 1
Forrest 2 (52, 62) Johnstone (69)

RANGERS: Ritchie; Provan, Caldow; Greig, McKinnon, Wood; Brand, Millar, Forrest, Baxter, Johnston

CELTIC: Fallon; Young, Gemmell; Clark, Cushley, Kennedy; Johnstone, Murdoch, Chalmers, Divers, Hughes

Attendance: 91,423. *Referee:* H. Phillips (Wishaw)

Behind Rangers' success was the influence of Baxter, who laid on the 2nd goal for Forrest after 62 minutes. The centre-forward, having 10 minutes earlier swooped on the ball after an indecisive clearance by Gemmell, again swept the ball into the net. When Johnstone scored for Celtic in 69 minutes after leading-up work by Clark and Chalmers, the stage was set for a grandstand finish which had the crowd of 91,000 in almost continuous uproar. This will be remembered as one of the great encounters between these 2 famous clubs. Hughes and Johnstone exchanged positions during the match but Baxter, Rangers' captain, cunningly countered by switching Provan and Caldow.

SCOTTISH CUP

First Round February 6th
ST MIRREN (0) 0 CELTIC (0) 3
Chalmers (49),
Lennox 2 (82, 87)

ST MIRREN: Liney; Murray, Riddell; Gray, Clunie, Wilson; McIntyre, Quinn, Carroll, Ross, Gemmill

CELTIC: Fallon; Young, Gemmell; Clark, McNeill, Brogan; Chalmers, Murdoch, Hughes, Lennox, Auld

Attendance: 28,300

Second Round February 20th
QUEENS PARK (0) 0 CELTIC (0) 1
Lennox (61)

QUEENS PARK: Clark; Gilmour, Pollatschek; Robertson, Neil, McLaughlin; Hopper, Millar, Buchanan, Mackay, Waddell

CELTIC: Fallon; Young, Gemmell; Clark, McNeill, Brogan; Chalmers, Murdoch, Hughes, Lennox, Auld

Attendance: 27,343

Third Round March 6th
CELTIC (1) 3 KILMARNOCK (0) 2
Lennox (15), Auld (60), McInally 2 (59, 73)
Hughes (67)

CELTIC: Fallon; Young, Gemmell; Clark, McNeill, Brogan; Chalmers, Murdoch, Hughes, Lennox, Auld

KILMARNOCK: Forsyth; King, Watson; Murray, McGrory, Beattie; Brown, McInally, Hamilton, McFadzean, McIlroy

Attendance: 47,000

Semi-Final at Hampden Park March 27th

MOTHERWELL (2) 2 CELTIC (1) 2
McBride 2 (10, 32) Lennox (28), Auld (60 pen)

MOTHERWELL: Wylie; Thomson, R. McCallum; Murray, Delaney, W. McCallum; Lindsay, McCann, McBride, Weir, Hunter

CELTIC: Fallon; Young, Gemmell; Murdoch, McNeill, Clark; Johnstone, Gallagher, Hughes, Lennox, Auld

Attendance: 52,000

Every Celtic supporter left Hampden convinced that Johnstone was not offside when in the dying seconds he gave the pass from which Auld stabbed the ball into the net. Celtic must be given credit for twice equalising when they were a goal down. The 2nd half was a story of almost continuous Celtic pressure. Motherwell relied almost entirely on McBride to shoulder the weight of their spasmodic attacks.

Semi-Final Replay at Hampden Park March 31st

MOTHERWELL (0) 0 CELTIC (1) 3
Chalmers (27), Hughes (68), Lennox (74)

MOTHERWELL: Wylie; Thomson, R. McCallum; Murray, Delaney, W. McCallum; Carlyle, McCann, McBride, Weir, Lindsay

CELTIC: Fallon; Young, Gemmell; Murdoch, McNeill, Clark, Chalmers, Gallagher, Hughes, Lennox, Auld

Attendance: 58,959

Celtic's power, aggression and speed were too much for Motherwell.

Final at Hampden Park April 24th

CELTIC (1) 3 DUNFERMLINE ATHLETIC (2) 2
Auld 2 (31, 52), McNeill (81) Melrose (15), McLaughlin (43)

CELTIC: Fallon; Young, Gemmell; Murdoch, McNeill, Clark; Chalmers, Gallagher, Hughes, Lennox, Auld

DUNFERMLINE: Herriot; W. Callaghan, Lunn; Thomson, McLean, T. Callaghan; Edwards, Smith, McLaughlin, Melrose, Sinclair

Attendance: 108,800. *Referee:* H. Phillips (Wishaw)

Twice Celtic were a goal down and twice they equalised. The climax of this unrelenting battle came 9 minutes from time when McNeill headed their winning goal to give them the Scottish Cup for the first time in 11 years. At the interval such an outcome seemed unlikely. Dunfermline, having faced the wind and an almost ceaseless battering from Celtic's anxious forwards, had nevertheless conceded only one goal and were leading 2-1. Celtic equalised for the 2nd time in 52 minutes. A fine interpassing movement between Lennox and Auld ended with a cross from the inside-forward being shot home by the winger from the inside-right position. Then came McNeill's goal, a brilliant header from an equally accurate corner-kick by Gallagher. It was a supreme moment for Celtic and their supporters.

FAIRS CITIES CUP

First Round First Leg September 23rd

LEIXOES (Portugal) (1) 1 CELTIC (1) 1
Esteves (6) Murdoch (31)

LEIXOES: Rosas; Geraldino, Raul; Pereira, Moreira, Marcal; Esteves, Wagner, Oliveira, Ventura, Mateus

CELTIC: Fallon; Young, Gemmell; Clark, Cushley, Kennedy; Johnstone, Murdoch, Chalmers, Gallagher, Lennox

Attendance: n.a. Chalmers, Young and Oliveira were ordered off

First Round Second Leg October 7th

CELTIC (1) 3 LEIXOES (0) 0
Chalmers 2 (14, 83), Murdoch (88 pen)

CELTIC: Fallon; Young, Gemmell; Clark, Cushley, Kennedy; Johnstone, Murdoch, Chalmers, Gallagher, Lennox

LEIXOES: Rosas; Geraldino, Raul; Pereira, Moreira, Marcal; Esteves, Wagner, Cambre, Ventura, Duarte Duarte

Attendance: 33,000. Murdoch missed a penalty

Celtic were subjected to some cruel and at times savage tackling. Yet they won handsomely – even with only 10 men in the second-half, Gallagher having been unable to resume after he had injured a leg 6 minutes before the interval. The home goalkeeper, Fallon, had only one direct shot to save in either half and was merely a spectator. Celtic won 4-1 on aggregate.

Second Round First Leg November 18th

BARCELONA (2) 3 CELTIC (0) 1
Zaldua (12), Seminario (22), Rife (83) Hughes (55)

BARCELONA: Sadurni; Foncho, Benitez; Torres, Eladio, Verges; Rife, Pereida, Zaldua, Seminario, Re

CELTIC: Simpson; Young, Gemmell; Clark, McNeill, Kennedy; Johnstone, Cushley, Chalmers, Murdoch, Hughes

Attendance: 25,000

A depleted but determined Celtic team won the admiration of the crowd for their 2nd-half performance. Clark limped on the wing a virtual passenger throughout the 2nd half, having hurt his right thigh in the 1st half. Murdoch dropped back to cover. In defence 7 players, marshalled by Cushley and McNeill, formed a wall of defiance in face of Barcelona.

Second Round Second Leg December 2nd
CELTIC 0 BARCELONA 0

CELTIC: Simpson; Young, Gemmell; Murdoch, McNeill, O'Neill; Johnstone, Chalmers, Hughes, Gallagher, Lennox

BARCELONA: Sadurni; Benitez, Eladio; Verges, Olivella, Garay; Goyvaerts, Kocsis, Re, Fuste, Seminario

Attendance: 43,000

Celtic were ignominiously eliminated from the Fairs Cup by a perfectly disciplined Barcelona machine. At scarcely any moment did they look capable of retrieving the deficit of 2 goals. Barcelona's use of the open space and their constant support of each other enabled them time and again to short-pass their way out of difficulty or into promising positions in front of goal. They were faster on the ball and to the ball and Celtic were reduced to a ragged battalion long before their forces were reduced when Chalmers was carried off with a leg injury 15 minutes from the end. Barcelona won 3-1 on aggregate.

APPEARANCES	League	League Cup	Scottish Cup	Fairs Cup
Fallon	26	10	6	2
Young	33	10	6	4
Gemmell	30	10	6	4
Clark	27	9	6	3
McNeill	22	6	6	2
Kennedy	22	8	–	3
Johnstone	24	10	1	4
Murdoch	32	9	6	4
Chalmers	23	10	5	4
Divers	10	2	–	–
Lennox	22	6	6	3
J. Brogan	13	3	3	–
Cushley	10	4	–	3
Gallagher	16	9	3	3
Hughes	29	4	6	2
McKay	1	–	–	–
Curley	1	–	–	–
Haverty	1	–	–	–
Maxwell	8	–	–	–
Simpson	8	–	–	2
O'Neill	4	–	–	1
Auld	12	–	6	–

GOALSCORERS:

League: Hughes 22, Chalmers 12, Auld 10 (4 pens), Lennox 9, Murdoch 8, Divers 3, Gemmell 3, Gallagher 3, Maxwell 2, Own Goals 2, J. Brogan 1, Johnstone 1

League Cup: Chalmers 10, Gallagher 6, Murdoch 5 (3 pens), Johnstone 3, Kennedy 2, Lennox 1

Scottish Cup: Lennox 6, Auld 4 (1 pen), Chalmers 2, Hughes 2, McNeill 1

Fairs Cities Cup: Chalmers 2, Murdoch 2 (1 pen), Hughes 1

The full Celtic squad in 1966. Back row: Connelly, Gemmell, Young, Cushley, Divers, Chalmers, Gallagher, Brogan. Middle row: Stein (manager), Hughes, McNeill, Martin, Kennedy, Simpson, Fallon, McCarron, Murdoch, O'Neil, Fallon (asst. manager). Front row: Rooney (trainer), Johnstone, McBride, Quinn, Cattenach, Clark, Auld, Lennox, Mochan (coach). Trophies: (left to right) The Glasgow Cup, The St. Mungo Cup, Scottish League Cup, Scottish F.A. Cup, Coronation Cup, Glasgow Exhibition Cup.

Season 1965-66

Celtic had a very successful first full season under the managership of Jock Stein – winning the League Championship and the League Cup and reaching the Final of the Scottish Cup and the Semi-Final of the European Cup Winners Cup.

They won their 21st Championship – their first for 12 years – finishing 2 points ahead of Rangers, who ran them close, and winning 27 of their 34 matches, scoring 106 goals in the process. They dropped only 1 point at home and recorded some notable wins over Aberdeen (7-1), Dundee (5-0), Hearts (5-2) and Morton (8-1). Undoubtedly their finest win was the 5-1 humiliation of Rangers in the New Year match after they had been a goal down inside 90 seconds. Away from home they lost only 4 matches – three of them in succession. The veteran Simpson made the goalkeeping position his own during the season. Gemmell and Clark played in all 34 matches, and in the free-scoring attack McBride scored 31 goals, with Chalmers, Lennox and Hughes all finishing on double figures. Jock Stein was named as both Scotland's and Britain's Manager of the Year.

Celtic won the League Cup for the 3rd time, beating Rangers by 2 controversial penalties – both converted by Hughes.

They reached their 31st Scottish Cup Final, beating, amongst others, Dundee at Dens Park, Hearts after a replay and Dunfermline comfortably in the Semi-Final. 4 days after defeat at Liverpool they faced Rangers in the Final. They went into the match as hot favourites but an exciting game finished goalless. Auld returned after suspension for the replay. Celtic had their chances but lost to a goal scored by Rangers' Danish full-back Johansen in the 70th minute.

They reached the Semi-Final of the Cup Winners Cup for the second time, losing in controversial fashion to Liverpool after two epic battles.

League:	Champions
League Cup:	Winners
Scottish Cup:	Runners-Up
Cup Winners Cup:	Semi-Finalists

SCOTTISH FIRST DIVISION

July 20th: Neil Mochan was appointed Trainer Coach.

July 31st: Brazilians Marco Di Sousa and Ayrton Inacio were at Parkhead for trials.

August 14th: Brazilians Fernando Consul and Yorge Fara arrived at Parkhead for trials.

August 19th: Henry Quinn was signed from St Mirren.

August 25th
DUNDEE UNITED (0) 0 CELTIC (1) 4
Divers (15),
McBride (52),
Young (56 pen),
Gemmell (65)

DUNDEE UNITED: Mackay; Millar, Briggs; Munro, Smith, Wing; Carroll, Gillespie, Dossing, Mitchell, Persson

CELTIC: Fallon; Young, Gemmell; Murdoch, McNeill, Clark; Chalmers, Divers, McBride, Lennox, Gallagher

Attendance: 18,000. Persson was ordered off.

September 11th
CELTIC (0) 2 — CLYDE (0) 1
Young (72 pen), Gemmell (76) — Stewart (84)

CELTIC: Fallon; Young, Gemmell; Murdoch, McNeill, Clark; Chalmers, Divers, McBride, Lennox, Hughes

CLYDE: Wright; Glasgow, Mulheron; McHugh, Fraser, White; Bryce, Gilroy, Staite, Stewart, Hastings

Attendance: 26,500

September 17th: Celtic decided to extend the trial period for Inacio and Fara.

September 18th
RANGERS (2) 2 — CELTIC (1) 1
Forrest (7), McLean (20 pen) — Hughes (18 pen)

RANGERS: Ritchie; Johansen, Provan; Watson, McKinnon, Greig; Henderson, Sorensen, Forrest, McLean, Johnston

CELTIC: Fallon; Young, Gemmell; Murdoch, McNeill, Clark; Johnstone, Divers, Hughes, Lennox, Auld

Attendance: 76,000

For the last 10 minutes of the game it was touch and go whether Rangers would be able to hold onto their narrow lead. In the last half-hour they were greatly indebted to Ritchie and McKinnon for holding together a defensive structure in which cracks began to appear. Celtic were handicapped in their 2nd-half rally by a leg injury to McNeill. Rangers also had to re-arrange their forces when Sorensen, also with a leg injury, switched to outside-left.

September 21st: Celtic released Inacio and Fara after they failed to reach terms.

September 25th
CELTIC (4) 7 — ABERDEEN (0) 1
Lennox 2 (3, 15), Johnstone 2 (12, 55), Hughes (43), Auld (70), McBride (74) — Winchester (61)

CELTIC: Simpson; Young, Gemmell; Murdoch, McNeill, Clark; Johnstone, Auld, McBride, Lennox, Hughes

ABERDEEN: Clark; Bennett, Shewan; Burns, McCormick, Smith; Wilson, Little, Ravn, Winchester, Mortensen

Attendance: 20,000

October 2nd: McNeill and Hughes were in the Scotland team which was beaten 3-2 by Northern Ireland in Belfast.

October 9th
CELTIC (3) 5 — HEARTS (0) 2
McBride 2 (11, 35), Lennox 2 (4, 57), Gallagher (69) — Gordon 2 (80, 85)

CELTIC: Simpson; Young, Gemmell; Murdoch, McNeill, Clark; Johnstone, Gallagher, McBride, Lennox, Hughes

HEARTS: Cruikshank; Ferguson, Shevlane; Polland, Anderson, Cumming; Jensen, Barry, Wallace, Gordon, Traynor

Attendance: 30,000

October 13th: Billy McNeill was in the Scotland team beaten 2-1 by Poland in a World Cup Qualifier at Hampden Park, McNeill scored Scotland's goal.

October 16th
FALKIRK (2) 3 — CELTIC (1) 4
Lambie (10), Wilson (36), Graham (67) — Lennox 2 (14, 84), Murdoch (60), Johnstone (68)

FALKIRK: Whigham; Lambie, Hunter; Rowan, Baillie, Scott; Lowrie, McManus, Wilson, Graham, Gourlay

CELTIC: Fallon; Young, Gemmell; Murdoch, McNeill, Clark; Johnstone, Gallagher, McBride, Lennox, Hughes

Attendance: 16,000

October 27th
DUNDEE (0) 1 — CELTIC (2) 2
Penman (55) — McBride (18), Lennox (23)

DUNDEE: Donaldson; Ryden, Cox; Cousin, Easton, Houston; Murray, Penman, Cameron, McLean, Cooke

CELTIC: Simpson; Young, Gemmell; Murdoch, McNeill, Clark; Johnstone, Gallagher, McBride, Lennox, Hughes

Attendance: 17,000

October 30th
CELTIC (3) 6 — STIRLING ALBION (1) 1
Murdoch (28), McBride 2 (32, 78), Hughes 3 (42, 50, 58) — Fyfe (43)

CELTIC: Simpson; Young, Gemmell; Murdoch, McNeill, Clark; Johnstone, Gallagher, McBride, Lennox, Hughes

STIRLING ALBION: Taylor; Cunningham, Murray; Reid, Rogerson, Robb; Fyfe, Anderson, Fleming, Thoms, Hall

Attendance: 17,000

November 6th
CELTIC (1) 1 — PARTICK THISTLE (0) 1
McBride (39) — Conway (54)

CELTIC: Simpson; Young, Gemmell; Murdoch, McNeill, Clark; Johnstone, Gallagher, McBride, Lennox, Hughes

PARTICK THISTLE: Gray; Campbell, Muir; Cunningham, Harvey, Gibb; Conway, Hainey, Roxburgh, McParland, Gallagher

Attendance: 26,000

League positions

	P	W	D	L	F	A	Pts
1 Rangers	10	8	2	0	33	8	18
2 CELTIC	9	7	1	1	32	12	15
3 Dundee United	10	7	1	2	34	16	15
4 Dunfermline	10	6	3	1	27	14	15
5 Hibernian	10	6	2	2	37	14	14

November 9th: Murdoch and Hughes were in the Scotland team which beat Italy 1-0 in a World Cup Qualifier at Hampden Park.

November 13th
ST JOHNSTONE (0) 1 — CELTIC (1) 4
Duffy (68) — McBride (36), Hughes 2 (54, 83), Johnstone (66)

ST JOHNSTONE: McVittie; Richmond, Coburn; Collumbine, McKinven, Renton; Cowan, Kerray, Anderson, Duffy, Kemp

CELTIC: Simpson; Craig, Gemmell; Murdoch, McNeill, Clark; Johnstone, Gallagher, McBride, Lennox, Hughes

Attendance: 11,700

November 20th
CELTIC (2) 5 — HAMILTON ACADEMICALS (0) 0
Auld (12), Johnstone (22), Gemmell (66), Murdoch (74), McBride (83)

CELTIC: Simpson; Craig, Gemmell; Murdoch, McNeill, Clark; Johnstone, Gallagher, McBride, Lennox, Auld

HAMILTON: Lamont; Gaughan, Holton; Hinshelwood, Small, Anderson; McClare, McCann, Forsyth, Gilmour, Frye

Attendance: 12,000

November 24th: Bobby Murdoch was in the Scotland team which beat Wales 4-1 at Hampden Park. Murdoch scored 2 goals.

November 27th
CELTIC (0) 2 — KILMARNOCK (0) 1
Hughes (67 pen), McBride (83) — McIlroy (57)

CELTIC: Simpson; Craig, Gemmell; Murdoch, Cushley, Clark; Johnstone, McBride, Chalmers, Lennox, Hughes

KILMARNOCK: Ferguson; King, Watson; Murray, McGrory, McFadzean; McLean, McInally, Hamilton, O'Connor, McIlroy

Attendance: 24,000

December 7th: Murdoch and Hughes were in the Scotland team beaten 3-0 by Italy in a World Cup Qualifier in Naples. Jock Stein gave up the position of temporary team manager after this match.

December 11th
CELTIC (1) 2 — HIBERNIAN (0) 0
Hughes (34), McBride (75)

CELTIC: Simpson; Young, Gemmell; Murdoch, Cushley, Clark; Johnstone, Gallagher, McBride, Lennox, Hughes

HIBERNIAN: Wilson; Simpson, Davis; Stanton, McNamee, Baxter; O'Rourke, Cousin, Scott, Cormack, Stevenson

Attendance: 23,000

December 18th
DUNFERMLINE (0) 0 — CELTIC (0) 2
Chalmers 2 (62, 67)

DUNFERMLINE: Martin; Callaghan, Lunn; Smith, McLean, Thomson; Edwards, Paton, Fleming, Ferguson, Robertson

CELTIC: Simpson; Craig, Gemmell; Murdoch, Cushley, Clark; Johnstone, Gallagher, McBride, Chalmers, Hughes

Attendance: 15,000

December 25th
CELTIC (7) 8 — MORTON (0) 1
McBride 3 (7, 25, 33), Chalmers 2 (11, 43), Hughes 2 (28, 80), Murdoch (35) — Watson (49)

CELTIC: Simpson; Craig, Gemmell; Murdoch, Cushley, Clark; Johnstone, Gallagher, McBride, Chalmers, Hughes

MORTON: Sorensen; Boyd, Loughlan; Gray, Strachan, Kennedy; McIntyre, McGraw, Harper, Stevenson, Watson

Attendance: 21,000

League positions

	P	W	D	L	F	A	Pts
1 CELTIC	15	13	1	1	55	15	27
2 Rangers	16	12	3	1	50	14	27
3 Dunfermline	16	10	4	2	48	25	24
4 Dundee United	16	10	3	3	45	21	23
5 Hibernian	16	9	3	4	49	23	21

December 27th: Aahrus goalkeeper Bent Martin arrived at Parkhead for a month's trial.

January 1st
CLYDE (1) 1 — CELTIC (2) 3
Bryce (4) — McBride 2 (38, 39), Lennox (80)

CLYDE: Wright; Glasgow, Soutar; McHugh, Fraser, White; Gilroy, Bryce, Knox, Stewart, Hastings

CELTIC: Simpson; Craig, Gemmell; Murdoch, Cushley, Clark; Johnstone, Lennox, McBride, Chalmers, Auld

Attendance: n.a.

January 3rd
CELTIC (0) 5 — RANGERS (1) 1
Chalmers 3 (49, 62, 90), Gallagher (68), Murdoch (79) — Wilson (1½)

CELTIC: Simpson; Craig, Gemmell; Murdoch, Cushley, Clark; Johnstone, Gallagher, McBride, Chalmers, Hughes

RANGERS: Ritchie; Provan, Johansen; Hynd, McKinnon, Greig; Wilson, Setterington, Forrest, McLean, Johnston

Attendance: 65,000

This was a humbling defeat for a poor Rangers team. Celtic, a goal down after 90 seconds, scored 5 times in the 2nd half. The deluge began in 49 minutes when McBride dummied Gemmell's cross and Chalmers shot home from 6 yards. In 62 minutes Chalmers put Celtic into the lead, heading in Gallagher's corner-kick. 6 minutes later Hughes slipped past Provan on the touch-line and cut the ball back to the edge of the area where Gallagher drove the ball past Ritchie off the underside of the crossbar. After 79 minutes Murdoch hammered a McBride pass into the net from 30 yards. Ritchie could do nothing to prevent Johnstone from hitting a post and Chalmers scoring the 5th goal in the final minute.

January 8th
CELTIC (0) 1 — DUNDEE UNITED (0) 0
Gallagher (57)

CELTIC: Simpson; Craig, Gemmell; Murdoch, Cushley, Clark; Johnstone, Gallagher, McBride, Chalmers, Hughes

DUNDEE UNITED: Mackay; Millar, Briggs; Neilson, Smith, Wing; Persson, Munro, Dossing, Gillespie, Mitchell

Attendance: 36,000

January 15th
ABERDEEN (2) 3 — CELTIC (1) 1
Ravn (23), Winchester (34), Little (71) — McBride (6)

ABERDEEN: Clark; Shewan, McCormick; Petersen, McMillan, Smith; Little, Melrose, Winchester, Ravn, Wilson

CELTIC: Simpson; Craig, Gemmell; Murdoch, Cushley, Clark; Johnstone, Gallagher, McBride, Chalmers, Hughes

Attendance: 20,000

January 22nd
CELTIC (1) 1 — MOTHERWELL (0) 0
McBride (15)

CELTIC: Simpson; Craig, Gemmell; Murdoch, Cushley, Clark; Johnstone, Lennox, McBride, Chalmers, Hughes

MOTHERWELL: McCloy; Delaney, R. McCallum; W. McCallum, Martis, Murray; Hunter, Campbell, McLaughlin, Thomson, Weir

Attendance: 27,000

January 29th
HEARTS (1) 3 — CELTIC (0) 2
Wallace 2 (36, 61), Kerrigan (68) — Hughes (48), McBride (78)

HEARTS: Cruikshank; Polland, Shevlane; Higgins, Anderson, Miller; Hamilton, Cumming, Wallace, Kerrigan, Traynor

CELTIC: Simpson; McNeill, Gemmell; Murdoch, Cushley, Clark; Johnstone, Gallagher, McBride, Lennox, Hughes

Attendance: 28,000

February 4th: Celtic signed Bent Martin.

February 12th
CELTIC (1) 6 — FALKIRK (0) 0
Auld 2 (20, 71), McBride 3 (51, 77, 89), Hughes (75)

CELTIC: Simpson; Craig, Gemmell; Murdoch, McNeill, Clark; Johnstone, McBride, Chalmers, Auld, Hughes

FALKIRK: Whigham; Lambie, Hunter; Rowan, Markie, Fulton; Haddock, Moran, Wilson, Graham, McKinney

Attendance: 19,500

February 26th
STIRLING ALBION (1) 1 — CELTIC (0) 0
Grant (37)

STIRLING ALBION: Taylor; Dickson, McGuinness; Reid, Rogerson, Thomson; Bowie, Grant, Fleming, McKinnon, Hall

CELTIC: Simpson; Young, Gemmell; Murdoch, McNeill, Clark; Johnstone, McBride, Chalmers, Auld, Hughes

Attendance: 17,000

League positions

	P	W	D	L	F	A	Pts
1 Rangers	23	18	3	2	70	20	39
2 CELTIC	24	19	1	4	79	24	39
3 Kilmarnock	25	16	2	7	60	35	34
4 Dunfermline	22	14	5	3	65	29	33
5 Hearts	23	11	8	4	42	32	30

February 28th
CELTIC (4) 5 DUNDEE (0) 0
Chalmers (8),
McBride 3 (25, 43, 89 pen)
Gemmell (35)

CELTIC: Simpson; McNeill, Gemmell; Murdoch, Cushley, Clark; Johnstone, McBride, Chalmers, Auld, Hughes

DUNDEE: Arrol; Ryden, Swan; Murray, Easton, Stuart; Penman, Bertelsen, Cameron, McLean, Harvey

Attendance: 23,000

March 12
CELTIC (1) 3 ST JOHNSTONE (1) 2
McBride (32 pen), Renton (25), Duffy (89)
Chalmers 2 (50, 55)

CELTIC: Simpson; McNeill, Gemmell; Murdoch, Cushley, Clark; Johnstone, Auld, Chalmers, McBride, Hughes

ST JOHNSTONE: McVittie; Michie, Coburn; McCarry, McKinven, Renton; Cowan, Duffy, Whitelaw, MacDonald, McGrogan

Attendance: 26,000

March 19th
HAMILTON ACADEMICALS (1) 1 CELTIC (3) 7
Gilmour (29)
Johnstone 2 (18, 30),
McBride 2 (44, 60 pen),
Lennox (52),
Chalmers 2 (65, 82)

HAMILTON: Lamont; Forrest, Holton; Gaughan, Small, King; McClare, Currie, Anderson, Gilmour, McCann

CELTIC: Simpson; Craig, Gemmell; Brogan, McNeill, Clark; Johnstone, McBride, Chalmers, Lennox, Auld

Attendance: 17,000

March 21st
PARTICK THISTLE (1) 2 CELTIC (1) 2
Duncan (36), Lennox (35), Auld (85)
Kilpatrick (60)

PARTICK THISTLE: Niven; West, Muir; Cunningham, McKinnon, Gibb; McLindon, McParland, Kilpatrick, Roxburgh, Duncan

CELTIC: Simpson; Young, Gemmell; Brogan, McNeill, Clark; Johnstone, McBride, Chalmers, Lennox, Auld

Attendance: 26,000

March 29th
KILMARNOCK (0) 0 CELTIC (2) 2
Lennox 2 (10, 35)

KILMARNOCK: Ferguson; King, McFadzean; Murray, Beattie, O'Connor; McLean, McInally, Black, Queen, McIlroy

CELTIC: Simpson; Young, Gemmell; Murdoch, McNeill, Clark; Johnstone, McBride, Chalmers, Lennox, Auld

Attendance: 25,000

April 2nd: Gemmell, Murdoch and Johnstone were in the Scotland team beaten 4-3 by England at Hampden Park. Johnstone scored 2 goals.

April 5th
ST MIRREN (0) 0 CELTIC (1) 3
Chalmers (32),
McBride 2 (48, 69)

ST MIRREN: Thorburn; Murray, Riddell; Pinkerton, Keirnan, Clark; Aird, Hamilton, Adamson, Robertson, Gemmill

CELTIC: Simpson; Young, Gemmell; Murdoch, McNeill, Clark; Johnstone, McBride, Chalmers, Lennox, Auld

Attendance: 10,000

April 9th
CELTIC (0) 5 ST MIRREN (0) 0
Gallagher (54),
Auld 2 (51, 81),
Chalmers 2 (74, 87)

CELTIC: Simpson; Young, Gemmell; Cattenach, McNeill, Clark; Johnstone, McBride, Chalmers, Gallagher, Auld

ST MIRREN: Thorburn; Murray, Riddell; Clark, Clunie, Keirnan; Adamson, McLaughlin, Hamilton, Pinkerton, Robertson

Attendance: 25,000

April 16th
HIBERNIAN (0) 0 CELTIC (0) 0

HIBERNIAN: Allan; Duncan, Davis; Stanton, McNamee, Cousin; Cormack, Stein, Scott, Quinn, Stevenson

CELTIC: Simpson; Young, Gemmell; Murdoch, McNeill, Clark; Johnstone, Lennox, McBride, Auld, Hughes

Attendance: 24,000

April 18th: Bertie Auld was suspended for 7 days which meant that he would miss the Scottish Cup Final unless it went to a replay.

April 30th
MORTON (0) 0 CELTIC (1) 2
Johnstone (45),
Lennox (90)

MORTON: Sorensen; Boyd, Loughlan; Gray, Madsen, Kennedy; Arentoft, Strachan, McGraw, Neilson, Watson

CELTIC: Simpson; Craig, Gemmell; Murdoch, McNeill, Clark; Johnstone, Gallagher, Chalmers, Lennox, Auld

Attendance: 18,000. Neilson missed a penalty – Morton were officially relegated after this match.

April 30th: Celtic freed Johnny Divers, Henry Quinn and Gerry Sweeney.

May 4th
CELTIC (1) 2 — DUNFERMLINE (1) 1
Lennox (34), Johnstone (59) — Ferguson (29)

CELTIC: Simpson; Craig, Gemmell; Murdoch, McNeill, Clark; Johnstone, Gallagher, Chalmers, Lennox, Auld

DUNFERMLINE: Martin; W. Callaghan, Lunn; Thomson, McLean, T. Callaghan; Edwards, Smith, Fleming, Ferguson, Robertson

Attendance: 30,000

May 7th
MOTHERWELL (0) 0 — CELTIC (0) 1
Lennox (89)

MOTHERWELL: McCloy; Thomson, R. McCallum; W. McCallum, Martis, Murray; Lindsay, Hunter, Delaney, Cairney, Campbell

CELTIC: Simpson; Craig, Gemmell; Murdoch, McNeill, Clark; Johnstone, Gallagher, Chalmers, Lennox, Auld

Attendance: 20,000. Celtic clinched the League Championship with this victory.

In the last minute of the last game on the last day of the season Lennox scored the goal which made Celtic Scottish League Champions on points instead of by the much less satisfying margin of goal average. So Celtic became Champs for the first time in 12 years and for the 21st time in the club's history.

Scottish First Division

	P	W	D	L	F	A	Pts
1 CELTIC	34	27	3	4	106	30	57
2 Rangers	34	25	5	4	91	29	55
3 Kilmarnock	34	20	5	9	73	46	45
4 Dunfermline	34	19	6	9	94	55	44
5 Dundee United	34	19	5	10	79	51	43
6 Hibernian	34	16	6	12	81	55	38
7 Hearts	34	13	12	9	56	48	38
8 Aberdeen	34	15	6	13	61	54	36
9 Dundee	34	14	6	14	61	61	34
10 Falkirk	34	15	1	18	48	72	31
11 Clyde	34	13	4	17	62	64	30
12 Partick Thistle	34	10	10	14	55	64	30
13 Motherwell	34	12	4	18	52	69	28
14 St Johnstone	34	9	8	17	58	81	26
15 Stirling Albion	34	9	8	17	40	68	26
16 St Mirren	34	9	4	21	44	82	22
17 Morton	34	8	5	21	42	84	21
18 Hamilton	34	3	2	29	27	117	8

May 11th: Jock Stein was named as Scotland's Manager of the Year.

May 17th: Jock Stein was named as Britain's Manager of the Year.

June 18th: Steve Chalmers came on as substitute for Alex Young in the Scotland v. Portugal Friendly at Hampden Park. Portugal won 1-0.

June 25th: Clark and Chalmers were in the Scotland team which drew 1-1 with Brazil at Hampden Park. Chalmers scored Scotland's goal in the 1st minute.

LEAGUE CUP

August 14th
DUNDEE UNITED (1) 2 — CELTIC (0) 1
Carroll (30), Gillespie (67) — Auld (66)

DUNDEE UNITED: Mackay; Millar, Briggs; Munro, Smith, Wing; Carroll, Gillespie, Dossing, Mitchell, Persson

CELTIC: Fallon; Young, Gemmell; Murdoch, McNeill, Clark; Johnstone, Gallagher, Chalmers, Lennox, Auld

Attendance: 25,000

August 18th
CELTIC (0) 1 — MOTHERWELL (0) 0
Divers (68)

CELTIC: Fallon; Young, Gemmell; Murdoch, McNeill, Clark; Johnstone, Divers, Chalmers, Lennox, Auld

MOTHERWELL: McCloy; M. Thomson, McCallum; Aitken, Martis, Murray; Lindsay, Hunter, Delaney, I. Thomson, Weir

Attendance: 32,000

August 21st
CELTIC (0) 0 — DUNDEE (0) 2
Cameron 2 (64, 73)

CELTIC: Fallon; Young, Gemmell; Murdoch, McNeill, Clark; Johnstone, Divers, McBride, Lennox, Auld

DUNDEE: Donaldson; Hamilton, Stuart; Cousin, Easton, Houston; Murray, Penman, Bertelsen, Cooke, Cameron

Attendance: 34,000

August 28th
CELTIC (2) 3 — DUNDEE UNITED (0) 0
Young (23 pen), Chalmers (28), McBride (86)

CELTIC: Fallon; Young, Gemmell; Murdoch, McNeill, Clark; Chalmers, Divers, McBride, Lennox, Hughes

DUNDEE UNITED: Mackay; Millar, Briggs; Munro, Smith, Neilson; Soutar, Gillespie, Rooney, Mitchell, Persson

Attendance: 36,000

September 1st
MOTHERWELL (1) 2 CELTIC (2) 3
Delaney (31), Murray (87) Lennox 2 (4, 52), Hughes (43 pen)

MOTHERWELL: McCloy; M. Thomson, McCallum; Aitken, Martis, Murray; I. Thomson, Howieson, Delaney, McLaughlin, Hunter

CELTIC: Fallon; Young, Gemmell; Murdoch, McNeill, Clark; Chalmers, Divers, Hughes, Lennox, Gallagher

Attendance: 22,000

September 4th
DUNDEE (1) 1 CELTIC (2) 3
Penman (42) Divers (11), Hughes (31), McBride (85)

DUNDEE: Donaldson; Hamilton, Stuart; Cousin, Easton, Houston; Murray, Penman, Cameron, Cooke, Bertelsen

CELTIC: Fallon; Young, Gemmell; Murdoch, McNeill, Clark; Chalmers, Divers, McBride, Lennox, Hughes

Attendance: 27,000

Section table

	P	W	D	L	F	A	Pts
CELTIC	6	4	0	2	11	7	8
Motherwell	6	3	0	3	9	11	6
Dundee	6	2	1	3	7	7	5
Dundee United	6	2	1	3	9	11	5

Qualifier: CELTIC

Quarter-Final First Leg September 15th
RAITH ROVERS (1) 1 CELTIC (3) 8
Richardson (21) McBride 3 (18, 67, 88), Lennox (19), Johnstone (44), Hughes 3 (58 pen, 78, 81)

RAITH ROVERS: Reid; McKeown, Gray; Stein, Evans, Porterfield; Hutchison, Gardner, Richardson, Lyall, McLean

CELTIC: Fallon; Young, Gemmell; Murdoch, McNeill, Clark; Johnstone, Gallagher, McBride, Lennox, Hughes

Attendance: 15,000

Quarter-Final Second Leg September 22nd
CELTIC (0) 4 RAITH ROVERS (0) 0
Murdoch (47), Auld 2 (48, 51), Chalmers (83)

CELTIC: Kennedy; Young, Gemmell; Murdocn, Cushley, Clark; Johnstone, Lennox, Chalmers, Auld, Hughes

RAITH ROVERS: Reid; Selfridge, Gray; Stein, Evans, Porterfield; Christie, Gardner, Richardson, Lyall, McLean

Attendance: 9,000. Celtic won 12-1 on aggregate.

Semi-Final at Ibrox Park October 4th
CELTIC (1) 2 HIBERNIAN (1) 2
McBride (8), Lennox (90) Martin 2 (16, 58)
After Extra Time

CELTIC: Simpson; Young, Gemmell; Murdoch, McNeill, Clark; Johnstone, Gallagher, McBride, Lennox, Hughes

HIBERNIAN: Wilson; Simpson, Davis; Stanton, McNamee, Baxter; Cormack, Quinn, Scott, Martin, Stevenson

Attendance: 50,000

Excitement was intense from start to finish of a great game in which the outcome was uncertain until the last kick of the ball. On a sodden pitch which severely tested stamina, both sets of players gave their all. As the 90 minutes neared the end it seemed likely that Hibs would scrape through to the Final. Then in the very last minute Wilson failed to hold Gemmell's shot from close range, and in the ensuing scramble Lennox prodded the ball into the net. Either side might have snatched a winning goal in extra time.

Semi-Final Replay at Ibrox Park October 18th
CELTIC (2) 4 HIBERNIAN (0) 0
McBride (17), Hughes (21), Lennox (69), Murdoch (83)

CELTIC: Simpson; Young, Gemmell; Murdoch, McNeill, Clark; Johnstone, Gallagher, McBride, Lennox, Hughes

HIBERNIAN: Wilson; Simpson, Davis; Stanton, McNamee, Baxter; Cormack, Quinn, Scott, Martin, Stevenson

Attendance: 51,423

Celtic made simple work of qualifying for the League Cup Final against Rangers. Hibs offered feeble resistance after Celtic had scored 2 goals inside 21 minutes. McNamee was ordered off 10 minutes from the end for dissent. Murdoch completed the scoring 3 minutes later.

Final at Hampden Park October 23rd
CELTIC (2) 2 RANGERS (0) 1
Hughes 2 (18 pen, 28 pen) Young o.g. (84)

CELTIC: Simpson; Young, Gemmell; Murdoch, McNeill, Clark; Johnstone, Gallagher, McBride, Lennox, Hughes

RANGERS: Ritchie; Johansen, Provan; Wood, McKinnon, Greig; Henderson, Willoughby, Forrest, Wilson, Johnston

Attendance: 107,600 *Referee:* H. Phillips (Wishaw)

Two penalty-kicks were scored in the 18th and 28th minutes by John Hughes and five players were booked in an untidy League Cup Final. Rangers scored a consolation goal late on with the assistance of an own goal by full-back Young.

SCOTTISH CUP

First Round February 5th
CELTIC (2) 4 STRANRAER (0) 0
Gallagher (8),
Murdoch (42),
McBride (62),
Lennox (82)

CELTIC: Simpson; Craig, Gemmell; Murdoch, McNeill, Clark; Johnstone, Gallagher, McBride, Lennox, Hughes

STRANRAER: Dine; Shanks, McNaught; W. King, Ferguson, S. King; McMurdo, Hanlon, McDonald, Logan, Bingham

Attendance: 15,500

Second Round February 23rd
DUNDEE (0) 0 CELTIC (2) 2
McBride (5),
Chalmers (44)

DUNDEE: Arrol; Hamilton, Ryden; Cooke, Easton, Stuart; Penman, Murray, Bertelsen, McLean, Cameron

CELTIC: Simpson; Craig, Gemmell; Murdoch, McNeill, Clark; Johnstone, McBride, Chalmers, Auld, Hughes

Attendance: 22,000

Third Round March 5th
HEARTS (2) 3 CELTIC (1) 3
Wallace (23), Auld (24, McBride (48),
Anderson (25), Chalmers (54)
Hamilton (84)

HEARTS: Cruikshank; Polland, Shevlane; Higgins, Anderson, Miller; Hamilton, Barry, Wallace, Kerrigan, Traynor

CELTIC: Simpson; McNeill, Gemmell; Murdoch, Cushley, Clark; Johnstone, McBride, Chalmers, Auld, Hughes

Attendance: 45,965

Third Round Replay March 9th
CELTIC (2) 3 HEARTS (0) 1
Johnstone (9), Wallace (83)
Murdoch (32),
Chalmers (50)

CELTIC: Simpson; Craig, Gemmell; Murdoch, McNeill, Clark; Johnstone, McBride, Chalmers, Gallagher, Hughes

HEARTS: Cruikshank; Polland, Shevlane; Higgins, Anderson, Miller; Hamilton, Barry, Wallace, Traynor, Ford

Attendance: 72,000. This was a record attendance for a mid-week game at Parkhead.

Semi-Final at Ibrox Park March 26th
CELTIC (1) 2 DUNFERMLINE (0) 0
Auld (37), Chalmers (66)

CELTIC: Simpson; Young, Gemmell; Murdoch, McNeill, Clark; Johnstone, McBride, Chalmers, Lennox, Auld

DUNFERMLINE: Martin; W. Callaghan, Lunn; Smith, McLean, Thomson; Fleming, Ferguson, Hunter, T. Callaghan, Robertson

Attendance: 53,900

The authority of Celtic's play was so far in advance of Dunfermline's that interest was kept alive largely by the lack of a correspondingly high rate of scoring.

Final at Hampden Park April 23rd
RANGERS (0) 0 CELTIC (0) 0

RANGERS: Ritchie; Johansen, Provan; Greig, McKinnon, Millar; Henderson, Watson, Forrest, Johnston, Wilson

CELTIC: Simpson; Young, Gemmell; Murdoch, McNeill, Clark; Johnstone, McBride, Chalmers, Gallagher, Hughes

Attendance: 126,599 *Referee:* T. Wharton (Clarkston)

Both forward lines had insufficient imagination to break down defences too sophisticated and practised in their art to be deceived by their naïve advances.

Final Replay at Hampden Park April 27th
RANGERS (0) 1 CELTIC (0) 0
Johansen (70)

RANGERS: Ritchie; Johansen, Provan; Greig, McKinnon, Millar; Henderson, Watson, McLean, Johnston, Wilson

CELTIC: Simpson; Craig, Gemmell; Murdoch, McNeill, Clark; Johnstone, McBride, Chalmers, Auld, Hughes

Attendance: 96,862 *Referee:* T. Wharton (Clarkston)

Rangers won the Scottish Cup for the 19th time in their history. Their triumph, against all the predicted odds, was built on a magnificent defence. The outstanding figure was Millar, always there when needed. This was Celtic's 4th successive game in which they failed to score. Johnstone made life a misery for Provan but Hughes was once more subdued. Auld, returning after suspension, laid on chances of which Chalmers missed 2 and Hughes the other.

CUP WINNERS CUP

First Round First Leg September 29th
GO AHEAD DEVENTER (Holland) (0) 0 — CELTIC (2) 6
Lennox 3 (26, 56, 70), Hughes (29), Johnstone 2 (48, 78)

GO AHEAD: Van Zoghel; Butter, Thiemann; Konselaar, Warnas, Somer; Grebing, Niehaus, Bockenstein, Veenstra, Adelaar

CELTIC: Simpson; Young, Gemmell; Murdoch, McNeill, Clark; Johnstone, Gallagher, Chalmers, Lennox, Hughes

Attendance: 25,000

Celtic completely outplayed Go Ahead and long before the finish they had the crowd of 25,000 laughing at their impudence on a football field.

First Round Second Leg October 7th
CELTIC (1) 1 — GO AHEAD (0) 0
McBride (12)

CELTIC: Simpson; Craig, Gemmell; Murdoch, McNeill, Clark; Johnstone, Chalmers, McBride, Lennox, Hughes

GO AHEAD: Van Zoghel; Butter, Thiemann; Konselaar, Warnas, Somer; Wustefeldt, Niehaus, Grebing, Veenstra, Adelaar

Attendance: 20,000

Go Ahead came out to save face and for almost all of the 90 minutes they had 11 players in their own half of the field intent on denying Celtic another big total. The match was memorable only for the sporting spirit displayed by the Dutch players. Celtic won 7-0 on aggregate.

Second Round First Leg November 3rd
A.G.F. AAHRUS (Denmark) (0) 0 — CELTIC (1) 1
McBride (22)

AAHRUS; Martin; A. Sorensen, Neilsen; Amidsen, Wolmar, Petersen; Jensen, Bjerregaard, Enoksen, O. Sorensen, Hermansen

CELTIC: Simpson; Young, Gemmell; Murdoch, McNeill, Clark; Johnstone, Gallagher, McBride, Lennox, Hughes

Attendance: 11,500

In a match of indifferent football Celtic were infinitely better than their Danish amateur opponents despite the fact that they scored only 1 goal.

Second Round Second Leg November 17th
CELTIC (2) 2 — A.G.F. AAHRUS (0) 0
McNeill (8), Johnstone (41)

CELTIC: Simpson; Craig, Gemmell; Murdoch, McNeill, Clark; Johnstone, Gallagher, McBride, Lennox, Hughes

AAHRUS: Martin; Laursen, A. Sorensen; Amidsen, Wolmar, Petersen; Bjerregaard, Jensen, Enoksen, O. Sorensen, Hermansen

Attendance: 27,000

The crowd who turned out on this miserable night deserved better than the display they were given. When McNeill scored from a Johnstone corner in 8 minutes the scene seemed set for a runaway home victory, but Celtic's play sagged thereafter. Celtic won 3-0 on aggregate.

Third Round First Leg January 12th
CELTIC (1) 3 — DYNAMO KIEV (0) 0
Gemmell (27), Murdoch 2 (64, 84)

CELTIC: Simpson; Craig, Gemmell; Murdoch, Cushley, Clark; Johnstone, Gallagher, McBride, Chalmers, Hughes

DYNAMO KIEV: Bannikov; Schegolkov, Sosnikhin; Ostrovsky, Medvid, Turyanchik; Bazilevich, Serebryannikov, Puzach, Biba, Khmelnitsky

Attendance: 64,000. Hughes missed a penalty.

2 goals scored by Murdoch within the last half-hour, added to Gemmell's of the 1st half, gave Celtic a satisfactory first-leg lead.

Third Round Second Leg January 26th
DYNAMO KIEV (1) 1 — CELTIC (1) 1
Sabo (22) — Gemmell (31)

DYNAMO KIEV: Bannikov; Schegolkov, Levchenko, Turyanchik, Sosnikhin; Bazilevich, Medvid, Sabo, Biba, Serebryannikov, Khmelnitsky

CELTIC: Simpson; Craig, Gemmell; McNeill, Cushley, Clark; Johnstone, Murdoch, McBride, Chalmers, Hughes

Attendance: 45,000

The second leg was a rough, bad-tempered match and Craig and Kiev left-winger Khmelnitsky were ordered off. Celtic started well but seemed momentarily stunned when the Russians went ahead in 22 minutes. Celtic had to wait only 9 minutes for the equaliser. Hughes burst through from his own half, rounded 2 Kiev defenders and pulled the ball back for Gemmell to shoot home from 20 yards. Celtic won 4-1 on aggregate.

Semi-Final First Leg April 14th
CELTIC (0) 1 — LIVERPOOL (0) 0
Lennox (51)

CELTIC: Simpson; Young, Gemmell; Murdoch, McNeill, Clark; Johnstone, McBride, Chalmers, Lennox, Auld

LIVERPOOL: Lawrence; Lawler, Byrne; Milne, Yeats, Stevenson; Callaghan, Chisnall, St John, Smith, Thompson

Attendance; 80,000

Liverpool were splendidly organised in defence but not impenetrable, and had Celtic taken advantage of 4 excellent chances in the 1st half the story would have been different. Only after Lennox's goal did Celtic, free from tension, move with more rhythm and evident confidence.

Semi-Final Second Leg April 19th
LIVERPOOL (0) 2 CELTIC (0) 0
Smith (60), Strong (65)

LIVERPOOL: Lawrence; Lawler, Byrne; Milne, Yeats, Stevenson; Callaghan, Strong, St John, Smith, Thompson

CELTIC: Simpson; Young, Gemmell; Murdoch, McNeill, Clark; Lennox, McBride, Chalmers, Auld, Hughes

Attendance: 54,000

After having fought a magnificent tactical battle for an hour to defend their slender lead Celtic were sent to defeat as Liverpool scored twice in 5 minutes. The game ended in controversy when Celtic had the ball in the net in the last minutes only to have the goal disallowed. Liverpool won 2-1 on aggregate.

APPEARANCES	League	League Cup	Scottish Cup	Cup Winners Cup
Fallon	4	7	–	–
Young	16	11	2	4
Gemmell	34	11	7	8
Murdoch	31	11	7	8
McNeill	25	10	7	7

APPEARANCES	League	League Cup	Scottish Cup	Cup Winners Cup
Clark	34	11	7	8
Chalmers	22	6	6	6
Divers	3	5	–	–
McBride	30	7	7	7
Lennox	24	11	2	6
Gallagher	19	6	3	4
Hughes	23	8	6	7
Johnstone	32	8	7	7
Auld	17	4	4	2
Simpson	30	3	7	8
Craig	15	–	4	4
Cushley	12	1	1	2
Brogan	2	–	–	–
Cattenach	1	–	–	–
John Kennedy	–	1	–	–

GOALSCORERS

League: McBride 31 (1 pen), Chalmers 15, Lennox 15, Hughes 13 (2 pens), Johnstone 9, Auld 7, Murdoch 5, Gallagher 4, Gemmell 4, Young 2 (2 pens), Divers 1

League Cup: Hughes 8 (3 pens), McBride 7, Lennox 5, Auld 3, Divers 2, Chalmers 2, Murdoch 2, Johnstone 1, Young 1 (pen)

Scottish Cup: Chalmers 4, McBride 3, Murdoch 2, Auld 2, Gallagher 1, Lennox 1, Johnstone 1

Cup Winners Cup: Lennox 4, Johnstone 3, Gemmell 2, Murdoch 2, McBride 2, McNeill 1, Hughes 1

On May 6th, 1967, Celtic have just drawn 2-2 with Rangers at Ibrox to gain the League Championship for the 22nd time.

Season 1966-67

In the most successful season in the clubs' history Celtic swept all before them and won every competition they entered, including the European Cup and their first domestic Treble.

Despite the close attentions of Rangers they won their 22nd League Championship by 3 points from the Ibrox club. They completed the double over 11 of the 17 teams, losing only 2 matches – both against Dundee United. Their defeat at Tannadice on 31st December was their first in the League since losing to Stirling Albion the previous February. They overcame the loss, through injury, of Joe McBride who had scored 18 goals in 14 matches. The signing of Willie Wallace from Hearts was an inspired one, and he went on to score 14 goals in his 21 matches, also scoring the goals which took Celtic into the European Cup Final and which won the Scottish Cup Final. Steve Chalmers finished as top scorer with 23 of their total of 111. Gemmell and Clark played in every game, and both Simpson and McNeill missed only one. 11 players received International recognition during the season and Jock Stein was voted as Britain's Manager of the Year for the 2nd successive season.

Celtic scored an incredible 34 goals to reach the Final of the League Cup in which they faced Rangers and although they were outplayed by their great rivals, a brilliant piece of opportunism by Lennox gave them the trophy for the 4th time.

They had a fairly easy passage to the Final of the Scottish Cup, and 2 goals from Wallace – one on either side of half-time – gave them the trophy for the 19th time against an Aberdeen team who played with unrealistic caution throughout.

In their first season in Europe's top tournament Celtic went all the way and became the first British side to win the trophy. In the Final in Lisbon against former winners Internazionale Milan they recovered from losing a goal in only the 7th minute to beat the ultra-defensive Italian side whose style of play had threatened the very future of the game as a mass spectator sport, and the whole football world immediately acknowledged the debt which they owed to Celtic.

League:	Champions
League Cup:	Winners
Scottish Cup:	Winners
European Cup:	Winners

SCOTTISH FIRST DIVISION

September 10th
CLYDE (0) 0 — CELTIC (2) 3
Chalmers (10),
McBride (18),
Hughes (75)

CLYDE: Wright; Glasgow, Mulheron; McHugh, Fraser, Staite; McFarlane, Anderson, Gilroy, Soutar, Hastings

CELTIC: Simpson; Gemmell, O'Neill; Murdoch, McNeill, Clark; Chalmers, Lennox, McBride, Auld, Hughes
Attendance: 16,500

September 17th
CELTIC (2) 2 — RANGERS (0) 0
Auld (1),
Murdoch (4)

CELTIC: Simpson; Gemmell, O'Neill; Murdoch, McNeill, Clark; Johnstone, Lennox, McBride, Auld, Hughes

RANGERS: Ritchie; Provan, Greig; Millar, McKinnon, D. Smith; Wilson, A. Smith, Forrest, McLean, Johnston
Attendance: 65,000

Rangers' defence was run through twice before they even took guard. Celtic moved with a smooth efficiency in both attack and defence which Rangers never achieved.

September 24th:
DUNDEE (1) 1 — CELTIC (1) 2
Penman (28) — Lennox (32), Chalmers (78)

DUNDEE: Donaldson; Wilson, Cox; Houston, Easton, Stuart; McKay, Penman, Cameron, Murray, Campbell

CELTIC: Simpson; Gemmell, O'Neill; Murdoch, McNeill, Clark; Johnstone, Lennox, McBride, Auld, Hughes
Attendance: 28,500

October 1st
CELTIC (2) 6 — ST JOHNSTONE (0) 1
Johnstone 2 (11, 52), Lennox 2 (38, 60), McBride 2 (65, 75) — Kilgannon (54)

CELTIC: Simpson; Gemmell, O'Neill; Murdoch, McNeill, Clark; Johnstone, Lennox, McBride, Auld, Hughes

ST JOHNSTONE: Donaldson; McCarry, Coburn; Townsend, Ryden, McPhee; O'Donnell, Whitelaw, Kilgannon, Duffy, Kemp
Attendance: 24,000

October 8th
HIBERNIAN (2) 3 — CELTIC (4) 5
Cormack (10), Davis (37 pen), McGraw (89) — McBride 4 (15, 41, 43, 74), Chalmers (30)

HIBERNIAN: Allan; Duncan, Davis; Stanton, Cousin, O'Rourke; Cormack, Stein, Scott, McGraw, Stevenson

CELTIC: Simpson; Gemmell, O'Neill; Murdoch, McNeill, Clark; Johnstone, McBride, Chalmers, Auld, Hughes
Attendance: 43,256

October 15th
CELTIC (0) 3 — AIRDRIE (0) 0
McBride (65), Lennox 2 (68, 87)

CELTIC: Simpson; Young, Gemmell; Clark, McNeill, O'Neill; Chalmers, Lennox, McBride, Gallagher, Hughes

AIRDRIE: McKenzie; Jonquin, Keenan; Goodwin, Black, Ramsey; Ferguson, McPheat, Marshall, Murray, Phillips
Attendance: 41,000

October 22nd: Gemmell, Clark, Johnstone and McBride were in the Scotland team which drew 1-1 with Wales in Cardiff.

October 24th
CELTIC (2) 5 — AYR UNITED (1) 1
Lennox (2), Hughes (45), Johnstone 2 (57, 88), Gemmell (69) — Black (40)

CELTIC: Simpson; Gemmell, O'Neill; Murdoch, McNeill, Clark; Johnstone, Lennox, Chalmers, Auld, Hughes

AYR UNITED: Millar; Malone, Murphy; Quinn, Monan, Mitchell; McMillan, McAnespie, Black, Hawkshaw, Brand
Attendance: 21,000

League positions

	P	W	D	L	F	A	Pts
1 CELTIC	7	7	0	0	26	6	14
2 Kilmarnock	7	5	1	1	12	7	11
3 Aberdeen	8	4	2	2	12	11	10
4 Rangers	6	4	1	1	18	6	9
5 Dunfermline	8	3	3	2	21	15	9

November 2nd
CELTIC (6) 7 — STIRLING ALBION (1) 3
McBride 3 (12, 41, 48), Chalmers 2 (19, 42), Johnstone (6), Auld (25) — McGuinness (43), Reid (65), Kerray (87)

CELTIC: Simpson; Gemmell, O'Neill; Murdoch, McNeill, Clark; Johnstone, Gallagher (Craig), McBride, Chalmers, Auld

STIRLING ALBION: Murray; Cunningham, Caldow; Reid, Rogerson, Thomson; Kerray, McKinnon, McGuinness, Peebles, Symington
Attendance: 21,000

November 5th
CELTIC (0) 1 — ST MIRREN (0) 1
Gemmell (47) — Treacy (54)

CELTIC: Simpson; Craig, O'Neill; Murdoch, Gemmell, Clark; Johnstone, McBride, Chalmers, Auld, Lennox

ST MIRREN: Connaghan; Murray, Gemmill; Clark, Kiernan, Pinkerton; Hutton, Hamilton, Taylor, McLaughlin, Treacy
Attendance: 24,000. Murdoch was ordered off

November 12th
FALKIRK (0) 0 — CELTIC (2) 3
McBride 2 (2, 43 pen), Auld (62)

FALKIRK: McDonald; Markie, Hunter; Smith, Baillie, Fulton; Vincent, Lambie, Moran, Baxter, McKinney

CELTIC: Simpson; Gemmell, O'Neill; Murdoch, McNeill, Clark; Chalmers, Gallagher, McBride, Lennox, Auld
Attendance: 12,000

November 16th: Gemmell, Clark, Murdoch, McBride, Chalmers and Lennox were all in the Scotland team which beat Northern Ireland 2-1 at Hampden Park. Murdoch and Lennox scored Scotland's goals.

November 19th
DUNFERMLINE (3) 4 — CELTIC (2) 5
Robertson (31), Delaney (33), Paton (38), Ferguson (48) — Murdoch (34), Johnstone (43), Auld (62), McBride 2 (69, 89 pen)

DUNFERMLINE: Martin; Callaghan, Totten; Thomson, McLean, Barry; Fleming, Paton, Delaney, Ferguson, Robertson

CELTIC: Simpson; Gemmell, O'Neill; Murdoch, McNeill, Clark; Johnstone, McBride, Chalmers, Auld, Lennox

Attendance: 22,000

November 26th
CELTIC (1) 3 — HEARTS (0) 0
Miller o.g. (12), McBride 2 (76, 89 pen)

CELTIC: Simpson; Gemmell, O'Neill; Murdoch, McNeill, Clark; Johnstone, Chalmers, McBride, Lennox, Auld

HEARTS: Cruikshank; Ferguson, Holt; McDonald, Anderson, Miller; Wallace, Kerrigan, Murphy, Gordon, Traynor

Attendance: 40,000

December 3rd
KILMARNOCK (0) 0 — CELTIC (0) 0

KILMARNOCK: Ferguson; King, McFadzean; O'Connor, McGrory, Beattie; McLean, McInally, Murray, Watson, McIlroy

CELTIC: Simpson; Gemmell, O'Neill; Murdoch, McNeill, Clark; Johnstone, Chalmers, McBride, Lennox, Auld

Attendance: 27,000

December 5th: It was reported that Celtic were ready to make a £60,000 bid for Ian Gibson of Coventry City.

December 6th: Celtic signed Willie Wallace from Hearts for £30,000.

December 10th
CELTIC (2) 4 — MOTHERWWELL (0) 2
Chalmers 3 (30, 41, 83), Murdoch (87) — Murray (78), Lindsay (84)

CELTIC: Simpson; Gemmell, O'Neill; Murdoch, McNeill, Clark; Johnstone, Wallace, Chalmers, Lennox, Auld

MOTHERWELL: McCloy; Whiteford, R. McCallum; W. McCallum, Martis, Campbell; Lindsay, Cairney, Deans, Murray, Hunter

Attendance: 40,000. Deans was sent off

December 17th
CELTIC (4) 6 — PARTICK THISTLE (1) 2
Wallace 2 (2, 24), Chalmers 2 (14, 74), Murdoch (32), McBride (56) — Duncan (36), Gibb (64)

CELTIC: Simpson; Gemmell, O'Neill; Murdoch, McNeill, Clark; Chalmers, Wallace, McBride, Lennox, Auld

PARTICK THISTLE: McFedries; Tinney, Muir; Gibb, McKinnon, Cunningham; McLindon, McParland, Divers, Flanagan, Duncan (Rae)

Attendance: 25,000

League positions

	P	W	D	L	F	A	Pts
1 CELTIC	15	13	2	0	55	19	28
2 Rangers	15	11	2	2	48	13	24
3 Aberdeen	15	10	2	3	34	20	22
4 Clyde	15	9	2	4	31	23	20
5 Dundee	15	8	3	4	30	19	19

December 24th
ABERDEEN (1) 1 — CELTIC (1) 1
Melrose (30) — Lennox (25)

ABERDEEN: Clark; Whyte, Shewan; Munro, McMillan, Petersen; Wilson, Melrose, Johnston, Smith, Taylor

CELTIC: Simpson; Gemmell, O'Neill; Murdoch, McNeill, Clark; Chalmers, Auld, McBride, Wallace, Lennox

Attendance: 31,000

December 31st
DUNDEE UNITED (1) 3 — CELTIC (2) 2
Dossing (22), Gillespie (72), Mitchell (75) — Lennox (12), Wallace (23)

DUNDEE UNITED: Davie; Miller, Briggs; Neilson, Smith, Wing; Dossing, Hainey, Mitchell, Gillespie, Persson

CELTIC: Simpson; Gemmell, O'Neill; Murdoch, McNeill, Clark; Chalmers, Lennox, Wallace, Auld, Hughes

Attendance: 25,000

January 7th
CELTIC (4) 5 — DUNDEE (0) 1
Wilson o.g. (4), Wallace 2 (5, 89), Johnstone (21), Gallagher (28) — Cameron (51)

CELTIC: Simpson; Craig, Gemmell; Murdoch, McNeill, Clark; Johnstone, Wallace, Chalmers, Gallagher, Lennox

DUNDEE: Arrol; Wilson, Cox; Murray, Easton, Houston; Bryce, Scott, Cameron, McLean, Kinninmonth

Attendance: 37,000

January 11th
CELTIC (1) 5 — CLYDE (1) 1
Chalmers 2 (12, 72), Gallagher (54), Gemmell (74), Lennox (75) — Gilroy (32)

CELTIC: Simpson; Craig, Gemmell; Murdoch, McNeill, Clark; Johnstone, Wallace, Chalmers, Gallagher, Lennox

CLYDE: McCulloch; Glasgow, Mulheron; Anderson, Staite, McHugh; McFarlane, Hood, Gilroy, Stewart, Hastings

Attendance: 38,000

January 14th
ST JOHNSTONE (0) 0 — CELTIC (0) 4
Johnstone 2 (63, 69), Chalmers (86), Lennox (90)

ST JOHNSTONE: Donaldson; McCarry (Clark), Smith; Townsend, Rooney, McPhee; Coburn, Whitelaw, Kilgannon, MacDonald, Johnston

CELTIC: Simpson; Craig, Gemmell; Murdoch, McNeill, Clark; Johnstone, Wallace, Chalmers, Auld, Lennox

Attendance: 19,000

January 21st
CELTIC (2) 2 — HIBERNIAN (0) 0
Wallace (12), Chalmers (38)

CELTIC: Simpson; Craig, Gemmell; Murdoch, McNeill, Clark; Johnstone, Wallace, Chalmers, Auld, Hughes

HIBERNIAN: Allan; Duncan, Davis; Stanton, Madsen, Cousin; Scott, Quinn, Cormack, O'Rourke, Stevenson

Attendance: 41,000

February 4th
AIRDRIE (0) 0 — CELTIC (1) 3
Johnstone (12), Chalmers (47), Auld (69)

AIRDRIE: McKenzie; Jonquin, Keenan; Goodwin, Black, Ramsey; Ferguson, McPheat, Fyfe, Murray, Marshall

CELTIC: Simpson; Craig, Gemmell; Murdoch, McNeill, Clark; Johnstone, Wallace, Chalmers, Auld, Hughes

Attendance: 23,000

February 11th
AYR UNITED (0) 0 — CELTIC (1) 5
Johnstone (41), Chalmers 3 (57, 62, 82), Hughes (59)

AYR UNITED: Millar; Malone, Murphy; Quinn, Monan, Thomson; Rutherford, McMillan, Ingram, Black, Oliphant

CELTIC: Simpson; Craig, Gemmell; Murdoch, McNeill, Clark; Johnstone, Wallace, Chalmers, Gallagher, Hughes

Attendance: 19,000

February 25th
STIRLING ALBION (1) 1 — CELTIC (0) 1
Peebles (23) — Hughes (52)

STIRLING ALBION: Murray; Dickson, McGuinness; McKinnon, Rogerson, Thomson; Peebles, Smith, Kerray, Laing, Symington

CELTIC: Simpson; Craig, Gemmell; Murdoch, McNeill, Clark; Johnstone, Wallace, Chalmers, Auld, Hughes

Attendance: 16,000

League positions

	P	W	D	L	F	A	Pts
1 CELTIC	24	19	4	1	83	25	42
2 Rangers	24	18	4	2	72	21	40
3 Aberdeen	25	14	4	7	58	31	32
4 Hibernian	25	15	2	8	50	40	32
5 Clyde	24	13	4	7	43	37	30

March 4th
ST MIRREN (0) 0 — CELTIC (1) 5
Wallace 2 (31, 88), Lennox (48), Hughes (53), Gemmell (82 pen)

ST MIRREN: Connaghan; Murray, Young; Kiernan, Hannah, Renton; Hutton, Bell, Kane, Hamilton (Pinkerton), Adamson

CELTIC: Simpson; Craig, Gemmell; Murdoch, McNeill, Clark; Hughes, Lennox, Wallace, Gallagher, Auld (Johnstone)

Attendance: 18,000

March 18th
CELTIC (3) 3 — DUNFERMLINE (1) 2
Chalmers (3), Gemmell (21 pen), Wallace (42) — Ferguson 2 (19, 87)

CELTIC: Simpson; Gemmell, O'Neill; Murdoch, McNeill, Clark; Hughes, Gallagher, Chalmers, Wallace, Lennox

DUNFERMLINE: Martin; Callaghan, Totten; Thomson, Fraser, Barry; Edwards, Kerrigan, Delaney, Ferguson, Robertson

Attendance: 41,000

March 20th
CELTIC (2) 5 FALKIRK (0) 0
Chalmers 2 (25, 74),
Auld (29),
Hughes (66),
Gemmell (67 pen)

CELTIC: Simpson; Craig, Gemmell; Murdoch, McNeill, Clark; Johnstone, Wallace, Chalmers, Auld, Hughes

FALKIRK: McDonald; Lambie, Hunter; Markie, Baillie, Fulton; McManus, Smith, Moran, Graham, McKinney

Attendance: 25,000

March 25th
HEARTS (0) 0 CELTIC (1) 3
Auld (42),
Wallace (62),
Gemmell (85 pen)

HEARTS: Cruikshank; Shevlane, Peden; Thomson, Anderson, Miller; Ford (Milne), Ferguson, Fleming, Murphy, Hamilton

CELTIC: Simpson; Craig, Gemmell; Murdoch (Lennox), McNeill, Clark; Johnstone, Wallace, Chalmers, Auld, Hughes

Attendance: n.a.

March 27th
PARTICK THISTLE (0) 1 CELTIC (1) 4
Flanagan (52)
Lennox (41),
Chalmers 2 (59, 86),
Wallace (67)

PARTICK THISTLE: Niven; Campbell, Muir; Cunningham, McKinnon, Gibb; Gallagher, McParland, Rae, Flanagan, Duncan

CELTIC: Simpson; Craig, Gemmell; Wallace, McNeill, Clark; Johnstone, Gallagher, Chalmers, Lennox, Hughes

Attendance: 30,000. Lennox scored Celtic's 100th League goal of the season

April 8th
MOTHERWELL (0) 0 CELTIC (0) 2
Wallace (57),
Gemmell (79 pen)

MOTHERWELL: McCloy; Whiteford, M. Thomson; I. Thomson, Martis (Murray), McCallum; Moffat, Hunter, Deans, Campbell, Weir

CELTIC: Simpson; Craig, Gemmell; Wallace, McNeill, Clark; Hughes, Lennox, Chalmers, Gallagher (Brogan), Auld

Attendance: 21,000

April 15th: Simpson, Gemmell, Wallace and Lennox were in the Scotland team which beat England 3-2 at Wembley. Lennox scored one of the goals.

April 19th
CELTIC (0) 0 ABERDEEN (0) 0

CELTIC: Simpson; Craig, Gemmell; Murdoch, McNeill, Clark; Johnstone, Wallace, Chalmers, Auld, Lennox

ABERDEEN: Clark; Whyte, Shewan; Munro, McMillan, Petersen; Wilson, Smith, Storrie, Melrose, Johnston

Attendance: 33,000

May 3rd
CELTIC (1) 2 DUNDEE UNITED (0) 3
Gemmell (27 pen)
Wallace (61)
Hainey (55),
Gillespie (68),
Graham (71)

CELTIC: Simpson; Craig, Gemmell; Murdoch, McNeill, Clark, Johnstone, Gallagher, Wallace, Lennox, Hughes

DUNDEE UNITED: Davie; Millar, Briggs; Neilson, Smith, Moore; Berg, Graham, Hainey, Gillespie, Persson

Attendance: 44,000

May 6th
RANGERS (1) 2 CELTIC (1) 2
Jardine (40),
Hynd (81)
Johnstone 2 (41, 74)

RANGERS: Martin; Johansen, Provan; Jardine, McKinnon, Greig; Henderson, A. Smith, Hynd, D. Smith, Johnston

CELTIC: Simpson; Craig, Gemmell; Murdoch, McNeill, Clark; Johnstone, Wallace, Chalmers, Auld, Lennox

Attendance: 78,000

Celtic attained the one point which won them the League Championship for the 22nd time. The 78,000 crowd included Mr Helenio Herrera, Manager of Internazionale of Milan, Celtic's opponents in the forthcoming European Cup Final. On a sodden pitch and in constant heavy rain the players gave their all. In 74 minutes Johnstone, having received the ball from a throw-in by Chalmers, made for the penalty-area, evading McKinnon's tackle, and in the process veered left as other defenders closed in and then smacked a glorious shot into the roof of the net. Hynd scored the equaliser for Rangers 9 minutes from time when he prodded home a Henderson cross.

May 10th: Simpson, Gemmell, McNeill, Clark, Johnstone and Lennox were all in the Scotland team which was beaten 2-0 by the U.S.S.R. at Hampden Park. Wallace made an appearance as substitute for Denis Law. Gemmell had the misfortune to score through his own goal.

Two pictures from the proudest season in Celtics' history. Top: Billy McNeill, the Celtic captain, holds aloft the European Cup after defeating Inter Milan by 2-1. The first British team to win Europe's major prize. Below: Celtic players salute their fans before the start of the match.

May 15th
CELTIC (1) 2 KILMARNOCK (0) 0
Lennox (25),
Wallace (76)

CELTIC: Fallon; Craig, Gemmell; Murdoch, Cushley, Clark; Johnstone, McNeill, Wallace, Auld, Lennox

KILMARNOCK: Ferguson; King, McFadzean; Murray, McGrory, Beattie; McLean, McInally, Bertelsen, Queen, C. Watson

Attendance: 21,000

Scottish First Division

	P	W	D	L	F	A	Pts
1 CELTIC	34	26	6	2	111	33	58
2 Rangers	34	24	7	3	92	31	55
3 Clyde	34	20	6	8	64	48	46
4 Aberdeen	34	17	8	9	72	38	42
5 Hibernian	34	19	4	11	72	49	42
6 Dundee	34	16	9	9	74	51	41
7 Kilmarnock	34	16	8	10	59	46	40
8 Dunfermline	34	14	10	10	72	52	38
9 Dundee United	34	14	9	11	68	62	37
10 Motherwell	34	10	11	13	59	60	31
11 Hearts	34	11	8	15	39	48	30
12 Partick Thistle	34	9	12	13	49	68	30
13 Airdrie	34	11	6	17	41	53	28
14 Falkirk	34	11	4	19	33	70	26
15 St Johnstone	34	10	5	19	53	73	25
16 Stirling Albion	34	5	9	20	31	85	19
17 St Mirren	34	4	7	23	25	81	15
18 Ayr United	34	1	7	26	20	86	9

May 18th: Jock Stein was named as Britain's Manager of the Year.

May 19th: Murdoch, Wallace and Lennox were all linked with Chicago Sting of the North American soccer league.

June 2nd: John Cushley was transferred to West Ham for £20,000.

June 18th: Willie Fernie returned to Celtic Park as a Coach.

June 21st: Chris Shevlane was signed on a free transfer from Hearts.

LEAGUE CUP

August 13th
HEARTS (0) 0 CELTIC (1) 2
McBride 2 (18 pen, 88)

HEARTS: Cruikshank; Polland, Holt; Barry, Anderson, Higgins; Hamilton, Gordon, Wallace, Kerrigan, Traynor

CELTIC: Simpson; Gemmell, O'Neill; Murdoch, McNeill, Clark; Johnstone, McBride, Chalmers, Lennox, Auld

Attendance: 25,000

August 17th
CELTIC (3) 6 CLYDE (0) 0
Lennox 2 (5, 60),
McBride 3 (30 pen, 44, 63)
Chalmers (83)

CELTIC: Simpson; Gemmell, O'Neill; Murdoch, McNeill, Clark; Johnstone, McBride, Chalmers, Lennox, Auld

CLYDE: Wright; Glasgow, Mulheron; McHugh, Staite, Anderson; McFarlane, Gilroy, Stewart, Fraser, Hastings

Attendance: 30,000

August 20th
CELTIC (4) 8 ST MIRREN (0) 2
Lennox 2 (10, 72), Treacy 2 (78, 82)
McBride 4 (24 pen, 26, 44, 46),
Auld (58),
Chalmers (86)

CELTIC: Simpson; Gemmell, O'Neill; Murdoch, McNeill, Clark; Johnstone, McBride, Chalmers, Lennox, Auld

ST MIRREN: Thorburn; Murray, Clark; Pinkerton, Kiernan, Wilson; Aird, Treacy, Adamson, Gemmill, Hamilton

Attendance: 31,500

August 27th
CELTIC (0) 3 HEARTS (0) 0
McBride 2 (54, 73),
Chalmers (68)

CELTIC: Simpson; Gemmell, O'Neill; Murdoch, McNeill, Clark; Johnstone, McBride, Chalmers, Hughes, Auld

HEARTS: Cruickshank; Shevlane, Holt; Barry, Anderson, Higgins; Jensen, Miller, Wallace, Kerrigan, Traynor

Attendance: 46,000

August 31st
CLYDE (1) 1 CELTIC (2) 3
Gilroy (35) McBride 2 (16, 38 pen),
Gemmell (86)

CLYDE: McCulloch; Glasgow, Mulheron; McHugh, Fraser, Staite; McFarlane, Gilroy, Knox, Anderson, Hastings

CELTIC: Simpson; Gemmell, O'Neill; Murdoch, McNeill, Clark; Johnstone, McBride, Chalmers, Lennox, Auld

Attendance: 18,000

September 3rd
ST MIRREN (0) 0 CELTIC (0) 1
Murdoch (53)

ST MIRREN: Thorburn; Murray, Brown; Bell, Kiernan, Clark; Hutton, Pinkerton, Hamilton, Treacy, Adamson

CELTIC: Simpson; Craig, Gemmell; Murdoch, McNeill, Clark; Johnstone (O'Neill), McBride, Chalmers, Lennox, Gallagher

Attendance: 20,000. O'Neill became Celtic's first-ever substitute in a competitive match.

Section table

	P	W	D	L	F	A	Pts
CELTIC	6	6	0	0	23	6	12
Hearts	6	3	1	2	10	10	7
Clyde	6	2	0	4	7	16	4
St Mirren	6	0	1	5	3	14	1

Qualifier: CELTIC

Quarter-Final First Leg September 14th

CELTIC (5) 6	DUNFERMLINE (1) 3
McNeill (30 secs),	Ferguson 2 (18, 85),
Hughes (4),	Hunter (62)
Auld 2 (11, 70)	
McBride (20 pen),	
Johnstone (23)	

CELTIC: Simpson; Gemmell, O'Neill; Murdoch, McNeill, Clark; Johnstone, McBride, Chalmers, Auld, Hughes

DUNFERMLINE: Anderson; W. Callaghan, Lunn; Delaney, McLean, Thomson (Paton); Fleming, Ferguson, Hunter, T. Callaghan, Robertson

Attendance: 36,000

Quarter-Final Second Leg September 21st

DUNFERMLINE (0) 1	CELTIC (2) 3
Fleming (70)	McNeill (32),
	Chalmers 2 (42, 54)

DUNFERMLINE: Martin; W. Callaghan, Lunn; Paton, Delaney, T. Callaghan; Edwards, Fleming, Hunter, Ferguson, Robertson

CELTIC: Simpson; Gemmell, O'Neill; Murdoch, McNeill, Clark; Johnstone, Chalmers, McBride, Auld, Hughes

Attendance: 20,000. Celtic won 9-4 on aggregate

Semi-Final at Hampden Park October 17th

CELTIC (0) 2	AIRDRIE (0) 0
Murdoch (64),	
McBride (75)	

CELTIC: Simpson; Gemmell, O'Neill; Murdoch, McNeill, Clark; Johnstone, McBride, Chalmers, Auld, Lennox. Sub: Hughes

AIRDRIE: McKenzie; Jonquin, Keenan; Goodwin, Black, Ramsey; Ferguson, McPheat, Marshall, Murray, Irvine. Sub: Reid

Attendance: 36,930

Celtic found Airdrie a tough nut to crack. But with 2 goals in 11 minutes in the 2nd half the task was accomplished and the holders went through to the Final for the third successive year.

Final at Hampden Park October 29th

CELTIC (1) 1	RANGERS (0) 0
Lennox (19)	

CELTIC: Simpson; Gemmell, O'Neill; Murdoch, McNeill, Clark; Johnstone, Lennox, McBride, Auld, Hughes (Chalmers)

RANGERS: Martin; Johansen, Provan; Greig, McKinnon, D. Smith; Henderson, Watson, McLean, A. Smith, Johnston. Sub: Wilson

Attendance: 94,532. *Referee:* T. Wharton (Clarkston)

Celtic were outplayed by Rangers but retained the League Cup. Their one opportunity was brilliantly taken, but for almost all of the remainder of the game Rangers outplayed them and pushed them relentlessly back into defence. Celtic's goal came after 19 minutes. Auld flighted a cross beyond the far post and McBride headed down and back for Lennox who hammered it past Martin into the net. Unfortunately for Rangers it is goals, not sweat and lost opportunities, that show in the record books.

SCOTTISH CUP

First Round January 28th

CELTIC (3) 4	ARBROATH (0) 0
Murdoch (13),	
Gemmell (19),	
Chalmers (33),	
Auld (80)	

CELTIC: Simpson; Craig, Gemmell; Murdoch, McNeill, Clark; Gallagher, Wallace, Chalmers, Auld, Hughes

ARBROATH: Williamson; Cameron, Hughes; Cargill, Stirling, Pierson; Easton, Sellars, Jack, Cant, Finnie

Attendance: 31,000

Second Round February 18th

CELTIC (3) 7	ELGIN CITY (0) 0
Chalmers (43),	
Lennox 3 (44, 45, 70),	
Hughes (62),	
Wallace 2 (83, 89)	

CELTIC: Simpson; Cattenach, Gemmell; Murdoch (Wallace), McNeill, Clark; Johnstone, Lennox, Chalmers, Gallagher, Hughes

ELGIN CITY: Connell; Gerrard, Laing; Sanderson, D. Grant, Smith; Graham, Gilbert, W. Grant, Middleton, Fraser

Attendance: 34,000

Third Round March 11th

CELTIC (4) 5	QUEENS PARK (2) 3
Gemmell (7 pen),	Gemmell o.g. (15 secs),
Chalmers (23),	Hopper 2 (31, 46)
Wallace (33),	
Murdoch (38),	
Lennox (84)	

CELTIC: Simpson; Cattenach, Gemmell; Murdoch, McNeill, Clark; Johnstone, Wallace, Chalmers, Auld, Lennox

QUEENS PARK: G. Wilson; T. Barr, C. Gilmour; I. Robertson, W. Neill, E. Hunter; C. Emery, N. Hopper, M. McKay, M. Hay, A. Watson
Attendance: 34,000

Semi-Final at Hampden Park April 1st
CELTIC (0) 0 CLYDE (0) 0

CELTIC: Simpson; Craig, Gemmell; Wallace, McNeill, Clark; Johnstone, Auld, Chalmers, Lennox, Hughes Sub: Gallagher

CLYDE: McCulloch; Glasgow, Soutar; Anderson, Staite, McHugh; McFarlane, Hood, Gilroy, Stewart, Knox. Sub: Fraser

Attendance: 56,704

Celtic were denied a penalty with 4 minutes to go when Soutar appeared to elbow away what looked like a scoring shot from Johnstone after a fast Lennox cross had caught the Clyde defence in two minds.

Semi-Final Replay at Hampden Park April 5th
CELTIC (2) 2 CLYDE (0) 0
Lennox (2),
Auld (24)

CELTIC: Simpson; Craig, Gemmell; Wallace, McNeill, Clark; Johnstone (Hughes), Lennox, Chalmers, Gallagher, Auld

CLYDE; McCulloch; Glasgow, Soutar; Anderson, Staite, McHugh; McFarlane, Gilroy, Knox, Stewart, Hastings. Sub: Fraser

Attendance: 55,138

Clyde offered feeble resistance after Celtic had scored their 2 goals in 24 minutes with the result that for long periods of the 2nd half the winners, with a heavy fixture list in front of them, were able to play at half pace.

Final at Hampden Park April 29th
CELTIC (1) 2 ABERDEEN (0) 0
Wallace 2 (42, 49)

CELTIC: Simpson; Craig, Gemmell; Murdoch, McNeill, Clark; Johnstone, Wallace, Chalmers, Auld, Lennox

ABERDEEN: Clark; Whyte, Shewan; Munro, McMillan, Petersen; Wilson, Smith, Storrie, Melrose, Johnston

Attendance: 126,102 *Referee:* W. Syme

Celtic thoroughly deserved to beat Aberdeen for their more positive approach to the game. Because of Aberdeen's unrealistic caution, play rarely reached a high level of entertainment or skill. Celtic's forwards always looked likely to inflict more damage than Aberdeen's depleted attack in which only Storrie, despite poor support, performed with any lasting effect. Celtic's decisive tactic was to move Chalmers almost immediately the game started out to the right wing and play Johnstone as a double spearhead with Wallace. Unfortunately Aberdeen's Manager Eddie Turnbull was unable to attend the match due to illness.

EUROPEAN CUP

First Round First Leg September 28th
CELTIC (0) 2 F.C. ZÜRICH
Gemmell (64), (Switzerland) (0) 0
McBride (69)

CELTIC: Simpson; Gemmell, O'Neill; Murdoch, McNeill, Clark; Johnstone, McBride, Chalmers, Auld, Hughes

F.C. ZÜRICH: Iten; Munsch, Leimgruber; Stierli, Neumann, Brodmann; Kuhn, Martinelli, Bani, Meyer, Kunzl

Attendance: 50,000

From start to finish Zürich put the emphasis on physical contact. Johnstone was the main target of abuse from defenders. For most of the game Celtic were on the offensive and in the last half hour they had Zürich more or less penned into their own half of the field.

First Round Second Leg October 5th
F.C. ZURICH (0) 0 CELTIC (2) 3
Gemmell 2 (22, 48 pen),
Chalmers (38)

F.C. ZÜRICH: Iten; Munsch, Kyburz; Neumann, Stierli, Leimgruber, Kuhn, Bani, Kunzl, Sturmer, Kubala

CELTIC: Simpson; Gemmell, O'Neill; Murdoch, McNeill, Clark; Johnstone, Lennox, Chalmers, Auld, Hughes

Attendance: 23,000

Only for the first 15 minutes did the Swiss pose a threat to Celtic. The longer the game went on, the more confident Celtic became. The match, dead at half-time, was buried after 48 minutes when Neumann brought down Lennox inside the penalty-area and Gemmell, from the spot, scored his 2nd and his side's 3rd. Celtic won 5-0 on aggregate.

Second Round First Leg November 30th
NANTES (France) (1) 1 CELTIC (1) 3
Magny (16) McBride (24),
Lennox (50),
Chalmers (67)

NANTES: Castel; Le Chenadec, Budzinski; Robin, De Michele, Kovacevik; Suaudeau, Blanchet, Simon, Magny, Michel

CELTIC: Simpson; Gemmell, O'Neill; Murdoch, McNeill, Clark; Johnstone, Chalmers, McBride, Lennox, Auld

Attendance: 25,000

Jock Stein has promised before the start that his team would not play defensive football and that promise was kept. As the French players wilted in the 2nd half Murdoch chipped a perfect ball through a gap in their defence and Lennox, racing in, scored. Chalmers made certain of victory with a 3rd goal in 67 minutes and Celtic coasted to the finish.

Second Round Second Leg December 7th
CELTIC (1) 3 NANTES (1) 1
Johnstone (13), Georgen (36)
Chalmers (56),
Lennox (78)

CELTIC: Simpson; Gemmell, O'Neill; Murdoch, McNeill, Clark; Johnstone, Gallagher, Chalmers, Auld, Lennox

NANTES: Georgin; Le Chenadec, Budzinski; Robin, Grabowski, Kovacevik; Georgen, Blanchet, Simon, Magny, Michel

Attendance: 41,000

Celtic were assured of a place in the Quarter-Finals as early as the 13th minute when Johnstone put them 3 ahead on aggregate. The French Champions of the past two seasons, like all continental sides, moved the ball attractively enough in midfield but they were much too deliberate in their method. It was Johnstone who engineered Celtic's 2nd and 3rd goals scored by Chalmers in 56 minutes and by Lennox 12 minutes from the end. The diminutive winger sent over crosses which left his colleagues with the simplest of chances to score. Celtic won 6-2 on aggregate.

Quarter-Final First Leg March 1st
VOJVODINA CELTIC (0) 0
(Yugoslavia) (0) 1
Stanic (69)

VOJVODINA: Pantelic; Aleksic, Radovic; Nesticki, Brzic, Dakic; Rakic, Radosav, Sekeres, Djordjic, Stanic

CELTIC: Simpson; Craig, Gemmell; Murdoch, McNeill, Clark; Johnstone, Lennox, Chalmers, Auld, Hughes

Attendance: 30,000

For 45 minutes Celtic had defended brilliantly against massive pressure from a big and strong Yugoslav team. Celtic appeared to be coasting to a draw when Gemmell made a careless mistake. He tried to pass back to Clark, mis-hit it, and Clark in turn was so surprised that he allowed the ball to run on to Stanic who had the easiest of jobs in scoring the only goal of the game.

Quarter-Final Second Leg March 8th
CELTIC (0) 2 VOJVODINA (0) 0
Chalmers (58),
McNeill (90)

CELTIC: Simpson; Craig, Gemmell; Murdoch, McNeill, Clark; Johnstone, Lennox, Chalmers, Gallagher, Hughes

VOJVODINA: Pantelic; Aleksic, Radovic; Sekeres, Brzic, Nesticki; Rakic, Dakic, Radsosav, Trivic, Pusibric

Attendance: 75,000

Celtic reached the Semi-Final in fairytale fashion – the goal that put them through came with only about 20 seconds remaining for play. A play-off in Rotterdam looked inevitable when Johnstone suddenly burst through on the right and won a corner. Gallagher crossed over to take the kick and flighted it perfectly into the heart of the Vojvodina penalty area where McNeill, timing his jump perfectly, headed cleanly outwith the reach of the diving Pantelic. As the referee signalled a goal the whole ground erupted. Yet it might have all been very different had Pusibric scored with a simple chance after only five minutes. Celtic won 2-1 on aggregate.

Semi-Final First Leg April 12th
CELTIC (1) 3 DULKA PRAGUE (1) 1
Johnstone (27), Strunc (44)
Wallace 2 (59, 65)

CELTIC: Simpson; Craig, Gemmell; Murdoch, McNeill, Clark; Johnstone, Wallace, Chalmers, Auld, Hughes

DUKLA: Viktor; Cmarada, Cadek; Taborsky, Zlocha, Geleta; Strunc, Dvorak, Masopust, Nedorost, Vacenovsky

Attendance: 75,000

2 brilliantly taken goals by Wallace within the space of 6 minutes in the 2nd half brought Celtic a well-deserved victory. Wallace might have had a 3rd goal in 72 minutes, the ball striking the face of the crossbar after he had stuck out a leg to a low cross by Chalmers.

Semi-Final Second Leg April 25th
DUKLA PRAGUE (0) 0 CELTIC (0) 0

DUKLA: Viktor; Cmarada, Novak; Taborsky, Zlocha, Geleta; Strunc, Pnebort, Masopust, Nedorost, Vacenovsky

CELTIC: Simpson; Craig, Gemmell; Murdoch, McNeill, Clark; Johnstone, Wallace, Chalmers, Auld, Lennox

Attendance: 22,000

Celtic became the first British team to reach the Final of the European Cup. Throughout the 90 minutes Simpson had only 1 worthwhile save to make from a Nedorost shot early on. So determinedly and so well did McNeill and all the other players give cover to their goalkeeper that he had one of the easiest matches of his long footballing career. McNeill was the outstanding player on the field and Dukla never managed to beat him in the air. He was the inspiration of the victory. Celtic won 3-1 on aggregate.

Final in Estadio Nacional, Lisbon May 25th
CELTIC (0) 2 INTERNAZIONALE
Gemmell (63), MILAN (1) 1
Chalmers (85) Mazzola (7 pen)

CELTIC: Simpson; Craig, Gemmell; Murdoch, McNeill, Clark; Johnstone, Wallace, Chalmers, Auld, Lennox

INTERNAZIONALE: Sarti; Burgnich, Facchetti; Bedin, Guarneri, Picchi; Domenghini, Cappellini, Mazzola, Bicicli, Corso

Attendance: 55,000 *Referee:* K. Tschescher (West Germany)

Celtic made football history when they completely outplayed Inter and brought the European Cup to Britain for the first time. The score makes a travesty of the facts. If justice had been done and Inter had not been so brilliantly served by their goalkeeper Sarti, Celtic would have scored 5 or 6. Celtic got off to the worst possible start. After only 7 minutes' play Craig chased Cappellini across the penalty area and was adjudged to have bodychecked the Italian striker. It seemed a harsh decision. Mazzola sent Simpson the wrong way from the resultant penalty. Celtic kept up a relentless assault on the Inter goal but for an hour their efforts were repelled. Gemmell and Auld hit the crossbar and the Italian goalkeeper made a series of brilliant saves. Celtic eventually equalised in the 63rd minute. Murdoch passed to right-back Craig on the overlap. He squared the ball to Gemmell just outside the penalty area and his tremendous shot from at least 20 yards flashed into the top right-hand corner of the net, giving Sarti no chance. Celtic continued to attack and their winning goal came with only 5 minutes remaining. Murdoch passed low across the face of the goal and Chalmers was there to push out his foot and score the goal which won the trophy. The era of Italian defensive football was dead. Football owed a great debt to Celtic. Some of the after match comments were as follows: Jock Stein: 'We won and we won on merit. This win gives us more satisfaction than anything.' Helenio Herrera (Manager of Internazionale): 'We can have no complaints. Celtic deserved their victory. We were beaten by Celtic's force. Although we lost, the match was a victory for sport'. Scot Symon (Manager of Rangers): 'Words just cannot express this achievement after such a wonderful season. This is a fitting climax'. Bill Shankly (Manager of Liverpool): 'Jock, you're immortal'.

APPEARANCES	League	League Cup	Scottish Cup	European Cup
Simpson	33	10	6	9
Gemmell	34	10	6	9
O'Neill	18	9+1S	–	4
Murdoch	31	10	4	9
McNeill	33	10	6	9
Clark	34	10	6	9
Chalmers	28	9+1S	5	9
Lennox	26+1S	7	5	7
McBride	14	10	–	2
Auld	27	9	5	8
Hughes	19	4	3+1S	5
Johnstone	25+1S	10	5	9
Young	1	–	–	–
Gallagher	11	1	4	2
Craig	17+1S	1	4	5
Wallace	21	–	5+1S	3
Fallon	1	–	–	–
Cushley	1	–	–	–
Brogan	0+1S	–	–	–
Cattenach	–	–	2	–

GOALSCORERS

League: Chalmers 23, McBride 18 (3 pens), Wallace 14, Lennox 13, Johnstone 13, Gemmell 9 (6 pens), Auld 7, Hughes 6, Murdoch 4, Gallagher 2, Own goals 2

League Cup: McBride 15 (5 pens), Lennox 5, Chalmers 5, Auld 3, Murdoch 2, McNeill 2, Gemmell 1, Hughes 1, Johnstone 1

Scottish Cup: Wallace 5, Lennox 5, Chalmers 3, Auld 2, Murdoch 2, Gemmell 2 (1 pen), Hughes 1

European Cup: Chalmers 5, Gemmell 4 (1 pen), McBride 2, Lennox 2, Johnstone 2, Wallace 2, McNeill 1

The goal that won the European Cup for Celtic. Chalmers is the scorer.

Season 1967-68

Celtic won the League Championship for the 3rd successive season with a record post-war points total of 63. They finished 2 points ahead of Rangers despite dropping 3 of the 4 points to the Ibrox team who had led the table for most of the season. Their only League defeat came against Rangers at Ibrox in only their 2nd match. Every other one of their away matches was won. They dropped only 3 points at home and did the double over 14 teams. Reserve goalkeeper John Fallon must have been especially relieved when the Championship was again won for it looked for a long time as if his two unfortunate mistakes in the Ne'erday match against Rangers would cost his team the title. Fortunately for him Rangers dropped 3 points in their final 3 matches to relinquish their leading position. The defence was positively miserly and conceded only 24 goals – a post-war club record. Gemmell, Murdoch and McNeill played in all 34 matches and for the 3rd season in a row the club scored over 100 League goals. Bobby Lennox led the field with 32, winning for him Europe's Bronze Boot Award, followed by Willie Wallace on 21.

The League Cup was won for the 5th time, but Dunfermline, who went on to win the Scottish Cup, caused a major upset by beating Celtic 2-0 at Parkhead in the first Round of the tournament.

Celtic's hopes of retaining the European Cup were dashed at the first hurdle by Russian Champions, Dynamo Kiev, who recorded a sensational win at Parkhead against a clearly off-form Celtic. They faced South American Champions Racing Club of Argentina in the Final of the World Club Championship. They were violently provoked in the first 2 matches in Glasgow and Buenos Aires and lost goalkeeper Ronnie Simpson, hit by a missile, even before the return match had begun. Not surprisingly the play-off in Montevideo boiled over and in a series of incidents 4 Celtic players and 2 Racing players were sent off by the Paraguayan referee, Racing winning the match by a goal from centre-forward Cardenas.

League:	Champions
League Cup:	Winners
Scottish Cup:	First Round
European Cup:	First Round

SCOTTISH FIRST DIVISION

August 14th: Morton signed Tony Taylor.

September 9th
CELTIC (3) 3 CLYDE (0) 0
McMahon (12),
Lennox (37), Auld (44)

CELTIC: Simpson; Shevlane, Gemmell; Murdoch, McNeill, Clark; Chalmers (Hughes), McMahon, Wallace, Auld, Lennox

CLYDE: Wright; Glasgow, Soutar; Anderson, Fraser, McHugh; McFarlane, Hood, Gilroy, Staite, Hastings
Attendance: 37,000

September 16th
RANGERS (0) 1 CELTIC (0) 0
Persson (47)

RANGERS: Sorensen; Johansen, Provan (Johnston); Jardine, McKinnon, Greig; Henderson, Penman, Ferguson, Smith, Persson

CELTIC: Simpson; Cattenach, Gemmell; Murdoch, McNeill, Clark; Johnstone, Wallace, Chalmers, Auld, Lennox

Attendance: 90,000

After the match it was confirmed that Rangers' Scottish Internationalist, left-back Provan, carried off after a tackle on Auld in 4 minutes, would be out of football for some 3 months with a broken leg. After the only goal of the match Rangers created – and scorned – more clear-cut chances than Celtic. Johnston, who had come on as a substitute, finished the game with a twisted ankle and Henderson required four stitches in a gash on his left shin.

September 23rd
CELTIC (0) 1 — ST JOHNSTONE (0) 1
Murdoch (74) — MacDonald (47)

CELTIC: Simpson; Craig, Gemmell; Murdoch, McNeill, Clark; Johnstone, McMahon (Cattenach), Wallace, Auld, Lennox

ST JOHNSTONE: Donaldson; McGillvray, Coburn; Miller, Rooney, McPhee; Aird, Whitelaw, McCarry, MacDonald, Wilson

Attendance: 31,000. Johnstone was ordered off in the 37th minute.

September 30th
STIRLING ALBION (0) 0 — CELTIC (1) 4
Wallace (43), Auld 2 (66, 78), Lennox (70)

STIRLING ALBION: Murray; Cunningham, McGuinness; Reid, Rogerson, Thomson; McPhee, Kerray, Grant, Peebles (McKinnon), Hall

CELTIC: Simpson; Craig, Gemmell; Murdoch, McNeill, Clark; Chalmers, Lennox, Wallace, Auld, Hughes

Attendance: 16,000

October 7th
CELTIC (1) 4 — HIBERNIAN (0) 0
Murdoch 2 (26, 65), Johnstone (48), Wallace (59)

CELTIC: Simpson; Craig, Gemmell; Murdoch, McNeill, Clark; Johnstone, Lennox, Wallace, Auld, Hughes

HIBERNIAN: Allan; Duncan, Davis; Stanton, Madsen, McGraw; Scott, Quinn, Stein, Cormack, Stevenson

Attendance: 40,000

October 14th
PARTICK THISTLE (0) 1 — CELTIC (1) 5
Duncan (78) — McNeill (42), Lennox 4 (52, 60, 71, 89)

PARTICK THISTLE: Niven; Campbell, Muir; O'Neill, McKinnon, Gibb; Rae, McParland, Coulston, Flanagan, Duncan

CELTIC: Simpson; Craig, Gemmell; Murdoch, McNeill, Clark (Brogan); Johnstone, Lennox, Wallace, Auld, Hughes

Attendance: 30,000. McParland was ordered off.

October 21st: Simpson, Gemmell, Murdoch and Wallace were in the Scotland team beaten 1-0 by Northern Ireland in Belfast. Simpson saved a penalty from Crossan.

October 24th
CELTIC (3) 4 — MOTHERWELL (1) 2
Wallace (12), McNeill (40), Lennox (42), Chalmers (58) — Campbell 2 (15, 48)

CELTIC: Simpson; Craig, Gemmell; Murdoch, McNeill, Clark; Chalmers, Lennox, Wallace, Auld, Hughes

MOTHERWELL: McCloy; Whiteford, McKay; Murray, Martis, McCallum; Lindsay (Forsyth), Thomson, Deans, Goldthorpe, Campbell

Attendance: 23,000

League positions

	P	W	D	L	F	A	Pts
1 Rangers	8	6	2	0	12	2	14
2 Hibernian	8	6	1	1	24	10	13
3 CELTIC	7	5	1	1	21	5	11
4 Hearts	8	5	1	2	19	14	11
5 St Johnstone	8	3	4	1	14	9	10

November 11th
AIRDRIE (0) 0 — CELTIC (1) 2
Brogan (18), Murdoch (56)

AIRDRIE: McKenzie; Jonquin, Caldwell; Goodwin, Black, Whiteford; McLellan, Ramsey, Marshall, Fyfe, Wilson

CELTIC: Simpson; Gemmell, O'Neill; Brogan, McNeill, Clark; Hughes, Wallace, Chalmers, Murdoch, Auld (McBride)

Attendance: 18,000

November 15th
CELTIC (1) 3 — KILMARNOCK (0) 0
Auld (44), Hughes (52), Chalmers (73)

CELTIC: Simpson; Gemmell, O'Neill; Murdoch, McNeill, Brogan; Johnstone, Chalmers, Wallace, Auld, Hughes

KILMARNOCK: McLaughlin; Arthur, McFadzean; Dickson, McGrory, Beattie; McLean, Cameron, Morrison, Queen, McIlroy

Attendance: 30,000. Gemmell missed a penalty.

November 18th
CELTIC (2) 3 — FALKIRK (0) 0
Chalmers 2 (21, 32),
Hughes (89)

CELTIC: Simpson; Gemmell, O'Neill; Murdoch, McNeill, Brogan; Johnstone, Chalmers, McBride, Auld, Hughes

FALKIRK: Devlin; Moreland, Hunter; Scott, Baillie, Gibson; Watson, Smith, Vincent, McLaughlin, Marshall

Attendance: 35,000. Chalmers missed a penalty.

November 22nd: Craig, Johnstone and Lennox were in the Scotland team which beat Wales 3-2 at Hampden Park.

November 25th
RAITH ROVERS (0) 0 — CELTIC (0) 2
Gemmell (56 pen),
Wallace (66)

RAITH ROVERS: Reid; Hislop, Gray; Stein, Davidson, Porterfield; Murphy, Sneddon, Wallace, Richardson, Falconer

CELTIC: Simpson; Gemmell, O'Neill; Murdoch, McNeill, Brogan (McBride); Johnstone, Wallace, Chalmers, Auld, Hughes

Attendance: 18,000. Gemmell missed a penalty.

December 2nd
CELTIC (0) 1 — DUNDEE UNITED (0) 1
Murdoch (73½) — Wilson (73)

CELTIC: Simpson; Shevlane (McBride), Gemmell; Murdoch, McNeill, Clark; Johnstone, Chalmers, Wallace, Auld, Hughes

DUNDEE UNITED: Mackay; Millar, Briggs; Wood, Smith, Gillespie; Seeman, Rolland, Hainey, Graham, Wilson

Attendance: 37,000. Wallace was ordered off.

December 9th
CELTIC (3) 3 — HEARTS (1) 1
G. Fleming o.g. (3), — J. Fleming (40)
Chalmers (12), Lennox (31)

CELTIC: Simpson; Craig, Gemmell; Murdoch, McNeill, Clark; Johnstone, Wallace, Chalmers, Lennox, Hughes

HEARTS: Cruikshank; Sneddon, Mann; Anderson, Thomson, Miller; Jensen (Kemp), G. Fleming, Ford, J. Fleming, Traynor

Attendance: 35,000

December 16th
DUNDEE (2) 4 — CELTIC (4) 5
G. McLean (8), — McNeill (5),
Scott (41), Campbell (76), — Lennox (26),
Wilson (85) — Johnstone (36),
Wallace 2 (38, 56)

DUNDEE: Donaldson; Wilson, Houston; Murray, Easton, Stewart; Scott, J. McLean, Wilson, G. McLean, Campbell

CELTIC: Simpson; Craig, Gemmell; Murdoch, McNeill, Clark; Johnstone, Wallace, Hughes, Lennox, Auld

Attendance: 16,000

December 23rd
MORTON (0) 0 — CELTIC (1) 4
McBride 3 (5, 76, 84),
Hughes (81)

MORTON: Russell; Murray, Loughlan; Arnetoft, Strachan, Rankin; Thorup (Taylor), Jensen, Allan, Stevenson, Sweeney

CELTIC: Simpson; Craig, Gemmell; Murdoch, McNeill, Clark; Johnstone, Lennox, McBride, Auld, Hughes

Attendance: 18,000

December 30th
CELTIC (2) 3 — DUNFERMLINE (1) 2
McNeill (21), — Gardner (40),
Chalmers 2 (22, 51) — Robertson (88 pen)

CELTIC: Simpson; Craig, Gemmell; Murdoch, McNeill, Clark; Johnstone, Chalmers, McBride, Auld, Hughes

DUNFERMLINE: Martin; W. Callaghan, Lunn; Fraser, Barry, Thomson; Edwards, Paton, Gardner, T. Callaghan, Robertson

Attendance: 36,000. Barry was ordered off.

League positions

	P	W	D	L	F	A	Pts
1 Rangers	16	14	2	0	42	12	30
2 CELTIC	16	13	2	1	47	13	28
3 Hearts	17	10	3	4	38	26	23
4 Hibernian	16	9	2	5	32	20	20
5 Clyde	16	9	1	6	28	23	19

January 1st
CLYDE (2) 2 — CELTIC (3) 3
Anderson (6), — Chalmers 2 (35, 45),
McFarlane (43) — McBride (38)

CLYDE: Wright; Glasgow, Soutar; Anderson, Fraser, McHugh; McFarlane, Hood, Staite, Stewart, Hastings

CELTIC: Simpson; Cattenach, Gemmell; Murdoch, McNeill, Brogan; Lennox, Chalmers, McBride, Auld, Hughes

Attendance: 15,000

January 2nd
CELTIC (1) 2 — RANGERS (0) 2
Auld (18), Murdoch (78) — Johnston (55),
Johansen (88)

CELTIC: Fallon; Gemmell, Cattenach; Brogan, McNeill, Clark; Johnstone, Murdoch, Hughes, Lennox, Auld (Quinn)

RANGERS: Sorensen; Johansen, Greig; Jardine, McKinnon, D. Smith; Penman, Watson (A. Smith), Hynd, Johnston, Persson

Attendance: 75,000

Rangers were harassed above all by Johnstone's tortuous dribbling. With 12 minutes remaining Celtic scored the goal they thought was the winner. Brogan found Murdoch in the area, and he drove a magnificent left-foot shot away from Sorensen. With only 2 minutes remaining Rangers scored an equaliser when Fallon blundered by allowing a speculative drive from Johansen to pass under his body.

January 20th
HIBERNIAN (0) 0 — CELTIC (2) 2
Duncan o.g. (2), Lennox (18)

HIBERNIAN: Wilson; Duncan (Cousin), Davis; Stanton, Madsen, McGraw; Marinello, Quinn, Stein, Cormack, Scott

CELTIC: Simpson; Cattenach, Gemmell; Murdoch, McNeill, Clark; Johnstone (Auld), Wallace, Chalmers, Lennox, Hughes

Attendance: 38,077

February 3rd
CELTIC (2) 4 — PARTICK THISTLE (0) 1
Lennox 2 (17, 21), McKinnon o.g. (49), Gemmell (65 pen) — O'Neill (57)

CELTIC: Simpson; Craig, Gemmell; Murdoch, McNeill, Clark; Johnstone, Wallace, Hughes, Auld, Lennox

PARTICK THISTLE: Niven; Campbell, Muir; O'Neill, McKinnon, Gibb; Rae, Roxburgh, Coulston, Flanagan, Gallagher

Attendance: 27,000

February 10th
MOTHERWELL (0) 0 — CELTIC (1) 1
Hughes (27)

MOTHERWELL: McCloy; Whiteford, McKay; Campbell, Martis, McCallum; Wilson, McInally, Deans, McCall, Murray

CELTIC: Simpson; Craig, Gemmell; Murdoch, McNeill, Clark; Johnstone, Wallace, Hughes (Chalmers), Auld, Lennox

Attendance: 20,000

February 14th
CELTIC (1) 2 — STIRLING ALBION (0) 0
Gemmell (16 pen), Wallace (60)

CELTIC: Simpson; Craig, Gemmell; Murdoch, McNeill, Clark; Johnstone, Wallace, Hughes, Gallagher, Lennox

STIRLING ALBION: Murray; Reid, Corrigan; Henderson, Rogerson, McKinnon; McPhee, Smith, Lynn, Peebles, Hall

Attendance: 17,000

February 24th: Simpson, Gemmell, McNeill, Hughes and Lennox were in the Scotland team which drew 1-1 with England in a European Nations Qualifier at Hampden Park. Hughes scored Scotland's goal.

March 2nd
KILMARNOCK (0) 0 — CELTIC (3) 6
Wallace 4 (2, 16, 72, 89), Lennox (42), Quinn (87)

KILMARNOCK: McLaughlin; Arthur, McFadzean; Rodman, McGrory, Beattie; McLean, Queen, Morrison, Gilmour, Cameron

CELTIC: Simpson; Gemmell, O'Neill; Murdoch (Quinn), McNeill, Brogan; Johnstone, Lennox, Wallace, Gallagher, Hughes

Attendance: 14,000

League positions

	P	W	D	L	F	A	Pts
1 Rangers	24	21	3	0	67	21	45
2 CELTIC	23	19	3	1	67	18	41
3 Hibernian	24	15	3	6	50	29	33
4 Dunfermline	24	11	5	8	46	30	27
5 Kilmarnock	26	11	5	10	48	48	27

March 6th
CELTIC (4) 4 — ABERDEEN (0) 1
Lennox 3 (3, 30, 35), McNeill (7) — Johnston (70)

CELTIC: Simpson; Gemmell, O'Neill; Murdoch, McNeill, Brogan; Johnstone, Lennox, Wallace, Gallagher (Hay), Hughes

ABERDEEN: Clark; Whyte, Shewan; Petersen, McMillan, Murray; Johnston, Smith, Watt, Buchan, Craig

Attendance: 28,000

March 13th
CELTIC (2) 4 — AIRDRIE (0) 0
Lennox (22), Wallace 3 (28, 48, 73)

CELTIC: Simpson; Craig, Gemmell; Murdoch, McNeill, Brogan; Johnstone, Gallagher, Wallace, Lennox, Hughes (Chalmers)

AIRDRIE: McKenzie; Jonquin, Keenan; Goodwin, Black, Whiteford; Madden, Ramsey, McPheat, Jarvie, Phillips

Attendance: 17,000

March 16th
FALKIRK (0) 0 — CELTIC (1) 3
Gemmell (20 pen), Wallace (49), Lennox (52)

FALKIRK: Devlin; Lambie, Hunter; Markie, Baillie, Gibson; McManus, Scott, Graham, McLaughlin, Watson

CELTIC: Simpson; Craig, Gemmell; Murdoch, McNeill, Brogan; Johnstone, Lennox, Wallace, Gallagher, Hughes

Attendance: n.a.

March 23rd
CELTIC (1) 5 RAITH ROVERS (0) 0
Wallace 3 (16, 70, 76),
Hughes (51), Lennox (54)

CELTIC: Simpson; Craig, Gemmell; Murdoch, McNeill, Brogan; Johnstone, Lennox, Wallace, Gallagher (Chalmers), Hughes

RAITH ROVERS: Reid; Hislop, Gray (Sneddon); Stein, Polland, Millar; Wilson, Falconer, Wallace, Judge, Gillespie

Attendance: 22,500

March 25th
ST JOHNSTONE (0) 1 CELTIC (3) 6
McPhee (74) Lennox 4 (4, 35, 44, 73),
Johnstone (78),
Wallace (89)

ST JOHNSTONE: Robertson; McGillivray, Coburn; Ryden, Rooney, McPhee; MacDonald, Gordon, Wilson, McCarry, Aitken

CELTIC: Simpson; Craig, Gemmell; Murdoch, McNeill, Brogan; Johnstone, Lennox, Wallace, Gallagher, Hughes

Attendance: 12,000

March 30th
DUNDEE UNITED (0) 0 CELTIC (2) 5
Johnstone (13),
Lennox 2 (35, 73),
Wallace (70),
Cattenach (89)

DUNDEE UNITED: Davie; Rolland, Cameron; Neilson, Smith, Wood; Seeman, Millar, Mitchell, Gillespie, Wilson

CELTIC: Simpson; Craig, Gemmell; Murdoch, McNeill, Brogan; Johnstone, Lennox, Wallace, Gallagher (Cattenach), Hughes

Attendance: 20,000

April 6th
HEARTS (0) 0 CELTIC (2) 2
Johnstone (29),
Lennox (38)

HEARTS: Cruikshank; Sneddon, Mann; Anderson, Thomson, Miller; J. Fleming, G. Fleming, Ford, Irvine, Traynor

CELTIC: Simpson; Craig, Gemmell; Murdoch, McNeill, Brogan; Johnstone, Lennox, Wallace, Gallagher, Hughes

Attendance: 27,000

April 10th
ABERDEEN (0) 0 CELTIC (0) 1
Lennox (60)

ABERDEEN: Clark; Whyte, Shewan; Petersen, McMillan, Buchan; Little, Smith, Johnston, Robb, Watson

CELTIC: Simpson; Craig, Gemmell; Murdoch, McNeill, Brogan; Johnstone, Lennox, Wallace, Gallagher, Hughes

Attendance: 25,000

April 13th
CELTIC (3) 5 DUNDEE (1) 2
Lennox 2 (4, 58), Scott (38),
Hughes 2 (9, 53), G. McLean (64)
Stewart o.g. (18)

CELTIC: Simpson; Craig, Gemmell; Murdoch, McNeill, Brogan; Johnstone, Lennox, Wallace, Gallagher, Hughes

DUNDEE: Donaldson; R. Wilson, Swan; Murray, Easton, Stewart; Campbell, J. McLean, S. Wilson, G. McLean, Scott

Attendance: 41,500

April 20th
CELTIC (1) 2 MORTON (1) 1
Wallace (14), Mason (45)
Lennox (90)

CELTIC: Simpson; Craig, Gemmell; Murdoch, McNeill, Brogan; Johnstone, Lennox, Wallace, Gallagher, Hughes

MORTON: Crawford; Thorup, Sweeney; Arnetoft, Strachan, Rankin; Jensen, Gray, Mason, Allan, Taylor

Attendance: 51,000

April 30th
DUMFERMLINE (1) 1 CELTIC (0) 2
Gardner (27) Lennox 2 (47, 72)

DUNFERMLINE: Martin; W. Callaghan, Lunn; McGarty, Barry, T. Callaghan; Lister, Paton, Gardner, Robertson, Edwards

CELTIC: Simpson; Craig, Gemmell; Murdoch, McNeill, Brogan; Johnstone, Lennox, Wallace, Gallagher, Hughes

Attendance: 30,000

Two of the Lisbon 'Lions', Jimmy Johnstone and Steve Chalmers.

Scottish First Division

	P	W	D	L	F	A	Pts
1 CELTIC	34	30	3	1	106	24	63
2 Rangers	34	28	5	1	93	34	61
3 Hibernian	34	20	5	9	67	49	45
4 Dunfermline	34	17	5	12	64	41	39
5 Aberdeen	34	16	5	13	63	38	37
6 Morton	34	15	6	13	57	53	36
7 Kilmarnock	34	13	8	13	59	57	34
8 Clyde	34	15	4	15	55	55	34
9 Dundee	34	13	7	14	62	59	33
10 Partick Thistle	34	12	7	15	51	67	31
11 Dundee United	34	10	11	13	53	72	31
12 Hearts	34	13	4	17	56	61	30
13 Airdrie	34	10	9	15	45	58	29
14 St Johnstone	34	10	7	17	43	52	27
15 Falkirk	34	7	12	15	36	50	26
16 Raith Rovers	34	9	7	18	58	86	25
17 Motherwell	34	6	7	21	40	66	19
18 Stirling Albion	34	4	4	26	29	105	12

May 1st: Ian Young and Chris Shevlane were given free transfers.

LEAGUE CUP

August 12th
CELTIC (0) 1 DUNDEE UNITED (0) 0
Johnstone (90)

CELTIC: Simpson; Craig, Gemmell; Murdoch, McNeill, Clark; Johnstone, Wallace, Chalmers, Auld, Lennox

DUNDEE UNITED: Mackay; T. Millar, Briggs; J. Millar, Smith, Wood; Berg, Gillespie, Hainey, Graham, Wilson

Attendance: 54,000

August 16th
RANGERS (0) 1 CELTIC (1) 1
Penman (88) Gemmell (38 pen)

RANGERS: Sorensen; Johansen, Provan; Jardine, McKinnon, Greig; Henderson, Penman, Ferguson, D. Smith, Persson

CELTIC: Simpson; Craig, Gemmell; Murdoch, McNeill, Clark; Johnstone, Wallace, Chalmers, Auld, Lennox

Attendance: 94,168

Although Rangers had most of the pressure and enough scoring chances to win the game, Celtic performed magnificently in defence. With just 2 minutes remaining Penman, who had earlier failed to score with a penalty kick, brought the Ibrox house down when he rammed the ball home directly from a free-kick awarded some 25 yards from goal.

August 19th
CELTIC (0) 3 ABERDEEN (0) 1
Gemmell (48 pen), Storrie (77)
Lennox (71, Auld (88 pen)

CELTIC: Simpson; Craig, Gemmell; Murdoch, McNeill, Clark; Johnstone, Wallace, Chalmers, Auld, Lennox

ABERDEEN: Clark; Whyte, Shewan; Munro, McMillan, Petersen; P. Wilson, Storrie, Robb, Buchan, Johnston

Attendance: 50,000

August 26th
DUNDEE UNITED (0) 0 CELTIC (0) 1
Lennox (60)

DUNDEE UNITED: Mackay; T. Millar, Briggs; J. Millar, Smith, Wood; Berg, Gillespie, Hainey, Mitchell, Wilson

CELTIC: Simpson; Craig, Gemmell; Murdoch, McNeill, Clark; Johnstone, Gallagher, Wallace, Auld, Lennox

Attendance: 30,000

August 30th
CELTIC (0) 3 RANGERS (1) 1
Wallace (78), Henderson (8)
Murdoch (83),
Lennox (89)

CELTIC: Simpson; Craig, Gemmell; Murdoch, McNeill, Clark; Johnstone, Wallace, Chalmers, Auld, Lennox

RANGERS: Sorensen; Johansen, Provan; Jardine, McKinnon, Greig; Henderson, Penman, Ferguson, D. Smith, Johnston

Attendance: 75,000

With 12 minutes to go Rangers were grimly holding onto their lead, but then came 3 Celtic goals in a rush. As vast empty spaces appeared on the terracing Lennox nipped in between hesitant Rangers defenders and cooly clipped in No 3. A Johnasen penalty miss for Rangers before Celtic scored was probably crucial to the outcome.

September 2nd
ABERDEEN (1) 1 CELTIC (2) 5
Smith (8) Gemmell (16 pen),
McMahon (32),
Johnstone (63),
Auld (87), Craig (89)

ABERDEEN: Clark; Whyte, Shewan; Petersen, McMillan, Buchan; J. Wilson, Munro, Storrie, Smith, Taylor

CELTIC: Simpson; Craig, Gemmell (Auld); Clark, McNeill, O'Neill; Johnstone, Wallace, Murdoch, McMahon, Lennox

Attendance: 23,000

League Cup Section table

	P	W	D	L	F	A	Pts
CELTIC	6	5	1	0	14	4	11
Rangers	6	3	2	1	10	5	8
Dundee United	6	1	1	4	7	8	3
Aberdeen	6	0	2	4	5	19	2

Quarter-Final First Leg September 13th
CELTIC (3) 6 AYR UNITED (1) 2
Lennox 2 (11, 22), Black 2 (30, 67)
Johnstone 2 (29, 68),
Murdoch (77),
McMahon (84)

CELTIC: Simpson; Gemmell, O'Neill (Cattenach); Murdoch, McNeill, Clark; Johnstone, McMahon, Wallace, Lennox, Hughes

AYR UNITED: Stewart; Malone, Murphy; Quinn, Monan, Walker; McMillan, Mitchell, Ingram, Hawkshaw, Black

Attendance: 26,000

Quarter-Final Second Leg September 27th
AYR UNITED (0) 0 CELTIC (1) 2
Brogan (17), Wallace (90)

AYR UNITED: Stewart; Quinn, Murphy; Thomson, Monan, Walker; McMillan, Mitchell, Ingram, Hawkshaw, Black

CELTIC: Fallon; Shevlane, O'Neill; Cattenach, McNeill, Brogan; Wallace, Gallagher, McBride, Auld (Macari), Hughes

Attendance: n.a. McBride missed a penalty. Celtic won 8-2 on aggregate.

Semi-Final at Hampden Park October 11th
CELTIC (5) 7 MORTON (1) 1
Hughes 2 (4, 66), Arnetoft (12)
Wallace (7),
Johnstone (18),
Lennox (20),
Craig 2 (21, 53)

CELTIC: Simpson; Craig, Gemmell; Murdoch, McNeill, Clark; Johnstone, Lennox, Wallace, Auld, Hughes. Sub: Chalmers

MORTON: Crawford; Loughlan, Kennedy; Arnetoft, Strachan, Gray; Jensen, Allan, Mason, Stevenson, Sweeney. Sub: Taylor

Attendance: 45,662

A goal ahead in 4 minutes, 2 up in 7, Celtic proceeded to completely demoralise Morton. It was left to Hughes, the game's outstanding attacker, to complete the scoring in 66 minutes with a glorious goal. He ran some 50 yards with the ball, shaking off one challenge after another before hammering it into the net.

Final at Hampden Park October 28th
CELTIC (2) 5 DUNDEE (1) 3
Chalmers 2 (6, 73), G. McLean 2 (23, 84),
Hughes (10), Lennox (79), J. McLean (77)
Wallace (88)

CELTIC: Simpson; Craig, Gemmell; Murdoch, McNeill, Clark; Chalmers, Lennox, Wallace, Auld (O'Neill), Hughes

DUNDEE: Arrol; Wilson, Houston; Murray, Stewart, Stuart; Campbell, J. McLean, Wilson, G. McLean, Bryce. Sub: Cox (not used)

Attendance: 66,600 *Referee:* R. H. Davidson (Airdrie)

Although beaten, Dundee took a lot of credit from the game. Two goals down after only 10 minutes – Chalmers and Hughes having scored spectacularly – the Dens Park team took fresh heart midway in the 1st half. 6 minutes from the end George McLean tricked McNeill and Craig before shooting past Simpson. Any hope Dundee had of snatching an equalising goal was however dispelled 2 minutes from the end when Chalmers and Wallace, running shoulder to shoulder, took full advantage of a slip-up in Dundee's defence and Wallace slipped the ball into an unguarded net. On several occasions Celtic's defence was caught flat-footed and indecisive, and it was obvious there would have to be a tightening up in the rear if the club were to return victorious from South America.

SCOTTISH CUP

First Round January 27th
CELTIC (0) 0 DUNFERMLINE (0) 2
Robertson (64),
Gardner (74)

CELTIC: Simpson; Cattenach, Gemmell; Murdoch, McNeill, Brogan; Johnstone, Wallace, McBride (Chalmers), Auld, Hughes

DUNFERMLINE: Martin; W. Callaghan, Lunn; Fraser (Hunter), Barry, Thomson; Edwards, Paton, Gardner, T. Callaghan, Robertson

Attendance: 47,000

EUROPEAN CUP

First Round First Leg September 20th
CELTIC (0) 1 DYNAMO KIEV (2) 2
Lennox (62) Pusach (4),
Bychevetz (29)

CELTIC: Simpson; Craig, Gemmell; Murdoch, McNeill, Clark; Johnstone, Wallace, Chalmers, Auld, Lennox

DYNAMO KIEV: Rudakov; Schegolkov, Sosnichin; Levchenko, Sabo, Krulikovsky; Turvanchik, Bychevetz, Medvid, Serebrianikov, Pusach

Attendance: 54,000

Celtic's worst display for many a long day led to unexpected defeat. A crowd of 54,000 saw an unsteady, easily penetrated rearguard, fumbling play at wing-half and an uninspired forward line. McNeill and Gemmell were out of touch and only Clark of the defence emerged with any credit. For practically the whole of the 2nd half Celtic set up camp in Kiev's half, but it would have been an injustice had they managed to snatch the match from the well-drilled Russians at the 11th hour.

First Round Second Leg October 4th
DYNAMO KIEV (0) 1 CELTIC (0) 1
Bychevetz (90) Lennox (61)

DYNAMO KIEV: Bannikov; Schegolkov, Sosnichin; Levchenko, Krulikovsky, Turvanchik; Bychevetz, Sabo, Medvid, Serebrianikov, Pusach

CELTIC: Simpson; Craig, Gemmell; Murdoch, McNeill, Clark; Johnstone, Lennox, Wallace, Auld, Hughes

Attendance: 85,000

Although Celtic fought hard, Kiev were obviously told to concentrate on defence. They played carefully and studiously throughout the 1st half and at half-time Celtic had failed to get a goal. In 59 minutes they suffered a shattering blow when Murdoch, who earlier had been cautioned, was ordered from the field for throwing the ball away in temper after his side had been penalised. That left Celtic a depleted side with only 31 minutes left to play and with 2 goals to score. Incredibly 2 minutes later they did, a free-kick by Auld being screwed into the net from a near-impossible angle by Lennox. Celtic now needed only 1 more goal to win the match and a Hughes goal was disallowed for a foul on the goalkeeper. When Bychevetz scored in the last minute Celtic had lost the Cup after the shortest possible tenure of office as European champions. Dynamo Kiev won 3-2 on aggregate.

WORLD CLUB CHAMPIONSHIP FINAL

First Leg at Hampden Park October 18th

CELTIC (0) 1 RACING CLUB (Argentina) (0) 0

McNeill (69)

CELTIC: Simpson; Craig, Gemmell; Murdoch, McNeill, Clark; Johnstone, Lennox, Wallace, Auld, Hughes

RACING: Cejas; Perfumo, Dias; Martin, Mori, Basile; Raffo, Rulli, Cardenas, Rodriguez, Maschio

Attendance: 90,000 *Referee:* J. Gardeazabal (Spain)

Celtic deservedly won their duel with Racing Club but the display of the Argentinians was a pointed reminder that it would take an extraordinary performance for Celtic to win on alien soil. Racing came to Hampden with no ambition other than to gain a draw – relying on massed defence to keep their goal intact and they were not too particular how they did so. In 69 minutes McNeill once again came to his side's rescue. Cejas pushed a shot from Hughes round the post and from the corner Hughes found the head of McNeill whose header flew into the far corner of the net.

November 1st

RACING CLUB (1) 2 CELTIC (1) 1

Raffo (33), Cardenas (48) Gemmell (22 pen)

RACING: Cejas; Perfumo, Chabay; Martin, Rulli, Basile; Raffo, Cardoso, Cardenas, Rodriguez, Maschio

CELTIC: Fallon; Craig, Gemmell; Murdoch, McNeill, Clark; Johnstone, Wallace, Chalmers, O'Neill, Lennox

Attendance: 120,000 *Referee:* E. Marinho (Uruguay)

Celtic lost goalkeeper Simpson seconds before the kick-off after he was felled by a missile from the crowd. The incident touched off pandemonium on the field with officials, players and photographers crowding around the goalkeeper who was finally led off holding his head, Fallon taking over in goal. Celtic, to their credit, did not play for a draw, and they stayed on the attack. Racing were the better team in the 2nd half and Celtic had Fallon to thank for saving them going further behind. The result meant that there would have to be a play-off in Montevideo, Uruguay.

Play-off in Montevideo November 5th

RACING CLUB (0) 1 CELTIC (0) 0

Cardenas (55)

RACING: Cejas; Perfumo, Chabay; Martin, Rulli, Basile; Cardoso, Maschio, Cardenas, Rodriguez, Raffo

CELTIC: Fallon; Craig, Gemmell; Murdoch, McNeill, Clark; Johnstone, Lennox, Wallace, Auld, Hughes

Attendance: 75,000 *Referee:* R. P. Osorio (Paraguay)

The future of the World Club Championship was cast in deep shadow after Racing beat Celtic with a goal by Cardenas in 55 minutes in a brutally fought match in which 6 players were sent off and police were twice called in to restore order on the field of play. Not a happy experience for anyone connected with the club.

APPEARANCES	League	League Cup	Scottish Cup	European Cup	World Club Champ
Simpson	33	9	1	2	1
Shevlane	2	1	–	–	–
Gemmell	34	9	1	2	3
Murdoch	34	9	1	2	3
McNeill	34	10	1	2	3
Clark	18	9	–	2	3
Chalmers	13+3S	5	0+1S	1	1
McMahon	2	2	–	–	–
Wallace	29	10	1	2	3
Auld	19+1S	8+1S	1	2	2
Lennox	28	9	–	2	3
Cattenach	4+2S	1+1S	1	–	–
Johnstone	29	8	1	2	3
Craig	22	8	–	2	3
Hughes	31+1S	4	1	1	2
O'Neill	6	3+1S	–	–	1
Brogan	18+1S	1	1	–	–
McBride	4+3S	1	1	–	–
Fallon	1	1	–	–	2
Gallagher	13	2	–	–	–
Quinn	0+2S	–	–	–	–
Hay	0+1S	–	–	–	–
Macari	–	0+1S	–	–	–

GOALSCORERS

League: Lennox 32, Wallace 21, Chalmers 9, Hughes 7, Murdoch 6, Auld 5, Johnstone 5, McNeill 5, McBride 4, Gemmell 4 (4 pens), Own Goals 4, McMahon 1, Quinn 1, Cattenach 1, Brogan 1

League Cup: Lennox 7, Johnstone 5, Wallace 4, Hughes 3, Craig 3, Gemmell 3 (3 pens), Murdoch 2, McMahon 2, Chalmers 2, Auld 2 (1 pen), Brogan 1

European Cup: Lennox 2

World Club Championship: McNeill 1, Gemmell 1 (pen)

The Celtic staff in Season 1968-69 pose for the camera. Back row: Brogan, McGrain, McBride, Cattanach, Connelly, Fallon, Simpson, Gallagher, Quinn, John Clark, Dalglish, O'Neill. Middle row: Wraith, Hughes, Hay, Craig, Jacky Clarke, Gemmell, McKellar, Murdoch, Murray, Chalmers, Livingstone. Front row: McMahon, Johnstone, Macari, Wallace, Davidson, McNeill, Wilson, Lennox, Jim Clarke, Auld and Gorman. The three trophies are the Glasgow Cup, the League Championship Cup and the Scottish League Cup.

Season 1968-69

In another glory-filled season Celtic won their 2nd treble and their 6th League and Cup double. They won their 4th consecutive Championship and were again trailed home by Rangers who had beaten them in both League encounters – 2 of only 3 defeats all season. They showed no signs of a drop in their high standards and added Tom Callaghan and Harry Hood to an already impressive player pool. Joe McBride left for Hibs, after almost 3½ years of valuable service. The form of Johnstone and Hughes throughout the season was phenomenal and both underlined their reputations as world-class players. Captain Billy McNeill was the only player to appear in all 34 matches and Willie Wallace finished as top scorer with 18 goals. Bobby Murdoch was named as Scotland's Player of the Year. Chairman Robert Kelly received a knighthood in the New Year's honours list.

Hibernian were destroyed in the long-delayed League Cup Final. Celtic, missing Hughes but inspired by Auld, were 6 goals up in 75 minutes before relaxing near the end to win the trophy for the 4th season in a row.

The Scottish Cup was won for the 20th time. In the Final against Rangers, Celtic were deprived of the services of both Johnstone and Hughes but they went on to thrash Rangers with their fine play and ruthless finishing. Young George Connelly, playing in his first-ever Scottish Cup tie, scored a fine goal just before half-time and was many people's man of the match.

Celtic led the protests against the Soviet bloc countries following the invasion of Czechoslovakia, and as a result the First Round draw which had paired them with Ferencvaros of Hungary was eventually scrapped and re-drawn. The Iron Curtain countries eventually withdrew from the competition in protest. The re-draw paired Celtic with St Etienne of France. Celtic eventually running out 4-0 winners against the best French team in years. Celtic went on to blitz Red Star of Belgrade 5-1 in Glasgow and returned from Belgrade with an impressive 1-1 draw to reach the quarter-finals. In atrocious conditions in Milan, Celtic held out for an impressive no-scoring draw against Italian Champions, A.C. Milan, in the San Siro Stadium where Hughes was particularly impressive. A rare slip-up by McNeill gave Prati an early goal in the return in Glasgow, and hard as they tried for the remaining 78 minutes, Celtic could not penetrate the massed Italian defence in which Anquiletti and Schnellinger were outstanding. It was little consolation when A.C. Milan went on to win the Cup against Ajax of Amsterdam in Madrid.

League:	Champions
League Cup:	Winners
Scottish Cup:	Winners
European Cup:	Quarter-Finalists

SCOTTISH FIRST DIVISION

July 27th: Jackie Clarke was signed for Shamrock Rovers.

September 7th
CLYDE (0) 0 CELTIC (1) 3
Brogan (25), Lennox (80), Gemmell (84 pen)

CLYDE: McCulloch; Glasgow, Mulheron; Burns, Fraser, McHugh; McFarlane, Hood, Staite, Stewart, McGregor

CELTIC: Simpson; Craig, Gemmell; Brogan, McNeill, Clark; Johnstone, Chalmers, Lennox, McBride, Connelly, Hughes

Attendance: 26,000

September 14th
CELTIC (1) 2 RANGERS (2) 4
Wallace 2 (28, 66) Johnston 2 (17, 89), Penman (65), Persson (15)

CELTIC: Simpson; Gemmell, O'Neill; Brogan, McNeill, Clark; Johnstone, Lennox, Wallace, Connelly (Chalmers), Hughes

RANGERS: Martin; Jackson, Mathieson; Greig, McKinnon, Hynd; Henderson, Penman, Jardine, Johnston, Persson

Attendance: 75,000

This was Rangers' 1st victory in an Old Firm match for exactly 12 months and their first at Parkhead since New Year's Day 1964, with Celtic having to give best to Penman and Greig in midfield. Rangers' strikers, Persson and Johnston, enjoyed a field day, Gemmell having an uncomfortable afternoon gainst the powerful Swede. Johnston produced several mesmeric runs.

September 21st
DUNFERMLINE (1) 1 CELTIC (0) 1
Fraser (33) Johnstone (66)

DUNFERMLINE: Martin; W. Callaghan, Lunn; Fraser, Barry, Renton; Robertson, Paton, Edwards, Gardner, Lister

CELTIC: Simpson; Craig, Gemmell; Murdoch, McNeill, Brogan; Johnstone, Wallace, Chalmers, Lennox, Hughes

Attendance: 25,000

September 28th
CELTIC (1) 2 ABERDEEN (1) 1
Connelly (2), Lennox (75) Rae (19)

CELTIC: Simpson; Craig, Gemmell; Murdoch, McNeili, Brogan; Johnstone, Lennox, Wallace, Connelly, Hughes

ABERDEEN: Clark; Hermiston, Shewan; Petersen, McMillan, Craig; Rae, Robb, Forrest, Smith, Taylor

Attendance: 37,000

October 5th
CELTIC (0) 2 DUNDEE UNITED (0) 0
Murdoch (48), Gemmell (81)

CELTIC: Simpson; Craig, Gemmell; Murdoch, McNeill, Clark; Johnstone (Connelly), Wallace, Chalmers, McBride, Hughes

DUNDEE UNITED: Makay; Rolland, Cameron; Gillespie, Smith, Wood; Hogg, Reid, K. Cameron, Mitchell, Wilson

Attendance: 46,000

Johnstone was substituted by Connelly. He was later suspensed for 7 days by the club for remarks to the dug-out on the way off.

October 12th
HEARTS (0) 0 CELTIC (0) 1
Chalmers (76)

HEARTS: Cruikshank; Sneddon, Mann; Townsend, E. Thomson, MacDonald; Ford, Traynor, Moller, Hamilton, G. Fleming

CELTIC: Simpson; Craig, Gemmell; Clark, McNeill, Brogan; Connelly, Wallace, McBride, Chalmers, Lennox

Attendance: 34,000

October 16th: Gemmell and Lennox were in the Scotland team which beat Denmark 1-0 in Copenhagen. Lennox scored the only goal.

October 19th
CELTIC (1) 2 ST JOHNSTONE (0) 1
Lennox (22), McNeill (50) W. Coburn (69)

CELTIC: Simpson; Craig, Gemmell; Clark, McNeill, Brogan; Johnstone, Connelly, Chalmers, Lennox, Hughes

ST JOHNSTONE: Robertson; Miller, Coburn; Gordon, Rooney, Rennie; Aird, Ryden, MacDonald, Whitelaw, Aitken

Attendance: 37,000

October 26th
MORTON (0) 1 CELTIC (1) 1
Harper (64) McBride (38)

MORTON: Russell; Thorup, Sweeney; Arnetoft, Gray, Rankin; Harper, Stevenson, Mason, Allan, Taylor

CELTIC: Simpson; Craig, Gemmell; Murdoch, McNeill, Brogan; Johnstone, McBride, Wallace, Lennox, Hughes

Attendance: 23,000

League positions

	P	W	D	L	F	A	Pts
1 CELTIC	8	5	2	1	14	8	12
2 St Mirren	8	3	5	0	10	6	11
3 Dundee United	8	5	1	2	15	11	11
4 Dunfermline	8	5	1	2	12	10	11
5 Rangers	8	4	2	2	17	12	10

November 2nd
CELTIC (2) 3 DUNDEE (1) 1
Johnstone (9), Chalmers 2 (17, 51) Campbell (32)

CELTIC: Simpson; Craig, Gemmell; Murdoch, McNeill, Brogan; Johnstone, Wallace, Chalmers, Lennox, Hughes

DUNDEE: Donaldson; Wilson, Houston; Murray, Easton, Stewart; Campbell, McLean, Gilroy, Kinninmonth, Scott

Attendance: 37,000

November 5th: Joe McBride joined Hibernian as a replacement for Colin Stein.

November 6th: Simpson, Gemmell, Johnstone, Lennox and Hughes were all in the Scotland team which beat Austria 2-1 in a World Cup qualifier at Hampden Park.

November 9th
ARBROATH (0) 0 CELTIC (2) 5
Chalmers 3 (12, 61, 89),
McNeill (15)
Wallace (53)

ARBROATH: Williamson; Booth, Riddle; Kennedy, Stirling, Hughes (Cant); Sellars, Reid, Jack, Bruce, Wilkie

CELTIC: Fallon; Craig, Gemmell; Murdoch, McNeill, Brogan; Johnstone, Wallace, Chalmers, Lennox (Auld), Hughes

Attendance: n.a.

November 16th
CELTIC (1) 2 RAITH ROVERS (0) 0
Murdoch 2 (11, 74)

CELTIC: Fallon; Craig, Gemmell; Murdoch, McNeill, Brogan; Johnstone, Lennox, Wallace, Auld, Hughes

RAITH ROVERS: Reid; Hislop, Gray; Miller, Polland, Bolton; Wilson, Falconer, Wallace, Sneddon, Gillespie

Attendance: 31,000. Goalkeeper Reid was ordered off for fouling Lennox

November 22nd: Tom Callaghan was signed from Dunfermline Athletic for £35,000.

November 23rd
PARTICK THISTLE (0) 0 CELTIC (2) 4
Hughes 2 (14, 68),
Callaghan (22),
Lennox (84)

PARTICK THISTLE: Ritchie; Campbell, McLindon; McParland, Gray, Hansen; Cunningham, Flanagan, Divers (Cumming), Bone, Duncan

CELTIC: Fallon; Craig, Gemmell; Murdoch, McNeill, Brogan; Johnstone, Lennox, Chalmers (Wallace), Callaghan, Hughes

Attendance: 29,300

November 30th
HIBERNIAN (1) 2 CELTIC (1) 5
McBride (23), Gemmell (8 pen),
Davis (74 pen) McNeill (79),
Hughes 2 (80, 84),
Lennox (82)

HIBERNIAN: Wilson; Shevlane, Davis; Cousin, Stanton, O'Rourke; Scott, Quinn, McBride, Cormack, Stevenson

CELTIC: Fallon; Craig, Gemmell; Murdoch, McNeill, Brogan; Johnstone, Callaghan, Wallace, (Chalmers), Lennox, Hughes

Attendance: 34,988

December 7th
CELTIC (0) 5 ST MIRREN (0) 0
Chalmers 2 (46, 63)
Johnstone (59),
Hughes (68),
Gemmell (78 pen)

CELTIC: Fallon; Craig, Gemmell; Murdoch, McNeill, Brogan; Johnstone, Lennox, Chalmers, Callaghan, Hughes (Wallace)

ST MIRREN: Connaghan; Murray, Connell; Fulton, McFadden, Murray; Adamson, Pinkerton (Hainey), Kane, Blair, Gilshan

Attendance: 47,000

December 11th: Bobby Murdoch scored 2 goals for Scotland in a 5-0 win over Cyrpus in Nicosia in a World Cup Qualifier.

December 14th
FALKIRK (0) 0 CELTIC (0) 0

FALKIRK: Rennie; Lambie, Hunter; Smith, Markie, Miller; Marshall, McLaughlin, Young, Gibson, Watson

CELTIC: Fallon; Craig, Gemmell; Murdoch, McNeill, Brogan; Johnstone, Lennox, Wallace, Callaghan, Hughes

Attendance: 17,000

December 21st
CELTIC (1) 1 KILMARNOCK (0) 1
Chalmers (35), McIlroy (60)

CELTIC: Fallon; Craig, Gemmell; Murdoch, McNeill, Brogan; Johnstone, Callaghan, Chalmers, Auld, Hughes

KILMARNOCK: McLaughlin; King, Dickson; Gilmour, McGrory, Beattie; McLean, Queen, Morrison, J. McLean, McIlroy

Attendance: 40,000

December 28th
AIRDRIE (0) 0 CELTIC (0) 0

AIRDRIE: McKenzie; Jonquin, Keenan; Goodwin, Black, Whiteford; Wilson, Fyfe, Mashall, McPheat, Jarvie

CELTIC: Fallon; Craig, Gemmell; Murdoch, McNeill, Brogan; Johnstone, Wallace, Hughes, Chalmers, Lennox

Attendance: 22,000

League positions

	P	W	D	L	F	A	Pts
1 CELTIC	17	11	5	1	39	12	27
2 Dundee United	17	11	3	3	32	21	25
3 Kilmarnock	17	10	4	3	31	16	24
4 Dunfermline	17	10	3	4	36	25	23
5 Rangers	16	9	4	3	37	18	22

January 1st: Celtic Chairman, Robert Kelly was knighted in the New Year's Honours List.

January 1st
CELTIC (3) 5 CLYDE (0) 0
Callaghan 2 (19, 40),
Gemmell (36 pen),
Wallace (78),
Lennox (80)

CELTIC: Fallon; Craig, Gemmell; Murdoch, McNeill, Brogan (Auld); Johnstone, Lennox, Wallace, Callaghan, Hughes

CLYDE: Wright; Glasgow, Mulheron; Anderson, Fraser, McHugh; McFarlane, Hood, Staite (Soutar), Burns, Hastings

Attendance: 31,000

January 2nd
RANGERS (0) 1 CELTIC (0) 0
Greig (60 pen)

RANGERS: Martin; Johansen, Provan (Jardine); Greig, McKinnon, Watson; Henderson, Penman, Stein, Johnston, Persson

CELTIC: Fallon; Craig, Gemmell; Brogan, McNeill, Clark; Johnstone, Murdoch, Wallace (Chalmers), Lennox, Hughes

Attendance: 85,000. 50 people were hurt when a barrier on a stairway collapsed. 24 had to be taken to hospital.

The goal came after exactly an hour's play, Greig scoring from the spot after McNeill had allegedly deflected a Henderson shot with a hand. In the opening minutes McNeill had to produce 2 brilliant tackles to frustrate the goal-hungry Stein.

January 4th
CELTIC (2) 3 DUNFERMLINE (1) 1
Wallace 2 (1, 9), Edwards (20)
Lennox (64)

CELTIC: Fallon; Craig, Gemmell; Murdoch, McNeill, Brogan; Hughes, Wallace, Chalmers, Callaghan, Lennox (Johnstone)

DUNFERMLINE; Duff; Callaghan, Lunn; Fraser, Barry, Renton; Robertson, Paton, Edwards, Gardner, Mitchell (Cowan)

Attendance: 43,500

January 9th: Jimmy Quinn was temporarily transferred to Clyde.

January 11th
ABERDEEN (0) 1 CELTIC (2) 3
Forrest (79) Hughes (3),
Wallace (7),
Boel o.g. (62)

ABERDEEN: McGarr; Whyte, Shewan; Petersen, Boel, Murray; Johnston, Smith, Forrest, Robb, Craig

CELTIC: Simpon; Craig, Gemmell; Murdoch, McNeill, Brogan; Johnstone, Callaghan, Wallace, Lennox, Hughes

Attendance: 31,000

January 18th
DUNDEE UNITED (0) 1 CELTIC (1) 3
Mitchell (80) Lennox (20),
Hughes (84),
McMahon (89)

DUNDEE UNITED: Mackay; Rolland, J. Cameron; Gillespie (Reid), Smith, Wood; Hogg, Millar, K. Cameron, Mitchell, Wilson

CELTIC: Simpson; Craig, Gemmell; Murdoch, McNeill, Brogan; Johnstone (McMahon), Callaghan, Wallace, Lennox, Hughes

Attendance: 23,000

February 1st
CELTIC (1) 5 HEARTS (0) 0
Lennox (13),
Wallace (55),
Murdoch (68),
Johnstone (77),
Brogan (89)

CELTIC: Simpson; Craig, Gemmell; Murdoch, McNeill, Brogan; Johnstone, Lennox, Wallace, Chalmers, Auld

HEARTS: Cruickshank; Holt, McAlpine; Anderson, E. Thomson, A. Thomson; Traynor, Hamilton, Ford, G. Fleming (MacDonald), Jensen

Attendance: 37,000

League positions

	P	W	D	L	F	A	Pts
1 CELTIC	23	16	5	2	58	16	37
2 Kilmarnock	26	13	9	4	43	26	35
3 Dunfermline	25	15	4	6	51	33	34
4 Rangers	22	14	5	3	51	21	33
5 Dundee United	23	13	4	6	43	36	30

March 5th
CELTIC (4) 7 ARBROATH (0) 1
Wallace 3 (7, 17, 46), Bruce (89)
Chalmers 2 (9, 55),
Johnstone (16),
Hughes (48)

CELTIC: Fallon; Craig, Gemmell; Murdoch (Auld), McNeill, Brogan; Johnstone, Wallace, Chalmers, Callaghan, Hughes

ARBROATH: Williamson; Booth, Hughes; Cargill, Stirling, Reid; Sellars, Cant, Jack, Bruce, Wilkie (Kennedy)

Attendance: 20,000

March 8th
RAITH ROVERS (0) 1 CELTIC (0) 3
Wallace (46) Wallace 2 (63, 88),
Auld (80)

RAITH ROVERS: Reid; McDonald, Gray; Millar, Polland, Bolton; Cunningham, Falconer, Wallace, Sneddon (Judge), Wilson

CELTIC: Fallon; Craig, Gemmell; Murdoch, McNeill, Brogan; Johnstone, Lennox, Wallace, Callaghan (Auld), Hughes

Attendance: 16,000

March 15th

CELTIC (1) 1	PARTICK THISTLE (0) 0
Hughes (42)	

CELTIC: Fallon; Craig, Gemmell; Murdoch, McNeill, Brogan; Johnstone, Chalmers, Wallace, Auld, Hughes

PARTICK THISTLE: Ritchie; Gray, McLindon; McParland, McKinnon, O'Neill; Coulston, Hansen, Flanagan, Bone, Duncan

Attendance: 29,000

March 16th: Harry Hood was signed from Clyde for £40,000.

March 24th

CELTIC (1) 1	HIBERNIAN (0) 1
Wallace (14)	McBride (73)

CELTIC: Fallon; Craig, O'Neill; Murdoch, McNeill, Brogan; Johnstone, Lennox, Wallace, Auld, Hughes

HIBERNIAN: Allan; Shevlane, Davis; Blackley, Madsen, Stanton; Marinello, McGraw (Grant), McBride, Cormack, Stevenson

Attendance: 30,000

March 29th

ST MIRREN (0) 0	CELTIC (1) 3
	Craig (41),
	Hughes (54),
	Hood (69)

ST MIRREN: Thorburn; Murray (Blair), Connell; Fulton, Young, Murray; Adamson, Urquhart, Kane, Pinkerton, Gilshan

CELTIC: Fallon; Craig, Gemmell; Murdoch, McNeill, Brogan; Johnstone, Hood, Wallace, Lennox, Hughes (Callaghan)

Attendance: 24,000

April 1st

ST JOHNSTONE (0) 2	CELTIC (2) 3
Hall (8),	Wallace (67),
Connelly (42)	Gemmell (75),
	Hood (90)

ST JOHNSTONE: Robertson; Miller, Coburn; Gordon, Rooney, McPhee; Aird (Rennie), Hall, McCarry, K. Wilson, Connelly

CELTIC: Fallon; Craig, Gemmell; Murdoch, McNeill, Brogan; Johnstone, Hood, Wallace, Lennox, Hughes (Clark)

Attendance: 13,000

April 9th

CELTIC (2) 5	FALKIRK (0) 2
Wallace 2 (25 pen, 88)	McLaughlin 2 (60, 72)
Hood (30),	
Lennox 2 (70, 81)	

CELTIC: Fallon; Craig, O'Neill; Murdoch, McNeill, Clark; Johnstone, Hood, Wallace, Auld (Callaghan), Lennox

FALKIRK: Rennie; Lambie, J. Hunter; Gibson, Markie, Miller; Graham, Smith, I. Hunter, McLaughlin, Watson

Attendance: 24,000

April 16th: Gemmell, Murdoch, Johnstone and Lennox were in the Scotland team which drew 1-1 with West Germany in a World Cup Qualifier at Hampden Park. Murdoch scored Scotland's goal.

April 19th

CELTIC (1) 2	AIRDRIE (0) 2
Gemmell (42 pen),	McPheat (55),
Lennox (79),	Marshall (67)

CELTIC: Fallon; Craig, Gemmell; Murdoch, McNeill, Brogan; Johnstone, Hood, Wallace, Auld, Lennox

AIRDRIE: McKenzie; Jonquin, Caldwell; Goodwin, Black, Whiteford; Bird, Fyfe, Marshall, McPheat, Wilson

Attendance: 34,000

April 21st

KILMARNOCK (2) 2	CELTIC (0) 2
Morrison (8),	Beattie o.g. (63),
Queen (30)	Gemmell (90)

KILMARNOCK: McLaughlin; King, Dickson; Evans, McGrory, Beattie; T. McLean, Queen, Morrison, J. McLean, McIlroy

CELTIC: Fallon; Craig, Gemmell; Murdoch, McNeill, Clark; Johnstone, Callaghan (Lennox), Wallace, Chalmers, Hood

Attendance: 18,000

April 21st: Jimmy Johnstone was suspended to the 6th of May and missed the Scottish Cup Final.

April 28th

CELTIC (1) 2	MORTON (3) 4
Wallace (6),	Bartram 3 (4, 5, 10),
Hood (64),	Harper (48)

CELTIC: Fallon; Cattenach, Gemmell; Murdoch, McNeill, Clark; Connelly (Callaghan), Chalmers, Wallace, Hood, Auld

MORTON: Neilsen; Ferguson, Kerr; Sweeney, Gray, Strachan; Coakley, Allan, Rankin, Harper (Mason), Bartram

Attendance: 31,000

April 20th; Bobby Murdoch was named Scotland's player of the year

April 30th
DUNDEE 1 — CELTIC 2
Murdoch o.g. — Macari, Hood

DUNDEE: Donaldson; Wilson, Swan; Murray, Easton, Houston; Steele, Scott, Gilroy, Kinninmonth, Bryce

CELTIC: Fallon; Craig, O'Neill; Murdoch, McNeill, Clark; Chalmers, Wallace, Hood, Auld, Macari
Attendance: n.a.

Scottish First Division

	P	W	D	L	F	A	Pts
1 CELTIC	34	23	8	3	89	32	54
2 Rangers	34	21	7	6	81	32	49
3 Dunfermline	34	19	7	8	63	45	45
4 Kilmarnock	34	15	14	5	50	32	44
5 Dundee United	34	17	9	8	61	49	43
6 St Johnstone	34	16	5	13	66	59	37
7 Airdrie	34	13	11	10	46	44	37
8 Hearts	34	14	8	12	52	54	36
9 Dundee	34	10	12	12	47	48	32
10 Morton	34	12	8	14	58	68	32
11 St Mirren	34	11	10	13	40	54	32
12 Hibernian	34	12	7	15	60	59	31
13 Clyde	34	9	13	12	35	50	31
14 Partick Thistle	34	9	10	15	39	53	28
15 Aberdeen	34	9	8	17	50	59	26
16 Raith Rovers	34	8	5	21	45	67	21
17 Falkirk	34	5	8	21	33	69	18
18 Arbroath	34	5	6	23	41	82	16

May 2nd: Celtic freed McMahon and Wraith.

May 3rd: Gemmell, McNeill and Murdoch were in the Scotland team which beat Wales 5-3 in Wrexham. McNeill scored Scotland's opening goal.

May 6th: Gemmell and Murdoch were in the Scotland team which drew 1-1 with Northern Ireland at Hampden Park.

May 10th: Gemmell, Murdoch and McNeill were in the Scotland team beaten 4-1 by England at Wembley. Wallace came on as a substitute for Alan Gilzean.

May 12th: Gemmell and McNeill were in the Scotland team which beat Cyprus 8-0 at Hampden Park. Both players scored.

May 13th: Willie O'Neill joined Carlisle for £10,000.

May 17th: Aberdeen failed in a bid to sign John Clark after the clubs had agreed terms.

May 19th: Celtic announced that Charlie Gallagher would be free to join another club.

LEAGUE CUP

August 10th
RANGERS (0) 0 — CELTIC (2) 2
Wallace 2 (9, 35)

RANGERS: Martin; Jackson, Mathieson; Greig, McKinnon, D. Smith; Henderson, A. Smith, Penman, Ferguson, Persson

CELTIC: Simpson; Gemmell, O'Neill; Murdoch, McNeill, Brogan; Connelly (Clark), Johnstone, Wallace, Lennox, Hughes
Attendance: 80,000

Greig's mistakes led to Celtic's 2 goals but Simpson had 3 phenomenal saves in the 2nd half and Hughes once headed off his own goal-line.

August 14th
CELTIC (2) 4 — MORTON (0) 1
Wallace (16), Hughes (21), Murdoch (50), Gemmell (69 pen) — Mason (67)

CELTIC: Simpson; Gemmell, O'Neill; Murdoch, McNeill, Brogan (Macari); Johnstone, Connelly, Wallace, Lennox, Hughes

MORTON: Russell; Thorup, Rankin; Arnetoft, Strachan (Harper), Gray; Stevenson, Allan, Mason, Sweeney, Taylor
Attendance: 41,000

August 17th
CELTIC (3) 4 — PARTICK THISTLE (0) 0
Wallace 4 (3, 28, 43, 75)

CELTIC: Simpson; Gemmell, O'Neill; Murdoch, McNeill, Brogan; Johnstone, Connelly (Auld), Wallace, Lennox, Hughes

PARTICK THISTLE: Ritchie; Cumming, Brown; Cunningham, McKinnon, O'Neill; McLindon, Bone, Coulston, Flanagan, Duncan
Attendance: 46,000

August 24th
CELTIC (0) 1 — RANGERS (0) 0
Wallace (55)

CELTIC: Simpson; Gemmell, O'Neill; Murdoch, McNeill, Brogan; Johnstone, Connelly, Wallace, Lennox, Hughes

RANGERS: Martin; Jackson, Mathieson; Greig, McKinnon, Hynd; Penman, Ferguson, Johnston, D. Smith, Persson
Attendance: 75,000

The game had gone 30 minutes when crudeness began to rear its ugly head, Jackson bringing down Lennox with a crushing tackle. Celtic deserved to win: what technique, ability and attacking ideas were on view belonged almost entirely to them, and but for some splendid goalkeeping by Martin they might have scored sooner than they did. He even saved a penalty by Gemmell awarded in 73 minutes when Mathieson rashly upended Wallace near the bye-line.

August 28th
MORTON (0) 0 — CELTIC (2) 3
Wallace (8), Lennox (33), Hughes (63)

MORTON: Crawford; Thorup, Loughlan; Arnetoft, Rankin, Gray; Bartram, Allan, Mason, Sweeney, Taylor

CELTIC: Fallon; Gemmell, O'Neill; Murdoch, McNeill, Brogan; Johnstone, Lennox, Wallace, Connelly, Hughes

Attendance: 25,000

August 31st
PARTICK THISTLE (0) 1 CELTIC (2) 6
O'Neill (74) Lennox 5 (15 sec, 46, 65, 78, 83), Cumming o.g. (8)

PARTICK THISTLE: Ritchie; Cumming, McLindon; McParland, McKinnon, O'Neill; Gallagher, Hansen, Bone, Flanagan, Duncan

CELTIC: Fallon; Craig, O'Neill; Murdoch, McNeill, Brogan; Johnstone, Lennox, Wallace, Connelly, Hughes

Attendance: 25,000

League Cup Section Table

	P	W	D	L	F	A	Pts
CELTIC	6	6	0	0	20	2	12
Rangers	6	4	0	2	14	5	8
Partick Thistle	6	2	0	4	8	18	4
Morton	6	0	0	6	2	19	0

Quarter-Final First Leg September 11th
CELTIC (4) 10 HAMILTON ACADEMICALS (0) 0
Chalmers 5 (26, 43, 61, 75, 87),
Lennox 5 (27, 37, 80, 83, 88)

CELTIC: Simpson; Craig, Gemmell; Brogan, McNeill, Clark; Macari, Lennox, McBride, Chalmers, Hughes (Johnstone)

HAMILTON: Lamont; Halpin, Hunter; Fraser, Small, Gaughan; Lawlor, Gilchrist, Thomson, Wardrope, Clifford

Attendance: 26,000

Quarter-Final Second Leg September 25th
HAMILTON ACADEMICALS (1) 2 CELTIC (2) 4
Lawlor (23), Halpin (79) McBride 2 (5, 56), McMahon (43), Clark (50)

HAMILTON: Lamont; Halpin, Hunter; Fraser, Small, Gaughan; Goodwin, Lawlor, Thomson (Gilchrist), Wardrope, Clifford

CELTIC: Wraith; Craig, Gorman; Connelly, Hay, Clark; McMahon, McBride, Quinn, Gallagher (Dalglish), Macari

Attendance: 4,000. Celtic won 14-2 on aggregate.

Semi-Final at Hampden Park October 9th
CELTIC (0) 1 CLYDE (0) 0
Connelly (75)

CELTIC: Simpson; Craig, Gemmell; Murdoch, McNeill, Brogan; Lennox, Wallace, Chalmers, McBride (Connelly), Hughes

CLYDE: Wright; Glasgow, Mulheron; Anderson, Fraser, McHugh; McFarlane, Hood, Staite (Stewart), Burns, Hastings

Attendance: 34,676

With the breaks going Clyde's way early in the game a sensational result did not appear out of the question. Simpson saved well from Hood in 8 minutes and shortly after the same player headed just wide from a Hastings cross. Celtic's forwards were having difficulty in striking a profitable game against Clyde's well-organised defence, and even when chances arose Wallace, Lennox and McBride in turn squandered them. Celtic switched Hughes and Lennox at the start of the 2nd half and in 75 minutes Hughes squared the ball from near the bye-line and Connelly, who had come on for McBride, promptly hammered it high into the net for a spectacular goal. Such was the valour of Clyde's performance that the issue remained in doubt till the final whistle.

Final at Hampden Park April 5th
CELTIC (3) 6 HIBERNIAN (0) 2
Wallace (23), Auld (30), Lennox 3 (45, 58, 73), Craig (75) O'Rourke (82), Stevenson (87)

CELTIC: Fallon; Craig, Gemmell (Clark); Murdoch, McNeill, Brogan; Johnstone, Wallace, Chalmers, Auld, Lennox

HIBERNIAN: Allan; Shevlane, Davis; Stanton, Madsen, Blackley; Marinello, Quinn, Cormack, O'Rourke, Stevenson. Sub: Hunter

Attendance: 74,000 *Referee:* W. M. Syme (Glasgow)

Not only did Celtic record their 4th consecutive League Cup triumph, but as Rangers slumped to an inglorious defeat at Tannadice Park Celtic were virtually assured of the League Championship for the 4th successive season. It took them 20 minutes to take Hibs' measure. Once they had done so there was no holding them. With Hughes out through injury Celtic took the opportunity to field their European Cup-winning attack and as in Lisbon two years previously they were well nigh unstoppable and Auld more than any other made this Celtic machine click. Hibs scored 2 late goals to make the score-line slightly more respectable.

SCOTTISH CUP

First Round January 25th
PARTICK THISTLE (0) 3 CELTIC (1) 3
Bone 2 (6, 89), Flanagan (71) Hughes (40), Wallace (56), Murdoch (62)

PARTICK THISTLE: Ritchie; Campbell, Gray; Hansen, McKinnon, O'Neill; McLindon, McParland, Flanagan, Bone, Duncan

CELTIC: Simpson; Craig, Gemmell; Murdoch, McNeill, Brogan; Johnstone, Callaghan, Wallace, Lennox, Hughes
Attendance: 35,867

First Round Replay January 29th
CELTIC (4) 8 PARTICK THISTLE (1) 1
McNeill (8), Gemmell o.g. (34)
Johnstone (12),
Wallace (23),
Callaghan 2 (44, 62),
Lennox (51),
Hughes (55),
Gemmell (76)

CELTIC: Simpson; Craig, Gemmell; Murdoch (Chalmers), McNeill, Brogan; Johnstone, Lennox, Wallace, Callaghan, Hughes

PARTICK THISTLE: Ritchie; Campbell, Gray; Hansen, McKinnon, O'Neill; McLindon, McParland, Flanagan, Bone, Duncan
Attendance: 48,000

Second Round February 12th
CLYDE (0) 0 CELTIC (0) 0

CLYDE: Wright; Glasgow, Mulheron; Anderson, Staite, McHugh; McFarlane, Hood, Quinn, Burns, Hastings

CELTIC: Simpson (Gemmell); Craig, Gemmell (Auld); Murdoch, McNeill, Brogan; Johnstone, Lennox, Wallace, Callaghan, Chalmers
Attendance: 25,000

Simpson had to go off with a dislocated shoulder and Gemmell had to go in goal for nearly all of the game.

Second Round Replay February 24th
CELTIC (1) 3 CLYDE (0) 0
Chalmers (24),
Hughes (74),
Murdoch (83)

CELTIC: Fallon; Gemmell, O'Neill; Murdoch, McNeill, Hay; Johnstone (Callaghan), Lennox, Wallace, Chalmers, Hughes

CLYDE: Wright; Glasgow, Mulheron; Anderson, Staite, McHugh; McFarlane (Stewart), Hood, Quinn, Burns, Hastings
Attendance: 38,000. Gemmell missed a penalty

Third Round March 1st
CELTIC (1) 3 ST JOHNSTONE (0) 2
Hughes (2), Connolly (59),
Lennox (75), Hall (85)
Chalmers (79)

CELTIC: Fallon; Craig, Gemmell; Murdoch, McNeill, Clark; Johnstone, Lennox, Wallace, Chalmers, Hughes

ST JOHNSTONE: Robertson; Miller, Coburn; Gordon, Rooney, McPhee; Aird, Hall, McCarry, Connolly, Aitken
Attendance: 39,000

Semi Final at Hampden Park March 22nd
CELTIC (2) 4 MORTON (1)
Wallace (12), Allan (2)
McNeill (43),
Chalmers (56),
Johnstone (65)

CELTIC: Fallon; Craig, Gemmell; Murdoch, McNeill, Brogan; Johnstone, Wallace, Chalmers, Auld (Callaghan), Hughes

MORTON: Neilsen; Ferguson, Rankin (Mason); Jensen, Gray, Strachan; Coakley, Allan, Harper, Sweeney, Bartram
Attendance: 48,349

After Morton scored in the 2nd minute Celtic settled down and drew level in the 12th minute, after which there was not much doubt that they would qualify for the Final. But the Greenock side contributed much to the entertainment of the afternoon. The standard of play was high and the sportsmanship excellent.

Final at Hampden Park April 26th
CELTIC (3) 4 RANGERS (0) 0
McNeill (2),
Lennox (44),
Connelly (45),
Chalmers (76)

CELTIC: Fallon; Craig, Gemmell; Murdoch, McNeill, Brogan (Clark); Connelly, Chalmers, Wallace, Lennox, Auld

RANGERS: Martin; Johansen, Mathieson; Greig, McKinnon, D. Smith; Henderson, Penman, Ferguson, Johnston, Persson. Sub: Jardine
Attendance: 132,870 *Referee:* J. Callaghan (Glasgow)

Celtic, with ruthless professionalism, took heavy toll of their opponents' defensive blunders and technical naïvety. In the 1st half tackles were intimidating, even brutal. The wonder of it all was that the game finished with 11 men in each team. This was Rangers' 1st defeat in a Scottish Cup Final for 40 years.

EUROPEAN CUP

First Round First Leg September 18th
ST ETIENNE (France) (2) 2 CELTIC (0) 0
Keita (15), Revelli (37)

ST ETIENNE: Carnus; Durkovic, Camerini; Mitoraj, Bosquier, Jacquet; Fefeu, Herbin, Revelli, Keita, Bereta

CELTIC: Simpson; Craig, O'Neill; Brogan, McNeill, Clark; Johnstone, Connelly, Wallace, Lennox, Hughes
Attendance: 34,000

Celtic, without Gemmell and Murdoch, were in grave trouble at half-time when they were down 0-2. They made a determined effort to knock off at least one of the goals in the 2nd half but they were foiled by Carnus who played brilliantly.

First Round Second Leg October 2nd
CELTIC (1) 4 ST ETIENNE (0) 0
Gemmell (45 pen),
Craig (59),
Chalmers (67),
McBride (87)

CELTIC: Simpson; Craig, Gemmell; Murdoch, McNeill, Brogan; Johnstone, Wallace, Chalmers, McBride, Hughes

ST ETIENNE: Carnus; Durkovic, Camerini; Mitoraj, Bosquier, Herbin; Fefeu, Jacquet, Revelli, Keita, Bereta
Attendance: 75,000

Until Gemmell scored with a penalty-kick just before the interval when McBride was brought down the issue seemed wide open. The goal was the tonic Celtic needed and Craig equalised the aggregate in the 59th minute. Anxiety vanished 8 minutes later when Chalmers, on the goal-line, whipped the ball into the net after Johnstone had completely foxed the French defence with a mazy run and in the dying minutes McBride capped his fine performance with an opportunist goal from close range. Johnstone was the architect of Celtic's victory. McNeill was a pillar of strength, cutting out dangerous balls with complete assurance, and behind him were two adventurous full-backs. Goalkeeper Simpson also had a great game, pulling off three fine saves. Celtic won 4-2 on aggregate.

Second Round First Leg November 13th
CELTIC (1) 5 RED STAR (Yugoslavia) (1) 1
Murdoch (3), Johnstone 2 (47, 81), Lennox (50), Wallace (75)
Lazervic (39)

CELTIC: Fallon; Craig, Gemmell; Murdoch, McNeill, Brogan; Johnstone, Wallace, Chalmers, Lennox, Hughes

RED STAR: Durkovic, Djoric, Krivocuka, Pavlovic, Dojcinovski; Klenkovski, Antonijevic, Ostojic, Lazervic, Acimovic, Ozajic
Attendance: 67,000

Few would disagree that it was the performances of Johnstone and Murdoch which saw Celtic through. 9 minutes from the end – running onto a long pass from Murdoch – Johnstone tore past all opposition and lashed the ball into the net for the most spectacular goal of the night.

Second Round Second Leg November 27th
RED STAR (0) 1 CELTIC (0) 1
Ostojic (88) Wallace (76)

RED STAR: Durkovic; Dokic, Krivocuka; Pavlovic, Dojcinovski, Klenkovski (Karadvic); Antonijevic, Ostojic, Lazervic, Acimovic, Dzajic

CELTIC: Fallon; Craig, Gemmell; Brogan, McNeill, Clark; Connelly, Lennox, Chalmers (Wallace), Murdoch, Hughes
Attendance: 40,000

Celtic won their way into the Quarter-Finals with almost impudent ease. Manager Stein said before the match that he was going to play this match on purely defensive lines, and his players held Red Star in total check right until 2 minutes from the end. Celtic won 6-2 on aggregate.

Third Round First Leg February 19th
A.C. MILAN (0) 0 CELTIC (0) 0

A.C. MILAN: Cudicini; Anquilletti, Schnellinger; Rosato, Malatrasi, Trapattoni; Hamrin (Rognani), Lodetti, Sormani, Rivera, Prati

CELTIC: Fallon; Craig, Gemmell; Clark, McNeill, Brogan (Auld); Johnstone, Murdoch, Wallace, Lennox, Hughes
Attendance: 72,402

In a snow blizzard Celtic got exactly the result they wanted for the Second Leg – a no-scoring draw.

Third Round Second Leg March 12th
CELTIC (0) 0 A. C. MILAN (1) 1
Prati (12)

CELTIC: Fallon; Craig, Gemmell; Clark, McNeill, Brogan (Auld); Johnstone, Wallace, Chalmers, Murdoch, Hughes

A.C. MILAN: Cudicini; Anquilletti, Schnellinger; Maldera, Malatrasi, Rosato; Hamrin, Lodetti, Prati, Rivera, Scala
Attendance: 75,000

Celtic were tense from the start and failed to establish any lasting rhythm to their game. Once Milan had snatched the psychologically important 1st goal they settled down to an Italian League-style defensive formation, using Prati as their sole spearhead. Celtic had several near misses and any number of shots blocked but there were rare glimpses of the incisiveness and ability to apply crushing pressure that had worn down many other sides. For this Anquilletti and Schnellinger, who changed places to mark Johnstone and Hughes, were very much responsible and the wingers were effectively blotted out. A. C. Milan won 1-0 on aggregate.

APPEARANCES	League	League Cup	Scottish Cup	European Cup
McNeill	34	9	7	6
Craig	32	5	6	6
Gemmell	31	8	7	5
Brogan	30	9	5	6
Johnstone	30+1S	7+1S	6	5
Murdoch	30	8	7	5
Wallace	29+1S	8	7	5+1S
Hughes	27	8	5	6
Lennox	27+1S	9	6	4
Fallon	22	3	4	4
Chalmers	17+4S	3	5+1S	4
Callaghan	12+3S	–	3+2S	–
Simpson	12	6	3	2
Auld	9+4S	1+1S	2+1S	0+2S
Clark	9+1S	2+2S	1+1S	4
Hood	7	–	–	–
Connelly	6+1S	7+1S	1	2
McBride	4	3	–	1
O'Neill	4	6	1	1
Cattenach	1	–	–	–
Macari	1	2+1S	–	–
McMahon	0+1S	1	–	
Hay	–	1	1	–

APPEARANCES	League	League Cup	Scottish Cup	European Cup
Gallagher	–	1	–	–
Wraith	–	1	–	–
Gorman	–	1	–	–
Quinn	–	1	–	–

GOALSCORERS: *League:* Wallace 18 (1 pen), Lennox 12, Chalmers 11, Hughes 10, Gemmell 8 (5 pens), Johnstone 5, Hood 5, Murdoch 4, Callaghan 3, McNeill 3, Brogan 2, Own Goals 2, Connelly 1, McBride 1, McMahon 1, Auld 1, Craig 1, Macari 1.

League Cup: Lennox 14, Wallace 10, Chalmers 5, Hughes 2, McBride 2, Auld 1, Craig 1, Murdoch 1, Gemmell 1 (pen), Clark 1, McMahon 1, Connelly 1, Own Goal 1.

Scottish Cup: Chalmers 4, Hughes 4, McNeill 3, Lennox 3, Wallace 3, Murdoch 2, Johnstone 2, Callaghan 2, Connelly 1, Gemmell 1.

European Cup: Johnstone 2, Wallace 2, Gemmell 1 (pen), Craig 1, Chalmers 1, McBride 1, Murdoch 1, Lennox 1.

The victorious Celtic players in the dressing-room after winning the 1967 League Cup, defeating Dundee 5-3 in the Final at Hampden Park.

Season 1969-70

Celtic just missed out on the domestic treble and, after beating Leeds United in the Semi-Final, reached the European Cup Final for the 2nd time only to lose to Holland's Feyenoord in extra-time in Milan

The Championship was won for the 25th time. They lost only 4 matches – 2 at home and 2 away – and took the title from Rangers by a massive 12 points. This was the 5th successive season that the Ibrox team had finished in the runners-up spot. Billy McNeill played in most matches (31) and Willie Wallace was top scorer with 16 of their 96 goals. Bertie Auld was runner-up to Hibs' Pat Stanton as Scotland's Player of the Year, and Manager Jock Stein received the C.B.E. for his outstanding achievements in the game. Veteran Ronnie Simpson announced his retirement at the end of the season at the age of 39.

Celtic overcame Rangers, Airdrie and Raith Rovers to win their League Cup Section. Their solitary defeat at Ibrox, by a Baxter-inspired Rangers, was their first in the competition for 4 years. Aberdeen were beaten 2-1 on aggregate in the Quarter-Finals and Ayr United provided a surprise package in the Semi-Final – twice going into the lead before a goal by Auld in Extra-Time earned Celtic a replay which they won despite losing Simpson with a shoulder injury 12 minutes from time. It was a goal from Auld in only 2 minutes which won the Cup for the 5th successive season against a very talented St Johnstone side.

Dunfermline, both Dundee clubs and Rangers were beaten in Celtic's run to the Scottish Cup Final. In the Final itself, Aberdeen were lucky to be ahead at half-time through a Joe Harper penalty but 2 goals from former Dundee winger Derek McKay in the last 8 minutes took the Cup to Pittodrie for the first time in 23 years.

League:	Champions
League Cup:	Winners
Scottish Cup:	Finalists
European Cup:	Finalists

SCOTTISH FIRST DIVISION

August 30th

CELTIC (1) 2	ST JOHNSTONE (1) 2
Chalmers (38), Hood (63)	McCarry (23), Aitken (57)

CELTIC: Fallon; Craig, Gemmell; Brogan, McNeill, Clark; Johnstone, Connelly (Macari), Wallace, Hood, Chalmers

ST JOHNSTONE: Donaldson; Lambie, Cockburn; Gordon, Rooney, McPhee; Aird, Hall, McCarry, Connolly, Aitken

Attendance: 60,000

September 3rd

KILMARNOCK (1) 2	CELTIC (2) 4
Mathie (45), Morrison (85)	Wallace 2 (11, 63), Lennox 2 (23, 88)

KILMARNOCK: McLaughlin; King, Dickson; W. Waddell, Strachan, Beattie; T. McLean, Mathie, Morrison, J. McLean, Cook

CELTIC: Fallon; Craig, Gemmell; Murdoch, McNeill, Clark; Johnstone, Hood, Wallace, Chalmers, Lennox

Attendance: 25,000

September 6th

DUNFERMLINE (2) 2	CELTIC (0) 1
Gardner (10), Craig o.g. (20)	Gemmell (55)

DUNFERMLINE: Duff; Callaghan, Lunn; McGarty, Barry, Renton; Mitchell, Paton, Edwards, Gardner, McLean

CELTIC: Fallon; Craig, Gemmell; Murdoch, McNeill, Clark (Callaghan); Johnstone, Hood, Wallace, Chalmers, Lennox

Attendance: 25,000. Both Wallace and Renton were ordered off in the 12th minute.

September 13th
CELTIC (1) 1 — HIBERNIAN (0) 2
Johnstone (21) — Hamilton (48), Stanton (82)

CELTIC: Fallon; Hay, Gemmell; Murdoch, McNeill, Clark; Johnstone, Hood (Callaghan), Wallace, Chalmers, Lennox

HIBERNIAN: Marshall; Shevlane, Jones; Blackley, Black, Stanton; Marinello, Hamilton, McBride, Cormack, Stevenson

Attendance: 45,000

September 20th
RANGERS (0) 0 — CELTIC (0) 1
Hood (49)

RANGERS: Neef; Johansen, Provan; Greig, McKinnon, Baxter; Henderson, Jardine (Watson), Stein, Smith, Johnston

CELTIC: Fallon; Craig, Gemmell; Clark, McNeill, Brogan; Johnstone, Hood, Wallace, Hay, Lennox

Attendance: 75,000

In the 67th minute Johnston and Craig chased the ball unavailingly to the touchline and the winger was in the process of retrieving it for the throw-in when he was tackled from behind. Craig was immediately ordered off and Celtic were left to defend a 1 goal lead for 23 minutes a man short. Their first League win at Ibrox for 12 years.

September 27th
CELTIC (1) 2 — CLYDE (0) 1
Lennox 2 (39, 65) — Hay (55)

CELTIC: Fallon; Hay, Gemmell; Brogan, McNeill, Clark; Johnstone, Hood (Craig), Wallace, Lennox, Hughes

CLYDE: Wright; Glasgow, Soutar; Anderson, McHugh, Burns; McFarlane, Hay, McBride, Hulston, Hastings

Attendance: 35,000

October 4th
CELTIC (4) 7 — RAITH ROVERS (1) 1
Johnstone 2 (12, 20), Lennox 2 (36, 63), Wallace (38), Callaghan (65), Hughes (73) — Sinclair (42)

CELTIC: Simpson; Hay, Gemmell; Dalglish, McNeill, Clark; Johnstone (Hood), Lennox, Wallace, Callaghan, Hughes

RAITH ROVERS: Reid; Gray, Lindsay; D. Millar, Polland, Cooper; A. Millar (Bolton), Falconer, Sinclair, Brand, Gillespie

Attendance: 32,000

October 11th
AIRDRIE (0) 0 — CELTIC (1) 2
Chalmers (43), Wallace (68)

AIRDRIE: McKenzie; Jonquin, Caldwell; Goodwin, Delaney, D. Whiteford; Bird (J. Whiteford), Jarvie, Marshall, McPheat, Stewart

CELTIC: Simpson; Craig, Gemmell; Brogan, Connelly, Callaghan; Johnstone (Hughes), Hood, Wallace, Chalmers, Lennox

Attendance: 20,000. Ronnie Simpson was made captain for the day to celebrate his 39th birthday.

October 14th: Evan Williams was signed from Wolves for a moderate fee. He had been on loan to Aston Villa.

October 22nd: Gemmell, McNeill and Johnstone were in the Scotland team beaten 3-2 by West Germany in a World Cup Qualifier in Hamburg. Johnstone scored one of the goals. Gemmell was ordered off near the end for deliberately kicking Haller.

October 29th
ABERDEEN (1) 2 — CELTIC (1) 3
Fallon o.g (34), Robb (55) — Murdoch (5), Johnstone (78), Brogan (83)

ABERDEEN: McGarr; Boel, Kirkland; Hermiston, McMillan, Murray; Harper (Petersen), Robb, Forrest, Willoughby, McIlroy

CELTIC: Fallon; Craig, Hay; Murdoch, McNeill, Clark; Johnstone, Callaghan, Hughes, Hood (Brogan), Auld

Attendance: 25,000

November 1st
AYR UNITED (1) 2 — CELTIC (1) 4
Ingram 2 (26, 56) — Johnstone 2 (15, 53), Murdoch 2 (75, 90)

AYR UNITED: Stewart; Malone, Murphy; Fleming, Quinn, Mitchell; Young, Hood (McFadzean), Ingram, McCulloch, Rough

CELTIC: Fallon; Craig, Hay; Murdoch, McNeill, Brogan; Johnstone, Callaghan, Hughes, Macari, Auld

Attendance: 20,000

League positions

	P	W	D	L	F	A	Pts
1 Dundee United	10	7	2	1	19	13	16
2 Dunfermline	11	7	2	2	15	11	16
3 CELTIC	10	7	1	2	27	14	15
4 Hibernian	10	7	1	2	20	10	15
5 Motherwell	11	5	4	2	21	13	14

November 5th: Bobby Murdoch was in the Scotland team beaten 2-0 by Austria in the World Cup Qualifier in Vienna.

November 8th
CELTIC (0) 0 — HEARTS (2) 2
Jensen (36), Ford (42)

CELTIC: Fallon; Craig, Gemmell; Murdoch, McNeill, Brogan; Johnstone, Dalglish, Hughes, Macari, Callaghan

HEARTS: Cruikshank; Clunie, Oliver; MacDonald, Anderson, Thomson; Jensen, Miller, Ford, Brown (Fleming), Lynch

Attendance: 35,000

November 15th
MOTHERWELL (1) 1 — CELTIC (1) 2
Deans (38) — Hood (6), Hughes (74)

MOTHERWELL: McCloy; Campbell, Wark; Forsyth, McCallum, Goldthorpe; Murphy, McInally, Deans, Wilson, Muir

CELTIC: Fallon; Craig, Gemmell; Murdoch, McNeill, Clark; Johnstone, Hood, Wallace, Auld (Hay), Hughes

Attendance: 23,000

November 29th
MORTON (0) 0 — CELTIC (1) 3
Macari (8), Hood (78), Wallace (86)

MORTON: Neilson; Murray, Laughton; McDerment, Gray, Rankin; Collins, Sweeney, Osborne, Mason, O'Neill

CELTIC: Fallon; Hay, Gemmell; Murdoch, McNeill, Brogan; Johnstone (Auld), Hood, Wallace, Macari, Hughes

Attendance: 22,000

December 1st
CELTIC (1) 2 — ST MIRREN (0) 0
Macari 2 (45, 46)

CELTIC: Williams; Hay, Gemmell; Murdoch, McNeill, Brogan; Hughes, Hood, Wallace, Macari, Auld

ST MIRREN: Connaghan; C. Murray, Connell; Cumming, McFadden, E. Murray; Gilshan, Lister, McLaughlin, Blair, Fulton

Attendance: 23,000

December 7th
CELTIC (0) 1 — DUNDEE (0) 0
Gemmell (51 pen)

CELTIC: Fallon; Hay, Gemmell; Murdoch, McNeill, Brogan; Johnstone, Hood, Wallace, Macari, Auld

DUNDEE: Donaldson; Wilson, Houston; Murray, Easton, Selway; Gilroy (Campbell), Kinninmonth, Wallace, Scott, Steele

Attendance: 31,000

December 14th
ST JOHNSTONE (0) 1 — CELTIC (2) 4
Aird (60) — Wallace 2 (30, 36), Gemmell (47), Hood (50)

ST JOHNSTONE: Donaldson; Lambie, Coburn; Gordon, Rooney, McPhee; Aird, Hall, McCarry (Whitelaw), Connolly, Aitken

CELTIC: Fallon; Hay, Gemmell; Murdoch, McNeill, Brogan; Johnstone, Hood, Wallace, Auld, Hughes

Attendance: 15,500

December 17th
CELTIC (4) 7 — DUNDEE UNITED (1) 2
Auld (2), Hood (16), Gemmell (40 pen), Hughes (42), Wallace 2 (46, 52), Murdoch (74) — Mitchell (25 pen), Gordon (65)

CELTIC: Fallon; Hay, Gemmell; Murdoch, McNeill, Brogan; Johnstone, Hood, Wallace, Auld (Craig), Hughes

DUNDEE UNITED: Mackay; Rolland, J. Cameron; Gillespie, Smith, Henry (K. Cameron); Wilson, Reid, Gordon, Mitchell, Scott

Attendance: 26,000

December 20th
CELTIC (2) 3 — KILMARNOCK (1) 1
Gemmell (28 pen), Hughes 2 (31, 66) — Morrison (24)

CELTIC: Fallon; Hay, Gemmell (Craig); Murdoch, McNeill, Brogan; Johnstone, Hood, Wallace, Auld, Hughes

KILMARNOCK: McLaughlin; King, Dickson; Gilmour, McGrory, Beattie (Strachan); McLean, Morrison, Mathie, Waddell, Cook

Attendance: 35,000

December 27th
CELTIC (3) 8 — PARTICK THISTLE 1
Hughes 3 (17, 60, 80), Auld (26), McNeill (44), Wallace 2 (51, 77 pen), Campbell o.g. (85) — Smith

CELTIC: Williams; Craig, Hay; Murdoch, McNeill, Brogan; Johnstone, Hood (Lennox), Wallace, Auld, Hughes

PARTICK THISTLE: Ritchie; Campbell, Holt; Johnston, McKinnon (Gray), Hansen; Rae, Smith, Bone, Flanagan, Duncan

Attendance: 30,000

League positions

	P	W	D	L	F	A	Pts
1 CELTIC	19	15	1	3	57	22	31
2 Rangers	19	13	3	4	41	21	29
3 Hibernian	17	12	2	3	33	16	26
4 Dundee United	18	9	5	4	30	29	23
5 Dunfermline	19	9	4	6	24	22	22

January 1st
CLYDE (0) 0 — CELTIC (1) 2
Hughes (36), Macari (90)

CLYDE: McCulloch; E. Anderson, Soutar; S. Anderson (Stewart), McHugh, Beattie; Glasgow, McFarlane, Staite, Burns, McLean

CELTIC: Williams; Craig, Hay; Murdoch, McNeill, Brogan; Macari, Hood, Wallace, Auld, Hughes

Attendance: 26,000

January 3rd
CELTIC (0) 0 RANGERS (0) 0

CELTIC: Williams; Hay, Gemmell; Murdoch, McNeill, Brogan; Johnstone, Hood, Wallace, Auld, Hughes

RANGERS: Neef; Johansen, Mathieson; Greig, McKinnon, Smith; Henderson (Jardine), Penman, Stein, Johnston, MacDonald

Attendance: 72,000

Rangers and Celtic were subdued by the frost-bound conditions. As a spectacle the greatest club match in the world shrunk to ordinary proportions. Williams was probably the busier of the 2 goalkeepers and showed plenty of agility in cutting out high crosses and, in the 1st-half, in turning a Johansen lob over the bar. Rangers' unsuccessful transfer move on the eve of the match for Bobby Clark, the Aberdeen goalkeeper, must have had an inspiring effect on Gerry Neef who displayed great confidence throughout.

January 17th
HIBERNIAN (0) 1 CELTIC (1) 2
Duncan (52) McNeill (13), Hughes (86)

HIBERNIAN: Marshall; Shevlane, Schaedler; Blackley, Black, Stanton; Duncan, McEwan, McBride (Hamilton), Graham, Stevenson

CELTIC: Williams; Hay, Gemmell; Murdoch (Craig), McNeill, Brogan; Johnstone, Hood, Wallace, Auld, Hughes

Attendance: 40,839

January 31st
CELTIC (1) 3 DUNFERMLINE (0) 1
Wallace (44), Macari (52), Lennox (74) Gillespie (61)

CELTIC: Williams; Craig, Gemmell; Murdoch, McNeill, Brogan; Macari, Lennox, Wallace, Hay, Hughes

DUNFERMLINE: Arrol; Callaghan, Lunn; McNichol, McGarty, Gardner; McKimmie, McLaren, Mitchell, McLean, Gillespie

Attendance: 36,000

February 16th
PARTICK THISTLE (0) 1 CELTIC (3) 5
Rae (67) Hood (12), Johnstone (14), Gemmell 2 (32, 58 pen), Macari (89)

PARTICK THISTLE: Ritchie; Reid, Holt; Clark, Gray, Johnston (Hansen); Rae, Smith, Flanagan, Bone, Lawrie

CELTIC: Williams; Craig, Gemmell; Brogan, McNeill, Hay; Johnstone, Hood, Wallace (Macari), Lennox, Hughes

Attendance: 20,000

February 25th
RAITH ROVERS (0) 0 CELTIC (1) 2
McNeill (2), Gemmell (59)

RAITH ROVERS: Whiteside; Hislop, Weir; Cooper, Bolton, Sneddon; Wilson, McCarthy, Sinclair, McGuire, Brand

CELTIC: Williams; Craig, Gemmell; Hay, McNeill, Brogan; Johnstone, Macari, Wallace, Hood (Auld), Lennox

Attendance: 11,000

February 28th
CELTIC (2) 4 AIRDRIE (1) 2
Johnstone 2 (3, 79), Lennox (43), Wallace (86) Marshall (44), Cowan (53)

CELTIC: Williams; Craig, Gemmell; Hay (Hood), McNeill, Brogan; Johnstone, Lennox, Wallace, Callaghan, Macari

AIRDRIE: McKenzie; Jonquin, Caldwell (McPheat); Menzies, Delaney, Whiteford; Wilson, Jarvie, Marshall, Goodwin, Cowan

Attendance: 31,000

League positions

	P	W	D	L	F	A	Pts
1 CELTIC	26	21	2	3	75	27	44
2 Rangers	25	17	5	3	56	25	39
3 Hibernian	24	14	5	5	45	25	33
4 Hearts	26	10	10	6	39	28	30
5 Dundee United	26	12	6	8	48	49	30

March 7th
DUNDEE UNITED (0) 0 CELTIC (1) 2
McNeill 2 (41, 56)

DUNDEE UNITED: Mackay; Rolland, Cameron; Gillespie, Smith, Henry; Wilson, Scott, Gordon, Mitchell, Dunne

CELTIC: Williams; Hay, Gemmell; Murdoch (Auld), McNeill, Brogan; Johnstone, Hood, Wallace, Callaghan, Lennox

Attendance: 20,500

March 10th
CELTIC (0) 4 MORTON (0) 0
Ferguson o.g. (47), Auld (49), Macari (55), Lenox (59)

CELTIC: Williams; Hay, Gemmell; Callaghan, McNeill, Brogan; Johnstone, Macari, Wallace, Auld (Murdoch), Lennox

MORTON: Neilson; Murray (Anderson), Laughton; Ferguson, Gray, Rankin; Coakley, Lavelle, Osborne, Mason, Campbell

Attendance: 21,000

March 21st
CELTIC (0) 3 — AYR UNITED (0) 0
Lennox (50),
Wallace 2 (61, 63)

CELTIC: Williams; Craig, Gemmell; Connelly, McNeill (Murdoch), Brogan; Macari, Wallace, Hood, Callaghan, Lennox

AYR UNITED: Stewart; Malone, Murphy; Fleming, Quinn, Mitchell; Young, Ferguson, Hood, Aitken, McCulloch

Attendance: 27,000

March 25th
CELTIC (0) 1 — ABERDEEN (0) 2
Gemmell (88) — G. Murray (50), Graham (65)

CELTIC: Williams; Craig, Gemmell; Murdoch, McNeill, Brogan; Johnstone, Connelly, Wallace, Lennox, Auld

ABERDEEN: Clark; Boel, G. Murray; S. Murray, McMillan, Buchan; McKay, Hermiston, Robb, Willoughby, Graham

Attendance: 33,000

March 28th
HEARTS (0) 0 — CELTIC (0) 0

HEARTS: Cruikshank; Clunie, Oliver; Veitch, Anderson, Thomson; Traynor, Winchester, Irvine, Townsend, Moller (Ford)

CELTIC: Williams; Hay, Gemmell; Murdoch, Connelly, Brogan; Callaghan, Wallace, Quinn (Hood), Macari, Lennox

Attendance: 26,000. Celtic clinched the League title but were deprived of a victory by Jim Cruikshank who saved a penalty from Gemmell.

April 4th
CELTIC (4) 6 — MOTHERWELL (0) 1
Lennox 3 (1, 34, 49),
Wallace (20 pen),
Johnstone (42),
Murdoch (65) — Deans (82)

CELTIC: Williams; Hay, Craig; Murdoch, McNeill, Brogan; Johnstone (Macari), Connelly, Wallace, Lennox, Hughes

MOTHERWELL: MacRae; Wark, Heron (McCabe); Forsyth, McCallum, Donnelly; Wilson, Muir, Deans, McInally, Murphy

Attendance: 30,000

April 6th
DUNDEE (1) 1 — CELTIC (2) 2
Wallace (16) — Auld (2), Lennox (41)

DUNDEE: Donaldson; Selway, Houston; Kinninmonth, Easton, Stewart; Campbell, Bryce, Wallace, Scott, Steele

CELTIC: Fallon; Craig, Gemmell; Murdoch, McNeill, Hay; Callaghan, Lennox (Wallace), Hood, Auld, Hughes

Attendance: 13,000

April 18th
ST MIRREN (1) 2 — CELTIC (2) 3
Blair 2 (10, 86) — Hood (39), Davidson (41), Callaghan (46)

ST MIRREN: McGann; C. Murray, Connell; E. Murray, McFadden, McLaughlin; Gilshan (Fulton), Lister, Hamilton, Blair, Pinkerton

CELTIC: Williams; Craig, Gemmell; Murdoch (Cattenach), Connelly, Brogan; Hood, Davidson, Hughes, Callaghan, Lennox

Attendance: 25,000

Scottish First Division

	P	W	D	L	F	A	Pts
1 CELTIC	34	27	3	4	96	33	57
2 Rangers	34	19	7	8	67	40	45
3 Hibernian	34	19	6	9	65	40	44
4 Hearts	34	13	12	9	50	36	38
5 Dundee United	34	16	6	12	62	64	38
6 Dundee	34	15	6	13	49	44	36
7 Kilmarnock	34	13	10	11	62	57	36
8 Aberdeen	34	14	7	13	55	45	35
9 Morton	34	13	9	12	52	52	35
10 Dunfermline	34	15	5	14	45	45	35
11 Motherwell	34	11	10	13	49	51	32
12 Airdrie	34	12	8	14	59	64	32
13 St Johnstone	34	11	9	14	50	62	31
14 Ayr United	34	12	6	16	37	52	30
15 St Mirren	34	8	9	17	39	54	25
16 Clyde	34	9	7	18	34	56	25
17 Raith Rovers	34	5	11	17	32	67	21
18 Partick Thistle	34	5	7	22	41	82	17

April 18th: David Hay was in the Scotland team which beat Northern Ireland 1-0 in Belfast.

April 22nd: Hay was in the Scotland team which drew 0-0 with Wales at Hampden Park. Lennox made an appearance as substitute.

April 25th: Hay, Gemmell and Johnstone were in the Scotland team whcih drew 0-0 with England at Hampden Park.

May 1st: Charlie Gallagher was given a free transfer.

May 7th: After the European Cup Final Ronnie Simpson announced his retirement. His career stretched back to June 3, 1945 when he first played for Queens Park at Hampden Park.

May 21st: Celtic announced that they would listen to offers for Gemmell and Johnstone.

LEAGUE CUP

August 9th
CELTIC (4) 6 AIRDRIE (0) 1
Hughes 2 (19, 36), Marshall (64)
Wallace (28),
Connelly (35), Hood (77),
Gemmell (82)

CELTIC: Fallon; Hay, Gemmell; Murdoch, McNeill, Clark; Connelly, Hood, Wallace, Lennox, Hughes

AIRDRIE: McKenzie; Jonquin, Caldwell; Menzies, Keenan, Whiteford; Jarvie, Fyfe, Marshall, McPhear, Cowan

Attendance: 40,000

August 13th
RANGERS (0) 2 CELTIC (1) 1
Persson (48), Hood (8)
Johnston (50)

RANGERS: Neef; Johansen, Provan; Greig, McKinnon, Baxter; Johnston, Watson, Stein, Jardine, Persson

CELTIC: Fallon; Hay, Gemmell; Murdoch (Auld), McNeill, Clark; Connelly, Hood, Wallace, Lennox, Hughes

Attendance: 71,645

Rangers' equaliser, scored by Persson, and the leading goal nodded by Johnston from Greig's service after a Baxter free-kick inspired the home side. Masterminds in Rangers triumph were Baxter and Johnston. Once his team had snatched the lead Baxter took command.

August 16th
CELTIC (3) 5 RAITH ROVERS (0) 0
Wallace 2 (9, 63),
Hood (15), McNeill (16),
Hughes (80)

CELTIC: Fallon; Craig, Gemmell; Brogan, McNeill, Clark; Connelly, Hood (Chalmers), Wallace, Lennox, Hughes

RAITH ROVERS: Reid; Hislop, Gray; D. Millar, Davidson, Polland; A. Millar, Sneddon (Watt), Wallace, Sinclair, Wilson

Attendance: 37,000

August 20th
CELTIC (0) 1 RANGERS (0) 0
Gemmell (67)

CELTIC: Fallon; Craig, Gemmell; Murdoch, McNeill, Clark; Johnstone, Hood, Wallace, Lennox (Brogan), Hughes

RANGERS: Neef; Johansen, Provan; Greig, McKinnon, Smith; Henderson (Penman), Jardine, Stein, Johnston, Persson

Attendance: 70,000

A blunder by goalkeeper Neef cost Rangers this League Cup Sectional tie. He failed to hold the ball after Murdoch had taken a free-kick from the angle of the penalty area and Gemmell bobbed up to head into the net. It was a hard game in which the tackling by several players on both sides was less than scrupulous but it was great entertainment for the 70,000 crowd. Rangers lodged a protest about the standard of the refereeing in this match – they claimed that Celtic's John Hughes should have been ordered off for downing Willie Johnston in an off-the-ball incident.

August 23rd
AIRDRIE (0) 0 CELTIC (2) 3
Wallace (6), Lennox (24),
McNeill (50)

AIRDRIE: Clark; Jonquin, Caldwell; Goodwin, Whiteford, Menzies; Bird, Jarvie, Marshall, McPheat, Stewart

CELTIC: Fallon; Craig, Gemmell; Murdoch (Chalmers), McNeill, Clark; Johnstone, Hood, Wallace, Lennox, Hughes

Attendance: 21,000

League Cup Section table

	P	W	D	L	F	A	Pts
CELTIC	6	5	0	1	21	5	10
Rangers	6	4	1	1	14	7	9
Raith Rovers	6	1	1	4	10	20	3
Airdrie	6	1	0	5	5	18	2

Quarter-Final First Leg September 10th
ABERDEEN (0) 0 CELTIC (0) 0

ABERDEEN: McGarr; Boel, Hermiston; Murray, McMillan, Petersen; Rae, Robb, Forrest, Wilson, Hamilton

CELTIC: Fallon; Hay, Gemmell; Murdoch, McNeill, Clark; Hood, Chalmers, Wallace, Callaghan, Lennox

Attendance: 32,000

Quarter-Final Second Leg September 24th
CELTIC (0) 2 ABERDEEN (1) 1
Lennox (52), Wallace (54) Forrest (31)

CELTIC: Fallon; Hay, Gemmell; Brogan, McNeill, Clark; Johnstone, Wallace, Chalmers, Hood, Lennox

ABERDEEN: McGarr; Boel, Hermiston; Murray, McMillan, Petersen; Adams, Robb, Forrest, Wilson, Hamilton

Attendance: 47,000

Semi-Final at Hampden Park October 8th
CELTIC (1) 3 AYR UNITED (1) 3
Hughes (41), Rough 2 (32, 95),
Gemmell (50 pen), McCulloch (61),
Auld (98) *After Extra Time*
(90 mins 2-2)

CELTIC: Fallon; Hay, Gemmell; Dalglish, McNeill, Clark; Hood (Auld), Lennox, Wallace, Callaghan, Hughes

AYR UNITED: Stewart; Malone, Murphy; Fleming, Quinn, Mitchell; Young, Ferguson, Ingram, McCulloch, Rough

Attendance: 33,110

This was previewed as a walkover but the spectators were quickly to change their minds. Ingram gave McNeill one of his unhappiest games for a long time. Dalglish, in only his 2nd game, did extremely well but Celtic clearly missed Johnstone who had to withdraw with ear trouble. The game see-sawed in extra-time after Auld was brought on for Hood and Ayr took the lead for the 2nd time in 95 minutes when Rough scored with another header from a Malone free-kick. 3 minutes later Auld justified his inclusion by equalising with a 20-yard shot.

Semi-Final Replay at Hampden Park October 13th

CELTIC (1) 2 AYR UNITED (1) 1
Hood (22), Chalmers (54) Ingram (14)

CELTIC: Simpson (Wallace); Craig, Gemmell; Dalglish, McNeill, Brogan; Johnstone, Hood, Chalmers, Callaghan, Hughes

AYR UNITED: Stewart; Malone, Murphy; Fleming, Quinn, Mitchell; Young, Ferguson, Ingram, McCulloch, Rough

Attendance: 47,831

Ronnie Simpson dislocated his shoulder again as Celtic edged their way uneasily into their 6th successive League Cup Final. He was injured making a fantastic save 12 minutes from the end from Ingram. Gemmell took over in goal and Wallace was brought on as an outfield sub.

Final at Hampden Park October 25th

CELTIC (1) 1 ST JOHNSTONE (0) 0
Auld (2)

CELTIC: Fallon; Craig, Hay; Murdoch, McNeill, Brogan; Callaghan, Hood, Hughes, Chalmers (Johnstone), Auld

ST JOHNSTONE: Donaldson; Lambie, Coburn; Gordon, Rooney, McPhee; Aird, Hall, McCarry (Whitelaw), Connolly, Aitken

Attendance: 73,067 *Referee:* J. W. Paterson (Bothwell)

Celtic were without Simpson, Gemmell, Lennox and Clark and, for a major part of this thrilling game, Johnstone. St Johnstone concentrated on playing stylishly and sportingly despite the loss of a 2nd-minute goal that eventually proved decisive. Celtic had a goal disallowed when Hughes dispossessed Donaldson and tapped into the empty net but the referee blew for an infringement against Hughes. It was the only real break St Johnstone had in the entire game, for shortly after, Fallon pulled off a masterly save from Rooney which would have taken the game into extra-time.

SCOTTISH CUP

First Round January 24th

CELTIC (0) 2 DUNFERMLINE (0) 1
Hughes (81), Hood (89) Gillespie (60)

CELTIC: Williams; Hay, Gemmell; Murdoch, McNeill, Brogan; Johnstone, Hood, Wallace, Auld (Craig), Hughes

DUNFERMLINE: Arrol; Callaghan, McLaren; McNichol, McGarty, Gardner; Edwards (Thomson), McKimmie, Mitchell, McLean, Gillespie

Attendance: 50,000

Second Round February 7th

CELTIC (2) 4 DUNDEE UNITED (0) 0
Hughes 2 (15, 43),
Macari (58), Wallace (77)

CELTIC: Williams; Hay, Gemmell; Murdoch (Craig), McNeill, Brogan; Macari, Hood, Wallace, Lennox, Hughes

DUNDEE UNITED: Mackay; Rolland, J. Cameron; Gillespie, Smith, Henry; K. Cameron (Markland), Smith, Gordon, Mitchell, Wilson

Attendance: 45,000

Third Round February 21st

CELTIC (1) 3 RANGERS (1) 1
Lennox (39), Hay (85), Craig o.g. (5)
Johnstone (88)

CELTIC: Williams; Craig, Gemmell; Murdoch, McNeill, Brogan; Johnstone, Lennox, Wallace, Hay, Hughes (Hood)

RANGERS: Neef; Johansen, Mathieson; Greig, McKinnon, Smith; Conn (Henderson), Penman, Stein, MacDonald, Johnston

Attendance: 75,000 *Referee:* T. Wharton

Rangers took an early lead by means of an own goal by Craig. Celtic deservedly equalised in 39 minutes with a Lennox shot that deflected off Neef into the net. Davie Hay was fielded at inside-left in place of Bertie Auld and he crowned his day by shooting the magnificent 25-yard match-winning 2nd goal 5 minutes from the end. Celtic's 3rd goal scored by Johnstone a couple of minutes from time merely emphasised the superiority of the Cup holders.

Semi-Final at Hampden Park March 14th

CELTIC (0) 2 DUNDEE (0) 1
Macari (58), Lennox (82) Wallace (64)

CELTIC: Williams; Hay, Gemmell; Murdoch, McNeill, Brogan; Johnstone, Macari, Wallace, Callaghan, Lennox. Sub: Auld

DUNDEE: Donaldson; Selway, Houston; Steele, Easton, Stewart; Bryce, Kinninmonth, Wallace, Scott, Campbell. Sub: Georgeson

Attendance: 64,546

Celtic, with a heavy domestic and European programme, were saved from a replay 8 minutes from the end when Donaldson erred and virtually dropped a high ball on to Lennox's feet for the winning goal, though until then he had been a giant in a 9-man defence that had looked composed against Celtic's superior power and speed. The most Dundee could have expected from their well-drilled resistance was the bonus of a 2nd game, for their tactics were never designed to beat Celtic.

Final at Hampden Park April 11th
ABERDEEN (1) 3 CELTIC (0) 1
Harper (27 pen), Lennox (89)
McKay 2 (82, 90)

ABERDEEN: Clark; Boel, Murray; Hermiston, McMillan, M. Buchan; McKay, Robb, Forrest, Harper, Graham. Sub: G. Buchan (not used)

CELTIC: Williams; Hay, Gemmell; Murdoch, McNeill, Brogan; Johnstone, Connelly, Wallace, Lennox, Hughes (Auld)

Attendance: 108,434 *Referee:* R. H. Davidson (Airdrie)

Celtic's mantle of invincibility was destroyed by Aberdeen who gambled on youth and were highly rewarded. Reassurance that they could repeat their recent League victory over Celtic was supplied in a crucial spell before the interval. McKay settled the destination of the Cup with the 3rd goal in the last 30 seconds of the match to take the Cup to Pittodrie for the first time in 23 years.

EUROPEAN CUP

First Round First Leg September 17th
BASLE (Switzerland) (0) 0 CELTIC (0) 0

BASLE: Kunz; Keifer, Fischli, Odermatt, Michaud; Siegenchaler, Balmer, Benthaus, Hauser, Ramseir (Rahmen), Wenger

CELTIC: Fallon; Hay, Gemmell; Brogan, McNeill, Clark; Johnstone, Lennox, Chalmers (Hood), Wallace, Hughes

Attendance: 38,000

First Round Second Leg October 1st
CELTIC (1) 2 BASLE (0) 0
Hood (1), Gemmell (65)

CELTIC: Fallon; Hay, Gemmell; Clark, McNeill, Callaghan; Johnstone, Wallace, Chalmers, Hood, Lennox

BASLE: Kunz; Kiefer, Michaud; Siegenchaler, Ramseir, Fischli; Balmer, Odermatt, Hauser (Demarmells), Benthaus, Wenger

Attendance: 52,000

Second Round First Leg November 12th
CELTIC (2) 3 BENFICA (Portugal) (0) 0
Gemmell (2), Wallace (41),
Hood (69)

CELTIC: Fallon; Craig, Gemmell; Murdoch, McNeill, Clark; Johnstone, Hood, Wallace, Auld, Hughes

BENFICA: Henrique; Malta, C. Humberto; Zeca, F. Humberto, Graca; Coluna, Simoes, Torres, Eusebio (Augusto), Diamentino (Jorge)

Attendance: 80,000

Celtic produced a devastating performance. Benfica, who withdrew Diamentino and Eusebio at the interval in an attempt to switch to a defensive game, could have gone home 7 or 8 goals in arrears.

Second Round Second Leg November 26th
BENFICA (2) 3 CELTIC (0) 0
Eusebio (36), Graca (40), *After Extra Time*
Diamentino (90)

BENFICA: Henrique; Da Silva, Messias; Coluna, Adolfo, Toni; Graca, Aguas (Diamentino), Jorge, Eusebio (Martins), Simoes

CELTIC: Fallon; Craig, Gemmell; Murdoch, McNeill, Brogan; Johnstone, Callaghan (Hood), Wallace, Auld (Connelly), Hughes

Attendance: 37,000

In a disastrous 4-minute spell shortly before the interval Celtic lost 2 unexpected goals and from that point on they were fighting for survival. With the official clock showing 2 minutes overtime Diamentino, a 2nd-half substitute, headed in from a corner-kick to send the match into extra-time. Aggregate 3-3; Celtic won on the toss of a coin.

Quarter-Final First Leg March 4th
CELTIC (1) 3 FIORENTINA (Italy)
Auld (30), (0) 0
Carpenetti o.g. (49),
Wallace (89)

CELTIC: Williams; Hay, Gemmell; Murdoch, McNeill, Brogan; Johnstone, Lennox, Wallace, Auld, Hughes (Hood)

FIORENTINA: Superchi; Rogora, Longoni; Carpenetti, Ferrante, Brizi; Eposito, Merlo (Rizzo), Maraschi, De Sisti, Amarildo

Attendance: 80,000

Fiorentina, one of the most famous teams in Europe, were beaten in probably the most one-sided European club match seen at Parkhead in years. Stein's master stroke was to bring back Auld after an absence of several weeks. The wily inside-forward scored the opening goal and shattered the Italians by making all the play for the two others. Celtic made brilliant use of the wings against a 9 man defence and their defenders were always aware of the Italians' potential to hit on the break.

Quarter-Final Second Leg March 18th
FIORENTINA (1) 1 CELTIC (0) 0
Chiarugi (36)

FIORENTINA: Superchi; Rogora, Longoni; Eposito, Ferrante, Brizi; Chiarugi, Merlo, Maraschi, De Sisti, Amarildo

CELTIC: Williams; Hay, Gemmell; Murdoch, McNeill, Brogan; Johnstone, Connelly, Wallace, Auld (Callaghan), Lennox

Attendance: 50,000

Celtic had to withstand the greatest pressure that had been exerted on them all season, yet they accomplished their work in a cool, orderly manner. They met an unknown force in Fiorentina's problem boy Chiarugi who proved to be an attacking player of International stamp. It was appropriate that he should score the game's only goal in 36 minutes with a close-range shot after the ball broke badly for Celtic, leaving the striker with a clear view of goal. Celtic won 3-1 on aggregate.

Semi-Final First Leg April 1st

LEEDS UNITED (0) 0	CELTIC (1) 1
	Connelly (45 secs)

LEEDS UNITED: Sprake; Reaney, Cooper; Bremner (Bates), Charlton, Madeley; Lorimer, Clarke, Jones, Giles, Gray

CELTIC: Williams; Hay, Gemmell; Murdoch, McNeill, Brogan; Johnstone, Connelly (Hughes), Wallace, Lennox, Auld

Attendance: 45,505

With a brilliant exhibition of cut and thrust football Celtic scored a 1st-minute goal and held the lead throughout. Johnstone continually shattered the best-drilled defence in England with his incredible dribbling skill at top speed. He could beat 4 or 5 players at a time, and only some heavy body checking by the Leeds full-backs stopped him.

Semi-Final Second Leg at Hampden Park April 15th

CELTIC (0) 2	LEEDS UNITED (1) 1
Hughes (47),	Bremner (14)
Murdoch (51)	

CELTIC: Williams; Hay, Gemmell; Murdoch, McNeill, Brogan; Johnstone, Connelly, Hughes, Auld, Lennox

LEEDS UNITED: Sprake (Harvey); Madeley, Cooper; Bremner, Charlton, Hunter; Lorimer, Clarke, Jones, Giles, Gray

Attendance: 136,505 (A European Cup record)

Celtic crowned themselves Champions of Britain. The fanatical crowd stayed for almost 20 minutes after the match, demanding a lap of honour from the side. McNeill passed a fitness test only 30 minutes before the kick-off but a late training injury put Wallace out of the game. Leeds unexpectedly took the lead in 14 minutes when Bremner took a pass from Giles and shot from almost 35 yards over the Celtic defence and beyond Williams. Hughes snatched a brilliant equalising goal soon after half-time when Auld crossed for the big centre to send a glancing header past Sprake. Sprake was carried off with a knee injury 6 minutes after half-time after a collision with Hughes, and substitute Harvey had hardly time to settle before Murdoch thundered a 2nd goal past him. Celtic remained very much in command for the rest of the match, winning 3-1 on aggregate.

Final at the San Siro Stadium in Milan May 6th

CELTIC (1) 1	FEYENOORD (Holland)
Gemmell (30)	(1) 2
	Israel (32),
	Kindvall (116)
	After Extra Time

CELTIC: Williams; Hay, Gemmell; Murdoch, McNeill, Brogan; Johnstone, Lennox, Wallace, Auld (Connelly), Hughes

FEYENOORD: Pieters Graafland; Romeyn (Haak), Laseroms; Israel, Van Duivenbode, Hasil; Jansen, Van Hanegem, Wery, Kindvall, Mouljin

Attendance: 53,187 *Referee:* Concetto Lo Bello (Italy)

After a season of almost non-stop success Celtic failed in the most crucial match of all. They were beaten by a much more competent and surprisingly good Dutch team. Celtic were never in command of the midfield and as a result their forwards never got off the mark. They were forced to hold on with tenacious grimness to take the game into extra-time, when McNeill deliberately handled a high ball deep in the penalty area. It was a clear penalty but Kindvall swept round him to lob the ball into the net. Jock Stein said after the match, 'The better team won. We had too many players off-form.'

APPEARANCES	League	League Cup	Scottish Cup	European Cup
McNeill	31	10	5	9
Gemmell	29	9	5	9
Wallace	29+1S	8+1S	5	8
Brogan	27+1S	4+1S	5	7
Johnstone	27	4+1S	4	9
Hood	25+3S	10	2+1S	2+3S
Hay	25+1S	6	5	7
Murdoch	24+2S	6	5	7
Hughes	20+1S	8	4	6+1S
Craig	20+4S	5	1+2S	2
Lennox	19+1S	8	4	7
Fallon	16	9	–	4
Williams	16	–	5	5
Auld	15+3S	1+2S	1+1S	7
Callaghan	12+2S	4	1	2+1S
Macari	12+3S	–	2	–
Clark	9	8	–	3
Connelly	7	3	1	3+2S
Chalmers	5	4+2S	–	2
Simpson	2	1	–	–
Dalglish	2	2	–	–
Davidson	1	–	–	–
Quinn	1	–	–	–
Cattenach	0+1S	–	–	–

GOALSCORERS

League: Wallace 16 (2 pens), Lennox 14, Johnstone 10, Hughes 10, Gemmell 9 (4 pens), Hood 8, Macari 7, Murdoch 5, McNeill 5, Auld 4, Chalmers 2, Callaghan 2, Own Goals 2, Davidson 1, Brogan

League Cup: Wallace 5, Hughes 4, Hood 4, Gemmell 3 (1 pen), Auld 2, Lennox 2, McNeill 2, Chalmers 1, Connelly 1

Scottish Cup: Hughes 3, Lennox 3, Macari 2, Hood 1, Wallace 1, Hay 1, Johnstone 1

European Cup: Gemmell 3, Hood 2, Wallace 2, Auld 1, Connelly 1, Murdoch 1, Hughes 1, Own Goals 1

Jubilant Celtic players celebrate Scottish Cup success in 1969 over their great rivals, Rangers. Celtic won 4-0 in a match played before almost 133,000 spectators at Hampden Park.

Season 1970-71

The season was overshadowed by the disaster at Ibrox on 2nd January in which 66 people died and 145 were injured.

Celtic won their 26th Championship and the League and Cup double for the 7th time, just missing out on the treble. Aberdeen led the table for much of the season but Celtic eventually took the title by a 2-point margin from the Dons to whom they had surrendered 3 points in their 2 meetings. They lost only 3 times – once at home and twice away. The Championship won, the Lisbon Lions played for the last time together against Clyde in the last match of the season and showed that they were still an exceptional combination by winning 6-1. Both Auld and Clark left the club at the end of the season, joining Hibs and Morton respectively. Jim Brogan finished as runner-up to Martin Buchan as Scotland's Player of the Year. Both Williams and McNeill played in 31 matches and Harry Hood topped the scoring list with 22 goals followed by Wallace on 19. Their average home gate for the season: 32,176.

In the League Cup Celtic went throught their Section matches undefeated, beat Dundee 7-3 on aggregate in the Quarter-Final but took almost 4 hours to overcome plucky Second Division Dumbarton in the Semi-Final before going down to Rangers in the final.

Celtic won the Scottish Cup for the 21st time. They looked to have the Final against Rangers won until young substitute Johnstone popped up to head an equaliser 3 minutes from time. However, they made no mistake in the replay.

In the European Cup Quarter-Finals Celtic faced Ajax of Amsterdam. A last-minute goal gave the Dutch team a 3-goal winning margin in the First Leg in Holland, and despite a great effort in the return at Hampden Park a solitary Johnstone goal was the most they could manage against a very talented side who went on to win the trophy.

League:	Champions
League Cup:	Finalists
Scottish Cup:	Winners
European Cup:	Quarter-Finalists

SCOTTISH FIRST DIVISION

July 14th: Tommy Gemmell withdrew his transfer request.

August 29th
CELTIC (1) 2 MORTON (0) 0
Lennox 2 (30, 49)

CELTIC: Williams; McGrain, Gemmell (Connelly); Murdoch, McNeill, Brogan; Johnstone, Hay, Hood, Lennox, Macari

MORTON: Sorensen; Murray, McDerment; Sweeney, Rankin, Gray; Booth (Jordan), Collins, Mason, Hannigan, Clark

Attendance: 35,000. Murdoch missed a penalty

September 5th
CLYDE (0) 0 CELTIC (2) 5
Macari 2 (10, 83), McHugh o.g. (50), May (23), Davidson (79)

CLYDE; McCulloch; Anderson, Mulheron; Beattie, McHugh, Burns; Hay, McFarlane, Hulston (Swan), Hastings, McColligan

CELTIC: Williams; McGrain, Hay; Murdoch (Davidson), McNeill, Brogan; Hughes, Connelly, Hood, Lennox, Macari

Attendance: 20,000. Beattie was ordered off

September 12th
CELTIC (1) 2 — RANGERS (0) 0
Hughes (6),
Murdoch (54)

CELTIC: Williams; McGrain, McNeill, Connelly, Brogan; Murdoch, Hay; Johnstone, Hood, Hughes, Lennox

RANGERS: McCloy; Jardine, McKinnon, Jackson, Miller; Greig, Conn, MacDonald; Fyfe (Penman), Stein, Johnston

Attendance: 73,000. Brogan missed a penalty

This was the 25th time Celtic had met Rangers since Jock Stein took over as Manager at Parkhead 5½ years before. The teams were poles apart in technique. McGrain, McNeill, Connelly and Brogan formed a seemingly impenetrable barrier in front of their goalkeeper.

September 19th
HIBERNIAN (0) 2 — CELTIC (0) 0
McBride 2 (51, 67)

HIBERNIAN: Marshall; Jones, Schaedler; Blackley, Black, Stanton; Hamilton, Blair, McBride, McEwan, Duncan

CELTIC: Williams; McGrain, Brogan; Murdoch, McNeill, Hay; Johnstone, Connelly, Hood, Lennox, Hughes

Attendance: 36,000

September 26th
CELTIC (0) 3 — DUNDEE (0) 0
Johnstone 2 (50, 89),
Macari (57)

CELTIC: Williams; McGrain, Hay; Murdoch, Connelly, Brogan; Johnstone, Callaghan, Hood, Macari, Wilson (Lennox)

DUNDEE: Donaldson; R. Wilson, Houston; Selway, Easton, Stewart (Johnston); Duncan, Kinninmonth, Wallace, Scott, Steele

Attendance: 30,000. Selway was ordered off

October 3rd
DUNFERMLINE (0) 0 — CELTIC (0) 2
Macari (67),
Wallace (83 pen)

DUNFERMLINE: Arrol; Callaghan, Lunn; Fraser, Cushley, Thomson; Gardner, Robertson, Mitchell, McNichol (Tracey), McKimmie

CELTIC: Williams; McGrain, Hay; Murdoch, McNeill, Connelly; Davidson (Hood), Johnstone, Wallace, Macari, Lennox

Attendance: 15,000

October 4th: Goalkeeper Tom Lally was signed from Sligo Rovers

October 10th
CELTIC (1) 1 — ST JOHNSTONE (0) 0
Wallace (39)

CELTIC: Williams; Hay, McGrain; Connelly, McNeill, Callaghan (Quinn); Johnstone, Wallace, Hood, Lennox, Macari

ST JOHNSTONE: Donaldson; Coburn, Argue (McCarry); Rooney, Gordon, Rennie; Muir, Hall, Connolly, McPhee, Aitken

Attendance: 37,000

October 17th
AIRDRIE (1) 1 — CELTIC (2) 3
Wilson (13) — Hood 2 (15, 68),
Lennox (23)

AIRDRIE: McKenzie; Jonquin, Caldwell; Menzies, Delaney, Goodwin; Wilson, Jarvie, Busby, McPheat, Cowan (Bird)

CELTIC: Williams; Craig, Hay; Murdoch, McNeill, Cattenach; Johnstone (Dalglish), Connelly, Wallace, Hood, Lennox

Attendance: 20,000

League positions

	P	W	D	L	F	A	Pts
1 CELTIC	8	7	0	1	18	3	14
2 Aberdeen	9	6	2	1	18	7	14
3 St Johnstone	9	5	3	1	18	8	13
4 Motherwell	9	6	0	3	16	10	12
5 Rangers	8	5	1	2	13	5	11

October 22nd: Clyde made an approach for Bertie Auld

October 28th
CELTIC (0) 3 — HEARTS (1) 2
Wallace 2 (66, 72) — Ford 2 (28, 53)
Hood (77)

CELTIC: Williams; Craig, Hay; Murdoch, McNeill, Cattenach; Johnstone, Hood, Wallace, Connelly, Lennox

HEARTS: Garland; Clunie, Oliver; Anderson, Thomson, Brown; Young, Townsend, Ford, Wood, Lynch

Attendance: 18,000

October 31st
MOTHERWELL (0) 0 — CELTIC (2) 5
Hood 3 (18, 37 pen, 52),
Connelly (47),
Johnstone (86)

MOTHERWELL: MacRae; Whiteford, Wark; Forsyth, McCallum, Donnelly; McInally, Watson (Campbell), Deans, Muir, Heron

CELTIC: Williams; Craig, Hay; Murdoch, McNeill, Cattenach; Johnstone, Hood (Macari), Wallace, Connelly, Lennox

Attendance: 13,000

November 7th
CELTIC (2) 3 — COWDENBEATH (0) 0
Connelly 2 (30, 44),
Wallace (75)

CELTIC: Williams; Craig, Brogan; Murdoch, McNeill, Cattenach; Johnstone, Hood, Wallace, Connelly, Hughes
COWDENBEATH: Wylie; McLaughlin, Bostock; Ferguson, Kinnell, Moore; Laing, Allan (Dickson), McCullie, Taylor, Ross
Attendance: 19,572

November 11th: Hay and Johnstone were in the Scotland team which beat Denmark 1-0 at Hampden Park.

November 14th
CELTIC (2) 3 KILMARNOCK (0) 0
Murdoch (19), Wallace (33), Johnstone (56)
CELTIC: Williams; Craig, Gemmell; Murdoch (Hood), McNeill, Brogan; Johnstone, Lennox, Wallace, Connelly, Hughes
KILMARNOCK: Hunter; Rodman, Dickson; Gilmour, McGrory, MacDonald; McLean, Maxwell (Mathie), Morrison, Cairns, Cook
Attendance: 27,000

November 21st
FALKIRK (0) 0 CELTIC (0) 0
FALKIRK: Rennie; Abel, McLaughlin; Markie, Miller, Gibson; Hoggan, Roxburgh, Ferguson, Shirra, Setterington
CELTIC: Williams; Craig, Gemmell; Murdoch, McNeill, Brogan; Johnstone, Connelly, Hughes, Hay, Lennox (Wallace)
Attendance: 18,700

November 28th
CELTIC (1) 3 ST MIRREN (0) 0
Gemmell (3), Davidson 2 (55, 68)
CELTIC: Fallon; Craig, Gemmell; Murdoch, McNeill, Brogan; Davidson, Hood (Connelly), Wallace, Hay, Hughes
ST MIRREN: Connaghan; C. Murray, Connell; Millar, Fulton, McLaughlin; Lister (McKean), Knox, Hamilton, Munro, Traynor
Attendance: 25,000

December 5th
DUNDEE UNITED (1) 1 CELTIC (0) 2
McNeill o.g. (20) Davidson (58), Markland o.g. (73)
DUNDEE UNITED: Mackay; Rolland, J. Cameron; Markland, Smith, Henry; Wilson, A. Reid, K. Cameron, Gordon, Stevenson
CELTIC: Fallon; Craig, Gemmell; Murdoch, McNeill, Brogan; Johnstone, Connelly, Macari, Davidson, Hughes
Attendance: 18,000

December 8th: Tommy Gemmell played for the Rest of Europe against Benfica in a testimonial match for Mario Coluna. Benfica won 3-2.

December 12th
CELTIC (0) 0 ABERDEEN (0) 1
Harper (53)
CELTIC: Fallon; Craig, Gemmell; Murdoch, McNeill, Brogan; Johnstone, Connelly (Hood), Macari, Hay, Hughes
ABERDEEN: Clark; Boel, Hermiston; Murray, McMillan, Buchan; Taylor, Robb, Forrest (Willoughby), Harper, Graham
Attendance: 63,000

December 19th
AYR UNITED (0) 1 CELTIC (1) 2
Flynn (55) Hughes (26), Hood (54)
AYR UNITED: Stewart; McFadzean, Murphy; Fleming, McAnespie, Mitchell; Young, Reynolds, McGovern, Whitehead (Flynn), McLean
CELTIC: Williams; Craig, Gemmell; Murdoch, McNeill, Hay; Johnstone, Lennox, Hood, Callaghan, Hughes (Macari)
Attendance: 15,000

December 26th
MORTON (0) 0 CELTIC (3) 3
Chalmers (12), Lennox (16), Wallace (35)
MORTON: Sorensen; Murray, McDerment; Sweeney, Gray, Rankin; Hannigan, Collins, Bartram (O'Neill), Thomson, Laughton
CELTIC: Williams; Craig, Gemmell; Murdoch, Connelly, Hay; Chalmers, Hood, Wallace, Callaghan, Lennox
Attendance: 18,0C0. Johnstone and McNeill were both dropped for this match.

League positions

	P	W	D	L	F	A	Pts
1 Aberdeen	18	15	2	1	42	7	32
2 CELTIC	18	15	1	2	42	8	31
3 Rangers	18	10	3	5	35	16	23
4 St Johnstone	18	9	4	5	34	28	22
5 Dundee	18	8	5	5	28	21	21

January 2nd
RANGERS (0) 1 CELTIC (0) 1
Stein (90) Johnstone (89)
RANGERS: Neef; Jardine, Mathieson; Greig, McKinnon, Jackson; Henderson (MacDonald), Conn, D. Johnstone, Smith, Stein
CELTIC: Williams; Craig, Gemmell; Brogan, Connelly, Hay; Johnstone, Hood, Wallace, Callaghan, Lennox
Attendance: 80,000

66 people died on Stairway 13 and 145 were injured at the end of this match. With a mere 15 seconds of the game remaining Colin Stein equalised for Rangers. Those down the exit steps made an attempt to clamber back into the ground and share the jubilation after Rangers' late equaliser. They were met by a floodtide of their happy fellow supporters sweeping down uncontrollably on top of them. In a good-natured match there had been only 2 arrests – for drunkenness – in an all-ticket crowd.

January 9th
CELTIC (1) 2 — HIBERNIAN (0) 1
Callaghan (35), Hood (49) — Stanton (89)

CELTIC: Williams; Craig, Gemmell; Murdoch, McNeill, Brogan; Johnstone, Wallace, Hood, Callaghan, Lennox

HIBERNIAN: Baines; Brownlie, Jones; Blackley, Black, Stanton; Blair, McEwan, Duncan, Hamilton, Davidson (Hazel)

Attendance: 28,000

January 16th
DUNDEE (0) 1 — CELTIC (2) 8
Duncan (80) — Hood 2 (18, 87), Wallace 2 (44, 57), Houston o.g. (67), Callaghan (75), Johnstone 2 (77, 85)

DUNDEE: Donaldson; Wilson (Johnston), Soutar; Steele, Phillip, Houston; Duncan, Gilroy, Wallace, Scott, Kinninmonth

CELTIC: Williams; Craig, Gemmell; Murdoch, McNeill, Brogan; Johnstone, Wallace, Hood, Callaghan, Auld

Attendance: 20,000

January 27th: Scotland beat an Old Firm Select 2-1 at Hampden Park in a match in aid of the Ibrox disaster victims. Attendance: 81,405.

January 30th
CELTIC (0) 1 — DUNFERMLINE (0) 0
Wallace (49)

CELTIC: Williams; Craig, Gemmell; Murdoch (Hay), McNeill, Brogan; Johnstone, Wallace, Hood, Callaghan, Auld

DUNFERMLINE: McGarr; Callaghan, Fraser, Cushley, Lunn; Thomson, McNichol (Robertson); Mitchell, McBride, Gardner, Millar

Attendance: 25,000

February 3rd: Hay and Gemmell were in the Scotland team beaten 3-0 by Belgium in Liège.

February 6th
ST JOHNSTONE (2) 3 — CELTIC (1) 2
Pearson (10), Hall (44), McPhee (76) — Hood (12), Wallace (81)

ST JOHNSTONE: Donaldson; Lambie, Argue; Rooney, Rennie, McPhee; Aird, Pearson, McCarry, Hall, Connolly

CELTIC: Williams; Craig, Gemmell; Brogan, McNeill, Hay; Johnstone, Wallace, Hood, Callaghan, Hughes (Chalmers)

Attendance: 19,000

February 20th
CELTIC (1) 4 — AIRDRIE (0) 1
Wallace 2 (2, 53), Hood (71), Macari (85) — Jarvie (79)

CELTIC: Williams; Hay, Gemmell; Connelly (Macari), McNeill, Brogan; Johnstone, Hood, Wallace, Callaghan, Lennox

AIRDRIE: Gourlay; Jonquin, McKay; Menzies, Delaney, Whiteford; Wilson, McKinlay, Busby, Jarvie, Cowan

Attendance: 27,000. Gemmell missed a penalty.

February 27th
HEARTS (1) 1 — CELTIC (1) 1
Carruthers (32) — Hood (29)

HEARTS: Cruikshank; Clunie, Hay; Thomson, Anderson, Brown; Young, Townsend, Ford, Wood, Carruthers

CELTIC: Williams; Hay, Gemmell; Connelly, McNeill, Brogan; Johnstone, Hood, Wallace, Callaghan, Lennox

Attendance: 24,000

League positions

	P	W	D	L	F	A	Pts
1 Aberdeen	26	19	4	3	54	12	42
2 CELTIC	25	19	3	3	61	16	41
3 St Johnstone	26	15	4	6	46	36	34
4 Ranger	25	12	7	6	42	23	31
5 Falkirk	25	10	8	7	34	30	28

March 13th
COWDENBEATH (1) 1 — CELTIC (2) 5
Hay o.g. (4) — Hughes (25), McNeill (36), Hood 2 (52, 60 pen), Lennox (76)

COWDENBEATH: McArthur; McLaughlin, Cairns; Taylor, Kinnell (Dickson), Moore; Bostock, McCullie, Laing, Kennedy, Ross

CELTIC: Williams; Craig, Hay; Callaghan, McNeill, Brogan; Chalmers, Hood, Wallace (Lennox), Davidson, Hughes

Attendance: 8,500. Jimmy Johnstone asked to be dropped from the team before this match.

March 20th
KILMARNOCK (1) 1 — CELTIC (1) 4
Morrison (2) — Hood 2 (49, 64), Hughes (60), Davidson (83)

KILMARNOCK: Hunter; Whyte, Dickson; Gilmour, McGrory, MacDonald; McLean, Morrison, McCulloch, Cairns (Rodman), Cook

CELTIC: Williams; Hay, Gemmell; Callaghan, McNeill, Brogan; Johnstone, Hood (Auld), Wallace, Davidson, Hughes

Attendance: 16,000. Gemmell missed a penalty.

March 27th
CELTIC (2) 4 FALKIRK (0) 0
Wallace (36),
Hughes (40),
Hood 2 (50, 51)

CELTIC: Williams; Hay, Gemmell; Callaghan, McNeill, Brogan (Murdoch); Johnstone, Hood, Wallace, Davidson, Hughes

FALKIRK: Devlin; Abel, McLaughlin; Markie, Miller, Gibson; Hoggan, Ford, Young, Ferguson (Setterington), Shirra

Attendance: 22,000

April 10th
CELTIC (0) 1 DUNDEE UNITED (1) 1
Wallace (72) Rolland (31)

CELTIC: Williams; Hay, Gemmell; Callaghan, McNeill; Brogan; Johnstone, Hood, Wallace, Dalglish, Auld

DUNDEE UNITED: McAlpine; Rolland, J. Cameron; W. Smith, D. Smith, Henry; Watson, Reid, K. Cameron, Gordon, Wilson

Attendance: 30,000

April 12th
CELTIC (2) 3 MOTHERWELL (0) 0
Wallace (36),
Johnstone (44),
Hood (71)

CELTIC: Williams; Craig, Brogan; Connelly, McNeill, Hay; Johnstone, Lennox, Wallace, Callaghan, Hood (Murdoch)

MOTHERWELL: MacRae; Whiteford, Wark; Forsyth, McCallum, Goldthorpe; Martin, Watson, Deans, Muir, Heron

Attendance: 23,000

April 17th
ABERDEEN (1) 1 CELTIC (1) 1
Willoughby (38) Hood (3)

ABERDEEN: Clark; Boel, Hermiston; S. Murray, McMillan, M. Buchan; Forrest, Willoughby, G. Buchan (Harper), Graham, Robb

CELTIC: Williams; Craig, Brogan; Connelly, McNeill, Hay; Johnstone, Lennox, Wallace, Callaghan, Hood (Quinn)

Attendance: 35,000

April 20th: Desmond White became Chairman of the club with Sir Bob Kelly becoming President.

April 21st: Hay and Brogan were in the Scotland team beaten 2-0 by Portugal in Lisbon.

April 27th
ST MIRREN (1) 2 CELTIC (1) 2
McLeod 2 (8, 59) Hood (21),
Lennox (60)

ST MIRREN: Connaghan; Murray, McLaughlin; Miller, McQueen, Fulton; Hamilton, McLeod, Knox, Blair, Gilshan

CELTIC: Williams; Craig, Brogan; Connelly, McNeill, Hay; Johnstone, Lennox, Wallace, Callaghan, Hood

Attendance: 20,000

April 29th at Hampden Park
CELTIC (1) 2 AYR UNITED (0) 0
Lennox (18),
Wallace (58)

CELTIC: Williams; Craig, Brogan; Connelly, McNeill, Hay; Johnstone, Lennox, Wallace (Dalglish), Callaghan, Macari

AYR UNITED: Stewart; McFadzean, Murphy; Fleming, Quinn, Mitchell; Young, McGovern, Ingram, Whitehead (Doyle), Reynolds

Attendance: 25,000. Celtic clinched the title.

April 30th: Bertie Auld was given a free transfer.

May 1st
CELTIC (4) 6 CLYDE (0) 1
Lennox 3 (11, 19, 61), McColligan (46)
Wallace 2 (13, 46),
Chalmers (78)

CELTIC: Simpson and Williams; Craig, Gemmell; Murdoch, McNeill, Clark; Johnstone, Wallace, Chalmers, Auld, Lennox

CLYDE: McCulloch; Anderson, Mulheron (McVie); Miller, McGoldrick, McHugh; Sullivan, Burns, Hay, Thomson, McColligan

Attendance: 35,000. This was the last appearance of the Lisbon Lions.

May 6th: Auld joined Hibernian.

May 15th: Hay and Brogan were in the Scotland team which drew 0-0 with Wales in Cardiff.

May 18th: Hay and Brogan were in the Scotland team beaten 1-0 by Northern Ireland at Hampden Park.

May 22nd: Brogan and Johnstone were in the Scotland team beaten 3-1 by England at Wembley.

June 12th: John Clark joined Morton.

June 15th: Billy Mitchell was signed from Raith Rovers for £1,000.

Scottish First Division

	P	W	D	L	F	A	Pts
1 CELTIC	34	25	6	3	89	23	56
2 Aberdeen	34	24	6	4	68	18	54
3 St Johnstone	34	19	6	8	59	44	44
4 Rangers	34	16	9	9	58	34	41
5 Dundee	34	14	10	10	53	45	38
6 Dundee United	34	14	8	12	53	54	36
7 Falkirk	34	13	9	12	46	53	35
8 Morton	34	13	8	13	44	44	34
9 Motherwell	34	13	8	13	43	47	34
10 Airdrie	34	13	8	13	60	65	34
11 Hearts	34	13	7	14	41	40	33
12 Hibernian	34	10	10	14	47	53	30
13 Kilmarnock	34	10	8	16	43	67	28
14 Ayr United	34	9	8	17	37	54	26
15 Clyde	34	8	10	16	33	59	26
16 Dunfermline	34	6	11	17	44	56	23
17 St Mirren	34	7	9	18	38	56	23
18 Cowdenbeath	34	7	3	24	33	77	17

LEAGUE CUP

August 8th
HEARTS (0) 1 — CELTIC (1) 2
Hegarty (72) — Hughes (36), Johnstone (76)

HEARTS: Cruikshank; Sneddon, Oliver; Veitch, Thomson, Wood; Ford, Clunie, Winchester (Hegarty), Fleming, Lynch

CELTIC: Fallon; Craig, Gemmell; Connelly, McNeill, Brogan; Johnstone, Lennox, Hood, Hay, Hughes

Attendance: n.a.

August 12th
CELTIC (3) 5 — CLYDE (0) 3
Lennox 3 (10, 22, 53), Johnstone 2 (28, 64) — Burns (n.a.), Hastings (66), Staite (82)

CELTIC: Williams; Craig, Gemmell; Hay, McNeill, Brogan; Johnstone, Hood, Connelly, Lennox, Hughes (Wallace)

CLYDE: McCulloch; Anderson, Mulheron; Beattie, McHugh, Burns; Hay, MacFarlane, Staite, Hulston, Hastings

Attendance: 25,000

August 15th
CELTIC (1) 2 — DUNDEE UNITED (0) 2
Callaghan (11), Lennox (70) — I. Reid (16), Gordon (89)

CELTIC: Fallon; Craig (Wallace), Gemmell; Hay, McNeill, Brogan; Callaghan, Hood, Connelly, Lennox, Hughes

DUNDEE UNITED: Mackay; Rolland, Cameron; Markland, Smith, Henry; Wilson, A. Reid, I. Reid, Gordon, Traynor

Attendance: 39,000

August 19th
CLYDE (0) 0 — CELTIC (0) 2
Gemmell 2 (47 pen, 77 pen)

CLYDE: McCulloch; Anderson, Mulheron; Beattie, McHugh, Burns; Hay, MacFarlane, Staite (McColligan), Hulston, Hastings

CELTIC: Williams; Hay, Gemmell; Murdoch (Macari), McNeill, Brogan; Callaghan, Connelly, Wallace, Hood, Lennox

Attendance: 24,000. Wallace was ordered off in the 41st minute.

August 22nd
CELTIC (1) 4 — HEARTS (1) 2
Hughes 2 (30 secs, 67), Connelly (83), Macari (86) — Hegarty 2 (16, 80)

CELTIC: Williams; Hay, Gemmell; Murdoch, McNeill, Brogan; Johnstone, Hood, Connelly, Lennox (Macari), Hughes

HEARTS: Cruikshank; Sneddon, Oliver; Veitch (Winchester), Thomson, Brown; Jensen, Clunie, Ford, Hegarty, Lynch

Attendance: 40,000

August 26th
DUNDEE UNITED (0) 2 — CELTIC (1) 2
Wilson (31), Gordon (89) — Hay (82), Macari (89½)

DUNDEE UNITED: Mackay; Rolland, Cameron; Markland, Smith, Henry; Wilson, A. Reid, I. Reid, Gordon, Traynor

CELTIC: Williams; Hay, Gemmell; Murdoch, Connelly, Brogan; Callaghan, Johnstone, Hood (McGrain), Macari, Hughes

Attendance: 16,000

Section Table

	P	W	D	L	F	A	Pts
CELTIC	6	4	2	0	17	10	10
Dundee United	6	1	5	0	8	7	7
Clyde	6	1	2	3	8	15	4
Hearts	6	1	1	4	10	11	3

Qualifier: CELTIC

Quarter-Final First Leg September 9th
DUNDEE (0) 2 — CELTIC (2) 2
Kinninmonth (60), Scott (65) — Johnstone 2 (20, 23)

DUNDEE: Donaldson; Selway, Houston; Kinninmonth, Easton, Stewart; J. Wilson, Steele, Wallace, Scott, Bryce

CELTIC: Williams; McGrain, Hay; Murdoch, McNeill, Brogan; Johnstone, Connelly, Hood, Macari, Hughes

Attendance: 23,000

Quarter-Final Second Leg September 23rd

CELTIC (3) 5	DUNDEE (0) 1
Macari 2 (8, 88),	
Hughes (31),	
Hood (42), Wilson (69)	

CELTIC: Williams; McGrain, Hay; Murdoch, McNeill, Brogan; Johnstone, Connelly, Hood, Macari, Hughes (Wilson)

DUNDEE: Donaldson; R. Wilson, Houston; Selway, Stewart, Steele; Gilroy (Duncan), Kinninmonth, Wallace, Scott, J. Wilson

Attendance: 41,000. Celtic won 7-3 on aggregate

Semi-Final at Hampden Park October 7th

CELTIC (0) 0	DUMBARTON (0)
	after extra time

CELTIC: Williams; Craig, McGrain; Murdoch, McNeill, Hay; Johnstone, Connelly, Hood, Macari, Lennox (Wallace)

DUMBARTON: Williams; Jenkins, Muir; Ferguson, Bolton, Graham; Coleman, C. Gallagher, McCormack, K. Wilson (Donnelly), B. Gallagher

Attendance: 25,838

Dumbarton bravely extended the Champions for a 0-0 draw over 120 action-packed minutes. Lawrie Williams made an amazing double save from Wallace after Celtic had been awarded a penalty kick in extra time after Johnstone had been brought down by Bolton's outstretched leg.

Semi-Final Replay at Hampden Park October 12th

CELTIC (2) 4	DUMBARTON (0) 3
Lennox 2 (13, 16),	C. Gallagher (65 pen)
Wallace (95),	Wilson (71),
Macari (113)	Graham (120)
	After extra time 90 mins 2-2.

CELTIC: Williams; Quinn, McGrain; Murdoch, McNeill, Hay; Johnstone, Connelly, Wallace, Lennox, Wilson (Macari)

DUMBARTON: Williams; Jenkins, Muir; Ferguson, Bolton, Graham; Coleman, C. Gallagher, McCormack, Wilson, B. Gallagher

Attendance: 32,913

Dumbarton, 2 down in the opening 16 minutes, played themselves back with an exciting verve which enabled them to take the League Cup holders into another 30 minutes of extra-time.

Final at Hampden Park October 24th

RANGERS (1) 1	CELTIC (0) 0
D. Johnstone (40)	

RANGERS: McCloy; Jardine, Miller; Conn, McKinnon, Jackson; Henderson, MacDonald, D. Johnstone, Stein, Johnston. Sub: Fyfe

CELTIC: Williams; Craig, Quinn; Murdoch, McNeill, Hay; Johnstone, Connelly, Wallace, Hood (Lennox), Macari

Attendance: 106,263 *Referee:* T. Wharton

Quicker to the ball and sharper to the tackle, Rangers fully extended Celtic's rearguard and but for some majestic goalkeeping by Williams might have had more than one goal to show for their ascendancy in the first 45 minutes. Stein, wearing the No. 10 jersey roamed all over the place in search of the ball and in the closing minutes he had the disappointment of seeing a ball driven strongly by him hit the inside of the far post, and rebound into Williams arms. A goal then would have been no more than he deserved for his persistence. What effect the absence of Greig of Rangers and Hughes of Celtic had on the result can only be a matter of speculation. Deputy skipper Ron McKinnon collected the trophy in Greig's absence.

SCOTTISH CUP

Third Round January 23rd

CELTIC (3) 5	QUEEN OF THE SOUTH (1) 1
Wallace (21),	Dempster (45)
Hood 2 (25, 70),	
Callaghan (35),	
McNeill (83)	

CELTIC: Williams; Craig, Gemmell; Murdoch (Brogan), McNeill, Hay; Johnstone, Wallace, Hood, Callaghan, Auld

QUEEN OF THE SOUTH: Ball; Gilmour, Barker; Kerr, Scott, Dickson; Dempster, Evans, McChesney, Law, Murray

Attendance: 25,900

Fourth Round February 13th

CELTIC (1) 1	DUNFERMLINE (0) 1
Wallace (39)	McBride (50)

CELTIC: Williams; Hay, Gemmell; Connelly, McNeill, Brogan; Johnstone, Wallace, Hood (Lennox), Callaghan, Auld

DUNFERMLINE: McGarr; Thomson, Lunn; Fraser, Cushley, McNichol; Edwards, Mitchell, McBride, Gardner, Robertson

Attendance: 35,000

Fourth Round Replay February 17th

DUNFERMLINE (0) 0	CELTIC (1) 1
	Hood (19)

DUNFERMLINE: McGarr; Thomson, Lunn; Fraser, Cushley, McNichol; Edwards (Millar), Mitchell, McBride, Gardner, Robertson

CELTIC: Williams; Hay, Gemmell; Connelly, McNeill, Brogan; Johnstone, Hood, Wallace, Callaghan, Lennox

Attendance: 22,728

Fifth Round March 6th

CELTIC (3) 7	RAITH ROVERS (0) 1
Lennox 3 (22, 27, 81)	Georgeson (64)
Gemmell (36 pen)	
Callaghan (52),	
Wallace (72),	
Davidson (74)	

CELTIC: Williams; Hay, Gemmell; Callaghan, McNeill, Brogan; Johnstone, Hood (Connelly), Wallace, Davidson, Lennox

RAITH ROVERS: McDermott; Hislop, Gray; Beveridge (Wilkinson), Thomson, Lindsay; Wallace, Sinclair, Innes, Georgeson, McGuire

Attendance: 32,000. John Hughes was sent home following a row with Stein after he had been left out of the team.

Semi-Final at Hampden Park April 3rd

CELTIC (2) 3	AIRDRIE (0) 3
Hood 2 (23, 52),	D. Whiteford (47),
Johnstone (43)	Wilson (54),
	Busby (67)

CELTIC: Williams; Hay, Gemmell; Callaghan, McNeill, Brogan; Johnstone, Hood, Wallace, Davidson, Hughes (Lennox)

AIRDRIE: McKenzie; Jonquin, Caldwell; Menzies, Goodwin, D. Whiteford; J. Whiteford, Cowan, Busby, Jarvie, Wilson. Sub: Delaney

Attendance: 39,404

The match had everything – skill, excitement, goals and sportsmanship. Johnstone and Jarvie contributed the largest portions of artistry and enjoyment, Johnstone, in the first half, jinking and dribbling at electrifying pace. John Whiteford had the mastery of Gemmell and Wilson kept Hay fully occupied.

Semi-Final Replay at Hampden Park April 7th

CELTIC (0) 2	AIRDRIE (0) 0
Johnstone (51),	
Hood (83)	

CELTIC: Williams, Hay, Gemmell; Callaghan, McNeill, Brogan; Johnstone, Hood, Wallace, Dalglish, Auld. Sub: Lennox

AIRDRIE: McKenzie; Jonquin, Caldwell; Menzies, Goodwin, D. Whiteford; J. Whiteford, Cowan, Busby, Jarvie, Wilson (Delaney)

Attendance: 47,184

Celtic marched on to the Cup Final after scoring two 2nd-half goals against a courageous Airdrie. The increased attendance had the fullest value for money as the entertainment did not flag for a moment. Airdrie's part-timers could claim justifiably that the result might have been reversed but for the unlucky break of the ball when they struck the crossbar in the 2nd minute and repeated it after the interval.

Final at Hampden Park May 8th

CELTIC (1) 1	RANGERS (0) 1
Lennox (40)	D. Johnstone (87)

CELTIC: Williams; Craig, Brogan; Connelly, McNeill, Hay; Johnstone, Lennox, Wallace, Callaghan, Hood. Sub: Macari

RANGERS: McCloy; Miller, Mathieson; Greig, McKinnon, Jackson; Henderson, Penman, (D. Johnstone), Stein, MacDonald, Johnston

Attendance: 120,092 *Referee:* T. Wharton

Derek Johnstone was brought into the team to replace Penman in the final 20 minutes and completed a modern football fairy tale by heading the vital equaliser to give his club another chance. Celtic had been thrown out of their stride in the 1st half by a passionately determined Rangers team who wanted to prove themselves anything but underdogs.

Final Replay at Hampden Park May 12th

CELTIC (2) 2	RANGERS (0) 1
Macari (24),	Craig o.g. (58)
Hood (25 pen)	

CELTIC: Williams; Craig, Brogan; Connelly, McNeill, Hay; Johnstone, Macari, Hood (Wallace), Callaghan, Lennox

RANGERS: McCloy; Denny, Mathieson; Greig, McKinnon, Jackson; Henderson, Penman, (D. Johnstone), Stein, MacDonald, Johnston

Attendance: 103,332 *Referee:* T. Wharton (Glasgow)

Lou Macari and Jimmy Johnstone held the key to Celtic's 21st Cup success. It was largely through their sharpness and trickery that Celtic established command before the interval. In a late rally Rangers almost forced extra-time when a Colin Stein shot hit Williams on the chest and rebounded clear.

EUROPEAN CUP

First Round First Leg September 16th

CELTIC (6) 9	KOKKOLA (Finland) (0) 0
Hood 3 (45 secs, 23, 36 pen),	
Wilson 2 (54, 70),	
Hughes (15),	
McNeill (22),	
Johnstone (38),	
Davidson (60)	

CELTIC: Williams; McGrain, Brogan; Murdoch, McNeill, Hay (Wilson); Johnstone, Connelly, Hood (Davidson), Lennox, Hughes

KOKKOLA: Isosaari; Korhonen, S. Makela; Makinen, Hautala, Ponkanen; Sorvisto, Raatikainen, A. Lamberg, Kallio, H. Lamberg

Attendance: 41,000

Celtic dominated the exchanges from start to finish although the pace and power of their game might have overwhelmed a much more experienced side than the Finns.

First Round Second Leg September 30th

KOKKOLA (0) 0	CELTIC (2) 5
	Wallace 2 (26, 46),
	Callaghan (35),
	Davidson (51),
	Lennox (72)

KOKKOLA: Isasaari, Korhonen, Malmuer; Hautala, Kangas, Sorosto; Raatikainen, A. Lamberg, Malesta, H. Lamberg, Kallio

CELTIC: Fallon; Craig (McGrain), Brogan; Murdoch (Dalglish), Connelly, Cattenach; Davidson, Wallace, Chalmers, Callaghan, Lennox

Attendance: 4,500

Celtic went through the formality of their Second-Leg European tie and scored 5 effortless goals. They won 14-0 on aggregate.

Second Round First Leg in Dublin October 21st

WATERFORT (Eire) (0) 0 CELTIC (4) 7
Wallace 3 (18 secs, 54, 56),
Murdoch 2 (26, 38),
Macari 2 (17, 86)

WATERFORD: Thomas; Bryan, Brennan; Maguire, Morrisey, McGeough; Casey, Hale, O'Neill, Buck (Power), Matthews

CELTIC: Williams; Craig, Quinn; Murdoch, McNeill, Hay; Connelly, Macari, Wallace (Davidson), Hood (Chalmers), Lennox

Attendance: 50,000

The 2nd half restarted 5 minutes late after the crowd invaded the pitch. Bottles were thrown onto the pitch and ugly violence continually erupted on the terracing. Celtic effortlessly swept their opponents aside and the referee might have invoked the U.E.F.A. law governing disorderly crowds and abandoned the match at half-time.

Second Round Second Leg November 4th

CELTIC (0) 3 WATERFORD (2) 2
Hughes (45), McNeill o.g. (18),
Johnstone 2 (56, 77) Matthews (30)

CELTIC: Williams; Craig, Gemmell; Murdoch (Brogan), McNeill, Hay; Johnstone, Lennox, Wallace (Hood), Connelly, Hughes

WATERFORD: Thomas; Bryan, Brennan; Maguire, Morrisey, McGeough; Casey, Hale, Kirkby, O'Neill, Matthews

Attendance: 19,000

Waterford unbelievably led 2-0 at the interval as they outplayed the home team. They obviously revelled in the unaccustomed wide green space at Parkhead. After half time the picture changed and Celtic ran out easy winners in the end. They won 10-2 on aggregate.

Quarter-Final First Leg March 10th

AJAX (Holland) (0) 3 CELTIC (0) 0
Cruyff (62),
Hulshoff (70), Keizer (90)

AJAX: Stuy; Vasovic, Suurbier; Hulshoff, Krol, Rijnders; Neeskens, Swart, Muhren, Cruyff, Keizer

CELTIC: Williams; Craig, Gemmell; Hay, McNeill, Brogan; Johnstone, Connelly, Wallace, Callaghan, Lennox

Attendance: 65,000

Celtic's hopes of keeping the score down were cruelly shattered by Keizer who gave his team a 3rd goal in the last minute. Celtic had held out defiantly against a siege on their goal, having prepared themselves for a fierce defensive encounter. Ajax swept into attack after attack, forcing innumerable corner-kicks.

Quarter-Final Second Leg at Hampden Park March 24th

CELTIC (1) 1 AJAX (0) 0
Johnstone (28)

CELTIC: Williams; Hay, Gemmell; Callaghan, McNeill, Brogan; Johnstone, Hood, Wallace (Davidson), Auld (Lennox), Hughes

AJAX: Stuy; Vasovic, Suurbier; Hulshoff, Krol, Rijnders; Neeskens, Blankenburg, Muhren, Cruyff, Keizer

Attendance: 83,684

The task of recovering three goals proved insurmountable. Celtic played to the best of their ability to pressurise Ajax all the way but their efforts were not good enough. In 28 minutes Johnstone scored his team's goal. Following a foul on the little winger by Krol, Auld flighted a free-kick into the goalmouth, Callaghan returned it smartly and Wallace touched it for Johnstone to prod it past Stuy. Celtic tried to step up the pace by taking off Auld in 62 minutes and substituting Lennox. 10 minutes later they brought on Davidson for Wallace. Stuy touched over a McNeill header in 72 minutes. 10 minutes from the end Hughes had a goal disallowed for offside. With victory near Ajax began time-wasting and Neeskens was booked by referee Lo Bello for feigning injury and play-acting. Ajax won 3-1 on aggregate.

David Hay, the present manager, a member of the Celtic squad in the early seventies.

APPEARANCES	League	League Cup	Scottish Cup	European Cup
Williams	31	8	8	5
McGrain	7	4+1S	–	1+1S
Gemmell	19	6	6	3
Murdoch	21+2S	8	1	4
McNeill	31	10	8	5
Brogan	26	8	7+1S	4+1S
Johnstone	30	9	8	4
Hay	27+1S	11	8	5
Hood	27+3S	10	8	3+1S
Lennox	22+2S	7+1S	4+2S	5+1S
Macari	8+3S	5+2S	1	1
Connelly	22+2S	11	4+1S	5
Hughes	14	7	1	3
Callaghan	19	3	8	3
Wilson	1	1+1S	–	–
Davidson	6+1S	–	2	1+3S
Wallace	25+1S	3+3S	7+1S	5
Craig	22	5	3	4
Cattenach	4	–	–	1
Fallon	3	3	–	1

APPEARANCES	League	League Cup	Scottish Cup	European Cup
Chalmers	3+1S	–	–	1+1S
Auld	4+1S	–	3	1
Dalglish	1+2S	–	1	–
Quinn	0+2S	2	–	1
Clark	1	–	–	–

GOALSCORERS:

League: Hood 22 (2 pens), Wallace 19 (1 pen), Lennox 10, Johnstone 8, Macari 5, Davidson 5, Hughes 5, Connelly 3, Own Goals 3, Murdoch 2, Chalmers 2, Callaghan 2, Hay 1, Gemmell 1, McNeill 1

League Cup: Lennox 6, Johnstone 5, Macari 5, Hughes 4, Gemmell 2 (2 pens), Callaghan 1, Connelly 1, Hay 1, Hood 1, Wilson 1, Wallace 1

Scottish Cup: Hood 7 (1 pen), Lennox 4, Wallace 3, Callaghan 2, Johnstone 2, McNeill 1, Gemmell 1 (pen), Davidson 1, Macari 1

European Cup: Wallace 5, Johnstone 4, Hood 3 (1 pen), Murdoch 2, Macari 2, Hughes 2, Wilson 2, Davidson 2, McNeill 1, Callaghan 1, Lennox 1.

The Celtic squad in 1970. Back row: George Connolly, David Hay, Tommy Gemmell, John Fallon, Billy McNeill (Captain), Evan Williams, Jim Craig, John Hughes, Tommy Callaghan. Front row: Jimmy Johnstone, Bobby Lennox, Bobby Murdoch, Harry Hood, Willie Wallace, Bertie Auld, Lou Macari and Jim Brogan.

Season 1971-72

Celtic's great run of success continued unabated with their 7th successive Championship win which set a new Scottish record. They finished a massive 10 points ahead of 2nd placed Aberdeen in the table, winning 28 of their 34 matches – their second best performance since the War. Billy McNeill was the only ever-present, and John 'Dixie' Deans, who was signed from Motherwell on the last day of October, was top scorer with 19 goals followed by Kenny Dalglish, who had not only established a 1st team place but had broken into the full International side, on 17. Lou Macari also made the full Scotland side during the season. Goalkeeper Denis Connaghan was signed from St Mirren and 5 players from the 'Lisbon Lions' era – Chalmers, Hughes, Wallace, Gemmell and Fallon – all departed for pastures new during the season. Another, Jim Craig, left for South Africa after the Cup Final win over Hibs. Old favourite Charlie Tully died, just after the start of the season, aged 47.

Celtic reached the League Cup Final for the 10th time. Their passage included two wins over Rangers at Ibrox, but despite starting the Final as odds-on favourites they were totally outplayed by a rampant Partick Thistle who created one of the biggest-ever Scottish football shocks by winning their first major trophy in 50 years.

Celtic, in their 4th successive Scottish Cup Final, ripped both their opponents, Hibs, and the football record books apart with the most convincing Scottish Cup Final win of the century. Deans atoned for his penalty-miss, which put them out of the European Cup, with a brilliant hat-trick which included one of the best solo goals ever seen at Hampden.

Celtic came close to making their 3rd European Cup Final. They gave a tremendous display in the First Leg of the Semi-Final in the San Siro Stadium, Milan to hold Internazionale to a no-scoring draw but despite almost constant pressure in the return in Glasgow they could not pierce the Italians' defence. 30 minutes of extra-time also failed to produce any goals, and so the match went to a nerve-jangling penalty tie-break. A miss by substitute Dixie Deans proved fatal and Inter scored with all 5 of their kicks to go into the Final.

League:	Champions
League Cup:	Finalists
Scottish Cup:	Winners
European Cup:	Semi-Finalists

SCOTTISH FIRST DIVISION

July 13th: Gordon Marshall was signed on a free transfer from Hibernian.

July 27th: Charlie Tully died aged 47.

September 4th
CELTIC (5) 9 — CLYDE (0) 1
Lennox 3 (28, 42, 87), Macari 2 (70, 76), Murdoch (5), Dalglish (7), McNeill (14), Callaghan (48) — Sullivan (83)

CELTIC: Williams; Hay, Gemmell; Murdoch, McNeill, Connelly; Johnstone, Lennox, Dalglish (Wallace), Callaghan, Macari

CLYDE: McCulloch; Mulheron, Swan; Burns, McVie, McHugh; Sullivan, McGrain, Flanagan, Hay, Hastings

Attendance: 30,000

September 9th: Steve Chalmers joined Morton.

September 11th
RANGERS (2) 2 — CELTIC (1) 3
W. Johnston (31 pen), Stein (45) — Macari (8), Dalglish (55), Johnstone (89)

RANGERS: McCloy; Jardine, Mathieson; Greig, Jackson, MacDonald; McLean (Henderson), Penman, Stein, Conn, Johnston

CELTIC: Williams; Brogan, Hay; Murdoch, McNeill, Connelly; Johnstone, Lennox, Dalglish, Callaghan, Macari

Attendance: 69,000

Rangers claimed that the game was won and lost midway through the 2nd half by the referee's decision to disallow a goal by Colin Stein for dangerous play. Only a moment or two earlier they had been left with only 10 men when Alfie Conn was ordered off for a foul on Tom Callaghan. In the last minute Jimmy Johnstone somehow managed to outjump the tall Rangers defenders and head the winner.

September 18th
CELTIC (2) 3 — MORTON (0) 1
Lennox (8), Clark o.g. (37), Hood (79) — Thorup (78)

CELTIC: Williams; Hay, Brogan; Murdoch, McNeill, Connelly; Hood, Lennox, Dalglish (Wallace), Callaghan, Macari

MORTON: Sorensen; Hayes, McDerment; Lumsden, Laughton, Clark; Thorup, Mason, Osborne, Murphy, Chalmers

Attendance: 35,000

September 25th
AIRDRIE (0) 0 — CELTIC (2) 5
Macari 3 (5, 28, 87), Lennox (61), Dalglish (65)

AIRDRIE: McKenzie; Jonquin, McKay; Delaney, Goodwin, Whiteford; Wilson, Menzies, Busby, Jarvie, Cowan (Young)

CELTIC: Williams; Craig (Hughes), Brogan; Hay, McNeill, Connelly; Wallace, Lennox, Dalglish, Callaghan, Macari

Attendance: 20,000

October 2nd
CELTIC (0) 0 — ST JOHNSTONE (1) 1
Connolly (32)

CELTIC: Williams; Craig, Brogan (Lennox); Hay, McNeill, Connelly; Johnstone, Dalglish, Wallace, Callaghan, Macari

ST JOHNSTONE: Donaldson; Lambie, Coburn; Rennie, Gordon, McPhee; Aird, Whitelaw, Pearson, Connolly, Aitken

Attendance: 38,000

October 9th
HIBERNIAN (0) 0 — CELTIC (0) 1
Macari (71)

HIBERNIAN: Herriot; Brownlie, Schaedler; Stanton, Black, Blackley; Duncan, Hamilton, Hazel, Auld, Cropley

CELTIC: Williams; Hay, Gemmell; Murdoch, McNeill, Connelly; Johnstone, Lennox, Hood, Macari, Callaghan

Attendance: 40,000

October 13th: Hay and Johnstone were in the Scotland team which beat Portugal 2-1 at Hampden Park.

October 16th
CELTIC (1) 3 — DUNDEE (0) 1
Dalglish 3 (35, 46, 51) — Duncan (47)

CELTIC: Williams; Hay, Gemmell; Murdoch, McNeill, Connelly; Johnstone, Dalglish, Hood, Callaghan, Macari

DUNDEE: Hewitt; R. Wilson, Johnston; Steele, Phillip, Houston; Duncan, Selway, Wallace, J. Scott (Kinninmonth), Lambie

Attendance: 32,000. Gemmell missed a penalty.

October 19th: John Hughes and Willie Wallace were transferred to Crystal Palace for a combined fee of £50,000.

October 25th: Denis Connaghan was signed from St Mirren for an undisclosed fee.

October 27th
DUNFERMLINE (1) 1 — CELTIC (0) 2
Gillespie (8) — McNeill (61), Lennox (82)

DUNFERMLINE: McGarr; Callaghan, Mercer; Fraser, McNichol, O'Neill; Paterson, Scott, Mitchell, Gardner, Gillespie

CELTIC: Connaghan; Craig, Hay; Murdoch (Brogan), McNeill, Connelly; Dalglish, Macari, Hood, Lennox, Callaghan

Attendance: 16,000

October 30th
AYR UNITED (0) 0 — CELTIC (1) 1
Dalglish (34)

AYR UNITED: Stewart; Fillipi, Murphy; Fleming, Quinn, Mitchell (Reynolds); Doyle, Graham, Ingram, McLean, Stevenson

CELTIC: Connaghan; Craig, Brogan; Hay, McNeill, Connelly; Dalglish, Macari, Davidson, Lennox, Hood

Attendance: 18,000

League positions

	P	W	D	L	F	A	Pts
1 Aberdeen	9	8	1	0	26	4	17
2 CELTIC	9	8	0	1	27	7	16
3 St Johnstone	9	5	2	2	18	11	12
4 Hearts	9	4	4	1	13	9	12
5 Hibernian	9	5	1	3	18	8	11

October 31st: Dixie Deans was signed from Motherwell for £17,500.

November 6th
CELTIC (0) 1 — ABERDEEN (0) 1
Hood (59) — McNeill o.g. (77)

CELTIC: Connaghan; Craig, Brogan; Hay, McNeill, Connelly; Johnstone, Hood, Dalglish, Macari, Callaghan

ABERDEEN: Clark; G. Murray, Hermiston; S. Murray, Young, Buchan; Forrest, Robb, Harper, Willoughby, Graham

Attendance: 64,000

November 10th: Hay and Johnstone were in the Scotland team which beat Belgium 1-0 at Pittodrie. Dalglish made an appearance as a substitute.

November 13th
DUNDEE UNITED (1) 1 CELTIC (0) 5
Gordon (19) — Hood 2 (49, 50), Macari (72), Dalglish (77), Lennox (80)

DUNDEE UNITED: McAlpine; Rolland, Cameron; W. Smith, D. Smith, Henry; Traynor, Reid, Copland, Gordon, Stevenson

CELTIC: Connaghan; Craig, Brogan; Hay, McNeill, Connelly; Johnstone, Hood, Dalglish (Lennox), Macari, Callaghan

Attendance: 18,500

November 20th
CELTIC (1) 2 FALKIRK (0) 0
Dalglish (5), McNeill (46)

CELTIC: Connaghan; Craig, Quinn; Callaghan, McNeill, Hay; Johnstone, Macari, Dalglish, Lennox, Hood

FALKIRK: Devlin; Abel, Jones; Markie, Miller, Shirra; Hoggan, Young, Somner, Ferguson, Roxburgh

Attendance: 20,000

November 27th
PARTICK THISTLE (1) 1 CELTIC (3) 5
Bone (42) — Hood (12), Johnstone (19), Dalglish (22), Strachan o.g. (83), Deans (86)

PARTICK THISTLE: Rough; Hansen, Forsyth; Glavin, Campbell, Strachan; McQuade, Coulston, Bone, Rae, Lawrie (Gibson)

CELTIC: Connaghan; Hay, Quinn; Callaghan, McNeill, Connelly; Johnstone, Dalglish, Deans, Macari, Hood

Attendance: 33,000

December 1st: Hay, Johnstone and Dalglish were in the Scotland team beaten 2-1 by Holland in Amsterdam.

December 4th
CELTIC (1) 5 KILMARNOCK (0) 1
Johnstone 2 (31, 65), Deans (55), Dalglish 2 (70, 86) — Mathie (57)

CELTIC: Connaghan; Hay, Quinn; Callaghan, McNeill, Connelly; Johnstone, Dalglish, Deans, Macari (Wilson), Hood

KILMARNOCK: Hunter; Whyte, Cairns; Maxwell, Rodman, McGrory; McSherry, Gilmour, Mathie, Morrison, Cook

Attendance: 28,000

December 11th
CELTIC (1) 2 EAST FIFE (1) 1
Deans 2 (12, 75) — Hughes (40)

CELTIC: Connaghan; Hay, Quinn; Callaghan, McNeill, Brogan; Johnstone, Dalglish, Deans, Hood, Wilson

EAST FIFE: Gorman; Duncan, McQuade; Cairns, Martis, Clarke; Love (Bernard), Honeyman, Hughes, Hamilton, McPhee

Attendance: 20,000. Cairns was ordered off.

December 17th: Tommy Gemmell was transferred to Nottingham Forest for £35,000.

December 18th
MOTHERWELL (1) 1 CELTIC (4) 5
McInally (33) — Deans (10), Dalglish 2 (31, 32), Lennox (41), Johnstone (62)

MOTHERWELL: Ritchie; Gillespie, Wark; John Muir, Whiteford, McInally; Campbell, Jim Muir, McCabe (Martin), Goldthorpe, Heron

CELTIC: Connaghan; Hay, Quinn; Dalglish, McNeill, Connelly; Johnstone, Lennox, Deans, Callaghan, Hood

Attendance: 19,000

December 25th
CELTIC (2) 3 HEARTS (1) 2
Hood (1), Johnstone (36), Deans (70) — Renton (31), Brown (77)

CELTIC: Connaghan; Hay, Quinn; Dalglish, McNeill, Connelly; Johnstone, Lennox, Deans, Callaghan, Hood

HEARTS: Cruikshank; Sneddon, Oliver; Brown, Veitch, Thomson; Fleming, Renton, Ford, Winchester, T. Murray

Attendance: 34,000

League positions

	P	W	D	L	F	A	Pts
1 CELTIC	17	15	1	1	55	15	31
2 Aberdeen	17	14	2	1	53	10	30
3 Rangers	17	12	0	5	40	18	24
4 Hibernian	17	10	3	4	30	14	23
5 Dundee	17	8	5	4	30	19	21

January 1st
CLYDE (0) 0 CELTIC (5) 7
Hood 2 (15, 74), Mulheron o.g. (19), Davidson (72), Deans 2 (24, 37), Dalglish (85)

CLYDE: Cairney; Anderson, Mulheron; Burns, McHugh, Glasgow (McVie); Sullivan, McGrain, Brown, Thomson, Aherne

CELTIC: Connaghan; Hay, Brogan; Dalglish, McNeill, Connelly; Davidson, Lennox, Deans (McGrain), Callaghan, Hood

Attendance: 20,000

January 3rd
CELTIC (1) 2 — RANGERS (0) 1
Johnstone (35), Brogan (90) — Stein (81)

CELTIC: Connaghan; Hay, Brogan; Dalglish, McNeill, Connelly; Johnstone, Lennox, Deans, Callaghan, Hood

RANGERS: McCloy; Jardine, Mathieson; Greig, Jackson, Smith; McLean, Johnstone, Stein, MacDonald, Johnston

Attendance: 70,000

Rangers were stunned by an injury-time winner from Brogan. With the game ebbing towards the draw, McNeill took a free-kick. The ball came to Hood and as he brought it under control, Brogan began a run into the area which he timed perfectly to meet Hood's lob and glance the ball home. Rangers hardly deserved to lose. Brogan's bolt from the blue left the masses at the Celtic end to exult over their rivals who stood in mute disbelief at the other end.

January 8th
MORTON (1) 1 — CELTIC (1) 1
Gillies (19) — Hood (32)

MORTON: Sorensen; Hayes, Shevlane; Lumsden, Anderson, Rankin (Thorup); Gillies, Mason, Osborne, Murphy, Chalmers

CELTIC: Connaghan; Hay, Brogan; Dalglish, McNeill, Connelly; Johnstone, Lennox, Deans, Callaghan, Hood

Attendance: 14,000

January 15th
CELTIC (1) 2 — AIRDRIE (0) 0
Dalglish (21), Lennox (77)

CELTIC: Connaghan; Hay, Brogan; Callaghan, McNeill, Connelly; Johnstone, Dalglish, Deans, Lennox, Hood

AIRDRIE: McKenzie; Jonquin, Clarke; Menzies, McKinlay, D. Whiteford; Wilson (J. Whiteford), Walker, Busby, Jarvie, Cowan

Attendance: 27,000

January 20th: Dave Cattenach joined Falkirk.

January 22nd
ST JOHNSTONE (0) 0 — CELTIC (1) 3
Dalglish (5), Deans 2 (71, 85)

ST JOHNSTONE: Robertson; Coburn, Argue; Rennie, Gordon, Rooney; Aird, Whitelaw (Pearson), Connolly, Hall, Aitken

CELTIC: Williams; Craig, Brogan; Hay, McNeill, Connelly; Johnstone, Dalglish, Deans, Lennox, Hood (Callaghan)

Attendance: 14,500

January 27th: Gordon Marshall joined Aberdeen for £1,000.

January 29th
CELTIC (0) 2 — HIBERNIAN (1) 1
Hood (54), Deans (74) — Hay o.g. (23)

CELTIC: Williams; Craig, Brogan; Hay, McNeill, Connelly; Johnstone, Dalglish, Deans, Lennox, Hood

HIBERNIAN: Herriot; Brownlie, Schaedler; Stanton, Black, Blackley; Edwards (Hazel), Hamilton, Gordon, Cropley, Duncan

Attendance: 38,500

February 19th
CELTIC (0) 1 — DUNFERMLINE (0) 0
Macari (63)

CELTIC: Williams; Hay, Brogan; Murdoch, McNeill, Connelly; Dalglish, Macari, Deans, Lennox, Hood

DUNFERMLINE: Arrol; Callaghan, Lunn; Fraser, Cushley, McNichol; Thomson (Gillespie), Mitchell, Scott, Mercer, O'Neill

Attendance: 25,000

League positions

	P	W	D	L	F	A	Pts
1 CELTIC	24	21	2	1	73	18	44
2 Aberdeen	25	18	5	2	67	19	41
3 Rangers	25	17	1	7	54	24	35
4 Hibernian	25	13	5	7	43	25	31
5 Dundee	24	10	10	4	43	25	30

February 29th: John Fallon joined Motherwell.

March 4th
CELTIC (0) 2 — AYR UNITED (0) 0
Deans 2 (57, 74)

CELTIC: Williams; Hay, Brogan; Murdoch, McNeill, Connelly; Hood, Dalglish (McCluskey), Deans, Callaghan, Lennox

AYR UNITED: Stewart; McFadzean, Murphy; McAnespie, Quinn, Fillipi; Doyle, Graham, Ingram, McGregor, Robertson (Mitchell)

Attendance: 25,000

March 11th
ABERDEEN (0) 1 — CELTIC (0) 1
Harper (81) — Lennox (73)

ABERDEEN: Marshall; Boel, Hermiston; S. Murray, Young, G. Murray; Forrest, Robb, Harper, Willoughby, Graham

CELTIC: Williams; McGrain, Brogan; Murdoch, McNeill, Connelly; Hood, Hay, Dalglish (Callaghan), Macari, Lennox

Attendance: 33,000

March 25th
FALKIRK (0) 0 CELTIC (0) 1
Davidson (86)

FALKIRK: Donaldson; Abel, Gibson; Cattenach, Markie, Kennedy; Hoggan, Harley, Jack, Ferguson, Somner

CELTIC: Williams; McGrain (Macari), Quinn; Hay, McNeill, Connelly; Davidson, Dalglish, Deans, Callaghan, Wilson

Attendance: 18,000. Danny McGrain fractured his skull after a collision with Somner.

March 28th: Former Morton goalkeeper Lief Neilsen was signed as cover for Williams and Connaghan.

April 1st
CELTIC (3) 3 PARTICK THISTLE (1) 1
Davidson 2 (20 secs, 14), Johnstone (25) Coulston (42)

CELTIC: Williams; Craig, Quinn; Murdoch, McNeill, Connelly; Johnstone, Davidson, Deans, Callaghan, Lennox

PARTICK THISTLE: Rough; Reid, Forsyth; Smith, Clark, Strachan; McQuade, Glavin, Coulston, A. Rae, Lawrie

Attendance: 27,000

April 8th
KILMARNOCK (0) 1 CELTIC (1) 3
Morrison (50) Deans (45), Davidson (64), Wilson (89)

KILMARNOCK: Hunter; Whyte (Cairns), Dickson; Maxwell, Rodman, McGrory; McSherry, Gilmour, Mathie, Morrison, Cook

CELTIC: Williams; Craig, McCluskey; Murdoch, McNeill, Connelly; Johnstone, Davidson, Deans, Callaghan, Lennox (Wilson)

Attendance: 15,000

April 15th
EAST FIFE (0) 0 CELTIC (2) 3
Deans 2 (39, 77), Hood (43)

EAST FIFE: Gorman; Duncan, McQuade; Walker, Martis, Clarke; Bernard (Honeyman), Borthwick, Hughes, Hamilton, McPhee

CELTIC: Williams; Craig, Quinn; Murdoch, McNeill, Connelly; Hood, Dalglish, Deans, Callaghan, Macari (McCluskey)

Attendance: 12,086. Celtic clinched the Championship with this win.

April 22nd
CELTIC (3) 5 MOTHERWELL (1) 2
Deans 2 (37, 75), Murdoch 2 (33 pen, 69 pen), Lennox (45) Muir (28), McInally (57)

CELTIC: Williams; Craig, McCluskey; Murdoch, McNeill, Connelly; Johnstone, Dalglish, Deans, Callaghan, Lennox

MOTHERWELL: Fallon; Whiteford, Wark; Forsyth, McCallum, Watson; McInally, Martin, Muir, Lawson, Heron

Attendance: 20,000

April 25th
CELTIC (0) 3 DUNDEE UNITED (0) 0
Johnstone (46), Lennox (51), Deans (83)

CELTIC: Williams; Craig, Brogan; Murdoch, McNeill, Connelly; Johnstone, Dalglish, Deans, Callaghan, Lennox

DUNDEE UNITED: McAlpine; Rolland, Cameron; Copland, Smith, Gray; Fleming, Kopel, Gardner (Knox), K. Cameron, Traynor

Attendance: 13,000

April 29th
HEARTS (2) 4 CELTIC (1) 1
Murray (22), Ford (34), Renton (54), Brown (76) Murdoch (9 pen)

HEARTS: Garland; Sneddon, Clunie; Thomson, Anderson, Wood; Murray, Brown, Ford, Renton, Lynch

CELTIC: Williams; Craig, Brogan; Murdoch, McNeill, Connelly; Hood, Hay, Deans, Macari, Dalglish

Attendance: 10,500

May 1st
DUNDEE (1) 1 CELTIC (0) 1
I. Scott (20) Macari (62)

DUNDEE: Hewitt; R. Wilson, Johnston; Phillip, Stewart, Houston; Wallace, Duncan, I. Scott, J. Scott, Ford

CELTIC: Williams; Craig, Brogan; Dalglish, McNeill, Connelly; Johnstone, Deans, Macari, Callaghan, Lennox

Attendance: 12,000

May 20th: McNeill and Johnstone were in the Scotland team which beat Northern Ireland 2-0 at Hampden Park.

May 24th: Billy McNeill was in the Scotland team which beat Wales 1-0 at Hampden Park. Lou Macari made an appearance as substitute.

May 27th: McNeill and Macari were in the Scotland team beaten 1-0 by England at Hampden Park. Johnstone made an appearance as substitute.

June 29th: Lou Macari scored both of Scotland's goals in a 2-2 draw with Yugoslavia in Belo Horizonte, Brazil.

July 2nd: Macari was in the Scotland team which drew 0-0 with Czechoslovakia in Porto Alegre, Brazil.

July 5th: Macari was in the Scotland team which was beaten 1-0 by Brazil in Rio de Janeiro, Brazil.

HEARTS: Garland; Sneddon (N. Murray), Jeffries; Thomson, Anderson, Wood; T. Murray, Brown, Ford, Renton, Lynch

CELTIC: Williams; Craig, Hay (Quinn), Murdoch, McNeill, Connelly; Hood, Macari, Dalglish, Callaghan, Lennox

Attendance: 40,029

Semi-Final at Hampden Park April 12th
KILMARNOCK (0) 1 CELTIC (1) 3
Cook (47) Deans 2 Macari

KILMARNOCK: Hunter; Dickson, Cairns; Maxwell, Rodman, McGrory; McSherry, Gilmour, Mathie, Morrison, Cook. Sub: Fleming

CELTIC: Williams; Craig, McCluskey; Murdoch, McNeill, Connelly; Johnstone, Macari, Deans, Callaghan, Lennox. Sub: Dalglish

Attendance: 48,398

Jimmy Johnstone hit the form that made him a world-class player and played a prominent role in all 3 Celtic goals in a game which was played in a sporting but typical Cup-tie atmosphere. Celtic were confronted by Alistair Hunter's outstanding goalkeeping, and it was certainly not his fault that Kilmarnock slid out of the competition.

Final at Hampden Park May 6th
CELTIC (2) 6 HIBERNIAN (1) 1
McNeill (2), Gordon (12)
Deans 3 (23, 54, 74),
Macari 2 (83, 87)

CELTIC: Williams; Craig, Brogan; Murdoch, McNeill, Connelly; Johnstone, Deans, Macari, Dalglish, Callaghan. Sub: Lennox

HIBERNIAN: Herriot; Brownlie, Schaedler; Stanton, Black, Blackley; Edwards, Hazel, Gordon, O'Rourke, Duncan (Auld)

Attendance: 106,102 *Referee:* A. MacKenzie (Larbert)

Celtic scored the most convincing Scottish Cup Final win this century. They went ahead through McNeill in only 2 minutes. Callaghan took the kick and McNeill, running in, took it in his stride and lashed it past Herriot. Hibs drew level 10 minutes later when Duncan smashed the ball low across goal and Gordon got a foot in ahead of Williams and McNeill. Celtic went back in front again in 23 minutes when Deans headed home a Murdoch free-kick. The same player scored a wonderful solo goal in 54 minutes. 3 times he might have lost the ball before he evaded Herriot for a 2nd time and shot emphatically into the net. Deans, whose penalty miss put Celtic out of the European Cup, clinched his hat-trick in 74 minutes when he ran onto a brilliant pass from Callaghan and beat the advancing Herriot. Lou Macari got into the act with 2 late goals to take the total to 6.

EUROPEAN CUP

First Round First Leg September 15th
BK 1903 COPENHAGEN CELTIC (1) 1
(Denmark) (2) 2 Macari (20)
Johansen 2 (13, 24)

BK 1903: Jensen; Nielsen, Petersen; Westergaard, Andressen, Sjoelberg; Thygesen, Mathiesen, Forssing, Aabling, Johansen

CELTIC: Marshall; Craig, Gemmell; Murdoch, McNeill, Connelly; Johnstone (Wallace), Lennox, Dalglish, Callaghan, Macari

Attendance: 6,600

Celtic were embarrassingly beaten by the Danish Champions whose successful tactics were to slow the game to their pace. Only Murdoch and the opportunist Macari appeared capable of turning the game.

First Round Second Leg September 29th
CELTIC (1) 3 BK 1903 COPENHAGEN
Wallace 2 (23, 85), (0) 0
Callaghan (79)

CELTIC: Williams; Craig, Brogan; Hay, McNeill, Connelly; Johnstone, Lennox (Hughes), Wallace, Callaghan, Macari

BK 1903: Jensen; E. Nielsen, Andressen; Petersen (Christiansen), Schoberg, Westergaard; T. Nielsen, Mathiesen, Aabling, Forssing, Johansen

Attendance: 53,000

Not unnaturally the crowd expected Celtic to run amok after Wallace had levelled the aggregate in 23 minutes, but the Danes put up a defiant stand and goalkeeper Jensen crowned a brilliant performance by saving an explosive penalty-kick from Hughes in 68 minutes after the substitute had been brought down in atempting to beat a 3rd defender. Celtic persevered and their skill was rewarded with 2 goals in the final 11 minutes. They won 4-2 on aggregate.

Second Round First Leg October 20th
CELTIC (4) 5 SLIEMA WANDERERS
Hood 2 (11, 26), (Malta) (0) 0
Gemmell (4), Brogan (62),
Macari (79)

CELTIC: Williams; Hay, Gemmell; Murdoch (Davidson), Connelly, Brogan; Johnstone, Hood (Lennox), Dalglish, Callaghan, Macari

SLIEMA: Pearson; Spiteri, J. Aquilina; Serge, Micallef, Briffa; Vella (Coruona), Darmanin, Cocks, E. Aquilina, Falzon

Attendance: 29,000

Had the score been doubled it would in no way have exaggerated the difference between the sides.

Second Round Second Leg November 3rd
SLIEMA WANDERERS CELTIC (1) 2
(1) 1 Hood (42), Lennox (55)
Cocks (1)

SLIEMA: Pearson; Borg, J. Aquilina; Serge, Micallef, Briffa; Vassalo, Darmanin, Cocks, Falzon, E. Aquilina

CELTIC: Williams; Craig, Gemmell; Dalglish, McNeill, Connelly; Callaghan, Macari, Hood, Davidson (Hancock), Lennox

Attendance: 10,000

Celtic found themselves a goal down in the 1st minute but they recovered to do all that was needed to win the match. They won 7-1 on aggregate.

Quarter-Final First Leg March 8th

UIJPEST DOSZA (Hungary) (0) 1 Horvath (64) — CELTIC (1) 2 Horvath o.g. (19), Macari (85)

UIJPEST: Szentmihalyi; Nosko, Horvath; Maurer, Juhasz, E. Dunai; Zambo, Fazekas, Bene, A. Dunai (Nagy), Toth

CELTIC: Williams; McGrain, Brogan; Murdoch, McNeill, Connelly; Hood, Hay, Dalglish, Macari, Lennox

Attendance: 31,000

Celtic produced one of their finest performances on the continent and brought high praise from Manager Stein who said, 'Considering the age of the team this was Celtic's best display at this level in Europe.' They did not allow Uijpest to build a rhythm, and little or nothing was seen of Bene, Antal Dunai or Fazekas, their feared strikers. Only after Horvath had redeemed an own goal with the equaliser did Celtic come under severe pressure, but they held out and with 5 minutes left Macari scored a deserved 2nd when he breasted down a Dalglish cross with his back to the goal and turned and slipped the ball into the net.

Quarter-Final Second Leg March 22nd

CELTIC (0) 1 Macari (64) — UIJPEST DOSZA (1) 1 A. Dunai (5)

CELTIC: Williams; McGrain, Brogan (Johnstone); Murdoch, McNeill, Connelly; Hood, Hay, Dalglish, Macari, Lennox

UIJPEST: Szentmihalyi; Kaposzta, Maurer; Juhasz, E. Dunai, Horvath; Fazekas, Bene, A. Dunai, Zambo, Toth (Gorocs)

Attendance: 75,000

The suspicion that the best of Uijpest had not been seen in the First Leg was all too soon confirmed when they took the lead in the 5th minute. In 64 minutes the Uijpest defence finally gave way. Maurer was short with a headed-back clearance to his goalkeeper and Macari, having anticipated the move, ran round Maurer and lobbed the ball over Szentmihalyi's head into the net. Only once did Uijpest threaten again when with 11 minutes to go Bene broke clear on the right, only to send his shot beyond the far post. Macari was Celtic's most dangerous forward; his harassing and running were a constant source of distraction to the tall and powerful Hungarian defence. Celtic won 3-2 on aggregate.

Semi-Final First Leg April 5th

INTERNAZIONALE MILAN (0) 0 — CELTIC (0) 0

INTER: Vieri; Bellugi, Facchetti; Bertini, Oriali, Burgnich; Jair, Pellizzaro (Ghio), Boninsegna, Mazzola, Frustalupi

CELTIC: Williams; Craig, Brogan (P. McCluskey); Murdoch, McNeill, Connelly; Johnstone, Dalglish, Macari, Callaghan, Lennox

Attendance: 80,000

Celtic gave a tremendous display of concentration and application to gain a draw in the San Siro Stadium although inexperienced in several positions. As a spectacle the match was not particularly entertaining or exciting for the 80,000 spectators. Inter seemed to rely almost completely on Mazzola to create openings and for Boninsegna to finish them off but they very seldom looked like scoring. As the 1st half developed it became clear that Celtic's tactics were to be the same safe and sensible ones they adopted in Budapest – Macari was the only constant target man, with Lennox and Callaghan coming through when they could. The closest the Italian Champions came to scoring was when Williams had to make a great save from Pellizzaro in the 1st half and when Connelly headed off the line in a furious period of activity in the 2nd, but eventually time ran out for Inter and Celtic's purpose had been achieved.

Semi-Final Second Leg April 19th

CELTIC (0) 0 — INTERNAZIONALE MILAN (0) 0

After Extra Time

CELTIC: Williams; Craig, McCluskey; Murdoch, McNeill, Connelly; Johnstone, Dalglish (Deans), Macari, Callaghan, Lennox

INTER: Vieri; Bellugi, Facchetti; Oriali, Giubertoni, Burgnich; Jair, Bedin, Bertini (Pellizzaro), Mazzola, Frustalupi

Attendance: 75,000

Having fought a war of attrition for 210 minutes of football in which neither side could pierce the other's defence, Inter went through to the Final when they scored 5 penalties to Celtic's 4. Celtic had made all the running, inspired by the abundant skills of Murdoch. Somehow Inter held out right through the extra 30 minutes and the match went to a penalty tie-breaker. Mazzola scored easily from the first penalty but Deans' kick flew over the crossbar, leaving him an inconsolable figure. Williams got to Facchetti's effort but could not stop it. Then in turn Craig, Frustalupi, Johnstone, Pellizzaro and McCluskey made no mistake, and when Jair scored the agony was over. Murdoch came up to complete the formalities. He too scored but Deans' miss had proved fatal and Inter went into the Final to face the mighty Ajax.

APPEARANCES	League	League Cup	Scottish Cup	European Cup
Williams	20	10	6	7
Connaghan	14	–	–	–
Brogan	20+1S	4	4	5
Craig	16	4+1S	3	5
Gemmell	3	4	–	3
McGrain	2+1S	4	1	2
Quinn	9	–	0+1S	–
Callaghan	28+2S	10	6	6
Connelly	32	10	5	8
Dalglish	31	7+1S	4	7
Hay	28	10	4	4
McNeill	34	8	6	7
Murdoch	15	6	6	6
Davidson	5	–	–	1+1S
Hood	24	4+2S	3	4
McCluskey	2+2S	–	1+1S	1+1S
Hughes	0+1S	4+1S	–	0+1S
Johnstone	23	8	2	5+1S
Lennox	24+2S	9	4	7+1S
Macari	19+1S	6	5	8
Wallace	2+2S	1+1S	–	1+1S
Wilson	2+2S	–	1	–
Deans	21	–	5	0+1S
McLaughlin	–	1	–	–
Marshall	–	–	–	1

GOALSCORERS

League: Deans 19, Dalglish 17, Lennox 12, Hood 11, Macari 10, Johnstone 9, Davidson 5, Murdoch 4 (3 pens), McNeill 3, Own Goals 3, Callaghan 1, Brogan 1, Wilson 1

League Cup: Dalglish 5 (1 pen), Macari 5, Hood 5, Lennox 4, Hay 3, Callaghan 2, Johnstone 1, Hughes 1, Wallace 1, Own Goals 1

Scottish Cup: Deans 8, Macari 5, Callaghan 2, Lennox 2, McNeill 1, Murdoch 1, Dalglish 1

European Cup: Macari 4, Hood 3, Wallace 2, Callaghan 1, Gemmell 1, Brogan 1, Lennox 1, Own Goals 1

Hibs have been defeated 6-2 and Celtic have just won the 1969 League Cup for the fourth time in succession.

Season 1972-73

Celtic managed to resist a strong challenge from Rangers to win their 8th successive League title. They were beaten only 3 times during the season – all away from home – and they put together a run of 14 unbeaten matches from the beginning of February to the end of the season when they clinched the title, in their final match, at Easter Road. As a result of ground alterations at Celtic Park their first 2 home matches – against Kilmarnock and Rangers – were played at Hampden. Lou Macari was transferred to Manchester United for a record £200,000 fee halfway through the season, and part of that money was used to strengthen the team with the signing of Ally Hunter from Kilmarnock and Andy Lynch from Hearts. Aberdeen midfield star Steve Murray was also signed at the end of the season for a fee of £50,000. George Connelly was named as Scotland's Footballer of the Year and Danny McGrain completed a remarkable recovery from a fractured skull to make the right-back position his own and also to break into the full International team. Dalglish and Connelly both played in 32 matches and Dalglish and Deans finished as joint top scorers with 21 goals each. The Charlton brothers paid Celtic a great tribute by inviting them to be their opponents in both of their testimonial matches, Celtic drawing 0-0 with Manchester United on September 18th and beating Leeds United 4-3 on May 7th.

Dundee and Aberdeen were again beaten in Celtic's run to their 11th League Cup Final in which their opponents were Hibs. The Easter Road team gained revenge for their humiliating defeat in the previous season's Scottish Cup Final. They dominated the midfield and 2 goals from Stanton and O'Rourke gave them their 1st major honour for 20 years. Hibs also beat Celtic in the Final of the Drybrough Cup at Hampden, winning 5-3 after extra time.

Celtic had 2 tough Fifth-Round matches with Aberdeen before a late goal from Billy McNeill at Pittodrie took them through to the Scottish Cup Semi-Final where they faced Dundee. They also needed a replay and extra-time to beat the Dens Parkers to reach their 37th final. It was fitting that their opponents in the Final should be Rangers. The match lived up to its pre-match billing but it was not to be Celtic's day. They surrendered an early lead and Rangers won 3-2 to take the trophy for the first time since 1966.

In the Second Round of the European Cup Uijpest Dosza gained revenge for their defeat the previous season with a devastating performance in the return in Budapest to win 4-2 on aggregate.

League:	Champions
League Cup:	Runners-Up
Scottish Cup:	Runners-Up
European Cup:	Second Round

SCOTTISH FIRST DIVISION

July 26th: Israeli International Mordechai Spiegler played for Celtic in a closed-door game against St Mirren.

September 2nd at Hampden Park

CELTIC (4) 6	KILMARNOCK (1) 2
Hood 3 (3, 15, 55), Deans 2 (7, 37), Murdoch (83 pen)	Cook (26), Morrison (66)

CELTIC: Connaghan; McGrain, Brogan (Lennox); Murdoch, McNeill, Connelly; Hood, Dalglish, Deans, Callaghan, Wilson

KILMARNOCK: Hunter; Whyte, Dickson; Gilmour, McGrory, Lee; Smith, Maxwell, Morrison, McSherry, Cook

Attendance: 11,651

September 9th
MORTON (0) 0 — CELTIC (2) 2
Murdoch 2 (13, 21 pen)

MORTON: Sorensen; Hayes, Shevlane; Rankin, Anderson, Clark; Gillies (Lumsden), Mason, Christiansen, Chalmers, Armstrong

CELTIC: Williams; McGrain, Callaghan (Macari); McCluskey, McNeill, Connelly; Hood, Dalglish, Deans, Murdoch, Lennox

Attendance: 15,000

September 16th at Hampden Park
CELTIC (2) 3 — RANGERS (0) 1
Dalglish (2), Johnstone (17), Macari (49) — Greig (90)

CELTIC: Williams; McGrain, McCluskey; Murdoch, McNeill, Connelly; Johnstone (Hood), Dalglish, Deans, Macari, Callaghan

RANGERS: McCloy; Jardine, Mathieson; Greig, Jackson, D. Smith; Stein, Denny, D. Johnstone, MacDonald, Johnston (Conn)

Attendance: 50,416

The final score gave little indication of Celtic's superiority. Celtic, announcing Jimmy Johnstone's return as outside-right issued him with shorts bearing the No. 7 and then played him at outside-left. After only 2 minutes a wide-arcing ball by Macari drew McCloy out to the right of his goal. Jimmy Johnstone headed the ball back over the goalkeeper and Dalglish touched it into goal. In 17 minutes the Johnstone-Dalglish double act again went into effective action. Dalglish cut along the goal-line and pushed the ball towards Johnstone. The winger's 1st attempt to meet the pass landed him flat on his back but he got a 2nd stab which put the ball into the net.3 minutes into the 2nd half Jardine passed back too softly for McCloy and Macari nipped in quickly to clip the ball into goal. So it went until, the last minute when a fine run and pass by Smith enabled Greig to score Rangers' goal and earn him a cheer from the Celtic support.

September 23rd
DUNDEE (2) 2 — CELTIC (0) 0
I. Scott (7), Gray (13)

DUNDEE: Hewitt; R. Wilson, Houston; Robinson, Phillip, Stewart; J. Wilson, Gray, Wallace (Pringle), J. Scott, I. Scott

CELTIC: Williams; McGrain, Quinn; Murdoch, McNeill, Connelly; Johnstone, McCluskey (Deans), Dalglish, Macari, Callaghan

Attendance: 18,300

September 30th
CELTIC (1) 1 — AYR UNITED (0) 0
Deans (15)

CELTIC: Williams; McGrain, McCluskey; Murdoch, McNeill, Callaghan; Johnstone, Dalglish, Deans, Macari, Hood

AYR UNITED: Stewart; Fillipi, Murphy; Fleming, Rogerson, McCulloch; Doyle, Stevenson, Ingram, McLean (McGovern), Graham

Attendance: 25,000

October 7th
CELTIC (1) 1 — AIRDRIE (1) 1
Lennox (36) — Fury (14)

CELTIC: Connaghan; McGrain, McCluskey; Murdoch, McNeill, Connelly; Hood (Davidson), Dalglish, Macari, Callaghan, Lennox

AIRDRIE: McKenzie; Caldwell, Jonquin; Menzies, McKinlay, D. Whiteford; Wilson, Walker, Busby, Fury, Cowan

Attendance: 20,000

October 14th
PARTICK THISTLE (0) 0 — CELTIC (1) 4
Hay (43), Deans (48), Lennox (66), Dalglish (86)

PARTICK THISTLE: Rough; Gray (Gibson), Forsyth; Smith, Clark, Strachan; Lawrie, Glavin, Coulston, A. Rae, McQuade

CELTIC: Williams; Hay, Brogan (Hood); Murdoch, McNeill, Connelly; Dalglish, Macari, Deans, Callaghan, Lennox

Attendance: 25,699

October 18th: Lou Macari was in the Scotland team which beat Denmark 4-1 in a World Cup Qualifying match in Copenhagen. He scored one of the goals. Dalglish made an appearance as a substitute.

October 21st
CELTIC (1) 3 — EAST FIFE (0) 0
Hood (45), Deans (80), Lennox (84)

CELTIC: Williams; McGrain, Hay; Murdoch (Hood), McNeill, Connelly; Dalglish, Macari, Deans, Callaghan, Lennox

EAST FIFE: Gorman; Duncan, McQuade; Hamilton, Martis, Clarke; Hegarty, Dailey, Green (Honeyman), Borthwick, McPhee

Attendance: 20,000

October 28th
ABERDEEN (1) 2 — CELTIC (2) 3
Varga 2 (25, 81) — Deans (13), Macari (15), Dalglish (67)

ABERDEEN: Clark; Willoughby, Hermiston; Murray, Young (Graham), Taylor; Varga, Robb, Harper, Jarvie, Mitchell

CELTIC: Williams; Hay, McGrain; Connelly, McNeill, McCluskey; Dalglish, Macari, Deans, Callaghan, Lennox

Attendance: 36,000

League positions

	P	W	D	L	F	A	Pts
1 CELTIC	9	7	1	1	23	8	15
2 Dundee United	9	7	0	2	19	11	14
3 Hibernian	9	6	1	2	19	10	13
4 Aberdeen	9	4	3	2	18	12	11
5 Rangers	9	5	1	3	16	11	11

November 4th
CELTIC (1) 3 — DUNDEE UNITED (1) 1
Johnstone (39), Dalglish (57), Macari (76) — Gardner (44)

CELTIC: Williams; Hay, Brogan; Connelly, McNeill, McCluskey; Johnstone, Dalglish, Deans (Hood), Macari, Callaghan

DUNDEE UNITED: McAlpine; Rolland, Kopel; Copland, Smith, Henry; Traynor, Fleming, Cameron, Gardner, White

Attendance: 32,000

November 11th
MOTHERWELL (0) 0 — CELTIC (3) 5
Hood 2 (7, 43), Dalglish 2 (37, 55), McCallum o.g. (68)

MOTHERWELL: McRae; Whiteford, Wark; Watson, McCallum, Muir; Gray (Jim Muir), Goodwin, Lawson, McCabe, Campbell

CELTIC: Williams; McGrain, Brogan; McCluskey, Connelly, Hay; Johnstone, Deans, Dalglish, Hood, Callaghan

Attendance: 11,000

November 15th: Kenny Dalglish scored his first goal for Scotland in a 2-0 win over Denmark in a World Cup Qualifier at Hampden Park.

November 18th
CELTIC (1) 4 — HEARTS (1) 2
Dalglish (40), Deans (65), Johnstone (73), Hood (83) — Ford 2 (13, 50)

CELTIC: Williams; McGrain, Quinn (Lennox); McCluskey, Hay, Brogan; Johnstone, Deans, Dalglish, Hood, Callaghan

HEARTS: Garland; Sneddon, Clunie; Thomson, Anderson, Brown; Park, Menmuir, Ford, Carruthers (Lynch), T. Murray

Attendance: 30,000

November 25th
FALKIRK (1) 2 — CELTIC (2) 3
McLeod 2 (21, 78) — Dalglish 2 (22, 44), Deans (49)

FALKIRK: Donaldson; Kennedy, Shirra (Cattenach); Markie, McMillan, McLeod; Hoggan, Harley, Scott, Young, Ferguson

CELTIC: Connaghan; McGrain, Brogan; McCluskey, Connelly, Hay; Hood, Deans, Dalglish, Lennox, Callaghan (Quinn)

Attendance: 15,000

December 2nd
DUMBARTON (0) 1 — CELTIC (4) 6
Wallace (84) — McCluskey 3 (15, 36, 78), Hood (4), Johnstone (23), Cushley o.g. (74)

DUMBARTON: Williams; Menzies, Wilkinson; Jenkins, Cushley (Coleman), Graham; Wallace, C. McAdam, McCormack, T. McAdam, Wilson

CELTIC: Connaghan; McGrain, Brogan; McCluskey, Connelly, Hay; Hood, Deans (Johnstone), Dalglish, Murdoch, Macari

Attendance: 15,000

December 6th: Jim Craig joined Sheffield Wednesday for £10,000 on his return from South Africa.

December 16th
ARBROATH (1) 1 — CELTIC (0) 2
Sellars (25 secs) — Hood 2 (21, 86)

ARBROATH: Marshall; Milne, Rylance; Cargill (Fletcher), Waddell, Winchester; Sellars, Cant, Pirie, Stanton, Payne

CELTIC: Williams; McGrain, Brogan; McCluskey (Lennox), McNeill, Hay; Johnstone, Connelly, Dalglish, Murdoch, Hood

Attendance: 5,481

December 23rd
CELTIC (0) 1 — HIBERNIAN (1) 1
Dalglish (78) — Gordon (37)

CELTIC: Williams; Hay, Brogan; McCluskey, McNeill, Connelly; Johnstone (Lennox), Deans, Dalglish, Callaghan, Hood

HIBERNIAN: Herriot; Brownlie, Schaedler; Stanton, Black, Blackley; Edwards, O'Rourke, Gordon, Cropley, Duncan

Attendance: 45,000

League positions

	P	W	D	L	F	A	Pts
1 CELTIC	16	13	2	1	47	16	28
2 Hibernian	17	12	2	3	45	19	26
3 Rangers	18	11	3	4	33	17	25
4 Dundee	18	9	5	4	32	20	23
5 Dundee United	18	11	1	6	32	30	23

January 4th: Celtic were interested in teenager George Anderson of Morton but no business was done.

January 6th
RANGERS (1) 2 — CELTIC (0) 1
Parlane (24), Conn (89) — Smith o.g. (51)

RANGERS: McCloy; Jardine, Mathieson; Greig, Johnstone, Smith; Conn, Forsyth, Parlane, MacDonald, Young

CELTIC: Williams; Hay, Brogan; McCluskey (Hood), McNeill, Connelly; Johnstone, Dalglish, Deans, Callaghan, Macari

Attendance: 67,000

Rangers controlled most of the game and their victory was hard-earned and well deserved. McCluskey rugby tackled MacDonald from behind and Parlane needed a lucky rebound from Williams' legs before the penalty ended in the back of the net. Celtic's equalising goal was fortunate because McCloy had Deans' shot covered before a wicked deflection off Smith carried it out of his reach. Conn's persistence finally brought him reward in the last minute when he headed home a Young cross. Hay, handicapped after an early injury, just could not rise to challenge him. The best defender on the field war Tom Forsyth. Rangers had started their Centenary Year with the one victory that really mattered.

January 6th: Celtic announced that they would listen to offers for Lou Macari.

January 13th
CELTIC (1) 2 — DUNDEE (1) 1
Johnstone (16), Dalglish (81) — Houston (29)

CELTIC: Williams; McGrain, Brogan; Murdoch, McNeill, Connelly; Johnstone, Dalglish, Deans (Lennox), Callaghan, Hood

DUNDEE: Allan; Ford, Johnston; Houston, Robinson, Pringle; R. Wilson, I. Scott (Semple), Duncan, Wallace, Lambie

Attendance: 27,000

January 18th: Lou Macari signed for Manchester United for a fee of £200,000.

January 20th
AYR UNITED (1) 1 — CELTIC (1) 3
Graham (10) — Dalglish 2 (78, 85), Deans (35)

AYR UNITED: Stewart; Wells, Murphy; McAnespie, Fleming, Fillipi; Doyle, Graham, Ingram, McLean, McCulloch

CELTIC: Williams; McGrain, Brogan; Murdoch, McNeill, Connelly; Johnstone, Deans (Lennox), Dalglish, Callaghan, Hood

Attendance: 11,500

January 24th: Goalkeeper Ally Hunter was signed from Kilmarnock for a fee of £40,000.

January 27th
AIRDRIE (0) 2 — CELTIC (0) 1
Hulston (61), McCann (89) — Deans (52)

AIRDRIE: McKenzie; Caldwell, Jonquin; Fraser, Menzies, Whiteford; McCann, Thomson (Clarke), Hulston, Cowan, Wilson

CELTIC: Hunter; McGrain, Brogan; Murdoch, McNeill, Connelly; Johnstone, Deans (Lennox), Dalglish, Callaghan, Hood

Attendance: 18,000. Murdoch missed a penalty.

February 7th
KILMARNOCK (0) 0 — CELTIC (2) 4
Johnstone (42), Dalglish 2 (30, 83), Callaghan (50)

KILMARNOCK: Stewart; Whyte, Cairns; Dickson, Rodman, Maxwell; McSherry, Smith, Morrison, McGovern, Cook

CELTIC: Hunter; McGrain, Quinn; Murdoch, McNeill, Connelly; Johnstone, Dalglish, Deans (Hood), Callaghan, Lennox

Attendance: 11,000. Dalglish missed an 88th minute penalty which would have been Celtic's 6,000th League goal.

February 7th: Andy Lynch was signed from Hearts for £35,000.

February 10th
CELTIC (0) 1 — PARTICK THISTLE (1) 1
Murdoch (71) — Lawrie (36)

CELTIC: Hunter; McGrain, Quinn; Murdoch, McNeill, Connelly; Johnstone, Dalglish, Deans, Callaghan, Lennox (Lynch)

PARTICK THISTLE: Rough; Hansen, Gray; Glavin, Campbell, Strachan; Chalmers, Craig, Coulston (McQuade), Rae, Lawrie

Attendance: 32,000. Murdoch's goal was Celtic's 6,000th in the League.

February 17th
EAST FIFE (0) 2 — CELTIC (1) 2
McPhee (48 pen), Borthwick (51) — Deans 2 (22, 87)

EAST FIFE: McGarr; Duncan, Printy; Borthwick, Martis, Clarke; Hegarty, Hamilton, Dailey, Love, McPhee

CELTIC: Hunter; McGrain, Quinn; Murdoch, McNeill, Connelly; Johnstone, Dalglish, Deans, Hood, Callaghan

Attendance: 11,557. Murdoch, Hood and Dalglish all missed penalties.

League positions

	P	W	D	L	F	A	Pts
1 Rangers	25	18	3	4	53	22	39
2 CELTIC	23	16	4	3	61	25	36
3 Hibernian	23	16	3	4	61	22	35
4 Aberdeen	24	12	7	5	48	26	31
5 Dundee	24	11	7	6	41	28	29

February 28th
CELTIC (1) 4 ST JOHNSTONE (0) 0
Lennox 2 (15, 85),
Hay (70), Dalglish (87)

CELTIC: Hunter; McGrain, Quinn; Murdoch, McNeill, Connelly; Johnstone (McLaughlin), Dalglish, Deans, Hay, Lennox

ST JOHNSTONE: Donaldson; McManus, Argue; Rennie, MacDonald, Rooney; Muir, Hall, Pearson, George, Aitken

Attendance: 19,000

March 3rd
CELTIC (0) 2 ABERDEEN (0) 0
Lennox (62 pen),
Dalglish (82)

CELTIC: Hunter; McGrain, Quinn; Murdoch (McCluskey), McNeill, Connelly; Johnstone, Dalglish, Deans, Hood, Lennox

ABERDEEN: Clark; Williamson, Hermiston; Murray, Young, Willoughby; Varga, Graham, Forrest, Jarvie, Purdie

Attendance: 38,000

March 6th
CELTIC (1) 1 MORTON (0) 0
Wilson (40)

CELTIC: Hunter; McGrain, Quinn; Hay, McNeill, Connelly; Dalglish, Wilson, Deans, Hood, Lennox

MORTON: Baines; Hayes, Ritchie; Lavelle, Anderson, Clark; Murray, Townsend, Gillies, Osborne, Murphy

Attendance: 23,000

March 10th
DUNDEE UNITED (2) 2 CELTIC (2) 2
Gardner (11), Lennox 2 (7, 25)
Cameron (24)

DUNDEE UNITED: Davie; Eddie, Kopel; Copland, D. Smith, W. Smith; Mitchell (Markland), Gardner, Cameron, Fleming, Traynor

CELTIC: Hunter; McGrain, Quinn; Hay, McNeill, Connelly; Johnstone, Dalglish, Deans, Hood (Wilson), Lennox

Attendance: 16,000

March 24th
HEARTS (0) 0 CELTIC (1) 2
Deans (7), Lennox (59)

HEARTS: Cruikshank; Sneddon, Oliver; Kay, Anderson, Brown; Aird, Menmuir, Ford, Carruthers, Murray (Renton)

CELTIC: Hunter; McGrain, Brogan; Murdoch, McNeill, Connelly; Hood (Wilson), Davidson, Deans, Hay, Lennox

Attendance: 22,000

March 31st
CELTIC (2) 4 FALKIRK (0) 0
Deans (28),
Lennox 2 (36 pen, 57),
Hood (61)

CELTIC: Hunter; McGrain, Brogan; Murdoch, McNeill, Connelly; Hood (McLaughlin), Lennox, Deans, Hay, Callaghan

FALKIRK: Donaldson; S. Kennedy, Young; Markie, McMillan, Wheatley; Scott, Hoggan, Harley, Cattenach, Jack

Attendance: 19,000

April 3rd
CELTIC (0) 2 MOTHERWELL (0) 0
Dalglish (60), Deans (68)

CELTIC: Hunter; McGrain, Brogan; Hay, McNeill, Connelly; Hood, Dalglish, Deans, Lennox, Callaghan

MOTHERWELL: MacRae; Whiteford, Wark; John Muir, McCallum, Goodwin; Martin, Watson, Goldthorpe, McInally, Millar

Attendance: 22,000. Muir was ordered off.

April 14th
ST JOHNSTONE (0) 1 CELTIC (1) 3
Pearson (77) McNeill (21),
Johnstone (56),
Dalglish (66)

ST JOHNSTONE: Donaldson; Lambie, Argue; Rennie, MacDonald, Smith; Hotson (Muir), Hall, Pearson, Rooney, Aitken

CELTIC: Hunter; McGrain, Brogan; Murdoch, McNeill, Connelly; Johnstone, Hood, Dalglish, Hay, Callaghan

Attendance: 14,000

April 18th
CELTIC (3) 5 DUMBARTON (0) 0
Deans 3 (12, 69, 84),
Callaghan (20),
Dalglish (38)

CELTIC: Hunter; McGrain, Brogan; Murdoch, McNeill, Connelly; Johnstone (Hood), Dalglish, Deans, Hay, Callaghan

DUMBARTON: Williams; Menzies, Wilkinson; Cushley, Bolton, Graham; Coleman, Wallace, McCormack, Mathie (Heron), Wilson

Attendance: 27,000

April 21st
CELTIC (0) 4 ARBROATH (0) 0
Hood (53), Hay (71),
Deans (75),
Winchester o.g. (89)

CELTIC: Hunter; McGrain, Brogan; Murdoch, McNeill, Connelly; Hood, Deans (Lennox), Dalglish, Hay, Callaghan

ARBROATH: Marshall; Milne, Rylance; Cargill, Waddell, Winchester; Sellars (Fletcher), Penman, Pirie, Cant, Payne

Attendance: 28,000

April 23rd: George Connelly was named Scotland's Footballer of the Year.

April 28th
HIBERNIAN (0) 0 — CELTIC (1) 3
Deans 2 (22, 80),
Dalglish (71)

HIBERNIAN: McArthur; Bremner, Schaedler; Stanton (Smith), Black, Spalding; Edwards, O'Rourke, Gordon, Cropley, Duncan

CELTIC: Hunter; McGrain, Brogan; Murdoch, McNeill, Connelly; Johnstone, Dalglish, Deans, Hay, Callaghan

Attendance: 45,000

Scottish First Division

	P	W	D	L	F	A	Pts
1 CELTIC	34	26	5	3	93	28	57
2 Rangers	34	26	4	4	74	30	56
3 Hibernian	34	19	7	8	74	33	45
4 Aberdeen	34	16	11	7	61	34	43
5 Dundee	34	17	9	8	68	43	43
6 Ayr United	34	16	8	10	50	51	40
7 Dundee United	34	17	5	12	56	51	39
8 Motherwell	34	11	9	14	38	48	31
9 East Fife	34	11	8	15	46	54	30
10 Hearts	34	12	6	16	39	50	30
11 St Johnstone	34	10	9	15	52	67	29
12 Morton	34	10	8	16	47	53	28
13 Partick Thistle	34	10	8	16	40	53	28
14 Falkirk	34	7	12	15	38	56	26
15 Arbroath	34	9	8	17	39	63	26
16 Dumbarton	34	6	11	17	43	72	23
17 Kilmarnock	34	7	8	19	40	71	22
18 Airdrie	34	4	8	22	34	75	16

May 1st: Steve Murray was signed from Aberdeen for £50,000.

May 12th: McGrain, Dalglish and Hay were in the Scotland team which beat Wales 2-0 at Wrexham.

May 16th: McGrain, Dalglish and Hay were in the Scotland team beaten 2-1 by Northern Ireland at Hampden Park.

May 19th: Hunter, McGrain, Dalglish and Hay were in the Scotland team beaten 1-0 by England at Wembley.

June 22nd: McGrain, Dalglish and Hay were in the Scotland team beaten 1-0 by Switzerland in Berne.

June 30th: McGrain, Hay and Dalglish were in the Scotland team beaten 1-0 by Brazil at Hampden Park.

LEAGUE CUP

August 12th
STIRLING ALBION (0) 0 CELTIC (2) 3
Macari 2 (19, 47),
Dalglish (33)

STIRLING ALBION: Young; McAleer, Jones; Henderson, McCarry, Carr; McPhee, Duffin, Steele, McMillan, Lawson

CELTIC: Connaghan; Brogan, Quinn; Murdoch, McNeill, Connelly; Johnstone, Dalglish, Macari, Callaghan, Wilson (Davidson)

Attendance: 18,000

August 16th
CELTIC (0) 1 — EAST FIFE (1) 1
Dalglish (70) — Hegarty (37)

CELTIC: Connaghan; McGrain, Quinn; Murdoch McNeill, Connelly; Johnstone, Dalglish, Macari, Callaghan, Davidson (Wilson)

EAST FIFE: Gorman; Duncan, McQuade; McIvor, Martis, Hamilton; Hegarty, Borthwick, Green, Hughes, McPhee

Attendance: 15,000

August 19th
ARBROATH (0) 0 — CELTIC (2) 5
Murdoch (14 pen),
Dalglish 2 (30, 48),
Deans 2 (79, 83)

ARBROATH: Marshall; Milne, Buchan; Cargill, Waddell, Winchester; Sellars, Cant, Rylance, Pirie (McAlpine), Payne

CELTIC: Connaghan; McGrain, Quinn; Murdoch, McNeill, Connelly; Hood, Dalglish, Deans, Macari (McLaughlin), Callaghan

Attendance: 7,607

August 23rd
EAST FIFE (0) 2 — CELTIC (1) 3
Hegarty 2 (79, 86) — Lennox (42),
Dalglish 2 (65, 75)

EAST FIFE: Gorman; Duncan, McQuade; Borthwick (Dailey), Martis, Clarke; Hegarty, Hughes, Green, Hamilton, McPhee

CELTIC: Connaghan; McGrain, Quinn; Hay, McNeill, Connelly; Hood, Dalglish, Deans, Callaghan (McCluskey), Lennox

Attendance: 9,152

August 26th
CELTIC (0) 3 — STIRLING ALBION (0) 0
Murdoch (62 pen),
Dalglish (72), Deans (89)

CELTIC: Connaghan; McGrain, Quinn; Murdoch, McNeill, Connelly; Hood, Deans, Dalglish, Hay, Lennox

STIRLING ALBION: Young; McAleer, Jones; Duffin, McCarry, Carr; McPhee, Christie, McMillan, Stevenson, Lawson

Attendance: 17,000

August 28th at Hampden Park

CELTIC (2) 3 — ARBROATH (1) 3

Cargill o.g. (33), Hood (42), Dalglish (57) — Rylance 3 (22, 68, 77)

CELTIC: Connaghan; McGrain, Quinn (McCluskey); Hay, McNeill, Connelly; McLaughlin, Deans, Dalglish, Hood, Lennox

ARBROATH: Marshall; Millar, McAlpine; Cargill, Waddell, Winchester (Robertson); Sellars, Cant, Pirie, Rylance, Payne

Attendance: 4,962

Section table

	P	W	D	L	F	A	Pts
CELTIC	6	4	2	0	18	6	10
East Fife	6	2	2	2	7	8	6
Stirling Albion	6	2	1	3	4	10	5
Arbroath	6	1	1	4	9	14	3

Qualifiers: CELTIC and East Fife

Second Round First Leg September 20th

STRANRAER (1) 1 — CELTIC (1) 2

Collings (4) — Davidson (6), Lennox (75)

STRANRAER: Whiteside; Hopkins, McAuley; Collings, Heap, Duffy; McCall, Evans, Meechan, Campbell, Traynor (Hay)

CELTIC: Connaghan; McGrain, McCluskey; Murdoch, McNeill, Connelly; McLaughlin, Davidson, Deans (Wilson), Lennox, Hood

Attendance: 4,500

Second Round Second Leg October 4th

CELTIC (3) 5 — STRANRAER (1) 2

Lennox 2 (37, 79), Deans (18), Davidson (23), Murdoch (70 pen) — Meechan (6), Campbell (53)

CELTIC: Williams; McCluskey, Quinn; Murdoch, McNeill, Callaghan; Johnstone (McLaughlin), Davidson, Deans, Lennox, Wilson

STRANRAER: Whiteside; Hopkins, McAuley; Collings, Heap, Hay; McColl, Duffy, Meechan, Campbell, Traynor

Attendance: 9,000. Celtic won 7-3 on aggregate.

Quarter-Final First Leg October 11th

DUNDEE (1) 1 — CELTIC (0) 0

Wallace (23)

DUNDEE: Allan; R. Wilson, Houston; Robinson, Stewart, Ford; J. Scott, Duncan, Wallace, J. Scott, Lambie

CELTIC: Williams; Hay, Brogan; Murdoch, McNeill, Connelly; Dalglish, Macari, Deans, Callaghan, Lennox

Attendance: 21,938

Quarter-Final Second Leg November 1st

CELTIC (3) 3 — DUNDEE (1) 2

Lennox (17), Macari 2 (32, 34) — Wallace (30), J. Scott (54)

After Extra Time

CELTIC: Williams; Hay, McGrain; McCluskey, Connelly, Callaghan; Johnstone, Dalglish (Hood), Deans, Macari, Lennox

DUNDEE: Allan; R. Wilson, Houston; Robinson, Stewart, Ford; J. Wilson, Duncan, Wallace (Gray), J. Scott, I. Scott

Attendance: 39,000

Quarter-Final Play-Off at Hampden Park November 20th

CELTIC (4) 4 — DUNDEE (1) 1

Hood (28), Dalglish (35), Deans 2 (38, 42) — J. Scott (18)

CELTIC: Williams; McGrain, Brogan; McCluskey, Connelly, Hay; Johnstone, Deans, Dalglish, Hood, Callaghan

DUNDEE: Allan; R. Wilson, Houston; Robinson, Stewart, Pringle; J. Wilson, Duncan, Wallace, J. Scott, I. Scott (Gray)

Attendance: 36,483

Semi-Final at Hampden Park November 27th

CELTIC (1) 3 — ABERDEEN (1) 2

Hood (33 pen), Johnstone (75), Callaghan (80) — Harper (30), Robb (74)

CELTIC: Williams; McGrain, Brogan; McCluskey, Connelly, Hay; Johnstone, Deans, Dalglish, Hood, Callaghan. Sub: Murdoch

ABERDEEN: Clark; Willoughby, Hermiston; Murray, Young, Taylor; Varga, Robb, Harper, Jarvie, Miller. Sub: G. Murray

Attendance: 39,687

Celtic were pushed long and hard by Aberdeen. 10 minutes from time Celtic scored the winning goal. Hood sent a high ball across the Aberdeen penalty area, Dalglish left it for Callaghan and Clark had only a glimpse of the ball as it flashed into the net. For the remainder of the match Aberdeen laid siege to the Celtic goal and both Harper and Varga hit the woodwork.

Final at Hampden Park December 9th

HIBERNIAN (0) 2 — CELTIC (0) 1

Stanton (60), O'Rourke (66) — Dalglish (77)

HIBERNIAN: Herriot; Brownlie, Schaedler; Stanton, Black, Blackley; Edwards, O'Rourke, Gordon, Cropley, Duncan. Sub: Hamilton

CELTIC: Williams; McGrain, Brogan; McCluskey, McNeill, Hay; Johnstone (Callaghan), Connelly, Dalglish, Hood, Macari

Attendance: 71,696 *Referee:* A. MacKenzie

Hibs won their 1st major trophy for 20 years. In a period between the 60th and 80th minutes Stanton scored a goal, made the cross for the 2nd and set up the easiest chance of the match which Gordon missed. Hibs won the midfield and erased their humiliating defeat in the Scottish Cup Final in May.

SCOTTISH CUP

Third Round February 3rd
CELTIC (2) 4 — EAST FIFE (0) 1
Deans 2 (23, 48), Dalglish 2 (26, 55) — McPhee (58)

CELTIC: Hunter; McGrain, Quinn; Murdoch, McNeill, Connelly; Johnstone, Dalglish, Deans, Callaghan (Hood), Lennox

EAST FIFE: Gorman; Duncan, Printy; Borthwick, Martis, Clarke; Hegarty, Hamilton, Honeyman (Cairns), Noble, McPhee

Attendance: 25,000

Fourth Round February 24th
MOTHERWELL (0) 0 — CELTIC (4) 4
Dalglish (6), Deans 2 (19, 24), Lennox (45)

MOTHERWELL: MacRae; Whiteford, Wark; Watson, McCallum, Goodwin; Campbell, McCabe, Muir, Lawson, Millar

CELTIC: Hunter; McGrain, Quinn; Murdoch, McNeill, Connelly; Johnstone, Dalglish, Deans, Hay (Hood), Lennox

Attendance: 24,764. Millar missed a penalty.

Fifth Round March 17th
CELTIC (0) 0 — ABERDEEN (0) 0

CELTIC: Hunter; McGrain, Brogan; Murdoch, McNeill, Connelly; Johnstone, Dalglish, Deans, Hay, Lennox

ABERDEEN: Clark; Williamson, Hermiston; Murray, Young, Smith; Varga (Jarvie), Robb, Forrest, Graham, Taylor

Attendance: 40,000. Johnstone was ordered off.

Fifth Round Replay March 21st
ABERDEEN (0) 0 — CELTIC (0) 1
McNeill (86)

ABERDEEN: Clark; Williamson, Hermiston; Murray, Young, Smith; Forrest, Robb (Buchan), Jarvie, Graham, Miller

CELTIC: Hunter; McGrain, Brogan; Murdoch, McNeill, Connelly; Johnstone (Davidson), Hood, Deans, Hay, Lennox

Attendance: 33,465

Semi-Final at Hampden Park April 7th
CELTIC (0) 0 — DUNDEE (0) 0

CELTIC: Hunter; McGrain, Brogan; Murdoch, McNeill, Connelly; Dalglish, Lennox, Deans (Johnstone), Hay, Callaghan

DUNDEE: Allan; R. Wilson, Johnston; Robinson, Stewart, Houston; J. Wilson (Ford), Wallace, Duncan, J. Scott, I. Scott

Attendance: 53,428

Dundee must shoulder most of the blame for making this Semi-Final an instantly forgettable one. Their negative tactics deprived the crowd of any entertainment value at all.

Semi-Final Replay at Hampden Park April 11th
CELTIC (0) 3 — DUNDEE (0) 0
Johnstone 2 (101, 110), Dalglish (102) — *After Extra Time*

CELTIC: Hunter; McGrain, Brogan; Murdoch, McNeill, Connelly; Johnstone, Dalglish (Hood), Deans, Lennox, Callaghan

DUNDEE: Allan; R. Wilson, Johnston; Robinson, Stewart, Houston; J. Wilson, Wallace (Semple), Duncan, J. Scott, I. Scott

Attendance: 47,384

Until the dramatic moments of extra-time this had been another dull meeting between the sides. Celtic eventually took the lead in the 101st minute. Dalglish headed a long punt out of defence into the path of Johnstone and he steered the ball wide of Allan. Seconds later Callaghan drove a return pass from a short corner across goal and Allan could only parry the ball to Dalglish who was left with the simple task of scoring. In the second period of extra-time McGrain laid a fine pass inside the full-back and Johnstone carried the ball before hitting a fierce shot from an acute angle past Allan.

Final at Hampden Park May 5th
CELTIC (1) 2 — RANGERS (1) 3
Dalglish (24), Connelly (54 pen) — Parlane (34), Conn (46), Forsyth (60)

CELTIC: Hunter; McGrain, Brogan (Lennox); Murdoch, McNeill, Connelly; Johnstone, Deans, Dalglish, Hay, Callaghan

RANGERS: McCloy; Jardine, Mathieson; Greig, Johnstone, MacDonald; McLean, Forsyth, Parlane, Conn, Young. Sub: Smith

Attendance: 122,714 *Referee:* J. R. P. Gordon

This was Rangers' first triumph in the competition since 1966. Celtic, attacking first, took the lead in 24 minutes. Dalglish, scampering on to a Deans pass, struck a shot past McCloy and turned in celebration. After 34 minutes Mathieson pushed a shrewd ball forward and MacDonald beat Connelly, drawn wide. His chipped centre to the near post brought Parlane away from his defender for the header that tied the match. 20 seconds after the interval Rangers took the lead. Young passed forward, Parlane flicked on and

Conn, left with a clear run at goal, shot past the advancing Hunter. In the 54th minute Celtic drew level, Greig handled a net-bound shot and Connelly, as cool as ever, struck the penalty home with authority. In the 60th minute McLean slanted over a free-kick, Johnstone headed against a post, and as the ball rolled agonisingly along the goal-line Forsyth stabbed it into the net. John Greig stood in tears at the end.

EUROPEAN CUP

First Round First Leg at Hampden Park September 13th
CELTIC (2) 2 — ROSENBURG (Norway) (0) 1
Macari (17), Deans (44) — Wirkola (49)

CELTIC: Williams; McGrain, Callaghan; Murdoch, McNeill, Connelly; Hood, Dalglish, Deans, Macari, Wilson (Lennox)

ROSENBURG: Karlsen (Torp); Warmdahl, Ronnes; Rime, Meirik, Christiansen; Ness, Sunde, Lindseth, Wirkola, Odegaard (Hansen)

Attendance: 18,797

Celtic maintained almost total domination in possession and territory but scored only twice and conceded a breakaway goal.

First Round Second Leg September 27th
ROSENBURG (1) 1 — CELTIC (0) 3
Christiansen (37) — Macari (56), Hood (82), Dalglish (89)

ROSENBURG: Torp; Meirik, Ronnes; Rime, Warmdahl, Christiansen; Ness, Lindseth, Sunde, Wirkola, Odegaard (Hansen)

CELTIC: Williams; McGrain, McCluskey; Murdoch, McNeill, Connelly; Johnstone, Dalglish, Macari, Hood, Callaghan

Attendance: 15,000

Celtic, down 0-1 at half time, came to life in the 2nd half, exerting tremendous pressure on the Norwegians' goal. With only a minute left for play Johnstone carried the ball the length of the field before giving a supreme pass to Dalglish, who scored. Celtic won 5-2 on aggregate.

Second Round First Leg October 25th
CELTIC (0) 2 — UIJPEST DOSZA (1) 1
Dalglish 2 (49, 74) — Bene (20)

CELTIC: Williams; Hay, McGrain; Connelly, McNeill, Callaghan; Johnstone (Lennox), Dalglish, Deans, Macari, Hood (McCluskey)

UIJPEST: Szentmihalyi; Kolar, Harsanyi; Toth, Dunai, Horvath; Fazekas, Juhasz (Nagy), Bene, A. Dunai, Zambo (Kellner)

Attendance: 55,000

Despite wave after wave of attack Celtic scored only twice. In 49 minutes Connelly swung over a low ball which Dalglish controlled and sidefooted home. In 74 minutes Stein pulled off Johnstone and sent on Lennox. With his first pass he sent over a curling cross which Dalglish glanced over the line. It was obvious that a repeat of the previous year's performance in Budapest, and nothing less, would be required to take Celtic through to the next round of the competition.

Second Round Second Leg November 8th
UIJPEST DOSZA (3) 3 — CELTIC (0) 0
Bene 2 (8, 22), Fazekas (16 pen)

UIJPEST: Borbely; Nosko (Kolar), Harsanyi; Toth, E. Dunai, Horvath; Fazekas, Juhasz (Nagy), Bene, A. Dunai, Zambo

CELTIC: Williams; McGrain (Deans), Brogan; Hay, McNeill, McCluskey; Johnstone, Connelly, Dalglish, Callaghan, Lennox (Hood)

Attendance: 20,000

Celtic were beaten by a much better side. Bene and A. Dunai did the damage, pulling the Celtic defence all over the field. As the match went on Williams increasingly became Celtic's busiest and best player. Celtic were arranged tactically to fight a semi-defensive battle and could not reshape after the shock opening. Uijpest Dosza won 4-2 on aggregate.

APPEARANCES	League	League Cup	Scottish Cup	European Cup
Connaghan	4	7	–	–
Williams	15	6	–	4
Brogan	20	5	5	1
Quinn	9+1S	7	2	–
Murdoch	24	7	7	2
McNeill	30	10	7	4
Connelly	32	12	7	4
Johnstone	21+1S	7	6+1S	3
Dalglish	32	11	6	4
Macari	10+1S	6	–	3
Callaghan	27	9+1S	4	4
Wilson	2+2S	2+2S	–	1
Davidson	1+1S	3+1S	0+1S	0+1S
McGrain	30	10	7	4
Hood	22+7S	8+1S	1+3S	3+1S
Deans	30+1S	10	7	2+1S
McLaughlin	0+2S	2+2S	–	–
Hay	21	8	5	2
Lennox	15+8S	7	6+1S	1+2S
McCluskey	14+1S	6+2S	–	2+1S
Hunter	15	–	7	–
Lynch	0+1S	–	–	–

GOALSCORERS

League: Deans 21, Dalglish 21, Hood 12, Lennox 11 (2 pens), Johnstone 7, Murdoch 4 (2 pens), Own Goals 4, Macari 3, Hay 3, McCluskey 3, Callaghan 2, Wilson 1, McNeill 1

League Cup: Dalglish 10, Deans 6, Lennox 5, Macari 4, Murdoch 3 (3 pens), Hood 3 (1 pen), Davidson 2, Johnstone 1, Callaghan 1, Own Goals 1

Scottish Cup: Dalglish 5, Deans 4, Johnstone 2, Connelly 1 (pen), Lennox 1, McNeill 1

European Cup: Dalglish 3, Macari 2, Deans 1, Hood 1

Season 1973-74

Celtic equalled the world record held by M.T.K. Budapest of Hungary and C.D.N.A. Sofia of Bulgaria by winning their 9th successive League Championship. They lost only 4 matches all season and finished with 53 points – 4 ahead of 2nd placed Hibernian. Rangers, who finished 3rd, were beaten twice and 'Dixie' Deans created a post-war club record when he scored 6 goals in a 7-0 win over Partick Thistle. 'Dixie' Deans finished as top scorer with 24 goals. Lisbon Lion Bobby Murdoch joined Middlesbrough on a free transfer in September, and goalkeeper Evan Williams was also freed at the end of the season.

It took Celtic 12 matches to reach the Final of the League Cup. They faced Rangers in the Semi-Final where a Harry Hood hat-trick gave them a much more comprehensive victory than they would have expected, but they were beaten by Gordon Wallace's 75th-minute goal in the Final against Dundee in a match which kicked off at 1.30 because of the power crisis and attracted a crowd of only 27,934. It was their 4th successive final defeat.

In the Scottish Cup a Deans goal took Celtic through in a Fifth Round Replay at Fir Park against his former club Motherwell. A Jimmy Johnstone volley saw off Dundee, for the 2nd successive year, in the Semi-Final, and 2 early goals from Hood and Murray and a late goal by Deans gave them the Cup for the 23rd time against a Dundee United side who froze on their biggest-ever day.

Celtic reached their 4th European Cup Semi-Final after victories over T.P.S. Turku of Finland, Vejle of Denmark and Basle of Switzerland. Their Semi-Final opponents, Atletico Madrid, came to Glasgow to secure a draw at any cost, and despite having 3 players sent off and 7 booked they achieved their objective. Johnstone was their main target throughout. The Spaniards, who were managed by the notorious Juan Carlos Lorenzo who was in charge of Argentina during the 1966 World Cup Finals and Racing Club in 1967, were warned about their future conduct by UEFA, fined £14,000 and had 6 players banned from the return which they won 2-0. Celtic's conduct was impeccable in both matches. Not surprisingly Johnstone was affected in Madrid by a pre-match death threat. Thankfully, for football. Atletico, having booted their way to the Final, were beaten by Bayern Munich after a replay.

League:	Champions
League Cup:	Runners-up
Scottish Cup:	Winners
European Cup:	Semi-Finalists

SCOTTISH FIRST DIVISION

August 11th: Celtic made a bid of £50,000 for John Duncan of Dundee.

September 1st

DUNFERMLINE (0) 2	CELTIC (1) 3
Kinninmonth (80),	Hood (20),
Sinclair (90),	Wilson (81),
	Leishman o.g. (89)

DUNFERMLINE: Arrol; Leishman, Wallace; Thomson, McNicoll, Kinninmonth; Nelson (Campbell), Scott, Mackie, Shaw, Sinclair

CELTIC: Hunter; McGrain, Brogan; Murray, McNeill, Connelly; McLaughlin (Wilson), Hood, Dalglish, Hay, Lennox

Attendance: 14,705

September 3rd: David Hay was reported to be heading to Manchester United for £250,000 with Alex Forsyth going to Parkhead as part of the deal.

September 8th
CELTIC (3) 5 CLYDE (0) 0
Lennox 3 (3 pen, 40, 84),
Dalglish (8),
McGrain (78)

CELTIC: Hunter; McGrain, Brogan; Murray, McNeill, Connelly; McLaughlin (Johnstone), Hood (Wilson), Dalglish, Hay, Lennox

CLYDE: Cairney; McHugh, Swan; Beattie, McVie, Aherne; Sullivan, Burns, Gillespie, McGrain, Miller

Attendance: 25,000

Every Celtic player had a No. 8 on his shorts to commemorate the club's 8 successive Championships. Brian McLaughlin was carried off with a serious injury.

September 15th
RANGERS (0) 0 CELTIC (0) 1
Johnstone (69)

RANGERS: McCloy; Jardine, Mathieson; Greig, Johnstone, MacDonald; McLean (Scott), Forsyth, Parlane, Conn, Young

CELTIC: Hunter; McGrain, Brogan; Murray, McNeill, Connelly; Johnstone, Hood (Callaghan), Dalglish, Hay, Wilson

Attendance: 60,000

After Young had a long swinging shot saved Hunter dived at the feet of McLean when he hesitated over the games' best opportunity. After 69 minutes Hay's low cross was headed underneath McCloy's body by Johnstone. Rangers were far too cautious, and Parlane was largely unsupported in attack. Johnstone's solitary goal had the Ibrox crowd spilling out of the stadium before the end of a poor match.

September 17th: Bobby Murdoch joined Middlesbrough on a free transfer.

September 26th: Hunter, McGrain, Connelly and Dalglish were all in the Scotland team which beat Czechoslovakia 2-1 in a World Cup Qualifier at Hampden Park.

September 29th
ST JOHNSTONE (1) 2 CELTIC (1) 1
Muir (5), Deans (2)
Pearson (84)

ST JOHNSTONE: Donaldson; Lambie, Argue; Rennie, MacDonald, Ritchie; Hall, Smith, Pearson, Muir, Aitken

CELTIC: Hunter; McGrain, Brogan; Murray, McNeill, Connelly; Johnstone, Dalglish, Deans, Hay, Hood (Callaghan)

Attendance: 12,000

October 6th
CELTIC (0) 2 MOTHERWELL (0) 0
Wilson (80),
Deans (87)

CELTIC: Hunter; McGrain, Brogan; Murray, McNeill, Connelly; Johnstone, Dalglish, Deans, Callaghan, Wilson

MOTHERWELL: MacRae; Millar, Wark; Watson Muir, Goodwin; McCabe, Graham, Goldthorpe (Lawson), McClymont, Martin

Attendance: 32,000

October 13th
DUNDEE (0) 0 CELTIC (1) 1
Callaghan (3)

DUNDEE: Allan, R. Wilson, Johnston; Ford, Gemmell, Pringle; J. Wilson (Semple), Robinson, Wallace, I. Scott, Lambie

CELTIC: Hunter; McGrain, Brogan; Murray, McNeill, Connelly; Hood, Deans (Wilson), Dalglish, Hay, Callaghan

Attendance: 17,433

October 14th: Celtic increased their bid for John Duncan to £60,000. Dundee put a price of £150,000 on the player.

October 17th: McGrain, Hay and Dalglish were in the Scotland team beaten 1-0 by Czechoslovakia in a World Cup Qualifier in Prague.

October 20th
CELTIC (0) 1 HIBERNIAN (0) 1
McCluskey (68) Gordon (57)

CELTIC: Hunter; McGrain, Brogan; Murray, McNeill (McCluskey), Connelly; Hood (Deans), Dalglish, Lennox, Hay, Callaghan

HIBERNIAN: McArthur; Bremner, Schaedler; Stanton, Black, Blackley; Edwards, Higgins, Gordon, Cropley, Duncan

Attendance: 34,000

October 27th
HEARTS (0) 1 CELTIC (3) 3
Ford (56) Connelly (7),
Dalglish 2 (29, 44)

HEARTS: Garland; Sneddon, Clunie; Cant, Anderson, Jeffries; Aird, Ford, Busby, Stevenson, Prentice

CELTIC: Hunter; McGrain, Brogan; McCluskey, MacDonald, Connelly; Johnstone, Murray, Deans, Hay, Dalglish

Attendance: 33,000

League positions

	P	W	D	L	F	A	Pts
1 CELTIC	8	6	1	1	17	6	13
2 Hearts	9	5	3	1	20	10	13
3 Aberdeen	8	4	4	0	10	4	12
4 Ayr United	9	5	2	2	17	11	12
5 Dundee United	8	5	0	3	13	11	10

Victory smiles from some of the Celtic players after defeating Dukla of Prague in April 1967.

November 3rd
CELTIC (2) 4 — EAST FIFE (0) 2
Deans 2 (6, 70), Dalglish (12), Hood (73) — Hamilton (81), Hegarty (87)

CELTIC: Hunter; McGrain, Brogan (Callaghan); McCluskey, McNeill, Connelly; Johnstone, Murray, Deans, Hood, Dalglish (Lynch)

EAST FIFE: Gorman; Duncan, Clarke; McIvor, Martis, Borthwick; Love, Hamilton, Honeyman, Rutherford, McPhee

Attendance: 23,000

November 10th
AYR UNITED (0) 0 — CELTIC (1) 1
Dalglish (41)

AYR UNITED: McLean; Wells, Murphy; McAnespie, Fleming, Fillipi; R. Ferguson, Graham, A. Ferguson (Ingram), McLean (Bell), McCulloch

CELTIC: Hunter; McGrain, Brogan; McCluskey, McNeill, Connelly; Lennox, Murray, Deans, Callaghan, Dalglish

Attendance: 16,000

November 14th: McGrain, Connelly and Dalglish were in the Scotland team which drew 1-1 with West Germany in a Friendly at Hampden Park.

November 17th
CELTIC (3) 7 — PARTICK THISTLE (0) 0
Deans 6 (8, 16, 24, 56, 74, 89), Lennox (64)

CELTIC: Hunter; McGrain, Quinn; McCluskey, McNeill, Murray; Lennox (McNamara), Hood, Deans, Callaghan, Dalglish (Wilson)

PARTICK THISTLE: Rough; Hansen, Kellachan; Glavin, Campbell, Clark; Gibson, Smith, Rae, Craig, Houston (Ralston)

Attendance: 22,000. Deans' 6 goals were a post-war club record for a competitive match.

November 24th
DUMBARTON (0) 0 — CELTIC (1) 2
Dalglish (11), Lennox (54 pen)

DUMBARTON: Williams; McKay (Paterson), Wilkinson; Menzies (McAdam), Cushley, Ruddy; Coleman, Wallace, McCormack, Graham, Heron

CELTIC: Hunter; McGrain, Brogan; McCluskey, McNeill, Murray; Lennox (Johnstone), Hood, Wilson, Callaghan, Dalglish

Attendance: 9,000.

Bobby Lennox set a post-war club scoring record, taking his goals total to 242, one ahead of Steve Chalmers

December 1st
ARBROATH (0) 1 — CELTIC (1) 2
Sellars (73) — Dalglish (5), Wilson (85)

ARBROATH: Marshall; Milne, Rylance; Cargill, Waddell, Murray; Sellars, Walker, Pirie, Penman, Fletcher

CELTIC: Hunter; McGrain, Brogan; McCluskey, McNeill, Murray; Johnstone, Hood, Wilson, Callaghan, Dalglish

Attendance: 5,708

December 8th
CELTIC (3) 3 — DUNDEE UNITED (1) 3
Hood (7), Callaghan (31), Dalglish (38) — Gray (17), Fleming (54), Knox (89)

CELTIC: Hunter; McGrain, Brogan; McCluskey, McNeill, Murray; Hood (Lennox), Hay, Wilson, Callaghan, Dalglish

DUNDEE UNITED: McAlpine; Rolland, Kopel; Copland, W. Smith, Narey (Cameron); Payne (Gardner), Knox, Gray, Fleming, Traynor

Attendance: 19,000

December 22nd
CELTIC (2) 6 — FALKIRK (0) 0
Dalglish (36), Lennox (43), Deans 4 (58, 66, 80, 88)

CELTIC: Hunter; McGrain, Brogan; McCluskey, McNeill, Hay; Hood, Murray, Deans, Dalglish, Lennox

FALKIRK: Donaldson; D. Whiteford, Cameron; Markie, Gibson, Wheatley; Hoggan, J. Whiteford, Lawson, Harley, McLeod (Shirra)

Attendance: 11,000

December 29th
CELTIC (3) 6 — DUNFERMLINE (0) 0
Deans 2 (26, 33), Dalglish 2 (30, 79), Hood 2 (63, 86)

CELTIC: Hunter; McGrain, Brogan; McCluskey, McNeill (Ritchie), Hay; Hood, Murray, Deans, Dalglish, Lennox (Wilson)

DUNFERMLINE: Karlsen; Thomson, Wallace; Baillie (Campbell), Leishman, Kinninmonth; Nelson, Scott, Mackie, Shaw, Sinclair

Attendance: 21,000

League positions

	P	W	D	L	F	A	Pts
1 CELTIC	16	13	2	1	48	12	28
2 Rangers	15	10	2	3	25	11	22
3 Hibernian	15	9	3	3	31	19	21
4 Hearts	17	8	5	4	30	21	21
5 Aberdeen	14	7	6	1	21	11	20

January 1st
CLYDE (0) 0 — CELTIC (2) 2
Dalglish
Lennox

CLYDE: Cairney; Anderson, Swan; McHugh, McVie, Jim Burns; Sullivan, Gillespie, Millar, McGrain, Boyle

CELTIC: Hunter; McGrain, Brogan; McCluskey, McNeill, Hay; Hood, Murray, Deans, Dalglish, Lennox

Attendance: 10,630

January 5th
CELTIC (1) 1 — RANGERS (0) 0
Lennox (27)

CELTIC: Hunter; McGrain, Brogan; McCluskey, McNeill, Hay; Hood, Murray, Deans, Dalglish, Lennox

RANGERS: McCloy; Jardine, Mathieson; Greig, Johnstone, Houston; Young, Forsyth, Parlane, MacDonald, Scott (Hamilton)

Attendance: 55,000

A goal by Bobby Lennox was all that separated the teams. Rangers showed remarkable stamina and spirit but were a collection of players without corporate understanding. They came closest to scoring when Greig sent Hunter scurrying to stop one low shot at the post. Murray and Hay were Celtic's guiding midfield lights, and Dalglish was a class attacker. Lennox and Deans might have scored the late goals that could have better reflected the difference in class.

January 19th
CELTIC (1) 3 — ST JOHNSTONE (0) 0
Argue o.g. (33),
Murray (77),
Lennox (79 pen)

CELTIC: Hunter; McGrain, Brogan; McCluskey, McNeill, Hay; Hood, Murray, Davidson, Dalglish, Lennox (Lynch)

ST JOHNSTONE: Donaldson; Ritchie, Argue; Rennie, MacDonald, Cramond; Muir, Smith, Pearson, Hall, Hotson

Attendance: 19,000

February 2nd
MOTHERWELL (0) 3 — CELTIC (1) 2
Martin (67), Graham (72), Goldthorpe (82) — Murray (28), Lennox (51)

MOTHERWELL: Rennie; W. Watson, Wark; R. Watson, Muir, Millar; Graham, McCabe, Goldthorpe, Martin, Kennedy

CELTIC: Hunter; McGrain, Brogan; McCluskey, McNeill, Hay; Hood, Murray, Deans, Dalglish, Lennox

Attendance: 16,669

February 2nd: A transfer request from George Connelly was granted and he was placed on the list at £200,000.

February 10th
CELTIC (1) 1 — DUNDEE (2) 2
Hay (35) — Lambie (23), Duncan (30)

CELTIC: Hunter; McGrain, Brogan; Connelly, McNeill, Hay; Hood (Callaghan), Murray, Deans, Dalglish, Lennox

DUNDEE: Allan; R. Wilson, Johnston (Pringle); Ford, Phillip, Gemmell; J. Wilson, Robinson, Duncan, J. Scott, Lambie

Attendance: 40,000. This was Celtic's 1st Sunday League match.

February 18th: Jimmy Bone was signed from Sheffield United for £25,000.

February 23rd
HIBERNIAN (1) 2 — CELTIC (2) 4
Duncan (23), O'Rourke (53) — Deans 2 (1, 89), Dalglish (37), Wilson (62)

HIBERNIAN: McArthur; Spalding, Schaedler; Stanton, Black, Blackley; Edwards, O'Rourke, Gordon, Cropley, Duncan

CELTIC: Hunter; McGrain, Brogan; Connelly, McNeill, Hay; Hood, Murray, Deans, Dalglish, Wilson

Attendance: 48,554

League positions

	P	W	D	L	F	A	Pts
1 CELTIC	22	17	2	3	61	19	36
2 Hibernian	22	13	5	4	46	27	31
3 Rangers	21	12	4	5	36	19	28
4 Ayr United	23	11	6	6	32	24	28
5 Aberdeen	20	8	9	3	28	18	25

March 2nd
CELTIC (1) 1 — HEARTS (0) 0
Deans (29)

CELTIC: Hunter; McGrain (McCluskey), Brogan; Connelly, MacDonald, Hay; Hood, Murray, Deans (Bone), Dalglish, Wilson

HEARTS: Cruikshank; Sneddon, Kay; Jeffries, Anderson, Brown; Aird, Gibson, Ford, Stevenson (Prentice), Murray

Attendance: 32,000

March 16th
CELTIC (1) 4 — AYR UNITED (0) 0
Johnstone 2 (56 pen, 71 pen),
Deans 2 (17, 75)

CELTIC: Connaghan; Hay, Brogan; Murray, McNeill, Connelly; Johnstone, Bone (Wilson), Deans, Callaghan, Dalglish (Hood)

AYR UNITED: McLean; Fillipi (Tait), Murphy; McAnespie, Fleming, Mitchell; Doyle, Graham, Ingram, R. Ferguson (A. Ferguson), McCulloch
Attendance: 26,000

March 23rd
PARTICK THISTLE (0) 2 CELTIC (0) 0
Glavin 2 (65, 69)

PARTICK THISTLE: Rough; Hansen, Kellachan; Glavin, Campbell, Anderson; Chalmers, Craig, Rae, Rooney, Lawrie

CELTIC: Connaghan; Hay, Brogan; Murray, McNeill, McCluskey; Johnstone (Wilson), Bone (Hood), Deans, Callaghan, Dalglish
Attendance: 20,000

March 27th: Hay and Dalglish were in the Scotland team beaten 2-1 by West Germany in Frankfurt. Hay captained the side and Dalglish scored Scotland's goal.

March 30th
CELTIC (1) 3 — DUMBARTON (2) 3
Wilson (7), Dalglish (61), Deans (83) — T. McAdam (9), C. McAdam (35), Coleman (76)

CELTIC: Hunter; McGrain, Brogan; Murray, McNeill, McCluskey; Johnstone, Hood, Deans, Callaghan (Dalglish), Wilson

DUMBARTON: Taylor; Mullen, Wilkinson; Ruddy, C. McAdam, Black; Coleman, Wallace, Bourke, T. McAdam, Heron
Attendance: 19,000

April 6th
CELTIC (0) 1 — ARBROATH (0) 0
Dalglish (61)

CELTIC: Connaghan; McGrain, Hay; Murray, McNeill, McCluskey; Johnstone, Hood (Wilson), Deans, Callaghan, Dalglish

ARBROATH: Marshall; Milne, Rylance; Cargill, Waddell, Murray; Sellars, Cant (Mitchell), Fletcher, Penman, Walker
Attendance: 22,000

April 13th
DUNDEE UNITED (0) 0 — CELTIC (2) 2
Murray (2), Hay (36)

DUNDEE UNITED: Davie; Gardner, Kopel; W. Smith, D. Smith, Narey; Payne (Rolland), Knox, Gray, Fleming, Traynor (White)

CELTIC: Connaghan; McGrain, Brogan; Murray, McNeill, McCluskey; Hood (Callaghan), Bone, Dalglish, Hay, Wilson
Attendance: 15,000

April 17th
EAST FIFE (1) 1 — CELTIC (3) 6
Miller (22) — Lennox (35), Dalglish 2 (37, 39) Deans (68), Hood 2 (62, 78)

EAST FIFE: McGarr; Walker (Rae), Gillies; Rutherford (McIvor), Martis, Clarke; Miller, Love, Kinnear, O'Connor, McPhee

CELTIC: Connaghan; McGrain, Quinn; Murray, McNeill, McCluskey; Hood, Dalglish (Wilson), Deans, Callaghan, Lennox
Attendance: 6,970. Lennox's goal was his 250th for the club.

April 20th
CELTIC (1) 2 — ABERDEEN (0) 0
Deans (5), Lennox (85)

CELTIC: Connaghan; McGrain, Brogan; Hay, McNeill, McCluskey; Johnstone (Callaghan), Murray, Deans (Lennox), Hood, Dalglish

ABERDEEN: Clark; Hermiston, McLelland; Thomson, Young, Miller (McCall); Smith, Hair, Pirie, Jarvie (Davidson), Graham
Attendance: 31,000

April 27th
FALKIRK (1) 1 — CELTIC (1) 1
Lawson (3) — Dalglish (19)

FALKIRK: Donaldson; Kennedy, McLeod; Markie, Gibson, D. Whiteford; Hoggan, Fowler, Lawson, J. Whiteford, Shirra

CELTIC: Connaghan; Hay, Brogan; Murray (McGrain), McNeill, McCluskey; Hood, Dalglish, Deans, Callaghan, Lennox
Attendance: 13,500

April 29th
ABERDEEN (0) 0 — CELTIC (0) 0

ABERDEEN: Clark; Hermiston, McLelland; Hair, Young, Miller; Smith, McCall, Pirie (Davidson), Jarvie Graham

CELTIC: Hunter; McGrain, Quinn; McCluskey, Welsh, Brogan; Dalglish, Hay, Deans (Hood), Davidson, Callaghan
Attendance: 10,500

April 30th
CELTIC (0) 1 — MORTON (0) 1
McLaughlin (67) — McGhee (59)

CELTIC: Hunter; McNamara, McCluskey; Hood, McNeill, Welsh; Johnstone, Wilson, Deans, Lennox, Lynch (McLaughlin)

MORTON: Baines; Hayes, Ritchie; Anderson, Nelson, Reid; McGhee, Townsend, McIlmoyle, Hegarty, Lavelle
Attendance: 9,000

May 6th
MORTON (0) 0 CELTIC (0) 0

MORTON: Baines; Hayes, Ritchie; Anderson, Nelson, Reid; McGhee, Townsend, McIlmoyle (O'Donnell) Hegarty, Hazel

CELTIC: Connaghan; Hay, Brogan; McCluskey, Welsh, Callaghan; Johnstone (Deans), Murray, Davidson (Dalglish), Hood, Lennox

Attendance: 6,500

Scottish First Division

	P	W	D	L	F	A	Pts
1 CELTIC	34	23	7	4	82	27	53
2 Hibernian	34	20	9	5	75	42	49
3 Rangers	34	21	6	7	67	34	48
4 Aberdeen	34	13	16	5	46	26	42
5 Dundee	34	16	7	11	67	48	39
6 Hearts	34	14	10	10	54	43	38
7 Ayr United	34	15	8	11	44	40	38
8 Dundee United	34	15	7	12	55	51	37
9 Motherwell	34	14	7	13	45	40	35
10 Dumbarton	34	11	7	16	43	58	29
11 Partick Thistle	34	9	10	15	33	46	28
12 St Johnstone	34	9	10	15	41	60	28
13 Arbroath	34	10	7	17	52	69	27
14 Morton	34	8	10	16	37	49	26
15 Clyde	34	8	9	17	29	65	25
16 Dunfermline	34	8	8	18	43	65	24
17 East Fife	34	9	6	19	26	51	24
18 Falkirk	34	4	14	16	33	58	22

May 6th: Evan Williams was freed.

May 11th: Hay and Dalglish were in the Scotland team beaten 1-0 by Northern Ireland at Hampden

May 14th: Hay, Johnstone and Dalglish were in the Scotland team which beat Wales 2-0 at Hampden Park. McGrain made an appearance as substitute. Dalglish scored one of the goals.

May 18th: McGrain, Johnstone, Dalglish and Hay were in the Scotland team which beat England 2-0 at Hampden Park.

June 1st: McGrain, Johnstone, Dalglish and Hay were in the Scotland team beaten 2-1 by Belgium in Bruges. Johnstone scored Scotland's goal.

June 6th: McGrain, Johnstone and Hay were in the Scotland team which beat Norway 2-1 in Oslo. Dalglish substituted for Johnstone and scored the winning goal.

June 14th: McGrain, Hay and Dalglish were in the Scotland team which beat Zaire 2-0 in the World Cup Finals in Dortmund.

June 18th: McGrain, Hay and Dalglish were in the Scotland team which drew 0-0 with Brazil in the World Cup Finals in Frankfurt.

June 22nd: McGrain, Hay and Dalglish were in the Scotland team which drew 1-1 with Yugoslavia in the World Cup Finals in Frankfurt.

LEAGUE CUP

August 11th
CELTIC (2) 2 ARBROATH (0) 1
Lennox (21), Butler (84)
Lynch (36)

CELTIC: Hunter; McGrain, Brogan; Murray, McNeill, Connelly; McLaughlin, Hood (Deans), Lennox, Hay, Lynch

ARBROATH: Marshall; Cant, Rylance; Cargill, Waddell, Murray; Sellars (Butler), Penman, Pirie, Fletcher, Reid (Donald)

Attendance: 19,000

August 15th
FALKIRK (0) 0 CELTIC (0) 2
Hay (46),
Lennox (58 pen)

FALKIRK: Donaldson; S. Kennedy, Young; Markie, Wheatley, Fowler; Hoggan, Whiteford, Somner, Shirra (Harley), McLeod (Mercer)

CELTIC: Hunter; McGrain, Brogan; Murray, McNeill, Connelly; Johnstone, McLaughlin (Callaghan), Deans (Hood), Hay, Lennox

Attendance: 12,000

August 18th
RANGERS (0) 1 CELTIC (0) 2
McNeill o.g. (89) Lennox (82),
Hood (86)

RANGERS: McCloy; Jardine, Mathieson; Greig, Johnstone, MacDonald; McLean (Scott), Forsyth, Parlane, Conn, Young (Smith)

CELTIC: Hunter; McGrain, Brogan; Murray, McNeill, Connelly; Johnstone, McLaughlin (Callaghan), Dalglish (Hood), Hay, Lennox

Attendance: 63,173

Missed chances proved costly for Rangers. 4 times Conn and Young mis-hit shots that should have guaranteed goals. Celtic accepted the fewer opportunities that came their way.

August 22nd
CELTIC (2) 2 FALKIRK (1) 1
Lennox 2 (12, 15 pen) Somner (9)

CELTIC: Hunter; McGrain, Brogan; Murray, McNeill, Connelly; Johnstone (Lynch), McLaughlin (Callaghan), Hood, Hay, Lennox

FALKIRK: Donaldson; Kennedy, Mercer; Markie, Wheatley, Fowler; Hoggan, Whiteford, Harley, Somner, McLeod

Attendance: 14,000

August 25th
CELTIC (1) 1 RANGERS (0) 3
Lennox (23) MacDonald (53),
Parlane (56),
Conn (82)

CELTIC: Hunter; McGrain, Brogan; Murray, McNeill, Connelly; Johnstone, McLaughlin (Hood), Dalglish, Hay, Lennox

RANGERS: McCloy; Jardine, Mathieson; Greig, Johnstone, MacDonald; McLean, Forsyth, Parlane, Conn, Young

Attendance: 57,000

It was Alex MacDonald who won the match for Rangers by scoring the first and making the 2nd and 3rd goals. After Johnstone was sent off and Celtic were reduced to 10 men Dalglish dredged the bottom of his stamina in trying to equalise and the whole side fought against impossible odds. Lennox had a goal disallowed.

August 29th
ARBROATH (1) 1 — CELTIC (1) 3
Yule (43) — Dalglish (35), Lennox (60), Wilson (75)

ARBROATH; Marshall; Milne, Rylance; Cargill, Waddell, Murray; Sellars, Cant, Fletcher, Penman, Yule

CELTIC: Hunter; McGrain, Brogan; Murdoch, MacDonald, Connelly; McLaughlin (Wilson), Hood, Dalglish, Callaghan, Lennox

Attendance: 5,101

Section table

	P	W	D	L	F	A	Pts
Rangers	6	5	0	1	17	6	10
CELTIC	6	5	0	1	12	7	10
Arbroath	6	2	0	4	9	13	4
Falkirk	6	0	0	6	6	18	0

Qualifiers: Rangers and CELTIC

Second Round First Leg September 12th
MOTHERWELL (0) 1 — CELTIC (2) 2
Goldthorpe (48) — Hood (21), Murray (44)

MOTHERWELL: MacRae; Millar, Wark; R. Watson, Jim Muir, Goodwin; Campbell, Graham, Goldthorpe, McCabe, McClymont (Lawson)

CELTIC: Hunter; McGrain, Brogan; Murray, McNeill, Connelly; Johnstone, Hood, Dalglish (Callaghan), Hay, Lennox (Wilson)

Attendance: 19,253

Second Round Second Leg October 10th
CELTIC (0) 0 — MOTHERWELL (1) 1
After extra time
Goldthorpe (38)

CELTIC: Hunter; McGrain, Brogan; Murray, McNeill, Connelly; Johnstone, Dalglish, Deans (McCluskey), Callaghan, Wilson (Hood)

MOTHERWELL; MacRae; Millar, Wark; W. Watson, Jim Muir, Goodwin; McCabe, Graham, Goldthorpe, McClymont, Martin

Attendance: 24,000

Second Round Play-Off October 29th
CELTIC (1) 3 — MOTHERWELL (0) 2
Murray (5), Deans (65), Johnstone (89) — McClymont (59), Graham (70)

CELTIC: Hunter; McGrain, Brogan; McCluskey (Wilson), MacDonald, Connelly; Johnstone, Murray, Deans, Callaghan, Dalglish

MOTHERWELL: Rennie; W. Watson, Wark; R. Watson, Jim Muir, Millar; Campbell, Graham, Goldthorpe, Martin, McClymont

Attendance: 26,000

Quarter-Final First Leg October 31st
CELTIC (2) 3 — ABERDEEN (1) 2
Dalglish 2 (15, 16), McCluskey (56) — Jarvie 2 (3, 55)

CELTIC: Hunter; McGrain, Brogan; McCluskey, McNeill, Connelly; Hood, Murray, Deans, Hay, Dalglish

ABERDEEN: Clark; Hair, Hermiston; Thomson, Young, W. Miller; Graham, Robb, Jarvie, Smith (Willoughby), Taylor (R. Miller)

Attendance: 28,000

Quarter-Final Second Leg November 21st
ABERDEEN (0) 0 — CELTIC (0) 0

ABERDEEN: Clark; Hair (Williamson), Hermiston; Thomson, Young, W. Miller; J. Miller, Robb, Jarvie, Craig, Graham (R. Miller)

CELTIC: Hunter; McGrain, Brogan; McCluskey, McNeill, Murray; Lennox, Hood, Deans (Johnstone), Callaghan, Dalglish

Attendance: 16,000. Celtic won 3-2 on aggregate

Semi-Final at Hampden Park December 5th
CELTIC (1) 3 — RANGERS (1) 1
Hood 3 (35, 55, 73) — MacDonald (38)

CELTIC: Hunter; McGrain, Brogan; McCluskey, McNeill, Murray; Hood, Hay, Wilson, Callaghan, Dalglish. Subs: Connelly and Johnstone

RANGERS: McCloy; Jardine, Mathieson; Greig, Jackson, Houston; McLean (Johnstone), Forsyth, Parlane, Conn, MacDonald. Other Sub: Smith

Attendance: 54,864

A Harry Hood hat-trick gave Celtic victory and a much more comfortable win than they could have expected. Celtic took the lead in the 35th minute when McCloy lost the ball and Dalglish crossed for Hood to score with a smart header. 3 minutes later Rangers equalised with a glorious goal – a terrific shot from MacDonald that gave Hunter no chance. In the 2nd half Rangers went to pieces. Hood scored Celtic's 2nd following a free-kick and in the 73rd minute he completed his hat-trick – although there was a suspicion of offside. After Rangers brought on Derek Johnstone for McLean, Hood had the ball in the net for the 4th time but he was ruled offside.

Final at Hampden Park December 15th
CELTIC (0) 0 DUNDEE (0) 1
Wallace (75)

CELTIC: Hunter; McGrain, Brogan; McCluskey, McNeill, Murray; Hood (Johnstone), Hay (Connelly), Wilson, Callaghan, Dalglish

DUNDEE: Allan; R. Wilson, Gemmell; Ford, Stewart, Phillip; Duncan, Robinson, Wallace, J. Scott, Lambie. Subs: Johnston, I. Scott

Attendance: 27,974 *Referee:* R. H. Davidson (Airdrie)

Dundee took the League Cup for the first time in 21 years. With the State of Emergency in force the match kicked off at 1.30. The hard pitch did not stop Dundee from displaying sufficient form to make them worthy winners.

Their defence never creaked despite the loss of Stewart for a time to have stitches inserted in a head wound. 15 minutes from time Wallace chested down a Wilson free-kick, turned sharply on the treacherous surface and shot past Hunter into the corner of the net. Celtic claimed a penalty in the dying minutes when Johnstone was bundled off the ball by Stewart but referee Davidson waved this aside.

SCOTTISH CUP

Third Round January 27th
CELTIC (4) 6 CLYDEBANK (0) 1
Deans 3 (4, 6, 39) Fallon (89 pen)
Lennox 2 (24, 55)
Davidson (64)

CELTIC: Hunter; McGrain (Davidson), Brogan; McCluskey, McNeill, Hay; Hood, Callaghan, Deans, Dalglish (Wilson), Lennox

CLYDEBANK: Gallagher; Mitchell, Abel; Fanning, Fallon, White; Roxburgh, Henderson, Larnach, McColl (Law), Currie (McCallan)

Attendance: 28,000. This was Celtic's first Sunday Scottish Cup match.

Fourth Round February 17th
CELTIC (4) 6 STIRLING ALBION (1) 1
Dalglish (9), Lawson (32)
Wilson (21)
Hood 2 (36, 45),
Murray 2 (55, 83)

CELTIC: Hunter; McGrain, Brogan; Connelly, McNeill (McCluskey), Hay; Hood (Davidson), Murray, Deans, Dalglish, Wilson

STIRLING ALBION: Young; Jones, McAlpine; Duffin, Stevenson, Carr; McPhee (Morrison), McMillan, Steele, Lawson, Murphy

Attendance: 23,000

Fifth Round March 10th
CELTIC (1) 2 MOTHERWELL (2) 2
Hood 2 (27, 47) Graham (16),
Kennedy (44)

CELTIC: Connaghan; Hay, Brogan; Connelly, MacDonald, McCluskey; Hood, Murray, Deans, Dalglish, Wilson

MOTHERWELL: Rennie; W. Watson, Wark; R. Watson, Jim Muir, Millar; Kennedy, Graham, Goldthorpe, Martin, McClymont

Attendance: 46,000

Fifth Round Replay March 13th
MOTHERWELL (0) 0 CELTIC (0) 1
Deans (60)

MOTHERWELL: Rennie; W. Watson, Wark; R. Watson, Jim Muir, Millar; Kennedy (Gray), Graham, Goldthorpe, Martin, McClymont

CELTIC: Connaghan; Hay, Brogan; Connelly, McNeill, McCluskey (Callaghan); Bone, Murray, Deans, Dalglish, Hood

Attendance: 24,875

Semi-Final at Hampden Park April 3rd
CELTIC (1) 1 DUNDEE (0) 0
Johnstone (43)

CELTIC: Connaghan; Hay, Brogan; Murray, McNeill, McCluskey; Johnstone, Hood, Deans, Callaghan, Dalglish. Subs: Wilson and McGrain

DUNDEE: Allan; R. Wilson, Gemmell; Ford, Stewart, Phillip; J. Wilson, Robinson, Duncan, J. Scott, Lambie (Wallace). Other Sub: Pringle

Attendance: 58,250

Celtic qualified for their 9th Scottish Cup Final in 10 years. 2 minutes from the interval Celtic finally made the breakthrough when Johnstone volleyed home McNeill's head flick from a Hood corner. All Dundee could muster in the 2nd half was a snap shot from substitute Wallace which went over the bar.

Final at Hampden Park May 4th
CELTIC (2) 3 DUNDEE UNITED (0) 0
Hood (20),
Murray (24),
Deans (89)

CELTIC: Connaghan; McGrain (Callaghan), Brogan; Murray, McNeill, McCluskey; Johnstone, Hood, Deans, Hay, Dalglish. Sub: Lennox

DUNDEE UNITED: Davie; Gardner, Kopel; Copland, D. Smith (Traynor), W. Smith, Payne (Rolland), Knox, Gray, Fleming, Houston

Attendance: 75,959 *Referee:* J.W. Paterson (Bothwell)

Celtic were 2 up after only 25 minutes' play. Only briefly after the interval did the Tannadice team revive. Connaghan saved point-blank from Gray and a shot from Knox hit McNeill involuntarily on the head. In the last moments Celtic took their total to 3 when Dalglish laid the ball back for Deans to scoop the ball past Davie.

EUROPEAN CUP

First Round First Leg September 19th

T.P.S. TURKU (Finland) (1) 1	CELTIC (2) 6
Andelmin (17 pen)	Callaghan 2 (1, 88), Hood (23), Johnstone (60), Connelly (78 pen), Deans (87)

TURKU: Enckelman (Kokkonen); Kymalainen, Saari; Nummi, Nummelin, Toivanen; Salama, Lindholm, Harittu, Andelmin, Suhonen

CELTIC: Hunter; McGrain, Brogan; Murray, McNeill, Connelly; Johnstone, Hay, Hood (Deans), Callaghan, Wilson (Davidson)

Attendance: 3,100

Celtic scored the goals that made the Second Leg at Parkhead no more then a formality.

First Round Second Leg October 3rd

CELTIC (2) 3	T.P.S. TURKU (0) 0
Deans (20), Johnstone 2 (24, 53)	

CELTIC: Hunter; McCluskey, Brogan; Murray, McNeill, Connelly; Johnstone, Davidson, Deans, Dalglish (McNamara), Wilson

TURKU: Enckleman; Kynatainer, Saari; Nummi, Salonen, Toivanen; Salama, Lindholm, Harittu, Andelmin, Saarinan

Attendance: 18,000

Celtic abused chances by the dozen but still won in a canter: 9-1 on aggregate.

Second Round Second Leg October 24th

CELTIC (0) 0	VEJLE (Denmark) (0) 0

CELTIC: Hunter; McGrain, Hay; Murray, Connelly, McCluskey; Johnstone, Hood (Wilson), Dalglish, Callaghan, Lennox

VEJLE: Woodsku; J. Jensen, F. Hansen; Serritslev, G. Jensen, Sorensen; T. Hansen, Markussen, Huttel, Pedersen, Norregard (Johansen)

Attendance: 30,000

This was amongst Celtic's poorest ever European performances. McNeill – injured – did not play and Johnstone was made captain for the night. They could not mount a charge against a side who defended with composure, skill and commitment.

Second Round Second Leg November 6th

VEJLE (0) 0	CELTIC (1) 1
	Lennox (36)

VEJLE: Wodsku; J. Jensen, F. Hansen; Serritslev, G. Jensen, Sorensen; Norregaard, T. Hansen, Markussen (Knudsen), Fritsen, Andersen (Huttel)

CELTIC: Hunter; McGrain, Brogan; McCluskey, McNeill, Connelly; Lennox, Murray, Deans, Hay, Dalglish

Attendance: 19,000

The Danes made little of the opportunity which their First Leg performance had given them and Celtic accomplished their task with ease. Before half-time Wodsku pulled off superb saves from Murray and Dalglish. The 2nd half was unexciting. The main highlight was a Dalglish goal which was disallowed for offside. Celtic won 1-0 on aggregate.

Quarter-Final First Leg February 27th

BASLE (Switzerland) (2) 3	CELTIC (1) 2
Hitzfeld 2 (28, 63 pen) Odermatt (30)	Wilson (20), Dalglish (54)

BASLE: Laufenburger; Mundschin, Fischli; Demarmels, Stohler, Hasler; Odermatt (Wampfler), Rahmen, Hitzfeld, Balmer, Wenger (Tanner)

CELTIC: Williams; McGrain, Brogan; Connelly, McNeill, Hay; Hood, Murray, Deans (Callaghan), Dalglish, Wilson

Attendance: 25,000

Celtic charitably presented the Swiss with their first goal and later conceded a penalty after they went ahead in the 20th minute. 9 minutes after half-time Celtic equalised. McGrain moved forward and pushed the ball into the path of Dalglish who cleverly chipped over the goalkeeper's head. In the 63rd minute Basle went ahead again when Hitzfeld scored from the spot after Connelly was beaten for pace and brought down Demarmels.

Quarter-Final Second Leg March 20th

CELTIC (2) 4	BASLE (2) 2
Dalglish (12), Deans (15), Callaghan (57), Murray (98)	Mundschin (33), Balmer (45) *After extra time, 90 mins 3-2 (5-5 on aggregate)*

CELTIC: Connaghan; Hay, Brogan; Murray, McNeill, Connelly (McCluskey); Johnstone, Hood, Deans, Dalglish, Callaghan

BASLE: Laufenburger (Kunz); Rahmen, Mundschin; Stohler, Fischli, Odermatt; Hasler, Wampfler, Balmer, Hitzfeld, Tanner

Attendance: 71,000

Celtic suffered an early setback when Connelly was carried off with a broken ankle after only 5 minutes, but it took them only 12 minutes to cancel out the First Leg deficit when Dalglish, unmarked, rose high to head Callaghan's kick into the net. Moments later Murray's pass left Deans with yards of space inside the penalty area and he beat the keeper on the run. After 30 minutes Basle replaced their goalkeeper with Kunz. Almost immediately Odermatt won a free-kick, took it himself, slanted the ball into the penalty area and Mundschin, the big defender came up to head past Connaghan. In time added on for injury in the first-half Odermatt hit a strong cross which Connaghan could not hold and Balmer eased the ball over the line for the equaliser. Celtic regained the lead in the 57th minute when Callaghan volleyed home following a Johnstone corner which had been played on by Deans. In extra time Celtic missed a great chance when Deans drove a shot straight at the goalkeeper when clean through, but in 98 minutes the winner arrived. Brogan pushed the ball down the wing to Hood, he crossed to the far post, the ball spun loose in the air and Murray rose to nod it high into the net and take Celtic into their 4th European Cup Semi-Final. They won 6-5 on aggregate.

Semi-Final First Leg April 10th
CELTIC (0) 0 ATLETICO MADRID (Spain) (0) 0

CELTIC: Connaghan; Hay, Brogan; Murray, McNeill, McCluskey; Johnstone, Hood, Deans (Wilson), Callaghan, Dalglish

ATLETICO: Reina; Melo, Diaz; Benegas, Overjero, Eusebio; Ayala, Adelardo, Garate (Quique), Irureta (Albert), Heredia

Attendance: 70,000

Atletico, managed by the notorious Juan Carlos Lorenzo, viciously kicked and maltreated Celtic especially Johnstone, in the First Leg of the Semi-Final at Parkhead. They had 3 players ordered off and 7 booked. Celtic were disciplined enough not to retaliate but were over-anxious and too hasty to allow their numerical advantage to count. Having secured the draw they came for, the Spaniards jumped for joy at the end.

Semi-Final Second Leg April 24th
ATLETICO MADRID (0) 2 CELTIC (0) 0
Garate (77)
Adelardo (86)

ATLETICO: Reina, Benegas, Capon; Adelardo, Heredia, Eusebio; Ufarte, Luis, Garate, Irureta, Becerra

CELTIC: Connaghan; McGrain, Brogan; Hay, McNeill, McCluskey; Johnstone, Murray, Dalglish, Hood, Lennox

Attendance: 64,000

The thugs of Atletico minus 6 of their players who were suspended by UEFA after their shocking conduct in Glasgow gradually wore down Celtic's resistance, and late goals from Garate and Adelardo took them through to the Final to face Bayern Munich. A tiring Celtic defence was finally beaten in the 77th minute when Becarra turned an orthodox cross into the penalty area and Garate tapped the ball home from close range. The Spaniards made sure of victory in the 86th minute. McNeill was caught out of position as he tried to encourage his forwards in a last rally. Atletico played the ball down the middle and Garate flicked it on to Adelardo who hit a punishing right-foot volley high into the net. Atletico Madrid won 2-0 on aggregate.

APPEARANCES	League	League Cup	Scottish Cup	European Cup
Hunter	26	13	2	4
Connaghan	8	–	4	3
McGrain	29+1S	13	3	5
Brogan	30	13	6	7
Murray	32	12	5	8
McCluskey	23+2S	5+1S	5+1S	5+1S
McNeill	30	11	5	7
Connelly	14	10+1S	3	6
Johnstone	13+2S	7+2S	2	6
McLaughlin	2+1S	6	–	–
Hood	28+3S	9+4S	6	6
Deans	24+2S	5	6	5+1S
Dalglish	31+2S	10	6	7
Lennox	17+2S	7	1	3
Hay	25	9	6	7
Lynch	1+2S	1+1S	–	–
Callaghan	16+6S	6+4S	2+2S	4+2S
MacDonald	2	2	1	–
Wilson	10+9S	3+2S	2+1S	3+2S
Quinn	3	–	–	–
McNamara	1+1S	–	–	0+1S
Ritchie	0+1S	–	–	–
Davidson	3	–	–	1
Bone	3+1S	–	1	–
Welsh	3	–	–	–
Williams	–	–	–	1
Murdoch	–	1	–	–

GOALSCORERS:

League: Deans 24, Dalglish 18, Lennox 12 (3 pens), Hood 7, Wilson 5, Murray 3, Johnstone 3 (2 pens), Hay 2, Callaghan 2, Own Goals 2, McLaughlin 1, McGrain 1, McCluskey 1, Connelly 1

League Cup: Lennox 7 (2 pens), Hood 5, Dalglish 3, Murray 2, Lynch 1, Hay 1, Wilson 1, Deans 1, Johnstone 1, McCluskey 1

Scottish Cup: Hood 5, Deans 5, Murray 3, Lennox 2, Davidson 1, Dalglish 1, Wilson 1, Johnstone 1

European Cup: Deans 3, Johnstone 3, Callaghan 3, Dalglish 2, Hood 1, Connelly 1 (pen), Lennox 1, Wilson 1, Murray 1

Jimmy Johnstone and Tommy Gemmell in Dukla strips after winning in Prague in 1967.

Season 1974-75

Celtic's long run of League Championship wins at last came to an end but they still monopolised other Scottish honours by winning both the Scottish Cup and the League Cup. They finished third in the table – 4 points behind Hibs and 11 behind Rangers who won the last-ever Scottish First Division Championship before re-construction and the formation of the Premier League. Celtic's form up until their meeting with Rangers on January 4th was superb with only 1 defeat in 19 matches but after the defeat by Rangers they went off the boil and won only 4 of their last 15 matches. Sadly, but inevitably, Billy McNeill announced his retirement after the Scottish Cup victory over Airdrie, and Jim Brogan and Jimmy Johnstone – one of Scotland's greatest ever players – also left the club having given tremendous service. David Hay left for Chelsea for £250,000 during the previous close season. New faces who arrived on the scene were Ronnie Glavin, an £80,000 capture from Partick Thistle, and England Under-23 goalkeeper Peter Latchford, who was signed following an initial loan period from West Bromwich Albion. Kenny Dalglish, now one of the elder statesmen, started in 33 matches and he finished as top scorer with 16 goals followed by Paul Wilson, who made 31 +2 substitute appearances, on 13. Jock Stein was offered the Scotland Manager's job at the end of the season but he opted to stay with Celtic.

The League Cup Final hoodoo was broken. In a classic encounter with Hibs Jimmy Johnstone produced one of his greatest performances and Celtic won 6-3 with their centre-forward Deans and Harper of Hibs both scoring hat-tricks.

Celtic beat Dundee, for the 3rd successive year, in the Semi-Final to reach their 39th Scottish Cup Final where their opponents, Airdrie, were contesting their first Final since 1924 and the days of Hughie Gallacher and Bob McPhail. The match ended with Celtic deservedly winning 3-1 and spoiling Airdrie's dreams of glory thanks mainly to the magic of Dalglish.

Celtic's European Cup challenge was their poorest yet and they went out meekly to Greek Champions Olympiakos in the First Round on a 1-3 aggregate.

League:	Third
League Cup:	Winners
Scottish Cup:	Winners
European Cup:	First Round

SCOTTISH FIRST DIVISION

July 18th: Clyde signed Evan Williams.

August 12th: Celtic drew 1-1 with Liverpool in a Billy McNeill Testimonial.

August 31st

CELTIC (1) 5 KILMARNOCK (0) 0
Davidson (37),
Johnstone (80),
Dalglish (84),
Wilson (88),
Murray (89 pen)

CELTIC: Connaghan; McGrain, Connelly, McNeill, McCluskey; Murray, Davidson, Callaghan; Johnstone, Dalglish, Wilson

KILMARNOCK: Stewart; Maxwell, Rodman, McDicken, Robertson; Cook, McCulloch, Sheed; Fleming, Morrison, Smith

Attendance: 27,000

September 7th
CLYDE (2) 2 — Marshall (25), Ferris (44)
CELTIC (0) 4 — Dalglish (52), Davidson (69), McCluskey (70), Lennox (84)

CLYDE: Williams; Jim Burns, Aherne, McVie, John Burns; Swan, Miller, Sullivan; Ferris, Marshall, Boyle

CELTIC: Connaghan; McGrain, McNeill, McCluskey, Brogan; Connelly, Murray, Davidson; Johnstone (Callaghan), Dalglish (Lennox), Wilson

Attendance: 15,000

September 14th
CELTIC (1) 1. — Dalglish (31)
RANGERS (0) 2 — McDougall (57), Jackson (75)

CELTIC: Connaghan; McGrain, McCluskey, McNeill, Brogan; Murray, Davidson, Callaghan; Johnstone (Hood), Dalglish, Wilson

RANGERS: Kennedy; Jardine, Jackson, Forsyth, Greig; McDougall (McLean), Johnstone, Young; Parlane, Fyfe, Scott

Attendance: 60,000

This was Rangers' first victory at Parkhead since September 1968. The referee should have awarded Celtic a penalty in the first minute when Forsyth blatantly pushed Dalglish off the ball in the area. He sent off Brogan after an incident with Parlane. Parlane was later sent off himself for dissent. Celtic should have won it in the 1st half. Dalglish's marvellously quick and instinctive goal after 31 minutes seemed to have put his side elegantly on their way to victory but Rangers fully deserved to win on their 2nd half performance.

September 14th: George Connelly announced his decision to quit football.

September 21st
MOTHERWELL (1) 1 — Taylor (20)
CELTIC (1) 2 — Lennox 2 (12 pen, 64 pen)

MOTHERWELL: Lloyd; Dickson, R. Watson, W. Watson, Wark; McCabe, Taylor, Stevens, Graham; Goldthorpe, McGuinness (Pettigrew)

CELTIC: Connaghan; McGrain, McNeill, McCluskey, Callaghan; Murray, Dalglish, Hood; Johnstone, Lennox, Wilson

Attendance: 13,113

September 28th
CELTIC (3) 5 — Deans (18), Wilson 2 (30, 47), Dalglish (42), Hood (53)
AYR UNITED (1) 3 — Somner (39), Dickson (56), Fillipi (89)

CELTIC: Connaghan; McGrain, McNeill, McCluskey, Brogan; Murray, Dalglish (Johnstone), Callaghan; Hood, Deans, Wilson (Lennox)

AYR UNITED: McLean; Wells, Fleming, McAnespie, Murphy; Doyle, Lannon, Fillipi; Ferguson (Graham), Dickson, Somner

Attendance: 20,000

October 5th
DUMBARTON (0) 1 — Wallace (70 pen)
CELTIC (2) 3 — Johnstone (3), Deans (40), Dalglish (82)

DUMBARTON: McGregor; Mullen, Cushley (Checkley), Muir, Watt; Ruddy, Wallace, Graham; Cook, McCormack, McAdam

CELTIC: Hunter; McGrain, McNeill (McCluskey), MacDonald, Brogan; Murray, Dalglish, Hood; Johnstone, Deans, Wilson

Attendance: 12,500

October 12th
CELTIC (0) 1 — Murray (55)
ARBROATH (0) 0

CELTIC: Hunter; McGrain, McCluskey, MacDonald, Brogan; Murray, Callaghan, Hood; Johnstone, Deans, Wilson

ARBROATH: Marshall; Milne, Carson, Murray, Ryland; Cargill, Cant, Penman (Buchan), Sellars (Reid), Fletcher, Yule

Attendance: 16,000

October 19th
CELTIC (3) 5 — Murray (15 pen), Johnstone (20), Deans 3 (24, 47, 76)
HIBERNIAN (0) 0

CELTIC: Hunter; McGrain, McNeill, McCluskey, Brogan (MacDonald); Murray, Dalglish, Hood; Wilson, Deans, Johnstone

HIBERNIAN: McArthur; Brownlie, Spalding, Blackley, Schaedler; Edwards (Duncan), Stanton, Cropley; Harper, Gordon, Munro

Attendance: 39,000

League positions

	P	W	D	L	F	A	Pts
1 Rangers	9	7	2	0	27	9	16
2 CELTIC	8	7	0	1	26	9	14
3 Aberdeen	9	7	0	2	22	9	14
4 Dundee United	9	4	3	2	19	10	11
5 Hibernian	8	5	1	2	19	12	11

October 30th: Dalglish, Johnstone and Deans were in the Scotland team which beat East Germany 3-0 at Hampden Park. Dalglish scored one of the goals.

November 2nd
CELTIC (1) 1 — Wilson (43)
ABERDEEN (0) 0

CELTIC: Hunter; Brogan, MacDonald, McNeill, McCluskey; Murray, Dalglish, Hood; Johnstone (Lennox), Deans, Wilson

ABERDEEN: Clark; Williamson, Young, Miller, McLelland; Smith, Purdie, Craig; Graham, McCall, Jarvie

Attendance: 29,000. Purdie missed a penalty.

November 6th
PARTICK THISTLE (0) 1 CELTIC (0) 2
Prudham (71) Deans (51), Dalglish (89)

PARTICK THISTLE: Rough; Hansen, Kellachan (Gray); Campbell, Clark, Anderson; Lawrie, Houston, Glavin, Prudham, McQuade

CELTIC: Hunter; MacDonald, Brogan; Murray, McNeill, McCluskey; Hood, Dalglish, Deans, Callaghan, Wilson

Attendance: 15,500. Houston was ordered off.

November 9th
DUNDEE UNITED (0) 0 CELTIC (0) 0

DUNDEE UNITED: McAlpine; Rolland, Copland, Smith (Knox), Kopel; Fleming, Houston, Narey; Traynor, Gray, MacDonald

CELTIC: Hunter; McCluskey, MacDonald, McNeill, Brogan; Murray, Hood, Dalglish; Deans, Davidson (Bone), Wilson

Attendance: 15,300. Murray missed a penalty.

November 15th: Ronnie Glavin was signed from Partick Thistle for £80,000.

November 16th
CELTIC (2) 6 AIRDRIE (0) 0
Murray 2 (20, 71),
McNeill (40), Glavin (62),
Lennox (78 pen),
Wilson (79)

CELTIC: Hunter; McGrain, McNeill (MacDonald), McCluskey, Brogan; Murray, Glavin, Dalglish (Johnstone); Deans, Lennox, Wilson

AIRDRIE: McWilliams; Jonquin, McKinlay, Black, Lapsley; Whiteford, Reynolds, McCann; Jones (Wilson), Franchetti, McCulloch

Attendance: 26,000

November 20th: Johnstone and Deans were in the Scotland team beaten 2-1 by Spain at Hampden Park. Dalglish made an appearance as substitute for Deans.

November 23rd
HEARTS (1) 1 CELTIC (1) 1
Busby (41) Wilson (14)

HEARTS: Cruikshank; Park, Anderson, Kay, Jeffries; Murray, Busby (Donaldson), Callachan; Carruthers, Gibson, Ford

CELTIC: Hunter; McGrain, McNeill, McCluskey, Brogan; Glavin, Dalglish, Murray; Wilson, Deans (Johnstone), Lennox (Callachan)

Attendance: 23,000. Lennox missed a penalty.

November 27th: George Connelly returned for Celtic reserves after quitting following the Clyde match on September 7th.

November 30th
MORTON (0) 0 CELTIC (1) 1
Murray (45)

MORTON: Baines; Hayes, Rankin, Anderson, Ritchie; Lumsden, Townsend, Reid; Skovdam (Taylor), McGhee, Harley (Osborne)

CELTIC: Connaghan; McGrain, McNeill, McCluskey, Brogan; Murray, Dalglish, Glavin; Wilson, Bone, Lennox

Attendance: 17,000

December 7th
CELTIC (1) 2 DUNFERMLINE (1) 1
Bone (16), Hood (89) Shaw (15)

CELTIC: Hunter; McGrain, McNeill, McCluskey (Welsh), Brogan; Murray, Dalglish, Glavin; Bone (Hood), Lennox, Wilson

DUNFERMLINE: Karlsen; Scott, Thomson, Evans, Markie; Kinninmonth, McNicoll, Cameron; Watson, Mackie, Shaw

Attendance: 20,000

December 11th: Celtic drew 3-3 with Benfica at Parkhead in a U.N.I.C.E.F. match. Benfica won 5-4 on penalties, McNeill being the only player to miss.

December 14th
DUNDEE (0) 0 CELTIC (4) 6
Johnstone 2 (5, 30),
Dalglish 3 (19, 67, 71),
Wilson (39)

DUNDEE: Allan; Wilson, Stewart, Phillip, Johnston; Ford, Caldwell (Gordon), Robinson; Hoggan, Hutchinson, J. Scott

CELTIC: Hunter; McGrain, McNeill, Connelly, McCluskey; Murray (MacDonald), Glavin (Hood), Callaghan; Johnstone, Dalglish, Wilson

Attendance: 14,901

December 14th: Jimmy Quinn was freed.

December 21st
CELTIC (1) 3 ST JOHNSTONE (1) 1
McCluskey (25 pen), O'Rourke (7)
Dalglish (57), Murray (85)

CELTIC: Hunter; McGrain, McNeill, Connelly, McCluskey; Murray, Hood, Callaghan; Johnstone, Dalglish (Lennox), Wilson

ST JOHNSTONE: Robertson; Smith, MacDonald, Kinnell, Argue; Rennie, Thomson, Cramond; Muir, O'Rourke, Lambie

Attendance: 20,000

December 28th
KILMARNOCK (0) 0 CELTIC (1) 1
Dalglish (38)

KILMARNOCK: Stewart; McLean, Rodman, McDicken, Robertson; McCulloch, Maxwell, Smith; Provan, Fleming, Morrison

CELTIC: Hunter; McGrain, McNeill, Connelly, Brogan; Glavin, Murray, Callaghan; Dalglish, Hood, Wilson

Attendance: 17,500

League positions

	P	W	D	L	F	A	Pts
1 CELTIC	18	15	2	1	49	13	32
2 Rangers	18	14	2	2	50	18	30
3 Hibernian	18	11	4	3	34	16	26
4 Dundee United	18	9	5	4	46	22	23
5 Aberdeen	18	8	4	6	31	24	20

January 1st
CELTIC (2) 5 — CLYDE (0) 1
Deans (7), Dalglish (49), Callaghan 2 (39, 55), Glavin (88) — Boyle (73)

CELTIC: Hunter; McGrain, McCluskey; Glavin, McNeill, Connelly (Brogan); Johnstone, Dalglish (Hood), Deans, Callaghan, Wilson

CLYDE: Cairney; Anderson, John Burns (Ferris); Aherne, McVie, Jim Burns; Sullivan, Millar, Boyle, Swan, Marshall (Ward)

Attendance: 20,000

January 4th
RANGERS (1) 3 — CELTIC (0) 0
Johnstone (6), McLean (50), Parlane (74)

RANGERS: Kennedy; Jardine, Forsyth, Jackson (Miller), Greig; McDougall, Johnstone, MacDonald; McLean, Parlane, Scott (Young)

CELTIC; Hunter; McGrain, McNeill, McCluskey, Brogan; Glavin, Hood (Johnstone), Murray; Callaghan, Dalglish, Wilson

Attendance: 70,000

Rangers won well and deservedly. Jock Wallace's match-winning stroke was to play without a left-back. Greig moved into a defensive midfield position, cutting off Dalglish's work at source. Both Glavin and Murray were bogged down in the mud and Wilson tired after a brilliant 1st half. Kennedy pulled off a remarkable save from McGrain, and a series of dives at Celtic feet was bravery in the extreme.

January 11th
CELTIC (1) 2 — MOTHERWELL (2) 3
Hood 2 (28, 57) — Pettigrew 2 (12, 76), Graham (21)

CELTIC: Hunter; McGrain, McNeill, McCluskey, MacDonald; Glavin, Dalglish, Murray; Hood, Deans (Johnstone), Wilson

MOTHERWELL: Rennie; W. Watson, R. Watson, McLaren, Wark; McIlwraith, Goodwin, Taylor; Pettigrew, Graham, Goldthorpe (Millar)

Attendance: 26,000

January 18th
AYR UNITED (1) 1 — CELTIC (1) 5
Ingram (32) — Murray (44), Hood (46), Deans 2 (60, 70), McDonald o.g. (77)

AYR UNITED: McGiffen; Fillipi, McDonald, Fleming, Murphy; Cairns (McAnespie), Graham, McCulloch; McVake (Bell), Ingram, Phillips

CELTIC: Hunter; McGrain, McNeill, Connelly, Brogan; Murray, Dalglish, Callaghan; Hood, Deans, Wilson

Attendance: 14,500

February 5th: McGrain and Dalglish were in the Scotland team which drew 1-1 with Spain in Valencia. Paul Wilson appeared as a substitute.

February 8th
ARBROATH (1) 2 — CELTIC (2) 2
Bone (9), Rylance (76) — Hood (17), Dalglish (42)

ARBROATH: Campbell; Murray, Carson, Smith, Milne; Penman, Cargill (Reid), Rylance; Fletcher, Bone, Sellars

CELTIC: Hunter; McGrain, McNeill, Connelly, Brogan; Murray, Dalglish, Callaghan; Hood, Deans (Glavin), Wilson (Lynch)

Attendance: 7,500

February 11th
CELTIC (2) 2 — DUMBARTON (0) 2
Hood (32), Wilson (37) — Bourke (56), T. McAdam (68)

CELTIC: Hunter; McGrain, Brogan; Murray, McNeill, Connelly; Hood, Glavin, Dalglish, Callaghan, Wilson (Johnstone)

DUMBARTON: McGregor; C. McAdam, Watt; Ruddy, Muir (Cushley), Graham; Coleman, Menmuir, T. McAdam, Bourke, Wallace

Attendance: 15,000

February 17th: Peter Latchford was signed on loan from West Bromwich Albion. Jock Stein was named as Assistant to Scotland Manager Willie Ormond.

February 22nd
HIBERNIAN (2) 2 — CELTIC (0) 1
Duncan 2 (11, 16) — Wilson (85)

HIBERNIAN: McArthur; Brownlie, Barry, Spalding, Schaedler; Stanton, Bremner, Munro; Carroll (Smith), Harper, Duncan

CELTIC: Latchford; Murray, MacDonald, Connelly, McCluskey; McGrain, McNamara, Dalglish; Hood, Deans, Wilson

Attendance: 31,000

March 1st
CELTIC (1) 3 — PARTICK THISTLE (2) 2
McCluskey (20 pen), Dalglish (69), Hood (89) — Craig (16), Kellachan (22)

CELTIC: Latchford; McGrain, McNeill, Connelly, McCluskey; Glavin, Dalglish, Murray; Hood, Deans, Wilson

PARTICK THISTLE: Rough; Campbell, A. Hansen, Anderson, Kellachan; Houston, Rooney, J. Hansen (Coulston); Craig, Somner, McQuade

Attendance: 21,000

League positions

	P	W	D	L	F	A	Pts
1 Rangers	26	20	4	2	72	25	44
2 CELTIC	26	18	4	4	69	29	40
3 Hibernian	26	14	7	5	46	29	35
4 Dundee United	25	12	6	7	54	33	30
5 Aberdeen	25	11	7	7	45	31	29

March 12th
ABERDEEN (1) 3
Williamson 3 (17, 57, 77) — Lynch 2 (53, 62)

ABERDEEN: Clark; Hair, McLelland; Thomson, Young, Miller; Purdie, Smith, Jarvie, Williamson, Graham

CELTIC: Latchford; McGrain, McCluskey; Glavin, McNeill, Connelly; Hood, Wilson, Dalglish, Callaghan, Lynch

Attendance: 16,000

March 15th
CELTIC (0) 0 — DUNDEE UNITED (1) 1
Gray (32)

CELTIC: Latchford; McGrain, MacDonald, McNeill, McCluskey (Wilson); Callaghan (Deans), Glavin, Hood; Johnstone, Dalglish, Lynch

DUNDEE UNITED: McAlpine; Rolland, D. Smith, Narey, Kopel (Forsyth); Houston, W. Smith, Hegarty; McLeod, Gray, Sturrock (MacDonald)

Attendance: 20,000

March 22nd
AIRDRIE (1) 1 — CELTIC (0) 0
McCulloch (38)

AIRDRIE: McWilliams; Jonquin, Menzies, Black, Lapsley; Whiteford, Reynolds, Walker (McKinlay); Wilson, McCulloch (Franchetti), McCann

CELTIC: Latchford; McCluskey, Welsh, Connelly, Brogan; Glavin (Hood), Dalglish, Callaghan; Johnstone, Deans (Wilson), Lennox

Attendance: 14,000

March 29th
CELTIC (0) 4 — HEARTS (0) 1
Dalglish 2 (48, 60), Wilson (61), Glavin (70) — Busby (80)

CELTIC: Latchford; McGrain, Connelly, McNeill, McCluskey; Callaghan, Glavin, Hood; Johnstone, Dalglish (Lynch), Wilson

HEARTS: Cruikshank; Kay, Anderson (Prentice), D. Murray, Clunie; Jeffries, Brown, Donaldson; Callachan, Gibson (T. Murray), Busby

Attendance: 21,000

April 5th
CELTIC (1) 1 — MORTON (0) 1
Wilson (6) — McGrain o.g. (50)

CELTIC: Latchford; McGrain, MacDonald, Connelly, McCluskey; Glavin, Hood, Dalglish; Lennox, Deans (Callaghan), Wilson (McLaughlin)

MORTON: Baines; Hayes, Thomson, Anderson, McNeill; Lumsden, Townsend, Reid; Osborne, Harley, Taylor (Flaherty)

Attendance: 13,000

April 12th
DUNFERMLINE (0) 1 — CELTIC (1) 3
Shaw (47) — Wilson 2 (34, 69), Lennox (71)

DUNFERMLINE: Karlsen; Hamilton, Evans, Thomson, Markie; Scott, Kinninmonth, Jenkins (Sinclair); Watson, Mackie, Shaw

CELTIC: Latchford; McCluskey; McGrain, McNeill, MacDonald, Lynch; Glavin, Murray; Wilson, Dalglish, Lennox

Attendance: 8,000

April 19th
CELTIC (0) 1 — DUNDEE (1) 2
Glavin (62) — Robinson (29), Hoggan (87)

CELTIC: Latchford; McCluskey; McGrain, MacDonald, McNeill, Lynch; Murray, Dalglish; Wilson (Burns), Glavin, Lennox

DUNDEE: Allan; Wilson, Ford, Gemmell, Johnston; Anderson, Robinson, J. Scott; Gordon, Hutchinson (I. Scott), Hoggan

Attendance: 12,000

April 26th
ST JOHNSTONE (1) 2 — CELTIC (1) 1
O'Rourke (42), G. Smith (67 pen) — Glavin (31)

ST JOHNSTONE: Robertson; G. Smith, Kinnell, MacDonald, S. Smith; Cramond, Thomson, Ritchie; Muir, O'Rourke, Lambie

CELTIC: Latchford; McGrain, McNeill, MacDonald, Lynch; Murray, Glavin, Callaghan; Johnstone (Hood), Deans (Lennox), Dalglish

Attendance: 11,000

Scottish First Division

	P	W	D	L	F	A	Pts
1 Rangers	34	25	6	3	86	33	56
2 Hibernian	34	20	9	5	69	37	49
3 CELTIC	34	20	5	9	81	41	45
4 Dundee United	34	19	7	8	72	43	45
5 Aberdeen	34	16	9	9	66	43	41
6 Dundee	34	16	6	12	48	42	38
7 Ayr United	34	14	8	11	50	61	36
8 Hearts	34	11	13	10	47	52	35
9 St Johnstone	34	11	12	11	41	44	34
10 Motherwell	34	14	5	15	52	57	33
11 Airdrie	34	11	9	14	43	55	31
12 Kilmarnock	34	8	15	11	52	68	31
13 Partick Thistle	34	10	10	14	48	62	30
14 Dumbarton	34	7	10	17	44	55	24
15 Dunfermline	34	7	9	18	46	66	23
16 Clyde	34	6	10	18	40	63	22
17 Morton	34	6	10	18	31	62	22
18 Arbroath	34	5	7	22	34	66	17

May 10th: Vic Davidson was given a free transfer.

May 17th: McGrain and Dalglish were in the Scotland team which drew 2-2 with Wales at Cardiff.

May 20th: Dalglish scored one of the goals in Scotland's 3-0 win over Northern Ireland at Hampden Park. McGrain was also in the team.

May 24th: Dalglish and McGrain were in the Scotland team beaten 5-1 by England at Wembley.

June 1st: McGrain and Dalglish were in the Scotland team which drew 1-1 with Rumania in Bucharest.

June 1st: Johnstone, Brogan and Davidson were given free transfers. Johnstone joined San Jose Earthquakes, returning to England in November to play for Sheffield United. Brogan joined Coventry City and Davidson joined Motherwell.

June 7th: Jock Stein was offered the Scotland Manager's job but opted to stay with Celtic.

LEAGUE CUP

August 10th
CELTIC (2) 2 — MOTHERWELL (0) 1
Dalglish (13), Wilson (45) — Martin (46)

CELTIC: Connaghan; McCluskey, Brogan; Murray, McNeill, Callaghan; Johnstone, Dalglish, Hood, Wilson, Lennox (Bone)

MOTHERWELL: Rennie; W. Watson, Wark; R. Watson, Muir (Dickson), Millar; Graham, Martin, Goldthorpe, Taylor, Kennedy

Attendance: 27,000

August 14th
AYR UNITED (2) 3 — CELTIC (1) 2
Somner (12), Mitchell (38 pen), Ingram (64) — Murray (25), Connelly (62)

AYR UNITED: A. McLean; Wells, Fillipi; Tait, Fleming, Somner; Doyle, Mitchell, Ingram, Dickson, McCulloch

CELTIC: Hunter; McGrain (Dalglish), McCluskey (McNamara); Murray, McNeill, Connelly; Johnstone, Hood, Wilson, Callaghan, Lennox

Attendance: 6,500

August 17th
CELTIC (1) 1 — DUNDEE UNITED (0) 0
McNamara (33)

CELTIC: Connaghan; McCluskey, Brogan; McNamara (Hood), McNeill, Connelly; Johnstone, Murray, Deans, Callaghan, Wilson

DUNDEE UNITED: McAlpine; Rolland, Kopel; Copland, D. Smith, Narey; Knox (Traynor), Gardner, Rankin (McLeod), Gray, MacDonald

Attendance: 26,000

August 21st
CELTIC (1) 5 — AYR UNITED (1) 2
Johnstone 2 (35, 71), Wilson 2 (55, 84), Lennox (51) — Doyle (4), Fleming (49)

CELTIC: Connaghan; McGrain (Hood), McCluskey; Connelly, McNeill, Callaghan; Johnstone (McNamara), Murray, Wilson, Dalglish, Lennox

AYR UNITED: A. McLean; Wells, Fillipi; Tait, Fleming, Somner; Doyle, Mitchell, Ingram, Dickson, McCulloch

Attendance: 16,000

August 24th
DUNDEE UNITED (0) 0 — CELTIC (1) 1
Wilson (7)

DUNDEE UNITED: McAlpine; Rolland, Kopel; Copland, D. Smith, Narey (White); Gardner, Fleming, Gray, Houston, MacDonald

CELTIC: Connaghan; McGrain, McCluskey; Connelly, McNeill, Callaghan; Johnstone, Murray, Wilson, Dalglish, Lennox

Attendance: 15,500

August 28th
MOTHERWELL (1) 2 — CELTIC (1) 2
Pettigrew (36), Taylor (53) — Dalglish 2 (38, 61)

MOTHERWELL: Rennie; Dickson, Wark; R. Watson, W. Watson, Millar (McClymont); Graham, Martin, Pettigrew, Taylor, Kennedy

CELTIC: Connaghan; McNamara, Brogan; McCluskey, MacDonald, Connelly; Hood, Dalglish, Bone, Davidson, Wilson

Attendance: 8,747

Section table

	P	W	D	L	F	A	Pts
CELTIC	6	4	1	1	13	8	9
Motherwell	6	2	2	2	11	5	6
Dundee United	6	2	2	2	6	5	6
Ayr United	6	1	1	4	8	20	3

Quarter-Final First Leg September 11th
CELTIC (1) 2 HAMILTON
Hood 2 (32, 49) ACADEMICALS (0) 0

CELTIC: Connaghan; McGrain, Brogan; McCluskey, McNeill, Callaghan (Lennox); Johnstone, Murray, Hood, Davidson, Wilson

HAMILTON: Ferguson; Frew, Grant; Hamilton, Bonnyman, Campbell; A. McMillan, Brand, Hegarty, Steven (O'Reilly), D. McMillan (Hood)

Attendance: 12,000

Quarter-Final Second Leg September 25th
HAMILTON ACADEMICALS (1) 2 CELTIC (1) 4
McNeill o.g. (5), Hegarty (65)
Deans (38), Callaghan (55 pen), McNamara (60), Lennox (62)

HAMILTON: Ferguson; Frew, Grant; Hamilton, Bonnyman, Campbell; Hunter, Brand, Hegarty, Hood, McInally

CELTIC: Hunter; McGrain, Brogan; McNamara, McNeill, McCluskey; Dalglish, Bone, Deans, Callaghan, Wilson (Lennox)

Attendance: 8,000. Celtic won 6-2 on aggregate.

Semi-Final at Hampden Park October 9th
AIRDRIE (0) 0 CELTIC (0) 1
Murray (62)

AIRDRIE: McWilliams; Jonquin, Lapsley; Black, McKinlay, Whiteford; Walker (Menzies), Cowan, McCulloch, Wallace, McCann. Sub: Franchetti

CELTIC: Hunter; McGrain, Brogan; McNamara, McNeill, McCluskey; Dalglish (Lennox), Murray, Deans, Hood, Wilson. Sub: MacDonald

Attendance: 19,332

Celtic won through to their 11th successive League Cup Final. The scoreline tells of a narrow win achieved with a solitary goal from Steve Murray, and there is little else to recall from a nervous Semi-Final.

Final at Hampden Park October 26th
CELTIC (2) 6 HIBERNIAN (1) 3
Johnstone (6), Deans 3 (34, 65, 67), Wilson (48), Murray (74)
Harper 3 (42, 61, 83)

CELTIC: Hunter; McGrain, Brogan; Murray, McNeill, McCluskey; Johnstone, Dalglish, Deans, Hood, Wilson. Subs: Lennox and MacDonald

HIBERNIAN: McArthur; Brownlie (Smith), Bremner; Stanton, Spalding, Blackley; Edwards, Cropley, Harper, Munro, Duncan (Murray)

Attendance: 53,848 *Referee:* J. R. P. Gordon

Celtic left Hibs 3 goals adrift and won the competition after a lapse of 4 years. Johnstone graced the stage with his entire repertoire and Deans, Murray and Dalglish also starred for the victors.

SCOTTISH CUP

Third Round January 25th
HIBERNIAN (0) 0 CELTIC (1) 2
Deans (12), Murray (80)

HIBERNIAN: Whyte; Brownlie, Stanton, Blackley, Schaedler; Spalding, Bremner, Munro; Duncan, Harper, Higgins

CELTIC: Hunter; McGrain, McNeill, Connelly, Brogan; Murray, Dalglish, Callaghan; Hood, Deans, Wilson (Glavin)

Attendance: 36,821

Fourth Round February 15th
CELTIC (3) 4 CLYDEBANK (1) 1
McNamara (37), Dalglish 2 (43, 44), MacDonald (83)
McCallan (26)

CELTIC: Barclay; McCluskey, MacDonald, Connelly, McGrain; Murray, McNamara, Hood; Dalglish, Deans, Wilson

CLYDEBANK: Gallagher; Hall, Fallon (Law), Fanning, Abel; Henderson, Hay; Cooper, Larnach, McCallan, Kane (Caskie)

Attendance: 21,000

Fifth Round March 8th
DUMBARTON (1) 1 CELTIC (1) 2
T. McAdam (8) Glavin (5), Wilson (61)

DUMBARTON: Williams; Muir (Coleman), Cushley, Ruddy, Watt; C. McAdam, Graham, Cook; Wallace, T. McAdam, Bourke

CELTIC: Latchford; McGrain, MacDonald, McNeill, McCluskey; Hood, Glavin, Callaghan; Dalglish, Lynch, Wilson

Attendance: 16,000

Semi-Final at Hampden Park April 2nd
CELTIC (0) 1 DUNDEE (0) 0
Glavin (59)

CELTIC: Latchford; McGrain, McCluskey; Connelly, McNeill, Callaghan; Hood, Glavin, Dalglish, Lennox, Wilson. Subs: MacDonald and Johnstone

DUNDEE: Allan; R. Wilson, Gemmell; Anderson, Stewart, Ford; Hoggan, Robinson, Wallace, J. Scott, Hutchinson (Gordon). Sub: Johnston

Attendance: 40,702

Celtic swept Dundee aside and theirs was a calm and measured victory against opponents who hardly made a chance in all of the 90 minutes. The only goal of the game came in the 59th minute and was the result of a mistake by former Lisbon Lion Tommy Gemmell. He received the ball deep inside his own penalty area and elected to walk it across the face of the goal. Glavin sprinted in, took the ball off his feet and neatly tucked it past Allan from 12 yards.

Final at Hampden Park May 3rd

CELTIC (2) 3 — AIRDRIE (1) 1

Wilson 2 (14, 43), McCluskey (53 pen) — McCann (42)

CELTIC: Latchford; McGrain, Lynch; Murray, McNeill, McCluskey; Hood, Glavin, Dalglish, Lennox, Wilson. Subs: Callaghan and MacDonald

AIRDRIE: McWilliams; Jonquin, Cowan; Menzies, Black, Whiteford; McCann, Walker, McCulloch (March), Lapsley (Reynolds), Wilson

Attendance: 75,457 *Referee:* I. M. D. Foote

Celtic took the lead in 14 minutes. McGrain poked the ball forward and Dalglish steadied and turned before dropping the ball onto the unmarked Wilson's head. Shortly after McCann hit the post with a header. Airdrie got the equaliser in the 42nd minute. McCulloch and Whiteford had shots charged down before the ball broke loose to McCann whose thunderous shot went high into the net. Within a minute Celtic were back in the lead when Wilson headed home a Lennox corner-kick and they made sure of winning the Cup in the 53rd minute when McCluskey scored from the spot after Jonquin had pushed Lennox off the ball. Billy McNeill collected the Cup and announced his retirement after 832 games with Celtic.

EUROPEAN CUP

First Round First Leg September 18th

CELTIC (0) 1 — OLYMPIAKOS (1) 1

Wilson (81) — Viera (36)

CELTIC: Connaghan; McGrain, Brogan (Lennox); Murray, McNeill, McCluskey; Johnstone, Hood, Dalglish, Callaghan, Wilson

OLYMPIAKOS: Kelesidis; Kyrastas, Aggelis; Sidkos, Glezos, Perssidis; Losanda, Viera, Kritikopoulos, Delikaris, Stavropoulos

Attendance: 40,000

Celtic tried hard and many played well but Olympiakos towered above them, tactically. They continually dropped into defensive positions and covered their goalkeeper well.

First Round Second Leg October 2nd

OLYMPIAKOS (2) 2 — CELTIC (0) 0

Kritikopoulos (3), Stavropoulos (23)

OLYMPIAKOS: Kelesidis; Liolios, Aggelis; Sidkos, Glezos, Perssidis; Losanda, Kyrastas, Kritikopoulos, Delikaris, Stavropoulos

CELTIC: Connaghan; McGrain, Brogan; Murray, McNeill, McCluskey; Johnstone (Lennox), Dalglish (Hood), Deans, Callaghan, Wilson

Attendance: 42,000

Celtic got off to the worst possible start when they lost a goal after only 3 minutes. Delikaris chipped a free-kick into the penalty area and Kritikopoulos ghosted away from McNeill and glanced a header past Connaghan into the far corner of the net. 20 minutes later they lost another goal. McNeill fouled Kritikopoulos as they challenged in mid-air. Stavropoulos fired through the defensive wall and the ball took a deflection and left Connaghan stranded. Celtic's night of misery was completed when Lennox was sent off late in the game. Olympiakos won 3-1 on aggregate.

APPEARANCES	League	League Cup	Scottish Cup	European Cup
Hunter	18	4	1	–
Connaghan	6	6	–	2
Latchford	10	–	3	–
McGrain	30	7	5	2
McCluskey	28+1S	10	4	2
Brogan	19+1S	7	1	2
Glavin	19+1S	–	3+1S	–
Murray	28	8	3	2
McNeill	30	9	4	2
Connelly	15	5	3	–
Callaghan	19+3S	7	3	2
Dalglish	33	7+1S	5	2
Johnstone	15+6S	7	–	2
Wilson	31+2S	10	5	2
Hood	21+6S	6+2S	5	1+1S
Davidson	4	2	–	–
Lennox	9+5S	4+3S	2	0+2S
McNamara	1	4+2S	1	–
Bone	2+1S	2+1S	–	–
Deans	18+1S	4	2	1
MacDonald	12+3S	1	2	–
Welsh	1+1S	–	–	–
Lynch	5+2S	–	2	–
McLaughlin	0+1S	–	–	–
Burns	0+1S	–	–	–
Barclay	–	–	1	–

GOALSCORERS

League: Dalglish 16, Wilson 13, Deans 9, Hood 8, Murray 8 (2 pens), Glavin 5, Lennox 5 (2 pens), Johnstone 5, McCluskey 3 (2 pens), Davidson 2, Callaghan 2, Lynch 2, Bone 1, McNeill 1. Own Goals 1.

League Cup: Wilson 5, Deans 4, Dalglish 3, Murray 3, Johnstone 3, McNamara 2, Lennox 2, Hood 2, Connelly 1, Callaghan 1 (pen)

Scottish Cup: Wilson 3, Glavin 2, Dalglish 2, Deans 1, Murray 1, McNamara 1, MacDonald 1, McCluskey 1 (pen)

European Cup: Wilson 1

Season 1975-76

Celtic had a very disappointing season by their standards. They finished 2nd to Rangers in the first-ever Premier Division Championship. But for a disastrous run-in, in which they won only 1 of their last 7 matches, the title could have been theirs. They lost Manager Jock Stein for the entire season while he recovered from injuries sustained in a car crash and were led by Irishman Sean Fallon in his absence. Midfield ace Steve Murray had to give up the game through injury although he did attempt a comeback which failed. Brighter news was the form of McGrain and Dalglish and the breakthrough of youngsters Roy Aitken, Tommy Burns and George McCluskey to first-team action. Johannes Edvaldsson also proved to be a good signing, but £90,000 buy from Ayr United, Johnny Doyle, did not have sufficient time to make any impression. Ally Hunter was transferred to Motherwell and Dixie Deans joined Luton Town. Another of the old guard, Harry Hood, was given a free transfer. Latchford, McGrain, Edvaldsson and Dalglish all played in 35 matches. Dalglish finished as top scorer with 24 goals and rounded off a fine season by scoring the winning goal for Scotland against England at Hampden. At the end of the season Davie McParland took over from Sean Fallon as assistant manager.

Celtic reached their 12th successive League Cup Final after wins over Aberdeen, Hearts and Partick Thistle amongst others but they lost to Rangers by a 67th-minute Alex MacDonald goal.

They conceded a 2-goal lead and lost out to a fast-improving Motherwell in the Third Round of the Scottish Cup – their poorest showing in the competition since 1968.

They overcame Valur of Iceland and Boavista of Portugal to reach the Quarter-Final of the Cup Winners Cup where they met the unknown East Germans Sachsenring Zwickau. The First Leg in Glasgow turned out to be an evening of bitter frustration for Celtic. Despite incessant attack they scored only one goal, missed a penalty and conceded a late equaliser. The loss of a 5th-minute goal in the return sealed their fate.

League:	Runners-up
League Cup:	Finalists
Scottish Cup:	Third Round
European Cup Winners Cup:	Quarter-Finalists

PREMIER DIVISION

August 5th: Kenney Dalglish asked for a transfer.
August 19th: Dalglish signed a new contract.

August 30th:

RANGERS (0) 2	CELTIC (1) 1
Johnstone (56), Young (68)	Dalglish (42)

RANGERS: McCloy; Forsyth, Greig; Jardine (O'Hara), Jackson, McKean; McLean, MacDonald, Stein, Johnstone, Young

CELTIC: Latchford; McGrain, MacDonald, McCluskey, Lynch; McNamara (Connelly), Dalglish, Edvaldsson; Callaghan, Wilson, Lennox (Ritchie)

Attendance: 69,594.

A record for the Premier League.

Dalglish was well patrolled in the 1st half by Jardine and brilliantly in the 2nd by O'Hara. McCloy kept Celtic from the equaliser in the last desperate stages when the substitutes Ritchie and Connelly inspired a rally against the 10-man Rangers (Alex MacDonald had been ordered off). In a coarse match there was too much shirt-pulling, pushing, high and late tackling and numerous off-the-ball incidents.

September 3rd: McGrain and Dalglish were in the Scotland team which beat Denmark 1-0 in Copenhagen.

September 6th
CELTIC (1) 4 — DUNDEE (0) 0
Lennox 3 (37, 70, 78),
McNamara (80)

CELTIC: Latchford; McGrain, Edvaldsson, McCluskey (Connelly), Lynch; Glavin, McNamara, Callaghan; Wilson, Dalglish, Lennox

DUNDEE: Allan; Wilson, Stewart, Phillips (Sinclair), Johnston; J. Martin, Anderson (Gemmell), Ford; Hoggan, Gordon, Purdie

Attendance: 25,000

September 6th: Steve Murray was forced to give up football through injury.

September 13th
MOTHERWELL (1) 1 — CELTIC (1) 1
Davidson (10) — Dalglish (42)

MOTHERWELL: Rennie; W. Watson, McVie, McLaren, Wark; Millar (Goldthorpe), R. Watson, McAdam (Stevens); Pettigrew, Graham, Davidson

CELTIC: Latchford; McGrain, Connelly, MacDonald, Edvaldsson; McNamara, Callaghan, Lynch; Lennox, Dalglish, Wilson (Hood)

Attendance: 18,612

September 20th
ST JOHNSTONE (0) 1 — CELTIC (1) 2
McCluskey o.g. (77) — McCluskey 2 (44 pen, 76 pen)

ST JOHNSTONE: Robertson; G. Smith, MacDonald, Kinnell, S. Smith; Hamilton (McGregor), Thomson, Cramond; Lambie, O'Rourke, Muir

CELTIC: Latchford; McGrain (Hood), McCluskey, MacDonald, Lynch; Edvaldsson, Dalglish, Callaghan; Wilson, Deans, Lennox

Attendance: 12,000

September 27th
CELTIC (0) 2 — DUNDEE UNITED (0) 1
Dalglish (53), — Payne (73 pen)
MacDonald (67)

CELTIC: Latchford; McGrain, McCluskey, MacDonald, Lynch; Glavin (Hood), Edvaldsson, Callaghan; Wilson, Dalglish, Lennox

DUNDEE UNITED: McAlpine; Rolland, Rennie, Narey, Kopel; Payne, Hall (MacDonald), Houston; Fleming, Sturrock, Hegarty

Attendance: 21,000

October 4th
CELTIC (3) 3 — HEARTS (0) 1
Deans (12), — Busby (71)
Hood (17),
Wilson (21)

CELTIC: Latchford; McGrain, MacDonald, McCluskey, Lynch; Dalglish, Edvaldsson, Callaghan; Wilson (Lennox), Deans, Hood

HEARTS: Cruikshank; Clunie, Anderson, Murray, Kay; Brown (Park), Callachan, Jeffries; Aird, Busby, Prentice (Gibson)

Attendance: 20,000

October 11th
ABERDEEN (0) 1 — CELTIC (2) 2
Scott (60) — Dalglish (15),
Deans (43)

ABERDEEN: Clark; Thomson, Ward (Pirie), Miller, McLelland (Williamson); Hair, Jarvie, Henry; Scott, Robb, Graham

CELTIC: Latchford; McGrain, McCluskey, MacDonald, Edvaldsson; Lynch, Dalglish, Callaghan, Hood (Ritchie), Wilson, Deans (Lennox)

Attendance: 18,000. Wilson was ordered off.

October 13th: There were newspaper reports that George Connelly was about to join Portsmouth in a straight exchange for Peter Marinello. No deal materialised.

October 19th: Celtic's home League match with Hibs had to be abandoned after 83 minutes owing to fog. Hibs were leading 2-0 with goals from Bremner (26 mins) and Harper (76 mins).

October 29th: McGrain and Dalglish were in the Scotland team which beat Denmark 3-1 at Hampden Park, Dalglish scored one of the goals.

November 1st
CELTIC (0) 1 — RANGERS (0) 1
Wilson (78) — Parlane (75)

CELTIC: Latchford; McGrain, P. McCluskey, MacDonald, Lynch; Dalglish, Edvaldsson, Callaghan; G. McCluskey (Hood), Deans, Wilson

RANGERS: Kennedy; Jardine, Forsyth, Jackson, Greig; McLean, MacDonald, Johnstone; Stein, Parlane, Young

Attendance: 55,000

In a good Old Firm match a draw was a fair result. Rangers took the lead in the 75th minute. Lynch took a short free-kick and Callaghan was dreaming. McLean stole in and pushed the ball to Parlane who may have been offside. Celtic waited for the whistle which never came and the centre-forward dribbled round Latchford to score his first Premier League goal. 3 minutes later Celtic equalised. Young McCluskey hit a fast cross and Wilson, running in at the far post, pushed the ball over the line with his stomach for the equaliser. Young's better form made Rangers a potent force coming forward, and Parlane hit the bar before the finish.

League positions

	P	W	D	L	F	A	Pts
1 CELTIC	8	5	2	1	16	8	12
2 Hibernian	9	4	3	2	13	9	11
3 Rangers	9	4	3	2	10	8	11
4 Motherwell	10	3	5	2	17	15	11
5 Hearts	10	4	3	3	12	13	11

November 8th
DUNDEE (0) 1 CELTIC (0) 0
Robinson (87)

DUNDEE: Allan; Caldwell, Stewart, Gemmell, Johnston; Ford, Robinson, Strachan; Wallace, Gordon, Purdie

CELTIC: Latchford; McGrain, Edvaldsson, P. McCluskey, MacDonald; Hood (G. McCluskey), McNamara, Lynch; Deans, Dalglish, Lennox

Attendance: 16,456

November 12th
AYR UNITED (1) 2 CELTIC (5) 7
Graham (42 pen), Doyle (55)
Edvaldsson 3 (5, 19, 75), Deans 2 (27, 83), Dalglish (31), MacDonald (34)

AYR UNITED: Sproat; McDonald, Murphy; McAnespie, Fleming, Fillipi; Doyle, Graham, Ingram, Phillips, McCulloch

CELTIC: Latchford; McGrain, Lynch; McCluskey, MacDonald, Edvaldsson; Wilson, Dalglish, Deans, McNamara, Callaghan

Attendance: 15,000

November 15th
CELTIC (0) 0 MOTHERWELL (1) 2
Pettigrew 2 (44, 52)

CELTIC: Latchford; McGrain, McCluskey, MacDonald, Lynch; McNamara, Dalglish, Edvaldsson, Callaghan (Lennox); Wilson, Deans

MOTHERWELL: Rennie; Millar, McVie, Stevens, Wark; McIlwraith, Watson, McLaren; Taylor (Davidson), Pettigrew, Graham

Attendance: 33,000

November 22nd
CELTIC (1) 3 ST JOHNSTONE (2) 2
Lennox 2 (24, 50) Dalglish (52)
O'Rourke (35), C. Smith (37)

CELTIC: Latchford; McGrain, P. McCluskey, MacDonald, Lynch; Dalglish, Edvaldsson, Callaghan; G. McCluskey, Deans, Lennox

ST JOHNSTONE: Nicoll; G. Smith, Roberts; MacDonald, Kinnell (Stevenson), Ritchie; C. Smith, Lambie, O'Rourke, Muir, Cramond

Attendance: 20,000

November 29th
DUNDEE UNITED (0) 1 CELTIC (1) 3
Hegarty (83)
Deans (3), Lennox (66), Lynch (71)

DUNDEE UNITED: McAlpine; Holt, Copland, Narey, Fleming; Payne, Rennie, Houston; McAdam (Steele), Sturrock, Hegarty

CELTIC: Latchford; McGrain, McCluskey, MacDonald, Lynch; Dalglish, Edvaldsson, Callaghan; Wilson, Deans, Lennox

Attendance: 11,000

December 6th
HEARTS (0) 0 CELTIC (0) 1
Deans (78)

HEARTS: Cruikshank; Clunie, Anderson, Murray, Jeffries; Brown, Busby, Park; Aird, Gibson, Callachan (Prentice)

CELTIC: Latchford; McGrain, McCluskey, MacDonald, Lynch; Edvaldsson, Dalglish, Callaghan; Hood (Wilson), Deans, Lennox

Attendance: 21,000

December 10th
CELTIC (0) 1 HIBERNIAN (0) 1
Deans (60) Harper (72)

CELTIC: Latchford; McGrain, Lynch; McCluskey, MacDonald, Edvaldsson; Hood (McNamara), Dalglish, Deans, Callaghan, Lennox

HIBERNIAN: McArthur; Brownlie, Schaedler; Stanton, Barry, Blackley; Edwards, Bremner, Harper, Munro, Duncan

Attendance: 33,000

December 13th
CELTIC (0) 0 ABERDEEN (2) 2
Jarvie (6), Graham (34)

CELTIC: Latchford; Edvaldsson; McGrain, McCluskey, MacDonald, Lynch; Dalglish, Callaghan; Wilson (Hood), Deans, Lennox

ABERDEEN: Geoghegan; Williamson, Thomson, Miller, McLelland; Robb, Smith (Hair), McMaster; Scott (Pirie), Jarvie, Graham

Attendance: 24,000

December 17th: Kenny Dalglish was in the Scotland team which drew 1-1 with Rumania at Hampden Park.

December 20th
HIBERNIAN (1) 1 CELTIC (2) 3
Duncan (19)
Deans (12), Edvaldsson (20), McNamara (89)

HIBERNIAN: McArthur; Brownlie, Barry, Blackley, Schaedler; Stanton, Edwards, Bremner; Harper, Duncan, Munro (Smith)

CELTIC: Latchford; McGrain, MacDonald, McCluskey, Lynch; Edvaldsson, McNamara, Callaghan; Dalglish, Deans, Lennox

Attendance: 21,136

December 27th
CELTIC (1) 3 — AYR UNITED (0) 1
Edvaldsson 2 (37, 63), Dalglish (84) — McCulloch (49)

CELTIC: Latchford; McGrain, MacDonald, McCluskey; Lynch; McNamara, Edvaldsson, Callaghan; Lennox, Deans, Dalglish

AYR UNITED: Sproat; McDonald, McAnespie, Fleming, Murphy; Graham (Wells), McSherry, McCulloch; Doyle, Ingram, Robertson (Cameron)

Attendance: 22,000

League positions

	P	W	D	L	F	A	Pts
1 CELTIC	18	11	3	4	37	21	25
2 Rangers	18	9	4	5	29	18	22
3 Motherwell	18	8	6	4	34	26	22
4 Hibernian	18	8	6	4	28	23	22
5 Hearts	18	7	7	4	22	20	21

January 1st
RANGERS (1) 1 — CELTIC (0) 0
Johnstone (30)

RANGERS: Kennedy; Miller, Greig; Forsyth, Jackson, MacDonald; McKean (Scott), Hamilton (O'Hara), Henderson, McLean, Johnstone

CELTIC: Latchford; McGrain, Lynch; Edvaldsson, MacDonald, McCluskey; McNamara, Dalglish, Deans (Wilson), Callaghan, Lennox (Hood)

Attendance: 57,839

January 3rd
CELTIC (2) 3 — DUNDEE (1) 3
Deans (18), Dalglish 2 (43, 51) — Lynch o.g. (13), Hoggan (59), McIntosh (82)

CELTIC: Latchford; McGrain, McCluskey, MacDonald (Murray), Lynch; McNamara, Edvaldsson, Callaghan; Wilson (Lennox), Deans, Dalglish

DUNDEE: Allan; McIntosh, Phillip, Stewart (Gordon), Mackie; Ford, Caldwell (Hoggan), Strachan; Laing, Wallace, Hutchinson

Attendance: 21,000

January 10th
MOTHERWELL (0) 1 — CELTIC (0) 3
Davidson (62) — Deans 2 (53, 60), Dalglish (82)

MOTHERWELL: Rennie; Millar (McAdam), W. Watson, Stevens, Wark; Gardner, R. Watson, MacLaren; Pettigrew, Davidson, Marinello

CELTIC: Latchford; Edvaldsson; McGrain, McCluskey, MacDonald, Lynch; Murray, Glavin; Dalglish, Deans, Lennox

Attendance: 17,000

January 17th
ST JOHNSTONE (2) 3 — CELTIC (2) 4
Lambie (17), Thomson (33), Cramond (46) — Dalglish (25), Deans (45), MacDonald (70), Edvaldsson (89)

ST JOHNSTONE; Robertson; Ritchie (Roberts), MacDonald, Anderson, S. Smith; Hotson (Muir), O'Rourke, Thomson; Cramond, McGregor, Lambie

CELTIC: Latchford; McGrain, MacDonald, McCluskey, Lynch; Murray, Edvaldsson, Glavin; Deans, Dalglish, Lennox

Attendance: 9,915

January 31st
CELTIC (2) 2 — DUNDEE UNITED (1) 1
Dalglish (13), Wilson (37) — Hall (1)

CELTIC: Hunter; McGrain, Edvaldsson, McCluskey, Lynch; Ritchie, McNamara, Callaghan (Hood); Dalglish, Wilson, Deans

DUNDEE UNITED: McAlpine; Rolland, Copland, Rennie, Smith; Hegarty, Holt, Houston; Hall, McAdam, Steele (Payne)

Attendance: 18,000

February 7th
CELTIC (0) 2 — HEARTS (0) 0
Dalglish 2 (59, 81)

CELTIC: Latchford; McGrain, Edvaldsson, Casey, Lynch; Ritchie, McCluskey, Dalglish; Glavin, Deans, Wilson

HEARTS: Cruikshank; Clunie, Gallacher, Murray, Jeffries; Busby, Brown, Callachan; Aird (Park), Ford, Shaw

Attendance: 22,000

February 21st
ABERDEEN (0) 0 — CELTIC (0) 1
Lennox (79)

ABERDEEN: Clark; Hair, Garner, Miller, McLelland; Smith, Williamson, McMaster; Graham, Pirie, Jarvie (Robb)

CELTIC: Latchford; McGrain, Aitken, Edvaldsson, Lynch; Ritchie (Lennox), McCluskey, Glavin; Wilson, Dalglish, Deans

Attendance: 18,221

February 28th
CELTIC (3) 4 — HIBERNIAN (0) 0
Deans (13 pen), Lennox (39), Wilson (44), Dalglish (65)

CELTIC: Latchford; McGrain, Edvaldsson, Aitken; Lynch; McCluskey, Glavin, Dalglish; Lennox, Deans, Wilson

HIBERNIAN: McDonald; Brownlie, Spalding, Blackley, Schaedler; Edwards, Bremner, Stanton; McLeod (Wilson), Duncan, Smith

Attendance: 33,000

League positions

	P	W	D	L	F	A	Pts
1 CELTIC	26	17	4	5	56	30	38
2 Rangers	26	16	5	5	43	21	37
3 Hibernian	25	13	6	6	44	29	32
4 Motherwell	26	12	7	7	45	33	31
5 Aberdeen	26	10	7	9	41	36	27

March 3rd: Jimmy Smith of Newcastle United joined Celtic on a month's loan.

March 15th: Johnny Doyle was signed from Ayr United for £90,000.

March 20th
DUNDEE (0) 0 CELTIC (0) 1
Dalglish (58)

DUNDEE: Allan; Wilson (Gemmell), Phillip, Caldwell, Johnston; Mackie, Robinson, Gordon; Wallace, Hutchinson, Laing

CELTIC: Latchford; McGrain, Aitken, Edvaldsson, Lynch; McNamara, McCluskey, Dalglish; Doyle (Wilson), MacDonald, Hood

Attendance: 14,830

March 23rd: Jimmy Smith was forced to quit Parkhead due to a knee injury.

March 27th
CELTIC (4) 4 MOTHERWELL (0) 0
Dalglish 2 (15, 34),
Deans (25),
Lennox (39)

CELTIC: Latchford; McGrain, Aitken, Edvaldsson, Lynch; McNamara, McCluskey, Dalglish; Deans, MacDonald (Wilson), Lennox

MOTHERWELL: Rennie; W. Watson, McLaren, Stevens, Wark; Millar (Gardner), R. Watson, Davidson; Pettigrew, Graham, Marinello (McAdam)

Attendance: 29,000

April 3rd
CELTIC (1) 1 ST JOHNSTONE (0) 0
Dalglish (21)

CELTIC: Latchford; McGrain, Aitken, Edvaldsson, Lynch; McCluskey, McNamara, Dalglish; Deans, MacDonald (Wilson), Lennox

ST JOHNSTONE: Nicoll; G. Smith, MacDonald, Kinnell, S. Smith; Anderson, Hamilton, McGregor; O'Rourke (Henderson), Thomson, Hotson

Attendance: 16,000

April 10th
DUNDEE UNITED (1) 3 CELTIC (0) 2
McAdam 2 (44, 85), Dalglish 2 (61, 87)
Fleming (63)

DUNDEE UNITED: McAlpine; Rolland, Forsyth, Narey, Kopel; Houston, Hegarty, Rennie; Hall, Fleming, McAdam

CELTIC: Latchford; McGrain, Aitken, Edvaldsson, Lynch; McCluskey, Glavin, Dalglish; Deans, Hood (Wilson), Lennox

Attendance: 12,771

April 15th: Ally Hunter joined Motherwell for £20,000

April 17th
CELTIC (1) 1 ABERDEEN (1) 1
Dalglish (25) Edvaldsson o.g. (40)

CELTIC: Latchford; McGrain, Aitken, Edvaldsson, Callaghan; Glavin, Dalglish, Burns; Doyle (Ritchie), Deans, Lennox (Wilson)

ABERDEEN: Clark; Hair, Thomson, Garner, Miller, McLelland; Williamson, Smith; Jarvie, Fleming, Robb

Attendance: 29,000. Miller was ordered off.

April 21st
HIBERNIAN (1) 2 CELTIC (0) 0
Smith (24),
McLeod (64 pen)

HIBERNIAN: McDonald; Smith, Schaedler; Stanton, Spalding, Blackley; Murray, Muir, McGhee, McLeod, Paterson

CELTIC: Latchford; McGrain, Lynch; P. McCluskey, Aitken, Edvaldsson; Wilson (G. McCluskey), Glavin, Deans, Dalglish, Lennox

Attendance: 19,076

April 24th
CELTIC (0) 1 AYR UNITED (0) 2
Deans (59 pen) Robertson 2 (47 pen, 58)

CELTIC: Latchford; McGrain, Evaldsson, Aitken, Lynch; McNamara, P. McCluskey, Burns; Doyle, Deans, Dalglish

AYR UNITED: Sproat; Fillipi, Fleming, Tait, Murphy (Kelly); Graham, McSherry, McCulloch; Cramond, Robertson, Phillips

Attendance: 16,000

April 26th
CELTIC (0) 0 RANGERS (0) 0

CELTIC: Latchford; McGrain, Lynch; P. McCluskey, Aitken, Edvaldsson (McNamara); Doyle, Dalglish, MacDonald, Burns, Lennox

RANGERS: McCloy; Miller, Greig; Jardine, Johnstone, MacDonald; McKean, Hamilton, Henderson, McLean, Parlane

Attendance: 51,000

Kenny Dalglish looked out of sorts all night but Tommy Burns the youngster with a career to carve, was busy in midfield. In the absence of Forsyth and Jackson, Derek Johnstone moved to centre-half to mark Edvaldsson. After only 6 seconds John Greig kicked an Edvaldsson shot off the line, and in 63 minutes Dalglish headed a Burns cross just an inch wide.

April 29th: Harry Hood was given a free transfer.

May 1st
AYR UNITED (2) 3 — CELTIC (1) 5
Graham (16), McCulloch (17), Phillips (55) — Ritchie (35), McCluskey (62 pen), Lennox (63), Dalglish 2 (67, 85)

AYR UNITED: Sproat; Fillipi, Fleming, Tait, Murphy; Graham, McSherry, McCulloch; Robertson, Phillips, Cramond (Ingram)

CELTIC: Latchford; McGrain, P. McCluskey, Aitken, MacDonald, Lynch; Dalglish, Burns (Hannah), Doyle, Ritchie, Lennox

Attendance: 6,800

May 3rd
HEARTS (0) 1 — CELTIC (0) 0
Brown (52)

HEARTS: Cruikshank; Brown, Burrell; Jeffries, Gallacher, Kay; Aird, Busby, Shaw, Callachan, Prentice

CELTIC: Latchford; P. McCluskey, Callaghan; McNamara, Aitken, MacDonald; Lennox, Ritchie, Deans (Wilson), Edvaldsson (Hannah), Burns

Attendance: 9,000

Premier division

	P	W	D	L	F	A	Pts
1 Rangers	36	23	8	5	60	24	54
2 CELTIC	36	21	6	9	71	42	48
3 Hibernian	36	20	7	9	55	43	43
4 Motherwell	36	16	8	12	56	48	40
5 Hearts	36	13	9	14	39	45	35
6 Ayr United	36	14	5	17	46	59	33
7 Aberdeen	36	11	10	15	49	50	32
8 Dundee United	36	12	8	16	46	48	32
9 Dundee	36	11	10	15	49	62	32
10 St Johnstone	36	3	5	28	29	79	11

May 6th: Danny McGrain was in the Scotland team which beat Wales 3-1 at Hampden Park.

May 18th: McGrain and Dalglish were in the Scotland team which beat Northern Ireland 3-0 at Hampden Park. Dalglish scored one of the goals.

May 15th: McGrain and Dalglish were in the Scotland team which beat England 2-1 at Hampden Park. Dalglish scored the winning goal.

May 17th: In the Bobby Lennox/Jimmie Johnstone Testimonial Celtic beat Manchester United 4-0.

May 22nd: Davie McParland, the former manager of Partick Thistle, joined Celtic as assistant manager.

June 3rd: Sean Fallon was put in charge of youth development.

June 17th: Dixie Deans joined Luton Town for £20,000.

LEAGUE CUP

August 9th
CELTIC (1) 1 — ABERDEEN (0) 0
Dalglish (11)

CELTIC: Latchford; McGrain, MacDonald, McCluskey, Edvaldsson, Lynch; Hood (McNamara), Dalglish; Wilson, Glavin, Lennox

ABERDEEN: Clark; Thomson (Williamson), Young, Miller, McLelland; Hair, Smith, Rougvie; Robb, Jarvie, Graham (Campbell)

Attendance: 32,000

August 13th
HEARTS (1) 2 — CELTIC (0) 0
Hancock (15), Ford (73 pen)

HEARTS: Cruikshank; Kay, Clunie; Jeffries, Anderson, Murray; Brown, Busby, Hancock, Ford, Prentice

CELTIC: Latchford; McGrain, Lynch; McCluskey, MacDonald, Edvaldsson; Hood, Glavin, Dalglish, Wilson, Lennox

Attendance: 19,000. McCluskey missed a penalty

August 16th
CELTIC (2) 3 — DUMBARTON (0) 1
Wilson (32), Lennox (35), Edvaldsson (84) — McAdam (62)

CELTIC: Latchford; McGrain, MacDonald, McCluskey, Edvaldsson, Lynch; McNamara (Hood), Glavin; Wilson, Dalglish, Lennox

DUMBARTON: Williams; Brown, Muir, Graham, Watt; Cushley (Cook), McLean, Ruddy; Bourke, Wallace, T. McAdam

Attendance: 23,000

August 20th
CELTIC (2) 3 — HEARTS (0) 1
Glavin (1½), Lynch (44), Edvaldsson (50) — Busby (76)

CELTIC: Latchford; McGrain, Lynch; McCluskey, MacDonald, Edvaldsson; Glavin, Wilson, Dalglish, McNamara, Hood

HEARTS: Cruikshank; Kay, Clunie; Jeffries, Anderson, Murray; Brown, Busby, Hancock (Park), Ford, Prentice

Attendance: 28,000

August 23rd
DUMBARTON (0) 0 CELTIC (2) 8
Hood 2 (3, 57),
Dalglish 2 (49, 62),
Wilson 2 (87, 89),
McGrain (20),
Callaghan (71)

DUMBARTON: McGregor; A. Brown (Mullen), Graham, McKinlay, Watt; Bennett, Cook, McLean; McAdam, Wallace, Coleman (J. Brown)

CELTIC: Latchford; McGrain, McCluskey, MacDonald, Edvaldsson, Lynch; Glavin (Callaghan), McNamara; Wilson, Dalglish, Hood (Lennox)

Attendance: 12,500

August 27th
ABERDEEN (0) 0 CELTIC (1) 2
Lennox (5),
Ritchie (87)

ABERDEEN: Clark; Hair, McLelland; Scott, Young, Miller; Smith (Rougvie), Robb, Pirie, McMaster, Graham

CELTIC: Latchford; McGrain, Lynch; McCluskey (Connelly), MacDonald, Edvaldsson; Dalglish, Wilson (Ritchie), McNamara, Callaghan, Lennox

Attendance: 13,000

Section table

	P	W	D	L	F	A	Pts
CELTIC	6	5	0	1	17	4	10
Hearts	6	4	0	2	13	8	8
Aberdeen	6	2	0	4	4	6	4
Dumbarton	6	1	0	5	5	21	2

Quarter-Final First Leg September 10th
STENHOUSEMUIR (0) 0 CELTIC (0) 2
Lennox (56),
Dalglish (80)

STENHOUSEMUIR: Dunlop; McCullie, Rose; Murdoch, Gordon, Sage; Sinclair, J. Scott (McPaul), Wight, Halliday, Simpson

CELTIC: Latchford; McGrain, Lynch; McNamara, Connelly, Edvaldsson (Aitken); Glavin, Wilson, Dalglish, Callaghan (Hood), Lennox

Attendance: 4,701

Quarter-Final Second Leg September 24th
CELTIC (0) 1 STENHOUSEMUIR (0) 0
Lynch (54)

CELTIC: Latchford; Aitken, Lynch; Edvaldsson (Casey), MacDonald, McCluskey; Dalglish, McNamara, Deans, Glavin, Lennox (Hood)

STENHOUSEMUIR: Dunlop; McCullie, Rose; Murdoch, Gordon, Sage; Sinclair, J. Scott (Fairley), Wight, Halliday (D. Scott), Simpson

Attendance: 6,000. Celtic won 3-0 on aggregate

Semi-Final at Hampden Park October 6th
CETIC (1) 1 PARTICK THISTLE (0) 0
Edvaldsson (28)

CELTIC: Latchford; McGrain, Lynch; McCluskey, MacDonald, Edvaldsson; Wilson, Dalglish, Deans, Callaghan, Hood (Lennox)

PARTICK THISTLE: Rough; J. Hansen, Kellachan; Campbell, A. Hansen (Fitzpatrick), Anderson; Houston, McQuade (Joe Craig), Marr, Somner, John Craig

Attendance: 31,421

The Semi-Final was dominated by one man, Johannes Edvaldsson. Only Alan Rough's brave goalkeeping defied him and many others from extending the scoreline.

Final at Hampden Park October 25th
RANGERS (0) 1 CELTIC (0) 0
MacDonald (67)

RANGERS: Kennedy; Jardine, Greig; Forsyth, Jackson, MacDonald; McLean, Stein, Parlane, Johnstone, Young. Subs: McKean, Miller

CELTIC: Latchford; McGrain, Lynch; McCluskey, MacDonald, Edvaldsson; Hood (McNamara), Dalglish, Wilson (Glavin), Callaghan, Lennox. *Attendance:* 50,806

The match kicked off at 1 pm as an anti-hooligan measure. Rangers were adequate most of the time and good in bits and pieces especially in the first part of the 2nd half. The only goal of the match came in the 67th minute. Parlane beat MacDonald well on the left bye-line and his cross was headed away by Edvaldsson in the general direction of Young. Young headed across goal and MacDonald dived forward to head strongly into the net. Forsyth marked Dalglish out of the match. This was the first time that John Greig had received the League Cup as captain.

SCOTTISH CUP

Third Round January 24th
MOTHERWELL (0) 3 CELTIC (2) 2
Graham (52), Dalglish (31),
Taylor (61), Lynch (39)
Pettigrew (70)

MOTHERWELL: Rennie; W. Watson, McVie, Stevens (Taylor), Wark; R. Watson (Millar), Davidson, McLaren; Pettigrew, Graham, Marinello

CELTIC: Latchford; McGrain, McNamara; McCluskey, MacDonald, Glavin; Edvaldsson, Lynch, Dalglish, Deans, Lennox

Attendance: 25,000

EUROPEAN CUP WINNERS CUP

First Round First Leg September 16th
VALUR (Iceland) (0) 0 CELTIC (1) 2
Wilson (7),
MacDonald (64)

VALUR: Dagsson; Alfonsson, Samundsen; Kjartanson, D. Gudmundsson, Berg; Porbjornsson, Hilmarsson, Gunnarsson, Albertsson, A. Edvaldsson

CELTIC: Latchford; McGrain, Lynch, McCluskey, MacDonald, Edvaldsson; Hood (Glavin), McNamara, Dalglish, Callaghan, Wilson

Attendance: 8,000. Edvaldsson missed a twice-taken penalty

Valur struggled to make a game of it, and even on a heavily sanded pitch Celtic's class was obvious.

First Round Second Leg October 1st
CELTIC (5) 7 — VALUR (0) 0
Edvaldsson (6),
Dalglish (12),
P. McCluskey (30 pen),
Hood 2 (37, 82),
Deans (42),
Callaghan (50)

CELTIC: Latchford; McGrain, Lynch; P. McCluskey, MacDonald, Edvaldsson, Wilson (G. McCluskey), Dalglish, Deans, Callaghan (Casey), Hood

VALUR: Dagsson; Alfonsson, Samundsen, Kjartsson, D. Gudmundsson, Berg; Porbjornsson, Hilmarsson, Gunnarsson, Albertsson, A. Edvaldsson

Attendance: 16,000

Celtic went on a goal spree and completely flattened the visitors. Celtic won 9-0 on aggregate.

Second Round First Leg October 22nd
BOAVISTA (Portugal) (0) 0 CELTIC (0) 0

BOAVISTA: Botelho; Trindade, Joao; Carolino, Tai, Celso; Alves, Acacio (Rufino), Mario, Mane, Salvador

CELTIC: Latchford; McGrain, Lynch; P. McCluskey, MacDonald, Edvaldsson; Callaghan, McNamara, Wilson, Hood, Lennox

Attendance: 25,000

Celtic's display puts them in with a wonderful chance of reaching the Quarter-Finals. Even without Kenny Dalglish they were much the better side and only in the later stages did they look unsteady. Latchford was the hero: he was unbeatable in goal. He had a series of wonderful saves, capping it all 5 minutes from time with a magnificent save from an Alves penalty-kick.

Second Round Second Leg November 5th
CELTIC (2) 3 — BOAVISTA (0) 1
Dalglish (35 secs), — Mane (36)
Edvaldsson (20),
Deans (85)

CELTIC: Latchford; McGrain, Lynch; P. McCluskey, MacDonald, Edvaldsson; G. McCluskey, Dalglish, Deans, McNamara, Callaghan (Lennox)

BOAVISTA: Botelho; Trindade, Mario Joao; Carolino, Tai, Barbosa (Rufino); Alves, Fransisco Mario, Mane, Salvador, Acacio (Zezinho)

Attendance: 37,000. Celtic wore numbers on their backs for the 1st time in their history.

George McCluskey, making his first full appearance in Europe, stamped his skill and personality throughout the 90 minutes. Boavista put themselves back into the tie in the 36th minute when Alves sent Mane away on the right and he hit a powerful drive past Latchford. Celtic sent on Lennox for Callaghan in the 2nd half. McGrain hit a post and Deans did the same before they wrapped up a tense match 5 minutes from time. Dalglish sent Deans away down the middle and, with the Boavista defence claiming offside, he took aim and lashed the ball past Botelho. Celtic won 3-1 on aggregate.

Quarter-Final First Leg March 3rd
CELTIC (1) 1 — SACHSENRING ZWICKAU (East Germany) (0) 1
Dalglish (40) — Blank (88)

CELTIC: Latchford; McGrain, Lynch; P. McCluskey, Aitken, Edvaldsson; Wilson, Dalglish, Deans, Hood, Lennox

SACHSENRING: Croy; Lippman, H. Schykowski; Stemmler, Reicheit, Leuschner; Schwemmer, Blank, J. Schykowski, Dietzch, Braun

Attendance: 46,000

This was an evening of bitter frustration for Celtic. Despite incessant attack they scored only one goal, missed a penalty (Lennox) and conceded a goal less than 2 minutes from the end. Zwickau made no attempt to win and concentrated all their efforts on not losing. Croy was immense in goal. Parkhead was silenced in the 88th minute when, with all Celtic forward, Blank took control of a ball inside the centre circle, slipped Aitken, ran forward, drew Latchford off his line and coolly put the ball into the net, leaving Celtic with a mountain to climb to make the Semi-Final.

Quarter-Final Second Leg March 17th
SACHSENRING ZWICKAU (1) 1 — CELTIC (0) 0
Blank (5)

SACHSENRING: Croy; Lippmann, H. Schykowski; Stemmler, J. Schykowski, Schwemmer; Lauschner, Blank, Brautigam (Eichelt), Dietzch, Braun

CELTIC: Latchford; McGrain, Callaghan; MacDonald, Aitken, McCluskey; Wilson (Casey), Glavin (McNamara), Edvaldsson, Dalglish, Hood

Attendance: 40,000

Andy Lynch failed a fitness test and Bobby Lennox dropped out with a leg strain. Within 5 minutes Celtic went a goal down. Aitken was beaten down the left by Brautigam and the ball was placed across an outstretched defence to Blank. He beat McCluskey and hit a wicked shot from the edge of the penalty-area which dipped over Latchford's head into the net. Celtic, with Roddie MacDonald at centre-forward, missed chances before half-time with Hood and MacDonald the culprits. Sachsenring Zwickau won 2-1 on aggregate.

APPEARANCES	League	League Cup	Scottish Cup	European Cup Winners Cup
Latchford	35	10	1	6
Hunter	1	–	–	–
McGrain	35	9	1	6
Lynch	34	10	1	5
P. McCluskey	34	9	1	6
Murray	2+1S	–	–	–
MacDonald	27	9	1	5
Edvaldsson	35	10	1	6
Connelly	1+2S	1+1S	–	–
Glavin	10	7+1S	1	1+1S
Hood	7+7S	6	–	5
McNamara	16+2S	6+2S	1	3+1S
Dalglish	35	10	1	5
Wilson	18+8S	9	–	5
Deans	29	2	1	3
Lennox	25+5S	7+2S	1	2+1S
Callaghan	22	4+1S	–	5
Ritchie	5+3S	0+1S	–	–
Aitken	12	1+1S	–	2
Casey	1	0+1S	–	0+2S
G. McCluskey	2+2S	–	–	1+1S
Doyle	5	–	–	–
Burns	5	–	–	–
Hannah	0+2S	–	–	–

GOALSCORERS:

League: Dalglish 24, Deans 15 (2 pens), Lennox 10, Edvaldsson 7, Wilson 4, MacDonald 3, P. McCluskey 3 (3 pens), McNamara 2, Hood 1, Lynch 1, Ritchie 1

League Cup: Dalglish 4, Lennox 3, Edvaldsson 3, Wilson 3, Lynch 2, Hood 2, Ritchie 1, Glavin 1, McGrain 1, Callaghan 1

Scottish Cup: Dalglish 1, Lennox 1

Cup Winners Cup: Dalglish 3, Hood 2, Deans 2, Edvaldsson 2, Wilson 1, MacDonald 1, Callaghan 1, P. McCluskey 1 (pen)

Celtic players on a lap of honour at Easter Road after defeating Hibs to clinch the 1966-67 Premier League Championship.

Season 1976-77

Celtic got back into their winning ways. Jock Stein, fit again, returned to full duty and he guided the club to their 10th League and Cup double. They remained unbeaten at home all season and lost only 4 matches away – twice at Pittodrie – finishing 9 points ahead of Rangers who finished in the runners-up spot. The Championship was clinched, with 4 matches in hand, with a 1-0 win at Easter Road courtesy of a Joe Craig goal. Celtic made a great signing in former Hibs captain, Pat Stanton and he played in every League and Scottish Cup match. Another ever-present (in all competitions), Danny McGrain, finished the season by being voted as Scotland's Player of the Year and he was commonly held to be the best player in his position in the world. Ronnie Glavin blossomed at last and finished as top scorer with 19 goals followed by his ex-Firhill team-mate Joe Craig, a £60,000 signing during the season, on 16. The club finally ran out of patience with George Connelly and he was freed. Former Ranger Alfie Conn was signed from Tottenham Hotspur for £65,000 and he went on to complete his own little bit of history before the end of the season. Tom Callaghan left the club and team captain, Kenny Dalglish, rounded off another outstanding season by scoring Scotland's winner over England at Wembley.

It was unlucky 13 for Celtic in the League Cup. They reached their 13th consecutive Final after two goals from Dalglish had given them victory in their Semi-Final with Hearts. They scored first through Dalglish but opponents Aberdeen, who had thrashed Rangers 5-1 in the Semi-Final, came back quickly with an equaliser. The Parkhead team dominated the second-half but couldn't score and an extra-time goal from substitute Davie Robb took the Cup to Pittodrie for the first time in 21 years.

Celtic had a fairly comfortable passage to their 40th Scottish Cup Final in which their opponents were Rangers. It was an undistinguished Final but not without a great deal of controversy about their 20th-minute penalty winner. Andy Lynch, who volunteered to take the kick, had taken only 2 penalties in his career – and had missed them both – but it was 3rd time lucky as he cracked the ball past Kennedy with his left foot.

Celtic's first sojourn in the U.E.F.A. Cup was brief. They lost to Polish side Wisla Krakow in the First Round which was no real surprise after they could only scrape a draw in their First-Leg home tie thanks to a last-minute goal from Dalglish.

League:	Champions
League Cup:	Finalists
Scottish Cup:	Winners
U.E.F.A Cup:	First Round

SCOTTISH PREMIER LEAGUE

July 14th: George Connelly was loaned out to Falkirk.
September 1st: Celtic signed Pat Stanton of Hibs in exchange for Jackie McNamara.

September 4th
CELTIC (0) 2 RANGERS (2) 2
Wilson 2 (54, 87) Johnstone (9), Parlane (34)
CELTIC: Latchford; McGrain; P. McCluskey, MacDonald, Lynch; Glavin, Stanton, Burns; Wilson Dalglish, Doyle

RANGERS: McCloy; Denny, Greig, Forsyth, Miller; Jardine, MacDonald, Munro, McLean, Parlane, Johnstone

Attendance: 57,000

In a great match Rangers took the lead in the 9th minute when McLean's free-kick and MacDonald's header gave Johnstone the present of the 1st goal. Celtic had hit the bar before Munro's pass to McLean's run gave Parlane a 2nd. Wilson's half-hit goal just after half-time gave some decency to the score. Celtic forced McCloy into serious saves for the next 20 minutes. In the last 10 minutes after Johnstone had abused two chances Burns' pass and Wilson's run and shot gave Celtic their 2nd goal. They had deserved no less.

September 8th: McGrain and Dalglish were in the Scotland team which beat Finland 6-0 in a Friendly at Hampden Park. Dalglish scored one of the goals.

September 11th
DUNDEE UNITED (1) 1 CELTIC (0) 0
Wallace (19)

DUNDEE UNITED: McAlpine; Rolland, Rennie, Narey, Kopel; Fleming, Hegarty, Payne; Sturrock, Wallace, McAdam

CELTIC: Latchford; McGrain, MacDonald, McCluskey, Lynch; Stanton, Glavin, Burns; Doyle, Dalglish, Wilson (Lennox)

Attendance: 13,000

September 17th: Joe Craig was signed from Partick Thistle for £60,000.

September 18th
CELTIC (1) 2 HEARTS (1) 2
Glavin (11), G. McCluskey (79) Busby (36 pen), Shaw (60)

CELTIC: Latchford; McGrain, Stanton, Aitken, Lynch; Glavin, Dalglish, Burns; Doyle, Craig, Wilson (G. McCluskey)

HEARTS: Cruikshank; Brown, Gallacher, Clunie, Kay; Callachan, Busby, Park; Aird (Fraser/Burrell), Gibson, Shaw

Attendance: 27,000

September 25th
KILMARNOCK (0) 0 CELTIC (2) 4
Craig (44), Glavin (45), Doyle (62), MacDonald (76)

KILMARNOCK: Stewart; S. McLean, Clarke, Welsh, Robertson; McCulloch, Murdoch, Maxwell; Provan, Fallis, Smith

CELTIC: Latchford; McGrain, MacDonald, Stanton, Lynch; Glavin, Aitken (Wilson), Burns (Callaghan), Dalglish, Craig, Doyle

Attendance: 14,900

October 2nd
CELTIC (0) 1 HIBERNIAN (1) 1
Dalglish (57 pen) Higgins (33)

CELTIC: Latchford; McGrain, MacDonald, Stanton, Lynch; Glavin, Aitken, Burns; Dalglish, Craig (Wilson), Doyle

HIBERNIAN: McDonald; Brownlie, Stewart, Blackley, Schaedler; Bremner, McNamara, Smith; Murray, Higgins, Scott

Attendance: 29,000

October 13th: McGrain and Dalglish were in the Scotland team beaten 2-0 by Czechoslovakia in a World Cup match in Bratislava.

October 16th
AYR UNITED (0) 0 CELTIC (0) 2
Glavin (69), Craig (88)

AYR UNITED: Geoghegan; McDonald, Fleming, Rodman, Murphy; Fillipi, McSherry, McCulloch; Ingram, McColl (Graham), Robertson

CELTIC: Latchford; McGrain, Stanton, MacDonald, Lynch; Aitken, Glavin, Dalglish; Doyle, Craig, Wilson

Attendance: 12,871

October 18th: George Connelly was freed.

October 20th
CELTIC (1) 5 DUNDEE UNITED (0) 1
Glavin 3 (1, 75, 80), Craig (68), Lennox (83) Sturrock (86)

CELTIC: Latchford; McGrain, Lynch; Stanton, MacDonald, Aitken; Doyle (Lennox), Glavin, Craig, Dalglish, Wilson (Burns)

DUNDEE UNITED: McAlpine; Rolland, Kopel; Fleming, Rennie (Holt), Narey; Sturrock, Wallace, Hegarty, McAdam (Hall), Payne

Attendance: 23,000

October 23rd
ABERDEEN (0) 2 CELTIC (0) 1
Harper 2 (63, 75 pen) Dalglish (56 pen)

ABERDEEN: Clark; Kennedy, Garner, Miller, Williamson; Sullivan (Jarvie), Smith, Shirra; Scott, Harper, Graham

CELTIC: Latchford; McGrain, Stanton, MacDonald, Lynch; Glavin, Aitken, Wilson; Doyle, Dalglish, Craig

Attendance: 19,370

October 27th: Celtic swopped Andy Ritchie for Roy Baines of Morton.

October 30th
CELTIC (0) 2 MOTHERWELL (0) 0
Dalglish 2 (57, 62)

CELTIC: Latchford; McGrain, Stanton, MacDonald, Lynch; Aitken, Glavin, Dalglish; Doyle, Craig, Wilson

MOTHERWELL: Rennie; McAdam (O'Rourke), McVie, Stevens, Wark; Millar, Davidson, Kennedy; Marinello (McLaren), Pettigrew, Graham

Attendance: 31,000

League positions

	P	W	D	L	F	A	Pts
1 Dundee United	8	6	0	2	16	12	12
2 CELTIC	9	4	3	2	19	9	11
3 Aberdeen	8	4	3	1	16	8	11
4 Partick Thistle	8	3	3	2	9	8	9
5 Hibernian	9	1	7	1	10	10	9

November 4th: Clydebank signed Tom Callaghan for £6,000.

November 17th: Dalglish and McGrain were in the Scotland team which beat Wales 1-0 in a World Cup Qualifier at Hampden Park.

November 20th
HEARTS (3) 3 — CELTIC (2) 4
Gibson 3 (8, 10, 33) — MacDonald (31), Lennox (36), Dalglish (60), Glavin (87)

HEARTS: Wilson; Brown, Gallacher, Clunie, Kay; Jeffries, Shaw, Park; Busby, Gibson, Prentice

CELTIC: Latchford; McGrain, Stanton, MacDonald, Lynch; Glavin, Dalglish, Aitken; Doyle, Craig, Lennox

Attendance: 20,500

November 24th
RANGERS (0) 0 — CELTIC (1) 1
Craig (36)

RANGERS: Kennedy; Jardine, Greig; Steele, Jackson, Watson; McLean, Hamilton, Parlane, MacDonald, McKean (Stein)

CELTIC: Latchford; McGrain, Lynch; Stanton, MacDonald, Aitken; Doyle, Glavin, Craig, Dalglish, Lennox (Wilson)

Attendance: 43,500

Celtic beat Rangers for the first time since January 1974. They were awarded a penalty in the 12th minute of the match when Greig brought down Lennox but the referee changed his mind after consulting his linesman. As a result of the tackle Lennox went off to hospital with a broken ankle. The only goal of the match came in the 36th minute. Dalglish started the move with a forward pass which Aitken nudged on to Craig who struck a vicious curling shot from 20 yards which flew high into the net well wide of Kennedy. McLean missed a chance to equalise in 55 minutes. He trapped and shot from a Parlane cross only for Latchford to fling himself sideways to make a thrilling save. Rangers brought on Colin Stein late in the match, for his first appearance in more than a year, but this made no real difference.

November 27th
CELTIC (2) 2 — KILMARNOCK (1) 1
Craig (44), Wilson (45) — McCulloch (5)

CELTIC: Latchford; McGrain, Stanton, MacDonald, Lynch; Glavin, Aitken, Dalglish; Doyle, Craig, Wilson

KILMARNOCK: Stewart; Maxwell, Clarke, Welsh, Robertson; Murdoch, McCulloch, Sheed (McDicken); Provan, Fallis, Smith

Attendance: 22,000

December 7th: Johnny Gibson was signed on a free transfer from St Mirren.

December 18th
CELTIC (3) 3 — AYR UNITED (0) 0
Doyle (10), Wilson (15), Dalglish (17)

CELTIC: Latchford; McGrain, MacDonald, Stanton, Lynch; Glavin (Edvaldsson), Aitken, Dalglish; Doyle (Gibson), Craig, Wilson

AYR UNITED: Geoghegan; McCulloch, Welsh, Fleming, McAnespie, Murphy; McSherry, Fillipi, Cramond; McCall (Masterton), Robertson

Attendance: 18,000

League positions

	P	W	D	L	F	A	Pts
1 CELTIC	13	8	3	2	29	13	19
2 Aberdeen	13	8	3	2	24	12	19
3 Dundee United	14	9	1	4	28	20	19
4 Rangers	13	5	5	3	20	13	15
5 Motherwell	14	5	3	6	24	25	13

December 26th
CELTIC (2) 2 — ABERDEEN (2) 2
Craig 2 (32, 44) — Jarvie 2 (23, 37)

CELTIC: Latchford; McGrain, Burns; Stanton, Macdonald, Aitken; Doyle, Glavin, Craig, Dalglish, Wilson

ABERDEEN: Clark; Kennedy, McLelland; Smith, Garner, Miller; Sullivan, Shirra, Harper, Jarvie, Graham

Attendance: 47,000

January 8th
DUNDEE UNITED (0) 1 — CELTIC (1) 2
McAdam (75) — Dalglish (13), Doyle (86)

DUNDEE UNITED: McAlpine; Fleming, Rennie, Narey, Kopel; Payne, Hegarty, Houston; Sturrock, Wallace (Addison), McAdam

CELTIC: Latchford; McGrain, Stanton, MacDonald, Lynch; Glavin, Dalglish, Aitken; Wilson, Craig, Doyle

Attendance: 16,000

January 11th
CELTIC (0) 1 — RANGERS (0) 0
Jackson o.g. (76)

CELTIC: Latchford; McGrain, Lynch; Stanton, MacDonald, Aitken; Doyle, Glavin, Craig, Dalglish, Wilson

RANGERS: Kennedy; Jardine, Miller; Forsyth, Jackson, Watson; McLean, O'Hara, Parlane, McKean, Johnstone

Attendance: 52,000

Celtic took the points that put them back on top of the Premier League. The victory came from an unlucky own goal by Colin Jackson. Doyle and Lynch worked the ball short from a corner, Lynch crossed on to the head of Roddie MacDonald and he struck the ball firmly if not decisively. Rangers goalkeeper Kennedy had it covered until the deflection by Jackson carried it into the net. Rangers might have equalised 2 minutes from the end when Aitken scrambled away a lob from McLean which had beaten Latchford.

January 22nd
KILMARNOCK (1) 1 — CELTIC (1) 3
Fallis (28) — Glavin 2 (38, 64 pen), Wilson (53)

KILMARNOCK: Stewart; Maxwell, Clarke, Welsh, Robertson; Murdoch, McCulloch, McDicken; Provan, Fallis, Smith (Sheed)

CELTIC: Latchford; McGrain, Stanton, MacDonald, Lynch; Aitken (P. McCluskey), Glavin, Dalglish; Doyle (Gibson), Craig, Wilson

Attendance: 14,363

February 5th
CELTIC (2) 4 — HIBERNIAN (1) 2
Edvaldsson (21), Glavin 2 (30, 72), Craig (57) — Smith (37), McLeod (85)

CELTIC: Latchford; McGrain, Stanton, MacDonald (Edvaldsson), Lynch; Glavin, Dalglish, Aitken; Doyle, Craig, Wilson

HIBERNIAN: McDonald; Brownlie, Stewart, Blackley, Spalding (Carroll); Edwards, Bremner, Smith; Murray (Scott), McLeod, Duncan

Attendance: 28,000

February 7th
CELTIC (2) 5 — HEARTS (0) 1
Edvaldsson (16), Craig (44), Glavin (46), Lynch (84), Dalglish (87) — Gibson (86)

CELTIC: Latchford; McGrain, Lynch; Stanton, Edvaldsson, Aitken (P. McCluskey); Doyle, Glavin, Craig (Burns), Dalglish, Wilson

HEARTS: Cruikshank; Clunie (Prentice), Burrell; Jeffries, Gallacher, Fraser; Bannon, Park, Gibson, Brown, Shaw

Attendance: 21,000

February 12th
CELTIC (0) 2 — PARTICK THISTLE (0) 0
Glavin (66), Dalglish (81)

CELTIC: Latchford; McGrain, Stanton, Edvaldsson, Lynch; Glavin, Dalglish, Aitken; Craig, Wilson (P. McCluskey), Doyle

PARTICK THISTLE: Rough; Mackie, Campbell, Marr, Whittaker; Anderson (Houston), J. Hansen, Love; Craig, Somner, Melrose

Attendance: 26,000

February 19th
AYR UNITED (2) 2 — CELTIC (1) 4
McCall (28), Masterton (41) — Craig (40), Lynch (63), Dalglish 2 (79, 82)

AYR UNITED: Sproat; Wells, Fleming, Tait, Murphy (McDonald); Fillipi, McSherry, McCulloch (Robertson); Cramond, McCall, Masterton

CELTIC: Latchford; McGrain, Stanton, Edvaldsson, Lynch; Aitken, Glavin, Dalglish; Doyle, Craig, Wilson (Burns)

Attendance: 13,684

February 22nd
PARTICK THISTLE (0) 2 — CELTIC (3) 4
McQuade (52), Edvaldsson o.g. (60) — Edvaldsson (3), Glavin (17 pen), Aitken (44), Craig (49)

PARTICK THISTLE: Rough; Mackie, Whittaker; J. Hansen, Campbell, A. Hansen; Houston, Somner, Marr, Craig, McQuade

CELTIC: Latchford; McGrain, Lynch; Stanton, Edvaldsson, Aitken; Doyle (Burns), Glavin, Craig, Dalglish, Wilson (P. McCluskey)

Attendance: 13,000

League positions

	P	W	D	L	F	A	Pts
1 CELTIC	22	16	4	2	56	24	36
2 Rangers	23	11	7	5	36	22	29
3 Dundee United	21	12	4	5	42	27	28
4 Aberdeen	22	10	8	4	37	22	28
5 Hibernian	23	4	14	5	20	23	22

March 1st: Former Ranger Alfie Conn was signed from Tottenham Hotspur for £65,000.

March 5th
ABERDEEN (1) 2 — CELTIC (0) 0
Graham (20), Harper (89)

ABERDEEN: Clark; Kennedy, Garner, Miller, McLelland; Smith, Fleming (Scott), Shirra; Davidson (Sullivan), Harper, Graham

CELTIC: Latchford; McGrain, Stanton, Edvaldsson, Lynch; Glavin, P. McCluskey (Conn), Aitken; Doyle, Craig, Dalglish

Attendance: 21,656

March 9th
CELTIC (1) 2 — PARTICK THISTLE (0) 1
Conn (41), Doyle (52) — Somner (89)

CELTIC: Latchford; McGrain, Burns; Stanton, Edvaldsson, Aitken; Doyle, Glavin, Craig, Dalglish, Conn

PARTICK THISTLE: Rough; J. Hansen, Whittaker; Campbell, Marr, A. Hansen; Houston, Love, Somner, Craig, McQuade

Attendance: 22,000. Somner missed a penalty.

March 16th
CELTIC (2) 2 — MOTHERWELL (1) 2
Glavin (1 pen) — Graham (45)
Edvaldsson (44) — Davidson (79)

CELTIC: Latchford; McGrain, Burns; Stanton, Edvaldsson, Aitken; Doyle, Glavin, Craig, Dalglish, Conn

MOTHERWELL: Rennie; Watson, Wark; McAdam, McLaren, Stevens; P. Millar, Pettigrew (J. Millar), Graham, Davidson, O'Rourke

Attendance: 23,000

March 19th
RANGERS (1) 2 — CELTIC (1) 2
Parlane 2 (21, 79) — Aitken 2 (12, 84)

RANGERS: Kennedy; Jardine, Forsyth, Jackson, Greig; McKean, MacDonald, Watson; McLean, Parlane, Johnstone

CELTIC: Latchford; McGrain, Stanton, Edvaldsson, Burns; Glavin, Aitken, Dalglish; Doyle, Craig, Conn

Attendance: 51,500

In the first 20 minutes Celtic's performance was almost brilliant. They scored through Roy Aitken in 12 minutes and should have had a couple more. Alfie Conn curled a shot round Stewart Kennedy after 15 minutes but the ball came back off the post and shortly after Rangers took over. Derek Parlane equalised with a great drive from the edge of the penalty area in 21 minutes. It was no real surprise when Parlane grabbed his second goal 11 minutes from time. A neat dummy from Johnstone, a slide-rule pass from McLean, and there was the Rangers striker in perfect position to hammer the ball past Latchford. 6 minutes from time Celtic equalised. Watson fouled Doyle on the right wing and when the winger's free-kick came over, Aitken met it in mid-air and sent a tremendous drive high into the Rangers net. Alex MacDonald scored what he thought was the winner but after signalling the goal, referee Paterson spotted his linesman with his flag in the air and the score was chalked off. The game finished with two wonder saves, Latchford touching a Greig pile-driver round the post and Kennedy throwing himself full length to palm away a Joe Craig shot.

March 26th
CELTIC (1) 2 — DUNDEE UNITED (0) 0
Craig (45), Glavin (50 pen)

CELTIC: Baines; McGrain, Stanton, Edvaldsson, Burns; Glavin, Dalglish, Aitken; Doyle, Craig, Conn

DUNDEE UNITED: McAlpine; Rolland, Smith (Williamson), Narey, Kopel; Payne, Fleming, Houston; McAdam, Sturrock, Hegarty

Attendance: 37,000

March 30th
HIBERNIAN (1) 1 — CELTIC (1) 1
McLeod (34) — Glavin (36)

HIBERNIAN: McDonald; Brownlie, Schaedler; Bremner, Spalding, Blackley; Edwards, McLeod, Scott, Smith, Duncan

CELTIC: Baines; McGrain, Burns; Stanton, Edvaldsson, McCluskey; Gibson, Glavin, Craig, Dalglish, Conn

Attendance: 11,841

April 2nd
HEARTS (0) 0 — CELTIC (2) 3
Aitken (10), Craig (28), Glavin (46)

HEARTS: Cruikshank; Kay, Clunie, Gallacher, Burrell; Busby, Fraser, Park; Bannon (Aird), Shaw, Robertson (Prentice)

CELTIC: Baines; McGrain, Stanton, MacDonald, Lynch; Glavin, Dalglish, Aitken; Doyle (Burns), Craig (Edvaldsson), Conn

Attendance: 17,000. Park was sent off.

April 9th
CELTIC (0) 1 — KILMARNOCK (0) 0
Craig (78)

CELTIC: Baines; McGrain, Stanton, MacDonald, Lynch; Edvaldsson, Glavin, Aitken (Burns); Doyle (Wilson), Craig, Conn

KILMARNOCK: Stewart; Maxwell, Clark, McDicken, Robertson; McCulloch, Jardine, Murdoch; Provan, Fallis, Smith

Attendance: 20,000

April 13th
MOTHERWELL (1) 3 — CELTIC (0) 0
Kennedy (42),
Lynch o.g. 2 (85, 87)

MOTHERWELL: Hunter; Watson, Wark; McAdam, McLaren, Stevens; J. Miller, Pettigrew, Graham, Davidson, Kennedy

CELTIC: Baines; McGrain, Lynch; Stanton, Edvaldsson, Aitken; Conn, Glavin, Craig, Dalglish, Burns

Attendance: 13,820

April 16th
HIBERNIAN (0) 0 — CELTIC (0) 1
Craig (63)

HIBERNIAN: McDonald; Brownlie, Brazil, Stewart, Schaedler; Bremner, Edwards, Smith; McLeod, Duncan, Scott

CELTIC: Latchford; McGrain, Stanton, MacDonald, Lynch; Glavin (Burns), Dalglish, Aitken; Conn, Craig, Doyle

Attendance: 22,306. Celtic clinched their 30th Championship.

April 20th
CELTIC (2) 4 — ABERDEEN (1) 1
Conn (19), Glavin (37), Craig (61), Dalglish (86) — Jarvie (30)

CELTIC: Latchford; McGrain, Lynch; Stanton, MacDonald, Aitken; Doyle, Glavin, Craig, Dalglish, Conn

ABERDEEN: McLean; Kennedy, McLelland; Smith (Rougvie), Garner, Miller; Sullivan, Davidson, Harper, Jarvie, Graham

Attendance: 27,000

April 23rd
PARTICK THISTLE (0) 1 CELTIC (1) 1
Somner (86) — Aitken (12)

PARTICK THISTLE: Rough; J. Hansen (Mackie), Marr, Campbell, Whittaker; McQuade (Frame), Gibson, A. Hansen; Craig, Somner, Melrose

CELTIC: Latchford; McGrain, Stanton, MacDonald, Lynch; Aitken, Glavin (Burns), Dalglish; Doyle (Wilson), Craig, Conn

Attendance: 18,000

April 27th: McGrain, Glavin and Dalglish were in the Scotland team which beat Sweden 3-1 in a Friendly International at Hampden Park. Joe Craig made an appearance as a substitute and he scored with his first touch of the ball. Dalglish was also on the scoresheet.

April 30th
CELTIC (1) 2 — AYR UNITED (0) 0
Dalglish (36), Edvaldsson (77)

CELTIC: Latchford; McGrain, MacDonald, Stanton, Lynch; Burns, Aitken, Conn (Edvaldsson); Doyle, Craig (Lennox), Dalglish

AYR UNITED: Geoghegan; Rodman, Fleming, McAnespie, Brogan, Murphy (Phillips); Fillipi, McCulloch (Hislop); Cramond, McCall, Masterton

Attendance: 17,000

April 30th: Henderson, Hannah and Barclay were given free transfers.

May 2nd: Danny McGrain was named as Scotland's Player of the Year.

May 10th
MOTHERWELL (2) 2 — CELTIC (0) 2
Stevens (42), Marinello (43) — Burns (60), Dalglish (69)

MOTHERWELL: Muir; Stevens, Wark; McAdam, McVie, McLaren; Miller, Pettigrew, Graham, Davidson (Kennedy), Marinello

CELTIC: Latchford; McGrain, Lynch; Stanton, MacDonald, Aitken; Dalglish, Edvaldsson (Burns), Craig, Conn, Wilson (Doyle)

Attendance: 12,500

Scottish Premier League

	P	W	D	L	F	A	Pts
1 CELTIC	36	23	9	4	79	39	55
2 Rangers	36	18	10	8	62	37	46
3 Aberdeen	36	16	11	9	56	42	43
4 Dundee United	36	16	9	11	54	45	41
5 Partick Thistle	36	11	13	12	40	44	35
6 Hibernian	36	8	18	10	34	35	34
7 Motherwell	36	10	12	14	57	60	32
8 Ayr United	36	11	8	17	44	68	30
9 Hearts	36	7	13	16	49	66	27
10 Kilmarnock	36	4	9	23	32	71	17

May 21st: Celtic signed Roy Kay on a free transfer from Hearts.

May 28th: McGrain and Dalglish were in the Scotland team which drew 0-0 with Wales in Wrexham.

June 1st: McGrain and Dalglish were in the Scotland team which beat Northern Ireland 3-0 at Hampden Park. Dalglish scored 2 goals.

June 4th: McGrain and Dalglish were in the Scotland team which beat England 2-1 at Wembley to win the Home International Championship for the 2nd succesive year. Dalglish scored the winning goal.

June 15th: McGrain and Dalglish were in the Scotland team which beat Chile 4-2 in Santiago. Dalglish scored a goal.

June 18th: McGrain and Dalglish were in the Scotland team which drew 1-1 with Argentina in Buenos Aires.

June 23rd: McGrain and Dalglish were in the Scotland team beaten 2-0 by Brazil in the Maracana Stadium in Rio de Janeiro.

LEAGUE CUP

August 14th
DUNDEE UNITED (0) 0 CELTIC (0) 1
Dalglish (69)

DUNDEE UNITED: McAlpine; Rolland, Kopel; Holt (Reid), Rennie, Narey; Hall, Fleming, Hegarty, McAdam, Payne

CELTIC: Latchford; McGrain, Lynch; P. McCluskey, MacDonald, Edvaldsson; Doyle, Glavin, G. McCluskey, Burns (Wilson), Dalglish

Attendance: 13,000

August 18th
CELTIC (1) 3 — DUMBARTON (0) 0
Doyle (25), Dalglish (80 pen, 88 pen)

CELTIC: Latchford; McGrain, Lynch; P. McCluskey, MacDonald, Edvaldsson; Doyle, Glavin, G. McCluskey (Lennox), Dalglish, Wilson

DUMBARTON: Williams; Sinclair, Watt; Smith, McKinlay, Muir; Cook (McLean), Brown (Mullen), Bourke, Wallace, Graham

Attendance: 15,000

August 21st
ARBROATH (0) 0 CELTIC (1) 5
Dalglish (18), Glavin (53), McGrain (57), Wilson (61), Edvaldsson (88)

ARBROATH: Marshall; Milne, Kidd; Murray, Carson, Rylance; Hendrie, McKenzie (Fettes), Bone, Gardner (Fletcher), Mitchell

CELTIC: Latchford; McGrain, Lynch; P. McCluskey, MacDonald, Edvaldsson; Doyle (G. McCluskey), Glavin, Dalglish, Burns (Lennox), Wilson

Attendance: 6,826

August 25th
DUMBARTON (3) 3 CELTIC (1) 3
Bourke 2 (8, 24), Wallace (34) Wilson (14), MacDonald (61), Doyle (84)

DUMBARTON: Williams; Sinclair, Watt; Smith, Muir, Graham; McLean, Brown, Bourke, Wallace, McLeod

CELTIC: Latchford; McGrain, Lynch; P. McCluskey, MacDonald, Edvaldsson; Doyle, Glavin, Dalglish, Burns, Wilson

Attendance: 12,000

August 28th
CELTIC (2) 2 ARBROATH (0) 1
Doyle (39), Wilson (41) Murray (87)

CELTIC: Latchford; McGrain, Lynch; Edvaldsson (P. McCluskey), MacDonald, Aitken; Doyle, Glavin, Dalglish, Burns, Wilson

ARBROATH: Marshall; Kidd, Milne; Murray, Carson, Fettes (Yule); Mitchell, Rylance, Bone, Gardner, Fletcher (McKenzie)

Attendance: 17,000

September 21st
CELTIC (0) 1 DUNDEE UNITED (0) 1
MacDonald (62) Hegarty (75)

CELTIC: Latchford; McGrain, Callaghan; Glavin, MacDonald, Aitken; Henderson, Dalglish, Wilson, Burns (P. McCluskey), Lennox

DUNDEE UNITED: McAlpine; Rolland, Kopel; Stewart, Rennie, Narey; Sturrock, Wallace, Hegarty, McAdam (Fleming), Payne

Attendance: 15,000

Section table

	P	W	D	L	F	A	Pts
CELTIC	6	4	2	0	15	5	10
Dundee United	6	3	2	1	9	5	8
Dumbarton	6	2	2	2	10	9	6
Arbroath	6	0	0	6	2	17	0

Quarter-Final First Leg September 22nd
ALBION ROVERS (0) 0 CELTIC (0) 1
Callaghan (47)

ALBION ROVERS: Thomson; McConville, Main; Franchetti, Shields, I. Doherty; Sermani, Muldoon, Brogan, McGuigan (J. Doherty), Coughlin

CELTIC: Connaghan; McGrain, Lynch; Aitken, MacDonald, P. McCluskey; Doyle (Edvaldsson), Glavin, G. McCluskey, Callaghan, Lennox

Attendance: 7,000

Quarter-Final Second Leg October 6th
CELTIC (2) 5 ALBION ROVERS (0) 0
Dalglish 3 (36 pen, 44, 66), Doyle 2 (87, 89)

CELTIC: Connaghan; McGrain (Aitken), Lynch; Edvaldsson, MacDonald, Callaghan; Doyle, Glavin, Wilson (Henderson), Dalglish, Lennox

ALBION ROVERS: Thomson; McConville, McCue; Franchetti, Shields, I. Doherty; Sermani, McGuigan, Brogan, Main, Muldoon

Attendance: 7,000. Celtic won 6-0 on aggregate.

Semi-Final at Hampden Park October 25th
CELTIC (1) 2 HEARTS (1) 1
Dalglish 2 (44, 72 pen) Brown (42)

CELTIC: Latchford; McGrain, Lynch; Edvaldsson, MacDonald, Aitken; Doyle, Glavin, Dalglish, Callaghan (P. McCluskey), Wilson

HEARTS: Wilson; Brown, Kay; Fraser, Gallagher, Clunie; Shaw, Busby, Gibson, Park, Prentice

Attendance: 21,706. Prentice was sent off.

Dalglish broke Hearts by equalising their opening goal and then gaining and converting the penalty which eventually won the match. Both Stanton and Joe Craig were ineligible for the match.

Final at Hampden Park November 6th
ABERDEEN (1) 2 CELTIC (1) 1
Jarvie (25), Robb (92) Dalglish (12 pen)
After Extra Time

ABERDEEN: Clark; Kennedy, Williamson; Smith, Garner, Miller; Sullivan, Scott, Harper, Jarvie (Robb), Graham. Other Sub: Fleming

CELTIC: Latchford; McGrain, Lynch; Edvaldsson, MacDonald, Aitken; Doyle, Glavin, Dalglish, Burns (Lennox), Wilson. Other Sub: McCluskey

Attendance: 69,707 *Referee:* J. Paterson

Aberdeen won the League Cup a year almost to the day after Ally McLeod took over as Manager. Jarvie's tackle on Dalglish gave Celtic the penalty which the captain himself converted to put his side ahead in the 12th minute. Aberdeen drew level 13 minutes later when Kennedy crossed the ball long, Harper screwed it back and Jarvie came in for a killing header. Celtic dominated the 2nd half. Both Doyle and Wilson missed chances and Lennox had a couple of shots which went just wide. The goal which gave Aberdeen the trophy came 2 minutes into extra-time. Graham took McGrain for a walk, Scott crossed, Graham miskicked in front of goal and Robb, brought on in the 2nd half, hit the ball past Latchford from a difficult angle.

SCOTTISH CUP

Third Round January 29th
AIRDRIE (1) 1 — CELTIC (1) 1
March (27) — Doyle (31)

AIRDRIE: Poulton; Jonquin, Black, March, Lapsley; Whiteford, Walker, McCulloch; Wilson, Clark, Cairney (Anderson)

CELTIC: Latchford; McGrain, Stanton, MacDonald, Lynch; Dalglish, Glavin, Aitken; Doyle, Craig, Wilson (Burns)

Attendance: 18,316

Third Round Replay February 2nd
CELTIC (4) 5 — AIRDRIE (0) 0
Craig 4 (8, 10, 38, 55), Glavin (12)

CELTIC: Latchford; McGrain, Lynch; Stanton, MacDonald (Burns), Aitken; Doyle, Glavin, Craig, Dalglish, Wilson

AIRDRIE: McWilliams; Jonquin, Lapsley; Anderson, March, Whiteford; Wilson, McCulloch, Cairney, Walker, Clark

Attendance: 20,000

Fourth Round February 27th
CELTIC (0) 1 — AYR UNITED (0) 1
Glavin (63) — Cramond (88)

CELTIC: Latchford; McGrain, Lynch; Stanton, MacDonald (Edvaldsson), Aitken; Doyle, Glavin, Craig, Dalglish, Wilson

AYR UNITED: Sproat; Wells, Fillipi; Fleming, Tait, Cramond; McSherry, McCall, Masterton, McCulloch (Kelly), Robertson

Attendance: 38,000

Fourth Round Replay March 2nd
AYR UNITED (1) 1 — CELTIC (1) 3
Masterton (25) — Glavin (7 pen), Doyle (47), Aitken (63)

AYR UNITED: Sproat; Wells, Kelly; Fleming, Tait, Fillipi; McSherry, McCall, Masterton, Cramond, Robertson

CELTIC: Latchford; McGrain, Lynch; Stanton, Edvaldsson, P. McCluskey; Doyle, Glavin, Craig, Aitken, Dalglish

Attendance: 13,100

Quarter-Final March 13th
CELTIC (3) 5 — QUEEN OF THE SOUTH (1) 1
Glavin 3 (27, 39 pen, 79 pen), Craig (44), Dalglish (89) — Dickson (29)

CELTIC: Latchford; McGrain, Burns; Stanton, Edvaldsson, Aitken; Doyle (Casey), Glavin, Craig, Dalglish, Wilson (Gibson)

QUEEN OF THE SOUTH: Ball; Millar, McChesney; McLaren, Clark, O'Hara; Dempster, Reid, Ferrie, P. Dickson, Balderstone

Attendance: 27,000

Semi-Final at Hampden Park April 6th
CELTIC (0) 2 — DUNDEE (0) 0
Craig 2 (79, 85)

CELTIC: Baines; McGrain, Lynch; Stanton, MacDonald, Aitken; Doyle, Glavin, Craig, Dalglish, Conn

DUNDEE: Donaldson; Gemmell, Johnston (Caldwell); Ford, Phillip, McPhail; Strachan, Sinclair, Pirie, Hutchinson, Purdie

Attendance: 29,900

Joe Craig scored both goals which took Celtic into their 40th Scottish Cup Final. The game was anything but a classic but it flowed from end to end.

Final at Hampden Park May 7th
CELTIC (1) 1 — RANGERS (0) 0
Lynch (20 pen)

CELTIC: Latchford; McGrain, Lynch; Stanton, MacDonald, Aitken; Dalglish, Edvaldsson, Craig, Wilson, Conn. Subs: Burns and Doyle

RANGERS: Kennedy; Jardine, Greig; Forsyth, Jackson, Watson (Robertson); McLean, Hamilton, Parlane, MacDonald, Johnstone. Other Sub: Miller

Attendance: 54,252 *Referee:* R. Valentine

Controversy raged over Celtic's Scottish Cup-winning goal. With 20 minutes gone Conn swung over a corner from the left. MacDonald headed back across goal and the ball was only partially cleared by Kennedy. Edvaldsson charged in and his shot beat the goalkeeper, but was handled on the line by Johnstone. Referee Valentine had no hesitation in pointing to the spot despite Rangers' furious protests. Andy Lynch, who volunteered to take the kick, had taken only 2 penalties in his career – both of them with Hearts – and had missed them. It was 3rd time lucky, however, as he cracked the ball past Kennedy with his left foot. Stein's surprise in bringing back Paul Wilson was a winner and Alfie Conn made history by gaining a winners' medal with both Rangers and Celtic.

U.E.F.A. CUP

First Round First Leg September 15th
CELTIC (1) 2 — WISLA KRAKOW (Poland) (0) 2
MacDonald (13), Dalglish (90) — Kmitcik (68), Wrobel (75)

CELTIC: Latchford; McGrain, Lynch; Glavin, MacDonald, Edvaldsson; Doyle, Dalglish, Wilson, Burns, Lennox

WISLA: Adamczyk; A. Szymanowski, Maculewicz; Budka (Gazda), Plaszewski, H. Szymanowski; Wrobel, Kapka, Nawalka, Kmiecik, Kusto

Attendance: 30,000

Celtic could only scrape a draw with the tough Poles. They made the best possible start with a goal in 13 minutes from MacDonald but they fell apart in the 2nd half. Even a last-gasp equaliser by Dalglish did little to raise the spirits of the fans who left disappointed.

First Round Second Leg September 29th
WISLA KRAKOW (0) 2 CELTIC (0) 0
Kmiecik 2 (54, 59)

WISLA: Gonet; Szymanowski, Maculewicz; Plaszewski, Budka, Jalocha; Lipka, Kapka, Kusto, Nawalka, Kmiecik

CELTIC: Latchford; McGrain, Lynch; P. McCluskey, Edvaldsson, MacDonald; Glavin, Aitken, Doyle (Lennox), Dalglish, Wilson

Attendance: 45,000

Celtic were hit by 2 great goals from World Cup striker Kmiecik just after half-time after having survived a Polish onslaught early on and finishing the 1st half on top. Celtic missed a great chance to go ahead in the 23rd minute. Aitken turned a ball inside to Wilson, who was on his own only 6 yards out. The winger hit it first time but Gonet managed to block the ball and it rebounded off the post. Wisla Krakow won 4-2 on aggregate.

APPEARANCES	League	League Cup	Scottish Cup	U.E.F.A Cup
Latchford	31	8	6	2
Baines	5	–	1	–
McGrain	36	10	7	2
Lynch	30	9	6	2
Aitken	33	5+1S	7	1
Stanton	36	–	7	–
MacDonald	24	10	5	2
Edvaldsson	13+4S	8+1S	3+1S	2
P. McCluskey	4+4S	5+3S	1	1
Doyle	33+1S	9	6	2
Glavin	34	10	6	2
Lennox	2+3S	3+3S	–	1+1S
Wilson	19+5S	8+1S	5	2
Burns	13+9S	6	1+2S	1
Dalglish	35	9	7	2
Joe Craig	34	–	7	–
Callaghan	0+1S	4	–	–
Gibson	1+2S	–	0+1S	–
Conn	13+1S	–	2	–
G.McCluskey	0+1S	3+1S	–	–
Casey	–	–	0+1S	–
Henderson	–	1+1S	–	–
Connaghan	–	2	–	–

GOALSCORERS

League: Glavin 19 (3 pens), Craig 16, Dalglish 14 (2 pens), Wilson 5, Aitken 5, Edvaldsson 5, Doyle 4, MacDonald 2, Lynch 2, Lennox 2, Conn 2, Own Goals 1, Burns 1, G. McCluskey 1

League Cup: Dalglish 10 (5 pens), Doyle 5, Wilson 3, MacDonald 2, McGrain 1, Edvaldsson 1, Callaghan 1, Glavin 1

Scottish Cup: Craig 7, Glavin 6 (3 pens), Doyle 2, Aitken 1, Dalglish 1, Lynch 1 (pen)

U.E.F.A. Cup: MacDonald 1, Dalglish 1

A happy Jock Stein at Hampden Park in May 1977 as Celtic celebrate winning the Scottish Cup against their 'old firm' rivals, Rangers.

Season 1977-78

Celtic had their poorest season for 13 years – finishing only 5th in the table and losing a post-war record-equalling 15 matches. They suffered 3 major blows right at the start. Kenny Dalglish left for Liverpool for a record fee between British clubs of £440,000. Pat Stanton received an injury in the first League match of the season against Dundee United which eventually forced his retirement and, worst of all, new captain Danny McGrain missed all but the opening 7 games through injury which also cost him a place in Scotland's World Cup team in Argentina. Unusually, Jock Stein was forced to buy. Tom McAdam was recruited from Dundee United for £60,000, John Dowie arrived from Fulham, Francis Munro was signed from Wolves after an initial trial period and Joe Fillipi came from Ayr United in exchange for Brian McLaughlin plus a cash adjustment, but the side never looked settled, and with the exception of McAdam all of the buys looked to be short-term investments. Only two of the first 9 matches were won and the team had another bad spell starting on December 31st which saw them suffer 5 straight defeats. Latchford, MacDonald and Edvaldsson played in all 36 matches and the latter finished as top scorer with 10 goals. At the end of the season former captain Billy McNeill, who had taken Aberdeen to 2nd place in the league and the Scottish Cup Final, was appointed as the new Team Manager. Under Stein's management Celtic had won 25 major trophies: The European Cup, The Scottish League Championship 10 times (including 9 in a row), The Scottish Cup 8 times and The Scottish League Cup 6 times. Their full League record under Stein was: Played 421 Won 296, Drew 66, lost 59, Goals for 1,111 and Goals Against 413.

His record excludes Season 1975-76, when he was recovering from injuries sustained in a car crash. His place in British football history was assured.

Celtic reached the Scottish League Cup Final for the 16th time after beating Motherwell, Stirling Albion, St Mirren and Hearts but they lost to Rangers after Extra-Time in an untidy Final.

They beat Dundee 7-1 in the Third Round of the Scottish Cup but were beaten by Second Division Kilmarnock in a Fourth Round Replay in which Roy Aitken ordered off.

They reached the Second Round of the European Cup but lost out to S.W.W. Innsbruck of Austria who wiped out their 1 goal First Leg lead within 4 minutes of the return and punished Celtic's defensive mistakes mercilessly.

League:	Fifth
League Cup:	Finalists
Scottish Cup:	Fourth Round
European Cup	Second Round

SCOTTISH PREMIER LEAGUE

July 30th: Ian McWilliams was signed from Queens Park.

August 10th: Kenny Dalglish joined Liverpool for £440,000.

August 12th: Pat McCluskey joined Dumbarton for £15,000.

August 13th
CELTIC (0) 0 DUNDEE UNITED (0) 0
CELTIC: Latchford; McGrain, MacDonald, Stanton (Doyle), Lynch; Glavin, Aitken, Burns; Craig, Edvaldsson, Conn (Lennox)
DUNDEE UNITED: McAlpine; Rolland, Hegarty, Narey, Kopel; Payne, Fleming, Addison; Sturrock (Dodds), Kirkwood, Wallace
Attendance: 34,000

August 20th
AYR UNITED (0) 2 CELTIC (1) 1
McCall 2 (56, 59) Craig (15)
AYR UNITED: Sproat; Rodman, Kelly, Fleming; McAnespie; Hannah, McCall, McSherry; Masterton, McCulloch, Cramond
CELTIC: Latchford; McGrain, Kay; Aitken, MacDonald, Burns; Glavin (Doyle), Edvaldsson, Craig, Lennox, Wilson (Casey)
Attendance: 14,500. Doyle was ordered off

August 27th
CELTIC (0) 0 MOTHERWELL (0) 1
Davidson (80)
CELTIC: Latchford; McGrain, Kay; Casey, MacDonald, Aitken; Glavin, Edvaldsson, Craig, Burns, Doyle
MOTHERWELL: Muir; Watson, Wark; McLaren, McVie (Miller), Millar, Stevens; Marinello (O'Neill), McAdam, Davidson, Purdie
Attendance: 29,000

September 6th: Celtic made a double signing: Tom McAdam from Dundee United for £60,000 and John Dowie from Fulham for £25,000.

September 7th: Danny McGrain was in the Scotland team beaten 1-0 by East Germany in East Berlin.

September 10th
RANGERS (0) 3 CELTIC (2) 2
Smith 2 (53, 81), Johnstone (65) Edvaldsson 2 (18, 31)
RANGERS: McCloy; Jardine, Miller; Forsyth, Johnstone, MacDonald (McLean); McKean, Russell, Parlane (Greig), Smith, Cooper
CELTIC: Latchford; McGrain, Lynch; Edvaldsson, MacDonald, Casey; Doyle, Dowie (McAdam), Glavin, Burns (Lennox), Wilson
Attendance: 48,788

Rangers gave their greatest rivals 2 goals of a start, sorted out their own problems at half-time and went on to win the points with a breathtaking display of attacking football. Rangers looked to have a bargain in Gordon Smith. He scored twice, bringing his total to 6 in the last 4 games.

September 17th
ABERDEEN (0) 2 CELTIC (0) 1
Fleming 2 (58, 67) Garner o.g. (49)
ABERDEEN: Clark; Kennedy, McLelland; Shirra, Garner, Miller; Davidson, Jarvie, Harper, Fleming, McMaster
CELTIC: Latchford; McGrain, Lynch; Edvaldsson, MacDonald, McWilliams; Glavin, McAdam, Craig (Doyle), Aitken, Wilson
Attendance: 25,800

September 21st: Danny McGrain was in the Scotland team which beat the European Champions Czechoslovakia 3-1 at Hampden Park.

September 24th
CELTIC (1) 1 CLYDEBANK (0) 0
McAdam (23)
CELTIC: Latchford; McGrain, MacDonald, Aitken, Lynch; Glavin, Burns (Dowie), Wilson; Doyle, McAdam, Edvaldsson
CLYDEBANK: Gallagher; Abel, Fallon, McCormack, McLaughlin (Houston); McNaughton, McColl, Hay; Colgan, Larnach, McCallan
Attendance: 20,000

October 1st
CELTIC (1) 3 HIBERNIAN (1) 1
Edvaldsson (45), Glavin (60), Craig (65) McKay (86)
CELTIC: Latchford; McGrain, Kay; Edvaldsson, MacDonald, Aitken; Glavin, Wilson, Craig, McAdam, Burns
HIBERNIAN: McDonald; McNamara, Schaedler; Brazil, Stewart, Blackley; McLeod, Bremner, McKay, Higgins, Duncan
Attendance: 26,000

October 8th
PARTICK THISTLE (0) 1 CELTIC (0) 0
Somner (61)
PARTICK THISTLE: Rough; Mackie, Whittaker; Marr (Love), Anderson, Campbell; Houston, Somner, Melrose (McQuade), Gibson, Craig
CELTIC: Latchford; Kay, Lynch; Glavin, MacDonald, Aitken; McLaughlin, McAdam, Craig (Edvaldsson), Burns, Wilson
Attendance: 19,500

October 14th: Celtic signed former Scottish International Francis Munro on a month's trial from Wolves.

October 15th
CELTIC (0) 1 ST MIRREN (0) 2
McAdam (64) Munro o.g. (59), Stark (69)
CELTIC: Latchford; Kay, Munro, MacDonald, Burns, Glavin, Edvaldsson, Aitken; Conn, Wilson, McAdam
ST MIRREN: Hunter; Young, Reid, Copland, Beckett; Fitzpatrick, Stark, Abercrombie; Richardson, McGarvey, Docherty (Sharp)
Attendance: 29,000

October 22nd
DUNDEE UNITED (1) 1 CELTIC (1) 2
Fleming (2) Glavin (37 pen), Wilson (79)

DUNDEE UNITED: McAlpine; Rolland, Kopel; Fleming, Hegarty, Narey; Sturrock, Wallace (Rennie), Bourke (Wallace), Robinson, Payne

CELTIC: Latchford; Aitken, Lynch; Glavin, MacDonald, Munro; Doyle, McAdam, Craig (Edvaldsson), Burns, Wilson

Attendance: 17,000

October 29th
CELTIC (1) 3 AYR UNITED (2) 2
McAdam (1), Glavin (66), MacDonald (83) Cramond (16), McCall (19)

CELTIC: Latchford; Aitken, Lynch; Glavin, MacDonald, Munro; Doyle, Edvaldsson, McAdam, Burns, Wilson

AYR UNITED: Sproat; Rodman, Kelly; Fleming, McAnespie, Fillipi; McCall, Hyslop, Masterton, Cramond, Christie (McCulloch)

Attendance: 20,000

League positions

	P	W	D	L	F	A	Pts
1 Rangers	11	8	1	2	26	13	17
2 Aberdeen	11	6	3	2	19	11	15
3 Dundee United	11	6	2	3	15	8	14
4 Partick Thistle	11	6	1	4	15	15	13
5 St Mirren	11	4	3	4	16	17	11
7 CELTIC	11	4	1	6	14	15	9

November 5th
MOTHERWELL (0) 2 CELTIC (0) 3
McAdam (54), O'Rourke (67) Craig 2 (51, 69), MacDonald (79)

MOTHERWELL: Rennie; Watson, Wark; J. Millar, McLaren (O'Rourke), Stevens; Marinello, P. Millar (Purdie), McAdam, Davidson, Robertson

CELTIC: Latchford; Fillipi, Lynch; Aitken, MacDonald, Munro; Doyle, McAdam, Craig, Burns (Edvaldsson), Wilson

Attendance: 16,547

November 4th: Joe Fillipi was signed from Ayr United in exchange for Brian McLaughlin and a cash adjustment of £15,000.

November 12th
CELTIC (0) 1 RANGERS (1) 1
McAdam (50) Johnstone (26)

CELTIC: Latchford; Fillipi, Edvaldsson, MacDonald, Lynch; Glavin, Aitken, Conn; Doyle, Craig (Wilson), McAdam

RANGERS: Kennedy; Jardine, Jackson, Forsyth, Greig; Russell, Smith, MacDonald; McLean, Johnstone, Cooper

Attendance: 56,000

Rangers were expected to win but, in the end, a draw was the right result. For all their first-half pressure Rangers went in at the interval only one goal ahead thanks mainly to the efforts of MacDonald and Edvaldsson in the Celtic defence. Celtic equalised in 50 minutes when Fillipi crossed and Craig headed down to McAdam who clipped it past Kennedy. In 66 minutes Joe Craig rounded Tom Forsyth and was sent sprawling but as the ball broke to McAdam the referee decided to play the advantage rule but the chance was lost.

November 14th: Francis Munro's trial period was extended for another month.

November 19th
CELTIC (1) 3 ABERDEEN (1) 2
Lynch (31 pen), Aitken (48), Edvaldsson (75) Jarvie (16), Harper (69 pen)

CELTIC: Latchford; Fillipi, Lynch; Munro, MacDonald, Aitken; Doyle, Edvaldsson, Craig (Wilson), McAdam, Conn

ABERDEEN: Clark; Kennedy, McLelland; Sullivan, Garner, Miller; Jarvie, Robb, Harper, Fleming (McMaster), Strachan

Attendance: 27,000

November 19th: Danny McGrain was reported to be in a Manchester hospital.

December 10th
CELTIC (2) 3 PARTICK THISTLE (0) 0
McAdam (10), MacDonald (41), Lynch (52 pen)

CELTIC: Latchford; Fillipi, MacDonald, Munro, Lynch; Aitken, Edvaldsson, Conn; Doyle, McAdam, Craig

PARTICK THISTLE: Rough; Mackie, Anderson (Campbell), Marr, Whittaker; Love, O'Hara, Gibson, Craig (Houston); Somner, Melrose

Attendance: 27,000

December 17th
ST MIRREN (1) 3 CELTIC (1) 3
Stark (11), McGarvey (70), Munro (77) McAdam (8), Lynch (80 pen), Craig (88)

ST MIRREN: A. Hunter; Young, Beckett; Fitzpatrick, Reid, Copland; Munro, Stark, McGarvey, Abercrombie, Hyslop

CELTIC: Latchford; Fillipi, Lynch; Edvaldsson, MacDonald, Aitken; Doyle, Glavin (Dowie), McAdam, Craig, Conn (Wilson)

Attendance: 17,000. Copland was sent off

December 24th
CELTIC (0) 1 DUNDEE UNITED (0) 0
Edvaldsson (82)

CELTIC: Latchford; Fillipi, Lynch; Aitken, MacDonald, Dowie; Doyle, Edvaldsson, McAdam, Craig, Conn (Wilson)

DUNDEE UNITED: McAlpine; Rolland, Kopel; Rennie, Hegarty, Narey; Sturrock, Kirkwood, Wallace (Addison), Fleming, Payne

Attendance: 21,000

League positions

	P	W	D	L	F	A	Pts
1 Rangers	18	12	3	3	42	23	27
2 Aberdeen	19	10	4	5	33	19	24
3 Partick Thistle	18	10	3	5	29	26	23
4 Dundee United	18	7	5	6	21	14	19
5 CELTIC	17	8	3	6	28	23	19

December 30th: Francis Munro was signed from Wolves for £20,000

December 31st
AYR UNITED (1) 2 — CELTIC (0) 1
Masterton, McLaughlin — Edvaldsson

AYR UNITED: Sproat; Rodman, Kelly; Fleming, Hyslop, McAnespie; McCall, McSherry, Masterton, McLaughlin, Cramond

CELTIC: Latchford; Fillipi, Lynch; Aitken, MacDonald, Munro; Doyle, Edvaldsson, McAdam, Craig (McCluskey), Conn

Attendance: 14,000

January 2nd
CELTIC (0) 0 — MOTHERWELL (1) 1
O'Rourke (24)

CELTIC: Latchford; Fillipi, Lynch; Edvaldsson, MacDonald, Munro; Doyle (G. McCluskey), Glavin, McAdam, Aitken, Wilson

MOTHERWELL: Rennie; Watson, Wark; Millar, McVie, Stevens; Marinello, Pettigrew, O'Rourke, McLaren, Mungall

Attendance: 23,000

January 7th
RANGERS (2) 3 — CELTIC (0) 1
Smith (35), Greig (37), Parlane (87) — Edvaldsson (64)

RANGERS: Kennedy; Jardine, Greig; Forsyth, Jackson, MacDonald; McLean (Parlane), Russell, Johnstone, Smith, Cooper (Miller)

CELTIC: Latchford; Fillipi, Lynch; Aitken, MacDonald, Munro; Glavin, Edvaldsson, Craig, McAdam, Wilson

Attendance: 51,000

Celtic were trailing to a brilliant Gordon Smith goal when Joe Craig was pushed in the back by Jackson as he tried to head the ball in at the far post. It looked a clear penalty but the referee said 'no' and was immediately beseiged by a posse of Celtic players. While the protests were going on Rangers took a quick free-kick and with only Latchford and Munro against a 5-man attack John Greig finished off the move by tapping the ball into the net to make it 2-0. Celtic had another penalty claim turned down when Alex MacDonald scooped an Aitken shot off the line with his arm. In the 64th minute Edvaldsson set the game alight when he shot past Kennedy from 12 yards after Aitken had touched on a Glavin free-kick. Shortly afterwards an Aitken shot cannoned back off a post with Kennedy beaten. 3 minutes from time Miller, who had replaced Cooper, took a throw on the right to Jardine whose shot was fumbled by Latchford, leaving Derek Parlane with an easy job of scoring.

January 14th
ABERDEEN (1) 2 — CELTIC (0) 1
Sullivan 2 (32, 71) — MacDonald (75)

ABERDEEN: Clark; Kennedy, McLelland; McMaster, Garner, Miller; Sullivan, Davidson, Gibson, Jarvie, Robb

CELTIC: Latchford; Fillipi, Lynch; Aitken, MacDonald, Munro; Glavin, Edvaldsson, G. McCluskey, McAdam, Wilson (Burns)

Attendance: 24,600

February 11th: It was revealed that Danny McGrain had diabetes.

February 25th
CELTIC (0) 1 — ST MIRREN (1) 2
McCluskey (72) — Bone (30), McGarvey (50)

CELTIC: Latchford; Sneddon, Munro, MacDonald, Fillipi; Edvaldsson (Casey), Aitken, Burns; G. McCluskey, McAdam, Conn (Wilson)

ST MIRREN: Hunter; Docherty, Reid, Copland, Beckett; Fitzpatrick, Abercrombie, Munro; McGarvey, Bone, Torrance

Attendance: 22,000

League positions

	P	W	D	L	F	A	Pts
1 Rangers	25	18	4	3	58	28	40
2 Aberdeen	25	14	6	5	41	21	34
3 Dundee United	23	10	6	7	27	17	26
4 Partick Thisle	23	10	4	9	31	35	24
5 Motherwell	25	9	5	11	33	34	23
8 CELTIC	22	8	3	11	32	33	19

March 4th
DUNDEE UNITED (0) 0 — CELTIC (0) 1
Narey o.g. (69)

DUNDEE UNITED: McAlpine; Rennie, Kopel; Fleming, Hegarty, Narey; Sturrock (Dodds), Holt; Bourke (Rolland), Kirkwood, Payne

CELTIC: Latchford; Sneddon, Dowie; Munro (Fillipi), MacDonald, Aitken; G. McCluskey, Edvaldsson, Craig, Burns, McAdam
Attendance: 12,771

March 4th: McGrain, Aitken and MacDonald were included in Scotland's World Cup 40 for Argentina.

March 11th
CELTIC (3) 3 — AYR UNITED (0) 0
Edvaldsson (30),
Glavin (36),
McCluskey (40)
CELTIC: Latchford; Sneddon, Munro, MacDonald, Dowie; Aitken, Glavin, Edvaldsson; G. McCluskey, McAdam, Burns
AYR UNITED: Sproat; Wells, Fleming; Hyslop, Cramond (McCutcheon), Sim; McLaughlin, McSherry, Walker (McDonald), McColl, Christie
Attendance: 15,000

March 12th: Houston Hurricanes offered £20,000 for John Dowie.

March 22nd
MOTHERWELL (0) 2 — CELTIC (1) 1
Marinello 2 (49, 54) — Craig (37)
MOTHERWELL: Rennie; Watson, Wark; Millar, McVie, Stevens; Marinello, Pettigrew, Clinging, Davidson, Mungall
CELTIC: Latchford; Sneddon, Lynch; Munro, MacDonald, Aitken (Burns); Glavin, Edvaldsson, Craig, Dowie, McAdam (Doyle)
Attendance: 9,613

March 25th
CELTIC (2) 2 — RANGERS (0) 0
Glavin (32),
MacDonald (39)
CELTIC: Latchford; Sneddon, MacDonald, Edvaldsson, Lynch; Glavin, Aitken, Dowie; Doyle, McAdam, Burns
RANGERS: Kennedy; Jardine, Jackson, Forsyth, Greig; Russell (Miller), Smith, MacDonald; McLean, Johnstone, Cooper (Parlane)
Attendance: 50,000

Celtic salvaged a lot of pride in this match and turned on some of their best football of the season. Rangers found themselves hustled and stretched right from the start. Rangers were 2 down at the interval but it could have been more. In 32 minutes Glavin hit a shot from 25 yards which dipped through Kennedy's arms. 7 minutes later Glavin sent a low free-kick into the heart of the Rangers goalmouth, Edvaldsson laid it off with a cheeky back heel pass and Roddie MacDonald steered the ball high past Kennedy. After the interval Rangers began to show some urgency and drive. Parlane and Miller replaced Cooper and Russell. Some fine saves from Latchford prevented any chance of a Rangers fightback.

March 25th: Danny McGrain had to withdraw from Scotland's World Cup pool.

March 27th: Bobby Lennox, the last of the Lisbon Lions, left Celtic to join Houston Hurricanes.

March 29th
PARTICK THISTLE (0) 0 — CELTIC (2) 4
Burns 2 (22, 29),
MacDonald (55),
McAdam (85)
PARTICK THISTLE: Rough; Mackie, Whittaker; Marr, McAdam, Anderson; Houston, Gibson, O'Hara, Somner, McQuade
CELTIC: Latchford; Sneddon, Lynch; Aitken, MacDonald, Dowie; Glavin, Edvaldsson, McAdam, Burns, Doyle
Attendance: 12,000. Glavin missed a penalty and Burns, McAdam and Houston were all sent off.

April 1st
CELTIC (1) 2 — ABERDEEN (0) 2
Glavin (33), — Davidson (57),
Edvaldsson (58) — Sullivan (67)
CELTIC: Latchford; Sneddon, MacDonald, Edvaldsson, Lynch; Aitken, Dowie, Glavin; Burns, Doyle (G. McCluskey), McAdam
ABERDEEN: Clark; Kennedy, Garner, Miller, Ritchie; Sullivan, McMaster, Jarvie; Harper, Archibald, Davidson
Attendance: 24,000

April 5th
CELTIC (0) 2 — HIBERNIAN (0) 1
McCluskey 2 (58, 67) — McLeod (51 pen)
CELTIC: Latchford; Sneddon, Aitken, Dowie, MacDonald, Burns; Glavin, Edvaldsson, G. McCluskey, McAdam, Doyle
HIBERNIAN: McDonald; Brownlie, Smith; McNamara, Stewart, Bremner; Murray, McLeod, Hutchinson, Duncan, Higgins
Attendance: 10,000

April 8th
CLYDEBANK (1) 3 — CELTIC (2) 2
McCormack (10), — McCluskey (14),
Lumsden (60), — Burns (16)
Colgan (86)
CLYDEBANK: Gallagher; Gourlay, Fallon; Hall, Abel, McCormack; Lumsden, Houston, O'Brien, McColl, Colgan
CELTIC: Latchford; Sneddon, Edvaldsson, MacDonald (Munro), Lynch (Doyle); Aitken, Glavin, Dowie, McAdam, G. McCluskey, Burns
Attendance: 8,500

April 12th
HIBERNIAN (1) 1 — CELTIC (1) 1
Higgins (19) — G. McCluskey (31)

HIBERNIAN: McDonald; Brownlie, Smith; McNamara, Stewart, Bremner; Murray, McLeod, Hutchinson, Duncan, Higgins

CELTIC: Latchford; Sneddon, Burns; Aitken, MacDonald, Dowie; Glavin, Edvaldsson, G. McCluskey, McAdam, Doyle (Wilson)

Attendance: 10,902

April 15th
HIBERNIAN (2) 4 — CELTIC (0) 1
Duncan (8), Higgins 2 (15, 84), McGhee (89) — Conroy (86)

HIBERNIAN: McDonald; Brownlie, McNamara, Stewart, Smith; McLeod, Bremner, Duncan; Murray, Hutchinson (McGhee), Higgins

CELTIC: Latchford; Sneddon, MacDonald, Edvaldsson, Burns; Aitken, Conroy, Dowie (Lynch); Wilson (Doyle), G. McCluskey, McAdam

Attendance: 16,286

April 17th
CELTIC (3) 5 — CLYDEBANK (0) 2
Edvaldsson (29), Glavin (40), MacDonald (41), McAdam (62), Aitken (77) — McColl (72), McCormack (74)

CELTIC: Latchford; Sneddon, Lynch; Aitken, MacDonald, Burns (Conn); Glavin, Edvaldsson, McAdam, Conroy, G. McCluskey

CLYDEBANK: Gallacher; Gourlay, Abel; Fallon, Hall, Houston; O'Brien, McCormack, McColl, Lumsden, Colgan

Attendance: 7,000

April 22nd
CELTIC (3) 5 — PARTICK THISTLE (0) 2
Glavin (17), Craig 2 (20, 63), Doyle 2 (22, 70) — Somner 2 (61, 65)

CELTIC: Latchford; Sneddon, MacDonald, Edvaldsson, Lynch; Doyle, Glavin, Conroy; McAdam, Craig, G. McCluskey

PARTICK THISTLE: Rough; Mackie, Marr, Campbell, Whittaker; McQuade, O'Hara, Love; Houston, Somner, McAdam

Attendance: 16,000

April 22nd: Johnny Gibson, Roy Kay, Willie Temperley and Ian McWilliams were also released.

April 26th
CLYDEBANK (0) 1 — CELTIC (0) 1
Houston (85) — Conroy (61)

CLYDEBANK: Gallacher; Gourlay, Abel; Fallon, McCormack, Houston; Geighan (Colgan), Lumsden, McNaughton, McColl, O'Brien

CELTIC: Latchford; Sneddon, Lynch; Edvaldsson, MacDonald, Conroy; G. McCluskey, Glavin, Craig, McAdam, Doyle (Mackie)

Attendance: 4,000

April 29th
ST MIRREN (1) 3 — CELTIC (1) 1
Fitzpatrick (36), McGarvey (65), Bell (86) — Glavin (31 pen)

ST MIRREN: McCulloch; Beckett, Dunlop, Copland, Munro; Fitzpatrick, Stark, Richardson (Bell); McGettrick, Bone, McGarvey

CELTIC: Latchford; Sneddon, Edvaldsson, MacDonald, Lynch (Craig); Aitken, Mackie, Conroy; Glavin, McAdam, G. McCluskey

Attendance: 13,026

Scottish Premier League

	P	W	D	L	F	A	Pts
1 Rangers	36	24	7	5	76	39	55
2 Aberdeen	36	22	9	5	68	29	53
3 Dundee United	36	16	8	12	42	32	40
4 Hibernian	36	15	7	14	51	43	37
5 CELTIC	36	15	6	15	63	54	36
6 Motherwell	36	13	7	16	45	52	33
7 Partick Thistle	36	14	5	17	52	64	33
8 St Mirren	36	11	8	17	52	63	30
9 Ayr United	36	9	6	21	36	68	24
10 Clydebank	36	6	7	23	23	64	19

May 28th: Billy McNeill, Manager of Aberdeen, was confirmed as the new Celtic Manager with another former Celtic player John Clark becoming his Assistant. Jock Stein was to be offered a Directorship with Davie McParland and Sean Fallon both leaving the club.

LEAGUE CUP

Second Round First Leg August 31st
CELTIC (0) 0 — MOTHERWELL (0) 0

CELTIC: Latchford; McGrain, Kay; Edvaldsson, MacDonald, Casey; Doyle, Lennox (Craig), Glavin, Burns, Wilson

MOTHERWELL: Muir; Watson, Wark; McLaren, McVie, Stevens; Kennedy (O'Neill), McAdam, Miller, Davidson, Purdie

Attendance: 23,000. Glavin missed a penalty

Second Round Second Leg September 3rd
MOTHERWELL (0) 2 — CELTIC (2) 4
Davidson 2 (74, 83) — Wilson (12), McLaren o.g. (26), Burns (66), Craig (89)

MOTHERWELL: Muir; Watson, Wark (Kennedy); McLaren, McVie, Stevens; Marinello (O'Neill), McAdam, Miller, Davidson, Purdie

CELTIC: Latchford; McGrain, Kay; Edvaldsson (Craig), MacDonald, Casey; Doyle, Lennox, Glavin, Burns, Wilson

Attendance: 20,494. Celtic won 4-2 on aggregate.

Third Round First Leg October 5th

STIRLING ALBION (0) 1	CELTIC (1) 2
Clark (54)	Doyle (30), Aitken (60)

STIRLING ALBION: Young; Nicol, Steedman; Browning (Gray), Kennedy, Moffat; McPhee, Duffin, Steele, Clark, Thomson (Burns)

CELTIC: Latchford; Kay, Casey, Aitken, MacDonald, Burns; Doyle, Edvaldsson, Glavin; Craig (Dowie), Lennox (G. McCluskey)

Attendance: 8,600

Third Round Second Leg October 26th

CELTIC (1) 1	STIRLING ALBION (0) 1
Kennedy o.g. (9)	McPhee (78)

CELTIC: Latchford; Kay, Lynch; Aitken, MacDonald, Munro (Mackie); Doyle, Glavin (Conn), Craig, Burns, Wilson

STIRLING ALBION: Young; Nicol, Steedman; Browning, Kennedy, Moffat; McPhee, Duffin, Steele, Thomson, Armstrong

Attendance: 12,000. Celtic won 3-2 on aggregate

Quarter-Final First Leg November 9th

ST MIRREN (0) 1	CELTIC (2) 3
Reid (57)	Craig 2 (17, 40), Edvaldsson (50)

ST MIRREN: D. Hunter; Young, Beckett; Fitzpatrick, Reid, Dunlop; McGarvey, Stark, Hyslop, Richardson, Munro

CELTIC: Latchford; Aitken, Lynch; McWilliams, MacDonald, Munro; Doyle, Edvaldsson, Craig (Glavin), Conn, Wilson

Attendance: 18,101

Quarter-Final Second Leg November 16th

CELTIC (0) 2	ST MIRREN (0) 0
Wilson (48), Doyle (65)	

CELTIC: Latchford; Mackie, Lynch; Edvaldsson, MacDonald, Munro; Doyle (Lennox), Wilson, Craig (McWilliams), Aitken, Conn

ST MIRREN: A. Hunter; McGettrick (Stark), Beckett; Fitzpatrick, Reid, Dunlop; Stevenson, Copland, Sharp, Richardson, Munro

Attendance: 17,000. Celtic won 5-1 on aggregate

Semi-Final at Hampden Park March 1st

CELTIC (2) 2	HEARTS (0) 0
Craig (16), McCluskey (36)	

CELTIC: Latchford; Sneddon, Dowie; Munro, MacDonald, Aitken; Wilson, Craig (Doyle), G. McCluskey, Burns, Conn (Edvaldsson)

HEARTS: Dunlop; Kidd, Fraser; Jeffries (Shaw), Rodger, Tierney; Park (Prentice), Bannon, Gibson, Busby, Robertson

Attendance: 18,840

By the interval Celtic had done enough to make the remainder of the match academic. They were denied a penalty in 5 minutes when McCluskey was brought down by Dunlop but 11 minutes later they went ahead. McCluskey cutely beat Fraser on the right and then slipped the ball into the path of Craig who made no mistake. Just on the half-hour Robertson missed a chance to equalise for Hearts when he was thwarted by Latchford. Celtic's 2nd goal came in the 36th minute. Jeffries was woefully short with a pass back to Dunlop and McCluskey nipped in and touched the ball away from the goalkeeper.

Final at Hampden Park March 18th

CELTIC (0) 1	RANGERS (1) 2
Edvaldsson (84)	*After extra time* Cooper (38), Smith (117)

CELTIC: Latchford; Sneddon, Munro, MacDonald, Lynch (Wilson); Glavin (Doyle), Dowie, Aitken; G. McCluskey, Edvaldsson, Burns

RANGERS: Kennedy; Jardine, Jackson, Forsyth, Greig; Hamilton (Miller), MacDonald, Smith; McLean, Johnstone, Cooper (Parlane)

Attendance: 60,168 *Referee:* D. Syme

In a tense, tight and untidy Final Rangers opened the scoring in the 38th minute. Glavin and Smith chased a ball to the byeline. The Celtic player decided to shield the ball and let it run for a goal-kick. Smith, however, managed to get a foot in and whipped the ball across goal for Cooper to send a tremendous drive high into the net. The score remained that way until 6 minutes from time when Edvaldsson headed in a Sneddon cross to send the match into extra-time. Jock Wallace decided to push on both substitutes in the Extra period and it was the drive and pace of Miller which brought the winning goal. 3 minutes from the end he crossed into the Celtic goalmouth. Alex MacDonald and Latchford both went for the ball, the Celtic goalkeeper could only palm it out and Smith headed it straight back into the net. Alan Sneddon gave a tremendous display of skill and composure just a month after making his senior debut. Jardine gave Russell, who had missed the Final with a virus, his winners' medal.

SCOTTISH CUP

Third Round February 6th

CELTIC (2) 7	DUNDEE (1) 1
G. McCluskey 3 (48, 63, 83), MacDonald (39), Burns (4), McAdam 2 (58, 73)	Schaedler (9)

CELTIC: Latchford; Sneddon, Burns; Munro, MacDonald, Aitken; Glavin, Edvaldsson, McCluskey, McAdam, Conn

DUNDEE: Donaldson; Caldwell, Schaedler; Shirra, McPhail, Phillip (McKinnon); McDougall, Sinclair (Redford), Pirie, Williamson, Scott

Attendance: 22,000

Fourth Round February 27th

CELTIC (0) 1	KILMARNOCK (1) 1
MacDonald (84)	McDowall (30)

CELTIC: Latchford; Sneddon, Aitken, Munro, MacDonald, Burns; Casey (Fillipi), Edvaldsson; G. McCluskey, McAdam, Conn (Craig)

KILMARNOCK: Stewart; McLean, Robertson; Jardine, Clarke, McDicken; Provan, McDowall, Doherty, Maxwell, Murdoch

Attendance: 25,000

Fourth Round Replay March 6th

KILMARNOCK (0) 1	CELTIC (0) 0
McDicken (83)	

KILMARNOCK: Stewart; McLean, Robertson; Jardine, Clarke, McDicken; Provan, McDowell (Doherty), Stein, Maxwell, McCulloch

CELTIC: Latchford; Sneddon, Dowie; Fillipi, MacDonald, Aitken; Edvaldsson, McAdam, G. McCluskey, Burns, Wilson

Attendance: 14,100. Aitken was ordered off.

EUROPEAN CUP

First Round First Leg September 14th

CELTIC (2) 5	JEUNESSE d'ESCH
MacDonald (20),	(Luxembourg) (0) 0
Wilson (37),	
Craig 2 (53, 60),	
McLaughlin (83)	

CELTIC: Latchford; McGrain, Lynch; Edvaldsson, MacDonald, McWilliams; Doyle (Lennox), Glavin (McLaughlin), Craig, Aitken, Wilson

JEUNESSE: Rogues; Pigat, Rohmann; Mond, Reding, Pentima (Richelli); Melde, Koster, Swally, Robert, Noel

Attendance: 22,000

Celtic ran the amateurs into the ground and they could have reached double figures but for a series of brilliant saves from Rogues. They also had 3 good penalty claims turned down.

First Round Second Leg September 28th

JEUNESSE d'ESCH (1) 1	CELTIC (1) 6
Giulana (40 secs)	Lennox (29),
	Glavin 2 (52, 60),
	Edvaldsson 2 (66, 76),
	Craig (57)

JEUNESSE; Rogues (Hoffman); Pigat, Rohmann; Mond, Cornado, Di Pentima; Melde, Koster (Reding), Swally, Giulana, Noel

CELTIC: Latchford; McGrain, Kay; Casey (McLaughlin), MacDonald, Aitken; Glavin, Wilson, Craig (J. McCluskey), Burns, Lennox

Attendance: 4,000

Celtic breezed into the 2nd round after a dismal 1st half in which they lost a goal in seconds when Glavin gave the ball away. Celtic won 11-1 on aggregate.

Second Round First Leg October 19th

CELTIC (0) 2	S.W.W. INNSBRUCK
Craig (49),	(Austria) (0) 1
Burns (78),	Kreiss (54)

CELTIC: Latchford; Aitken, Lynch; Edvaldsson, MacDonald, Casey; Doyle, Glavin, Craig, Burns, Wilson (Conn, Lennox)

S.W.W. INNSBRUCK: Koncillia; Kreiss, Constantini; P. Schwarz, Pezzey, Stering; Zanon, Forstinger, Welzl, W. Schwarz, Oberacher

Attendance: 30,000

Celtic started with Aitken at right-back in place of the injured McGrain. In 12 minutes Aitken headed a shot from Welzl off the line with Latchford beaten. Soon after a header from Edvaldsson crashed off the post. In 36 minutes Craig had an incredible miss when Burns left him in the clear only a yard out only for him to scoop the ball over the bar. Celtic eventually went ahead 4 minutes after the restart when Edvaldsson headed on a Doyle corner and Craig shot home from close range. Their lead however, was short lived for 5 minutes later Oberacher sent over a free-kick and Kreiss was all on his own to head past Latchford. Celtic immediately sent on Conn for Wilson but he lasted only 17 minutes before being injured in a tackle with Schwarz and was replaced by Lennox. Celtic never gave up trying and in 78 minutes they got their just reward when Burns scored with a glorious drive when Lynch's shot broke to him off a defender. They fought like furies to increase their lead and in doing so left gaps at the back, and twice Latchford had to come out and block Welzl.

Second Round Second Leg in Salzburg November 2nd

S.W.W. INNSBRUCK (3) 3	CELTIC (0) 0
Welzl (4),	
Stering (22),	
Oberacher (27)	

S.W.W. INNSBRUCK: Koncillia; Kreiss, Constantini; P. Schwarz, Pezzey, Stering; Zanon, Forstinger, Welzl, W. Schwarz, Oberacher

CELTIC: Latchford; Aitken, Lynch; Glavin, MacDonald, Casey; Doyle, Edvaldsson, Craig, Burns, Wilson

Attendance: 22,500

Celtic made defensive mistakes and were punished mercilessly by the Austrian champions. Their one-goal lead was wiped out in only 4 minutes when Oberacher fired over a cross from the left and Welzl stretched out a foot to touch it away from Latchford. The Austrians took the lead 18 minutes later when Oberacher took the ball to the bye-line and his cross was touched on by Welzl to Stering who was completely unmarked and had the easiest of tasks in shooting into the net. 5 minutes later they struck again. With Casey lying injured, Stering sent the ball into open space and Oberacher ran on to hit a tremendous shot past Latchford. The 2nd half saw a slight improvement from Celtic but in a match which was punctuated by nasty incidents and crude tackles from both sides Andy Lynch was sent off in 80 minutes for allegedly punching Rinker. S.W.W. Innsbruck won 4-2 on aggregate.

APPEARANCES	League	League Cup	Scottish Cup	European Cup
Latchford	36	8	3	4
McGrain	7	2	–	2
Lynch	26+1S	4	–	3
Kay	5	4	–	1
Stanton	1	–	–	–
MacDonald	36	8	3	4
Aitken	33	6	3	4
Casey	2+2S	3	1	3
Glavin	28	5+1S	1	4
Doyle	20+6S	6+2S	–	3
Edvaldsson	33+3S	6+1S	3	3
Wilson	14+6S	6+1S	1	4
Craig	19+1S	5+2S	0+1S	4
Burns	22+2S	6	3	3
Conn	9+1S	3+1S	2	0+1S
Lennox	1+2S	3+1S	–	1+2S
Dowie	12+2S	2+1S	1	–
McAdam	32+1S	–	3	–
McWilliams	1	1+1S	–	1
McLaughlin	1	–	–	0+2S
Munro	14+1S	5	2	–
Fillipi	11+1S	–	1+1S	–
G. McCluskey	12+3S	2+1S	3	–
Sneddon	15	2	3	–
Conroy	5	–	–	–
Mackie	1+1S	1+1S	–	–
J. McCluskey	–	–	–	0+1S

GOALSCORERS:

League: Edvaldsson 10, Glavin 9 (2 pens), Craig 8, McAdam 8, MacDonald 7, G. McCluskey 6, Burns 3, Lynch 3 (3 pens), Conroy 2, Doyle 2, Aitken 2, Own Goals 2, Wilson 1

League Cup: Craig 4, Wilson 2, Doyle 2, Own Goals 2, Edvaldsson 2, G. McCluskey 1, Burns 1, Aitken 1

Scottish Cup: G. McCluskey 3, MacDonald 2, McAdam 2, Burns 1

European Cup: Craig 4, Glavin 2, Edvaldsson 2, MacDonald 1, Wilson 1, McLaughlin 1, Lennox 1, Burns 1

Mrs Jock Stein unfurls the 1977 League Championship flag at Parkhead watched by Desmond White, the Club Chairman.

Season 1978-79

Billy McNeill brought the League Championship back to Parkhead in his first season as Manager. He spent big and well – bringing Davie Provan from Kilmarnock for £120,000 and Murdo MacLeod from Dumbarton, also for a 6 figure fee, and those two buys plus the return to first-team action of Danny McGrain in the New Year inspired Celtic to a late push which saw them snatch the League Championship from Rangers in the very last match of the season. It was a famous victory and gave them the League flag for the 31st time. The enforced break in mid-season because of the weather was a Godsend as Celtic recorded only 7 wins in their first 18 matches. From the resumption at the beginning of March until the end of the season they dropped only 7 points from 36. Roy Aitken was the only ever-present, and Andy Lynch and Tom McAdam finished as joint top scorers with 7 goals each. Bobby Lennox re-joined the club after a spell in America, and another old boy from the Stein days, Vic Davidson, was re-signed from Blackpool. Both played an important part in the League title win. Wilson, Craig and Glavin were all transferred. Jock Stein enjoyed a well-deserved Testimonial against Liverpool and left shortly after, to take up the job as Manager of Leeds United. Within 45 days he was to become Scotland's new International Team Manager.

Celtic beat both Dundee teams, Motherwell and Montrose to reach the Semi-Final of the League Cup but an own goal by young substitute Jim Casey 7 minutes from the end of extra-time of their tie with Rangers ended their record run of 155 successive Scottish League Cup matches without elimination from the competition which stretched back to season 1964-65.

They reached the Quarter-Final of the Scottish Cup but lost to Aberdeen, at home, after a replay.

In the absence of European football – for the first time since season 1961/62 – Celtic took part in the Anglo-Scottish Cup. They easily beat Clyde in the First Round but rather embarrasingly lost to Burnley, home and away, in the Quarter-Final.

League:	Champions
League Cup:	Semi-Finalists
Scottish Cup:	Quarter-Finalists
Anglo-Scottish Cup:	Quarter-Finalists

SCOTTISH PREMIER LEAGUE

July 7th: Jimmy Lumsden was recruited from Clydebank to bring on the 2nd team youngsters.

August 4th: Pat Stanton announced his retirement through injury.

August 12th

MORTON (0) 1	CELTIC (1) 2
Ritchie (75)	Glavin (32), MacDonald (70)

MORTON: Connaghan; Hayes, Evans, Orr, Holmes; Rooney, Miller, Rae; Ritchie, Russell, Scott

CELTIC: Latchford; Fillipi, Edvaldsson, MacDonald, Sneddon; Glavin, Aitken, Burns; Doyle (Casey), McAdam, Conn

Attendance: 12,000

August 16th: Pat Stanton joined Aberdeen as Assistant Manager.

August 19th
CELTIC (2) 4 — HEARTS (0) 0
McAdam (8), Burns (18), Conn 2 (75, 77)

CELTIC: Latchford; Fillipi, MacDonald, Edvaldsson, Lynch; Glavin, Aitken, Burns (Casey); Doyle (Wilson), McAdam, Conn

HEARTS: Dunlop; Kidd, McNicol, Liddell, Jeffries; Bannon, Fraser, Shaw (Tierney); Robertson (Park), Gibson, Prentice

Attendance: 24,000

August 21st: Jock Stein joined Leeds United as Manager at a reported salary of £30,000 per year.

August 26th
MOTHERWELL (1) 1 — CELTIC (1) 5
Edvaldsson o.g. (41) — Conn 2 (25, 78), Aitken 2 (50, 86), McAdam (53)

MOTHERWELL: Latchford; Millar, Mackin, Stevens, Wark; Boyd, Marinello, McLaren; Pettigrew, Larnach, Lindsay

CELTIC: Latchford; Fillipi, MacDonald, Edvaldsson, Lynch; Aitken, Glavin, Burns; Doyle, McAdam, Conn

Attendance: 19,710

September 9th
CELTIC (2) 3 — RANGERS (0) 1
McAdam 2 (2, 76), McCluskey (14) — Parlane (49)

CELTIC: Latchford; Fillipi, Edvaldsson, Aitken, Lynch; Glavin, Conroy, Burns (Casey), Doyle, McAdam, McCluskey (Craig)

RANGERS: McCloy; Jardine, Jackson, T. Forsyth, A. Forsyth; Russell, A. MacDonald (Miller), Johnstone; McLean (Cooper), Parlane, Smith

Attendance: 60,000

Rangers were caught cold at Parkhead. In 2 minutes Glavin half-hit a free-kick into the penalty area, Edvaldsson tapped it back to McAdam and the big striker fired a great shot high into the net. In 14 minutes McCluskey left Forsyth stranded and shot from a tight angle from just inside the box. McCloy seemed to go down in instalments and the ball shot under him and into the net. Rangers pulled a goal back in the 49th minute when Parlane scored. With 14 minutes left for play substitute Joe Craig set up the clincher with a tenacious run down the right and towards the penalty area. McAdam backed up well and was on the spot to steer the ball past McCloy when Craig released the pass. 7 minutes from time Latchford brilliantly saved an Alex Miller penalty.

September 14th: Bobby Lennox re-joined Celtic from U.S. soccer.

September 16th
CELTIC (0) 0 — HIBERNIAN (1) 1
Temperley (25)

CELTIC: Latchford; Fillipi, Aitken, Edvaldsson, Lynch; Conroy, Glavin (Doyle), Burns; McAdam, Conn, McCluskey

HIBERNIAN: McDonald; McNamara, Duncan; Fleming, Stewart, Smith; McLeod, Rae, Callachan, Higgins, Temperley

Attendance: 27,000

September 18th: Celtic signed Davie Provan from Kilmarnock for £120,000 – a record between Scottish clubs.

September 20th: Paul Wilson joined Motherwell for £50,000.

September 23rd
PARTICK THISTLE (2) 2 — CELTIC (1) 3
Melrose (35), Somner (39 pen) — Aitken (70), Lynch (48 pen), MacDonald (50)

PARTICK THISTLE: Rough; McKinnon, Campbell, Marr, Whittaker; Park, Gibson, Love (O'Hara); Houston, Melrose, Somner

CELTIC: Latchford; Fillipi, MacDonald, Edvaldsson, Lynch; Aitken, Burns, Provan; Conn, McAdam, McCluskey (Conroy)

Attendance: 22,000

September 28th: Joe Craig joined Blackburn Rovers for £40,000.

September 30th
CELTIC (1) 2 — ST MIRREN (0) 1
Lynch (35 pen), Conn (75) — Hyslop (81)

CELTIC: Latchford; Fillipi, Aitken, Edvaldsson, Lynch; Glavin, Conroy, Burns; Provan, McAdam, Conn

ST MIRREN: Thomson; Beckett, Dunlop, Copland, Munro; Fitzpatrick, Stark, Abercrombie (Richardson); Hyslop, Bone, McGarvey

Attendance: 26,000

October 4th: Jock Stein quit the Leeds job to become Scotland's International team Manager. He had been at the club only 45 days.

October 7th
ABERDEEN (3) 4 — CELTIC (1) 1
Archibald 2 (22, 54), Harper (23), Jarvie (32) — McAdam (43)

ABERDEEN: Leighton; Kennedy, McLeish, Miller, McLelland; Strachan, Sullivan, McMaster; Jarvie, Harper, Archibald

CELTIC: Latchford; Fillipi, MacDonald, Edvaldsson (Glavin), Sneddon; Aitken, Conroy, Burns (Lennox); Provan, McCluskey, McAdam

Attendance: 26,000

October 14th
DUNDEE UNITED (1) 1
Kopel (2)

DUNDEE UNITED: McAlpine; Stewart, Kopel; Fleming, Hegarty, Narey; Smith, Sturrock, Payne, Kirkwood, Addison

CELTIC: Latchford; Fillipi, Burns; Aitken, MacDonald, Edvaldsson (Mackie); Provan, Conroy, McAdam, Conn (McCluskey), Lennox

Attendance: 17,700

October 21st
CELTIC (0) 0 . MORTON (0) 0

CELTIC: Latchford; Fillipi, Sneddon; Aitken, MacDonald, Edvaldsson; Provan, Conroy, McAdam, Burns (McCluskey), Lennox

MORTON: Connaghan; Hayes, Holmes; Evans, Orr, Rooney; Russell, Miller, Thomson, Scott, Ritchie

Attendance: 24,000

October 28th
HEARTS (0) 2 CELTIC (0) 0
Busby 2 (53, 68)

HEARTS: Dunlop; Brown, Jeffries, McNicoll, Liddell; Fraser (Tierney), Gibson, Bannon; O'Connor, Busby, Robertson

CELTIC: Latchford; Fillipi, Lynch; Aitken, MacDonald, Edvaldsson; Provan, Conn, McAdam, Burns (Mackie), McCluskey

Attendance: 18,500. Robertson was ordered off.

League positions

	P	W	D	L	F	A	Pts
1 Dundee United	11	5	5	1	15	8	15
2 CELTIC	11	6	1	4	20	14	13
3 Hibernian	11	4	5	2	12	10	13
4 Rangers	11	3	6	2	12	10	12
5 Aberdeen	11	4	3	4	22	14	11

November 1st: Burns and McAdam were in the Scottish League team which drew 1-1 with the Irish League at Fir Park, Motherwell.

November 2nd: Murdo MacLeod was signed from Dumbarton for £100,000.

November 4th
CELTIC (1) 1 MOTHERWELL (1) 2
McAdam (12) Stevens (39), McLaren (82)

CELTIC: Baines; Sneddon, MacDonald, Edvaldsson, Lynch; Aitken, MacLeod, Burns; Provan, McAdam, Conn

MOTHERWELL: Rennie; Carr, McVie, Stevens, Wark; Marinello, McLaren, Pettigrew; Clinging (Lindsay), Larnach, Wilson

Attendance: 21,000

November 11th at Hampden Park
RANGERS (0) 1 CELTIC (0) 1
A. Forsyth (55 pen) Lynch (52)

RANGERS: McCloy; Miller, Jardine, T. Forsyth, A. Forsyth; McLean, Russell, A. MacDonald; Watson, Johnstone, Smith

CELTIC: Baines; Fillipi, MacDonald, Edvaldsson, Lynch; Aitken, MacLeod, Burns; Provan, McAdam, Doyle

Attendance: 52,330

Celtic had the edge in attack. Rangers were much the better organised at the back. Rangers sprang a couple of surprises at the start. They had Johnstone up front and Alex Miller at right-back and Sandy Jardine sweeping behind Tom Forsyth. Celtic had three Old Firm debutants in their side – MacLeod, Provan and Baines. They opened the scoring with a brilliant effort involving MacLeod and Andy Lynch. MacLeod split the Ibrox defence with a perfect pass inside the box, and there was Lynch in the open space to steer the ball past McCloy. Rangers hit back furiously and 3 minutes later they were level from the penalty spot. Edvaldsson handled a Johnstone header and Alex Forsyth stepped up to score his 4th penalty goal of the season.

November 18th
HIBERNIAN (1) 2 CELTIC (1) 2
Hutchinson (31), Callaghan (83) Provan (39), MacLeod (81)

HIBERNIAN: McDonald; Duncan, Fleming, McNamara, Smith; Bremner, McLeod, Callachan; Mathiesen, Refvik, Hutchinson

CELTIC: Baines; Fillipi (Casey), MacDonald, Edvaldsson, Lynch; Aitken, McAdam, MacLeod; Provan, McCluskey (Lennox), Doyle

Attendance: 22,000

November 25th
CELTIC (0) 1 PARTICK THISTLE (0) 0
McAdam (47)

CELTIC: Baines; Fillipi, MacDonald, Edvaldsson, Lynch; Aitken, Casey, MacLeod; Provan, McAdam, Doyle

PARTICK THISTLE: Rough; McKinnon, Campbell (Love), Anderson, Whittaker; Park, O'Hara, Marr; Houston, Somner, Melrose

Attendance: 26,000

December 9th
CELTIC (0) 0 ABERDEEN (0) 0

CELTIC: Baines; Fillipi, Edvaldsson, MacDonald, Lynch; Aitken, MacLeod, Burns; Provan, McAdam (Conn), Doyle

ABERDEEN: Clark; Kennedy, Miller, Rougvie, McLelland; Sullivan, Strachan, McMaster (Archibald), Jarvie; Harper, Fleming

Attendance: 24,000

December 16th
CELTIC (1) 1 DUNDEE UNITED (0) 1
Lynch (45 pen) Narey (74)

CELTIC: Baines; Fillipi, MacDonald, Edvaldsson, Lynch; Aitken, MacLeod, Glavin; Conn, McAdam (Lennox), Doyle

DUNDEE UNITED: McAlpine; Stewart, Hegarty, Narey, Stark; Holt, Payne, Fleming; Addison, Dodds (Phillip), Kirkwood

Attendance: 21,000

December 23rd
MORTON (0) 1 CELTIC (0) 0
Ritchie (89 pen)

MORTON: Brcic; Hayes, McLaren, Orr, Holmes; Rooney, Hutchinson, Thomson; McNeill, Ritchie, Scott

CELTIC: Baines; Fillipi, MacDonald, Edvaldsson, Lynch; Aitken, McAdam, Burns (Lennox); Provan, McAdam, Conn

Attendance: 16,000

Leading positions

	P	W	D	L	F	A	Pts
1 Dundee United	18	8	7	3	25	16	23
2 Partick Thistle	18	8	5	5	19	16	21
3 Aberdeen	19	6	8	5	30	19	20
4 Rangers	18	6	8	4	22	18	20
5 Morton	19	7	6	6	24	26	20
6 CELTIC	18	7	5	6	26	21	19

January 16th: Danny McGrain made his first-team comeback in the 4-0 win over Estoril in a Friendly match in Portugal.

March 3rd
CELTIC (0) 1 ABERDEEN (0) 0
Conn (65)

CELTIC: Latchford; McGrain, MacDonald, Edvaldsson, Lynch; Aitken, MacLeod, Burns (Fillipi); Provan, Conn, Doyle

ABERDEEN: Clark; Kennedy, Rougvie, Miller, McLelland; Sullivan, McMaster, Strachan (Considine); Archibald, Scanlon, Jarvie (Harper)

Attendance: 26,000

March 8th: Roy Baines re-joined Morton for a fee of £12,000.

March 17th
CELTIC (1) 2 MOTHERWELL (0) 1
Lennox 2 (13, 50) Donnelly (63)

CELTIC: Bonner; McGrain, MacDonald, Edvaldsson, Lynch; Aitken, MacLeod (McAdam), Burns; Provan, Lennox, Doyle

MOTHERWELL: Rennie; Kennedy, Dempsey, McLeod, Wark; Rafferty (Mungall), Kane, Donnelly (Sommerville); Clinging, Larnach, Wilson

Attendance: 16,000

March 28th
CELTIC (2) 3 MORTON (0) 0
Provan (6), Burns (43),
Glavin (80)

CELTIC: Latchford; McGrain, Fillipi; Aitken, MacDonald (McCluskey), Edvaldsson; Provan, Glavin, Lennox, Burns, Doyle

MORTON: Baines; Hayes, Holmes; Anderson, Orr, Thomson; McNeill, Miller, Hutchinson, Tolmie, Ritchie

Attendance: 16,000

March 31st
HIBERNIAN (2) 2 CELTIC (0) 1
Stewart (3), Rae (16) Glavin (82 pen)

HIBERNIAN: McArthur; Brazil, Stewart, McNamara, Duncan; Callachan, Bremner, MacLeod; Rae, Campbell, Brown

CELTIC: Latchford; McGrain, Edvaldsson, Aitken, Fillipi; Conroy (Lennox), Glavin, Burns; Provan (McCluskey), Davidson, Doyle

Attendance: 17,000

March 31st: Vic Davidson rejoined Celtic from Blackpool for a fee of £30,000.

April 4th
MOTHERWELL (1) 3 CELTIC (3) 4
Clinging (20), McGrain (23),
Stevens (79), Doyle (32),
Larnach (85) Davidson (43),
Lennox (79 pen)

MOTHERWELL: Rennie; McLeod, Wark; Carberry, Dempsey, Stevens; Smith, Pettigrew, Clinging, Irvine, Donnelly (Larnach)

CELTIC: Bonner; McGrain, MacLeod; Aitken, Edvaldsson, Conroy; Provan, Lennox, Davidson, Burns, Doyle

Attendance: 8,744

April 7th
CELTIC (1) 2 PARTICK THISTLE (0) 0
Conroy (7), Lynch (60)

CELTIC: Latchford; McGrain, Edvaldsson, Aitken, Lynch; Conroy, MacLeod, Burns; Provan, Davidson, Doyle

PARTICK THISTLE: Rough; McKinnon, Campbell (Houston), Anderson, Whittaker; O'Hara, Gibson, Love; Melrose (Somner), McAdam, Park

Attendance: 19,000

April 7th: Celtic announced that they would listen to offers for Alfie Conn.

April 11th
DUNDEE UNITED (1) 2 CELTIC (1) 1
Holt (38), Dodds (71) Davidson (21)

DUNDEE UNITED: McAlpine; Stewart, Stark; Fleming, Hegarty, Narey; Addison, Sturrock, Dodds, Holt, Kirkwood

CELTIC: Latchford; McGrain, Lynch; Aitken, Edvaldsson, MacLeod; Provan, Conroy (McCluskey), Davidson, Burns, Lennox (McAdam)

Attendance: 14,424

April 14th
ST MIRREN (0) 0 — CELTIC (1) 1
McCluskey (44)

ST MIRREN: Thomson; Young, Copland, Dunlop, Munro; Richardson, Fitzpatrick, Abercrombie (Weir); Stark (Torrance), Bone, McGarvey

CELTIC: Latchford; McGrain, Edvaldsson, Aitken, Lynch; Davidson, Conroy, MacLeod; Provan, McAdam, McCluskey

Attendance: 19,721

April 18th
HEARTS (0) 0 — CELTIC (1) 3
MacLeod (11), Conroy (61), Burns (76)

HEARTS: Allan; Kidd, Brown, Tierney, Liddell; Craig, Gibson, Fraser; Robertson, Busby, Prentice

CELTIC: Latchford; McGrain, Lynch; Aitken, Edvaldsson, MacLeod; Provan (Burns), Conroy, McAdam, Davidson, McCluskey

Attendance: 11,000

April 21st
ABERDEEN (1) 1 — CELTIC (1) 1
Strachan (24) — Lynch (40 pen)

ABERDEEN: Clark; Kennedy, Garner, Miller, Hamilton; Sullivan, McLeish, Strachan; Archibald, McGhee, Scanlon

CELTIC: Latchford; McGrain, Aitken, Edvaldsson, Lynch; Conroy, Burns, Davidson (McAdam), MacLeod; Provan, McCluskey (Doyle)

Attendance: 18,400

April 25th
CELTIC (0) 2 — ST MIRREN (0) 1
Edvaldsson (75), Aitken (88) — McGarvey (24)

CELTIC: Latchford; McGrain, Lynch; Aitken, Edvaldsson, MacLeod; Provan, Conroy, Davidson, Burns, Doyle

ST MIRREN: Thomson; Young, Munro; Fitzpatrick, Dunlop, Copland; Weir, Torrance, Bone, Abercrombie, McGarvey

Attendance: 18,000

April 28th
CELTIC (0) 2 — DUNDEE UNITED (1) 1
Doyle (58), Lynch (68 pen) — Dodds (43)

CELTIC: Latchford; McGrain, Edvaldsson, Aitken, Lynch; Conroy, Burns, MacLeod; Provan, McCluskey, Doyle

DUNDEE UNITED: McAlpine; Stewart, Hegarty, Narey, Stark; Addison, Fleming, Holt; Kirkwood (Payne), Sturrock (Kopel), Dodds

Attendance: 37,000

April 30th: Celtic freed Alfie Conn and John Dowie.

May 2nd
CELTIC (1) 3 — HIBERNIAN (1) 1
Conroy (32), Provan (67), McGrain (69) — Callachan (86)

CELTIC: Latchford; McGrain, MacLeod; Aitken, Edvaldsson, Conroy; Provan, Davidson, McCluskey, Burns, Doyle

HIBERNIAN: McArthur; Brazil, Duncan; Bremner, Stewart, McNamara; Rae, McLeod, Campbell, Callachan, Brown

Attendance: 23,000

May 5th at Hampden Park
RANGERS (0) 1 — CELTIC (0) 0
MacDonald (57)

RANGERS: McCloy; Jardine, Johnstone, Jackson, Dawson; A. MacDonald, Russell, Smith; McLean, Parlane, Cooper

CELTIC: Latchford; McGrain, Aitken, Edvaldsson, MacLeod; Davidson (McAdam), Conroy, Burns (Lynch); Provan, McCluskey, Doyle

Attendance: 52,841

This game was another triumph for Davie Cooper. He was in the mood and gave Danny McGrain more trouble than he had had since his return to the first team. The only goal of the game came in the 57th minute. McLean sent over a low cross. Russell dummied and MacDonald scooped the ball into the net. With Lynch and McAdam on for Burns and Davidson, Celtic found more power and they were desperately unlucky to see a Johnny Doyle shot come off a post. Throughout the match Rangers created many more chances and they were undoubtedly the more positive side throughout. As a result of their victory they now had a 1 point advantage over their opponents.

May 7th
PARTICK THISTLE (1) 1 — CELTIC (1) 2
Somner (3) — Provan (14), McCluskey (71)

PARTICK THISTLE: Rough; McKinnon, Whittaker; Campbell, McAdam, Marr; Melrose, Gibson, O'Hara, Somner, Park

CELTIC: Latchford; McGrain, Lynch; Aitken, McAdam, MacLeod; Provan, Conroy, McCluskey, Davidson, Doyle

Attendance: 17,000

May 10th: Kenny Dalglish was named as England's Footballer of the Year.

May 11th at Ibrox Park
ST MIRREN (0) 0 — CELTIC (0) 2
McCluskey (68), Lennox (80)

ST MIRREN: Thomson; Young, Munro; Fitzpatrick, Dunlop, Copland; Stark, Richardson, Torrance, Abercrombie, Docherty

CELTIC: Latchford; McGrain, Lynch; Aitken, McAdam, MacLeod; Provan, Davidson (Lennox), McCluskey, Burns, Doyle

Attendance: 22,000

May 8th: Alfie Conn signed for Derby County. Three days later Derby Manager Tommy Docherty moved on to Queens Park Rangers and the deal was cancelled.

May 14th
CELTIC (0) 1 HEARTS (0) 0
Conroy (55)

CELTIC: Latchford; McGrain, Lynch (Lennox); Aitken, McAdam, Edvaldsson; Provan, Conroy, McCluskey, MacLeod, Doyle

HEARTS: Allan; Kidd, Black; Moore, Liddell, Brown; O'Sullivan (Jeffries), Fraser, Gibson, Stewart, McLeod (Scott)

Attendance: 18,000

May 21st
CELTIC (0) 4 RANGERS (1) 2
Aitken (66), McCluskey (74), Jackson o.g. (85), MacLeod (90)
Russell (9), MacDonald (76)

CELTIC: Latchford; McGrain, Lynch; Aitken, McAdam, Edvaldsson; Provan, Conroy (Lennox), McCluskey, MacLeod, Doyle

RANGERS: McCloy; Jardine, Dawson; Johnstone, Jackson, A. MacDonald; McLean (Miller), Russell, Parlane, Smith, Cooper

Attendance: 52,000

Celtic were the Champions. Needing a victory to snatch the prize from Rangers, they found themselves a goal down and reduced to 10 men when Johnny Doyle was sent off 10 minutes after half-time. Spurred on by Roy Aitken, they fought back to win the match in the most dramatic style. Rangers had gone ahead in 9 minutes. Cooper went on a sweet run on the left, beat 2 men and sent over a perfect cross for Alex MacDonald to knock the ball past Latchford. 10 minutes after the restart Doyle foolishly aimed a kick at the prone figure of MacDonald who had been fouled by Conroy. After consultation with the linesman, the referee, who did not see the incident, gave him his marching orders. Celtic drew level in the 66th minute when a cute flick from Provan was turned into the net by Aitken. Celtic then sent on Lennox for Conroy and Rangers Miller for McLean. 9 minutes later an Aitken drive was blocked, the ball broke to McCluskey and he simply hammered it into the net. Within 2 minutes Rangers equalised. A Cooper corner broke to Russell who smashed a low drive through a posse of players and into the net. With only 5 minutes left Celtic sensationally took the lead when Jackson involuntarily headed the ball into his own net after a McCluskey cross had been pushed out by McCloy. Murdo MacLeod slammed in a 4th right on time.

Scottish Premier League

	P	W	D	L	F	A	Pts
1 CELTIC	36	21	6	9	61	37	48
2 Rangers	36	18	9	9	52	35	45
3 Dundee United	36	18	8	10	56	37	44
4 Aberdeen	36	13	14	9	59	36	40
5 Hibernian	36	12	13	11	44	48	37
6 St Mirren	36	15	6	15	45	41	36
7 Morton	36	12	12	12	52	53	36
8 Partick Thistle	36	13	8	15	42	39	34
9 Hearts	36	8	7	21	39	71	23
10 Motherwell	36	5	7	24	33	86	17

June 5th: Ronnie Glavin was transferred to Barnsley for £50,000.

June 11th: Celtic bid £100,000 for Frank McDougall of Clydebank.

LEAGUE CUP

First Round First Leg August 16th
CELTIC (0) 3 DUNDEE (0) 1
McAdam 2 (52, 84), Glavin (73)
Sinclair (64)

CELTIC: Latchford; Fillipi, Sneddon; Aitken, MacDonald, Edvaldsson; Doyle, Glavin, McAdam, Burns, Conn

DUNDEE: Donaldson; Barr, Watson; McDougall, Glennie, McPhail; Lambie (Shirra), McKinnon, Sinclair, McGhee, Redford

Attendance: 12,000

First Round Second Leg August 23rd
DUNDEE (0) 0 CELTIC (2) 3
Doyle 2 (23, 31), Conn (67)

DUNDEE: Donaldson; Barr, Watson; Lamb, Glennie, Phillip; McGhee, Shirra, Pirie, Sinclair, Redford

CELTIC: Latchford; Fillipi, Lynch; Aitken, MacDonald, Edvaldsson; Doyle (Casey), Glavin, McAdam, Burns, Conn

Attendance: 12,698. Celtic won 6-1 on aggregate.

Second Round First Leg August 30th
DUNDEE UNITED (1) 2 CELTIC (1) 3
Fleming (42), Sturrock (68)
Lynch (32), MacDonald (58), Conroy (67)

DUNDEE UNITED: McAlpine; Stewart, Kopel; Fleming, Hegarty, Narey; Sturrock, Addison, Frye (Kirkwood), Holt, Payne

CELTIC: Latchford; Fillipi, Lynch; Aitken, MacDonald, Edvaldsson; Doyle, Conroy, McAdam, Burns, Conn (Wilson)

Attendance: 12,648

Second Round Second Leg September 2nd
CELTIC (0) 1 DUNDEE UNITED (0) 0
Glavin (83 pen)

CELTIC: Latchford; Fillipi, Lynch; Aitken, MacDonald (Glavin), Edvaldsson; Doyle, Conroy, McAdam, Burns, Wilson (McCluskey)

DUNDEE UNITED: McAlpine; Kopel, Stewart; Fleming, Hegarty, Narey; Sturrock, Addison, Frye (Kirkwood), Holt, Payne

Attendance: 30,000. Celtic won 4-2 on aggregate.

Third Round First Leg October 4th

CELTIC (0) 0	MOTHERWELL (0) 1
	Pettigrew (68)

CELTIC: Latchford; Fillipi, Lynch; Aitken, MacDonald, Edvaldsson; Provan, Conroy (Glavin), McAdam (McCluskey), Burns, Conn

MOTHERWELL: Latchford; Shanks, Boyd; Capaldi (Larnach), McVie, Stevens; Marinello, Pettigrew, Clinging (McLeod), McLaren, Lindsay

Attendance: 19,000. McLaren and Conn were ordered off.

Third Round Second Leg October 11th

MOTHERWELL (0) 1	CELTIC (2) 4
Pettigrew (76)	McAdam 2 (17, 32), Lennox (83), Aitken (87)

MOTHERWELL: Latchford; Carr (McLeod), Wark; McLaren, McVie, Stevens; Marinello, Pettigrew, Larnach (Kennedy), Clinging, Lindsay

CELTIC: Latchford; Fillipi, Burns; Aitken, MacDonald, Edvaldsson; Provan, Conroy, McAdam, Glavin, Conn (Lennox)

Attendance: 17,911. Celtic won 4-2 on aggregate.

Quarter-Final First Leg November 8th

MONTROSE (1) 1	CELTIC (1) 1
Hair (23)	Lynch (28 pen)

MONTROSE: Gorman; Lowe, B. D'Arcy; Ford, D. D'Arcy, Taylor; McIntosh (Georgeson), Robb, Livingstone, Hair, Miller

CELTIC: Baines; Fillipi, Lynch; Aitken, MacDonald, Edvaldsson; Provan (Doyle), Glavin (Casey), McAdam, Burns, McCluskey

Attendance: 3,872

Quarter-Final Second Leg November 15th

CELTIC (3) 3	MONTROSE (0) 1
McAdam (5), Lynch (11 pen), Edvaldsson (37)	Georgeson (54)

CELTIC: Baines; McGrain, Lynch; Aitken, MacDonald, Edvaldsson; Provan, Casey, McAdam (McCluskey), Lennox, Doyle

MONTROSE: Gorman; Lowe, B. D'Arcy; Ford, D. D'Arcy, Hair; McIntosh, Robb, Georgeson, Walker, Livingstone (Murray)

Attendance: 10,000. Celtic won 4-2 on aggregate.

Semi-Final at Hampden Park December 13th

RANGERS (1) 3	CELTIC (1) 2
Jardine (26 pen), Jackson (80) Casey o.g. (113)	Doyle (10), McAdam (65) *After Extra Time*

RANGERS: McCloy; Miller, Dawson; Jardine, Jackson, MacDonald; McLean, Russell, Johnstone, Watson, Cooper (Smith). Sub: Parlane

CELTIC: Baines; Fillipi, Lynch; Aitken, MacDonald, Edvaldsson; Provan, Conroy (Casey), McAdam, Burns, Doyle. Sub: Conn

Attendance: 49,432

This was a tragic night for young Celtic substitute Jim Casey who put through his own goal just 7 minutes from the end of extra time to end his club's glorious record which has seen them take part in the last 14 Finals of the competition. Tommy Burns set up Celtic's 1st goal and looked in the mood before being sent off in the 26th minute. He picked up a bad Alex MacDonald pass deep in his own half and ran 50 yards before splitting the Ibrox defence with a brilliant pass to Doyle, who turned and beat McCloy with a low shot. In 26 minutes Cooper went down in the box when challenged by Edvaldsson and despite angry protests the referee awarded a penalty. Before the kick could be taken Burns was called over and sent off, presumably for saying something out of turn. Just a minute into the 2nd half Miller clashed with Doyle and was also given his marching orders. Rangers brought on Smith for Cooper in 61 minutes. 4 minutes after this Celtic took the lead. Doyle, a brilliant player on the night, left Roy Aitken with a chance. McCloy could only parry the ball to McAdam, who knocked it into the empty net. With 10 minutes remaining Rangers equalised. Johnstone won the ball in the air, and when Russell pushed it across goal Jackson hit a shot which was deflected past Baines. With only 7 minutes of extra-time remaining Rangers scored the goal which won the match. Baines blocked a shot from Johnstone but Casey, who had come on for Conroy, could not get out of the way and the ball cannoned off him and into the net.

SCOTTISH CUP

Third Round January 31st

MONTROSE (1) 2	CELTIC (0) 4
Miller (13), Murray (85)	McCluskey 3 (46, 55, 84), Lynch (88 pen)

MONTROSE: Gorman; B. D'Arcy, Johnston; Ford, D. D'Arcy, Hair; McIntosh, Robb, Livingstone (Murray), Lowe, Miller

CELTIC: Latchford; McGrain, Lynch; Fillipi, MacDonald, Edvaldsson; Provan, MacLeod, McCluskey, Lennox, Doyle

Attendance: 3,060

February 26th
CELTIC (1) 3 BERWICK RANGERS (0) 0
Lynch (9 pen),
Burns (64),
McDowell o.g. (86)

CELTIC: Latchford; McGrain, Lynch; Aitken, MacDonald, Edvaldsson; Provan, MacLeod, McCluskey (McAdam), Burns, Doyle

BERWICK: Frame; Rutherford, McLeod; D. Smith, McDowell, Jobson; Davidson, Moyes, G. Smith, Tait, Wheatley

Attendance: 13,000

Quarter-Final March 10th
ABERDEEN (1) 1 CELTIC (1) 1
Harper (26) Doyle (25)

ABERDEEN: Clark; Kennedy, McLeish, Miller, McLelland; Sullivan, McMaster, Strachan; Archibald, Harper, Scanlon (Davidson)

CELTIC: Latchford; McGrain, MacDonald, Edvaldsson, Lynch; Aitken, Burns, MacLeod; Provan, Conn, Doyle

Attendance: 24,000

Quarter-Final Replay March 14th
CELTIC (0) 1 ABERDEEN (2) 2
Lennox (64) Davidson (1),
Archibald (12)

CELTIC: Latchford; McGrain, Lynch; Aitken, MacDonald, Edvaldsson; Provan, MacLeod, Conn (Lennox), Burns, Doyle

ABERDEEN: Clark; Kennedy, McLelland; McMaster Rougvie, Miller; Sullivan (McLeish), Archibald, Harper (Scanlon), Jarvie, Davidson

Attendance: 37,000

ANGLO-SCOTTISH CUP

First Round First Leg August 3rd
CELTIC (0) 2 CLYDE (1) 1
Conn (53), Burns (87) Ward (4)

CELTIC: Latchford; Sneddon, Aitken, Edvaldsson, MacDonald, Burns; Conn, Lumsden, McAdam; Glavin McCluskey

CLYDE: Arrol; Anderson, Boyd; Clougherty, Kinnear, Aherne; Brogan, O'Neill, Marshall, McCabe, Ward

Attendance: 10,000

First Round Second Leg August 5th
CLYDE (0) 1 CELTIC (0) 6
O'Neill (68) Conn 2 (48, 85),
McAdam 2 (55, 80),
Glavin 2 (75, 86)

CLYDE: Arrol; Anderson, Kinnear; Clougherty, Boyd (Martin), O'Neill; Aherne, McCabe, Marshall, Ward, Hood (McNaughton)

CELTIC: Latchford; Sneddon, Edvaldsson, MacDonald, Lynch; Glavin, Aitken, Burns; Conn, McAdam, McCluskey (Wilson)

Attendance: n.a. Celtic won 8-2 on aggregate.

Quarter-Final First Leg September 12th
BURNLEY (0) 1 CELTIC (0) 0
Kindon (55)

BURNLEY: Stevenson; Scott, Brennan; Noble, Thomson, Rodaway; Cochrane, Hall, Fletcher, Kindon James

CELTIC: Latchford; Fillipi, Lynch; Aitken, Edvaldsson, Glavin; Doyle, Conroy, McAdam, Burns, McCluskey

Attendance: 25,000

Quarter-Final Second Leg September 27th
CELTIC (0) 1 BURNLEY (2) 2
Lynch (68 pen) Brennan (21)
Kindon (26)

CELTIC: Latchford; McGrain, Lynch; Aitken, Edvaldsson, Conroy; Provan, Conn, McAdam, Burns, Lennox

BURNLEY: Stevenson; Scott, Brennan; Noble, Thomson, Rodaway; Ingham, Smith, Fletcher, Kindon, James

Attendance: 28,000. Burnley won 3-1 on aggregate.

APPEARANCES	League	League Cup	Scottish Cup	Anglo-Scottish Cup
Latchford	27	6	4	4
Baines	7	3	–	–
Bonnar	2	–	–	–
McGrain	18	1	4	1
Lynch	27+1S	7	4	3
Sneddon	4	1	–	2
Fillipi	19+1S	8	1	1
MacDonald	18	9	4	2
Aitken	36	9	3	4
Casey	1+4S	1+3S	–	–
Glavin	9+1S	4+2S	–	3
Doyle	23+2S	6+1S	4	1
Edvaldsson	34	9	4	4
Wilson	0+1S	1+1S	–	0+1S
Provan	30	5	4	1
Burns	28+1S	8	3	4
Conn	12+1S	5	2	3
McAdam	24+4S	9	0+1S	4
Conroy	20+1S	5	–	2
G. McCluskey	16+5S	1+3S	2	3
Lennox	6+8S	1+1S	1	1+1S
Mackie	0+2S	–	–	–
Craig	0+1S	–	–	–
MacLeod	23	–	4	–
Davidson	12	–	–	–
Lumsden	–	–	–	1

GOALSCORERS

League: McAdam 7, Lynch 7 (5 pens), Conn 6, Aitken 5, McCluskey 5, Provan 4, Lennox 4 (1 pen), Conroy 4, Glavin 3 (1 pen), Burns 3, MacLeod 3, MacDonald 2, McGrain 2, Doyle 2, Davidson 2, Edvaldsson 1, Own Goals 1

League Cup: McAdam 6, Doyle 3, Lynch 3 (2 pens), Glavin 2 (2 pens), Conn 1, MacDonald 1, Conroy 1, Lennox 1, Aitken 1, Edvaldsson 1

Scottish Cup: McCluskey 3, Lynch 2 (2 pens), Burns 1, Doyle 1, Lennox 1, Own Goals 1

Anglo-Scottish Cup: Conn 3, McAdam 2, Glavin 2, Burns 1, Lynch 1 (pen)

The Celtic line-up for season 1978-79. Back row: F. Connor (coach), B. Wilson, A. Sneddon, J. Filippi, J. Edvaldsson, J. Casey, R. MacDonald, R. Aitken, R. Ward. Middle row: B. McNeill (manager), N. Mochan (trainer), I. McPhee, J. Weir, B. Coyne, B. Godzik, P. Bonner, P. Latchford, R. Baines, A. Lynch, P. Stanton, A. Conn, J. O'Donnell, J. Lumsden, B. Rooney (physiotherapist). Front row: M. Conroy, T. McAdam, P. Mackie, T. Burns, G. McCluskey, J. Craig, D. McGrain, P. Wilson, J. Doyle and R. Glavin.

Season 1979-80

Celtic would consider that they threw the Championship away. They had led the table on March 1st by 8 points from the field and were fully 10 points ahead of Aberdeen although the Dons had 2 games in hand. But in a disastrous run-in they were beaten by both Dundee teams and lost twice to Aberdeen in front of their own fans. Careless points were also dropped in a series of 7 draws in 9 matches, and Aberdeen eventually took the title by one point. Some consolation was the fact that they did not suffer a defeat at the hands of Rangers and took 6 of the 8 available points from them. Both Peter Latchford and Murdo MacLeod played in all 36 matches and George McCluskey finished as top scorer with 10 goals. Billy McNeill further strengthened his player pool by the acquisition of Dom Sullivan from Aberdeen for £80,000 and of Frank McGarvey for a record £250,000 fee from Liverpool. Both Provan and Aitken broke through to the full International side during the season and Davie Provan won the Scottish P.F.A. Players' Player of the Year Award. Andy Lynch joined the soccer exodus to the U.S.A.

Celtic reached the Quarter-Final of the Bell's League Cup but were beaten by Aberdeen home and away. They also reached the Final of the Drybrough Cup after beating Dundee United in extra time but lost 3-1 to Rangers. Their only defeat all season at the hands of their great rivals.

They beat Raith Rovers, St Mirren (in extra time of a replay), Morton and Hibs to reach their 41st Scottish Cup Final. They had to face Rangers in the Final without MacDonald and McAdam who were both suspended but they won a match which appeared to be heading for a goal-less draw when George McCluskey stuck out his left foot to deflect a first-time shot from Danny McGrain past McCloy 13 minutes from the end of extra time.

Partizan Tirana and Dundalk were early victims in the European Cup although both ties were not without their worrying moments. Celtic looked to have a great chance of reaching their 5th Semi-Final when they beat Real Madrid 2-0 in the First Leg of the Quarter-Final thanks to goals from McCluskey and Doyle which were both set up by young full-back Alan Sneddon. Unfortunately, they found, like many teams before, that a 2 goal lead was not enough to guarantee success at the Bernabeau Stadium, especially after McCluskey missed a great early chance. Their defence held out against the Real onslaught until a minute before half-time when Santillano made the breakthrough. 2nd half goals from Stielike and Juanito won the Tie for Real although Celtic were denied a clear penalty and a chance of victory when Benito handled in the box.

League:	Runners-Up
League Cup:	Quarter-Finalists
Scottish Cup:	Winners
European Cup:	Quarter-Finalists

SCOTTISH PREMIER LEAGUE

August 11th
CELTIC (2) 3 — MORTON (0) 2
McCluskey (30), Provan (32), MacLeod (68 pen) — Ritchie 2 (66, 86)

CELTIC: Latchford; Sneddon, MacDonald, McAdam, McGrain; Aitken, MacLeod, Conroy; Burns (Lennox), Provan, McCluskey

MORTON: Baines; Hayes, Orr, McLaren, Holmes; Hutchinson, Thomson, Ritchie, Rooney; Tolmie (McNeill), Russell (Scott)

Attendance: 26,000

August 18th
RANGERS (0) 2 — CELTIC (0) 2
J. MacDonald (49), Russell (53) — Sneddon (84), McAdam (87)

RANGER: McCloy; Miller, Jardine, Jackson, Dawson; Russell (Smith), Watson, A. MacDonald; Cooper, Johnsone, J. MacDonald

CELTIC: Latchford; Sneddon, MacDonald, Aitken, McGrain; Conroy, Edvaldsson (Lennox), MacLeod; Provan, McCluskey (Doyle), McAdam

Attendance: 36,000

After making a double substitution Celtic grabbed 2 goals in the last 6 minutes of a match which saw Roy Aitken ordered off in the 36th minute. Rangers took the lead in the 49th minute with a brilliant header. 4 minutes later a blistering drive from Bobby Russell put them further ahead. They should have added to that tally as they carved holes in the depleted Celtic ranks. Celtic, inspired by a magnificent Danny McGrain and utilising the pace and sharpness of substitutes Doyle and Lennox to the full, roared back for Alan Sneddon to score with a diving header in 84 minutes and for Tom McAdam to hammer in the equaliser 3 minutes later. As with the last season's Championship decider Rangers failed to win against 10 men.

August 21st: Celtic were reported to be ready to bid for Hamish McAlpine of Dundee United.

August 25th
CELTIC (3) 5 — KILMARNOCK (0) 0
McCluskey 3 (2, 46, 52 pen), Davidson 2 (29, 33)

CELTIC: Latchford; Sneddon, McGrain; Aitken (Lennox), MacDonald, McAdam; Provan, Davidson, McCluskey, MacLeod, Doyle

KILMARNOCK: McCulloch; McLean, Robertson; Jardine, Clarke, McDicken; Gibson, Maxwell, Bourke (Docherty), Clark, Street (Hughes)

Attendance: 26,000

September 8th
CELTIC (1) 2 — DUNDEE UNITED (1) 2
McCluskey 2 (21, 58) — Pettigrew (45 pen), Milne (76)

CELTIC: Latchford; Sneddon, Aitken, McAdam, McGrain; Davidson, Conroy (Lennox), MacLeod; Provan, McCluskey, Doyle

DUNDEE UNITED: McAlpine; Kirkwood, Stark, Narey, Kopel; Fleming, Phillip (Milne), Addison; Pettigrew, Payne, Sturrock

Attendance: 27,000

September 12th: Roy Aitken was in the Scotland team which drew 1-1 with Peru at Hampden Park.

September 15th
HIBERNIAN (1) 1 — CELTIC (1) 3
Higgins (20) — Lennox (38), Conroy (57), MacLeod (75 pen)

HIBERNIAN: McArthur; Brazil, Paterson, McNamara, Duncan; Bremner, Rae, MacLeod; Callachan (Hutchinson), Campbell, Higgins

CELTIC: Latchford; Sneddon, McAdam, Aitken, McGrain; Davidson, Conroy, MacLeod; Provan, McCluskey (MacDonald), Lennox

Attendance: 20,000

September 22nd
ABERDEEN (1) 1 — CELTIC (1) 2
Strachan (2) — Aitken (39), Doyle (74)

ABERDEEN: Clark; Kennedy, Garner, Miller, Considine (Rougvie); McLeish, Jarvie (Davidson), Strachan; McMaster, Archibald, Scanlon

CELTIC: Latchford; Sneddon, MacDonald, McAdam, McGrain; Aitken, Conroy, MacLeod; Doyle, Lennox, Burns

Attendance: 23,000. Burns was ordered off.

Celtic displayed all of their character when they played for 56 minutes with only 10 men and came back from a goal down to win both points. In the 34th minute Burns was ordered off but 10-man Celtic equalised five minutes later. Lennox fell in the box after a challenge by Kennedy. Clark blocked MacLeod's penalty kick but could not hold it and Aitken was on the spot to knock in the rebound. Celtic's winner came in 74 minutes and resulted from a bad throw-out from Clark to Miller. Lennox nipped in, took the ball from Miller and squared it across the face of the goal to give Doyle the easiest of chances.

September 29th
CELTIC (2) 3 — ST MIRREN (0) 1
MacLeod (2), MacDonald (29), McAdam (90) — Stark (76)

CELTIC: Latchford; Sneddon, McAdam, MacDonald, McGrain; Aitken, Davidson, MacLeod; Provan, McCluskey (Lennox), Doyle

ST MIRREN: Thomson; Beckett (Weir), Dunlop, Copland, Munro; Stark, Docherty, Richardson; McDougall, Bone, Somner

Attendance: 29,000. MacDonald and Somner were both ordered off.

October 6th
PARTICK THISTLE (0) 0 CELTIC (0) 0

PARTICK THISTLE: Rough; McKinnon, Campbell, Marr, Whittaker; Gibson (Jardine), O'Hara, Doyle; Park, McAdam, Melrose

CELTIC: Latchford; Sneddon, Edvaldsson, Aitken, McGrain (Casey); Conroy, Davidson (Lennox), MacLeod; Provan, McCluskey, Doyle

Attendance: 21,000

October 13th
CELTIC (1) 3 DUNDEE (0) 0
MacLeod (40 pen),
McAdam 2 (56, 82)

CELTIC: Latchford; Sneddon, MacDonald, McAdam, McGrain; Aitken, MacLeod, Burns; Provan, McCluskey, Doyle (Lennox)

DUNDEE: Donaldson; Turnbull (Barr), Glennie, McGeachie, Schaedler; Millar, McLaren, Fletcher (Shirra); Redford, Sinclair, Murphy

Attendance: 25,000

October 20th
MORTON (1) 1 CELTIC (0) 0
Thomson (32)

MORTON: Baines; Hayes, Anderson, Orr, Holmes; Brown, McLaren, Hutchinson (Tolmie); McNeill, Thomson, Ritchie

CELTIC: Latchford; Sneddon, MacDonald, McAdam, Lynch; Aitken, MacLeod, Burns; Provan (Conroy), McCluskey, Lennox

Attendance: 18,000

October 26th: Celtic signed Dom Sullivan from Aberdeen for £80,000.

October 27th
CELTIC (0) 1 RANGERS (0) 0
MacDonald (76)

CELTIC: Latchford; Sneddon, Aitken, MacDonald, McGrain; Sullivan, MacLeod, Burns (Conroy); Provan, McCluskey (Edvaldsson), McAdam

RANGERS: McCloy; Stevens, Jardine, Johnstone, A. Forsyth; Miller, McLean (Smith), A. MacDonald; Watson, Urquhart, Cooper

Attendance: 56,000

After their dismal result against Dundalk in the European Cup, Celtic restored Alan Sneddon to right-back with McGrain moving over to the left. New signing Dom Sullivan brought a silky-smooth touch to midfield. Celtic, with Davie Provan in the mood, spent most of the match in the Rangers half but due to fine work in the Ibrox defence they were allowed to create few chances. After an hour's play they began to find the gaps more easily and with 14 minutes left Provan flighted a perfect corner-kick, and there was MacDonald soaring high above everyone to head a fine goal. Rangers gave the Celtic defence more problems in the final 10 minutes than they did in the first 80.

League positions

	P	W	D	L	F	A	Pts
1 CELTIC	11	7	3	1	24	10	17
2 Morton	11	7	2	2	28	16	16
3 Aberdeen	11	5	3	3	23	13	13
4 Partick Thistle	11	4	4	3	13	14	12
5 Rangers	11	4	3	4	17	14	11

November 3rd
KILMARNOCK (1) 2 CELTIC (0) 0
Street (11), Gibson (59)

KILMARNOCK: McCulloch; McLean, Clark, McDicken, Robertson; Clark, Maxwell, Mauchlen; Street, Gibson, Bourke

CELTIC: Latchford; Sneddon, MacDonald, Aitken, McGrain; Sullivan, MacLeod, Burns; Provan, McAdam (Conroy), Doyle (Edvaldsson)

Attendance: 18,000

November 10th
DUNDEE UNITED (0) 0 CELTIC (0) 1
Edvaldsson (77)

DUNDEE UNITED: McAlpine; Stark, Hegarty, Narey, Kopel; Bannon, Phillip, Payne; Fleming, Pettigrew, Sturrock

CELTIC: Latchford; Sneddon, McAdam, Aitken, McGrain; Conroy, Sullivan, MacLeod; Provan, Edvaldsson, Lennox

Attendance: 17,000

November 17th
CELTIC (2) 3 HIBERNIAN (0) 0
Lennox (32),
Edvaldsson 2 (43, 63)

CELTIC: Latchford; Sneddon, Aitken, McAdam, McGrain; Sullivan, Conroy, MacLeod; Provan, Edvaldsson, Lennox

HIBERNIAN: McArthur; Brazil, Paterson, McNamara, McGlinchey; Rae, Callachan, McLeod; Ward, Duncan, Higgins

Attendance: 25,000

November 17th: Roddie MacDonald turned down a move to Dundee.

November 21st: Davie Provan made an appearance as substitute for Scotland in a match against Belgium in Brussels. Belgium won 2-0.

December 1st
ST MIRREN (1) 2 CELTIC (0) 1
Somner (2), MacDonald (78)
McDougall (55)

ST MIRREN: Thomson; Young, Fulton, Copland, Munro; Stark, Richardson, Bone; Weir, McDougall, Somner

CELTIC: Latchford; Sneddon, McAdam, Aitken, McGrain; Conroy (MacDonald), Sullivan, MacLeod; Provan, Edvaldsson (Lennox), McCluskey

Attendance: 20,500

December 15th
CELTIC (2) 5 — PARTICK THISTLE (0) 1
McAdam 2 (9, 21), MacDonald (65), Lennox (70), Sullivan (77) — Park (82)

CELTIC: Latchford; Sneddon, McAdam, MacDonald, McGrain; Sullivan, Aitken, MacLeod; Provan (Conroy), McCluskey, Lennox

PARTICK THISTLE: Rough; Mackie, Campbell, Anderson, Whittaker; Doyle, Park, Jardine; O'Hara, Melrose, McGregor (Wilson)

Attendance: 19,000

December 19th: McGrain and Aitken were in the Scotland team beaten 3-1 by Belgium at Hampden Park. Provan made an appearance as a substitute.

December 22nd
CELTIC (1) 3 — MORTON (0) 1
McAdam (44), Sullivan (70), Doyle (89) — Tolmie (46)

CELTIC: Latchford; Sneddon, MacDonald, McAdam, McGrain; Sullivan, Aitken, MacLeod; Provan, McCluskey (Doyle), Lennox

MORTON: Baines; Miller (Brown), Anderson, McLaughlin, Orr, Holmes; Hutchinson, McLaren, Ritchie; Scott, Tolmie

Attendance: 27,000. Holmes was ordered off.

December 29th
RANGERS (0) 1 — CELTIC (0) 1
Johnstone (73) — Lennox (74)

RANGERS: McCloy; Jardine, T. Forsyth, Jackson, Dawson; Russell (Miller), Stevens, A. MacDonald; McLean, Johnstone, J. MacDonald

CELTIC: Latchford; Sneddon, MacDonald, McAdam, McGrain; Sullivan, Aitken, MacLeod; Doyle, Lennox, Provan

Attendance: 34,000

Rangers produced their best performance for some time and should have been in front at half-time. Latchford denied them a lead 3 times in that first-half with a wonderful save from a Colin Jackson header and 2 great interceptions as Derek Johnstone looked all set to score. Latchford was out of luck when Rangers took the lead in the 73rd minute when Tommy McLean crossed from the right – the keeper slipped and had no chance with Johnstone's header. Celtic's reply was immediate and deadly. A Dom Sullivan free-kick was headed inside by Roy Aitken and Lennox ended the decade as he had started it – in scoring mood. Rangers appealed for offside but to no avail. Celtic were denied a 2nd-half penalty when an Aitken shot hit Stevens on the arm.

League positions

	P	W	D	L	F	A	Pts
1 CELTIC	18	11	4	3	38	17	26
2 Morton	18	10	3	5	36	24	23
3 Rangers	18	8	4	8	28	26	20
4 Aberdeen	15	7	3	5	27	18	17
5 Dundee United	18	6	5	7	24	19	17

January 5th
CELTIC (1) 1 — DUNDEE UNITED (0) 0
McLeod (36 pen)

CELTIC: Latchford; Sneddon, MacDonald, McAdam, McGrain; Sullivan, Aitken, MacLeod; Provan, Lennox, Doyle (Edvaldsson)

DUNDEE UNITED: McAlpine; Stark, Hegarty, Narey, Kopel; Fleming, Bannon, Holt; Kirkwood (Dodds), Sturrock, Pettigrew

Attendance: 25,000

January 12th
HIBERNIAN (1) 1 — CELTIC (1) 1
Best (26) — Aitken (36)

HIBERNIAN: McArthur; Brazil, Rae, Paterson, Lambie; McNamara, Callachan, MacLeod; Higgins, Campbell, Best

CELTIC: Latchford; Sneddon, MacDonald, McAdam, McGrain; Aitken, Sullivan, MacLeod; Provan, Lennox, Doyle

Attendance: 21,936. McLeod of Hibs missed a penalty.

January 19th
ABERDEEN (0) 0 — CELTIC (0) 0

ABERDEEN: Clark; Kennedy, Garner, Rougvie, Considine; McLeish, Strachan, McMaster; Archibald, Hamilton, Scanlon (Jarvie)

CELTIC: Latchford; Sneddon, MacDonald, McAdam, McGrain; Aitken, Sullivan, MacLeod; Provan, Lennox, Doyle

Attendance: 24,000

Celtic gave away nothing at the back and cancelled out Aberdeen's abundant skills in midfield with some class of their own. The 2 best chances of the match fell to Celtic. In 12 minutes Sullivan left Doyle in the clear 6 yards out. He took the ball on his chest but before he could move, Clark was off his line in a flash. In the 2nd half the keeper again came to Aberdeen's rescue when Celtic broke quickly and Aitken was left running in on goal.

February 9th
PARTICK THISTLE (0) 1 — CELTIC (0) 1
Melrose (89) — MacLeod (75)

PARTICK THISTLE: Rough; McKinnon, Campbell, Anderson (Wilson), Whittaker; Jardine (Gibson), Doyle, O'Hara; Park, McAdam, Melrose

CELTIC: Latchford; Sneddon, MacDonald, McAdam, McGrain; Aitken, Sullivan (Conroy), MacLeod; Provan, Lennox, Doyle

Attendance: 17,000

February 23rd
CELTIC (2) 2 — DUNDEE (1) 2
McCluskey (20), MacLeod (21) — Murphy (14), Aitken o.g. (82)

CELTIC: Latchford; Sneddon, Aitken, MacDonald, McGrain; Sullivan, McLeod, Provan; Doyle, McCluskey, Lennox

DUNDEE: Donaldson; Millar, McGeachie, Glennie, Schaedler; Fletcher (Barr), Mackie, Shirra; Sinclair, Fleming, Murphy

Attendance: 23,000

March 1st
MORTON (0) 0 — CELTIC (1) 1
Doyle (9)

MORTON: Baines; Miller, Orr, McLaughlin, Anderson, Holmes; Ritchie, Brown, Thomson; McNeill (Tolmie), Hutchinson

CELTIC: Latchford; Sneddon, MacDonald, McAdam, McGrain; Provan, Casey, MacLeod; Lennox, McCluskey, Doyle

Attendance: 20,000

League positions

	P	W	D	L	F	A	Pts
1 CELTIC	24	13	8	3	44	21	34
2 Morton	25	11	4	10	43	36	26
3 St Mirren	23	9	8	6	35	35	26
4 Aberdeen	22	9	6	7	36	26	24
5 Rangers	24	10	4	10	35	32	24

March 11th: Frank McGarvey was signed from Liverpool for a record £250,000 fee.

March 12th
CELTIC (1) 2 — ST MIRREN (0) 2
McCluskey (20), Doyle (52) — Somner 2 (69 pen, 75)

CELTIC: Latchford; Sneddon, McGrain; Aitken, MacDonald, McAdam; Provan, McCluskey, McGarvey, MacLeod, Doyle

ST MIRREN: Thomson; Beckett, Munro; Richardson, Fulton, Copland; Bone, Stark, Somner, Weir, Logan

Attendance: 30,000

March 15th
KILMARNOCK (1) 1 — CELTIC (0) 1
Street (1) — Lennox (86)

KILMARNOCK: McCulloch; Welsh, Clarke, McDicken, McLean; Clark, Mauchlen, Cramond; Houston, Gibson (Docherty), Street

CELTIC: Latchford; Sneddon, MacDonald, McAdam, McGrain; Aitken, MacLeod, Provan; McCluskey (Lennox), McGarvey, Doyle

Attendance: 15,000

March 23rd: Davie Provan was named as Players' Player of the year.

March 26th: McGrain was in the Scotland team which beat Portugal 4-1 at Hampden Park. Provan made an appearance as a substitute.

March 29th
CELTIC (0) 4 — HIBERNIAN (0) 0
Lennox (46 pen), McGarvey (63), Doyle (67), MacDonald (70)

CELTIC: Latchford; McGrain, MacDonald, McAdam, MacLeod; Casey (Burns), Aitken, Lennox; Provan, McGarvey, Doyle (McCluskey)

HIBERNIAN: McArthur; Brazil, McNamara (Hutchinson), Rae, Duncan; Tierney (Callachan), Cormack, Campbell; Murray, Best, Torrance

Attendance: 22,000

April 2nd
CELTIC (0) 1 — RANGERS (0) 0
McGarvey (85)

CELTIC: Latchford; Sneddon, McGrain; Aitken, MacDonald, McAdam; Provan, Lennox, McGarvey, MacLeod, Doyle

RANGERS: McCloy; Jardine, Dawson; T. Forsyth, Jackson, Smith; Cooper, Miller, Johnstone, Redford, J. MacDonald

Attendance: 52,000

This was a magic night for Frank McGarvey, Scotland's most expensive footballer, who headed the only goal of the match with just 5 minutes left. It looked odds on a no-scoring draw when McGarvey, playing in his first Old Firm match, pounced on a Roy Aitken cross at the far post and knocked it past McCloy. The match was untidy and bad-tempered but also thrilling, and both sides had penalty claims turned down. There was controversy in the 34th minute when Rangers broke down the right and Miller sent Smith clear. As the Rangers man turned inside MacDonald he was sent tumbling. It was a clear penalty but referee Anderson waved play on. In the 2nd half McCloy had 2 brilliant saves: a magnificent diving save when MacDonald met a Lennox corner with his head and an even better one when he touched over a McGarvey header from point-blank range.

April 5th
CELTIC (1) 1 — ABERDEEN (1) 2
Doyle (23) — Jarvie (19), McGhee (56)

CELTIC: Latchford; Sneddon, MacDonald, McAdam (Lennox), McGrain; Aitken, McLeod, Burns; Provan, McGarvey, Doyle

ABERDEEN: Clark; Kennedy, McLeish, Miller, Rougvie; Strachan, Watson, Jarvie (McMaster); Archibald, McGhee, Scanlon

Attendance: 40,000

McAdam had to be taken off at the start of the second-half suffering from concussion after clashing with McGhee. Aitken moved into the back four and Lennox came on but Celtic immediately missed Aitken's strength and drive in midfield. Celtic missed a great chance to equalise in 64 minutes when Clark was adjudged to have fouled McGarvey on the byeline. Lennox took the penalty but Clark saved easily.

April 8th
DUNDEE UNITED (0) 3 — CELTIC (0) 0
Dodds 2 (49, 61), Holt (78)

DUNDEE UNITED: McAlpine; Stark, Kopel; Phillip, Hegarty, Narey; Bannon, Sturrock, Pettigrew, Holt, Dodds

CELTIC: Latchford; Sneddon, McGrain; Aitken, MacDonald, McAdam; Provan, McCluskey (Burns), McGarvey (Edvaldsson), MacLeod, Lennox

Attendance: 14,616

April 16th
CELTIC (1) 2 — KILMARNOCK (0) 0
MacDonald (1), — Doyle (46)

CELTIC: Latchford; Sneddon, MacLeod; Aitken, MacDonald, McAdam; Provan, Lennox, McGarvey, Burns, Doyle

KILMARNOCK: McCulloch; Welsh, Robertson; J. Clarke, P. Clarke, McDicken; Houston, Mauchlen, Cramond, Bourke, McLean, Street

Attendance: 18,000

April 9th
DUNDEE (3) 5 — CELTIC (1) 1
Ferguson 2 (15, 26 pen), Fleming (43), Sinclair (58), Mackie (71) — Aitken (7)

DUNDEE: Donaldson; Barr, McGeachie, Glennie, Schaedler; Millar, Fleming, Shirra; Mackie, Sinclair, Ferguson

CELTIC: Latchford; Sneddon (Burns), MacDonald, McAdam, McGrain; Aitken, MacLeod, Provan; Lennox, McGarvey, Doyle

Attendance: 14,633

April 23rd
CELTIC (1) 1 — ABERDEEN (2) 3
McCluskey (10 pen) — Archibald (8), McGhee (45), Strachan (64)

CELTIC: Latchford; McGrain, MacLeod; Aitken, MacDonald, McAdam; Provan, Conroy (McGarvey), McCluskey, Burns, Doyle

ABERDEEN: Clark; Kennedy, Rougvie; Watson, McLeish, Miller; Strachan, Archibald, McGhee, McMaster, Scanlon

Attendance: 48,000. Strachan missed a penalty.

The Celtic defence looked shaky and the Dons punished them severely.

April 26th
CELTIC (0) 2 — PARTICK THISTLE (0) 1
McCluskey (46), McAdam (56) — Melrose (88)

CELTIC: Latchford; McGrain, McAdam, Aitken, MacLeod; Sullivan, Conroy, Burns; Provan, McCluskey, McGarvey

PARTICK THISTLE: Rough; Doyle, Campbell, Whittaker, Lapsley; Gibson (Park), O'Hara (McKinnon), Higgins, McDonald; Melrose, McAdam

Attendance: 20,000

April 30th
DUNDEE (0) — CELTIC (0) 2
Conroy (62), Sullivan (88)

DUNDEE: Donaldson; Barr, Schaedler; Millar, Glennie, McGeachie; Mackie, Sinclair, Fleming, Shirra, Ferguson

CELTIC: Latchford; McGrain, MacLeod; Aitken, McAdam, Conroy; Provan, Sullivan, McCluskey, Burns, McGarvey

Attendance: 10,200

May 3rd
ST MIRREN (0) 0 — CELTIC (0) 0

ST MIRREN: Thomson; Young, Copland, Fulton, Beckett; Stark, Abercrombie, Munro; Weir, Bone, Somner

CELTIC: Latchford; Sneddon, McAdam, Aitken, McGrain; Conroy, MacLeod, Burns; Provan, McGarvey, McCluskey

Attendance: 20,166

Scottish Premier League

	P	W	D	L	F	A	Pts
1 Aberdeen	36	19	10	7	68	36	48
2 CELTIC	36	18	11	7	61	38	47
3 St Mirren	36	15	12	9	56	49	42
4 Dundee United	36	12	13	11	43	30	37
5 Rangers	36	15	7	14	50	46	37
6 Morton	36	14	8	14	51	46	36
7 Partick Thistle	36	11	14	11	43	47	36
8 Kilmarnock	36	11	11	14	36	52	33
9 Dundee	36	10	6	20	47	73	26
10 Hibernian	36	6	6	24	29	67	18

May 16th: Danny McGrain was in the Scotland team beaten 1-0 by Northern Ireland in Belfast. Provan made an appearance as a substitute.

May 21st: Danny McGrain was in the Scotland team which beat Wales 1-0 at Hampden Park. Roy Aitken made an appearance as a substitute.

May 24th: McGrain and Aitken were in the Scotland team beaten 2-0 by England at Hampden Park.

May 28th: McGrain and Aitken were in the Scotland team beaten 1-0 by Poland in Poznan.

May 31st: Danny McGrain was in the Scotland team beaten 3-1 by Hungary in Budapest.

June 6th: Celtic made a bid of £200,000 for Jim Melrose of Partick Thistle.

June 10th: Melrose signed for Leicester City.

BELL'S LEAGUE CUP

Second Round First Leg August 29th
FALKIRK (0) 1 CELTIC (1) 2
Hay (63 pen) McCluskey (16), Provan (73)

FALKIRK: McKell; Johnston, Burrell; Stevenson, Brown, Hay; Perry, McRoberts, McDowall, Mitchell, Leetion

CELTIC: Latchford; Sneddon, McGrain; Aitken, MacDonald (Lennox), McAdam; Provan, Davidson, McCluskey, MacLeod, Doyle (Conroy)

Attendance: 9,000

Second Round Second Leg September 1st
CELTIC (0) 4 FALKIRK (1) 1
Lennox (63), Conroy 2 (64, 76), Doyle (70) Leetion (10)

CELTIC: Latchford; Sneddon, Aitken, McAdam, McGrain; Davidson, Conroy, MacLeod; Provan, Lennox, McCluskey (Doyle)

FALKIRK: McKell; Johnston, Brown, Meakin, Burrell; McRoberts, Mitchell, Leetion (Watson); Perry, McDowall (Paterson), McCallan

Attendance: 17,000. Celtic won 6-2 on aggregate.

Third Round First Leg September 26th
STIRLING ALBION (0) 1 CELTIC (0) 2
Armstrong (51 pen) McAdam (63), Doyle (78)

STIRLING ALBION: Arthur; Skilling, Steedman; Duffin, Nicol, Moffat; McPhee, Gray, A. Kennedy, Irvine, Armstrong

CELTIC: Latchford; Sneddon, McGrain; Aitken, MacDonald, McAdam; McCluskey, Davidson, Lennox, MacLeod, Doyle

Attendance: 8,000. Moffat was ordered off.

Third Round Second Leg October 10th
CELTIC (0) 2 STIRLING ALBION (0) 0
MacLeod (54 pen), Doyle (63)

CELTIC: Latchford; Sneddon, McGrain; Aitken, MacDonald, McAdam; Provan, Davidson, McCluskey, MacLeod (Lennox), Doyle

STIRLING ALBION: Arthur; Nicol, Steedman; Irvine, Kennedy, J. Moffat; McPhee, Duffin, A. Kennedy (Heggie), Skilling, Armstrong

Attendance: 11,000. Celtic won 4-1 on aggregate.

Quarter-Final First Leg October 31st
ABERDEEN (2) 3 CELTIC (1) 2
Archibald 3 (6, 30, 60) Edvaldsson (1), Provan (70)

ABERDEEN: Clark; Kennedy, Considine; McLeish, Garner, Miller; Strachan, Archibald, Harper (Jarvie), McMaster, Scanlon (Bell)

CELTIC: Latchford; Sneddon, McGrain; Aitken, MacDonald, MacLeod; Provan, Edvaldsson, Doyle (Lennox), Conroy, McAdam

Attendance: 24,000

Quarter-Final Second Leg November 24th
CELTIC (0) 0 ABERDEEN (0) 1
McGhee (50)

CELTIC: Latchford; Sneddon, Aitken, McAdam, McGrain; Conroy, MacLeod, Provan, Edvaldsson; McCluskey (MacDonald), Lennox

ABERDEEN: Clark; Kennedy, Garner, Miller, Rougvie; McLeish, Strachan, McMaster (Jarvie); Archibald, Harper (McGhee), Scanlon

Attendance: 39,000. Aberdeen won 4-2 on aggregate.

SCOTTISH CUP

Third Round January 26th
CELTIC (2) 2 RAITH ROVERS (0) 1
Lennox (15), Doyle (34) Ballantyne (57)

CELTIC: Latchford; Sneddon, MacDonald, McAdam, McGrain; Aitken, Edvaldsson (Conroy), MacLeod; Provan, Lennox, Doyle

RAITH ROVERS: McDermott; Houston, Forsyth; D. Thomson, Candlish, Ford; Urquhart, McFarlane, R. Thomson, Ballantyne, Miller (Duncan)

Attendance: 18,000

Fourth Round February 16th
CELTIC (0) 1 ST MIRREN (1) 1
MacLeod (88) McDougall (37)

CELTIC: Latchford; Sneddon, MacDonald, McAdam, McGrain; Aitken, Sullivan (McCluskey), MacLeod; Provan, Doyle, Lennox

ST MIRREN: Thomson; Young, Copland, Fulton, Munro; Stark, Bone, Richardson, Weir; McDougall, Somner

Attendance: 32,000

Fourth Round Replay February 20th
ST MIRREN (1) 2 CELTIC (1) 3
Bone (11), Somner (59 pen) Doyle 2 (30, 91), Lennox (72 pen)
After Extra Time

ST MIRREN: Thomson; Young, Munro; Richardson, Fulton, Copland; Bone, Stark, Somner, McDougall (Docherty), Weir

CELTIC: Latchford; Sneddon, McGrain; Aitken, MacDonald, McAdam; Provan, McCluskey, Lennox, MacLeod, Doyle

Attendance: 27,166. McAdam was ordered off.

Quarter-Final March 8th
CELTIC (2) 2 MORTON (0) 0
Casey (40), McCluskey (44)

CELTIC: Latchford; Sneddon, MacDonald, McAdam, McGrain; Casey, Lennox, MacLeod; Provan, McCluskey, Doyle

MORTON: Baines; Miller, Anderson, McLaughlin, Orr, Holmes; Brown, Ritchie, Thomson; Hutchinson (McLaren), McNeill (Tolmie)

Attendance: 35,000

Semi-Final at Hampden Park April 12th
CELTIC (1) 5 HIBERNIAN (0) 0
Lennox (9), Provan (48), Doyle (54), MacLeod (79), McAdam (86)

CELTIC: Latchford; Sneddon, MacDonald, McAdam, McGrain; Aitken, MacLeod, Lennox (Burns); Provan, McGarvey, Doyle (McCluskey)

HIBERNIAN: McArthur; Brazil, McNamara, Stewart, Duncan; Callachan, Rae, Best; Torrance, Hutchinson, Lambie. Subs: Campbell, Paterson

Attendance: 32,925

Celtic coasted into the final when they easily overcame a poor Hibs side and scored 5 without reply.

Final at Hampden Park May 10th
CELTIC (0) 1 RANGERS (0) 0
McCluskey (107) *After Extra Time*

CELTIC: Latchford; Sneddon, McGrain; Aitken, Conroy, MacLeod; Provan, Doyle (Lennox), McCluskey, Burns, McGarvey (Davidson)

RANGERS: McCloy; Jardine, Dawson; T. Forsyth (Miller), Jackson, Stevens; Cooper, Russell, Johnstone, Smith, J. MacDonald (McLean)

Attendance: 70,303

This was an enthralling match with both sides playing open football. The longer the game went, the better it appeared for Celtic. 17 minutes into extra time Ally Dawson headed out a corner from the right and Danny McGrain met the clearance first time to sent it back towards goal. McCloy had the ball covered but George McCluskey stuck out his left foot and deflected it towards the other corner. This was cruel luck for Rangers who deserved another chance. Rangers best chance had come in extra time. A McLean cross from the right caught Roy Aitken stranded. Johnstone was clear at the far post but he seemed paralysed at the chance. Peter Latchford was absolutely helpless but the Rangers skipper allowed the ball to bounce harmlessly past him and out of play. Miller replaced Tom Forsyth for the final 8 minutes.

EUROPEAN CUP

First Round First Leg September 19th
PARTIZAN TIRANA (ALBANIA) (1) 1 CELTIC (0) 0
Murati (35)

PARTIZAN: Musta; Millani, Hyfi; Spiro, Berisha, Ragami; Satedini, Lame, Breta, Murati, Shyqyriu

CELTIC: Latchford; Sneddon, McGrain; Aitken, McAdam, Conroy; Provan, Davidson, McCluskey (Doyle), MacLeod, Lennox

Attendance: 25,000

Celtic, a goal down after 35 minutes, came back and by the finish were unlucky not to equalise.

First Round Second Leg October 3rd
CELTIC (4) 4 PARTIZAN TIRANA (1) 1
MacDonald (20), Aitken 2 (22, 44), Davidson (30)
Sneddon o.g. (15)

CELTIC: Latchford; Sneddon, McGrain; Aitken, MacDonald, McAdam; Provan, Davidson, McCluskey (Lennox), MacLeod, Doyle

PARTIZAN: Musta; Bachi, Cocoli; Starova, Berisha, Ahmeti; Braho, Lame, Breta, Murati, Ballghini (Hado)

Attendance: 51,000

Celtic were knocked back on their heels when the Albanians took a shock early lead through an own goal by Alan Sneddon but MacDonald quickly put them back in the match – the first in a 4-goal burst over 24 minutes. In 15 minutes Berisha, from deep in his own half, sent a long lob into the Celtic penalty area. Latchford and Sneddon got themselves mixed up and the full-back's headed pass back eluded the keeper who had come off his line. Then came 2 goals inside 2 minutes for Celtic. The first came when McAdam won a ball at the far post and knocked it back for MacDonald to head home. Two minutes later Doyle played a short corner to Provan whose cross was headed in by Aitken. In the 30th minute Celtic took the lead in the tie. Davidson popped up at the far post to tap home a Provan corner. 4 minutes later McCluskey lashed a penalty-kick, awarded for a foul on himself, high and wide but a 4th goal did arrive, a minute before half-time, when Provan pierced the Partizan defence with a brilliant run and his cross was headed in by Aitken. Celtic won 4-2 on aggregate.

Second Round First Leg October 24th
CELTIC (3) 3 DUNDALK (1) 2
MacDonald (3), McCluskey (30), Burns (33)
Muckian (32), Mick Lawlor (66)

CELTIC: Latchford; McGrain, McAdam, MacDonald, Lynch; Aitken, MacLeod, Davidson (Lennox); Provan, McCluskey, Burns

DUNDALK: Blackmore; McConville, Keely; Dunning, Martin Lawlor, Dainty; Byrne, Devine, Flanagan, Muckian, Daly (Mick Lawlor)

Attendance: 33,000

Brave Dundalk defied all the odds and came close to pulling off a major shock.

Second Round Second Leg November 7th
DUNDALK (0) 0 CELTIC (0) 0

DUNDALK: Blackmore; McConville, Martin Lawlor (McKenna); Keely, Dunning, Flanagan; Mick Lawlor (Daly), Devine, Muckian, Byrne, Dainty

CELTIC: Latchford; McGrain, Aitken; McAdam, MacDonald, MacLeod; Provan, Conroy, Edvaldsson, Lennox, Burns (Davidson)

Attendance: 16,300

Celtic headed rather uneasily into the Quarter-Finals in a match which was nailbiting, frustrating and all too close for comfort. No goals came and although Celtic managed to hang onto their slender First-Leg lead the final minutes were shear agony for their supporters. Celtic won 3-2 on aggregate.

Quarter-Final First Leg March 5th
CELTIC (0) 2 REAL MADRID (0) 0
McCluskey (52),
Doyle (74)

CELTIC: Latchford; Sneddon, McGrain; Aitken, McAdam, MacDonald; MacLeod, Provan, Lennox, McCluskey, Doyle

REAL MADRID: Garcia Ramon; Sabido, Camacho; Garcia Hernandez, Benito, Del Bosque; Juanito (Roberto Martinez), Angel, Santillana, Stielike, Cunningham

Attendance: 67,000

Celtic thundered their way to victory. George McCluskey pounced on a blunder by the Real keeper to open the scoring in 52 minutes, and with 16 minutes remaining Doyle scored the 2nd with a brilliant header. McCluskey almost produced the perfect start when he cut past 2 defenders and hit a powerful shot that brought Ramon to his knees, saving at only the 2nd attempt. In 22 minutes Real almost went ahead when Cunningham's blistering drive cracked off the left-hand post and bounced to safety. 11 minutes later Doyle's cross clearly hit Del Bosque on the arm but the referee waved away Celtic's demands for a penalty. Celtic did not have a weakness in the 2nd half, and in 52 minutes Sneddon sent in a grounder which the keeper could not hold. The ball bounced off his chest and McCluskey was on the spot to hammer it into the net. Shortly after Sabido headed a header from McAdam off the line. Celtic kept up the pressure and in 74 minutes they scored again. MacLeod found Sneddon free on the right, he sent over a cross to the far post and Doyle leapt high to head past Ramon.

Quarter-Final Second Leg March 19th
REAL MADRID (1) 3 CELTIC (0) 0
Santillana (44),
Stielike (56), Juanito (83)

REAL MADRID: Garcia Ramon; Sabido (Isido), Benito; Pirri, Camacho, Santos; Stielike (Garcia Hernandez), Del Bosque, Juanito, Santillana, Cunningham

CELTIC: Latchford; Sneddon, McAdam, MacDonald, McGrain; Provan, Aitken, Doyle; MacLeod, McCluskey (Burns), Lennox

Attendance: 110,000

Celtic crashed out to the super skills of Real Madrid after they missed a great chance to go ahead in 5 minutes. MacLeod won the ball in the midfield and laid it off to Doyle. He left McCluskey clear in front of goal, but with only the keeper to beat he shot weakly past. In 18 minutes Latchford had a great save from Juanito, and 6 minutes later he pulled off another superb save from Del Bosque. A minute from half-time the worst possible thing happened. Latchford missed a Cunningham corner, and with the ball bobbing about Santillana hammered it in off a Celtic defender. Within seconds of the restart Santillana got his head to another Cunningham corner and headed against the underside of the bar – MacDonald saved Celtic by heading clear. Real did eventually equalise in 56 minutes. Cunningham crossed from the left, Juanito headed it down and Stielike hit a glorious drive low past Latchford. Celtic began to take the match to Real, and they were unlucky not to be given a penalty when Benito handled in the box and Pirri almost put through his own goal with a pass back. Seven minutes from time Real scored the decisive goal. Angel burst to the byeline and sent over a powerful cross which Juanito headed past Latchford. Celtic's European dream was over for another season. Real Madrid won 3-2 on aggregate.

APPEARANCES	League	League Cup	Scottish Cup	European Cup
Latchford	36	6	6	6
McGrain	34	6	6	6
Lynch	1	–	–	1
Sneddon	32	6	6	4
Aitken	35	6	5	6
MacDonald	27+2S	4+1S	5	5
Edvaldsson	5+4S	2	1	1
Casey	2+1S	–	1	–
McAdam	34	6	5	6
Provan	35	5	6	6
Conroy	13+5S	3+1S	1+1S	2
Sullivan	15	–	1	–
McCluskey	22+1S	5	3+2S	5
MacLeod	36	6	6	6
Burns	12+3S	–	1+1S	2+1S
McGarvey	11+1S	–	2	–
Doyle	22+2S	4+1S	6	3+1S
Lennox	19+10	3+3S	5+1S	4+2S
Davidson	5	4	–	3+1S

GOALSCORERS

League: McCluskey 10 (2 pens), McAdam 8, Doyle 7, MacLeod 7 (4 pens), Lennox 6 (1 pen), MacDonald 6, Edvaldsson 3, Sullivan 3, Aitken 3, McGarvey 2, Conroy 2, Davidson 2, Provan 1, Sneddon 1

League Cup: Doyle 3, Provan 2, Conroy 2, McCluskey 1, Lennox 1, McAdam 1, MacLeod 1, Edvaldsson 1

Scottish Cup: Doyle 4, Lennox 3 (1 pen), MacLeod 2, McCluskey 2, Casey 1, Provan 1, McAdam 1

European Cup: McCluskey 2, MacDonald 2, Aitken 2, Davidson 1, Doyle 1, Burns 1

Celtic had just clinched their 30th League Championship by defeating Hibs at Easter Road. Here Kenny Dalglish is chaired by his happy teammates.

Season 1980-81

Celtic won their 2nd Premier Division Championship under the managership of Billy McNeill. They had a record number of wins (26), they lost only 6 matches (3 of them in a particularly bad November) and took the title by 7 points from Aberdeen with Rangers 12 points away in 3rd place. Following the reverse at Pittodrie on December 27th they went 15 matches without defeat until they were eventually beaten by St Mirren in the last match of the season, by which time the title had already been won. Curiously, Dundee United, who put them out of both Cup competitions, were beaten in all 4 league meetings. Celtic had unearthed a real gem in young Charlie Nicholas, a product of the Celtic Boys Club, and he contributed 16 of their 84 goals and quickly became one of the most feared strikers in the country. Young Full-back Mark Reid also broke into the first team and made such good progress that Alan Sneddon was sold to Hibs for £60,000. Pat Bonner, who had made the goalkeeping position his own, was the only ever-present in the side. Frank McGarvey repaid a large chunk of his transfer fee with the 23 goals which made him the Premier League's top scorer. Danny McGrain had a well-earned Testimonial match against Manchester United at the beginning of the season. Celtic also provided the opposition for Arsenal's Sammy Nelson in his Testimonial.

Celtic were twice taken to extra-time in the early rounds of the League Cup but they won through and eventually faced Dundee United in the two-legged Semi-Final. A late goal from substitute Charlie Nicholas gave them a rather fortuitous draw at Tannadice and they looked all set for the Final. United, however, had other ideas. They played magnificently on the heavy Parkhead pitch and ran out winners by three clear goals. United then went on to win the Cup for the second successive season by beating near neighbours Dundee 3-0 in the Final at Dens Park.

Celtic had a fairly easy passage to the Semi-Final of the Scottish Cup. Their first meeting with Dundee United ended in a goal-less draw but the replay was a five goal thriller. Charlie Nicholas twice gave them the lead but United were not going to be denied and a late goal from inspirational captain Paul Hegarty gave them victory and took them through to only their 2nd ever Scottish Cup Final.

After struggling during the first-half of their First Round First Leg Cup Winners Cup tie with Diosgyeori of Hungary Celtic went on a 2nd half goal spree scoring 6 without reply. This made the trip to Hungary a mere formality. They drew another Iron Curtain country in the Second Round – the unknown Rumanians of Politechnica Timisoara. Unfortunately it was to be an old familiar story. Although they were far superior in the First Leg in Glasgow, the return turned out to be a fiasco. Both MacDonald and McGarvey together with a Rumanian defender were sent off. Peter Latchford, playing in only his first competitive first-team game of the season for the injured Bonner, was clearly fouled before the Rumanians scored their late goal, but the Greek referee turned a blind eye and Celtic were eliminated on the away goals rule.

League:	Champions
League Cup:	Semi-Finalists
Scottish Cup:	Semi-Finalists
Cup Winners Cup:	Second Round

SCOTTISH PREMIER LEAGUE

August 9th:
CELTIC (0) 2 — MORTON (0) 1
McCluskey (67), MacLeod (81) — Ritchie (76)

CELTIC: Bonner; Sneddon, Aitken, McAdam, McGrain; Conroy (Burns), Sullivan, MacLeod; Provan, McGarvey, McCluskey

MORTON: Baines; Orr, Anderson, McLaughlin, Holmes; Rooney, Hutchinson (McNeill), McLaren; Scott, Tolmie, Ritchie

Attendance: 20,000

August 16th
KILMARNOCK (0) 0 — CELTIC (3) 3
Sullivan (28), McGarvey 2 (29, 35)

KILMARNOCK: McCulloch; McLean, Clarke, McDicken, Robertson; Mauchlen, Gibson, Cramond; Street, Bourke, Cairney (Doherty)

CELTIC: Bonner; Sneddon, Aitken, McAdam, McGrain; Sullivan, MacLeod, Burns; Provan, McCluskey, McGarvey (Nicholas)

Attendance: 13,800

August 23rd
CELTIC (0) 1 — RANGERS (0) 2
Burns (47) — Bett (61), Miller (89)

CELTIC: Bonner; Sneddon, Aitken, McAdam, McGrain; Sullivan, MacLeod, Burns; Provan, McGarvey, McCluskey

RANGERS: McCloy; Jardine, Forsyth, Jackson, Miller; Russell (Johnstone), Bett, Redford; MacDonald (Cooper), McAdam, Johnston

Attendance: 58,000. The McAdam brothers were in opposition for the first time in an Old Firm match.

Celtic had most of the pressure and Rangers were rather fortunate to be going into the last 15 minutes level, but Rangers refused to settle for a draw and kept going at Celtic until Alex Miller scored a magnificent goal 30 seconds from time.

September 6th
CELTIC (2) 4 — PARTICK THISTLE (1) 1
McGarvey (23), MacLeod (25 pen) Nicholas 2 (69, 80) — Gibson (33)

CELTIC: Bonner; Sneddon, McAdam, Aitken, McGrain; Sullivan, MacLeod, Burns; Provan, Nicholas, McGarvey (McCluskey)

PARTICK THISTLE: Rough; Doyle, Welsh, Campbell (Lapsley), Whittaker; Park (Scott), Gibson, Jardine; Watson, Higgins, O'Hara

Attendance: 20,000

September 10th: Danny McGrain was in the Scotland team which beat Sweden 1-0 in a World Cup match in Stockholm.

September 13th
HEARTS (0) 0 — CELTIC (1) 2
Provan (34), Nicholas (53)

HEARTS: Brough; Robinson, Jeffries, Boyd, Liddell; Kidd, Bowman (Conn), Gibson; O'Connor, C. Robertson, MacDonald

CELTIC: Bonner; Sneddon, Aitken, McAdam, McGrain; Sullivan, MacLeod (Conroy), Burns; Provan, McCluskey, Nicholas

Attendance: 17,169. Aitken was ordered off in the 70th minute.

September 20th
CELTIC (0) 1 — AIRDRIE (0) 1
Nicholas (83 pen) — Clark (57)

CELTIC: Bonner; Sneddon, McGrain; Conroy, McAdam, Weir; Provan, Sullivan, McCluskey (Doyle), Burns, Nicholas

AIRDRIE; Martin; Erwin, Rodger; Walker, G. Anderson, N. Anderson; Thompson (McGuire), Clark, McVeigh, Gordon, McCulloch

Attendance: 18,000

September 27th
ABERDEEN (0) 2 — CELTIC (2) 2
McGhee (71), McAdam (o.g. 73) — Nicholas (6 pen), Burns (17)

ABERDEEN: Leighton; Kennedy, Rougvie, Miller, Hamilton (Scanlon); Watson, Strachan, McMaster; Bell, McGhee, Hewitt (McCall)

CELTIC: Bonner; Sneddon, McAdam, MacDonald, McGrain; Provan, Sullivan, Conroy, Burns (MacLeod); McGarvey (Doyle), Nicholas

Attendance: 24,000

October 4th
CELTIC (1) 2 — DUNDEE UNITED (0) 0
McGarvey (24), Nicholas (56)

CELTIC: Bonner; Sneddon, MacDonald, McAdam, McGrain; Sullivan, MacLeod, Conroy; McCluskey, McGarvey, Nicholas

DUNDEE UNITED: McAlpine; Stark, Phillip (Kirkwood), Hegarty, Kopel; Sturrock, Payne, Narey; Holt, Pettigrew, Dodds (Campbell)

Attendance: 21,000

October 11th
ST MIRREN (0) 0 — CELTIC (2) 2
McCormack o.g. (42), Stark o.g. (43)

ST MIRREN: Thomson; Young (Curran), McCormack, Copland, McAveety; Stark (Logan), Richardson, Abercrombie; Weir, McDougall, Somner

CELTIC: Bonner; Sneddon, McAdam, MacDonald, McGrain; Provan, Sullivan, Aitken; McCluskey, Nicholas, McGarvey

Attendance: 18,601. McGarvey was ordered off.

October 15th: Danny McGrain was in the Scotland team which drew 0-0 with Portugal in a World Cup match at Hampden Park.

October 18th
MORTON (0) 2 — Ritchie (76), Cochrane (86)
CELTIC (2) 3 — Provan (9), Aitken (27), Nicholas (47)

MORTON: Baines; Hayes, McLaughlin, Orr, Holmes; Rooney, Busby, Ritchie, McNeill (Tolmie), Cochrane, Thomson

CELTIC: Bonner; Sneddon, MacDonald, McAdam, McGrain; Aitken, Sullivan, Provan (MacLeod), Doyle, Nicholas, McCluskey

Attendance: 16,000

October 25th
CELTIC (2) 4 — Nicholas 2 (36, 51 pen), McGarvey 2 (44, 86)
KILMARNOCK (1) 1 — Cramond (15)

CELTIC: Bonner; Sneddon, McAdam, MacDonald, McGrain; Sullivan, Aitken, Burns; Provan, McGarvey, Nicholas

KILMARNOCK: Brown; Robertson, Clarke, McDicken, Cockburn; Clark, Mauchlen, Cramond; Doherty (McLean), McBride, Houston

Attendance: 18,000

League positions

	P	W	D	L	F	A	Pts
1 Aberdeen	11	8	3	0	25	7	19
2 CELTIC	11	8	2	1	26	10	18
3 Rangers	11	6	5	0	28	10	17
4 Airdrie	11	4	5	2	12	10	13
5 Partick Thistle	11	5	2	4	11	15	12

November 1st
RANGERS (2) 3 — McAdam 2 (21, 75), MacDonald (36)
CELTIC (0) 0

RANGERS: McCloy; Jardine, Johnstone, Jackson, Dawson; McLean, Bett, Redford, McAdam, MacDonald, Johnston

CELTIC: Bonner; Sneddon, MacDonald, McAdam, McGrain; Sullivan, Aitken, Burns; Provan, McGarvey (McCluskey), Nicholas (Doyle)

Attendance: 33,000

The return of Ally Dawson seemed to stabilise the Rangers defence, and Willie Johnstone turned back the clock to produce some vintage stuff on the left flank. Celtic began well and created 2 good chances in the opening 10 minutes but Dom Sullivan missed them both.

November 8th
CELTIC (0) 0
ABERDEEN (1) 2 — McCall 2 (32, 57)

CELTIC: Bonner; Sneddon, McAdam, Conroy (McCluskey), McGrain; Aitken, Sullivan, Burns; Provan, McGarvey (Doyle), Nicholas

ABERDEEN: Leighton; Dornan (Considine), McLeish, Cooper, Rougvie; Strachan, Watson, Bell; McCall (Hewitt), McGhee, Scanlon

Attendance: 29,000

November 8th: Bobby Lennox was put in charge of the Celtic second team.

November 15th
AIRDRIE (0) 1 — McGuire (89)
CELTIC (3) 4 — Aitken (12), McGarvey (15), Nicholas (25), McAdam (84)

AIRDRIE: Martin; Erwin, G. Anderson, N. Anderson, Rodger (McCulloch); McKeown, Walker, McCluskey (Russell); Gordon, McGuire, Clark

CELTIC: Bonner; McGrain, Aitken, McAdam, Reid; McCluskey, Provan, Weir, Burns; Nicholas, McGarvey

Attendance: 16,000

November 22nd
CELTIC (0) 1 — McCluskey (85 pen)
ST MIRREN (0) 2 — Richardson (84), Beckett (88)

CELTIC: Bonner; McGrain, MacDonald, McAdam, Reid; Sullivan, Aitken, Weir, Burns; Nicholas (McCluskey), McGarvey

ST MIRREN: Thomson; Beckett, Fulton, Copland, Abercrombie; Richardson, McCormack, Weir; Stark, Bone, Somner

Attendance: 16,000

November 29th
DUNDEE UNITED (0) 0
CELTIC (0) 3 — McAdam (58), Weir (78), Hegarty o.g. (89)

DUNDEE UNITED: McAlpine; Holt, Hegarty, Narey, Kopel; Addison (Kirkwood), Phillip (Payne), Bannon; Pettigrew, Sturrock, Dodds

CELTIC: Bonner; McGrain, MacDonald, McAdam; Aitken, Sullivan, Weir, Burns; McGarvey, McCluskey

Attendance: 15,000

December 1st: John Clark rejected the Partick Thistle manager's job to stay with Celtic as assistant manager.

December 6th
PARTICK THISTLE (0) 0
CELTIC (0) 1 — McCluskey (84)

PARTICK THISTLE: Rough; Doyle, Campbell, Anderson, Whittaker; Jardine, Watson, Lapsley; Park, Clark, O'Hara

CELTIC: Bonner; Sneddon, MacDonald, McAdam, Reid; Sullivan (Provan), Aitken, Weir, Burns; McGarvey, McCluskey

Attendance: 12,436

December 13th
CELTIC (2) 3 — HEARTS (1) 2
MacDonald (29), McGarvey (35), — MacDonald (6), Gibson (56)

CELTIC: Bonner; Sneddon, MacDonald, McAdam, Reid; Aitken, Proven, Weir, Burns; McGarvey, McCluskey

HEARTS: Brough; More, Denny, McVie, Shields; Robinson, Gibson, MacDonald; Hamill, Conn (Masterton), O'Brien (O'Connor)

Attendance: 13,800

December 20th
CELTIC (1) 2 — AIRDRIE (0) 1
McAdam (19), McCluskey (55) — Clark (80 pen)

CELTIC: Bonner; McGrain, MacDonald, McAdam, Reid; Aitken, Weir, Burns; Provan, McGarvey, McCluskey

AIRDRIE: Martin; Cairney, N. Anderson, G. Anderson, McCluskey; Rodger, Walker (McCulloch), McKeown (McGuire), Gordon; Russell, Clark

Attendance: 11,900

League positions

	P	W	D	L	F	A	Pts
1 Aberdeen	19	13	5	1	41	13	31
2 CELTIC	20	13	2	5	41	25	28
3 Rangers	18	8	8	2	34	14	24
4 Dundee United	19	7	7	5	27	25	21
5 St Mirren	19	7	5	7	29	25	19

December 27th
ABERDEEN (2) 4 — CELTIC (0) 1
McLeish (9), Miller (41), McCall (46), Strachan (69 pen) — Nicholas (72)

ABERDEEN: Leighton; Kennedy, McLeish, Miller, Considine; Strachan, Watson, Bell (Rougvie); McCall, McGhee, Scanlon

CELTIC: Bonner; McGrain, MacDonald, McAdam, Reid; Aitken, Conroy (Provan), Weir, Burns; McGarvey, McCluskey (Nicholas)

Attendance: 23,500

January 1st
KILMARNOCK (1) 1 — CELTIC (2) 2
Hughes (2) — McGarvey 2 (4, 43)

KILMARNOCK: A. Wilson, McLean, Cockburn; McClurg, Armstrong, Clarke; Houston, Gibson, Bourke, G. Wilson, Hughes

CELTIC: Bonner; McGrain, Reid; Sullivan, McAdam, Aitken; Provan, Weir, McGarvey, Burns, Nicholas

Attendance: 8,000

January 3rd
CELTIC (3) 3 — MORTON (0) 0
McGarvey 2 (12, 44), Provan (15)

CELTIC: Bonner; McGrain, Aitken, McAdam, Reid; Sullivan, Weir, Burns; Provan, McGarvey, Nicholas

MORTON: Baines; Hayes, McLaughlin, Orr, Holmes; Rooney, Busby, Thomson; McNeill (Bryce), Tolmie, Hutchinson (Ritchie)

Attendance: 14,900

January 9th: Alan Sneddon was transferred to Hibernian for £60,000.

January 10th
CELTIC (2) 2 — DUNDEE UNITED (0) 1
Nicholas (27), McGarvey (42) — Milne (82)

CELTIC: Bonner; McGrain, Aitken, McAdam, Reid; Sullivan, Weir, Burns; Provan, McGarvey, Nicholas

DUNDEE UNITED: McAlpine; Kirkwood, Narey, Hegarty, Kopel; Phillip, Gibson (Addison), Bannon; Sturrock, Pettigrew (Milne), Dodds

Attendance: 27,000

January 31st
HEARTS (0) 0 — CELTIC (1) 3
McGarvey (31), Burns (50), Sullivan (69)

HEARTS: Brough; Hamilton, More, Liddell, Shields; Mackay (White), Kidd, MacDonald; Hamill, Gibson (McShane), O'Brien

CELTIC: Bonner; McGrain, McAdam, Aitken, Reid; Sullivan, Conroy, Burns; Provan, McGarvey, Nicholas (McCluskey)

Attendance: 14,596

February 21st
CELTIC (0) 3 — RANGERS (1) 1
Nicholas 2 (57, 73), Aitken (87) — Johnstone (11)

CELTIC: Bonner; McGrain, Aitken, McAdam, Reid; Sullivan, Burns, Conroy; Provan, McGarvey, Nicholas

RANGERS: McCloy; Miller (MacDonald), Jardine, Jackson, Dawson; Cooper (Russell), Bett, Redford; Johnstone, McAdam, Johnston

Attendance: 52,800

After giving Rangers a goal start Celtic turned on one of their best displays of the season. a 2nd-half 1-2 from

Nicholas put the result right. Davie Provan was outstanding, McGarvey a constant menace and Nicholas a clinical assassin. In the 2nd half the Parkhead men proved they wanted to win the match more than their rivals. With 3 minutes left and with Rangers pushing forward to try and save the game, Aitken caught them on the break with a powerful run from the half-way line. He tried to cut the ball across to McGarvey but when it struck Jackson on the foot the big Celtic defender hammered the rebound high into the net.

February 25th: Danny McGrain was in the Scotland team which beat Israel 1-0 in a World Cup match in Tel Aviv.

February 28th
MORTON (0) 0 — CELTIC (2) 3
McGarvey 2 (32, 44),
Provan (75)

MORTON: Baines; Hayes, McLaughlin, Orr, Holmes; Rooney, Marr, Busby; Houston (McNeill), Tolmie, Ritchie

CELTIC: Bonner; McGrain, McAdam, Aitken, Reid; Sullivan, Conroy, Burns; Provan, McGarvey, Nicholas

Attendance: 14,000

League positions

	P	W	D	L	F	A	Pts
1 CELTIC	26	19	2	5	57	28	40
2 Aberdeen	26	14	8	4	46	19	36
3 Rangers	25	11	10	4	43	21	32
4 Dundee United	26	12	8	6	45	29	32
5 St Mirren	25	10	7	8	37	31	27

March 14th
CELTIC (3) 7 — ST MIRREN (0) 0
Aitken (12),
McGarvey 3 (37, 45, 57),
Nicholas (47),
McCluskey 2 (88, 90)

CELTIC: Bonner; McGrain, Aitken, McAdam, Reid; Sullivan, Conroy (MacLeod), Burns; Provan, McGarvey, Nicholas (McCluskey)

ST MIRREN: Thomson; Beckett (McAveety), Young, Fulton, McCormack; Stark, Abercrombie, Weir; Bone, McDougall (Logan), Speirs

Attendance: 18,100

March 18th
CELTIC (1) 4 — PARTICK THISTLE (0) 1
Sullivan (35) — Park (55)
MacLeod 2 (68, 89),
McGarvey (88)

CELTIC: Bonner; McGrain, Reid; Sullivan, McAdam; Provan, Conroy (MacLeod), McGarvey, Burns, Nicholas

PARTICK THISTLE: Rough; Welsh, Whittaker; Campbell, Anderson, Lapsley; Park, McDonald, Higgins, O'Hara, Clark

Attendance: 15,000. Whittaker was ordered off

March 21st
AIRDRIE (0) 1 — CELTIC (1) 2
Thompson (73) — McGarvey (31),
MacLeod (46)

AIRDRIE: Gardiner; G. Anderson, McCluskey, March, Rodger; Erwin, Walker (McKeown), N. Anderson; Flood, Clark, McGuire (Thompson)

CELTIC: Bonner; McGrain, McAdam, Aitken, Reid; Sullivan, MacLeod, Burns; Provan, McGarvey, Nicholas

Attendance: 13,000. March was ordered off

March 25th: Danny McGrain was in the Scotland team which drew 1-1 with Northern Ireland in a World Cup match at Hampden Park.

March 28th
CELTIC (0) 1 — ABERDEEN (1) 1
McCluskey (85) — Harrow (17)

CELTIC: Bonner; McGrain, McAdam, Aitken, Reid; Sullivan, MacLeod, Burns; Provan, McGarvey, Nicholas (McCluskey)

ABERDEEN: Leighton; Kennedy, McLeish, Miller, Rougvie; Simpson, Watson, Bell (Jarvie); McGhee, Harrow (McCall), Scanlon

Attendance: 35,200

April 1st
CELTIC (3) 6 — HEARTS (0) 0
McCluskey 2 (23 pen, 48),
Provan (24),
McGarvey (29),
MacLeod 2 (62, 75)

CELTIC: Bonner; McGrain, Reid; Sullivan, McAdam, Aitken; Provan, MacLeod, McGarvey, Burns, McCluskey

HEARTS: Brough; Denny, Shields; Kidd, More, Hamill; Mackay, Gibson, Liddell, Bowman, MacDonald

Attendance: 13,300

April 5th
PARTICK THISTLE (0) 0 — CELTIC (0) 1
McAdam (87)

PARTICK THISTLE: McNab; Welsh, Whittaker; Campbell, Anderson, Doyle; Park, McDonald, Higgins, Lapsley, Clark

CELTIC: Bonner; MacLeod, Reid; Sullivan, McAdam, Aitken; Provan, Conroy, McGarvey (Nicholas), Burns, McCluskey

Attendance: 17,196. McCluskey missed a penalty

April 18th
RANGERS (0) 0 — CELTIC (0) 1
Nicholas (55)

RANGERS: Stewart; Miller, Jackson, Johnstone, Dawson; Bett (MacDonald), Russell, McLean; Johnston (Jardine), McAdam, Redford

CELTIC: Bonner; McGrain, MacDonald, McAdam, Aitken; Conroy, Burns, MacLeod; Provan, McGarvey, Nicholas

Attendance: 34,000

Celtic were in full control of a quiet Old Firm game. It did not require anything special to beat a Rangers side who created only 2 genuine chances throughout the 90 minutes. MacDonald's command in the air nullified the dangerous flighted passes of McLean, and Aitken mastered the ground attacks.

April 22nd
DUNDEE UNITED (1) 2 CELTIC (2) 3
Pettigrew (29), Sturrock (72) — MacLeod (3), McGarvey (35), Burns (60)

DUNDEE UNITED: McAlpine; Holt, Kopel; Phillip, Hegarty, Stark; Bannon, Milne, Pettigrew, Sturrock, Addison

CELTIC: Bonner; McGrain, Reid; MacLeod, McAdam, Aitken; Provan, Conroy, McGarvey, Burns, Nicholas

Attendance: 15,349. Celtic clinched the title

April 25th
CELTIC (1) 1 KILMARNOCK (0) 1
Provan (20) — Eadie (63)

CELTIC: Bonner; McGrain, Aitken, McAdam, Reid; Sullivan, MacLeod, Burns; Provan, Nicholas, McGarvey

KILMARNOCK: McCulloch; Robin, McDicken, Armstrong, Robertson; Clark, McLean, Cockburn; McCreadie, Bourke, Eadie

Attendance: 23,200

April 28th: McGrain and Provan were in the Scotland team which beat Israel 3-1 in a World Cup match at Hampden Park. Provan scored one of the goals.

May 2nd
ST MIRREN (1) 3 CELTIC (0) 1
McDougall 2 (30, 89), Richardson (57) — Provan (63)

ST MIRREN: Thomson; Young, Fulton, Copland, Beckett; McCormack, Stark, Richardson; Bone, McDougall, Abercrombie

CELTIC: Bonner; McGrain, Aitken, MacDonald, Reid; Sullivan, MacLeod, Burns; Provan, McGarvey, Nicholas

Attendance: 14,806.

May 16th: McGrain and Provan were in the Scotland team beaten 2-0 by Wales in Swansea.

May 19th: McGrain and Burns were in the Scotland team which beat Northern Ireland 2-0 at Hampden Park.

May 23rd: McGrain and Provan were in the Scotland team which beat England 1-0 at Wembley.

Scottish Premier League

	P	W	D	L	F	A	Pts
1 CELTIC	36	26	4	6	84	37	56
2 Aberdeen	36	19	11	6	61	26	49
3 Rangers	36	16	12	8	60	32	44
4 St Mirren	36	18	8	10	56	47	44
5 Dundee United	36	17	9	10	66	42	43
6 Partick Thistle	36	10	10	16	32	48	30
7 Airdrie	36	10	9	17	36	55	29
8 Morton	36	10	8	18	36	58	28
9 Kilmarnock	36	5	9	22	23	65	19
10 Hearts	36	6	6	24	27	71	18

SCOTTISH LEAGUE CUP

Second Round First Leg August 27th
STIRLING ALBION (0) 1 CELTIC (0) 0
Irvine (65)

STIRLING ALBION: Arthur; Nicol, Steedman; Farmer, J. Kennedy, Young; McPhee, Gray, A. Kennedy, Beaton, Irvine

CELTIC: Bonner; Sneddon, McGrain; Aitken, McAdam, MacLeod (Conroy); Provan, Sullivan, McGarvey, Burns, McCluskey

Attendance: 6,000

Second Round Second Leg August 31st
CELTIC (1) 6 STIRLING ALBION (1) 1
Sullivan (22), Burns 2 (87, 100), Provan (93), Nicholas 2 (97, 109) — McPhee (12)
After extra tme

CELTIC: Bonner; Sneddon, Aitken, McAdam, McGrain; Sullivan, MacLeod, Burns; Provan, McGarvey (Conroy), McCluskey (Nicholas)

STIRLING ALBION: Arthur; Farmer (Moffat), Nicol, Young, F. Kennedy; Steedman, Gray, Beaton; McPhee, A. Kennedy, Irvine (McGregor)

Attendance: 16,000. Celtic won 7-2 on aggregate.

Third Round First Leg September 24th
CELTIC (2) 4 HAMILTON ACADEMICALS (0) 1
Nicholas (26), Burns (43), McGarvey 2 (59, 89) — McManus (89)

CELTIC: Bonner; Sneddon, McGrain; Aitken, MacDonald, McAdam; Provan, Sullivan, Doyle, Burns, Nicholas (McGarvey)

HAMILTON: Ferguson; Frew, Marshall; Gormley, McDougall, Alexander; McDowall, Graham, Fairlie, Wright, P. McAdam. Sub: McManus

Attendance: 10,000

Third Round Second Leg September 22nd
HAMILTON ACADEMICALS (0) 1 CELTIC (2) 3
McDowall (77) — Doyle (13), Nicholas (24), Burns (89)

HAMILTON: Ferguson; Frew, Brown; Alexander, McDougall, Marshall; McDowall, Graham, Fairlie, Wright, McGrogan

CELTIC: Bonner; Sneddon, McGrain; Aitken, MacDonald, McAdam; Provan, Sullivan, Doyle, Burns, Nicholas

Attendance: 12,000. Celtic won 7-2 on aggregate

Quarter-Final First Leg October 8th
PARTICK THISTLE (0) 0 CELTIC (0) 1
Nicholas (49 pen)

PARTICK THISTLE: Rough; Doyle, Whittaker; Gibson (McLeod), Campbell, Welsh; Park (Marr), O'Hara, Higgins, Watson, Jardine.

CELTIC: Bonner; Sneddon, McGrain; Aitken, MacDonald, McAdam; McCluskey, Sullivan, McGarvey, MacLeod, Nicholas

Attendance: 15,000

Quarter-Final Second Leg October 20th
CELTIC (0) 2 PARTICK THISTLE (1) 1
Burns (94), O'Hara (42)
MacDonald (113) *After extra time*

CELTIC: Bonner; Sneddon, McGrain (Conroy); Aitken, MacDonald, McAdam; Provan, Sullivan, Doyle, Burns, Nicholas

PARTICK THISTLE: Rough; Murray, Lapsley, Campbell (McDonald), Whittaker; Welsh, Park, O'Hara; Clark, Watson, Jardine

Attendance: 12,000

Semi-Final First Leg November 12th
DUNDEE UNITED (1) 1 CELTIC (0) 1
Bannon (23) Nicholas (82)

DUNDEE UNITED: McAlpine; Stark, Kopel; Phillip, Hegarty, Narey; Bannon, Kirkwood, Pettigrew, Sturrock, Dodds

CELTIC: Bonner; McGrain, Reid; Aitken, MacDonald, McAdam; Provan, Weir, McCluskey (McGarvey), Burns, Doyle (Nicholas)

Attendance: 14,000

Celtic, who were outplayed for most of the match, were rescued by substitute Charlie Nicholas. In 23 minutes United's more varied attacking strategy paid off. The busy Sturrock cut the ball back from the byeline, Bonner couldn't hold it, Pettigrew chipped cleverly to the left and Bannon volleyed home. In 80 minutes Phillip had a miraculous clearance off the line from Nicholas following a Burns cross. 2 minutes later hero Phillip became villain when he knocked a cross into the path of Nicholas who smacked it in off Stark's despairing legs.

Semi-Final Second Leg November 19th
CELTIC (0) 0 DUNDEE UNITED (1) 3
Pettigrew (4),
Sturrock (54),
Dodds (80)

CELTIC: Bonner; McGrain, Reid; Aitken, McAdam, Weir; Provan, McCluskey (MacDonald), McGarvey (Doyle), Burns, Nicholas

DUNDEE UNITED: McAlpine; Holt, Kopel; Phillip, Hegarty, Narey; Bannon, Payne, Pettigrew, Sturrock, Dodds

Attendance: 21,000

United played magnificently from start to finish. The slick, quick football of the Tannadice side on the heavy pitch had Celtic's defence in serious trouble right from the start. In 4 minutes Bannon passed to Payne on the left and his cross was whipped into the net by Pettigrew. Before half-time McAdam went close with a header and McAlpine blocked a McGarvey shot with his foot. 9 minutes after the interval United went 2 up when Bannon's low cross was brilliantly flicked into the net by Sturrock. Seconds later Payne headed onto the bar. United's 3rd goal came 10 minutes from time when Dodds headed in a perfectly flighted cross from Sturrock. Dundee United won 4-1 on aggregate.

SCOTTISH CUP

Third Round January 24th
BERWICK RANGERS (0) 0 CELTIC (1) 2
Nicholas (19),
Burns (81)

BERWICK RANGERS: McDonald; Moyes, Marshall, Muir, McCann; McGlynn, Hamilton, Black; Tait (Brown), Romanes, Davidson (McLeod)

CELTIC: Bonner; McGrain, McAdam, Aitken, Reid; Sullivan (McLeod), Weir, Burns; Provan, McGarvey, Nicholas

Attendance: 9,676

Fourth Round February 14th
CELTIC (1) 3 STIRLING ALBION (0) 0
McGarvey (4),
McCluskey (80),
Burns (87)

CELTIC: Bonner; McGrain, McAdam, Aitken, Reid; Sullivan, Conroy, Burns; Provan, McGarvey (McCluskey), Nicholas

STIRLING ALBION: Arthur; Young, Nicol; Moffat, Skilling, Philliben; Duffin, Gray, McPhee (Colquhoun), Steele, Armstrong (McNeill)

Attendance: 14,200

Quarter-Final March 8th
CELTIC (1) 2 EAST STIRLING (0) 0
Conroy (26),
MacLeod (71)

CELTIC: Bonner; McGrain, Reid; Sullivan, McAdam, Aitken; Provan, Conroy, McGarvey, Burns (MacLeod), Nicholas

EAST STIRLING: Kelly; Blair, Renwick; Watt, Rennie, Lamont; Grant, Gourlay, Ashwood, McCulley, Robertson

Attendance: 18,500

Semi-Final at Hampden Park April 11th
CELTIC (0) 0 DUNDEE UNITED (0) 0

CELTIC: Bonner; MacLeod, Aitken, McAdam, Reid; Sullivan, Conroy, Burns; Provan, McCluskey (Doyle), Nicholas. Sub: MacDonald

DUNDEE UNITED: McAlpine; Holt, Hegarty (Stark), Narey, Kopel; Phillip, Kirkwood, Bannon; Sturrock, Milne, Dodds

Attendance: 40,337

Despite the lack of goals there was plenty of excitement for the fans. Dundee United took the initiative and dominated for long spells. They were denied a possible penalty in 20 minutes when Sturrock was brought down by Aitken. They were also unlucky in the 74th minute when a Dodds shot was deflected and smacked off the face of a post. Hegarty was taken off with a knee injury and McCluskey took a bad knock on the ankle and was replaced by Doyle. Celtic could now call on Frank McGarvey for the replay after his one-match suspension.

Semi-Final Replay April 15th
CELTIC (2) 2 DUNDEE UNITED (2) 3
Nicholas 2 (5 pen, 44) Bannon (8), Hegarty 2 (10, 75)

CELTIC: Bonner; MacLeod, Reid; Sullivan (Doyle), McAdam, Aitken; Provan, Conroy, McGarvey, Burns, Nicholas. Sub: MacDonald

DUNDEE UNITED: McAlpine; Holt, Kopel; Phillip, Hegarty, Narey; Bannon, Milne, Kirkwood, Sturrock, Dodds

Attendance: 32,328

Dundee United took control of the midfield and after going behind to a Charlie Nicholas penalty in only 5 minutes showed their character by bouncing back quickly and scoring 2 goals within 2 minutes.

A minute before half-time Celtic scored a wonderful equaliser. McGarvey challenged McAlpine for a high cross and when the United keeper punched it out Nicholas met it first time from 18 yards and cracked in a grounder. Dundee United's winner came 15 minutes from time. The Celtic defence was caught napping when a long free-kick from the right sailed over everyone, Bannon met it with his head at the far post and Hegarty knocked it over the line to take Jim McLean's men through to the final against Rangers.

CUP WINNERS CUP

First Round First Leg August 20th
CELTIC (0) 6 DIOSGYEORI (Hungary) (0) 0
McGarvey 3 (52, 65, 70), McCluskey 2 (59, 79), Sullivan (71)

CELTIC: Bonner; Sneddon, McGrain; Aitken, McAdam, MacLeod (Doyle); Provan (Nicholas), Sullivan, McGarvey, Burns, McCluskey

DIOSGYOERI: Szabo; Szanto, Neder; Kadar, Olah, Kerekes; Szlifka, Fuko, Teodory, Gorgei, Borostyon

Attendance: 28,000

This was indeed a game of two halves. Celtic had no luck in the first 45 minutes but the picture changed completely in the 2nd half and they went on a goal spree.

First Round Second Leg September 3rd
DIOSGYEORI (1) 2 CELTIC (1) 1
Gorgei 2 (25, 64) Nicholas (24)

DIOSGYEORI: Szabo; Szanto, Neder; Kerekes, Teodory, Olah; Fuko, Gorgei, Szlifka, Magyar, Borostyon

CELTIC: Bonner; Sneddon, McGrain; Aitken, McAdam, Macleod; Provan, Sullivan, McGarvey, Burns, Nicholas

Attendance: 8,000

Charlie Nicholas put Celtic ahead in the 24th minute with a marvellous volley, making amends for 2 missed chances before then. Diosgyeori equalised inside a minute when Bonner pushed a shot from Gorgei onto the underside of the bar and the referee ruled that the ball was over the line. The Hungarians' winning goal came in 64 minutes when Gorgei smashed in a left-foot shot. The home side put in a fighting finish in an effort to make the aggregate scoreline a bit more respectable and Czel, a substitute, missed a great chance in the 81st minute. Celtic won 7-2 on aggregate.

Second Round First Leg September 17
CELTIC (2) 2 POLITECHNICA TIMISOARA (0) 1
Nicholas 2 (19, 42) Adrian (78)

CELTIC: Bonner; Sneddon, McGrain; Aitken, McAdam, MacLeod (Conroy); Provan (Doyle), Sullivan, McCluskey, Burns, Nicholas

POLITECHNICA: Moise; Nadu, Paltinisan; Sunda, Manea, Serbaniov; Anghel, Dembrovski, Adrian, Dumitru, Nedelcu

Attendance: 32,000

Celtic were far superior for a large proportion of the game and they should have made the Second Leg a formality but they now faced an extremely hazardous trip behind the Iron Curtain. In the 15th minute Provan missed a wonderful chance when he shot past an empty goal. Four minutes later Celtic went ahead when Provan sent in a strong cross which Moise held and then dropped; Nicholas pounced and hooked the ball home. The scoreline became much more realistic when they scored again 3 minutes before half-time. Provan lofted a free-kick to MacLeod whose return chip was tailor-made for Nicholas to head out of the goalkeeper's reach. 7 minutes after half-time McCluskey rounded Nadu and touched inside to Burns but his left-foot shot bounced off the bar. 12 minutes from time the Celtic defence got into a terrible tangle and they nearly lost a goal. Seconds later the Rumanians grabbed a valuable away goal when Adrian hit a vicious shot which cannoned off Bonner's hand and into the net. It was a real sickener.

Second Round Second Leg October 1st
POLITECHNICA TIMISOARA (0) 1 CELTIC (0) 0
Paltinisan (81)

POLITECHNICA: Moise; Nadu, Paltinisan; Sunda, Manea, Serbaniov; Anghel, Dembrovski, Visan, Dumitru, Nedelcu

CELTIC: Latchford; Sneddon, McAdam, MacDonald, McGrain; Sullivan, Aitken, MacLeod; McGarvey, Nicholas, Provan

Attendance: 50,000

Celtic had the best of the 2nd half and set up more genuine scoring opportunities than their opponents. MacDonald was dismissed with Manea in the 17th minute. The big defender tried to get in a shot as the goalkeeper went down on his feet. Manea remonstrated with MacDonald and the Greek referee surprised everyone when he ordered both off. The only goal of the game came in the 81st minute. Latchford caught a cross from the right but was heftily pushed by Paltinisan and dropped the ball. Aitken tried to clear but Paltinisan shot into the net and the referee, who had a poor match, surprised no one when he allowed the score. 3 minutes later McGarvey, who had previously been booked, was sent off for arguing. Aggregate 2-2. Poltechnica won on away goals.

APPEARANCES	League	League Cup	Scottish Cup	Cup Winners Cup
Bonner	36	8	5	3
McAdam	35	8	5	4
McGrain	33	8	3	4
Aitken	33	8	5	4
McGarvey	33	4+2S	4	4
Burns	32+1S	7	5	3
Provan	31+2S	7	5	4
Sullivan	30	6	5	4
Nicholas	26+3S	5+2S	5	3+1S
Reid	22	2	5	–
McCluskey	16+6S	5	1+1S	1
Sneddon	15	6	–	4
Conroy	14+1S	0+3S	4	0+1S
MacDonald	14	5+1S	–	1
MacLeod	14+4S	3	2+2S	4
Weir	11	2	1	–
Doyle	1+4S	4+1S	0+2S	0+2S
Latchford	–	–	–	1

GOALSCORERS:

League: McGarvey 23, Nicholas 16 (3 pens), McCluskey 10 (2 pens), MacLeod 8 (1 pen), Provan 7, Burns 4, Aitken 4, McAdam 4, Sullivan 3, Own Goals 3, Weir 1, MacDonald 1

League Cup: Nicholas 6 (1 pen), Burns 5, McGarvey 2, Sullivan 1, Provan 1, Doyle 1, MacDonald 1

Scottish Cup: Nicholas 3 (1 pen), Burns 2, McGarvey 1, McCluskey 1, Conroy 1, MacLeod 1

Cup Winners Cup: Nicholas 3, McGarvey 3, McCluskey 2, Sullivan 1

The Celtic squad in season 1981-82. Back row: Nicholas, Sullivan, McAdam, Latchford, Bonner, Aitken, Garner, Burns. Front row: Reid, McGarvey, McCluskey, McGrain, Provan, McLeod, Doyle and Conroy.

Season 1981-82

Celtic were at the top of the Premier Division throughout the season and deservedly won their 33rd Championship. They started with 7 straight wins which included away victories over Aberdeen and Rangers and they eventually won the title by 2 points from the Dons whom they had beaten 3 times in their 4 meetings. One of the highlights was the home match against Rangers in November which was one of the most thrilling Old Firm encounters in years. Celtic overcame the loss of both Nicholas and McGarvey with broken legs and George McCluskey went on to establish himself as the club's top striker with 21 goals. Murdo MacLeod contributed 10 and young Danny Crainie also scored some important goals. The side was very settled, which showed in the play, and Bonner, Reid and MacLeod started every match. It was particularly interesting to note Manager McNeill's positively spartan use of substitutes throughout the campaign. Young Paul McStay looked to be a bright prospect in his few outings. On the transfer front, Airdrie rejected an offer of £200,000 for striker Sandy Clark, and Roddie MacDonald and Jim Duffy both left for pastures new. Although the season ended with triumph, it was marred by the sad death of Johnny Doyle.

Celtic got off to the worst possible start to the season when they lost their first 2 League Cup ties against St Mirren and St Johnstone. They recovered well in the remaining 4 Section matches but failed to reach the Final stages of the Competition for the first time since season 1963/64.

Eventual winners Aberdeen put them out of the Scottish Cup in the Fourth Round at Pittodrie, although this did allow them to concentrate on the League title race.

Celtic were unfortunate to draw Juventus in the First Round of the European Cup. A Murdo MacLeod goal did give them a memorable win at Parkhead but only a magnificent display by Pat Bonner prevented a much bigger defeat in Turin.

They played a large number of Friendly matches throughout the season. They finished 3rd in a tournament in the U.S.A. and won the prestigious Feyenoord Tournament, beating Dukla Prague 2-1 in the Final. They also travelled to Hong Kong during the season for a match against the local Rangers.

League:	Champions
League Cup:	Failed to qualify from section
Scottish Cup:	Fourth Round
European Cup:	First Round

SCOTTISH PREMIER LEAGUE

July 1st: Willie Garner was signed from Aberdeen for £45,000.

July 7th: Roddie MacDonald joined Hearts for £55,000.

August 29th

CELTIC (1) 5	AIRDRIE (1) 2
Burns (40 secs), McCluskey 2 (48, 76), McGarvey (62), Nicholas (83)	Clark 2 (36, 78)

CELTIC: Bonner; McGrain, Reid; Aitken, Moyes, MacLeod; Provan, Sullivan, McGarvey (Nicholas), Burns, McCluskey

AIRDRIE: Martin; Erwin, Rodger; McCluskey, March, Kerr (T. Walker); McKeown, Clark, N. Anderson, Gordon, McGuire

Attendance: 21,100

September 4th: Johnny Doyle turned down a move to Motherwell after turning down a move to Hearts.

September 5th

ABERDEEN (1) 1	CELTIC (2) 3
Strachan (2 pen)	Burns (7), McGarvey 2 (25, 54)

ABERDEEN: Leighton; Kennedy, McLeish, Miller, Cooper; Strachan, Watson, Bell (McMaster); McCall, McGhee (Cowan), Hewitt

CELTIC: Bonner; McGrain, Aitken, McAdam, Reid; Sullivan, MacLeod, Burns; Provan, McGarvey, McCluskey

Attendance: 18,825

September 9th: McGrain and Provan were in the Scotland team which beat Sweden 2-0 in a World Cup match at Hampden Park.

September 12th

CELTIC (0) 2	MORTON (0) 1
MacLeod (51), McAdam (58)	Thomson (73)

CELTIC: Bonner; McGrain, Aitken, McAdam, Reid; Sullivan, MacLeod, Burns; Provan, McGarvey, McCluskey

MORTON: Baines; Hayes, McLaughlin, Orr, Holmes; Rooney, Docherty, Hutchinson; Houston, Busby (Cochrane), Thomson

Attendance: 19,900

September 19th

RANGERS (0) 0	CELTIC (1) 2
	McAdam (11), MacLeod (86)

RANGERS: McCloy; Jardine (McAdam), Forsyth, Stevens, Dawson; Miller, Bett, Redford, Cooper, Johnstone, Johnston (MacDonald)

RANGERS: Bonner; McGrain, Aitken, McAdam, Reid; Sullivan, MacLeod, Burns; Provan, McGarvey, McCluskey

Attendance: 40,900

Rangers never threatened any danger on the day on which they opened their new £4 million stand. Only captain Ally Dawson and Davie Cooper earned pass marks while Celtic did not have a failure in their side. They had outstanding performers in Provan, MacLeod, McGarvey, McAdam and Reid.

September 26th

CELTIC (0) 2	PARTICK THISTLE (0) 0
Nicholas (60), Burns (79)	

CELTIC: Bonner; McGrain (Moyes), Aitken, McAdam, Reid; Sullivan, MacLeod, Burns; Nicholas, McGarvey, McCluskey

PARTICK THISTLE: Rough; McKinnon (McDonald), Dunlop, Anderson, Whittaker; Lapsley, Jardine, Park (O'Hara); Doyle, Watson, Clark

Attendance: 15,200

October 3rd

DUNDEE (0) 1	CELTIC (1) 3
McGeachie (61)	McCluskey 2 (27, 57), McGarvey (70)

DUNDEE: Geddes; Barr, MacDonald, Glennie, Cameron; Fraser, Bell, McGeachie (Mackie); Ferguson, Sinclair, Fleming (Scrimgeour)

CELTIC: Bonner; Moyes, Aitken, McAdam, Reid; Sullivan, Burns, MacLeod; Nicholas, McCluskey, McGarvey

Attendance: 13,254

October 10th

ST MIRREN (0) 1	CELTIC (2) 2
Scanlon (49 pen)	Nicholas (21), McCluskey (42)

ST MIRREN: Thomson; Young (Logan), Beckett; McCormack, Fulton, Copland; McAvennie, Stark, Bone, Abercrombie, Scanlon

CELTIC: Bonner; McGrain, Reid; Aitken, McAdam, MacLeod; Nicholas, Sullivan, McGarvey, Burns, McCluskey

Attendance: 16,441

October 17th

CELTIC (0) 1	DUNDEE UNITED (1) 1
McCluskey (50)	Milne (90 secs)

CELTIC: Bonner; Moyes, McAdam, Aitken, Reid; Sullivan, MacLeod, Burns; McGarvey, McCluskey, Nicholas

DUNDEE UNITED: McAlpine; Kopel, Hegarty, Narey, Murray; Bannon, Phillip, Holt; Kirkwood, Dodds, Bannon

Attendance: 23,000

October 19th: Johnny Doyle died in an accident at his home.

October 24th

HIBERNIAN (1) 1	CELTIC (0) 0
McLeod (45 pen)	

HIBERNIAN: McArthur; Sneddon, McNamara, Paterson, Turnbull; Callachan, Flavell, Duncan; Rae, Murray, McLeod

CELTIC: Bonner; Moyes, Aitken, Garner, Reid; Sullivan, MacLeod, Burns; McGarvey, McCluskey, Nicholas

Attendance: 18,000. Nicholas missed a penalty.

October 31st
AIRDRIE (1) 1 — CELTIC (1) 3
Clark (5 pen) — Sullivan (40), McCluskey (56 pen), Burns (86)

AIRDRIE: Davidson; Erwin (Thomson/Kerr), March, Anderson, Rodger; McKeown, Walker, Gordon; Flood, Clark, McGuire

CELTIC: Bonner; Moyes, Aitken, McAdam, Reid; Sullivan, MacLeod, Burns; McGarvey, McCluskey, Nicholas

Attendance: 13,500

League positions

	P	W	D	L	F	A	Pts
1 CELTIC	10	8	1	1	23	9	17
2 Aberdeen	10	6	2	2	16	10	14
3 St Mirren	10	5	2	3	15	12	12
4 Hibernian	10	3	4	3	11	7	10
5 Rangers	9	3	4	2	12	11	10

November 7th
CELTIC (1) 2 — ABERDEEN (0) 1
McGarvey (39), McCluskey (72) — Strachan (89)

CELTIC: Bonner; Moyes, McAdam, Aitken, Reid; Sullivan, MacLeod, Burns (Conroy); Provan, McCluskey, McGarvey

ABERDEEN: Leighton; Kennedy, McLeish, Miller, Cooper; Strachan, Watson (Hewitt), Simpson; Black (McMaster), McGhee, Weir

Attendance: 29,326

November 14th
MORTON (0) 1 — CELTIC (0) 1
Ritchie (89 pen) — McCluskey (58)

MORTON: Baines; Hayes, Orr, McLaughlin, Holmes; Docherty, Cochrane, Ritchie; Slaven, McNeill, Hutchinson (Houston)

CELTIC: Bonner; Moyes, Aitken, McAdam, Reid; Sullivan, Conroy, MacLeod; Provan, McGarvey (Nicholas), McCluskey

Attendance: 14,500

November 19th: Davie Provan was in the Scotland team beaten 2-1 by Portugal in a World Cup match in Lisbon.

November 21st
CELTIC (2) 3 — RANGERS (3) 3
McAdam (3), McGarvey (10), MacLeod (51) — Dalziel (5), Bett (20), MacDonald (21)

CELTIC: Bonner; Moyes, McAdam, Aitken, Reid; Sullivan, MacLeod, Conroy; Provan, McGarvey, McCluskey

RANGERS: McCloy; Jardine, Jackson, Stevens, Miller; Russell, MacDonald, Bett; Cooper (Mackay), Johnstone, Dalziel (Redford)

Attendance: 48,600

Rangers can take great credit from twice coming from behind. Peter McCloy made a tremendous diving save from Dom Sullivan in 3 minutes. From the resultant corner Moyes headed towards McCloy – the ball was deflected – and McAdam provided the final touch to put Celtic ahead. 2 minutes later young Gordon Dalziel, playing in his first Old Firm match, went on hands and knees to guide the ball past Bonner with his head following a Derek Johnstone knockdown. Celtic regained the lead in the 10th minute following a great move. Provan sent Moyes down the right on the overlap and the young full-back sent in a precision cross which McGarvey headed high over McCloy. Rangers again equalised 9 minutes later. Dalziel took a pass from MacDonald and jinked his way to the bye-line before crossing to the far post for Jim Bett to head home. A minute later another Dalziel cross had the Celtic defence in all sorts of trouble and MacDonald slipped in to put Rangers in front. Six minutes after half-time Moyes again leaped high to knock down a Provan corner and Murdo MacLeod thundered a tremendous drive past McCloy. The action roared on but the defences finally got on top and there was no further scoring.

November 28th
PARTICK THISTLE (0) 0 — CELTIC (1) 2
McCluskey (24), Provan (59)

PARTICK THISTLE: Rough; Murray, Anderson, Dunlop, Whittaker; Park (McDowall), McDonald, Doyle; Watson, Johnston, Clark (Lapsley)

CELTIC: Bonner; Moyes, Aitken, McAdam, Reid; Sullivan (Nicholas), Conroy, MacLeod; Provan, McGarvey, McCluskey

Attendance: 13,073

December 5th
CELTIC (0) 3 — DUNDEE (0) 1
McGarvey 2 (59, 84), Conroy (81) — Sinclair (89)

CELTIC: Bonner; McGrain, Aitken, McAdam, Reid; Conroy, Burns, MacLeod; Provan, McCluskey, McGarvey

DUNDEE: Blair; Barr, Glennie, MacDonald, McLelland; Cameron, Fraser, Bell (Kidd); Sinclair, Ferguson, Mackie

Attendance: 14,570

League positions

	P	W	D	L	F	A	Pts
1 CELTIC	15	11	3	1	34	15	25
2 Dundee United	14	7	4	3	26	12	18
3 St Mirren	15	7	4	4	23	18	18
4 Aberdeen	15	7	4	4	21	16	18
5 Rangers	15	6	6	3	25	21	18

December 21st: Toronto Blizzard made an approach to Billy McNeill.

January 9th
RANGERS (0) 1 CELTIC (0) 0
Bett (72 pen)

RANGERS: Stewart; Jardine, Jackson, Stevens, Dawson; Russell, MacDonald, Bett; Cooper (McAdam), Johnstone, Dalziel

CELTIC: Bonner; McGrain, McAdam, Aitken, Reid; Conroy (Moyes), MacLeod, Burns; Provan (McGarvey), Nicholas, McCluskey

Attendance: 42,000

A penalty by Jim Bett was all that separated the sides. Had Johnstone been in sharper scoring form the issue would not have been clouded in any way. He had a chance from a MacDonald cross in 37 minutes which he squandered, and in 48 minutes, following a beautiful run down the right and cross by Dalziel, he had a fine chance close in and unmarked but this time he sliced it wide. In 72 minutes Stewart punted a long ball forward. Cooper sprinted on and was tripped up by Bonner coming off his line. Bett struck the penalty well out of Bonner's reach.

January 18th: Charlie Nicholas broke a leg playing for the reserves against Morton at Cappielow.

January 26th: Celtic had a £200,000 bid for Sandy Clark of Airdrie turned down.

January 30th
ABERDEEN (1) 1 CELTIC (1) 3
McMaster (1) McCluskey (27 pen), MacLeod (71), McStay (77)

ABERDEEN: Leighton; Kennedy, McLeish, Miller, Rougvie; Strachan, Bell, McMaster; Hewitt, McGhee (Black), Weir

CELTIC: Bonner; McGrain, McAdam, Aitken, Reid; Sullivan, MacLeod, Burns; McStay, McGarvey, McCluskey

Attendance: 19,000

February 4th: Morton signed Jim Duffy for £25,000.

February 2nd
CELTIC (0) 0 HIBERNIAN (0) 0

CELTIC: Bonner; McGrain, Reid; Aitken, McAdam, MacLeod; Sullivan (Halpin), McStay, McGarvey, Burns, McCluskey

HIBERNIAN: McArthur; Sneddon, Schaedler; Brazil, Paterson, McNamara; Callachan, Flavell, MacLeod, Murray, Duncan

Attendance: 16,700

February 6th
DUNDEE (0) 1 CELTIC (1) 3
Kidd (75) MacLeod 2 (9, 66), McGarvey (74)

DUNDEE: Blair; Cameron (Mackie), Glennie, McGeachie, McLelland; Scrimgeour, Kidd, McKimmie; Stephen, Sinclair (Fleming), Ferguson

CELTIC: Bonner; McGrain, Aitken, McAdam, Reid; Sullivan, McStay, MacLeod, Burns; McGarvey, McCluskey

Attendance: 11,373

February 20th
CELTIC (0) 2 PARTICK THISTLE (0) 2
McCluskey (75), Aitken (77) Jardine (52), Watson (72 pen)

CELTIC: Bonner; McGrain, Aitken, McAdam, Reid; McStay, MacLeod (Conroy), Burns; McCluskey, McGarvey, Halpin (Crainie)

PARTICK THISTLE: Rough; McKinnon, Anderson, Dunlop, Whittaker; Jardine, Doyle, Watson; Park (McDonald), Johnston, Higgins

Attendance: 14,200

February 24th: Danny McGrain was in the Scotland team beaten 3-0 by Spain in Valencia.

February 27th
HIBERNIAN (1) 1 CELTIC (0) 0
Rae (18)

HIBERNIAN: McArthur; Sneddon, Paterson, Brazil, Schaedler; Callachan, McNamara, Duncan; Rae, Murray (Flavell), MacLeod

CELTIC: Bonner; McGrain, McAdam, Moyes, Reid; McStay (Crainie), Conroy, MacLeod, Burns; McGarvey, McCluskey

Attendance: 15,914

League positions

	P	W	D	L	F	A	Pts
1 CELTIC	21	13	5	3	42	21	31
2 St Mirren	21	10	7	4	32	22	27
3 Rangers	21	9	8	4	33	25	26
4 Aberdeen	20	8	7	5	25	19	23
5 Hibernian	23	7	9	7	24	19	23

March 3rd
CELTIC (0) 1 MORTON (0) 0
McGarvey (82)

CELTIC: Bonner; McGrain, Reid; Moyes, McAdam, MacLeod; Sullivan, McCluskey, McGarvey, Burns, Halpin

MORTON: Baines; Hayes, Holmes; Rooney, McLaughlin, Duffy, McNeill, McNab, Busby, Hutchinson, Ritchie

Attendance: 9,000. McCluskey missed a penalty.

March 13th
ST MIRREN (0) 2 CELTIC (4) 5
McDougall 2 (48, 61) MacLeod 2 (17, 50), Burns (30), Sullivan (37), McCluskey (44)

ST MIRREN: Thomson; McCormack, Fulton, Copland, Beckett; Stark, Abercrombie, Richardson; Boag (MacDougall), Bone, Scanlon

CELTIC: Bonner; McGrain, Moyes, McAdam, Reid; Sullivan, MacLeod, Burns; Crainie, McGarvey (McStay), McCluskey
Attendance: 17,084

March 20th
CELTIC (2) 2 — AIRDRIE (0) 0
Sullivan (21), Burns (43)
CELTIC: Bonner; McGrain, Aitken, Moyes, Reid; Sullivan, MacLeod, Burns; Crainie, McGarvey, McCluskey (McAdam)
AIRDRIE: Martin; Cairney, N. Anderson, G. Anderson, Rodger; McKeown, Campbell, Gordon, Kerr (March); Thomson (McGuire), C. Walker
Attendance: 12,000

March 23rd: Danny McGrain was in the Scotland team which beat Holland 2-1 at Hampden Park. Tommy Burns made an appearance as substitute.

March 27th
CELTIC (0) 0 — ABERDEEN (0) 1
Kennedy (68)
CELTIC: Bonner; McGrain, Aitken, McAdam, Reid (Moyes); Crainie, Sullivan, MacLeod, Burns; McCluskey, McGarvey
ABERDEEN: Leighton; Kennedy, McLeish, Miller, Rougvie (McMaster); Simpson, Cooper, Strachan, Weir; McGhee, Hewitt (Cowan)
Attendance: 30,080

March 31st
DUNDEE UNITED (0) 0 — CELTIC (1) 2
Burns 2 (2, 84)
DUNDEE UNITED: McAlpine; Stark, Malpas; Gough, Hegarty, Narey; Kirkwood, Milne, Holt, Sturrock, Dodds
CELTIC: Bonner; McGrain, Reid; Aitken, McAdam, MacLeod; Crainie, Sullivan, McGarvey (McStay), McCluskey, Burns
Attendance: 15,143. McGarvey was carried off with a broken leg.

April 3rd
MORTON (0) 1 — CELTIC (1) 1
Ritchie (53) — Crainie (43)
MORTON: Baines; Hayes, McLaughlin, Duffy, Holmes; Rooney, Cochrane, Docherty; Ring (McNeill), Hutchinson, Ritchie
CELTIC: Bonner; Moyes, Aitken, McAdam, Reid; Sullivan (Provan), McStay, MacLeod, Burns; Crainie, McCluskey
Attendance: 10,500

April 10th
CELTIC (1) 2 — RANGERS (0) 1
Crainie (1), McAdam (50) — Johnstone (75)
CELTIC: Bonner; McGrain, Aitken, Moyes, Reid; Sullivan, MacLeod, Burns; Provan, McAdam, Crainie
RANGERS: Stewart; Jardine, McClelland, Jackson, Dawson; Russell, Bett, Redford (Dalziel); Cooper, Johnstone, MacDonald
Attendance: 40,144

Burns fashioned the 1st goal with a lethal pass inside Dawson. Sullivan had spotted the pass early and ran into the empty space. His shot was parried by Stewart. McAdam flicked the rebound on and Crainie, in his first Old Firm match, edged the ball over the line to give his side a sensational 1st minute lead. In 17 minutes a Cooper through ball left Russell clear and his thunderous volley rebounded off the bar. In 49 minutes Johnstone rose at the far post to head a Cooper free kick strongly against the woodwork. In the 50th minute Celtic went further ahead after a McClelland foul on Crainie. Burns' long free kick headed for the back post and as MacLeod took the defence for a little decoy run McAdam appeared on the blind side to score. Rangers pulled a goal back in the 75th minute when Johnstone chest trapped the ball before hitting a right-foot shot past Bonner.

April 14th
AIRDRIE (1) 1 — CELTIC (2) 5
Clark (29 pen) — Aitken (2), Crainie (9), McCluskey (56), Provan (60), Reid (76 pen)
AIRDRIE: Martin; T. Walker, Rodger; G. Anderson, March, N. Anderson; Flood, Clark, C. Walker, Campbell, Gordon
CELTIC: Bonner; McGrain, Reid; Aitken, McAdam, MacLeod; Provan, Sullivan, McCluskey, Crainie, Burns
Attendance: 12,000

April 17th
CELTIC (0) 4 — DUNDEE (1) 2
Reid (56 pen), McCluskey 2 (67, 83), Provan (77) — Smith (3), Ferguson (78)
CELTIC: Bonner; McGrain, Reid; Aitken, McAdam, MacLeod; Provan, Sullivan, McCluskey, Burns, Crainie
DUNDEE: Geddes; Barr, McKimmie; Fraser, Smith, Glennie; Ferguson, Kidd (Mackie), Sinclair, Scrimgeour (McGeachie), Stephen
Attendance: 14,288

April 21st
CELTIC (1) 3 — DUNDEE UNITED (0) 1
McCluskey 2 (39, 54), Provan (80) — Dodds (87)
CELTIC: Bonner; McGrain, Reid; Aitken, McAdam, MacLeod; Provan, Sullivan, McCluskey, Burns, Crainie
DUNDEE UNITED: McAlpine; Malpas, Murray (Holt); Gough, Hegarty, Narey; Bannon, Milne, Kirkwood, Sturrock, Dodds
Attendance: 14,659

April 24th
PARTICK THISTLE (0) 0 CELTIC (0) 3
Crainie 3 (51, 75, 85)

PARTICK THISTLE: Rough; McKinnon, Whittaker, Dunlop, Lapsley; Jardine, Doyle, Watson (McDonald); Park, Johnston, O'Hara (Clark)

CELTIC: Bonner; McGrain, Aitken, McAdam, Reid; Sullivan, MacLeod, Burns; Provan, McCluskey, Crainie

Attendance: 14,200

April 28th: McGrain and Provan were in the Scotland team which drew 1-1 with Northern Ireland in Belfast.

May 1st
CELTIC (4) 6 HIBERNIAN (0) 0
Burns (15), Crainie (19), Aitken (32), MacLeod 2 (41, 57), McCluskey (60)

CELTIC: Bonner; McGrain, McAdam, Aitken, Reid; Sullivan, MacLeod, Burns; Provan, Crainie, McCluskey

HIBERNIAN: McArthur; Sneddon, Paterson, Brazil (Schaedler), McLaren; McNamara, Flavell, Turnbull; MacLeod (Jamieson), Murray, Rodier

Attendance: 16,064

May 3rd
CELTIC (0) 0 ST MIRREN (0) 0

CELTIC: Bonner; McGrain, Reid; Aitken, McAdam, MacLeod; Provan, Sullivan, McCluskey, Burns, Crainie

ST MIRREN: Thomson; Walker (Somner), Beckett; Curran, Fulton, Copland; McEachran, Stark, McDougall, McAvennie (Logan), Abercrombie

Attendance: 27,395

May 8th
DUNDEE UNITED (1) 3 CELTIC (0) 0
Hegarty (18), Sturrock (46), Milne (80)

DUNDEE UNITED: McAlpine; Gough, Hegarty, Narey, Malpas; Bannon, Phillip, Holt; Milne (Reilly), Sturrock, Dodds

CELTIC: Bonner; McGrain, Aitken, McAdam, Reid; Sullivan (McStay), MacLeod, Burns; Provan, McCluskey (Moyes), Crainie

Attendance: 16,779

May 15th
CELTIC (0) 3 ST MIRREN (0) 0
McCluskey 2 (63, 76), McAdam (72)

CELTIC: Bonner; McGrain, McAdam, Aitken, Reid; McStay, MacLeod, Burns; Provan, McCluskey, Crainie

ST MIRREN: Thomson; Beckett, Fulton, Copland, Walker; Stark, Fitzpatrick, Richardson (Speirs); McAvennie, McDougall (Logan), Somner

Attendance: 39,669. Celtic clinched the title.

Scottish Premier League

	P	W	D	L	F	A	Pts
1 CELTIC	36	24	7	5	79	33	55
2 Aberdeen	36	23	7	6	71	29	53
3 Rangers	36	16	11	9	57	45	43
4 Dundee United	36	15	10	11	61	38	40
5 St Mirren	36	14	9	13	49	52	37
6 Hibernian	36	11	14	11	38	40	36
7 Morton	36	9	12	15	31	54	30
8 Dundee	36	11	4	21	46	72	26
9 Partick Thistle	36	6	10	20	35	59	22
10 Airdrie	36	5	8	23	31	76	18

May 14th: McGrain, Aitken, Burns, McCluskey and Provan were all included in Scotland's pool of 40 players for the World Cup Finals.

May 24th: Tommy Burns was in the Scotland team which beat Wales 1-0 at Hampden Park.

May 24th: John Weir was given a free transfer.

May 29th: Danny McGrain was in the Scotland team which was beaten 1-0 by England at Hampden Park.

June 15th: Danny McGrain was in the Scotland team which beat New Zealand 5-2 in the World Cup Finals in Malaga, Spain.

June 22nd: Danny McGrain made an appearance as a substitute for Scotland in the match against U.S.S.R. in Malaga which ended 2-2. It was his 62nd and last appearance for Scotland.

SCOTTISH LEAGUE CUP

August 8th
CELTIC (1) 1 ST MIRREN (1) 3
McGarvey (31) McDougall (33), Garner o.g. (61), McCormack (81)

CELTIC: Bonner; McGrain, Garner, Aitken, Reid; Sullivan, MacLeod (Conroy), Burns; Provan, Nicholas (McCluskey), McGarvey

ST MIRREN: Thomson; Beckett, McCormack, Copland, Abercrombie; Stark, Fitzpatrick, Richardson; McDougall (Logan), Bone, Scanlon

Attendance: 26,100

August 12th
ST JOHNSTONE (1) 2 CELTIC (0) 0
McCoist (37), Morton (81 pen)

ST JOHNSTONE: Tulloch; Mackay, Kilgour; Weir, Rutherford, Caldwell; Pelosi, McCoist, Beedie (Morton), Fleming, Brogan

CELTIC: Bonner; McGrain, McAdam; Aitken, Garner, MacLeod; Provan, Sullivan, McGarvey, Burns, McCluskey

Attendance: 10,406

August 15th
CELTIC (2) 4 HIBERNIAN (0) 1
McLeod 2 (90 secs, 83), Nicholas 2 (27, 65) Duncan (75)

CELTIC: Bonner; McGrain, Reid; Aitken, McAdam (Moyes), MacLeod; Provan, Sullivan, McGarvey, Burns, Nicholas

HIBERNIAN: Donaldson; Sneddon, Turnbull; McLaren, Paterson, McNamara; MacLeod (Murray), Flavell, Connolly, Rae, Duncan

Attendance: 19,200

August 19th
CELTIC (2) 4 — ST JOHNSTONE (0) 1
McGarvey (17), Provan 2 (21, 48), Nicholas (65) — McCoist (78)

CELTIC: Bonner; McGrain, Reid; Aitken, Moyes, MacLeod; Provan, Sullivan, McGarvey, Burns, Nicholas

ST JOHNSTONE: Tulloch; Mackay, Kilgour; Weir, Rutherford, Caldwell; Pelosi, McCoist, Fleming, Morton (Brannigan), Brogan

Attendance: 14,600. Pelosi was ordered off.

August 22nd
ST MIRREN (1) 1 — CELTIC (2) 5
Stark (10 pen) — MacLeod 2 (28, 75), McCluskey 3 (35, 55, 85)

ST MIRREN: Thomson; Young, McCormack, Copland, Abercrombie; Fitzpatrick, Stark, Richardson; Bone, McDougall (Logan), Scanlon

CELTIC: Bonner; McGrain, Aitken, Moyes, Reid; Sullivan, MacLeod, Burns; Provan, McGarvey, McCluskey

Attendance: 18,065

August 26th
HIBERNIAN (0) 1 — CELTIC (0) 4
Paterson (46) — McGarvey 2 (56, 78), Sullivan (57), MacLeod (65)

HIBERNIAN: Donaldson; Sneddon, Flavell; McLaren, Docherty, Paterson; McNamara, Callachan, Rae, Rodier, Duncan

CELTIC: Bonner; McAdam, Reid; Aitken, Moyes, MacLeod; Provan, Sullivan, McGarvey, Burns, McCluskey

Attendance: 13,685. Celtic failed to qualify for the Quarter-Finals.

Section Table

	P	W	D	L	F	A	Pts
St Mirren	6	4	1	1	10	8	9
CELTIC	6	4	0	2	18	9	8
St Johnstone	6	2	0	4	8	12	4
Hibernian	6	1	1	4	5	12	3

SCOTTISH CUP

Third Round January 23rd
CELTIC (3) 4 — QUEEN OF THE SOUTH (0) 0
McGarvey (19), McGrain (21), McCluskey (39 pen), Halpin (85)

CELTIC: Bonner; McGrain, Aitken, McAdam, Reid; McStay, Burns, MacLeod; McGarvey, McCluskey, Halpin

QUEEN OF THE SOUTH: Ball; Dickson, Clark, Boyd, Cloy; Miller, Alexander, McCall; G. Robertson, Phillips, J. Robertson

Attendance: 11,281

Fourth Round February 13th
ABERDEEN (1) 1 — CELTIC (0) 0
Hewitt (19)

ABERDEEN: Leighton; Kennedy, Rougvie, Miller, McMaster; Strachan, McLeish, Simpson (Bell); Weir, McGhee, Hewitt

CELTIC: Bonner; McGrain, Aitken, McAdam, Reid; Sullivan (Halpin), MacLeod, McStay, Burns; McGarvey, McCluskey

Attendance: 24,000

EUROPEAN CUP

First Round First Leg September 16th
CELTIC (0) 1 — JUVENTUS (0) 0
MacLeod (65)

CELTIC: Bonner; McGrain, Reid; Aitken, McAdam, MacLeod; Provan, Sullivan, Nicholas, Burns, McCluskey

JUVENTUS: Zoff; Gentile, Cabrini; Furino, Brio, Scirea; Marocchino (Fanna), Tardelli, Bettega, Brady, Bonini

Attendance: 60,017

Bonner came to Celtic's rescue in 21 minutes with a magnificent save after Aitken brought down Brady. The Irishman touched the free-kick to Tardelli and Bonner dived low to touch his shot round the post. Soon after Bettega sliced a shot wide. Twice in the last 5 minutes of the 1st half McCluskey was sent crashing in the box but the referee waved away Celtic's pleas for a penalty. The only goal of the game came in the 65th minute. The Italian defence, for once, could not get a corner cleared. Aitken's shot hit against a defender's arm, but rather than risk another penalty claim being turned down MacLeod lashed in a shot which hit Scirea and flew past Zoff.

First Round Second Leg September 30th
JUVENTUS (2) 2 — CELTIC (0) 0
Virdis (28), Bettega (40)

JUVENTUS: Zoff; Gentile, Cabrini; Furino, Brio, Scirea; Marocchino, Tardelli, Bettega, Brady (Bonini), Virdis (Fanna)

CELTIC: Bonner; Moyes, Reid; Aitken, McAdam, MacLeod; Provan, Sullivan, McGarvey, Burns, McCluskey

Attendance: 70,000

Liam Brady inspired Juventus to a deserved victory. Only a magnificent display by Bonner prevented a much bigger defeat. Celtic badly missed injured captain Danny McGrain. In 28 minutes Juventus hit Celtic a stunning blow on the break. Aitken hit a poor free kick to the edge of the Italians' penalty area. With the Celtic defence caught upfield Gentile sent the ball forward to Virdis who ran 60 yards before beating Bonner. 12 minutes later Juventus took the overall lead in the tie when Bettega killed a cross on his knee, swivelled and beat Bonner from 12 yards. In the 55th minute only a last-ditch tackle by Moyes stopped Marocchino scoring. In 72 minutes Bonner had 2 fine saves in quick succession. The first came when he stopped Brio's header from Brady's cross and the 2nd when he came out to block Virdis. Juventus won 2-1 on aggregate.

APPEARANCES	League	League Cup	Scottish Cup	European Cup
Bonner	36	6	2	2
McGrain	27	5	2	1
Reid	36	5	2	2

APPEARANCES	League	League Cup	Scottish Cup Cup	Cup Winners
Moyes	15+4S	3+1S	–	1
Aitken	33	6	2	2
McAdam	33+1S	3	2	2
MacLeod	36	6	2	2
P. McStay	7+3S	–	2	–
Halpin	2+1S	–	1+1S	–
Conroy	6+2S	–	–	–
Provan	19+1S	6	–	2
Sullivan	31	6	1	2
Burns	33	6	2	2
McGarvey	25+1S	6	2	1
McCluskey	35	3+1S	2	2
Nicholas	7+3S	3	–	1
Crainie	14+2S	–	–	–
Garner	1	2	–	–

GOALSCORERS

League: McCluskey 21 (2 pens), MacLeod 10, McGarvey 10, Burns 9, Crainie 7, McAdam 5, Provan 4, Aitken 3, Sullivan 3, Nicholas 3, Reid 2 (2 pens), Conroy 1, P. McStay 1

League Cup: McGarvey 4, MacLeod 3, Nicholas 3, McCluskey 3, Provan 2, MacLeod 2, Sullivan 1

Scottish Cup: McGarvey 1, McGrain 1, Halpin 1, McCluskey 1 (pen)

European Cup: MacLeod 1

Celtic clinched the League Championship in season 1981-82 when they defeated St Mirren 3-0 at Parkhead. Here Danny McGrain and Roy Aitken celebrate in style.

Season 1982-83

In one of the closest and most exciting League title races for years Celtic were pipped by one point by Dundee United who took their first ever Championship. Aberdeen finished with the same number of points as Celtic (55) but with an inferior goal difference. Celtic had led the table for most of the season but 2 defeats by Dundee United and Aberdeen within the space of 3 days at the end of April meant that they had to rely on United slipping up, but they never did and they clinched the title on the last day of the season at Dens Park. Meanwhile Celtic were taking their 7th League point of the season from Rangers by beating them 4-2 at Ibrox and the Celtic fans were seeing Charlie Nicholas for the last time in the Green and White Hoops before he took his talents to Arsenal for a £750,000 fee. Some of that money was used immediately to sign Brian McClair from Motherwell. Nicholas scored 29 of their 90 goals during the campaign and was deservedly voted Scotland's Player of the Year. He also won the P.F.A. award. Pat Bonner, Tom McAdam and Paul McStay played in every League match. In a sensational ending to the season, which stunned the Scottish football public, Manager Billy McNeill quit to take up the reigns at Manchester City. In his 5 seasons as Manager he had taken Celtic to 3 Premier Division Titles and had won the Scottish Cup once and the League Cup once. They had played 180 League matches under McNeill, winning 114, drawing 33 and losing 33.

Celtic won the League Cup and scored an amazing 41 goals in their 11 matches. They won their Section without dropping a point. Partick Thistle were beaten 7-0 on aggregate in the Quarter-Final and a late Nicholas goal at Tannadice gave them a 3-2 aggregate victory over Dundee United in the Semi-Final. They met Rangers in the Final and on a drab, rainy afternoon 2 first-half goals from Nicholas and MacLeod set them up for a deserved victory.

They reached the Semi-Final of the Scottish Cup without conceding a goal. However, top scorer Charlie Nicholas failed a late fitness test and the goal machine dried up for once, and Aberdeen went on to win an extremely physical match by a 65th-minute goal from substitute Peter Weir.

Celtic faced 3 times winners Ajax in the First Round of the European Cup. They were rather fortunate to gain a draw at Parkhead against the Dutch side who played their special brand of open, entertaining football and the return leg looked perilous, but a mixture of determination, skill and courage gave them a well-earned victory in Amsterdam. They were drawn against Real Sociedad in the Second Round, and just when it looked as if they were strolling to a 0-0 draw in Spain the home side hit them with a devastating double blow with 2 goals in 4 minutes. Although beaten, the winning of the tie overall did not look beyond Celtic, but that changed when they gifted Sociedad a first-half goal at Parkhead. They then needed 4 goals to win through to the Quarter-Finals. 2 great goals from Murdo MacLeod gave them victory on the night but they were out of Europe for another year.

League:	Runners-up
League Cup:	Winners
Scottish Cup:	Semi-Finalists
European Cup:	Second Round

SCOTTISH PREMIER LEAGUE

June 20th: Brian McClair was signed from Motherwell for £70,000.

August 12th: Graeme Sinclair was signed from Dumbarton for £60,000

September 4th
CELTIC (2) 2 DUNDEE (0) 0
Provan (34),
Aitken (41)

CELTIC: Bonner; McGrain, McAdam, Aitken, Reid; McStay, MacLeod, Burns; Provan, McCluskey, Nicholas

DUNDEE: Kelly; McGeachie, Smith, Glennie, McKimmie; Fraser, Bell, Fleming; Kidd (Sinclair), Davidson, Mackie

Attendance: 19,122

September 11th
ST MIRREN (1) 1 CELTIC (0) 2
Richardson (12) Nicholas 2
(64 pen, 87 pen)

ST MIRREN: Thomson; Wilson, McCormack, Copland, Clarke; Richardson, Fitzpatrick, Stark; McAvennie, McDougall (Logan), Scanlon

CELTIC: Bonner; McGrain, Aitken, McAdam, Reid; P. McStay, Burns, MacLeod; Crainie, McCluskey (McGarvey), Nicholas

Attendance: 15,449

September 18th
MOTHERWELL (0) 0 CELTIC (3) 7
Nicholas 3 (26, 61, 70),
McGarvey (32),
MacLeod (41),
Aitken 2 (57, 66)

MOTHERWELL: Sproat; McLelland, Wark; Carson, Rafferty, Forbes; McClair, O'Hara, Conn, Edvaldsson, Gahagan

CELTIC: Bonner; McGrain, Moyes, McAdam, Reid; McStay, Aitken, MacLeod; Provan, McGarvey (Crainie), Nicholas (McCluskey)

Attendance: 17,092

September 25th
CELTIC (1) 2 HIBERNIAN (0) 0
MacLeod (13),
McStay (60)

CELTIC: Bonner, McGrain, Aitken, McAdam, Reid; Sullivan, McStay, MacLeod; Provan, McGarvey (McCluskey), Nicholas

HIBERNIAN: McArthur; Sneddon, McNamara, Rae, Schaedler (Turnbull); Flavell, Callachan, Brazil (Duncan), Thomson; Jamieson, Murray

Attendance: 16,371

October 2nd
DUNDEE UNITED (0) 2 CELTIC (1) 2
Dodds (76), McStay (20),
Milne (85) Aitken (46)

DUNDEE UNITED: McAlpine; Gough, Hegarty, Narey, Stark; Kirkwood, Malpas, Bannon (Holt/Britton); Sturrock, Dodds, Milne

CELTIC: Bonner; McGrain, McAdam, Sinclair, Reid; Aitken, McStay, MacLeod; Provan, McGarvey (McCluskey), Nicholas

Attendance: 20,000

Celtic were coasting along on a 2 goal lead with only 14 minutes left when United produced a fightback which enabled them to snatch a draw.

October 9th
CELTIC (0) 1 ABERDEEN (0) 3
Nicholas (68) Strachan (54 pen),
Simpson (58),
McGhee (87)

CELTIC: Bonner; McGrain, McAdam, Sinclair, Reid; McStay, Aitken, MacLeod (Crainie); Provan, McGarvey, Nicholas

ABERDEEN: Leighton; Cooper, McLeish, Miller, Rougvie; Bell (Watson), McMaster, Simpson; Strachan, McGhee, Weir

Attendance: 29,733. McGrain was ordered off

October 11th: Mike Conroy was transferred to Hibernian for £40,000.

October 16th
CELTIC (0) 2 KILMARNOCK (0) 1
Nicholas 2 (78, 84) Clarke (51)

CELTIC: Bonner; Sinclair (McGarvey), McAdam, Aitken, Reid; McStay, Aitken, MacLeod; Provan, Crainie, Nicholas

KILMARNOCK: McCulloch; McDicken, Armstrong, Clarke; McLean, McClurg (Bourke), Bryson; McGivern, Gallagher

Attendance: 11,063

October 20th: Jimmy McGrory died aged 78.

October 23rd
MORTON (0) 1 CELTIC (2) 2
Rooney (70) McGarvey (22),
Nicholas (40 pen)

MORTON: Baines; Houston, McLaughlin, Duffy, Holmes; Rooney, Cochrane, Docherty (Gavigan); McNab, Hutchinson, Ritchie (McNeill)

CELTIC: Bonner; McGrain, Aitken, McAdam, Reid; McStay, Sinclair, MacLeod; Provan, McGarvey (Crainie), Nicholas

Attendance: 15,500

October 30th
CELTIC (1) 3 RANGERS (2) 2
McStay (18), Prytz (16),
McGarvey (67), Cooper (40)
MacLeod (87)

CELTIC: Bonner; McGrain, Aitken, McAdam, Reid; McStay, Sinclair, MacLeod; Provan, McGarvey, Nicholas

RANGERS: Stewart; McKinnon, McClelland, Stevens, Dawson; Russell (MacDonald), Prytz (McAdam); Cooper, Johnstone, Redford

Attendance: 60,408

Celtic broke Rangers' 20-match unbeaten run. The main features of the match were the power of Murdo MacLeod and the delicate touches and astute passing of Paul McStay.

League positions

	P	W	D	L	F	A	Pts
1 CELTIC	9	7	1	1	23	10	15
2 Dundee United	9	5	4	0	17	3	14
3 Aberdeen	9	5	2	2	15	9	12
4 Rangers	9	3	5	1	17	11	11
5 Dundee	9	3	3	3	9	8	9

November 6th

DUNDEE (0) 2 — Fraser 2 (64, 76)
CELTIC (3) 3 — Nicholas (23 pen), Burns (38), McGarvey (45)

DUNDEE: Kelly; Glennie, Smith, MacDonald, McKimmie (Bell); Fraser, Scrimgeour, Stephen; Ferguson (Kidd), Davidson, Mackie

CELTIC: Bonner; McGrain, Aitken, McAdam, Sinclair; McStay, MacLeod, Burns; Provan, McGarvey, Nicholas

Attendance: 11,681

November 13th

CELTIC (4) 5 — Nicholas 3 (20 pen, 22, 26), Burns (23), Aitken (88)
ST MIRREN (0) 0

CELTIC: Bonner; McGrain, Aitken, McAdam, Sinclair; McStay, MacLeod, Burns; Provan, McGarvey (McCluskey), Nicholas

ST MIRREN: Thomson; Wilson, Copland, Fulton, Clarke; Fitzpatrick, Stark (McDougall), Richardson; Somner, McAvennie, Abercrombie

Attendance: 15,044

November 20th

CELTIC (0) 3 — McStay (60), Nicholas (64), Burns (83)
MOTHERWELL (0) 1 — Flavell (85)

CELTIC: Bonner; McGrain, Aitken, McAdam, Sinclair; McStay, Macleod, Burns; Provan, McGarvey (McCluskey), Nicholas

MOTHERWELL: Sproat; McLeod, Carson, Edvaldsson, Forsyth; Flavell, Rafferty, O'Hara (Forbes); McLelland (Clinging); McClair, Gahagan

Attendance: 14,963. Nicholas missed a penalty

November 27th

HIBERNIAN (0) 2 — Murray 2 (65, 85)
CELTIC (1) 3 — McGarvey 2 (32, 82), McStay (57)

HIBERNIAN: Rough; Sneddon, Conroy, Rae, Duncan; Callaghan (Welsh), Turnbull, Thomson, Smith; Jamieson, Murray

CELTIC: Bonner; McGrain, McAdam, Moyes, Sinclair; Aitken, McStay, Burns; Provan, McGarvey, Nicholas

Attendance: 17,121

December 11th

ABERDEEN (1) 1 — McGhee (18)
CELTIC (1) 2 — MacLeod (16), Provan (59)

ABERDEEN: Leighton; Kennedy, McLeish, Miller, Rougvie (Hewitt); Strachan, Cooper, Bell (Black); Simpson, McGhee, Weir

CELTIC: Bonner; McGrain, Aitken, McAdam, Sinclair; McStay, MacLeod, Burns; Provan, McGarvey, Nicholas

Attendance: 25,000

December 15th: Roy Aitken was in the Scotland team beaten 3-2 by Belgium in Brussels. Tommy Burns made an appearance as a substitute.

December 18th

KILMARNOCK (0) 0
CELTIC (1) 4 — Provan (1), McAdam (55), McGarvey (75), Burns (80)

KILMARNOCK: McCulloch; Robertson, Clarke, McDicken, Cockburn; Clark, McClurg (R. Clark), MacLeod; McGivern, Callagher, Bryson (McKinna)

CELTIC: Bonner; McGrain, Aitken, McAdam, Sinclair; McStay, MacLeod, Burns; Provan (McCluskey), McGarvey, Nicholas

Attendance: 9,000

League positions

	P	W	D	L	F	A	Pts
1 CELTIC	15	13	1	1	43	16	27
2 Dundee United	15	10	4	1	36	11	24
3 Aberdeen	16	10	3	3	31	13	23
4 Rangers	15	5	7	3	25	17	17
5 Dundee	15	5	4	6	19	18	14

December 27th

CELTIC (1) 5 — Nicholas (41 pen), MacLeod (53), McGarvey 2 (60, 80), Reid (82)
MORTON (1) 1 — MacLeod o.g. (30)

CELTIC: Bonner; McGrain, Sinclair; Moyes (Reid), McAdam, MacLeod; Provan, McStay, McGarvey (McCluskey), Burns, Nicholas

MORTON: Baines; Houston, Holmes; Rooney, McLaughlin, Duffy; McNeill, Slavin, Hutchinson, Cochrane, McNab

Attendance: 19,953

January 1st
RANGERS (1) 1 — CELTIC (1) 2
Black (24) — McStay (13), Nicholas (67)

RANGERS: Stewart; McKinnon, McClelland; Stevens, Paterson, Bett; Cooper, Russell, Kennedy, Black (Redford), MacDonald

CELTIC: Bonner; McGrain, Reid; Sinclair, McAdam, MacLeod; Provan, McStay, McGarvey, Burns, Nicholas

Attendance: 44,000

Celtic started with the upper hand, and throughout the first 10 minutes Rangers could do little to contain their strong attacks. Throughout the 2nd half each team had their share of attacks, near misses and close shaves. In the 67th minute Celtic scored what proved to be the winner. Nicholas picked up the ball from a MacLeod throw-in and as he moved from the centre of the park towards his left-hand side he took off past the Rangers defence by using his pace and clever stops and starts. Suddenly he let loose with a tremendous shot that ended up in the back of the net to give Celtic the points.

January 3rd
CELTIC (1) 2 — DUNDEE (0) 2
Burns (25), Nicholas (56) — Sinclair 2 (62, 78)

CELTIC: Bonner; McGrain, Reid; Sinclair, McAdam, MacLeod; Provan, P. McStay, McGarvey, Burns, Nicholas

DUNDEE: Kelly; Glennie, Scrimgeour; Bell, Smith, MacDonald; Ferguson, Stephen, Sinclair, Mackie, Murphy

Attendance: 16,615

January 8th
ST MIRREN (0) 0 — CELTIC (1) 1
MacLeod (16)

ST MIRREN: Thomson; Wilson, Walker, Fulton, Clarke; Stark, Richardson, Abercrombie; McAvennie; McDougall, Logan (Somner)

CELTIC: Bonner; McGrain, Sinclair, McAdam, Reid; McStay, Aitken, MacLeod; Provan (McCluskey), McGarvey, Nicholas (Sullivan)

Attendance: 14,748

January 15th
MOTHERWELL (0) 2 — CELTIC (1) 1
McClair 2 (47 pen, 89) — McLeod (23)

MOTHERWELL: Walker; Dornan, McLeod (Coyne); Carson, Edvaldsson, Mauchlen; McClair, Rafferty, Harrow, Forbes, O'Hara

CELTIC: Bonner; McGrain, Reid; Aitken, Sinclair, Sullivan; Provan, McStay, McGarvey, MacLeod, McCluskey

Attendance: 15,290

January 22nd
CELTIC (1) 4 — HIBERNIAN (1) 1
Nicholas (4), McCluskey (47), McGarvey 2 (57, 74) — McAdam o.g. (43)

CELTIC: Bonner; McGrain, Aitken, McAdam, Reid; McStay, MacLeod; Provan, Nicholas, McCluskey, McGarvey

HIBERNIAN: Rough; Sneddon, Rae, McNamara, Turnbull; Conroy, Welsh, Duncan; Rice, Irvine, Murray (Jamieson)

Attendance: 17,106

February 5th
DUNDEE UNITED (1) 1 — CELTIC (1) 1
Dodds (40) — Nicholas (4)

DUNDEE UNITED: McAlpine; Gough, Hegarty, Narey, Malpas; Kirkwood, Stark, Holt; Dodds, Sturrock, Bannon

CELTIC: Bonner; McGrain, McAdam, Sinclair, Reid; McStay, Aitken, MacLeod; Provan, Nicholas, McCluskey

Attendance: 17,289

Celtic took the lead in only 4 minutes when the United defence could not clear a Mark Reid cross and Paul McStay lobbed the ball on for Nicholas to score from close range. For the rest of the 1st-half United laid siege to the Celtic goal. It took them until 5 minutes from half-time to equalise. Stark sent in an up and under, Bonner did not come to clear and Dodds accepted the free shot at goal. 2 minutes from time United were awarded a penalty when Sinclair handled in the box. Bonner made a tremendous leap to the right to turn away Bannon's spot-kick.

February 12th
CELTIC (1) 1 — ABERDEEN (2) 3
Nicholas (35) — Black 3 (44, 45, 71)

CELTIC: Bonner; McGrain, McAdam, Sinclair, Reid (McCluskey); Aitken, McStay, MacLeod; Provan, McGarvey, Nicholas

ABERDEEN: Leighton; Kennedy, McLeish, Miller, Rougvie; Cooper, Simpson, Bell; Black, McGhee, Weir

Attendance: 42,831

February 26th
CELTIC (1) 4 — KILMARNOCK (0) 0
Nicholas (24 pen), McGarvey 2 (52, 81), MacLeod (70)

CELTIC: Bonner; McGrain, Aitken, McAdam, Sinclair; Sullivan, McStay, MacLeod; Provan (McInally), Nicholas (McCluskey), McGarvey

KILMARNOCK: McCulloch; McDicken, P. Clarke, R. Clark, Cockburn; J. Clark, MacLeod, Simpson; Gallagher, Bourke, McGivern (McClurg)

Attendance: 10,691. Clarke was ordered off.

League positions

	P	W	D	L	F	A	Pts
1 Aberdeen	25	18	4	3	54	17	40
2 CELTIC	24	18	3	3	64	27	39
3 Dundee United	24	14	7	3	54	20	35
4 Rangers	24	7	10	7	35	28	24
5 Hibernian	25	5	11	9	21	31	21

March 5th
MORTON (0) 0 CELTIC (1) 3
Sullivan (9),
MacLeod (14),
McCluskey (89)

MORTON: Baines; Hayes, Holmes; Rooney, McLaughlin, Doak; Payne, McNeill, Hutchinson (Houston), Docherty, McNab (Gavin)

CELTIC: Bonner; McGrain, Sinclair; Aitken, McAdam, Sullivan; McCluskey, McStay, Nicholas, MacLeod, McGarvey

Attendance: 8,500

March 19th
DUNDEE (2) 2 CELTIC (1) 1
Kidd (22), McGarvey (37)
Scrimgeour (35)

DUNDEE: Kelly; McGeachie, Smith, MacDonald (McKimmie), Fraser, Bell, Scrimgeour; Mackie, Sinclair, Kidd (Ferguson)

CELTIC: Bonner; McGrain, McAdam, Aitken, Sinclair (Reid); Sullivan (McCluskey), McStay, MacLeod; Provan, Nicholas, McGarvey

Attendance: 11,196

March 23rd
CELTIC (0) 0 RANGERS (0) 0

CELTIC: Bonner; McGrain, Reid; Aitken, McAdam, Sullivan; Provan (McCluskey), McStay, Nicholas, MacLeod, McGarvey

RANGERS: McCloy; Dawson, McClelland; McPherson, Paterson, Bett; Cooper, McKinnon, Clark, Redford (Prytz), MacDonald (Dalziel)

Attendance: 51,062

Despite the blank score sheet more than 51,000 fans were thoroughly entertained. It was end-to-end stuff with tackles fierce and uncompromising. In 16 minutes Celtic missed a great chance to go ahead. Sullivan robbed Redford in midfield and sent McGarvey galloping down the left. When his low cross reached the near post Nicholas was first to it but he shot against McCloy. Next Sullivan charged forward and hit a tremendous shot which cannoned off the keepers' chest before being cleared. Bonner had a tremendous save at the end of the 1st half when he palmed away a flashing drive from McKinnon, then leapt to cover the rebound. In 73 minutes McCloy had a tremendous save from Nicholas and with only 7 minutes remaining he had another magnificent save from a MacLeod thunderbolt.

March 26th
CELTIC (0) 1 ST MIRREN (0) 1
Provan (82) Fulton (68)

CELTIC: Bonner; McGrain, Aitken, McAdam, Reid; Sullivan (McCluskey), McStay, MacLeod; Provan, McGarvey, Nicholas

ST MIRREN: Thomson; Wilson, McCormack, Fulton, Clarke; Fitzpatrick, Stark, Abercrombie; McAvennie, Logan, Somner (Wardrop)

Attendance: 15,935

March 30th: Charlie Nicholas scored on his debut for Scotland in a 2-2 draw with Switzerland at Hampden Park.

April 2nd
CELTIC (2) 3 MOTHERWELL (0) 0
McGarvey (17),
Harrow o.g. (36),
McAdam (80)

CELTIC: Bonner; McGrain, Aitken, McAdam, Reid; Provan, McStay, MacLeod; Crainie, Nicholas, McGarvey (W. McStay)

MOTHERWELL: Walker; Dornan, Wark; Harrow, MacLeod, Mauchlen; Coyne, O'Hara (Rafferty), Flavell, McClair, Gahagan
McClair, Gahagan

Attendance: 15,454

April 6th
CELTIC (0) 2 DUNDEE UNITED (0) 0
McGarvey (60),
Nicholas (78)

CELTIC: Bonner; McGrain, Reid; Aitken, McAdam, MacLeod; Provan, McStay, Nicholas, Burns, McGarvey

DUNDEE UNITED: McAlpine; Stark, Malpas; Gough, Hegarty, Narey (Reilly); Bannon, Milne, Holt, Sturrock, Dodds

Attendance: 34,508

This was a hard-fought victory for Celtic. In only 3 minutes McStay drove a marvellous right-foot shot from 25 yards which beat McAlpine but came back off the far post. In 18 minutes Celtic were denied what looked a clear penalty when Narey chopped down Nicholas in the box. It was a bad mistake by Hegarty in 60 minutes which allowed McGarvey to open the scoring. McStay sent a superb long ball through the middle. Hegarty reached it first but mis-hit his passback and McGarvey nipped in to score. 12 minutes from time Nicholas wrapped up the points for Celtic. Aitken made an exhilarating run upfield, passed to McGarvey whose shot was blocked and the ball came out to Nicholas who chipped it high into the net.

April 9th
HIBERNIAN (0) 0 CELTIC (2) 3
Nicholas 2 (6, 51),
Provan (28)

HIBERNIAN: Rough; Sneddon, McNamara, Rae, Duncan; Callachan, Rice, Turnbull; Harvey (Brazil), Thomson, Irvine (Murray)

CELTIC: Bonner; Sinclair, Aitken, McAdam, Reid; McStay, MacLeod, Burns; Provan, Nicholas, McGarvey

Attendance: 15,000. McNamara was ordered off

April 20th
CELTIC (1) 2 — DUNDEE UNITED (1) 3
Nicholas (38 pen), Burns (73) — Hegarty (14), Bannon (52 pen), Milne (84)

CELTIC: Bonner; Sinclair (McCluskey), Reid; Aitken, McAdam, MacLeod; Provan, McStay, Nicholas, Burns, McGarvey

DUNDEE UNITED: McAlpine; Stark, Malpas; Gough, Hegarty, Narey; Bannon, Milne, Holt, Sturrock, Dodds

Attendance: 23,965.

Sinclair was carried off with concussion after a clash of heads with Bannon. McCluskey substituted and MacLeod went to full-back. Celtic equalised in 38 minutes through a Nicholas penalty after Stark had impeded Burns. 7 minutes after half-time United went ahead from the penalty spot courtesy of Bannon after MacLeod pushed Dodds. In 58 minutes Gough was sensationally ordered off after a confrontation with Provan. Celtic then took the initiative and they had a number of chances before Burns eventually scored the equaliser in the 73rd minute. Still United refused to capitulate and 6 minutes from time they scored a classic winner. Bannon crossed from the left and Ralph Milne controlled the ball and cheekily lobbed it over the advancing Bonner.

April 23rd
ABERDEEN (1) 1 — CELTIC (0) 0
McGhee (34)

ABERDEFN: Leighton; Cooper, McLeish, Miller, Rougvie; Strachan, McMaster, Watson; McGhee, Hewitt (Falconer), Weir (Simpson)

CELTIC: Bonner; McGrain, Aitken, McAdam, Reid (Moyes); McStay, MacLeod, Burns; Provan, Nicholas, McGarvey (McCluskey)

Attendance: 24,500

April 25th: Charlie Nicholas was named as Scotland's Player of the Year.

April 30th
KILMARNOCK (0) 0 — CELTIC (2) 5
McGrain (7), MacLeod 2 (15, 75), Nicholas (62), Burns (79)

KILMARNOCK: McCulloch; Cockburn, McDicken, P. Clarke, R. Clark; MacLeod, J. Clark, Simpson; McGivern (Muir), Bryson, Gallagher

CELTIC: Bonner; McGrain, Aitken, McAdam, Sinclair; McStay, MacLeod, Burns; Provan, McGarvey, Nicholas

Attendance: 7,900

May 7th
CELTIC (2) 2 — MORTON (0) 0
Aitken (23), Nicholas (42 pen)

CELTIC: Bonner; McGrain, McAdam, Sinclair, Reid; Aitken, P. McStay, MacLeod; McCluskey, Nicholas, McGarvey (Crainie)

MORTON: Kyle; Hayes, McLaughlin, Duffy, Holmes; Payne, Rooney, Cochrane; Gavigan, Houston, Ritchie

Attendance: 12,610

May 14th
RANGERS (2) 2 — CELTIC (0) 4
Cooper (16), Clark (23) — Nicholas 2 (48 pen, 86 pen) McAdam (61), McGarvey (73)

RANGERS; McCloy; Dawson, McClelland; McPherson, Paterson, Bett; Cooper, McKinnon, (Russell), Clark, Redford, MacDonald (Dalziel)

CELTIC: Bonner; McGrain, Sinclair; Aitken, McAdam, MacLeod; Provan, McStay, Nicholas, Burns, McGarvey

Attendance: 39,000

Rangers were 2 goals up at half-time and looking to be well on the way to victory. Cooper's free-kick was splendidly taken but it appeared to touch someone in the crowded goal area before swerving past the baffled Bonner. They went two up in 23 minutes when McKinnon's shot cannoned off Clark's head with Bonner going the other way. There were doubts whether Provan and MacLeod were fouled in the area but the refree had no misgivings and Nicholas converted both penalty awards. Sandwiched between Nicholas's penalties were brilliant goals by McAdam and McGarvey – both of them headers. Rangers can be criticised for playing for only 45 minutes and Celtic can be congratulated for playing for the full 90.

Premier League

	P	W	D	L	F	A	Pts
1 Dundee United	36	24	8	4	90	35	56
2 CELTIC	36	25	5	6	90	36	55
3 Aberdeen	36	25	5	7	76	24	55
4 Rangers	36	13	12	11	52	41	38
5 St Mirren	36	11	12	13	47	51	34
6 Dundee	36	9	11	16	42	53	29
7 Hibernian	36	7	15	14	35	51	29
8 Motherwell	36	11	5	20	39	73	27
9 Morton	36	6	8	22	30	74	20
10 Kilmarnock	36	3	11	22	28	91	17

May 24th: Burns and Nicholas were in the Scotland team which drew 0-0 with Northern Ireland at Hampden Park.

May 29th: Manchester United made a bid of £600,000 for Charlie Nicholas.

June 1st: Charlie Nicholas was in the Scotland team beaten 2-0 by England at Wembley.

June 9th: Nicholas ended all the press speculation when he decided to join Arsenal.

June 22nd: Nicholas went to Highbury to complete his £750,000 move.

June 28th: Dom Sullivan was given a free transfer.

June 30th: Billy McNeill left Celtic to become Manager of Manchester City on a 3-year contract.

LEAGUE CUP

August 14th
CELTIC (1) 6 — DUNFERMLINE (0) 0
Reid (34 pen),
McGarvey (53),
McCluskey 2 (58, 61),
Provan 2 (77, 87)

CELTIC: Bonner; McGrain, Aitken, Moyes, Reid; McStay, Burns, MacLeod; Provan, McCluskey (Nicholas), McGarvey (Crainie)

DUNFERMLINE: Whyte; Ford, Dall, Considine, Wilcox; Hegarty, Robertson (Nicol), McCathie; Jenkins (McNaughton), Morrison, Forrest

Attendance: 14,500

August 18th
ALLOA ATHLETIC (0) 0 — CELTIC (3) 5
McCluskey (26),
McGrain (34),
Reid (44 pen),
McStay (47),
Burns (60)

ALLOA; Hunter; Thomson, Haggart; Purdie, Gray, Munro; Paterson, Smith, McComb, Houston, Grant

CELTIC: Bonner; McGrain, Reid; Aitken, Moyes, MacLeod; Provan, McStay, McCluskey, Burns, McGarvey

Attendance: 4,374. Munro missed a penalty

August 21st
ARBROATH (0) 0 — CELTIC (0) 3
McCluskey (56),
Nicholas (74),
Crainie (76)

ARBROATH: Robertson; McKenzie, Young, Glover, Kopel; Hill, Burke, Shaw; Lees, Steele, Robb (Yule)

CELTIC: Bonner; McGrain, Moyes, Aitken, Reid; McStay, Crainie, MacLeod; Provan, McCluskey (Nicholas), McGarvey

Attendance: 5,275

August 25th
CELTIC (1) 4 — ALLOA ATHLETIC (1) 1
Nicholas (13),
MacLeod (66),
Aitken (81),
Burns (82)
Gray (44 pen)

CELTIC: Bonner; McGrain, Reid; Aitken, Moyes, MacLeod; Provan, McStay, Nicholas, Burns, McGarvey

ALLOA: Hunter; Thomson, McKenzie; Purdie, Gray, Munro; Paterson (Haggart), Smith (Murray), McComb, Houston, Grant

Attendance: 6,100. Reid missed a penalty

August 28th
DUNFERMLINE (0) 1 — CELTIC (4) 7
Morrison (57)
McCluskey (19),
Burns (23),
R. Dall o.g. (41),
Nicholas 4 (43, 51, 53 pen, 76)

DUNFERMLINE: Whyte; Ford, Hegarty; Considine, R. Dall, Hepburn (Robertson); Bowie, Hamill, Morrison, Jenkins (S. Dall), Forrest

CELTIC: Bonner; McGrain (Sinclair), McInally; Aitken, McAdam, MacLeod; Provan (Halpin), Conroy, McCluskey, Burns, Nicholas

Attendance: 7,000

September 1st
CELTIC (3) 4 — ABROATH (0) 1
MacLeod (6),
McCluskey (25),
Nicholas (21),
Dobbin (55)
Yule (77)

CELTIC: Bonner; McGrain, Reid; Aitken, McAdam, MacLeod; Buckley, Dobbin, McCluskey (McGarvey), Burns, Nicholas (Crainie)

ARBROATH: Robertson; McKenzie, Kopel; Durno (T. Hill), Young (Davey), Gavine; Harley, Docherty, Powell, H. Hill, Yule

Attendance: 5,200

Section Table

	P	W	D	L	F	A	Pts
CELTIC	6	6	0	0	29	3	12
Arbroath	6	2	1	3	4	9	5
Alloa Athletic	6	2	0	4	7	13	4
Dunfermline	6	1	1	4	3	18	3

Quarter-Final First Leg September 8th
CELTIC (1) 4 — PARTICK THISTLE (0) 0
Provan (9),
Nicholas (56),
MacLeod (61),
McGarvey (85)

CELTIC: Bonner; McGrain, Reid; Aitken, McAdam, MacLeod; Provan, McStay, McCluskey (McGarvey), ɪrns, Nicholas

PARTICK THISTLE: Rough; Murray, Kay; G. Doyle (McDonald), Whittaker; Lapsley, Park, Clark; Johnston, J. Doyle, Kenny

Attendance: 9,248

Quarter-Final Second Leg September 22nd
PARTICK THISTLE (0) 0 CELTIC (1) 3
MacLeod (23),
Nicholas 2 (56, 86)

PARTICK THISTLE: Rough; Murray, Whittaker; Kay, Scott, Jardine; Docherty, McDowall, Johnston, J. Doyle, McDonald

CELTIC: Latchford; Sinclair, Reid; Aitken, McAdam, Moyes (Sullivan); Provan, McStay, McGarvey, MacLeod, Nicholas

Attendance: 8,000. Celtic won 7-0 on aggregate.

Semi-Final First Leg October 27th
CELTIC (2) 2 DUNDEE UNITED (0) 0
Nicholas (39 pen),
McGarvey (44)

CELTIC: Bonner; McGrain, Reid; Aitken, McAdam, Sinclair; Provan, McStay, McGarvey (Crainie), MacLeod, Nicholas. Sub: Moyes

DUNDEE UNITED: McAlpine; Phillip, Stark; Gough, Hegarty, Narey; Holt, Milne, Kirkwood, Payne (Reilly), Dodds. Sub: Malpas

Attendance: 19,100

Celtic hit Dundee United with a 2-goal burst just before half-time. In the 39th minute Provan was tripped inside the box by Stark, and Nicholas blasted the penalty past McAlpine. Almost on the stroke of half-time Provan crossed to the near post, Nicholas back-headed and McGarvey nicked in between 2 defenders to hook the ball past McAlpine. United, who had hit the post in only 5 minutes through Dodds, put in a great effort in the closing stages trying to pull a goal back and Bonner had to show top form to save shots from Gough and Holt.

Semi-Final Second Leg November 10th
DUNDEE UNITED (0) 2 CELTIC (0) 1
Sturrock 2 (52, 65) Nicholas (88)

DUNDEE UNITED: McAlpine; Holt, Malpas; Gough, Hegarty, Narey; Bannon, Milne, Kirkwood, Sturrock, Dodds. Subs: Stark and Reilly

CELTIC: Bonner; McGrain, Sinclair; Aitken, McAdam, Burns; Provan (McCluskey), McStay, McGarvey, MacLeod, Nicholas. Sub: Reid

Attendance: 15,400

United cut back the deficit in the 52nd minute when Dodds got in a cross which Sturrock blasted against Bonner. Aitken got in the way of the rebound shot from Sturrock and knocked the ball over the line. Sturrock set the tie alight when he scored and levelled the tie 13 minutes later. A free-kick from Narey beat the Celtic defence, Bonner hesitated and Sturrock raced in to flick the ball into the net. United's John Holt was sensationally ordered off in the 78th minute after a foul on Burns (he had been booked previously). With only 2 minutes remaining United were caught on the break. Burns pushed the ball into open space and Nicholas, with only McAlpine to beat, hammered the ball past him to put Celtic in the Final. Celtic won 3-2 on aggregate.

Final at Hampden Park December 4th
CELTIC (2) 2 RANGERS (0) 1
Nicholas (22), Bett (46)
MacLeod (31)

CELTIC: Bonner; McGrain, Sinclair; Aitken, McAdam, McLeod; Provan, McStay (Reid), McGarvey, Burns, Nicholas. Sub: McCluskey

RANGERS: Stewart; McKinnon, Redford; McClelland, Paterson, Bett; Cooper, Prytz (Dawson), Johnstone, Russell (MacDonald), Smith

Attendance: 55,372. *Referee:* K. Hope (Clarkston)

On a drab, rainy afternoon Celtic dominated the 1st-half, scoring 2 goals, but Rangers scored immediately after the interval and battled to the finish. Celtic went ahead in 23 minutes. Provan bustled down the right and when his route to the byeline was blocked he turned inside and squeezed the ball to Nicholas who shot fast and accurately away out of Stewart's reach. 8 minutes later they went 2 up with a spectacular Murdo MacLeod goal. Provan forced a corner, and he swung it across to McAdam at the far post who headed back across the face of the goal. McKinnon made only a half-clearance of the awkward ball, it bounced well for MacLeod on the edge of the penalty area and he sent a thunderous shot past Stewart. Rangers scored immediately on the restart. McAdam fouled Smith on the edge of the box and Bett swept the free-kick through the line of defenders low into the corner of the net.

Bobby Lennox, a regular in the seventies and a member of their European Cup Winning side.

SCOTTISH CUP

Third Round January 28th
CLYDEBANK (0) 0 — CELTIC (1) 3
McCluskey (20),
Nicholas 2 (64, 86)

CLYDEBANK: Gallacher; Treanor, Fallon; McGhie, Given, Gervaise; Ronald, Hughes, McCabe, Williamson, Coyne

CELTIC: Bonner; McGrain, Aitken, McAdam, Reid; MacLeod, McStay (Sullivan); Provan, Nicholas, McCluskey, McGarvey

Attendance: 9,800

Fourth Round February 19th
CELTIC (0) 3 — DUNFERMLINE (0) 0
McGarvey 2 (66, 80),
McCluskey (89)

CELTIC: Bonner; McGrain, Aitken, McAdam, McInally; McStay, Sinclair (McCluskey), MacLeod; Provan, McGarvey, Nicholas

DUNFERMLINE: Whyte; Crawford, Wilcox, Smith, Robertson; Bowie, Rodier, McCathie; Forrest, Tait, Jenkins (Stewart)

Attendance: 12,374

Quarter-Final March 12th
CELTIC (1) 4 — HEARTS (0) 1
MacLeod (12), — MacDonald (88)
McGarvey (53),
Nicholas 2 (67, 81)

CELTIC: Bonner; McGrain, Sinclair; Aitken, McAdam, Sullivan; Provan, McStay, Nicholas, MacLeod, McGarvey

HEARTS: Smith; Kidd, Shields (McLaren); Bowman, MacDonald, Jardine; Mackay, Robertson, O'Connor (Pettigrew), MacDonald, Johnston

Attendance: 25,458. Johnston was ordered off.

Semi-Final at Hampden Park April 16th
CELTIC (0) 0 — ABERDEEN (0) 1
Weir (65)

CELTIC: Bonner; Sinclair, McAdam, Aitken, Reid; McStay, MacLeod, Burns; Provan, McCluskey (Crainie), McGarvey. Sub: Moyes

ABERDEEN: Leighton; Kennedy, McLeish, Miller, Rougvie; Cooper (Weir), Simpson, Bell; Strachan, McGhee, Black (Watson)

Attendance: 51,152

Charlie Nicholas failed a late fitness test and he was badly missed. Aberdeen took a gamble by giving Weir, who had struggled all week with a groin injury, pain killers and put him on the bench. He came on as a substitute for Cooper and scored the 65th-minute goal which gave Aberdeen victory when he headed a cross from Black past Bonner. The match was extremely physical. Neil Cooper went off with a broken nose and concussion, Doug Bell suffered badly torn ankle ligaments and Eric Black had to go off with an ankle injury.

EUROPEAN CUP

First Round First Leg September 15th
CELTIC (2) 2 — AJAX (Holland) (2) 2
Nicholas (14 pen), — Olsen (4),
McGarvey (27) — Lerby (18)

CELTIC: Bonner; McGrain, McAdam, Moyes, Reid; McStay, Burns (Sullivan), MacLeod; Provan, Nicholas, McGarvey

AJAZ: Galje; Molenaar, Van Veen, Molby, Boeve; Schoenaker, Ophof, Cryuff; Lerby, Olsen, Vanenburg

Attendance: 56,229

Ajax went into a shock 4-minute lead when Olsen made straight for goal, leaving McGrain and Moyes standing before shooting between Bonner and the right-hand post. In the 12th minute Galje made a great save from a Provan free-kick from 30 yards, but 2 minutes later Cruyff, back defending, gave away a penalty when he pulled Burns down and Nicholas scored from the spot. In the 18th minute Ajax regained the lead. Cruyff took a pass from Olsen and pushed it through a gaping Celtic defence to the unmarked Lerby who chipped the ball over Bonner. Celtic equalised for the 2nd time 9 minutes later. A powerful Moyes header flashed past the defence and McGarvey shot under the goalkeeper as he came off his line. Only 6 minutes later a header from Schoenaker came back off the crossbar. Celtic were denied a certain penalty in the 2nd half when Burns was sent tumbling by Olsen.

First Round Second Leg September 29th
AJAX (0) 1 — CELTIC (1) 2
Vanenburg (65) — Nicholas (33),
McCluskey (88)

AJAZ: Galje; Monenaar, Van Veen, Molby, Boeve; Shoenaker, Vanenburg, Cruyff (Molenaar); Lerby, Olsen, Kieft

CELTIC: Bonner; McGrain, Aitken, McAdam, Reid; Provan (McCluskey), Sinclair, McStay (Moyes), MacLeod; McGarvey, Nicholas

Attendance: 65,000

Celtic were asked to come up with a miracle, and they did just that with determination, skill and a great deal of courage. They took the game to Ajax right from the start and forced a couple of early corners. They rocked the Dutch side in the 33rd minute with a wonderful goal. A devastating pass from McStay and then a strong run from Sinclair up the left moved the ball onto Nicholas. He beat 2 men, passed to McGarvey, was in place for the return and swerved a shot around the keeper. Bonner saved the day for Celtic just after the restart. McStay gave away a free-kick 20 yards out. Cruyff swerved the kick around the defensive wall and the big Irishman launched himself low to the left to touch it onto a post. However, the Dutch did score in

65 minutes. They played the ball about in a series of short passes and Vanenburg squeezed the ball past Bonner and in off a post from 12 yards. With only 2 minutes remaining Celtic substitute George McCluskey took a pass wide on the left, raced inside the box and fired a low shot under Schrijvers to give Celtic a well earned victory. Celtic won 4-3 on aggregate.

Second Round First Leg October 20th
REAL SOCIEDAD (Spain) (0) 2 — CELTIC (0) 0
Satrustegui (74), Uralde (78)

REAL SOCIEDAD: Arconada; Celayeta, Gorriz, Cortabarria, Olaizola; Diego, Zubillaga, Zamora; Uralde, Satrustegui, Lopez Ufarte

CELTIC: Bonner; McGrain, Aitken, McAdam, Reid; Sinclair, Provan, McStay, MacLeod; Nicholas, McGarvey

Attendance: 31,000

The Spanish Champions transformed the match with 2 goals in 4 minutes just when it seemed that the Parkhead team has taken the sting out of them and were strolling to a 0-0 draw. In the 74th minute Ufarte took the ball wide on the left, pushed it inside to Satrustegui and he shot past Bonner. 4 minutes later Uralde picked up the ball outside the penalty area With everyone expecting a pass the striker shot low and the ball was deflected out of Bonner's reach. Pat Bonner had a fine match and Celtic had come close to scoring several times themselves before the Spaniards' devastating double strike.

Second Round Second Leg November 3rd
CELTIC (1) 2 — REAL SOCIEDAD (1) 1
MacLeod 2 (44, 88) — Uralde (25)

CELTIC: Bonner; McGrain, Reid (Burns); Aitken, McAdam, MacLeod; Provan (McCluskey), McStay, McGarvey, Sinclair, Nicholas

REAL SOCIEDAD: Arconada; Celayeta, Olaizola; Zubillaga, Gorriz, Cortabarria; Uralde, Diego (Larranaga), Satrustegui, Zamora, Lopez Ufarte

Attendance: 54,874

Billy McNeill's men mounted a brave effort to wipe out the 2-goal lead, but as they did they committed football suicide by gifting the Spaniards a goal in 25 minutes. Sociedad were well disciplined and were not giving away possession easily. They shocked the large crowd when Ufarte crossed to the far post and Uralde rose unchallenged to head past Bonner. This meant that Celtic now had to score 4 goals to win the tie. Just before half-time Cortabarria scythed down Provan just outside the box. Provan touched the ball into the path of MacLeod and he hit a glorious drive from 25 yards which screamed past Arconada and into the roof of the net. Murdo MacLeod came close with 2 other fine efforts in the 2nd half. With only 2 minutes remaining McStay set up a chance with a pass to MacLeod and he cracked a left-foot shot away from Arconada to give Celtic a win on the night, but they were out of Europe for another season. Real Sociedad won 3-2 on aggregate.

APPEARANCES	League	League Cup	Scottish Cup	European Cup
Bonner	36	10	4	4
McGrain	34	10	3	4
Reid	24+2S	8+1S	2	4
Aitken	33	11	4	3
McAdam	36	7	4	4
MacLeod	35	11	4	4
Provan	33	10	4	4
P. McStay	36	9	4	4
McCluskey	7+15S	6+1S	2+1S	0+2S
Burns	17	8	1	1+1S
Nicholas	35	8+2S	3	4
Crainie	3+4S	1+3S	0+1S	–
Moyes	4+1S	5	–	1+1S
McGarvey	31+2S	8+2S	4	4
Sullivan	7+1S	0+1S	1+1S	0+1S
Sinclair	25	4+1S	3	3
J. McInally	0+1S	1	1	–
W. McStay	0+1S	–	–	–
Conroy	–	1	–	–
Buckley	–	1	–	–
Dobbin	–	1	–	–
Latchford	–	1	–	–
Halpin	–	0+1S	–	–

GOALSCORERS:

League: Nicholas 29 (11 pens), McGarvey 17, MacLeod 11, Burns 7, Aitken 6, McStay 6, Provan 5, McAdam 3, McCluskey 2, Reid 1, Sullivan 1, McGrain 1, Own Goals 1

League Cup: Nicholas 13 (2 pens), McCluskey 6, MacLeod 5, Provan 3, McGarvey 3, Burns, 3, Reid 2 (2 pens), McGrain 1, McStay 1, Crainie 1, Aitken 1, Dobbin 1, Own Goal 1

Scottish Cup: McGarvey 3, McCluskey 2, Nicholas 2, MacLeod 1

European Cup: MacLeod 2, Nicholas 2 (1 pen), McGarvey 1, McCluskey 1

John Hughes, a great favourite with the fans in the sixties.

Season 1983-84

Celtic, led by the new management team of David Hay and Frank Connor, finished the season as runners-up in the League behind Aberdeen who had led from start to finish. Following the departure of Billy McNeill and John Clark and the new appointments there was a fair amount of transfer activity — George McCluskey, Jim McInally, Crainie, Dobbin and Buckley all left the club and Jim Melrose, John Colquhoun and Alan McInally were all signed. Brian Whittaker came and went within 10 months. One player who stayed was Paul McStay who made his full international debut during the season and was the subject of a £2 million bid by Internazionale Milan. 23 players were used over the course of the League programme. Paul McStay and Murdo MacLeod started 34 matches although Brian McClair appeared in 35 (28 + 7 sub). They scored 80 goals, the highest in the League, and McClair finished as top scorer with 23 goals in his first season with the club.

Celtic met Rangers in the Final of the League Cup. They looked down and out at one stage but came battling back from 2 down to equalise with a last-gasp penalty from Mark Reid which sent the game into extra time. Just before the end of the first 15-minute period Aitken sent McCoist crashing in the box, and although Pat Bonner blocked McCoist's spot-kick, the Rangers striker followed up to score and the Cup went to Ibrox.

They reached the Final of the Scottish Cup, beating St Mirren in the Semi-Final and going through to face Aberdeen who were bidding for their 3rd successive Scottish Cup win. The 1st half was a nightmare for Celtic. They lost a controversial early goal and then had Roy Aitken ordered off for a foul on McGhee in the 38th minute. However, they reorganised quickly and the 2nd half belonged almost entirely to them. 5 minutes from time Paul McStay scored a magnificent and deserved equaliser and the match went into extra time. Aberdeen proved to be the stronger side in the extra 30 minutes and a first-time drive from McGhee gave them a hat-trick of Cup wins, although all the glory on the day belonged to the magnificet 10 men of Celtic.

As the previous season's League Cup winners Celtic took part in the U.E.F.A. Cup competition. They beat Aahrus of Denmark in the First Round, recovering well after a difficult home leg. They were drawn against Sporting Lisbon in the next round and returned from Lisbon with a worrying 2 goal deficit, but they hit peak performance in Glasgow and swept their opponents aside, scoring 5 goals without reply. Brian Clough's Nottingham Forest were their Third Round opponents. The First Leg was in Nottingham and they achieved the result they had planned for on the hard, frosty pitch. However, they were far below their best in the return and Forest's European-style game and smash-and-grab tactics took them through to the Quarter-Finals.

League:	Runners-Up
League Cup:	Finalists
Scottish Cup:	Finalists
European Cup:	Third Round

SCOTTISH PREMIER LEAGUE

July 4th: David Hay and Frank Connor were named as Celtic's new management team.

July 5th: Billy McNeill's assistant, John Clark left.

July 14th: George McCluskey was transferred to Leeds United. A tribunal had to decide the fee of £140,000 + VAT.

August 11th: Jim Melrose was signed from Coventry City for £100,000.

August 19th: Brian Whittaker of Partick Thistle came to Parkhead in exchange for John Buckley in a deal valued at £50,000.

August 20th
HIBERNIAN (0) 0 — CELTIC (0) 2
MacLeod (49), Melrose (67)

HIBERNIAN: Rough; McKee, Sneddon; Brazil, Rae, McNamara; Conroy (Duncan), Rice, Irvine, Thomson, Callachan (Murray)

CELTIC: Bonner; McGrain, Reid; Aitken, McAdam, MacLeod; Provan, McStay, McGarvey (Crainie), Burns, Melrose

Attendance: 14,750

August 30th: Jimmy Johnstone went back to Parkhead as a part-time coach.

September 3rd
CELTIC (1) 2 — RANGERS (1) 1
Aitken (8), McGarvey (86) — McCoist (33 secs)

CELTIC: Bonner; McGrain, Whittaker; Aitken, W. McStay, MacLeod; Provan, P. McStay, McGarvey, Burns, Melrose (McClair)

RANGERS: McCloy; McKinnon, Dawson; McPherson, McClelland, Redford; Prytz, McCoist, Clark, Russell, Mitchell

Attendance: 50,662

Rangers got off to a sensational start when McCoist scored with only 33 seconds on the clock. Celtic equalised through Aitken in 8 minutes. Dawson committed a foul on Melrose. Provan took the free-kick, McGarvey knocked it down and Aitken, up with the attack, shot home from close range. With only 4 minutes remaining for play Celtic hit Rangers on the break. Burns shot against McCloy, Provan did the same and even while on the ground the little winger showed marvellous reflexes to push the ball back for McGarvey to shoot into the net for the winner and Celtic's 50th Premier League goal against their old rivals.

September 10th
CELTIC (3) 5 — ST JOHNSTONE (1) 2
Morton o.g. (11), Melrose (38), Burns 2 (44, 80), McGarvey (50) — Brogan 2 (9, 82)

CELTIC: Bonner; McGrain, Aitken, W. McStay, Reid; MacLeod, P. McStay, Burns; Provan (Crainie), Melrose, McGarvey (McClair)

ST JOHNSTONE: McDonald; Kilgour, Caldwell; Rutherford, McVicar, Gibson; Addison, Morton, Brogan, Blair (Pelosi), Beedie

Attendance: 11,161

September 17th
MOTHERWELL (0) 0 — CELTIC (1) 3
McGarvey (5), McStay (76), Burns (84)

MOTHERWELL: Walker; Dornan, Wark; Carson, Edvaldsson, Mauchlen; Gahagan, Rafferty, Gillespie (Flavell), Ritchie, Forbes (Cormack)

CELTIC: Bonner; McGrain, Whittaker; Aitken, McAdam, MacLeod; Provan, McStay, McGarvey (Melrose), Burns, McClair

Attendance: 14,202

September 24th
DUNDEE (1) 2 — CELTIC (2) 6
Ferguson 2 (19 pen, 81 pen) — Burns (12), McClair 4 (38, 52, 72, 73), Melrose (80)

DUNDEE: Kelly; McGeachie, Glennie, MacDonald, McKinlay; Fraser, McKimmie (Mackie), Richardson; Ferguson, McCall (Smith), Kidd

CELTIC: Bonner; McGrain, McAdam, Aitken, Whittaker (Sinclair); McStay, MacLeod, Burns; Provan (Halpin), Melrose, McClair

Attendance: 11,467. Fraser was ordered off.

October 1st
CELTIC (0) 1 — ST MIRREN (1) 1
Whittaker (64) — McDougall (34)

CELTIC: Bonner; McGrain, McAdam, Aitken, Whittaker; McStay, MacLeod, Burns; Provan, Melrose (McClair), McGarvey

ST MIRREN: Thomson; Walker, McAveety (Cousar), McCormack, Clarke; McAvennie, Fitzpatrick, Abercrombie; Sinclair (Cameron), McDougall, Scanlon

Attendance: 15,289

October 8th
DUNDEE UNITED (1) 2 — CELTIC (0) 1
Kirkwood (27), Gough (63) — Melrose (84)

DUNDEE UNITED: McAlpine; Kirkwood, Malpas; Gough, Hegarty, Narey; Bannon, Milne, Reilly (Stark), Holt, Dodds

CELTIC: Bonner; McGrain, Whittaker (McClair); Aitken, McAdam, Sinclair; McStay, Melrose, McGarvey, MacLeod, Burns

Attendance: 20,741

October 12th: McStay was in the Scotland team which drew 1-1 with Belgium at Hampden Park.

McGarvey and Aitken made appearances as substitutes.

October 15th
CELTIC (1) 1 — HEARTS (0) 1
McGarvey (44) — Bone (48)

CELTIC: Bonner; McGrain, Aitken, McAdam, Sinclair; McStay, MacLeod, Burns; Provan, McGarvey, Melrose (McClair)

HEARTS: Smith; Kidd, Jardine, R. MacDonald, Cowie; Park, Bowman, A. MacDonald; McLaren (Mackay), Bone, Robertson

Attendance: 20,207. Smith saved a MacLeod penalty.

October 22nd
ABERDEEN (1) 3 — CELTIC (0) 1
Hewitt (43), McLeish (55), Strachan (74 pen) — Aitken (87)

ABERDEEN: Leighton; McIntyre, Miller, McLeish, Rougvie; Strachan (Simpson), Cooper, Bell; Hewitt, McGhee, Weir

CELTIC: Bonner; McGrain, Aitken, McAdam, Sinclair; P. McStay, MacLeod (Reid), Burns; Provan, McGarvey, McClair

Attendance: 22,000

After Aberdeen took the lead 2 minutes before half-time they never looked back. Bell set up the goal with a strong run and a cross which John Hewitt headed down and past Bonner. Alex McLeish made it 2-0 with another header in 55 minutes with Bonner looking suspect. Aberdeen continued to play with rhythm and earned 2 penalties within a couple of minutes. McAdam handled a Strachan cross in 72 minutes but Bonner saved the spot-kick. However, when McStay then tripped McGhee, Strachan made a perfect job of the 2nd penalty. With 3 minutes left Aitken scored from close range with Aberdeen appealing for offside.

October 29th
CELTIC (1) 5 — HIBERNIAN (0) 1
McClair 2 (8, 86), Provan (48), Whittaker (60), MacLeod (78) — Thomson (77)

CELTIC: Latchford; McGrain (Sinclair), Aitken, McAdam, Whittaker; MacLeod, McStay, Burns; Provan, McGarvey (Melrose), McClair

HIBERNIAN: Rough; Sneddon, Rae, Jamieson, Schaedler; Brazil, Turnbull, Duncan; Rice (McKee), Thomson, Irvine

Attendance: 13,777

League positions

	P	W	D	L	F	A	Pts
1 Aberdeen	10	7	1	2	26	7	15
2 Dundee United	9	7	1	1	22	7	15
3 CELTIC	10	6	2	2	27	13	14
4 Hearts	10	6	2	2	13	8	14
5 Hibernian	10	5	0	5	15	20	10

November 5th
RANGERS (0) 1 — CELTIC (0) 2
Clark (86) — McGarvey (53), Burns (75)

RANGERS: McCloy; McKinnon, Paterson, McClelland, Dawson; Nicholl, McPherson, Redford; McCoist (Cooper), Clark, Mitchell (MacDonald)

CELTIC: Bonner; McGrain, McAdam, W. McStay, Whittaker; P. McStay, MacLeod, Burns; Provan (Melrose), McGarvey, McClair

Attendance: 40,000

Rangers had the slight edge in the 1st half but Celtic's class told in the end. Paul McStay set up the first goal in 53 minutes when he released the ball at the right time to the feet of McGarvey who drove low inside McCloy's right-hand post. Celtic scored a 2nd magnificent goal in 75 minutes. Burns tried a 1-2 with McGarvey, changed his mind, and took the ball back off the striker and shot past Peter McCloy. Sandy Clark managed a consolation goal with only 4 minutes left. Celtic missed the influence of Roy Aitken but Willie McStay and McAdam were outstanding.

November 12th
CELTIC (2) 4 — MOTHERWELL (0) 0
MacLeod (29), McClair 2 (40, 81), McGarvey (64)

CELTIC: Bonner; McGrain, Whittaker (Sinclair); W. McStay, McAdam, MacLeod; McClair, P. McStay, McGarvey, Burns, Halpin

MOTHERWELL: Walker; Dornan, Wark; Carson, Edvaldsson, Forbes; Gahagan, Cormack, Alexander, Friar (McAllister), Harrow

Attendance: 13,408

November 16th: Paul McStay was in the Scotland team beaten 2-1 by East Germany in Halle. McGarvey made an appearance as a substitute.

November 18th: Wolves signed Danny Crainie for £20,000.

November 19th
ST MIRREN (3) 4 — CELTIC (2) 2
Clarke (26), McCormack (32), McDougall (45), Scanlon (88) — Burns (9), Aitken (19)

ST MIRREN: Thomson; Clark, Hamilton; McCormack (Jarvie), Cooper, Fulton; Fitzpatrick, McAvennie (Alexander), McDougall, Abercrombie, Scanlon

CELTIC: Bonner; McGrain, Sinclair; Aitken, McAdam, W. McStay (Halpin); McClair, P. McStay, McGarvey, MacLeod, Burns

Attendance: 13,062

November 21st: John Colquhoun was signed from Stirling Albion for £60,000.

November 26th
CELTIC (0) 1 — DUNDEE (0) 0
Reid (67 pen)

CELTIC: Bonner; McGrain, Reid; Aitken, Sinclair, MacLeod; McClair, P. McStay, McGarvey, Melrose, Burns

DUNDEE: Geddes; McWinnie, McKinlay; Fraser, Smith, Glennie; Mackie, Richardson, Ferguson, McCall, Stephen (McGlashan)

Attendance: 14,583

December 3rd
ST JOHNSTONE (0) 0 — CELTIC (1) 3
Dobbin (8), Melrose (48), Aitken (69)

ST JOHNSTONE: Baines; Kilgour, McVicar; Addison, Kennedy, Rutherford; Gibson (Brannigan), Lyons, Blair, Morton, Beedie

CELTIC: Bonner; McGrain, Reid; Aitken, Sinclair, MacLeod (W. McStay); McClair (Halpin), Dobbin, McGarvey, Melrose, Burns

Attendance: 8,153

December 10th
CELTIC (0) 0 — ABERDEEN (0) 0

CELTIC: Bonner; McGrain, Reid; Aitken, McAdam, MacLeod; McClair, McStay, McGarvey, Burns, Melrose

ABERDEEN: Leighton; Cooper (Angus), Rougvie; Simpson, McLeish, Miller; Strachan, Hewitt (Falconer), McGhee, Bell, Weir

Attendance: 25,867

Celtic were extremely unlucky not to win. David Hay's men bounced back after their shattering U.E.F.A. Cup defeat by Nottingham Forest and even when down to 10 men after the ordering off of Jim Melrose still showed a willingness to go forward. Aberdeen came to Parkhead favourites to open up a 5-point gap but were not allowed to show the form which had earned them such a reputation throughout Europe.

December 13th: Aitken, McStay and McGarvey were in the Scotland team beaten 2-0 by Northern Ireland in Belfast.

December 17th
HEARTS (0) 1 — CELTIC (1) 3
Robertson (75) — McClair 2 (26, 81), Dobbin (63)

HEARTS: Smith; Kidd, Jardine, R. MacDonald, Cowie; Bowman, Mackay, Levein; Robertson, Bone, Park, Johnston

CELTIC: Bonner; McGrain, Aitken, McAdam, Reid; McStay, Sinclair, MacLeod (Dobbin); Colquhoun, McClair, McGarvey

Attendance: 15,298

League positions

	P	W	D	L	F	A	Pts
1 Aberdeen	17	13	2	2	43	9	28
2 CELTIC	17	11	3	3	42	19	25
3 Dundee United	16	9	3	4	31	15	21
4 Hibernian	17	8	1	8	27	29	17
5 Hearts	17	6	5	6	18	22	17

December 27th
CELTIC (1) 1 — DUNDEE UNITED (0) 1
McClair (45) — Bannon (68 pen)

CELTIC: Bonner; McGrain, Reid; Aitken, McAdam (Dobbin), Sinclair; Colquhoun, P. McStay, McGarvey, MacLeod, McClair

DUNDEE UNITED: McAlpine; Stark, Malpas; Gough, Hegarty, Holt; Bannon, Milne, Kirkwood, Sturrock, Dodds

Attendance: 25,982

December 31st
HIBERNIAN (0) 0 — CELTIC (0) 1
Blackley o.g. (77)

HIBERNIAN: Rough; Sneddon, Schaedler; Brazil, Jamieson, Blackley; Callachan, Conroy, Irvine, Harvey, Duncan

CELTIC: Bonner; McGrain, Reid; Aitken, W. McStay, MacLeod; Colquhoun, P. McStay, McGarvey, Sinclair, McClair

Attendance: 11,234

January 7th
MOTHERWELL (1) 2 — CELTIC (1) 2
Rafferty (11), Dornan (82) — McGarvey (22), P. McStay (80)

MOTHERWELL: Sproat; McLeod, Forbes, Edvaldsson, Black; Dornan, Lyall (McAllister), Mauchlen (Gahagan); Harrow, Rafferty, Gillespie

CELTIC: Bonner; McGrain, Aitken, W. McStay, Reid; MacLeod, P. McStay, Burns; McClair (Colquhoun), McGarvey (Sinclair), Melrose

Attendance: 11,268

January 18th: Internazionale Milan were reported to be ready to bid £2 million for Paul McStay.

February 4th
ABERDEEN (1) 1 — CELTIC (0) 0
Hewitt (19)

ABERDEEN: Leighton; McKimmie, Rougvie; Cooper, McLeish, Miller; Strachan, Simpson (Falconer), McGhee, Hewitt (Bell), Weir

CELTIC: Bonner; McGrain (W. McStay), Reid; Aitken, McAdam, Sinclair; McClair, P. McStay, McGarvey, MacLeod, Burns (Melrose)

Attendance: 23,000

Although Leighton looked very uncomfortable in his handling of the cross ball, his instantaneous reactions enabled him to make the 2 or 3 great saves necessary to thwart Celtic's attempts at scoring. McClair and McGarvey soldiered manfully up front but the absence of a real winger continued to disrupt Celtic's ambitions. The only goal of the match came in 19 minutes when Strachan and Weir combined and left Hewitt to push the ball into the net.

February 11th
CELTIC (3) 5 — ST JOHNSTONE (0) 2
McClair 2 (18, 44), MacLeod 2 (35, 72), McGarvey (46) — Scott (50), Blair (87)

CELTIC: Bonner; McGrain, Aitken, McAdam, Reid; McStay, Sinclair (Burns), MacLeod; Colquhoun, McGarvey (Melrose), McClair

ST JOHNSTONE: Baines; McVicar, Caldwell, Rutherford, Morton; Gibson (Barron), Beedie, Lyons; Scott, Brogan, Brannigan (Blair)

Attendance: 9,439

February 14th
CELTIC (0) 2 — ST MIRREN (0) 0
McGarvey 2 (59, 81)

CELTIC: Bonner; McGrain, Reid; Aitken, McAdam, Sinclair; Colquhoun, McStay, McGarvey, MacLeod, McClair

ST MIRREN: Thomson; Hamilton, Clarke; Cooper, Fulton, McCormack; Fitzpatrick, McAvennie, McDougall, Abercrombie, Scanlon

Attendance: 9,835

February 25th
CELTIC (2) 4 — HEARTS (0) 1
McClair 3 (22, 37, 80), Colquhoun (73) — Park (86)

CELTIC: Bonner; McGrain, Reid; Aitken, McAdam, MacLeod; Colquhoun, McStay, McGarvey (Melrose), Burns, McClair

HEARTS: Smith; Kidd, Cowie; Jardine, Stevens, Levein (Johnston); McLaren, Bowman, Mackay, Park, Robertson

Attendance: 17,950

League positions

	P	W	D	L	F	A	Pts
1 Aberdeen	23	18	3	2	59	12	39
2 CELTIC	24	15	5	4	57	26	35
3 Dundee United	21	12	5	4	40	20	29
4 Rangers	24	11	5	8	38	31	27
5 St Mirren	24	6	11	7	35	35	23

February 28th: McStay and McGarvey were in the Scotland team which beat Wales 2-1 at Hampden Park. Aitken made an appearance as substitute for McStay.

March 3rd
DUNDEE UNITED (1) 3 — CELTIC (0) 1
Bannon (10), Kirkwood (51), Dodds (69) — Aitken (87)

DUNDEE UNITED: McAlpine; Stark, Malpas; Gough, Hegarty, Narey; Bannon (Holt), Kirkwood, Coyne, Sturrock (Milne), Dodds

CELTIC: Bonner; Sinclair, Whittaker; Aitken, McAdam, MacLeod; Colquhoun, P. McStay, McGarvey (Melrose), Burns, McClair

Attendance: 15,326

March 6th: Jim Dobbin was loaned to Motherwell for a month.

March 15th: Doncaster Rovers signed Jim Dobbin for £25,000.

March 20th
DUNDEE (0) 3 — CELTIC (1) 2
McCall 2 (50, 77), Stephen (56) — Burns (44), Reid (81 pen)

DUNDEE: Kelly; McGeachie, McKinlay; Fraser, Smith, MacDonald; Kidd, Ferguson, McCall, Richardson, Stephen

CELTIC: Bonner; McGrain, Reid; Aitken, McAdam, MacLeod; Provan, McStay, McGarvey (Melrose), Burns, McClair

Attendance: 7,746

March 31st
CELTIC (1) 1 — ABERDEEN (0) 0
Melrose (35)

CELTIC: Bonner; McGrain, Reid; Aitken, McAdam, W. McStay; McClair, P. McStay (Provan), Melrose, MacLeod, Burns

ABERDEEN: Leighton; McKimmie, Rougvie; Cooper, McLeish, Miller; Strachan, Black (Mitchell), McGhee, Angus (Porteous), Hewitt

Attendance: 19,193

Despite Celtic's win Aberdeen still had a comfortable cushion at the top of the table. Young defender Willie McStay and striker Jim Melrose were both drafted in to freshen up the Celtic side and justified their selection with first-rate performances. Celtic's goal in 35 minutes was a classic. A tremendous defence-splitting pass from Burns did the damage. Melrose, for once, got to it before his shadow Miller and he beat Leighton with a delicate little touch. That was the first League goal the Dons have lost since the 1-1 draw with Rangers on January 7th.

April 2nd
CELTIC (1) 3 — RANGERS (0) 0
P. McStay (31), W. McStay (69), Provan (84)

CELTIC: Bonner; McGrain, Reid; Aitken, McAdam, W. McStay; McClair, P. McStay, Melrose (McGarvey), MacLeod, Burns (Provan)

RANGERS: McCloy; Nicholl, Dawson; McClelland, Paterson, McPherson; Russell (Redford), McCoist, Clark, Williamson, Cooper (Burns)

Attendance: 53,229

Just 8 days after having lost in extra time in the Final of the League Cup Celtic produced some devastating form. Paul McStay opened the scoring with a magnificent solo goal in the 31st minute. He collected the ball midway inside the opposition's half and set off on a tremendous run which carried him through the entire Rangers defence to the byeline where he somehow managed to squeeze the ball past McCloy. In 55 minutes Rangers almost equalised when McPherson headed just past from a Cooper free-kick. 13 minutes later Bonner pulled off a brilliant save from a Paterson header, touching the ball over the bar. A minute later Celtic went 2 up. Willie McStay ran on to a loose ball 25 yards out and hit a first-time drive which the keeper looked to have covered. He missed it, however, and the ball shot in off a post. With 6 minutes remaining Provan, who had come on for Burns, scored a brilliant 3rd goal. 2 back-heelers from Paul McStay and McGarvey set it up and Provan scored with a left-foot drive just inside the left-hand post.

April 7th

ST JOHNSTONE (0) 0	CELTIC (0) 0

ST JOHNSTONE: Baines; Kilgour, Morton; Barron, Caldwell, Rutherford; Gibson, Brogan (Lyons), Reid (Sludden), Blair, Beedie

CELTIC: Bonner; McGrain, Reid; Aitken, McAdam, McStay; Provan, McGarvey (McClair), Melrose, MacLeod, Burns

Attendance: 6,667

April 10th

CELTIC (1) 4	MOTHERWELL (1) 2
McClair 2 (31, 48),	Gahagan (34),
MacLeod (57),	Forbes (81)
Archdeacon (89)	

CELTIC: Bonner; McGrain, Reid; W. McStay, McAdam (Sinclair), MacLeod; Provan, P. McStay, Melrose, Burns (Archdeacon), McClair

MOTHERWELL: Maxwell; Kennedy, Boyd; Wishart, Forbes, McLeod; Rafferty, Black, Harrow, Lyall, Gahagan

Attendance: 5,673

April 18th

ST MIRREN (2) 2	CELTIC (1) 4
Scanlon 2 (3, 32)	Burns (31),
	McClair 2 (75, 82),
	Sinclair (76)

ST MIRREN: Thomson; Clarke, Hamilton; McCormack, Cooper, McGregor; Fitzpatrick (Logan), McAvennie, McDougall, Abercrombie, Scanlon

CELTIC: Bonner; McGrain, Reid; W. McStay, McAdam, Sinclair; Provan, P. McStay, Melrose (McClair), Burns, McGarvey

Attendance: 6,122

April 21st

RANGERS (0) 1	CELTIC (0) 0
Williamson (55)	

RANGERS: McCloy; Nichol, McClelland; McPherson, Paterson, Redford; Russell, Prytz (McKinnon), Williamson (MacDonald), McCoist, Cooper

CELTIC: Bonner; McGrain, Reid; Grant (Provan), McAdam, W. McStay; McClair, P. McStay, McGarvey (Melrose), MacLeod, Burns

Attendance: 40,260

Williamson's opportunism gave Rangers the edge and his goal was worthy of winning any match. Rangers had to play for almost half an hour with only 10 men when Jimmy Nicholl, playing his last game for the club before returning to Toronto Blizzard, was sent off for retaliation against McClair. He had been booked in the 1st half. Rangers' goal came in the 55th minute. Cooper sent in a corner from the right. McGrain failed to head clear. MacLeod mis hit the clearance and Williamson, facing his own goal, scored with a spectacular overhead kick. Despite their handicap Rangers' defence stood firm with Paterson and McPherson immense and McClelland organising brilliantly.

April 24th

CELTIC (2) 3	DUNDEE (0) 0
Melrose (7),	
McClair (25),	
McAdam (77)	

CELTIC: Bonner; W. McStay, Reid; Aitken, McAdam, MacLeod (Grant); Colquhoun, P. McStay, Melrose, Burns, McClair

DUNDEE: Geddes; McInally, McKinlay; Kidd (Shannon), Smith, McGeachie; Mackie, Ferguson, McCall, Harris, McGlashan (Hendry)

Attendance: 4,956

April 28th

CELTIC (1) 3	HIBERNIAN (1) 2
McClair 2 (2, 47),	Callachan (33), Rice (81)
Colquhoun (60)	

CELTIC: Latchford; McGrain, Reid; Aitken, McGugan (W. McStay), Grant; Colquhoun, P. McStay (McGarvey), Melrose, Burns, McClair

HIBERNIAN: Rough; Brazil (McKee), Schaedler; Sneddon, Rae, Blackley; Callachan, Jamieson, Irvine, Rice, McGeachie

Attendance: 9,553

May 5th

HEARTS (0) 1	CELTIC (1) 1
Johnston (74)	Burns (45)

HEARTS: Smith; Kidd, Cowie; Jardine, R. MacDonald, Levein; Bowman, Mackay, Bone, Robertson, A. MacDonald (Johnston)

CELTIC: Latchford; Sinclair, Whittaker; Aitken, McAdam, MacLeod; Colquhoun, P. McStay, Melrose, Burns, McClair

Attendance: 12,281

May 12th
CELTIC (0) 1 — DUNDEE UNITED (0) 1
MacLeod (75) — Sturrock (78)

CELTIC: Bonner; McGrain, Reid; Aitken, W. McStay, MacLeod; Colquhoun (Provan), P. McStay, McClair, Burns, Melrose

DUNDEE UNITED: McAlpine; Gough, Munro; Malpas, Hegarty, Narey; Bannon, Holt, Coyne, Sturrock (Clark), Taylor

Attendance: 10,281

Scottish Premier Division

	P	W	D	L	F	A	Pts
1 Aberdeen	36	25	7	4	78	21	57
2 CELTIC	36	21	8	7	80	41	50
3 Dundee United	36	18	11	7	67	39	47
4 Rangers	36	15	12	9	53	41	42
5 Hearts	36	10	16	10	38	47	36
6 St Mirren	36	9	14	13	55	59	32
7 Hibernian	36	12	7	17	45	55	31
8 Dundee	36	11	5	20	50	74	27
9 St Johnstone	36	10	3	23	36	81	23
10 Motherwell	36	4	7	25	31	75	15

May 12th: Celtic signed Alan McInally from Ayr United. The fee was £70,000 plus an additional £20,000 if he established himself in the first team plus another £20,000 if he got a Scottish cap.

May 13th: In the Lou Macari Testimonial, Manchester United drew with Celtic 1-1. Macari played the last 15 minutes for Celtic.

May 18th: Jim McInally, who had been on loan to Dundee, was transferred to Nottingham Forest for £40,000.

May 22nd: Brian Whittaker was transferred to Hearts for £25,000.

May 26th: Paul McStay made an appearance as a substitute for Scotland in a 1-1 draw with England at Hampden Park.

May 27th: Celtic's bid of £275,000 for Dave Narey of Dundee United was rejected.

June 1st: Aberdeen and Celtic both bid around £350,000 for homesick Watford striker Mo Johnston.

June 8th: Celtic made an inquiry for Joe Jordan of Verona.

LEAGUE CUP

Second Round First Leg August 24th
BRECHIN CITY (0) 0 — CELTIC (0) 1
Melrose (85)

BRECHIN: Neilson; Watt, Reid; Leslie, Hay, Scott; Campbell, Elvin, Eadie, Young, Stewart

CELTIC: Bonner; McGrain, Reid; Aitken, McAdam, MacLeod; Provan, P. McStay, McClair (Crainie), Burns, Melrose

Attendance: 3,000

Second Round Second Leg August 27th
CELTIC (0) 0 — BRECHIN CITY (0) 0

CELTIC: Bonner; McGrain, Whittaker; Aitken, W. McStay, MacLeod; Crainie, Dobbin, McGarvey, Burns, Melrose

BRECHIN: Neilson; Watt, Reid; Leslie, Hay (Alexander), Scott; Campbell, Elvin (Mackie), Paterson, Young, Stewart

Attendance: 8,502. Celtic won 1-0 on aggregate.

August 31st
AIRDRIE (0) 1 — CELTIC (1) 6
B. Miller (69) — McGarvey (43), MacLeod (50 pen), Provan (68), Whittaker (78), P. McStay (84), MacLauchlan (o.g. 89)

AIRDRIE: Martin; McKeown, Rodger; MacLauchlan, B. March, Gordon; Walker, McCafferty, B.Miller, Jarvie (S. Miller), Slaven

CELTIC: Bonner; McGrain, Whittaker; Aitken, W. McStay, MacLeod; Provan, P. McStay, McGarvey, Burns, Melrose (McClair)

Attendance: 7,000. Martin saved a MacLeod penalty.

September 7th
CELTIC (1) 5 — HIBERNIAN (1) 1
Reid 2 (43, 62 pen), Melrose (58), McGarvey (78), P. McStay (86) — Conroy (41)

CELTIC: Bonner; McGrain, Whittaker (Reid); Aitken, W. McStay, MacLeod; Provan, P. McStay, McGarvey, Burns, Melrose

HIBERNIAN: Rough; Sneddon, Schaedler; Brazil, Jamieson, McNamara; Callachan, Conroy, Irvine, Duncan (Rice), Murray

Attendance: 11,046

October 5th
CELTIC (0) 1 — KILMARNOCK (0) 1
MacLeod (63 pen) — Gallagher (64)

CELTIC: Bonner; W. McStay, Whittaker; Aitken, McAdam, MacLeod; Provan (Halpin), Dobbin, McGarvey, Burns, McClair

KILMARNOCK: McCulloch; Robertson, Cockburn; J. Clark, P. Clarke, R. Clark; McGivern, Simpson, Gallagher, MacLeod, Bryson

Attendance: 5,435

October 26th
HIBERNIAN (0) 0 CELTIC (0) 0

HIBERNIAN: Rough; Sneddon, Schaedler; Brazil, Jamieson, McNamara (Rae); McKee, Rice, Irvine, Thomson, Duncan

CELTIC: Bonner; McGrain, Whittaker; Aitken, McAdam, Sinclair; McClair, McStay, McGarvey, Burns, Halpin

Attendance: 8,000

November 9th
CELTIC (0) 0 AIRDRIE (0) 0

CELTIC: Bonner; McGrain, Whittaker; W. McStay, McAdam, MacLeod; McClair, Dobbin, McGarvey, Burns, Melrose (Halpin)

AIRDRIE: Martin; Black, Rodger; McLauchlan, March, Gordon; McKeown (McCafferty), N. Anderson, Flood, Walker, McGuire

Attendance: 5,216

November 30th
KILMARNOCK (0) 0 CELTIC (1) 1
Melrose (20)

KILMARNOCK: McCulloch; Robertson, Cockburn; Simpson, Clarke, R. Clark; McGivern (McKenna), McDicken, Gallagher, MacLeod, Bryson

CELTIC: Bonner; McGrain, Reid; Aitken, Sinclair, MacLeod; McClair, P. McStay (Halpin), McGarvey, Melrose, Burns

Attendance: 9,000

Section table

	P	W	D	L	F	A	Pts
CELTIC	6	3	3	0	13	3	9
Kilmarnock	6	3	1	2	9	6	7
Hibernian	6	2	2	2	7	9	6
Airdrie	6	0	2	4	3	14	2

Semi-Final February 22nd
ABERDEEN (0) 0 CELTIC (0) 0

ABERDEEN: Leighton; Rougvie, McMaster (Mitchell); Cooper, McLeish, Miller; Strachan, Black, McGhee, Angus, Weir (Hewitt)

CELTIC: Bonner; McGrain, Reid; Aitken, McAdam, Sinclair; McClair, P. McStay, McGarvey, MacLeod, Burns

Attendance: 23,000

Celtic were entitled to be well satisfied with a splendid performance. They were undoubtedly the better side, and had Frank McGarvey put 1 or 2 excellent first-half chances into the net, Celtic would have had the kind of result their play merited. Leighton saved from McGarvey inside 30 seconds but a minute later Aberdeen were unlucky when a 20-yard drive from Strachan crashed off the bar. In 20 minutes McMaster failed to clear properly, allowing McStay to send over a low cross which was dummied by McClair but McGarvey only 15 yards out, did not hit the shot powerfully enough and Leighton made the save. Leighton remained the busier keeper in the 2nd half as Celtic continued to dominate the game.

Semi-Final Second Leg March 10th
CELTIC (0) 1 ABERDEEN (0) 0
Reid (54 pen)

CELTIC: Bonner; McGrain, Reid; Aitken, McAdam, Sinclair (Provan); McClair, McStay, McGarvey, MacLeod, Burns

ABERDEEN: Leighton; Cooper, Rougvie; Simpson (Falconer), McLeish, Miller; Strachan, Bell, Black, Angus, Hewitt

Attendance: 41,169

Celtic were awarded a penalty in 54 minutes when Burns accepted a Provan pass and beautifully turned Bell who tripped him in attempting to recover. Reid showed great composure in smacking the ball into the net to give Celtic their first win of the season over Aberdeen and to take them into the Final of the League Cup. Celtic did not have a failure and their defence looked solid. Bonner played his part by saving a late shot from Hewitt. The return of Davie Provan as a 2nd half substitute was most encouraging. Referee Valentine booked 6 players. Celtic won 1-0 on aggregate.

Final at Hampden Park March 25th
RANGERS (1) 3 CELTIC (0) 2
McCoist 3 (44 pen, 61, 104) McClair (67), Reid (89 pen)
After Extra Time

RANGERS: McCloy; Nicholl, Dawson; McClelland, Paterson, McPherson; Russell, McCoist, Clark (McAdam), MacDonald (Burns), Cooper

CELTIC: Bonner; McGrain, Reid; Aitken, McAdam, MacLeod; Provan (Sinclair), P. McStay, McGarvey (Melrose), Burns, McClair

Attendance: 66,369 *Referee:* R. B. Valentine (Dundee)

This was an amazing Final, with Celtic looking down and out only to come back battling from 2 down to equalise with a last-gasp penalty from Mark Reid which sent the game into extra time. Celtic pulled a goal back through McClair in the 67th minute. McClelland was booked for fouling Burns on the edge of the box. Burns took the kick himself, lobbing it over the defence to McClair who met it on the volley and beat McCloy. With full-time approaching Celtic mounted a final assault and MacLeod looked certain to score, as he had only McCloy to beat from a few yards, but he was pulled down by McCoist and a penalty was given. Reid hammered the ball into the net in fine style. 10 minutes into extra-time Sinclair came on for Provan. 4 minutes later McCoist was sent crashing by Aitken. This time Bonner blocked McCoist's kick but the Rangers striker followed up to score.

SCOTTISH CUP

Third Round January 28th
BERWICK RANGERS (0) 0 — CELTIC (2) 4
McClair 2 (4, 34), McGarvey (78), Melrose (80)

BERWICK: Watson; McCann, Morgan; Flavell, Steedman, Muir; Davidson, Romaines, Tait, Rodier, Tomassi

CELTIC: Bonner; McGrain, Reid; Aitken, McAdam, MacLeod; McClair, McStay, McGarvey, Burns, Melrose

Attendance: 5,510

Fourth Round 18th February
EAST FIFE (0) 0 — CELTIC (1) 6
MacLeod (28), McGarvey (46), Colquhoun (70), Burns 2 (75, 78), McClair (84)

EAST FIFE: Marshall; Clarke (Stalker), McLaren, Harley, Jenkins; Durie, Kirk, Hutt; McCafferty, Pryde (O'Brien), Burt

CELTIC: Bonner; McGrain, Aitken, McAdam, Reid; P. McStay, MacLeod, Burns; Colquhoun, McGarvey, McClair

Attendance: 10,000

Fifth Round March 17th
MOTHERWELL (0) 0 — CELTIC (3) 6
Reid (3), Burns (32), McClair 2 (38, 65), MacLeod (54), McGarvey (78)

MOTHERWELL: Sproat; McLeod, Lyall; Boyd, Forbes, Edvaldsson (Dornan); McAllister, Rafferty, Harrow, Grant, McFadden (Gillespie)

CELTIC: Bonner; McGrain (Sinclair), Reid; Aitken, McAdam, MacLeod; Provan (Melrose), McStay, McGarvey, Burns, McClair

Attendance: 14,795

Semi-Final at Hampden Park April 14th
CELTIC (1) 2 — ST MIRREN (1) 1
McClair (29), P. McStay (81) — McDougall (38)

CELTIC: Bonner; McGrain, Reid; W. McStay, McAdam, MacLeod; Provan, P. McStay, McClair, Melrose (McGarvey), Burns. Sub: Sinclair

ST MIRREN: Thomson; Clarke, Hamilton; Cooper, Fulton, McCormack; Fitzpatrick, McAvennie, McDougall, McGregor, Scanlon (Logan). Sub: Abercrombie

Attendance: 24,690

Celtic were the hungrier and more professional side and the final scoreline rather flattered St Mirren. The Love Street side could not settle and with an almost gale force wind behind them in the 1st half most of their passes went astray. Celtic adapted better to the conditions and deserved to be in the Final.

Final at Hampden Park May 19th
ABERDEEN (1) 2 — CELTIC (0) 1
Black (24), McGhee (98) — P. McStay (85)
After Extra Time

ABERDEEN: Leighton; McKimmie, Rougvie (Stark); Cooper, McLeish, Miller; Strachan, Simpson, McGhee, Black, Weir (Bell)

CELTIC: Bonner; McGrain, Reid (Melrose); Aitken, W. McStay, MacLeod; Provan, P. McStay, McGarvey, Burns, McClair (Sinclair)

Attendance: 58,900 — *Referee:* R. B. Valentine (Dundee)

Aitken was ordered off in the 38th minute. Celtic played for 82 minutes with 10 men and battled magnificently in a bid to finish the season with one major honour. The match began at a cracking pace with MacLeod twice coming close for Celtic. However, in 24 minutes it was Aberdeen who scored. Strachan took a corner on the right and McLeish headed the ball towards Black who looked offside as he hooked the ball past Bonner but the linesman kept his flag down, and despite Celtic's protests the goal stood. In the 38th minute Roy Aitken hit McGhee with a crunching tackle and the Celtic man became the first player since 1929 to be ordered off in a Scottish Cup Final. Celtic had to reorganise quickly and they put MacLeod into the centre of the defence. The 2nd half belonged almost entirely to Celtic, and 5 minutes from the end of normal time they were rewarded for their efforts when Sinclair, Provan and McGrain combined to set up a magnificent equaliser for Paul McStay. As expected Aberdeen were the stronger side in extra time, and 8 minutes into the extra period they scored the winning goal. Substitute Bell showing great pace and skill made an opening and thundered a tremendous drive off a post. The ball carried to the unmarked Strachan out on the right, and when Bonner failed to cut out his cross McGhee was at the far post to hit a first-time drive into the net to give Aberdeen a hat-trick of Cup wins and possibly their least deserved success. All the glory on the day belonged to Celtic.

U.E.F.A. CUP

First Round First Leg September 14th
CELTIC (0) 1 — AAHRUS (Denmark) (0) 0
Aitken (63)

CELTIC: Bonner; McGrain, Reid; Aitken, W. McStay, MacLeod; Provan, P. McStay, McGarvey, Burns, Melrose (McClair)

AAHRUS: Rasmussen; Wachmann, Stampe; B. Kristensen, Olsen, Duedahl; Scheepers, Hansen, Andersen (Sander), Lundkvist (T. Christiansen), K. Christiansen

Attendance: 23,569. Stampe missed a 29th minute penalty.

Celtic found the task of opening up the Danish defence rather more difficult than they had hoped, and even when they did they were far too inaccurate with their finishing. Aahrus held out until the 63rd minute when Provan, who was involved in just about everything, sent over a corner from the right. Aitken headed it strongly and Rasmussen allowed the ball to slip through his hands and into the net.

First Round Second Leg September 28th
AAHRUS (0) 1 CELTIC (2) 4
Scheepers (76) MacLeod (21), McGarvey (27), Aitken (47), Provan (81)

AAHRUS: Rasmussen; Wachmann, B. Kristensen; Stampe, Olsen, Scheepers; Ziegler, Andersen, Duedahl, Lundkvist, K. Kristensen. Sub: T. Christiansen

CELTIC: Bonner; McGrain, Reid; Aitken, McAdam, MacLeod; Provan, P. McStay, McGarvey (Halpin), Burns, Melrose (McClair)

Attendance: 15,000

Celtic demolished the Danes and cruised into the Second round of the competition. They did not have a poor player in their side on the night and fully redeemed their dented reputation following the First Leg. Celtic won 5-1 on aggregate.

Second Round First Leg October 19th
SPORTING LISBON (Portugal) (1) 2 CELTIC (0) 0
Jordao 2 (30, 68)

SPORTING: Katzirz; Gabriel, Jorge; Kostov, Virgilio (Carlos Xavier), Zexinho; Lieto, Romeu (Futre), Fernandez, Olivera, Jordao

CELTIC: Bonner; McGrain, Sinclair; Aitken, McAdam, MacLeod; Provan, P. McStay, McGarvey, Burns, Melrose (McClair)

Attendance: 57,500

Celtic did not play at all badly but they failed to cope with the lightning strikes of the Sporting dangermen.

Second Round Second Leg November 2nd
CELTIC (3) 5 SPORTING LISBON (0) 0
Burns (17), McAdam (43), McClair (45), MacLeod (57), McGarvey (59)

CELTIC: Bonner; McGrain, Sinclair; Aitken, McAdam, MacLeod; Provan, P. McStay, McGarvey (Melrose), Burns (Reid), McClair

SPORTING: Katzirz; Gabriel, Jorge (Carlos Xavier); Kostov, Virgilio, Zezinho; Lieto, Romeu, Fernandez, Olivera, Jordao

Attendance: 39,183

Facing a worrying 2-goal deficit from the First Leg, Celtic disdainfully swept aside their opponents, scoring 5 goals and hitting a peak they had not previously approached this season. Celtic won 5-2 on aggregate.

Third Round First Leg November 23rd
NOTTINGHAM FOREST (0) 0 CELTIC (0) 0

NOTTINGHAM FOREST: Sutton; Anderson, Swain; Fairclough, Hart, Bowyer; Wigley, Davenport (Wallace), Birtles, Hodge, Walsh

CELTIC: Bonner; McGrain, Reid; Aitken, McAdam (Melrose), Sinclair; McClair, McStay, McGarvey, MacLeod, Burns

Attendance: 32,017

Celtic went to Nottingham and achieved the result they had planned for. They adapted to the hard, frosty surface better than their opponents whose preference for the short-passing build-up was clearly the wrong tactic in the conditions. Celtic decided it was not the occasion for frills, and their uncompromising defence dealt competently with Forest's attacks.

Third Round Second Leg December 7th
CELTIC (0) 1 NOTTINGHAM FOREST (0) 2
MacLeod (80) Hodge (54), Walsh (74)

CELTIC: Bonner; McGrain, Reid; Aitken, McAdam, Sinclair (Melrose); McClair, P. McStay, McGarvey, MacLeod, Burns

NOTTINGHAM FOREST: Van Breukelen; Anderson, Swain; Fairclough, Hart, Bowyer; Wigley, Hodge, Birtles, Davenport, Walsh

Attendance: 66,938

A splendid display of disciplined defence and accurate counter-attacking took Forest through to the Quarter-Finals although they were assisted by the fact that Celtic played well below their best. Celtic badly missed Davie Provan, and they rarely provided proper service to their front players – McGarvey and McClair. Forest always looked threatening on the break, and 9 minutes after half-time they went ahead. Wigley took advantage of a slack pass from Burns and ran 50 yards, beating both Reid and Aitken en route. His low cross went to Davenport and he pushed it into the path of Hodge who slipped it past Bonner. The home fans were further stunned when Davenport laid on a 2nd goal in 74 minutes. He went past McAdam down the left, then beat Aitken before cutting the ball back for Walsh who touched it into the net. 6 minutes later Celtic gained some consolation when MacLeod headed a McStay corner past Van'Breukelen, but by then the match had slipped away. Nottingham Forest won 2-1 on aggregate.

APPEARANCES	League	League Cup	Scottish Cup	U.E.F.A Cup
Bonner	33	11	5	6
McGrain	33	10	5	6
Reid	23+1S	5+1S	5	4+1S
Aitken	31	10	4	6
McAdam	28	7	4	5
MacLeod	34	10	5	6
Provan	14+4S	5+1S	3	4
P. McStay	34	8	5	6
McGarvey	28+2S	10	4+1S	6
Burns	31+1S	11	5	6
Melrose	20+9S	6+1S	2+2S	3+3S
Crainie	0+2S	1+1S	–	–
Whittaker	10	6	–	–
W. McStay	15+3S	5	2	1
McClair	28+7S	8+1S	5	3+3S
Sinclair	15+5S	4+1S	0+2S	4
Halpin	1+3S	1+3S	–	0+1S
Latchford	3	–	–	–
Dobbin	1+2S	3	–	–
Colquhoun	11+1S	–	1	–

APPEARANCES	League	League Cup	Scottish Cup	U.E.F.A Cup
Archdeacon	0+1S	–	–	–
Grant	2+1S	–	–	–
McGugan	1	–	–	–

GOALSCORERS

League: McClair 23, McGarvey 10, Burns 9, MacLeod 7, Melrose 7, Aitken 5, P. McStay 3, Whittaker 2, Provan 2, Dobbin 2, Colquhoun 2, Reid 2 (2 pens), Own Goals 2, W. McStay 1, Archdeacon 1, Sinclair 1, McAdam 1

League Cup: Reid 4 (3 pens), Melrose 3, McGarvey 2, MacLeod 2 (2 pens), P. McStay 2, McClair 1, Provan 1, Whittaker 1, Own Goals 1

Scottish Cup: McClair 6, McGarvey 3, Burns 3, P. McStay 2, MacLeod 2, Melrose 1, Colquhoun 1, Reid 1

U.E.F.A. Cup: MacLeod 3, Aitken 2, McGarvey 2, Provan 1, Burns 1, McAdam 1, McClair 1

Celtic won the 1982 League Cup, defeating old rivals Rangers by 2 goals to 1. Frank McGarvey shows the Cup to the supporters.

Season 1984-85

Celtic had a fine league season, finishing in 2nd place in the table behind run-away winners Aberdeen. One consolation was that they managed to inflict 2 of only 4 defeats suffered by the Champions. They just had the edge in their league encounters with Rangers. In the most ambitious move made by a Scottish club in years they paid a record £400,000 fee to bring Maurice Johnston back to Scotland, and he repaid part of that fee by scoring 14 goals in his 27 matches. Jim Melrose and Mark Reid were both transferred to English clubs and Frank McGarvey also left the club at the end of the season. Pat Bonner played in 34 matches and Brian McClair finished as top scorer for the 2nd successive season with 18 goals followed by McGarvey on 15. Sadly, Chairman Desmond White died while on holiday. Tom Devlin was later named as his successor.

Celtic had one or two frights on their way to their 43rd Scottish Cup Final. Things looked ominous when opponents Dundee United went ahead 8 minutes after half-time, but an astute tactical switch by Manager David Hay transformed the match and a magnificent free-kick goal from Davie Provan and a spectacular diving header by Frank McGarvey gave Celtic the silverware and gave David Hay his first major prize as Celtic Manager. The Scottish Cup victory was revenge for a defeat in extra-time at the hands of the Tannadice team in the Skol Cup Quarter-Final.

Celtic beat the Belgian Cup holders K.A.A. Ghent 3-1 on aggregate in the First Round of the Cup Winners cup. The draw paired them with Rapid Vienna in the Second Round. They lost the away leg 1-3 and had substitute Alan McInally ordered off but they staged a remarkable comeback to win the return in Glasgow by 3-0 against the Austrians who had one of their players ordered off. But their opponents protested that a bottle and coins had been thrown onto the field and claimed that their player Weinhofer had been hit by a missile although T.V. evidence suggested otherwise. U.E.F.A. at first fined both teams but an appeals committee later ruled that the Second Leg would have to be replayed, more than 100 hundred miles from Glasgow. Old Trafford was chosen as the venue and a crowd of almost 52,000 packed in to see if Celtic could repeat their previous performance, but sadly they could not – they lost 0-1.

League:	Runners-up
Skol Cup:	Quarter-Finalists
Scottish Cup:	Winners
Cup Winners' Cup:	Second Round

SCOTTISH PREMIER LEAGUE

July 1st: Celtic showed interest in Neale Cooper of Aberdeen.

July 6th: Celtic won their appeal against the pitch invasion fine at Nottingham Forest. Their £2,000 fine was refunded less £160 for a shoe and a toilet roll being thrown onto the pitch.

July 25th: Cooper rejected a move to Parkhead.

July 27th: Chelsea offered £125,000 for Tommy Burns.

August 11th
HIBERNIAN (0) 0 CELTIC (0) 0

HIBERNIAN: Rough; McKee, Schaedler; Sneddon, Rae, McNamara; Callachan, Jamieson (McCachie), Irvine, Rice (Brazil), Thomson

CELTIC: Bonner; Sinclair, Reid; McAdam, McGugan, MacLeod; Colquhoun, Grant, McClair (McInally), Burns, McGarvey (McKechnie)

Attendance: 15,500

August 18th
CELTIC (0) 1 DUNDEE UNITED (1) 1
McClair (59) Beedie (7)

CELTIC: Bonner; Sinclair, Reid; Aitken, McAdam, Macleod (McInally); Colquhoun (Provan), McClair, McGarvey, Grant, Burns

DUNDEE UNITED: Thomson; Holt, Malpas; Narey, Hegarty, Gough; Bannon, Milne (Clark), Kirkwood, Sturrock, Beedie

Attendance: 19,000

August 25th
RANGERS (0) 0 CELTIC (0) 0

RANGERS: Walker; McKinnon, Dawson; McClelland, Paterson, Redford; Russell (Burns), Fraser, Clark (McCoist), I. Ferguson, Cooper

CELTIC: Bonner; McGrain, Sinclair; Aitken, McAdam, Grant; Colquhoun, P. McStay (W. McStay), McClair, Burns, McInally (McGarvey)

Attendance: 44,000

This was one of the tamer Old Firm confrontations with both sides having their moments. Rangers would regret missing chances when they were clearly on top early in the second-half. Redford should have scored instead of blasting high over after getting the break of the ball of Roy Aitken and Iain Ferguson should have done better than send a header against Pat Bonner. Celtic were clearly missing the drive of Murdo MacLeod although Peter Grant looked a bright prospect. At the end of the day a draw was perhaps the proper result.

September 1st
CELTIC (4) 5 MORTON (0) 0
McClair 2 (1½, 50),
McGarvey 2 (11, 15),
Grant (23)

CELTIC: Bonner; McGrain, McAdam, Aitken, Sinclair; P. McStay (McInally), Burns, Grant; Provan, McClair, McGarvey

MORTON: McDermott; McClurg, Dunlop, Duffy, Holmes; Sullivan, O'Hara, Docherty; Robertson, Pettigrew (Wilson), McNeill (Clinging)

Attendance: 12,123

September 6th: Jim Melrose went to Wolves on a month's loan.

September 8th
DUMBARTON (0) 1 CELTIC (1) 1
J. Coyle (77 pen) McGarvey (32)

DUMBARTON: Arthur; Kay, McGowan; T. Coyle, McNeill, Clougherty; Ashwood, Craig, P. McGowan, Crawley, J. Coyle

CELTIC: Bonner; McGrain, Sinclair (Reid); Aitken, McAdam, Grant; Provan, P. McStay, McClair (McInally), Burns, McGarvey

Attendance: 8,416

September 12th: Paul McStay made an appearance as a substitute in the Scotland team which beat Yugoslavia 6-1 at Hampden Park.

September 13th: Double glazing firm C.R. Smith signed a £500,000 sponsorship deal with both Celtic and Rangers.

September 15th
CELTIC (0) 1 HEARTS (0) 0
McGarvey (58)

CELTIC: Bonner; McGrain, McAdam, Aitken, Reid; Grant, P. McStay, Burns; Colquhoun, McClair, McGarvey (McInally)

HEARTS: Smith; Kidd (Whittaker), Jardine, MacDonald, Cowie; Bowman, Mackay, Levein, A. MacDonald (Park); Bone, Robertson

Attendance: 18,411. Whittaker was sent off 3 minutes after coming on as a substitute

September 22nd
ST MIRREN (0) 1 CELTIC (0) 2
McAvennie (85) McClair (73),
Colquhoun (84)

ST MIRREN: Money; Wilson, Winnie; Rooney, Cooper, Clarke; Fitzpatrick, McAvennie, Gallagher (McDowall), Abercrombie, Scanlon

CELTIC: Bonner; McGrain, Reid; Aitken, McAdam, Grant; Colquhoun, P. McStay, McGarvey, Burns, McInally (McClair)

Attendance: 12,550

September 29th
DUNDEE (1) 2 CELTIC (2) 3
McCormack (41), Grant (21 pen),
Stephen (59) Colquhoun (26),
Burns (81)

DUNDEE: Carson; McGeachie, McKinlay; Rafferty, McCormack, Glennie; Stephen, Brown, McCall (Kidd), Connor, Harris (Richardson)

CELTIC: Bonner; McGrain, Reid (MacLeod); Aitken, McAdam, Grant; Colquhoun, McStay, McClair, Burns, McGarvey

Attendance: 13,761. Reid and Brown both missed penalties

October 4th: Celtic offered £300,000 for Davie Dodds of Dundee United.

October 6th

CELTIC (1) 2	ABERDEEN (0) 1
McGarvey (30),	McDougall (47)
Provan (80)	

CELTIC: Bonner; McGrain, Reid; Aitken, McAdam, Grant; Colquhoun (Provan), P. McStay, McClair, MacLeod, McGarvey

ABERDEEN: Leighton; McKimmie, McQueen; Cooper, McLeish, Miller; Black, Simpson, McDougall, Angus (Hewitt), Stark, Porteous

Attendance: 31,418

After being outplayed for most of the 1st-half and having gone in at the interval trailing to a Frank McGarvey goal, the Dons needed an early strike in the 2nd half and they got it after just 2 minutes when McDougall scored with a marvellous 20-yard drive. Shortly after, McDougall was hauled down by Reid when he looked certain to score. Stark shot weakly to the right from the spot and Bonner saved. That was the turning point. Celtic got back into their stride and staged a tremendous finish to snatch the points.

October 10th: Celtic bid £400,000 for Maurice Johnston of Watford.

October 11th: Celtic got Johnston for a record Scottish transfer fee of £400,000 after the player rejected a move to Spurs.

October 13th

CELTIC (0) 3	HIBERNIAN (0) 0
Grant (72 pen),	
Burns (82)	
McClair (87)	

CELTIC: Bonner; McGrain, MacLeod; Aitken, McAdam, Grant; Provan, P. McStay, Johnston, Burns, McGarvey (McClair)

HIBERNIAN: Rough; Sneddon, Schaedler; Brazil, Rae, McNamara; Callachan, Kane (Brogan), Irvine, Thomson, Rice

Attendance: 27,863

October 17th: McStay and Johnston were in the Scotland team which beat Iceland 3-0 in a World Cup match at Hampden Park. Paul McStay scored 2 goals.

October 20th

DUNDEE UNITED (0) 1	CELTIC (1) 3
Bannon (56)	MacLeod (36),
	Johnston (52),
	Grant (67)

DUNDEE UNITED: McAlpine; Gough, Munro (McGinnis); Malpas, Hegarty, Narey; Bannon, Coyne, Kirkwood (Taylor), Sturrock, Dodds

CELTIC: Bonner; McGrain, MacLeod; Aitken, McAdam, Grant; Provan, McStay, Johnston, Burns (McClair), McGarvey

Attendance: 16,738

League positions

	P	W	D	L	F	A	Pts
1 Aberdeen	11	9	1	1	27	6	19
2 CELTIC	11	7	4	0	21	7	18
3 Rangers	11	6	4	1	11	2	16
4 St Mirren	12	6	1	5	13	14	13
5 Hearts	12	5	1	6	11	16	11

November 3rd

MORTON (1) 2	CELTIC (1) 1
Gillespie 2 (36, 83)	Johnston (9)

MORTON: McDermott; Wilson, Holmes; Sullivan (Doak), Mackin, Duffy; Robertson (O'Hara), Docherty, Gillespie, Clinging, Pettigrew

CELTIC: Bonner; McGrain, Reid; Aitken, McAdam, Grant; Provan, McStay, Johnston, MacLeod, McGarvey (McClair)

Attendance: 8,500

November 6th: Jim Melrose was transferred to Manchester City for £40,000. He has scored 4 goals in 4 games while on loan to Wolves.

November 10th

CELTIC (1) 2	DUMBARTON (0) 0
McGarvey (33),	
Johnston (55)	

CELTIC: Bonner; McGrain, MacLeod; Aitken, McAdam, Grant; Provan (Colquhoun), McStay, Johnston, McGarvey, McClair

DUMBARTON; Arthur; Kay, McGowan; McCahill, McNeill, Clougherty; Bourke (Simpson), Robertson (Crawley), Craig, T. Coyle, J. Coyle

Attendance: 13,791

November 14th: McStay and Johnston were in the Scotland team which beat Spain 3-1 at Hampden Park in a World Cup Group match. Johnston scored 2 goals and former Celt Kenny Dalglish equalled the Scottish International scoring record of 30 goals held by Denis Law.

November 17th

HEARTS (0) 1	CELTIC (1) 5
Johnston (89)	Johnston (33),
	McClair 3 (48, 49, 82),
	Burns (60)

HEARTS: Smith; Kidd, Whittaker; Jardine, R. MacDonald, Levein; Park (Johnston), Bone, Clark, A. MacDonald (Bowman), Black

CELTIC: Bonner; McGrain, MacLeod; Aitken, McAdam, McClair; Provan, P. McStay, Johnston (McInally), Burns, McGarvey

Attendance: 20,117

November 17th: Graeme Sinclair joined Manchester City on loan for 4 weeks.

November 24th

CELTIC (1) 7	ST MIRREN (1) 1
P. McStay (20), McGarvey 3 (47, 60,72) Burns (50), Provan (55), McClair (81)	Gallagher (11)

CELTIC: Bonner; McGrain, Aitken, McAdam (W. McStay); MacLeod; P. McStay, McClair, Burns; Provan (Colquhoun), Johnston, McGarvey

ST MIRREN: Money; Wilson, Clarke, Winnie, Hamilton (Cameron); Abercrombie, Rooney, Fitzpatrick; McAvennie, Gallagher, Scanlon (McDowall)

Attendance: 16,418

November 29th: Pierce O'Leary was signed from Vancouver Whitecaps.

December 1st

CELTIC (1) 5	DUNDEE (1) 1
Johnston 3 (28, 73, 78) Burns (65), McGarvey (79)	Connor (26)

CELTIC: Bonner; McGrain, Aitken, McAdam, MacLeod; McClair, McStay, Burns; Provan, Johnston, McGarvey

DUNDEE: Geddes; McGeachie, Glennie, Smith, McKinlay; Rafferty, Brown (Forsyth), Richardson (McCall), Connor; Stephen, Harris

Attendance: 15,887. McGarvey missed a penalty

December 8th

ABERDEEN (2) 4	CELTIC (0) 2
Black 2 (33, 61), McKimmie (45), McDougall (86)	Johnston (57 pen), McGarvey (84)

ABERDEEN: Leighton; McKimmie, McQueen; Stark, McLeish, Miller; Black, Simpson, McDougall, Angus, Weir

CELTIC: Bonner; McGrain, MacLeod; Aitken, McAdam (W. McStay/Colquhoun), McClair; Provan, P. McStay, Johnston, Burns, McGarvey

Attendance: 23,000

Aberdeen swept aside Celtic's challenge in a thrilling match. Eric Black in particular was a constant menace and it was he who headed in a Weir free-kick in the 33rd minute as the Celtic defence stood still. Just before half-time Burns cleared to McKimmie 35 yards out. There seemed no danger but the full-back hit a cracking first time drive which took a deflection off McAdam and landed in the back of the net. Celtic pulled a goal back in the 57th minute from a Mo Johnston penalty after Black had pushed McAdam. 4 minutes later Weir took a free-kick and Black got in an early header to beat Bonner. In the 84th minute McGarvey gave Celtic some hope when he headed in a Provan cross but it took the Dons only two minutes to reply when McDougall headed home from a cross supplied by Black. The referee booked 8 players bringing the total to 32 in the last 6 matches between the teams.

December 15th

HIBERNIAN (0) 0	CELTIC (0) 1
	Johnston (78)

HIBERNIAN: Rough; Sneddon, Schaedler; Brazil, Rae, Hunter; Craig (Thomson), Durie, Irvine, Kane, Rice

CELTIC: Bonner; McGrain, Reid; Aitken, McAdam, MacLeod; Colquhoun (Provan), McStay, Johnston, McClair, McGarvey

Attendance: 10,000

December 22nd

CELTIC (1) 1	RANGERS (0) 1
McClair (9)	Cooper (85)

CELTIC: Bonner; McGrain (Sinclair), Reid; McClair, Aitken, MacLeod; Colquhoun (Provan), McStay, Johnston, Burns, McGarvey

RANGERS: McCloy; Burns, Munro; McPherson, McKinnon, Redford (Prytz), MacDonald, Fraser, Mitchell (McMinn), D. Ferguson, Cooper

Attendance: 43,748. Bonner saved Fraser's 50th minute penalty

Celtic got off to a fine start with a goal in 9 minutes. McClair cleverly set up the chance for Mo Johnston and when the strikers' shot came off the legs of McCloy, McClair was first to the rebound. In the 50th minute Reid fouled Cooper in the box. Fraser hit the penalty well but Bonner made a magnificent save. Sadly for him that was overshadowed by his late lapse which brought the game level.

With 5 minutes left the big Irishman came running off his line to cut out a Ted McMinn cross which was almost out of his reach. He could only palm it weakly down and Davie Cooper rifled in a left-foot drive for the equaliser. Normally reliable Paul McStay was wayward with his passes but 17-year old Derek Ferguson showed all the touches to suggest that he was one of the best young Scottish players to emerge in years.

December 29th

CELTIC (1) 1	DUNDEE UNITED (0) 2
Burns (22)	Sturrock (64), Gough (72)

CELTIC: Bonner; McGrain, Reid; McClair, Aitken, MacLeod; Provan, McStay, Johnston, Burns, McGarvey

DUNDEE UNITED: McAlpine; Malpas, Holt; Gough, Hegarty, Narey; Bannon, Taylor (Sturrock), Coyne, Beedie, Dodds

Attendance: 22,894. Mo Johnston missed a penalty

League positions

	P	W	D	L	F	A	Pts
1 Aberdeen	20	15	3	2	44	14	33
2 CELTIC	20	12	5	3	46	19	29
3 Rangers	20	9	9	2	26	12	27
4 Dundee United	20	10	4	6	36	23	24
5 St Mirren	20	8	3	9	25	34	19

January 1st
RANGERS (1) 1 — CELTIC (0) 2
Cooper (33) — Johnston (46), McClair (55)

RANGERS: McCloy; Burns, Munro; McPherson, McKinnon, Redford; McMinn (MacDonald), D. Ferguson (Dawson), I. Ferguson, Prytz, Cooper

CELTIC: Bonner; McGrain, Reid; McClair, Aitken, MacLeod; Colquhoun, McStay, Johnston, Burns, McGarvey

Attendance: 45,000

Rangers had started badly but, after McCloy had saved a 17th-minute penalty from Maurice Johnston, they gained the upper hand and dominated the play with skilful football. They took the lead in 33 minutes with a glorious 20-yard drive from Davie Cooper after good work by Iain Ferguson and young Derek Ferguson. Rangers kicked-off the 2nd-half but astonishingly within 50 seconds of the restart Celtic were back level when Johnston was left unmarked and headed home easily from 6 yards, 9 minutes later McClair scored what proved to be the winner. He collected the ball on the edge of the box and fired in a low shot which caught McCloy wrong-footed and trundled into the far corner of the net.

February 2nd
ST MIRREN (0) 0 — CELTIC (0) 2
Johnston (57), Burns (74)

ST MIRREN: Money; Wilson, Hamilton; Rooney (Winnie), Godfrey, Clarke; Fitzpatrick, McDowall (Mackie), Gallagher, Abercrombie, Spiers

CELTIC: Bonner; McGrain, Reid; MacLeod, McAdam, O'Leary; Colquhoun, McStay, Johnston, Burns, McGarvey (McInally)

Attendance: 14,025

February 9th
DUNDEE (0) 2 — CELTIC (0) 0
Stephen (81), Connor (89 pen)

DUNDEE: Geddes; McGeachie, McKinlay; McCormack, Smith, Glennie; Stephen, Brown, Harvey (Rafferty), Connor, Kidd (McCall)

CELTIC: Bonner; McGrain, Reid; MacLeod, McAdam, O'Leary; Colquhoun, P. McStay, Johnston (McInally), Burns, McGarvey

Attendance: 12,087

February 19th
CELTIC (2) 4 — MORTON (0) 0
P. McStay (20), McGarvey (34), Provan (50), Chalmers (78)

CELTIC: Latchford; W. McStay, McGrain; Grant, Aitken, O'Leary; Provan, P. McStay (Burns), Johnston (Chalmers), MacLeod, McGarvey

MORTON: McDermott; Welsh, Holmes; Docherty, Boag, Duffy; Wilson, Doak, Pettigrew, O'Hara, Clinging

Attendance: 10,197. This was Roy Aitken's 300th League appearance

February 23rd
CELTIC (0) 2 — ABERDEEN (0) 0
Johnston (68), P. McStay (90 pen)

CELTIC: Bonner; W. McStay, McGrain; Aitken, McAdam, O'Leary; Grant (Provan), P. McStay, Johnston, MacLeod, McGarvey

ABERDEEN: Leighton; McKimmie, McQueen; Cooper, McLeish, Miller; Black, Simpson (Bell), Cowan (Hewitt), Angus, Weir

Celtic opened up the Championship with this win. The match was stalemate until Provan came on in with 25 minutes to go and within 3 minutes Celtic were in the lead. Provan sent a corner-kick to the far post and when Alex McLeish hesitated, Aitken made a huge leap to knock the ball down and Mo Johnston beat Leighton with a close-range hook shot. It was Celtic all the way in the closing stages, and in injury time another Provan cross beat the Dons' defence. Neale Cooper barged into Johnston as he was about to connect with his head and the referee had no hesitation in pointing to the spot. Paul McStay, who had a magnificent match, sent the kick just inside Leighton's right-hand post.

League positions

	P	W	D	L	F	A	Pts
1 Aberdeen	27	19	4	4	61	21	42
2 CELTIC	25	16	5	4	56	22	37
3 Dundee United	25	13	5	7	44	25	31
4 Rangers	27	10	11	6	33	25	31
5 St Mirren	27	12	4	11	32	39	28

February 27th: McStay and Johnston were in the Scotland team which was beaten 1-0 by Spain in a World Cup match in Seville.

March 2nd
DUNDEE UNITED (0) 0 — CELTIC (0) 0

DUNDEE UNITED: McAlpine; Malpas, Holt; Gough, Hegarty, Narey; Bannon, Milne, Kirkwood (Beedie), Coyne (Reilly), Dodds

CELTIC; Bonner; W. McStay, McGrain; Grant, Aitken, O'Leary; Provan, McGarvey, Johnston (McClair), MacLeod, Burns

Attendance: 16,493. Grant missed a penalty

March 16th
CELTIC (0) 0 — HIBERNIAN (1) 1
Kane (21)

CELTIC: Bonner; W. McStay (Burns), McAdam, O'Leary, McGrain; P. McStay, Aitken, MacLeod; Colquhoun, Johnston, McClair (McGarvey)

HIBERNIAN: Rough; McKee, Rae, Brazil, Schaedler; Sneddon, Callachan, Rice; McBride, Kane, Irvine

Attendance: 15,820

March 20th
CELTIC (1) 3 — HEARTS (2) 2
Johnston (37), MacLeod (78), McClair (80) — Robertson (4), Watson (29)

CELTIC: Bonner; W. McStay, McGrain; Aitken, O'Leary, MacLeod; Provan, P. McStay, Johnston, Burns, McGarvey (McClair)

HEARTS: Smith; Kidd, Cowie; Whittaker, Jardine, R. MacDonald, Levein; Watson, Clark, Robertson, Black

Attendance: 11,522

March 23rd
MORTON (1) 2 — CELTIC (5) 7
O'Leary o.g. (19), Doak (47) — McClair 4 (10, 15, 21, 66), McGarvey 2 (20, 40), Archdeacon (64)

MORTON: McDermott; Welsh (Docherty), Holmes; Doak, Boag, Duffy; McCurdy, Sullivan, Alexander (McNeill), Thomson, Clinging

CELTIC: Bonner; W. McStay, McGrain (Grant); Aitken, O'Leary, MacLeod; Provan (Archdeacon), P. McStay, Johnston, McClair, McGarvey

Attendance: 8,000

March 27th: Johnston and McStay were in the Scotland team beaten 1-0 by Wales in a World Cup match at Hampden Park.

April 3rd
DUMBARTON (0) 0 — CELTIC (2) 2
Johnston (33), McClair (43)

DUMBARTON: Arthur; Kay, Montgomery; T. Coyle, McNeill, Clougherty; Ashwood, Craig, Bourke, Robertson, Simpson

CELTIC: Bonner; McGrain, Reid; Aitken, O'Leary, MacLeod; Provan, McStay (McGarvey), Johnston, Burns, McClair

Attendance: 7,000

April 6th
HEARTS (0) 0 — CELTIC (1) 2
McStay (10), McClair (65)

HEARTS: Smith; Levein, Jardine, R. MacDonald, Whittaker; Kidd, Mackay, Watson; Black, Clark, Robertson (Park)

CELTIC: Bonner; McGrain (McAdam), Aitken, O'Leary, Reid; McStay, MacLeod, Burns; Provan, Johnston, McClair

Attendance: 14,883

April 20th
CELTIC (1) 3 — ST MIRREN (0) 0
Aitken 2 (38 pen, 57 pen), McGarvey (51)

CELTIC: Bonner; W. McStay, MacLeod; Aitken, McAdam, McClair; Provan (Colquhoun), P. McStay, Johnston, Burns, McGarvey

ST MIRREN: Money; Wilson, Winnie; Clarke, Godfrey, Abercrombie; Fitzpatrick, McAvennie, Gallagher, McDowell, Speirs

Attendance: 11,746

April 27th
ABERDEEN (0) 1 — CELTIC (1) 1
Miller (62) — Aitken (39 pen)

ABERDEEN: Leighton; McKimmie, McQueen; Stark, McLeish, Miller; Porteous, Simpson, McDougall (Cowan), Bell (Cooper), Hewitt

CELTIC: Bonner; W. McStay, McGrain; Aitken, McAdam, MacLeod; Grant (Provan), P. McStay, Johnston (McClair), Burns, McGarvey

Attendance: 23,000

Celtic took the lead in 39 minutes in controversial fashion. McGarvey squeezed past Miller and sent over a cross which seemed too high for Johnston. However the striker was nudged in the back by Stark and the referee pointed to the spot. Despite Aberdeen protests Aitken scored with a blistering drive. Celtic seemed quite content to sit on their lead when in the 62nd minute Porteous sent a free-kick bending away from Bonner and with the Celtic defence at sixes and sevens Miller leapt high to head the ball just inside the left-hand post. The match ended in controversy when 3 minutes from time McGarvey had a goal disallowed when the referee ruled that he had fouled Leighton in the process of scoring. Aberdeen, who had never clinched the Championship on their own ground before, celebrated immediately the final whistle sounded.

April 29th: Mark Reid was transferred to Charlton Athletic for £40,000.

May 1st
CELTIC (0) 1 — RANGERS (0) 1
McInally (60) — McCoist (77 pen)

CELTIC: Latchford; W. McStay, MacLeod; Aitken, McGugan, Grant; Provan, P. McStay, Johnston, McClair, McInally (Colquhoun)

RANGERS: McCloy; Dawson, Munro; McPherson, Johnstone, Durrant; Russell (Burns), McKinnon, E. Ferguson (I. Ferguson), McCoist, Cooper

Attendance: 40.079

In only 2 minutes McPherson quite blatantly whipped the legs from Johnston inside the area. Aitken smacked the ball into the net from the penalty but referee Valentine ordered a retake on the grounds that it had moved, and Aitken's 2nd effort crashed off the legs of McCloy to safety. 7 minutes after the interval Cooper, who had been booked earlier, was sent off for fouling Grant. In the 60th minute Celtic took the lead, McCloy saved a shot from Johnston but could not hold it and McInally managed to touch it over a couple of despairing defenders. In 71 minutes Dawson was ordered off following an off-the-ball incident with Johnston. In 77 minutes Rangers were awarded a penalty for hands against Aitken. McCoist levelled the score with the kick.

May 4th
CELTIC (0) 0 — DUNDEE (0) 1
Brown (52)

CELTIC: Bonner; W. McStay, MacLeod; Aitken, McGugan, Grant; Colquhoun (Archdeacon), McClair, Johnston, McKechnie (Coyle), McInally

DUNDEE: Geddes, McGeachie (McWilliams), McKinlay; McCormack, Glennie, Shannon; Rafferty, Brown, McCall, Connor, Stephen (Kidd)

Attendance: 8,815

May 11th
CELTIC (0) 2 — DUMBARTON (0) 0
McClair (74),
W. McStay (85)

CELTIC: Bonner; W. McStay, O'Leary; Aitken, McAdam, MacLeod; McClair, P. McStay, Johnston, McGarvey, Archdeacon

DUMBARTON: Arthur; Kay, McGowan; T. Coyle, McCahill, Montgomerie; Moore, Crawley (Simpson), Bourke, Craig, J. Coyle

Premier League

	P	W	D	L	F	A	Pts
1 Aberdeen	36	27	5	4	89	26	59
2 CELTIC	36	22	8	6	77	30	52
3 Dundee United	36	20	7	9	67	33	47
4 Rangers	36	13	12	11	47	38	38
5 St Mirren	36	17	4	15	51	56	38
6 Dundee	36	15	7	14	48	50	37
7 Hearts	36	13	5	18	47	64	31
8 Hibernian	36	10	7	19	38	61	27
9 Dumbarton	36	6	7	23	29	64	19
10 Morton	36	5	2	29	29	100	12

June 21st: Celtic Chairman Desmond White died while on holiday in Crete. He was 73.

June 29th: Tom Devlin was named as new Celtic Chairman.

May 25th: Roy Aitken was in the Scotland team which beat England 1-0 at Hampden Park to win the inaugural Rous Cup. Murdo MacLeod made an appearance as a substitute.

May 28th: Roy Aitken was in the Scotland team which beat Iceland 1-0 in a World Cup match in Reykjavick.

June 12th: Frank McGarvey joined St Mirren for £80,000.

SKOL LEAGUE CUP

Second Round August 22nd
DUNFERMLINE (1) 2 — CELTIC (0) 3
Watson 2 (26, 69) — McClair 2 (64, 84), McInally (68)

DUNFERMLINE: Whyte; Robertson, Forrest; Rodgers (T. Smith), Young, McCathie; Perry, Hamilton, Watson, Morrison, Jenkins

CELTIC: Bonner; McGrain, Reid; Aitken, McAdam, Grant; Colquhoun, W. McStay (Melrose), McClair, Burns, McInally

Attendance: 9,000

Third Round August 29th
AIRDRIE (0) 0 — CELTIC (3) 4
Burns (23), McInally (32), Grant (40), McClair (79)

AIRDRIE: Martin; Steven, Rodger; Black, Lawrie, Gillies; Yule (Christie), Fairlie, McCabe, Hood, Paterson

CELTIC: Bonner; McGrain (W. McStay), Sinclair; Aitken, McAdam, Grant; Colquhoun, P. McStay, McClair, Burns, McInally (McGarvey)

Attendance: 11,411

Quarter-Final September 4th
DUNDEE UNITED (0) 2 — CELTIC (1) 1
Sturrock (61), Clark (92) — McInally (82)
After extra time

DUNDEE UNITED: Thomson; Holt (Beedie), Malpas; Gough, Hegarty, Narey; Bannon, Milne, Kirkwood, Sturrock, Dodds (Clark)

CELTIC: Bonner; McGrain, Sinclair; Aitken, McAdam, Grant; Colquhoun (McInally), P. McStay, McClair, Burns, McGarvey

Attendance: 21,182

SCOTTISH CUP

Third Round January 30th
HAMILTON ACADEMICALS (1) 1 — CELTIC (0) 2
Forsyth (27) — McGarvey 2 (61, 86)

HAMILTON: Ferguson; Gervaise, Hamill; Forsyth, Speirs, Mitchell (McCurdy); McNaught, Clarke, Phillips, Wright, Brogan

CELTIC: Bonner; McGrain, Reid; MacLeod, McAdam, O'Leary; Provan, P. McStay, Johnston, Burns, McClair (McGarvey)

Attendance: 10,000

Fourth Round February 16th

CELTIC (3) 6 — INVERNESS THISTLE (0) 0

McGarvey (9), P. McStay 3 (15, 63, 85), Johnston (30), MacLeod (80)

CELTIC: Latchford; W. McStay, McGrain; Grant (Archdeacon), McAdam, O'Leary; Provan, P. McStay, Johnston, MacLeod, McGarvey (McInally)

INVERNESS THISTLE: Fridge; Skinner, Wilson; Sanderson (Fraser), Milroy, Andrew; Black, Hay, MacDonald, Oliver, McLean (Calder)

Attendance: 14,927

Quarter-Final March 9th

DUNDEE (0) 1 — CELTIC (0) 1

Brown (72) — Johnston (67)

DUNDEE: Geddes; McGeachie, Smith, Glennie, McKinlay; McCormack, Brown, Connor; Stephen, Harvey (McCall), Rafferty

CELTIC: Bonner; McGrain, Aitken, McAdam (Burns), Reid; Provan, Grant, McStay, MacLeod; McGarvey (McClair), Johnston

Attendance: 21,301

Quarter-Final Replay March 13th

CELTIC (1) 2 — DUNDEE (0) 1

McGarvey (34), Johnston (68) — Stephen (47)

CELTIC: Bonner; W. McStay, McGrain (Burns), Aitken, McAdam, O'Leary; Provan, P. McStay, Johnston, MacLeod, McGarvey (McClair)

DUNDEE: Geddes; McGeachie, McKinlay; McCormack, Smith, Glennie; Rafferty, Brown, Forsyth (McCall), Connor, Stephen

Attendance: 37,390

Semi Final at Hampden Park April 13th

MOTHERWELL (1) 1 — CELTIC (1) 1

McAllister (12) — Burns (23)

MOTHERWELL: Gardiner; McLeod, Murray; Doyle, Forbes, Boyd; Stewart (Walker/Gahagan), McAllister, Harrow, Mauchlen, Blair

CELTIC: Bonner; McGrain, Reid (McAdam); Aitken, O'Leary, MacLeod; Provan, McStay (McGarvey), Johnston, Burns, McClair

Attendance: 30,536

Manager Tommy McLean obviously prepared his side well and Motherwell ended up unlucky to be held to a draw. After having withstood the opening thrust from Celtic the underdogs began making more and better passes themselves. Celtic had to sweat out a series of corners in the closing stages.

Semi-Final Replay April 17th

MOTHERWELL (0) 0 — CELTIC (0) 3

Aitken (73), Johnston 2 (81, 89)

MOTHERWELL: Gardiner; McLeod, Murray; Doyle, Forbes, Boyd; Walker, McAllister, Harrow, Mauchlen, Blair. Subs: Gahagan, Clark

CELTIC: Bonner; W. McStay, McGrain (Grant); Aitken, McAdam, MacLeod; Provan, P. McStay, Johnston, Burns, McClair (McGarvey)

Attendance: 25,677

For 73 minutes Motherwell refused to buckle under immense Celtic pressure. Provan was a perpetual pest to their defence. In the 73rd minute he touched the ball inside to Burns who pushed it forward to Aitken, who deceived Forbes with a body swerve before turning and knocking the ball into the corner of the net. In the 81st minute Celtic went 2 up. Burns strode away down the middle and sent Johnston through on the left and the Scotland striker whipped the ball past Gardiner. Just before the end Johnston struck again when he headed in a carefully flighted McGarvey cross to take Celtic into their 43rd Scottish Cup Final.

Final at Hampden Park May 18th

CELTIC (0) 2 — DUNDEE UNITED (0) 1

Provan (76), McGarvey (84) — Beedie (54)

CELTIC: Bonner; W. McStay, McGrain; Aitken, McAdam, MacLeod; Provan, P. McStay (O'Leary), Johnston, Burns (McClair), McGarvey

DUNDEE UNITED: McAlpine; Malpas, Beedie (Holt); Gough, Hegarty, Narey; Bannon, Milne, Kirkwood, Sturrock, Dodds. Sub: Coyne

Attendance: 60,346 — *Referee:* B.R. McGinlay (Balfron)

Davie Provan and Frank McGarvey grabbed the glory goals for Celtic in the 100th Scottish Cup Final at Hampden. Dundee United, leading by a Beedie goal, looked to have their name written on the Cup. Then David Hay made a switch, pushing Roy Aitken forward from the centre of defence and he quickly became the most effective midfield man on the field. With 14 minutes remaining, Bannon fouled MacLeod just outside the penalty area. Provan sent a great free-kick into the top left-hand corner, giving McAlpine no chance. Hampden erupted. 6 minutes from time Celtic grabbed a stunning winner. Aitken charged down the right, shrugged off a challenge and sent a cross over and McGarvey threw himself forward to score with a spectacular diving header. It was a goal fit to win any match.

CUP WINNERS CUP

First Round First Leg September 19th

K.A.A. GHENT (Belgium) (0) 1 — CELTIC (0) 0
Cordiez (81)

K.A.A. GHENT: Laurijssen; Busk, Criel; Hansens, De Wolf, Ruzic; Van Looy, Quipor, Martens, Schapendonk, Cordiez

CELTIC: Bonner; McGrain, Reid; Aitken, McAdam, MacLeod; Grant, P. McStay, McClair, Burns, McGarvey

Attendance: 22,500

Celtic came within 9 minutes of getting a result before losing to a simple goal from Cordiez. Until Ghent scored Celtic had strolled through the First Leg of this Cup Winners Cup tie, playing with discipline and a confidence which seldom saw them in any danger.

First Round Second Leg October 3rd

CELTIC (1) 3 — K.A.A. GHENT (0) 0
McGarvey 2 (40, 61), McStay (89)

CELTIC: Bonner; McGrain, MacLeod; Aitken, McAdam, Grant; Colquhoun (Provan), P. McStay, McClair, Burns, McGarvey

K.A.A. GHENT: Laurijssen; Hansens, Criel; Busk, De Wolf, Cordiez; De Kneef (Todoki), Quipor (Van Looy), Martens, Schapendonk, Bouvy

Attendance: 32,749

Celtic overcame a stubborn Belgian side to earn a place in the Second Round. They stormed into action from the first while but it was not until 5 minutes from the interval that they made the breakthrough which levelled the tie. Ghent were still far from finished. They occasionally broke from defence and when they did they were not afraid to shoot. The home crowd were therefore greatly relieved when Paul McStay headed in a 3rd from a Provan cross a minute from time. Celtic won 3-1 on aggregate.

Second Round First Leg October 24th

VIENNA RAPID (Austria) (0) 3 — CELTIC (0) 1
Pacult (53), Lainer (66), Krankl (87) — McClair (57)

RAPID VIENNA: Feurer; Lainer, Brauneder; Pregesbauer; Weber; Kienast, Kranjcar, Panenka, Krankl, Brucic, Pacult

CELTIC: Bonner; McGrain, Reid; Aitken, W. McStay, Grant; Provan, P. McStay, McClair, MacLeod, McGarvey (McInally)

Attendance: 16,000

Celtic not only lost a goal soon after the interval but also were deprived of the injured McGarvey before half-time and then had his replacement Alan McInally sent off 16 minutes from the end for his one and only questionable tackle. Captain Danny McGrain was also booked and would also miss the return through suspension.

Second Round Second Leg November 7th

CELTIC (2) 3 — RAPID VIENNA (0) 0
McClair (32), MacLeod (44), Burns (68)

CELTIC: Bonner; W. McStay, MacLeod; Aitken, McAdam, Grant; Provan, P. McStay, McClair, Burns (Reid), McGarvey

RAPID VIENNA; Ehn; Lainer, Pregesbauer, Garger, Weber; Kienast, Brauneder (Willfurth), Brucic, Krankl, Pacult (Weinhofer), Kranjcar

Attendance: 48,813

Parkhead witnessed one of the most dramatic European ties of all time. Celtic reduced the 2 goal First leg deficit in the 32nd minute. Paul McStay started the move with a marvellous pass to Provan who sent over a well-judged cross for McClair to knock past Ehn. In injury time in the 1st-half a Provan corner caused panic in the Austrian penalty area and MacLeod hammered a left-foot shot into the corner of the net to put Celtic 2 up. Celtic's tie-clinching 3rd goal proved the seed of the trouble to come. Burns chased a good pass from McGarvey and slid towards the ball as the Austrian keeper raced out. The ball bounced from Ehn's body and Burns touched the rebound into the net. The Austrians protested furiously but the referee was unmoved. A few minutes later Kienast felled Burns out of sight of the referee. However, the far-side linesman saw the incident. Kienast was ordered from the field. Shortly afterwards Celtic were awarded a penalty but young Grant sent it wide. 14 minutes from time a bottle and some coins were thrown onto the field and the Austrian player Weinhofer went down as if poleaxed, obviously indicating that he had been hit by a missile. Television evidence suggested otherwise. Celtic won 4-3 on aggregate, but U.E.F.A. subsequently ordered the second leg to be replayed.

Second Round Second Leg Replay at Old Trafford December 12th

CELTIC (0) 0 — RAPID VIENNA (1) 1
Pacult (17)

CELTIC: Bonner; McGrain, MacLeod; Aitken, McAdam (Colquhoun), Grant; Provan, McStay, McGarvey, Burns, McClair

RAPID VIENNA: Feurer; Lainer, Garger; Weinhofer, Weber, Braunender; Kranjcar, Willfurth, Gross, Brucic, Pacult

Attendance: 51,500

In a match which was too emotional Celtic could not find the form which destroyed Rapid in the original Second leg. In the 9th minute Aitken blasted a great chance over the bar. 8 minutes later Celtic in their efforts to score were caught cold at the back. Roy Aitken hit a post at one end and Rapid raced upfield for Pacult to cut past Bonner and score a killing goal. Celtic expended as much energy as any side has ever done to get back into the match but their raids lacked imagination and in retrospect the tie was lost as soon as the Austrians scored. Rapid won 4-1 on aggregate.

APPEARANCES	League	Skol Cup	Scottish Cup	Cup Winners Cup
Bonner	34	3	6	5
McGrain	30	3	7	4
Reid	15+1S	1	3	2+1S
McAdam	25+1S	3	6+1S	4
MacLeod	30+1S	–	7	5
Colquhoun	14+5S	3	–	1+1S
Grant	19+1S	3	2+1S	5
McClair	25+7S	3	3+3S	5
Burns	25+2S	3	4+2S	4
McGarvey	30+3S	1+1S	4+3S	5
McInally	4+8S	2+1S	0+1S	0+1S
Aitken	33	3	5	5
Provan	19+6S	–	7	3+1S
P. McStay	32	2	7	5
W. McStay	11+3S	1+1S	4	2

APPEARANCES	League	Skol Cup	Scottish Cup	Cup Winners Cup
Johnston	27	–	7	–
O'Leary	11	–	4+1S	–
Latchford	2	–	1	–
Sinclair	5+1S	2	–	–
McGugan	3	–	–	–
McKechnie	1+1S	–	–	–
Chalmers	0+1S	–	–	–
Archdeacon	1+2S	–	0+1S	–
Coyle	0+1S	–	–	–
Melrose	–	0+1S	–	–

GOALSCORERS:

League: McClair 19, McGarvey 15, Johnston 14 (1 pen), Burns 7, Grant 4 (2 pens), P. McStay 4 (1 pen), Provan 3, Aitken 3 (3 pens), MacLeod 2, Colquhoun 2, Chalmers 1, Archdeacon 1, McInally 1, W. McStay 1

Skol Cup: McClair 3, McInally 3, Grant 1, Burns 1

Scottish Cup: McGarvey 5, Johnston 5, P. McStay 3, MacLeod 1, Burns 1, Aitken 1, Provan 1

Cup Winners Cup: McGarvey 2, McClair 2, P. McStay 1, MacLeod 1, Burns 1

The Celtic squad in season 1982-83. Back row: C. Nicholas. T. McAdam, D. Crainie, P. McStay, P. Bonner, P. Latchford, D. Moyes, M. Conroy, D. Sullivan, J. Halpin. Front row: M. Reid, D. Provan, F. McGarvey, R. Aitken, G. McCluskey, M. MacLeod and T. Burns.

Season 1985-86

While all eyes were focused on surprise team Hearts, Celtic put together an unbeaten 16-match run including 8 straight wins and took their 5th Premier Division Championship at Love Street in the last match of the season. No one had given David Hay's men much chance of taking the Title, but with Burns restored to midfield they kept on winning. Hearts lost their last match at Dens Park and Celtic, having demolished St Mirren, took the title on goal difference. It was a personal triumph for Hay. Another milestone was reached when Brian McClair scored the club's 7,000th League goal against Hibs on April 19th. Former Aberdeen striker Mark McGhee was signed from S.V. Hamburg in November for £150,000 but injury and loss of form restricted him to 13 appearances. Roy Aitken was the only ever-present in the side and Brian McClair again finished as top scorer with 22 goals. Aitken and Paul McStay both took part in the World Cup Finals in Mexico but there was no place in Scotland's 22 for Mo Johnston. Tragically Jock Stein died of a heart attack at the end of Scotland's World Cup match in Cardiff on September 10th.

Celtic lost to Hibs in the Quarter-Final of the Scottish Cup. A thrilling match looked to be heading for a replay until substitute Eddie May popped up with a last-minute winner to put them out of the competition. Earlier in the season the Edinburgh team had also halted Celtic's Skol Cup progress, putting them out in a penalty shoot-out at the end of extra time after the teams had finished level at 4 all in their Quarter-Final match.

Mo Johnston and Pat Bonner were the men mainly responsible for Celtic's fine 1-1 draw against Atletico Madrid in Spain in the First Round of the Cup Winners Cup, Johnston heading a 69th-minute equaliser, and Bonner saving a penalty 7 minutes later. As punishment for the hooligan behaviour of two English 'fans' at Old Trafford Celtic were ordered to play their home match with Atletico behind closed doors. The lack of atmosphere badly affected them. They looked edgy and unsure from the start and their Spanish opponents, without the incessant noise of 60,000+ Celtic fans to contend with, went on to win the match 2-1.

League:	Champions
League Cup:	Quarter-Finalists
Scottish Cup:	Quarter-Finalists
Cup Winners' Cup:	First Round

SCOTTISH PREMIER DIVISION

July 13th: Celtic made a move for Frank Gray of Leeds United. No business was done.

August 10th
HEARTS (1) 1 — CELTIC (0) 1
Colquhoun (27) — P. McStay (89½)

HEARTS: Smith; Berry (Cherry), Jardine, Levein, Whittaker; Sandison, Watson, Mackay; Colquhoun, Clark, Robertson

CELTIC: Bonner; W. McStay, Aitken, McAdam, Burns; Grant, P. McStay, MacLeod; Provan, Johnston, McClair (McInally)

Attendance: 21,786

August 17th
CELTIC (0) 2 — MOTHERWELL (0) 1
McClair (58), Provan (74) — Blair (85)

CELTIC: Bonner; W. McStay, Aitken, O'Leary, Burns; Grant, P. McStay, MacLeod; Provan, McClair, Johnston

Paul McStay, influential for Celtic in midfield.

MOTHERWELL: Gardiner; McLeod, Boyd, Kennedy, Murray; Dornan, Clark (McCart), Doyle; J. McStay, Harrow (Walker), Blair

Attendance: 10,189

August 24th
CLYDEBANK (0) 0 CELTIC (1) 2
Johnston 2 (25, 62)

CLYDEBANK: Gallacher; Dickson, Fallon, Treanor, Given; Ronald, Shanks, Moore (Hughes); McCabe, Larnach, Conroy

CELTIC: Bonner; McGrain, Aitken, McAdam (O'Leary), Burns; Grant, McClair, MacLeod; Provan, Johnston, McInally

Attendance: 9,100

August 31st
CELTIC (0) 1 RANGERS (1) 1
P. McStay (52) McCoist (35)

CELTIC: Bonner; McGrain, Aitken, McAdam, Burns; P. McStay, Grant (McInally), MacLeod; Provan, Johnston, McClair

RANGERS: Walker; Burns, McPherson, Paterson, Munro; Russell (Dawson), Bell, McKinnon; McCoist, Williamson, Cooper (Fleck)

Attendance: 58,365

Celtic outplayed Rangers for most of the match, conducted brilliantly by Paul McStay. There was a magnificent display of goalkeeping by Nicky Walker but Celtic still managed to miss enough genuine chances to have won 2 or 3 matches. It was almost 20 minutes before Rangers mounted a serious attack and by that time Celtic had seen a McAdam goal disallowed, Walker save brilliantly from MacLeod and McClair send a header just over. Against the run of play Rangers scored in 35 minutes. It was fitting that Paul McStay should get the equaliser. There appeared to be little danger when Celtic won a free-kick well outside the penalty area. MacLeod pushed the ball to McStay who strode forward to crack a great drive past Walker from 22 yards.

September 7th
HIBERNIAN (0) 0 CELTIC (2) 5
McClair 2 (10, 89), Johnston (17), Fulton o.g. (64), Archdeacon (79)

HIBERNIAN: Rough; Brazil, Rae, Hunter, Fulton; Sneddon, Weir (McKee), Munro; Harris (Collins), Cowan, Durie

CELTIC: Bonner; McGrain, Aitken, McGugan, Burns; McClair, Grant (Archdeacon), McStay, MacLeod; Johnston, McInally

Attendance: 13,150

September 10th: Roy Aitken was in the Scotland team which drew 1-1 with Wales in a World Cup match in Cardiff. Tragically, Scotland Manager Jock Stein died of a heart attack just after the final whistle.

September 14th
CELTIC (1) 2 ABERDEEN (0) 1
McClair 2 (32, 88) McDougall (85)

CELTIC: Bonner; McGrain, Aitken, McGugan, Burns; P. McStay, Grant, MacLeod; Provan, Johnston, McClair

ABERDEEN: Leighton; McKimmie, McLeish, Miller, Mitchell; Stark (Cooper), Simpson, Bett; Black, McDougall, Hewitt (Weir)

Attendance: 39,450

September 28th
DUNDEE (0) 0 CELTIC (2) 2
McClair (31), Johnston (43)

DUNDEE: Geddes; Smith (Hendry), Duffy, Glennie, Shannon; Rafferty, McCormack, Brown, Connor; Harvey (Jack), Stephen

CELTIC: Bonner; McGrain, Aitken, McGugan, Burns; Grant, McStay, MacLeod (McInally); Provan, Johnston, McClair

Attendance: 15,387

October 5th
CELTIC (2) 2 ST MIRREN (0) 0
McClair (17), McGugan (39)

CELTIC: Bonner; McGrain, Aitken, McGugan, Burns; P. McStay (McInally), Grant, MacLeod; Provan, Johnston, McClair

ST MIRREN: Money; Wilson, Godfrey, Clarke, Hamilton; Rooney, Cooper, Speirs (Abercrombie); Mackie, McGarvey, Gallagher (McDowall)

Attendance: 25,651. This was Danny McGrain's 600th match for the club.

October 12th
CELTIC (0) 0 HEARTS (1) 1
Robertson (32)

CELTIC: Bonner; McGrain, Aitken, McGugan, Burns; Grant, McStay, MacLeod; Provan, Johnston, McClair

HEARTS: Smith; Kidd, W. Jardine, Levein, Whittaker; I. Jardine, Berry, Mackay; Colquhoun (Black), Clark, Robertson (Watson)

Attendance: 26,683

October 16th: Paul McStay came on for Roy Aitken in Scotland's 0-0 draw with East Germany at Hampden Park.

October 19th
MOTHERWELL (1) 1 CELTIC (1) 2
Walker (44) P. McStay 2 (10, 80 pen)

MOTHERWELL: Gardiner; Kennedy, Forbes, Boyd, Wishart; Dornan, MacLeod, Wright; Blair, Gahagan (Reilly), Walker

Mo Johnston, scorer of 15 league goals in season 1985-86.

CELTIC: Bonner; McGrain, Aitken, McGugan, Burns; Grant (W. McStay), P. McStay, MacLeod; Provan (Chalmers), Johnston, McClair
Attendance: 13,902

October 26th
CELTIC (0) 0 — DUNDEE UNITED (2) 3
Dodds (6), Bannon 2 (42, 68)

CELTIC: Bonner; McGrain, Aitken, McGugan, Burns; P. McStay, Grant, MacLeod; McClair, Johnston (W. McStay), McInally (Chalmers)
DUNDEE UNITED: Thomson; Gough, Hegarty, Narey, Holt; Dodds, Malpas, Bannon; Milne, Redford (Coyne), Sturrock
Attendance: 25,976

League positions

	P	W	D	L	F	A	Pts
1 Aberdeen	11	6	4	1	23	10	16
2 CELTIC	11	7	2	2	19	9	16
3 Rangers	12	6	2	4	18	12	14
4 St Mirren	12	6	1	5	19	19	13
5 Dundee	12	6	1	5	14	16	13

November 2nd
ABERDEEN (1) 4 — CELTIC (1) 1
McDougall 4 (27, 48, 55, 64) — Provan (43)

ABERDEEN: Leighton; McKimmie, McLeish, Cooper, Miller, Mitchell; Stark (Bett), Simpson; Black, McDougall, Hewitt (Wright)
CELTIC: Bonner; W. McStay, Aitken, McAdam (McGugan), McGrain; P. McStay, Grant, Burns; Provan, McClair, McInally (Chalmers)
Attendance: 23,000

November 6th: Mark McGhee was signed from Hamburg for £150,000.

November 9th
RANGERS (1) 3 — CELTIC (0) 0
Durrant (30), Cooper (80), McMinn (84)

RANGERS: Walker; Dawson, McPherson, McKinnon, Munro; D. Ferguson (Russell), Bell, Durrant; McCoist, Williamson (McMinn), Cooper
CELTIC: Bonner; W. McStay (McGrain), McAdam, McGugan, Burns; Aitken, Provan, P. McStay, Grant; McGhee, McClair (Johnston)
Attendance: 42,045

Rangers were ahead in every aspect of the game, and the final scoreline did not flatter them. Head and shoulders above everyone else on the field was Ian Durrant whose overall contribution was tremendous. Derek Ferguson was also outstanding in midfield until he was taken off injured. Weeks of misery for the Ibrox faithful were blown away by this performance.

November 16th
CELTIC (1) 2 — CLYDEBANK (0) 0
McGhee 2 (37, 85)

CELTIC: Bonner; W. McStay, Aitken, McGugan, Burns; Grant, P. McStay, MacLeod; McGhee, Johnston, Archdeacon
CLYDEBANK: Gallacher; McGhie, Auld, Maher, Given; Dickson, Treanor, Hughes; Ronald, Larnach, Lloyd (Gibson)
Attendance: 14,148

November 20th: Roy Aitken was in the Scotland team which beat Australia 2-0 at Hampden Park in a World Cup Play-off.

November 23rd
CELTIC (1) 1 — HIBERNIAN (0) 1
Johnston (13) — Chisholm (76)

CELTIC: Bonner; W. McStay, Aitken, McGugan, Burns; P. McStay, Grant, MacLeod; McGhee (McClair), Johnston, Archdeacon
HIBERNIAN: Rough; Sneddon, Rae, Fulton, Hunter, Munro; Chisholm, Kane; Durie, Cowan, McBride (Callachan)
Attendance: 21,510

December 4th: McStay and Aitken were in the Scotland team which drew 0-0 with Australia in Melbourne to reach the World Cup Finals in Mexico.

December 14th
HEARTS (1) 1 — CELTIC (0) 1
Robertson (9) — McGhee (66)

HEARTS: Smith; Kidd, Levein, W. Jardine, Black; I. Jardine, Mackay, Berry; Colquhoun, Robertson (Watson), Clark
CELTIC: Bonner; Grant, Aitken, McGugan, Burns; McClair, McStay, MacLeod; Johnston, McGhee, Archdeacon
Attendance: 22,163

December 23rd
DUNDEE UNITED (1) 1 — CELTIC (0) 0
Bannon (42 pen)

DUNDEE UNITED: Thomson; Malpas, Holt; Gough, Hegarty, Narey; Bannon, Gallacher, Sturrock, Redford, Dodds
CELTIC: Bonner; Grant, Aitken, McGugan (W. McStay), MacLeod; McClair (McInally), P. McStay; McGhee, Johnston, Archdeacon
Attendance: 15,400

December 28th
CELTIC (1) 2 — CLYDEBANK (0) 0
Johnston (11), P. McStay (49 pen)

Archdeacon, a break-through in season 1985-86. He made 19 league appearances and came on as a substitute on 4 occasions.

CELTIC: Bonner; Grant, McGrain; Aitken, McGugan, MacLeod; P. McStay, Johnston, McGhee, Burns, Archdeacon

CLYDEBANK: Gallacher; Dickson, Given; Fallon, Auld, Treanor; Shanks, Hughes, Larnach, Gibson (Bain), Lloyd

Attendance: 13,822

League positions

	P	W	D	L	F	A	Pts
1 Hearts	21	10	6	5	31	22	26
2 Dundee United	19	9	6	4	27	16	24
3 Aberdeen	19	9	5	5	38	19	23
4 CELTIC	18	9	4	5	26	19	22
5 Rangers	20	8	5	7	26	22	21

January 1st
CELTIC (1) 2 — RANGERS (0) 0
McGugan (9), McClair (49)

CELTIC: Bonner; W. McStay, McGrain; Aitken, McGugan, Grant; McClair, P McStay, McGhee, Burns, Archdeacon

RANGERS: Walker; Dawson, Munro; McPherson, Paterson, Durrant; McCoist, Russell, Williamson, D. Ferguson (Bell), Cooper (McMinn)

Attendance: 49,812

Celtic fully deserved their victory in the 100th League meeting between the teams at Parkhead and the 199th overall. With the 1st scoring chance of the game the home side took the lead. Dawson obstructed Archdeacon on the left wing. Archdeacon sent over a lovely flighted free-kick which found McGugan unmarked 12 yards out and he headed powerfully down and into the corner of the net. Rangers had 3 chances to get back on level terms but McCoist (twice) and Russell squandered these. After the spell of pressure from the Ibrox team Celtic became more dominant and after Grant had wasted two chances they went into a 2 goal lead 4 minutes after the break. Paul McStay crossed from the right, Munro managed to block it but it went back to the Celtic midfielder, and this time his cross was met by McClair who headed home from 3 yards.

January 4th
DUNDEE UNITED (4) 4 — CELTIC (1) 2
Dodds 2 (14, 17), Bannon (32 pen), Gallacher (34) — McClair 2 (26, 87)

DUNDEE UNITED: Thomson; Malpas, Holt; Gough, Hegarty, Narey; Bannon, Gallacher, Kirkwood (Redford), Sturrock, Dodds

CELTIC: Bonner; W. McStay, McGrain; Aitken, Coyle, Grant; McClair, P. McStay, McGhee, Burns, Archdeacon (McInally)

Attendance: 16,113

January 11th
CELTIC (1) 1 — ABERDEEN (1) 1
Grant (19) — J. Miller (14)

CELTIC: Latchford; W. McStay, McGrain; Aitken, O'Leary, Grant; McClair, P. McStay, McGhee (McInally), MacLeod (Archdeacon), Johnston

ABERDEEN: Leighton; McKimmie, McQueen; Bett, McLeish, W. Miller; Black, Simpson, J. Miller (McDougall), Cooper, Weir (Stark)

Attendance: 31,305

January 15th
CELTIC (1) 3 — MOTHERWELL (1) 2
McGhee (31), Johnston (49), McClair (86) — Reilly (12), Doyle (89)

CELTIC: Latchford; W. McStay, McGrain; Aitken, O'Leary, Grant; McClair, P. McStay, Johnston, McGhee, Archdeacon (Provan)

MOTHERWELL: Gardiner; Dornan, Murray; Doyle, Forbes, Boyd; Baptie, McLeod, Reilly, Wright, Blair

Attendance: 12,002

January 18th
HIBERNIAN (0) 2 — CELTIC (0) 2
Durie (52), Cowan (77) — Archdeacon (64), Burns (73)

HIBERNIAN: Rough; Sneddon, Munro; Milne, Fulton (Rae), Chisholm; Kane, May, Cowan, Durie, Collins

CELTIC: Latchford; W. McStay, McGrain; Aitken, O'Leary, Grant; McClair (Archdeacon), P. McStay, Johnston, McGhee, Burns

Attendance: 13,500

January 27th: Paul Chalmers joined Bradford City on loan.

January 28th: Paul McStay scored Scotland's goal in a 1-0 win over Israel in Tel Aviv. Roy Aitken was also in the team.

February 1st
DUNDEE (1) 1 — CELTIC (1) 3
Stephen (9 pen) — Johnston (44), McStay (50), McClair (83)

DUNDEE: Geddes; Forsyth, McKinlay; Kidd (Rafferty), Glennie, Duffy; Shannon (McCormack), Mennie, Harvey, Connor, Stephen

CELTIC: Latchford; McGrain, Burns; Aitken, O'Leary, Grant (McGhee); McClair, P. McStay, Johnston, MacLeod, Archdeacon

Attendance: 12,295. Geddes saved a Paul McStay penalty.

February 2nd: Assistant Manager Frank Connor parted company with the Club.

February 8th
CELTIC (0) 1 — ST MIRREN (0) 1
Burns (47) — Clarke (75)

CELTIC: Latchford; McGrain, Burns; Aitken, O'Leary, MacLeod; McClair, P. McStay (W. McStay), Johnston, McGhee (McInally), Archdeacon

ST MIRREN: Money; Clarke, Abercrombie; Hamilton (Wilson), Godfrey, Cooper; Fitzpatrick, Winnie, McGarvey, Gallagher, Speirs

Attendance: 18,102

February 22nd

CELTIC (1) 1	HEARTS (1) 1
Johnston (31)	Robertson (45)

CELTIC: Latchford; McStay, McGrain; Aitken, McGugan, MacLeod; McClair, McGhee (Shepherd), Johnston, Whyte, Burns

HEARTS: Smith; Kidd, Black; W. Jardine, Berry, Levein; Colquhoun, I. Jardine, Clark, G. Mackay, Robertson (W. Mackay)

Attendance: 45,346

League positions

	P	W	D	L	F	A	Pts
1 Hearts	28	14	9	5	44	28	37
2 Dundee United	26	13	9	4	43	21	35
3 Aberdeen	27	13	8	6	49	24	34
4 CELTIC	26	12	8	6	41	31	32
5 Rangers	29	12	7	10	42	31	31

February 26th: Tom McAdam was given a free transfer.

March 8th: Celtic and Bradford City failed to agree a fee for Chalmers and he returned to Parkhead after playing 2 games for the Yorkshire Club.

March 15th

CELTIC (0) 1	DUNDEE UNITED (1) 1
MacLeod (82)	Dodds (38)

CELTIC: Bonner; W. McStay, Whyte; Aitken, O'Leary (MacLeod), Grant; McClair (McGhee), P. McStay, Johnston, Burns, Archdeacon

DUNDEE UNITED: Thomson; Malpas, Holt; Gough, Hegarty, Narey; Bannon, Gallacher, Clark (Redford), Beedie, Dodds

Attendance: 21,600. Holt was ordered off.

March 22nd

RANGERS (1) 4	CELTIC (2) 4
Fraser 2 (34, 63), McCoist (52), Fleck (59)	Johnston (21), McClair (29), Burns (47), MacLeod (70)

RANGERS: Walker; Burns (D. Ferguson), Munro; McPherson, McKinnon, Durrant; McMinn (Cooper), Russell, Fleck, Fraser, McCoist

CELTIC: Bonner; W. McStay, Whyte; Aitken, O'Leary, MacLeod; McClair, P. McStay (McInally), Johnston, Burns, Archdeacon (Grant)

Attendance: 41,006

Rangers had been much the better side in the opening 20 minutes during which they could reasonably have been a goal or two ahead, but as so often happens in Old Firm meetings it was the team under pressure who produced the goal. Mo Johnston was alert and accurate when McClair mis-hit his shot following a great Paul McStay run and Owen Archdeacon cross. Archdeacon was again involved when Celtic went 2 up in the 29th minute, his cross being pushed on by MacLeod for McClair to steer it wide of Walker. Willie McStay was sensationally ordered off in the 33rd minute for a foul on McMinn. Celtic were still regrouping when Rangers reduced the gap, Cammy Fraser heading home following a good move on the left. Celtic resumed after the break with Peter Grant on for Archdeacon to cover the gap left by Willie McStay. Within 3 minutes the 10 men had gone 2 goals clear again when Tommy Burns, taking a beautifully weighted pass from Johnston, slipped the ball past Walker. Rangers then took command and in a pulsating 11-minute spell scored 3 times. Celtic refused to lie down and 20 minutes from time MacLeod sent a right-foot drive screaming into the net from all of 30 yards to level the match.

March 29th

CLYDEBANK (0) 0	CELTIC (0) 5
	McClair 3 (50 pen, 54, 67 pen), Burns (58), McInally (82)

CLYDEBANK: Gallacher; Dickson, Maher; Treanor, Auld, Moore (Hughes); Shanks, Gordon, Conroy, Ronald, McCabe

CELTIC: Bonner; McGrain, Whyte; Aitken, O'Leary, MacLeod; McClair, P. McStay, Johnston, Burns, Archdeacon (McInally)

Attendance: 7,969

April 2nd

CELTIC (1) 2	DUNDEE (0) 1
Johnston (18), Burns (47)	Stephen (86)

CELTIC: Bonner; McGrain, Whyte; Aitken, O'Leary, MacLeod; McClair, P. McStay, Johnston, Burns, Archdeacon (McInally)

DUNDEE: Geddes; Shannon, Glennie; Rafferty, Hendry, Duffy; Stephen, Mennie, Harvey, Connor, Campbell

Attendance: 12,506

April 5th

ST MIRREN (0) 1	CELTIC (1) 2
Mackie (56)	MacLeod (26), P. McStay (87)

ST MIRREN: Money; Wilson, Hamilton; Clarke, Godfrey, Cooper; Fitzpatrick, Mackie (Rooney), McGarvey, Cameron, Speirs

CELTIC: Bonner; McGrain, Whyte; Aitken, O'Leary, MacLeod; McClair, P. McStay, McInally (Grant), Burns, Archdeacon (McGugan)

Attendance: 11,284

April 12th
ABERDEEN (0) 0 — CELTIC (0) 1
Johnston (49)

ABERDEEN: Gunn; McKimmie, McQueen (McMaster); Stark, McLeish, W. Miller; Black, Mitchell, J. Miller, Bett, Hewitt (Falconer)

CELTIC: Bonner; McGrain, Whyte; Aitken, O'Leary (Archdeacon), Grant; McClair, P. McStay, Johnston, MacLeod, Burns

Attendance: 22,000

April 19th
CELTIC (0) 2 — HIBERNIAN (0) 0
Archdeacon (80),
McClair (87)

CELTIC: Bonner; McGrain, Whyte; Aitken, McGugan, MacLeod; McClair, McStay (McGhee), Johnston, Burns, Archdeacon

HIBERNIAN: Rough; Sneddon, Brazil; Harris, Fulton, Rae; Tortolano (May), Chisholm, Cowan, Kane, Collins

Attendance: 15,966. Brian McClair's goal was Celtic's 7,000th in the League.

April 23rd: Roy Aitken was in the Scotland team beaten 2-1 by England at Wembley.

April 26th
CELTIC (0) 2 — DUNDEE (0) 0
McClair (56),
Johnston (85)

CELTIC: Bonner; McGrain (Grant), Whyte (McGhee); Aitken, McGugan, MacLeod; McClair, P. McStay, Johnston, Burns, Archdeacon

DUNDEE: Geddes; Forsyth, McKinlay (McCormack); Glennie, Smith, Duffy; Rafferty, Brown, Mennie (Harvey), Connor, Stephen

Attendance: 14,511. Stephen was ordered off in the 22nd minute.

April 30th
MOTHERWELL (0) 0 — CELTIC (1) 2
McClair 2 (32, 64 pen)

MOTHERWELL: Maxwell; Wishart, Murray; Dornan, Kennedy, Boyd; Baptie, MacLeod, Reilly, Wright, Walker

CELTIC: Bonner; McGrain, Whyte; Aitken, McGugan, MacLeod; McClair, P. McStay, Johnston, Burns, Archdeacon (McGhee)

Attendance: 10,545

May 3rd
ST MIRREN (0) 0 — CELTIC (4) 5
McClair 2 (6, 54),
Johnston 2 (32, 33),
P. McStay (38)

ST MIRREN: Stewart; Wilson, D. Hamilton; B. Hamilton, Godfrey, Cooper; Fitzpatrick, Abercrombie, McGarvey, Gallagher (Speirs), Mackie

CELTIC: Bonner; McGrain (Grant), Whyte; Aitken, McGugan, MacLeod; McClair, P. McStay, Johnston, Burns, Archdeacon

Attendance: 17,557

Premier Division

	P	W	D	L	F	A	Pts	
1 CELTIC	36	20	10	6	67	38	50	+29 Goal Diff.
2 Hearts	36	20	10	6	59	33	50	+26 Goal Diff.
3 Dundee United	36	18	11	7	59	31	47	
4 Aberdeen	36	16	12	8	62	31	44	
5 Rangers	36	13	9	14	53	45	35	
6 Dundee	36	14	7	15	45	51	35	
7 St Mirren	36	13	5	18	42	63	31	
8 Hibernian	36	11	6	19	49	63	28	
9 Motherwell	36	7	6	23	33	66	20	
10 Clydebank	36	6	8	22	29	77	20	

May 16th: Danny McGrain did not, as expected, become Player-Manager of Airdrie. He returned to Parkhead and was given a 12-month contract.

June 4th: Roy Aitken was in the Scotland team beaten 1-0 by Denmark in Mexico.

June 8th: Roy Aitken was in the Scotland team beaten 2-1 by West Germany in Mexico.

June 13th: Aitken and McStay were in the Scotland team which drew 0-0 with Uruguay in Mexico.

SKOL CUP

Second Round August 21st
QUEEN OF THE SOUTH (1) 1 — CELTIC (1) 4
Bryce (32) — McClair (30), Johnston 2 (46, 52), McInally (87)

QUEEN OF THE SOUTH: Davidson; Robertson, Gervaise (Muir); Parker, Hetherington, Cloy; Reid, Cochrane, Bryce, Dick, J. Robertson

CELTIC: Bonner; W. McStay (McAdam), Burns; Aitken, O'Leary, Grant; Provan, McClair, Johnston, MacLeod, McInally

Attendance: 6,400

Third Round August 28th
CELTIC (3) 7 — BRECHIN CITY (0) 0
Aitken (8 pen),
Johnston 2 (21, 62),
McStay (40),
McInally (53),
Provan (60), Burns (70)

CELTIC: Bonner; McGrain, Burns; Atiken, McAdam (O'Leary), Grant; Provan, McStay, Johnston, MacLeod (McInally), McClair

BRECHIN: Neilson; Watt, Kerr; Hay, Fleming (Brown), Scott; Lees (Payne), Stewart, Eadie, Powell, Reid

Attendance: 9,292

Quarter-Final September 4th
HIBERNIAN (2) 4 CELTIC (2) 4
Cowan (30), Durie (39), Harris (58), McGrain o.g. (101)
Johnston 2 (3, 59), Provan (40), Aitken (100)
After Extra Time

HIBERNIAN: Rough; Sneddon, Brazil; Fulton, Rae, Hunter; Weir (McKee), Munro, Cowan, Durie, Collins (Harris)

CELTIC: Bonner; McGrain, Burns; Aitken, McAdam (O'Leary) Grant; Provan, McStay, Johnston (McInally), MacLeod, McClair

Attendance: 15,500. Hibernian won 4-3 on penalties.

SCOTTISH CUP

Third Round January 25th
CELTIC (2) 2 ST JOHNSTONE (0) 0
Grant (28), Johnston (44)

CELTIC: Latchford; McGrain, Burns; Aitken, O'Leary, Grant; McGhee (McClair), P. McStay, Johnston, MacLeod, Archdeacon

ST JOHNSTONE: Balvage; Millen, Winter; Barron, Liddle, Morton; Johnston (Adam), McGurn, Brown, Evans, Gibson (Ward)

Attendance: 15,006

Fourth Round February 15th
CELTIC (0) 2 QUEENS PARK (0) 1
McClair (54), Aitken (61)
Boyle (50 pen)

CELTIC: Latchford; W. McStay, McGrain; Aitken, McAdam, Burns; Shepherd, McGhee, Johnston, McClair, Archdeacon

QUEENS PARK: Ross; Boyle, McLaughlin; McNamee, Brannigan, Walker; Cairns, Fraser, Smith, Caven, Crooks

Attendance: 11,656

Quarter-Final March 8th
HIBERNIAN (0) 4 CELTIC (1) 3
Cowan 2 (51, 84 pen), Chisholm (76), May (89)
McClair 2 (42, 86 pen), McGhee (60)

HIBERNIAN: Rough; Milne; Brazil (Harris), Rae, Fulton; Tortolano, Chisholm, Cowan, Durie, Collins (May)

CELTIC: Latchford; Grant, Burns; Aitken, McGugan, MacLeod; McClair, P. McStay, Johnston, McGhee, Archdeacon

Attendance: 20,000

CUP WINNERS CUP

First Round First Leg September 18th
ATLETICO MADRID (Spain) (1) 1 CELTIC (0) 1
Setien (35)
Johnston (69)

ATLETICO: Fillol; Julio Prieta (Rubio), Tomas; Arteche, Ruiz; Setien; Cabrera, Quique, Da Silva, Landaburu, Marina

CELTIC: Bonner; McGrain, Burns; Aitken, McGugan, Grant; Provan, McStay, Johnston, MacLeod, McClair

Attendance: 55,000. Bonner saved a 76th minute penalty from Rubio.

Celtic had gone a goal down in 35 minutes against a very useful Spanish team and had survived some sticky moments when Johnston headed in a superb Provan cross midway through the 2nd half. Bonner had no chance with Atletico's goal. It was engineered beautifully with two rapid 1-2's on the left involving Cabrera and Da Silva and was clinically finished off by Setien.

First Round Second Leg October 2nd
CELTIC (0) 1 ATLETICO MADRID (1) 2
Aitken (73)
Setion (38), Quique (71)

CELTIC: Bonner; McGrain (McInally), Burns; Aitken, McGugan, Grant; Provan, McStay (McAdam), Johnston, MacLeod, McClair

ATLETICO: Fillol; Tomas, Clemente; Arteche, Ruiz, Setien; Cabrera (Rubio), Quique, Da Silva, Landaburu, Marina (Julio Prieta)

Played behind closed doors as ordered by U.E.F.A.

Celtic went out of Europe after one of their poorer performances. The Spaniards were much the more composed team throughout. From the beginning Celtic looked edgy and unsure of themselves. Landaburu headed onto Bonner's bar in 13 minutes. Murdo MacLeod missed a real opportunity when from Grant's pass no more than 3 or 4 yards out he managed to hit the bar. It was a real surprise when Atletico went into the lead in the 38th minute. In the 2nd half Celtic took off Paul McStay, bringing on McAdam, and pushed Aitken into midfield. But Atletico delivered the killer blow 19 minutes from time when Quique drew McAdam, whipped the ball around him, flashed past to retake possession again and calmly hit the ball out of Bonner's reach. Celtic did pull a goal back 2 minutes later when McGrain put McClair through and his cut-back was flicked into goal by Aitken. Although that gave them brief hope, Celtic never really looked like getting the 2 further goals they needed to win the tie. Atletico Madrid won 3-2 on aggregate.

APPEARANCES	League	Skol Cup	Scottish Cup	Cup Winners Cup
Bonner	30	3	–	2
W. McStay	14+4S	1	1	–
Burns	34	3	3	2
Aitken	36	3	3	2
McAdam	5	2+1S	1	0+1S
Grant	26+4S	3	2	2
Provan	11+1S	3	–	2
P. McStay	34	2	2	2
Jonnston	31+1S	3	3	2
MacLeod	29+1S	3	2	2
McClair	33+1S	3	2+1S	2
McGrain	27+1S	2	2	2
McInally	5+11S	1+2S	–	0+1S
O'Leary	12+1S	1+2S	1	–
Archdeacon	19+4S	–	3	–
McGugan	19+2S	–	1	2
Chalmers	0+3S	–	–	–
McGhee	13+5S	–	3	–
Latchford	6	–	3	–
Shepherd	0+1S	–	1	–
Whyte	11	–	–	–
Coyle	1	–	–	–

GOALSCORERS

League: McClair 22 (1 pen), Johnston 15, P. McStay 8 (2 pens), Burns 5, McGhee 4, Archdeacon 3, MacLeod 3, Provan 2, McGugan 2, Grant 1, McInally 1, Own goals 1

Skol Cup: Johnston 6, McInally 2, Provan 2, Aitken 2 (1 pen), McClair 1, P. McStay 1, Burns 1

Scottish Cup: McClair 3 (1 pen), Grant 1, Johnston 1, Aitken 1, McGhee 1

Cup Winners Cup: Johnston 1, Aitken 1

Tommy Burns, with over 40 first team appearances to his credit in season 1985-86.

Brian McClair, scorer of 22 league goals in season 1985-86, in action against Dundee.

The Vital Statistics

League Champions (34 times)
1893, 1894, 1896, 1898, 1905, 1906, 1907, 1908, 1909, 1910, 1914, 1915, 1916, 1917, 1919, 1922, 1926, 1936, 1938, 1954, 1966, 1967, 1968, 1969, 1970, 1971, 1972, 1973, 1974, 1977, 1979, 1981, 1982, 1986

Scottish Cup Winners (27 times)
1892, 1899, 1900, 1904, 1907, 1908, 1911, 1912, 1914, 1923, 1925, 1927, 1931, 1933, 1937, 1951, 1954, 1965, 1967, 1969, 1971, 1972, 1974, 1975, 1977, 1980, 1985

Scottish League Cup Winners (9 times)
1956-57, 1957-58, 1965-66, 1966-67, 1967-68, 1968-69, 1969-70, 1974-75, 1982-83

European Cup Winners 1967

Coronation Cup Winners 1953

St Mungo's Cup Winners 1951

Glasgow Cup Winners (29 times including once as joint winners)

Empire Exhibition Cup Winners 1938

Summary of European Results

1962-63 *Fairs Cities Cup:* Valencia (2-4, 2-2)

1963-64 *Cup Winners Cup:* Basle (5-1, 5-0), Dinamo Zagreb (3-0, 1-2), Slovan Bratislava (1-0, 1-0), M.T.K. Budapest (3-0, 0-4)

1964-65 *Fairs Cities Cup:* Leixoes (1-1, 3-0), Barcelona (1-3, 0-0)

1965-66 *Cup Winners Cup:* Go Ahead Deventer (6-0, 1-0), A.G.F. Aarhus (1-0, 2-0), Dynamo Kiev (3-0, 1-1), Liverpool (1-0, 0-2)

1966-67 *European Cup:* Zürich (2-0, 3-0), Nantes (3-1, 3-1), Vojvodina (0-1, 2-0), Dukla Prague (3-1, 0-0), Internazionale Milan (2-1)

1967-68 *European Cup:* Dynamo Kiev (1-2, 1-1)

1968-69 *European Cup:* St Etienne (0-2, 4-0), Red Star Belgrade (5-1, 1-1), A.C. Milan (0-0, 0-1)

1969-70 *European Cup:* Basle (0-0, 2-0), Benfica (3-0, 0-3†), Fiorentina (3-0, 0-1), Leeds United (1-0, 2-1), Feyenoord (1-2)

1970-71 *European Cup:* Kokkola (9-0, 5-0), Waterford (7-0, 3-2), Ajax (0-3, 1-0)

1971-72 *European Cup:* Boldklub 1903 (1-2), 3-0), Sliema Wanderers (5-0, 2-1), Ujpest Dosza (2-1, 1-1), Internazionale Milan (0-0, 0-0†)

1972-73 *European Cup:* Rosenberg Trondheim (2-1, 3-1), Ujpest Dosza (2-1, 0-3)

1973-74 *European Cup:* T.P.S. Turku (6-1, 3-0), Vejle B.K. (0-0, 1-0), Basle (2-3, 4-2), Atletico Madrid (0-0, 0-2)

1974-75 *European Cup:* Olympiakos (1-1, 0-2)

1975-76 *Cup Winners Cup:* Valur (2-0, 7-0), Boavista (0-0, 3-1), Sachsenring Zwickau (1-1, 0-1)

1976-77 *U.E.F.A. Cup:* Wisla Krakow (2-2, 0-2)

1977-78 *European Cup:* Jeunesse d'Esch (5-0, 6-1), S.W.W. Innsbruck (2-1, 0-3)

1979-80 *European Cup:* Partizan Tirana (0-1, 4-1), Dundalk (3-2, 0-0), Real Madrid (2-0, 0-3)
1980-81 *Cup Winners Cup:* Diosgyeori Miskolc (6-0, 1-2), Politechnica Timisoara (2-1, 0-1★)
1981-82 *European Cup:* Juventus (1-0, 0-2)
1982-83 *European Cup:* Ajax (2-2, 2-1), Real Sociedad (0-2, 2-1)
1983-84 *U.E.F.A. Cup:* A.G.F. Aarhus (1-0, 4-1), Sporting Lisbon (0-2, 5-0), Nottingham Forest (0-0, 1-2)
1984-85 *Cup Winners Cup:* K.A.A. Ghent (0-1, 3-0), Rapid Vienna (1-3, 3-0,° 0-1)
1985-86 *Cup Winners Cup:* Atletico Madrid (1-1, 1-2)

† Lost on penalties
\+ Won on toss of Coin
★ Lost on Away Goals Rule
° U.E.F.A. ordered match to be replayed

Scottish Football Writers Player of the Year
1965 Billy McNeill, 1967 Ronnie Simpson, 1969 Bobby Murdoch, 1973 George Connelly, 1977 Danny McGrain, 1983 Charlie Nicholas

Scottish P.F.A. Player of the Year
1980 Davie Provan, 1983 Charlie Nicholas

Scottish P.F.A. Young Player of the Year
1982 Charlie Nicholas

Scottish Cup Winning Teams

1950-51 (beat Motherwell 1-0)
Hunter; Fallon, Rollo; Evans, Boden, Baillie; Weir, Collins, J. McPhail, Peacock, Tully
1953-54 (beat Aberdeen 2-1)
Bonnar; Haughney, Meechan; Evans, Stein, Peacock; Higgins, Fernie, Fallon, Tully, Mochan
1964-65 (beat Dunfermline 3-2)
Fallon; Young, Gemmell; Murdoch, McNeill, Clark; Chalmers, Gallacher, Hughes, Lennox, Auld
1966-67 (beat Aberdeen 2-0)
Simpson; Craig, Gemmell; Murdoch, McNeill, Clark; Johnstone, Wallace, Chalmers, Auld, Lennox
1968-69 (beat Rangers 4-0)
Fallon; Craig, Gemmell; Murdoch, McNeill, Brogan (Clark); Connelly, Chalmers, Wallace, Lennox, Auld
1970-71 (beat Rangers 2-1 after a 1-1 draw)
Williams; Craig, Brogan; Connelly, McNeill, Hay; Johnstone, Macari, Hood (Wallace), Callaghan, Lennox

1971-72 (beat Hibernian 6-1)
Williams; Craig, Brogan; Murdoch, McNeill, Connelly; Johnstone, Deans, Macari, Dalglish, Callaghan Substitute: Lennox (not used)
1973-74 (beat Dundee United 3-0)
Connaghan; McGrain (Callaghan), Brogan; Murray, McNeill, P. McCluskey; Johnstone, Hood, Deans, Hay, Dalglish Substitute: Lennox (not used)
1974-75 (beat Airdrie 3-1)
Latchford; McGrain, Lynch; Murray, McNeill, P. McCluskey; Hood, Glavin, Dalglish, Lennox, Wilson Substitutes: Callaghan and MacDonald (not used)
1976-77 (beat Rangers 1-0)
Latchford; McGrain, Lynch; Stanton, MacDonald, Aitken; Dalglish, Edvaldsson, Craig, Conn, Wilson Substitutes: Burns and Doyle (not used)
1979-80 (beat Rangers 1-0)
Latchford; Sneddon, McGrain; Aitken, Conroy, MacLeod; Provan, Doyle (Lennox), G. McCluskey, Burns, McGarvey Substitute: Davidson (not used)
1984-85 (beat Dundee United 2-1)
Bonner; W. McStay, McGrain; Aitken, McAdam, MacLeod; Provan, P. McStay (O'Leary), Johnston, Burns (McClair), McGarvey

Scottish League Cup Winning Teams

1956-57 (beat Partick Thistle 3-0 after 0-0 draw)
Beattie; Haughney, Fallon; Evans, Jack, Peacock; Tully, Collins, W. McPhail, Fernie, Mochan
1957-58 (beat Rangers 7-1)
Beattie; Donnelly, Fallon; Fernie, Evans, Peacock; Tully, Collins, W. McPhail, Wilson, Mochan
1965-66 (beat Rangers 2-1)
Simpson; Young, Gemmell; Murdoch, McNeill, Clark; Johnstone, Gallagher, McBride, Lennox, Hughes
1966-67 (beat Rangers 1-0)
Simpson; Gemmell, O'Neill; Murdoch, McNeill, Clark; Johnstone, Lennox, McBride, Auld, Hughes (Chalmers)
1967-68 (beat Dundee 5-3)
Simpson; Craig, Gemmell; Murdoch, McNeill, Clark; Chalmers, Lennox, Wallace, Auld (O'Neill), Hughes
1968-69 (beat Hibernian 6-2)
Fallon; Craig, Gemmell (Clark); Murdoch, McNeill, Brogan; Johnstone, Wallace, Chalmers, Auld, Lennox
1969-70 (beat St Johnstone 1-0)
Fallon; Craig, Hay; Murdoch, McNeill, Brogan; Callaghan, Hood, Hughes, Chalmers (Johnstone), Auld
1974-75 (beat Hibernian 6-3)
Hunter; McGrain, Brogan; Murray, McNeill, P. McCluskey; Johnstone, Dalglish, Deans, Hood, Wilson Substitutes: Lennox and MacDonald (not used)
1982-83 (beat Rangers 2-1)
Bonner; McGrain, Sinclair; Aitken, McAdam, MacLeod; Provan, P. McStay (Reid), McGarvey, Burns, Nicholas Substitute: G. McCluskey

League Record Year by Year

Season	*Played*	*Won*	*Drew*	*Lost*	*For*	*Against*	*Points*	*Pos*
1946-47	30	13	6	11	53	55	32	7th
1947-48	30	10	5	15	41	56	25	12th
1948-49	30	12	7	11	48	40	31	6th
1949-50	30	14	7	9	51	50	35	5th
1950-51	30	12	5	13	48	46	29	7th
1951-52	30	10	8	12	52	55	28	9th
1952-53	30	11	7	12	51	54	29	8th
1953-54	30	20	3	7	72	29	43	1st
1954-55	30	19	8	3	76	37	46	2nd
1955-56	34	16	9	9	55	39	41	5th
1956-57	34	15	8	11	58	43	38	5th
1957-58	34	19	8	7	84	47	46	3rd
1958-59	34	14	8	12	70	53	36	6th
1959-60	34	12	9	13	73	59	33	9th
1960-61	34	15	9	10	64	46	39	4th
1961-62	34	19	8	7	81	37	46	3rd
1962-63	34	19	6	9	76	44	44	4th
1963-64	34	19	9	6	89	34	47	3rd
1964-65	34	16	5	13	76	57	37	8th
1965-66	34	27	3	4	106	30	57	1st
1966-67	34	26	6	2	111	33	58	1st
1967-68	34	30	3	1	106	24	63	1st
1968-69	34	23	8	3	89	32	54	1st
1969-70	34	27	3	4	96	33	57	1st
1970-71	34	25	6	3	89	23	56	1st
1971-72	34	28	4	2	96	28	60	1st
1972-73	34	26	5	3	93	28	57	1st
1973-74	34	23	7	4	82	27	53	1st
1974-75	34	20	5	9	81	41	45	3rd
1975-76	36	21	6	9	71	42	48	2nd
1976-77	36	23	9	4	79	39	55	1st
1977-78	36	15	6	15	63	54	36	5th
1978-79	36	21	6	9	61	37	48	1st
1979-80	36	18	11	7	61	38	47	2nd
1980-81	36	26	4	6	84	37	56	1st
1981-82	36	24	7	5	79	33	55	1st
1982-83	36	25	5	6	90	36	55	2nd
1983-84	36	21	8	7	80	41	50	2nd
1984-85	36	22	8	6	77	30	52	2nd
1985-86	36	20	10	6	67	38	50	1st+

+ Won on Goal Difference

Scottish International Appearances (up to v. Bulgaria, September 1986)

R. Aitken	24	M. Johnston	7(10)
R. Auld	3	J. Johnstone	23
J. Brogan	4	J. Kennedy	6
T. Burns	7	R. Lennox	10
S. Chalmers	5	J. McBride	2
J. Clark	4	F. McGarvey	5(7)
R. Collins	22(31)	D. McGrain	62
G. Connelly	2	D. McKay	14
Joe Craig	1	M. MacLeod	1
Jim Craig	1	W. McNeill	29
P. Crerand	11(16)	J. McPhail	5
K. Dalglish	47(101)	P. McStay	15
J. Deans	2	L. Macari	6(24)
R. Evans	45(48)	W. Miller	6
W. Fernie	12	N. Mochan	3
T. Gemmell	18	R. Murdoch	12
R. Glavin	1	C. Nicholas	6(18)
F. Haffey	2	D. Provan	10
M. Haughney	1	R. Simpson	5
D. Hay	27	E. Smith	2
J. Hughes	8	W. Wallace	4(7)
A. Hunter	2(4)	P. Wilson	1

Republic of Ireland Internationalists: S. Fallon, C. Gallagher, P. Turner, J. Haverty, P. Bonner

Icelandic Internationalist: J. Edvaldsson

Totals in brackets indicate total caps won.
Players such as Pat Stanton who did not win any caps as a Celtic player have not been included in the above list.

Scottish League Internationalists:
R. Auld, J. Baillie, R. Beattie, T. Bogan, J. Brogan, T. Callaghan, S. Chalmers, J. Clark, R. Collins, G. Connelly, P. Crerand, J. Divers, R. Evans, W. Fernie, T. Gemmell, M. Haughney, D. Hay, J. Higgins, H. Hood, J. Hughes, J. Johnstone, J. Kennedy, T. Kiernan, R. Lennox, P. McAuley, J. McBride, D. McGrain, W. McNeill, J. McPhail, J. Mallan, W. Miller, R. Murdoch, W. O'Neill, A. Rollo, R. Simpson, J. Stein, W. Wallace.

Top League Scorers

1946-47	Jerry McAloon	12
1947-48	Tommy McDonald	7
1948-49	Jackie Gallacher	12
1949-50	Mike Haughney	12
	John McPhail	12
1950-51	Bobby Collins	15
1951-52	Bobby Collins	12
1952-53	Bertie Peacock	8
1953-54	Neil Mochan	20
1954-55	Jimmy Walsh	19
1955-56	Neil Mochan	15
1956-57	Neil Mochan	11
1957-58	Sammy Wilson	23
1958-59	John Colrain	14
1959-60	Steve Chalmers	14
1960-61	Steve Chalmers	20
1961-62	John Divers	19
1962-63	Bobby Craig	13
1963-64	Steve Chalmers	28
1964-65	John Hughes	22
1965-66	Joe McBride	31
1966-67	Steve Chalmers	23
1967-68	Bobby Lennox	32
1968-69	Willie Wallace	18
1969-70	Willie Wallace	16
1970-71	Harry Hood	22
1971-72	Dixie Deans	19
1972-73	Dixie Deans	21
	Kenny Dalglish	21
1973-74	Dixie Deans	24
1974-75	Kenny Dalglish	16
1975-76	Kenny Dalglish	24
1976-77	Ronnie Glavin	19
1977-78	Jo Edvaldsson	10
1978-79	Tom McAdam	7
	Andy Lynch	7
1979-80	George McCluskey	10
1980-81	Frank McGarvey	23
1981-82	George McCluskey	21
1982-83	Charlie Nicholas	29
1983-84	Brian McClair	23
1984-85	Brian McClair	19
1985-86	Brian McClair	22

Celtic Players with 200+ League Appearances 1946-86

1.	Billy McNeill	486
2.	Danny McGrain	412 + 3 Sub
3.	Bobby Evans	385
4.	Roy Aitken	348
5.	Bertie Peacock	318
6.	Jimmy Johnstone	298 + 11 Sub
7.	Bobby Lennox	296 + 50 Sub
8.	Bobby Murdoch	287 + 4 Sub
9.	John Hughes	254 + 3 Sub
10.	Steve Chalmers	253 + 7 Sub
11.	Tommy Burns	252 + 20 Sub
12.	Tom McAdam	252 + 7 Sub
13.	Tommy Gemmell	247
14.	Murdo MacLeod	237 + 6 Sub
15.	Bobby Collins	220
16.	Willie Fernie	219
17.	Charlie Tully	213
18.	Jim Brogan	208 + 5 Sub
19.	Kenny Dalglish	200 + 4 Sub

Celtic Players with 100+ League Goals 1946-86

1.	Bobby Lennox	168
2.	Steve Chalmers	158
3.	John Hughes	116
4.	Kenny Dalglish	112